LENIN REVISITED
HIS ENTIRE THINKING PROCESS
ON MARXIST PHILOSOPHY

A POST-TEXTOLOGICAL READING OF
PHILOSOPHICAL NOTES

LENIN REVISITED
HIS ENTIRE THINKING PROCESS
ON MARXIST PHILOSOPHY

A POST-TEXTOLOGICAL READING OF PHILOSOPHICAL NOTES

By Zhang Yibing

Translated by Thomas Mitchell

CANUT INTERNATIONAL PUBLISHERS
Berlin, London

Originally published as Back to Lenin- A Post-textological Reading on Philosophical Notes in 2008 by Jiangsu People's Press Press.

Original Chinese Edition Copyright © September 2008

ISBN: 978-7-214-0487-07

English Print edition: Lenin Revisited- His Entire Thinking Process on Marxist Philoophy. A Post-Textological Reading of Philosophical Notes, December 2011

ISBN: 978-605-87737-0-7

English Digital Edition:

ISBN: 978-605-87737-1-4

Published by
Canut International Publishers
Yorck Street. 66
10965 Kreuzberg Berlin-Germany

Canut International-London
12a Guernsey Road E11
London 4BJ –England-UK
URL: http://www.leftreader.com
E-Mail: canut@leftreader.com

I dedicate this book to my
Alma mater – Nanjing University

CONTENTS

Publisher's Foreword   *xi*
Author's Preface   *xiii*

INTRODUCTION
1 *The heterogeneity of Lenin's thought*   *34*
2 *What kind of a "book" is made up of Lenin's Philosophical Notebooks?*   *42*
3 *The basic layout of Philosophical Notebooks*   *49*
4 *The textual structure of the Bern Notebooks*   *55*
5 *Overview of past research on Lenin's Philosophical Notebooks*   *60*
6 *Reconsidering the issue from another perspective*   *75*
7 *Bern Notebooks: The historical process of Lenin's philosophical shift*
   that took place in his study of Hegel's thought   *92*

PART I
LENIN ON THE PATH TO PHILOSOPHICAL ENLIGHTENMENT

CHAPTER ONE
YOUNG LENIN IN REVOLUTIONARY PRACTICE AND
THE SUBJECTIVE DIMENSION OF HISTORICAL REALITY   *109*

1 *Young Lenin and the objective dimension of historical dialectics*   *110*
2 *Young Lenin and his philosophy teacher, Plekhanov*   *122*
3 *Young Lenin reads The Holy Family*   *132*
4 *The subjective dimension: The earliest changes in young Lenin's thought*   *139*
5 *Class consciousness and the dynamism of the revolution*   *148*

CHAPTER TWO
LENIN, PLEKHANOV AND PHILOSOPHICAL MATERIALISM   *155*

1 *The background of Lenin's first systematic study of philosophical theory*   *156*
2 *Draft text: Reading notes and their interpretation*   *165*
3 *Annotations to Plekhanov's Fundamental Problems of Marxism*   *168*
ADDENDUM 1
THE FETISHISM OF MATERIAL RELATIONS:
A FORGOTTEN PHILOSOPHICAL CONTEST   *177*

CHAPTER THREE
READINGS ON DIETZGEN'S PHILOSOPHICAL MATERIALISM   *193*

1 *Lenin studies Dietzgen's Philosophical materialism*   *194*
2 *Dietzgen: "Comrade" of Marx and Lenin*   *199*
3 *On "dialectical materialism" and epistemology*   *204*

CHAPTER FOUR
LENIN BEGINS TO UNDERSTAND MODERN WESTERN PHILOSOPHY   211

1 *A strange aberration in Lenin's reading*   *212*
2 *Commentary on Rey's Modern Philosophy*   *219*
3 *A broad philosophical research scope:*
Reading notes on Western philosophy and science   *226*

CHAPTER FIVE
LENIN'S EXCERPTED NOTES ON FEUERBACHIAN PHILOSOPHY   231

1 *Nature and religion*   *232*
2 *Materialism, or materialism*   *237*
3 *"A germ of historical materialism"*   *241*

CHAPTER SIX
RUSSIAN THINKERS: STILL MATERIALISM   247

1 *Material substantive ontology: Commentary on Deborin's*
Dialectical Materialism   *248*
2 *Understanding Chernyshevsky*   *253*

CHAPTER SEVEN
COMPREHENSIVE UNDERSTANDING AND PROPAGATION OF MARXISM   261

1 *Marxism as a guide to action*   *262*
2 *The philosophical views in Karl Marx*   *266*
3 *Marxist philosophical historical thread*   *272*

CHAPTER EIGHT
LENIN'S OUTLINE ON THE CORRESPONDENCE BETWEEN MARX AND ENGELS   277

1 *Dialectics: Why Hegel?*   *278*
2 *It is a mistake to not understand Hegel's dialectic*   *285*
3 *Dialectics: The spirit of Marxist philosophy*   *291*

PART II
BERN NOTEBOOKS:
LENIN ON THE SHOULDERS OF PHILOSOPHICAL GIANTS

CHAPTER NINE
LENIN'S PERSPECTIVE AS HE BEGINS
TO READ HEGEL'S PHILOSOPHY   301

   1   *Why did Lenin read Hegel?*   302
   2   *Three foundational elements of Lenin's early reading framework*   306
   3   *Was Lenin really able to easily read Hegel?*   316
   4   *From "incomprehensible" to the first signs of mental activity*   323

CHAPTER TEN
THE SUDDEN EMERGENCE OF A NEW INTERPRETIVE FRAMEWORK
AND DÉTOURNEMENT OF THEORETICAL LOGIC   333

   1   *Criticism and affirmation within Lenin's consternation:*
      Logical contradictions in his reading   334
   2   *The revolutionary leap in Lenin's research line of thought*   338
   3   *The three "aphorisms" of Lenin's cognitive breakthrough*   347

CHAPTER ELEVEN
ESSENTIALLY PRACTICAL MATERIALIST DIALECTICS   355

   1   *Lenin's early understanding of dialectical thought in the process of his reading*   356
   2   *Practical dialectics: Lenin's new understanding on materialist dialectics*   362
   3   *Practice: Drawing a diagram of the objective world*   371

ADDENDUM
A DELETED TEXT: THE CONCEPT OF HISTORY
IN THE CONTEXT OF MARXIST PHILOSOPHY   381

CHAPTER TWELVE
THE UNITY OF IDENTICAL LOGIC, EPISTEMOLOGY, AND
SUBJECTIVE DIALECTICS IN OBJECTIVE PRACTICAL DIALECTICS   399

   1   *"Triple identity" and Hegel's line of philosophical thought*   400
   2   *The discovery of the "dual identity" of epistemology and logic*   406
   3   *Practical dialectics: The sole foundation point of "triple identity"*   410

CHAPTER THIRTEEN
DESANCTIFICATION:
LENIN'S "SIXTEEN ELEMENTS" OF DIALECTICS   417

   1   *Logical analysis of textual structure*   418
   2   *The dialectical and epistemological thought in the "sixteen elements"*   425
   3   *A general review*   439

CHAPTER FOURTEEN
THE CONCLUSION OF LENIN'S STUDY ON HEGELIAN PHILOSOPHY   441

   1   *Confirming practical dialectics in the history of philosophy*   442
   2   *An important reading summary and record of thoughts*   450
   3   *"On the Question of Dialectics":*
      The major achievement of Lenin's study of dialectics   458

About the Author   467

PUBLISHER'S FOREWORD

Lenin Revisited is another meticulous textological research into Marxist philosophy by Professor Zhang Yibing. In *Lenin Revisited*, Professor Zhang proposes a new research method, *i.e.*, the theory of philosophical situating. With this method, he attempts a constructive interpretation of Lenin's complete study and reading notes (including draft texts), and establishes a historical shift model that examines Lenin's development from mirroring others to situating his own philosophy. In his treatment of the central text to be interpreted–the most important of Lenin's *Philosophical Notebooks*, namely the *Bern Notebooks*– Zhang completely abandons the traditional method of analysis that is employed by textbook systems which amputated and grafted in new notes to classical texts.

In particular, Professor Zhang abandons the model that proceeds from the *a priori* "conception" model in the study of Lenin's notebooks on Hegelian philosophy. Zhang Yibing begins with a broad vision of Lenin's entire 20-year historical process of studying philosophy, reconstructing the constantly-evolving progression of logic developed in Lenin's "thought laboratory," basing his analysis on actual texts.

Professor Zhang accords special attention to the many important philosophical and logical twists and turns in Lenin's reading and note-taking process. The material discussed in Lenin Revisited is extensive with the unique method, it can be considered a new, pioneering, original work in the research of classical Marxist texts.

Unfortunately, after the Second International Lenin's philosophical facet have been an object of misleading interpretations by both Soviet scholars and Western-Marxist critics. The fact that Young Lenin was a staunch Marxist when he started his political struggle has led to a serious negligence of the historical, actual context of Lenin's philosophical investigations, especially its merely political-oriented and practical character. Zhang Yibing's interpretation of *Philosophical Notebooks* is developed from a textual fact that has long been ignored despite its truth. This is that Philosophical Notebooks are not a "book," but rather a collection of notes and outlines collected after the death of the author.

Therefore, Lenin's Philosophical Notebooks should be interpreted as a series of documents that reflect the theoretical and political conflicts of the time, including his numerous backtrackings and aimless wandering.

In this book Zhang Yibing discloses serious falsehoods, myths, and also traces of irresponsible scholarship resulting from subjective, arbitrary, indiscriminate, linear, and homogeneous conclusions. Zhang Yibing carefully uncovers Lenin's penetration process of Marxist dialectics by analyzing any of his particular reading.

In his analysis we can clearly observe that Lenin has indeed arrived at the total logical line of practical dialectics- which was formerly achieved by Marx and Engels; and that Lenin was neither a philosopher by birth nor a patient thinker awaiting his philosophical masterpiece, but a real practical philosopher. Zhang Yibing's methodology enables him to let the text speak for itself by abandoning the practice of directly equating interpretations with Lenin's original ideas.

In this book the readers will also find first hand materials and analysis on the history of Russian and Soviet Marxist philosophy, its major debates and shifts.

This line of interpretation reveals to us, in a truly miraculous fashion that has never before been duplicated, a Lenin who survives the existential test, who is interpreted with the newest philosophical experiments. Lenin, in Yibing's eyes as a contemporary thinker and practicer extends to us the call to continue his critical line of thought. For us today, the words "Lenin revisited" actually mean to step into the future in the company of this great historical thinker. I thank Thomas Mitchell for his outstanding efforts by the translation of this book. Finally I would like to thank China Renmin University Press, and their encouragement to our publishing house for the realization of this book.

Daivya Jindal

December 2011, London

AUTHOR'S PREFACE

In the modern research of Marxist philosophy in China, Marx's philosophical thought has been brought to life and magnified by textual research that focuses on careful study of first-hand documents and a completely new thinking context. This was my vision for the future when I published *Marx Revisited* 10 years ago. It is significant for the whole world that Marx's philosophical thought has thrown off its dogmatic constraints and is again a relevant philosophical subject in the modern Chinese scholarly world.[1] However, I soon realized that outside the light thrown on the subject by these positive developments, we had forgotten Lenin as an important Marxist philosopher. It is my view that in the history of Marxist philosophy, Lenin is a historical link that cannot be forgotten; without Lenin, there would never have been the October Revolution, nor would there have been a Chinese tradition of Marxism that extends to the present day. However, it is regrettable that with the exception of non-scholarly bourgeois ideological backlash, after the fall of the Soviet Union, scholars from Russia and the states of the former Soviet Union seemed to attempt to delete the history of Russian communists and the entire genesis and development of Soviet philosophical thought, whether they did so consciously or unconsciously.[2] In terms of the logical thread of philosophical history, this is a nihilist illusion that could never be. I believe that insomuch as Marxism is the ideological base of our nation-state, the historical task of studying Marxism logically and inevitably falls to us to begin and complete.[3]

---

1   In discussing this development of the Chinese scholarly world with the British professors Carver, Jessop, and Callinicos, the American professors Anderson, Kellner, Derick, Brenner, and the Slovenian professor Slavoj Zizek, this was also their sentiment.
2   In May 2008, I led representatives of the Nanjing University Marxist Social Research Center to Russia, my second visit to Russia. During this trip, I read and copied a large number of important scholarly texts, photographs, and audiovisual materials from Lenin's former home, the Russian National Archives, and the National Social Historical Museum. In Moscow, we participated in a symposium organized by the University of Moscow and the Russian Institute; we were able to exchange ideas with such Russian Marxist experts as Georg Bagaturija. During this important scholarly visit, we were able to directly experience this historical, scholarly rupture.
3   During the May 2007 China-Russian philosophical symposium held in Suzhou, China, I frankly discussed these thoughts of mine in front of the delegation of Russian scholars. This obviously came as a great shock to them.

Let us revisit Lenin! Let us bring new methods and our new circumstances to the analysis and understanding of the history of Lenin's philosophical thought, and thus more perfectly step towards our present day. This is a historical duty that we cannot but come to grips with today. In fact, with *Lenin Revisited*, as with my book *Marx Revisited* from a decade ago, I am not advocating a laughably superficial return from today to the past, from real life to dusty old tomes[4]; so doing would only be the logical method of, to borrow the concept of Husserl and Heidegger, returning to "things in themselves" in a phenomenological sense. Rather, with these two books, it has always been my goal to deconstruct the ideological facade and pseudo-scholarly framework forced onto the classical texts of Marx and Lenin by Soviet and Eastern European scholars after the Second International, nothing more.

My progression from *Marx Revisited* to *Lenin Revisited* was not random. Rather, it was a constitutive part of the movement to use independent research approaches and models to truly undertake the great work of studying the classic texts of Marxist philosophy that came after us Chinese Marxist philosophers departed from the ideological dogmas of the Soviet and Eastern European interpretative framework[5]. Of course, the theoretical purpose of Lenin Revisited was to establish a new method that would be even truer than the textological interpretation contained in Marx Revisited: the method of philosophical **situating**. This method is employed to **simulate** the historical, actual circumstances of Lenin's philosophical thought, bringing it from out of the dense ideological fog of traditional Soviet dogmas. I use this irregular interpretative method because the primary object of study in Lenin Revisited is reading notes and commentaries: in other words, **draft texts** and

---

4 I am baffled by the fact that there have been articles written on the non-scholarly question of using "revisited" versus using "progress beyond" or "surpass."

5 I must emphasize that we must not become caught up in endless debate and empty discussion over such words as "textology," "Marx revisited," and "historical relations." If we could all spend the necessary time to carefully interpret important texts, in the not too distant future we would have a large body of independent theoretical work written by Chinese scholars who truly examine the classic Marxist texts; this are the true scholarly glories and achievements that we should garner as Chinese Marxist philosophers. It is my understanding that such young scholars as Han Lixin of Qinghua University, Wei Xiaoping of the Philosophy Department of the Chinese Social Science Institute, and Xia Fan of Nanjing University are undertaking serious, scientific study of Marx's classical texts based on the original German manuscripts. These scholars represent our hope for the future. I believe that this research is much more meaningful than the so-called "textology" that merely parrots Western Marxologie, Western Leninism, and Western Maoist Studies while non-critically accepting the results of others, without understanding the original text.

sub-texts or **generative texts**. More specifically, my primary object of study is the Bern Notebooks, which were important near the end of the philosophical development of Lenin's thought[6]. I am of the opinion that these texts were never truly opened in the subjective, forced interpretive discourse and theoretical falsehoods of the traditional research in the former Soviet Union and Eastern Europe.

Of course, I did not just now begin to study Lenin's *Philosophical Notebooks*. This is actually the fourth time I have studied and interpreted this important group of classic texts. I remember discussing at several instances my general experiences in studying these texts in a topical introduction for my "personal anthology"[7]. My first exposure to Lenin's *Philosophical Notebooks* came in the late 1970s, when I was just a sophomore at the Philosophy Department of Nanjing University. I can still remember dimly that Professor Hu Fuming led the class in reading and interpreting, page by page and line by line, the important parts of "Conspectus of Hegel's book *The Science of Logic*," one of the texts in Lenin's *Philosophical Notebooks*. For us, sitting below and listening to the lectures of Professor Hu, the abstruse words and recondite views of the Philosophical Notebooks bombarded us like artillery shells, filling our hearts with dread before the mysterious temple of philosophy. One day as class ended, a junior classmate, sounding quite mysterious and pleased with himself, informed us that Hegel's statement that "the more abstract a thing is, the more concrete it becomes" would take us our whole lives to understand. Later, this "thesis," along with one teacher's only half-joking remark that students "take in a bowl of noodles and take out a ball of befuddlement" would become famous warnings from the older philosophy students. I must confess that the first time I read Philosophical Notebooks, I could make sense of nothing beyond recording a few unfamiliar and decidedly strange nouns. Though I would often carry volume 38 of the *Collected Works of Lenin* around with me, my heart felt empty. There was even one night that I felt overwhelmed with despair that I would never understand Lenin. I am happy to say that as I studied Hegel the next year, many of Lenin's conclusions in *Philosophical Notebooks* became clearer.

---

6 I refer to the notes written by Lenin between 1914 and 1915 in the Swiss city of Bern as the *Bern Notebooks*. In these eight notebooks of excerpts, the central content is made up of Lenin's notes and thoughts as he came to understand Hegel's philosophy; it was not, as my predecessors have claimed, an unfinished manuscript for a work on materialist dialectics.

7 *Zhang Yibing's Personal Anthology*, Guangxi Normal University Press, 1999.

The second time I systematically studied the *Philosophical Notebooks* was during my last year as a graduate student, around 1981. For my dissertation I chose to write on a "philosophical principle," a topic that none of the other students was willing approach: the "negation of the negation." Unfortunately for me, my painstakingly completed, 200,000 character first draft was "shot down"; Professor Sun Bokui, who was in charge of graduate students, was not pleased with my long and dull "logical construct." He told me he would rather read some a more practical piece on the theoretical history of the dialectic. Thus my gargantuan piece on the logical structure of the dialectic was painfully condensed to a fraction of its original length, and at the end of my last chapter (on the line of development of the dialectic in the history of Marxist philosophy), I included an index of readings on such texts as Lenin's "Materialism and *Machism*" and *Philosophical Notebooks*. In this selective study, I originally planned on finding Lenin's writings on the negation of the negation, because under the influence of Professor Sun Bokui's thoughts on **underlying historical logic** in the research methods into Marxist philosophical history, I began to consciously look myself to see **whether or not** Lenin's own philosophical thinking **had changed**. Surprisingly enough, my conclusion was that it had. In fact, my conclusion here had already differentiated me from the dogmatic cognitive model of "Leninist Philosophy" expounded in the former Soviet Union and Eastern Europe; this was a static and non-historical theory of absolute truth. While this was not a comprehensive or pro-found investigation of Lenin's Philosophical Notebooks, nevertheless in the process of sifting through and organizing materials, I had dis-covered quite by accident that there really was a process of **change** and **development** in Lenin's thoughts on the dialectic. Although Lenin's philosophical thought did not experience the kind of sudden, revolu-tionary, and holistic shift that Marx and Engels' did, his philosophical understanding was always moving forward. This can primarily be seen in the fact that Lenin's philosophical ideas in "What is the Friend of the People?" and "Materialism and Empirio-Criticism" are not entirely **homogenous** with his understanding of the dialectic as he read Hegel's philosophical works on the eve of the October Revolution. As a gradu-ate student, I was astounded to find that not a single Soviet or Eastern European scholar had even mentioned this change! I provided a simple explanation of this point at the end of my dissertation. In that piece, however, I merely pointed out the differences between Lenin's thoughts on the dialectic at different points in time, I did not delve more deeply to find the line of theoretical logic connecting those points. Nevertheless, I always knew that I would return to this topic at a later point in time.

In 1990, I returned again to Lenin's *Philosophical Notebooks,* with the goal of interpreting his "Conspectus of Hegel's book *The Science of Logic,*" the most important text in those notebooks. Armed with the newest Chinese translation of the Philosophical Notebooks, I was prepared to concentrate on purposeful, meticulous study. At this time, I had recently enjoyed the experience of textual interpretation of the new translation of the manuscript of *The German Ideology* (1988 version), and although I had not yet established my own interpretive methods for the *Philosophical Notebooks*, I was quite ambitious. Thus I first shelved the traditional line of interpretation used to explain the Philosophical Notebooks, and the *Bern Notebooks* in particular, a line of thought that annotated classical texts using the systems of philosophy textbooks. Instead, I directly turned to Hegel's *The Science of Logic, Small Logic,* and *Lectures on the History of Philosophy*, etc., moving with Lenin page by page. At the same time, I paid meticulous attention to each fragment written by Lenin as he read Hegel's work; thus I felt that I had experienced, for the first time in a reduced sense, the true circumstances of Lenin's research. This was the method that I would later use to interpret Marx's excerpted notes in the *Paris Notebooks*, however, I now realize that this is a modern textological illusion. Following this, I began to study the many materials that made up Lenin's subsidiary awareness. Finally, I turned to secondary research texts. After repeating this process several times, I developed a new topical line of thought, writing some of the first Chinese essays on Lenin's *Bern Notebooks*, diverging, in terms of logical development, from the theoretical framework of Soviet and Eastern European scholars[8]. At the time, in one of my essays I emphasized the topic of "investigation," primarily wishing to express the idea that I did not believe that my understanding of Lenin's *Philosophical Notebooks* was absolute and eternally true. Through the writing of these essays, I wished to provide a new logic in the study of classic Marxist texts, *i.e.*, **to use a historical perspective of Marxism to truly investigate the classic texts**. By then I had already realized that Lenin had begun to come into contact with Marxism from an early age (here he was different from Marx and Engels). Thus he was able to gradually come to understand some of the most important basic theoretical qualifications of Marxist philosophy. Later, in the course of the actual revolution and in theoretical research, he was able to more deeply grasp the important content of this scientific theory. This should

---

8   Zhang Yibing: "The True Logic of Lenin's Deepening of the Materialist Dialectic," *Philosophical Studies*, 1992, volume 5; "A New Investigation of Lenin's 'Sixteen Essential Elements,'" *Investigation*, 1992, volume 3; "The Ultimate Formation of Lenin's Thinking on Practical Dialectics," *Nanjing Social Science*, 1993, volume 2; "The Unification of Identical Epistemologies, Logics, and Dialectic Theories in Practical Dialectics," *Nanjing University Newspaper*, 1993, volume 2.

have been an extremely normal thought process. However, our traditional philosophical interpretive framework insists on non-historically unifying this process, as if Lenin was always a great Marxist thinker from the very beginning, as if each sentence he ever wrote was absolutely correct and conformed exactly to each sentence he later wrote. Though this seems to protect the supremacy and wholeness of the classic authors, this interpretive framework in fact causes a layer of non-scientific mist to obscure these great philosophers from future readers. I firmly believe that this old logic, inherited from the theoretical research of the former Soviet Union, must be broken to pieces (in terms of Lenin's *Philosophical Notebooks*, the most representative of these old theories is Kedrov's "planned conception" theory, which is also the interpretive model that this book focuses on refuting and opposing). *Philosophical Notebooks* is truly an important collection of philosophical texts by Lenin; however, it is also an original group of documents that truly records the developmental process and leaps in understanding that Lenin experienced as he came to understand the essence of Marx's practical dialectic through the study of philosophical materialism and Hegel's philosophy. As such, it is my understanding that the most important aspect of the study of this group of documents is not to make each of Lenin's sentences appear incomparably heroic, but rather to truly understand how Lenin grasped the standpoint of philosophical materialism, and thus enter Hegel's philosophy gradually and with great difficulty, before finally standing with Marx on the summit of Hegel's logic, grasping the total logical line of thought of **practical dialectics**. I believe that what we must learn from the great teachers are not external words and sentences, but rather living, breathing standpoints, views, and methods! I must explain that in this study, I committed a mistake that placed me on par with the traditional research on Lenin's *Philosophical Notebooks*, *i.e.*, I merely focused on the *Bern Notebooks*, instead of placing the entire historical process of Lenin's philosophical study and research into an internally connected logical line of thought. In so doing, I left the *Bern Notebooks* as an isolated interpretive object. I did not overcome this mistake until my most recent research.

About 10 years later, in 2004, I received a national social science research project to study Lenin's philosophy. Before long, this topic was confirmed as a major research project by the Ministry of Education. I had the task of studying Lenin's *Philosophical Notebooks*[9]. Thus began

---

9   This topic was divided into three sub-topics: **first**, a study on Lenin's *Materialism and Empirical Criticism* led by Professor Liu Huaiyu; **second**, a study on Lenin's *Philosophical Notebooks* led by myself; **third**, a study on Western "Leninism" led by Professor Zhang Chuanping.

my fourth foray into the study of Lenin's *Philosophical Notebooks*. This was my most systematic and most comprehensive study of Lenin's Philosophical Notebooks. In 2005, after writing on Lacan's research and completing the second volume of *A Deep Plough: Unscrambling Major Post-marxist Texts from Adorno to Zizek* (textual interpretation of the post-Marxist Western schools of thought), I began to prepare my own materials and organize my thoughts. In this study, I systematically reconsidered my understanding of Lenin's philosophy, developed 15 years prior. I transformed my past point-by-point study of Bern Notebooks into a comprehensive view of Lenin's philosophical thought through analysis of primary material. Thus I had no choice but to re-read *The Collected Works of Lenin*. Of course, I primarily focused on the various documents left by Lenin before 1915, and I was thus able to acquire many of the primary lines of thought and logical thinking points in the development of Lenin's philosophical thought prior to the *Bern Notebooks*. In my research at this time, I consciously differentiated my research from Western Leninism, *i.e.*, I did not simply oppose young Lenin (especially *Materialism and Empirio-Criticism*) to the later Bern Notes. Rather, I concretely investigated the theoretical and practical connections between Lenin and Georg Plekhanov, the scholarly connections between Lenin and philosophical materialism, and the philosophical connections between Lenin and the reading of *Marx and Engels Correspondence*: these were all more focused in scale, more profound links in philosophical history, and they allowed me to reach new levels of understanding, thus providing me with an important subsidiary awareness in establishing my correct logical placement of the *Bern Notebooks*. In comparison with my own research in the early 1990s, my fourth study of Lenin's *Philosophical Notebooks* and especially my study of the *Bern Notebooks*, progressed in terms of research methods, profundity of thought, and the accurate interpretation of text. Of particular importance is the fact that through this systematic study, I was able to reach several new and extremely important conclusions in my overall understanding of Lenin's philosophical thought.

My **first** conclusion was the realization that in the research of all the past Soviet and Western "Leninologists," they all, whether consciously or unconsciously, viewed the *Philosophical Notebooks* as a "book." However, in reality, this "book" known as the *Philosophical Notebooks* does not exist; what does exist is only a varied and heterogeneous collection of excerpted notes, reading notes, thoughts, and commentaries. There are several important aspects to this new understanding:

First, Lenin's texts are not homogenous in terms of the profundity of thought. Importantly, unlike young Marx and young Engels, Lenin did not have a **non-Marxist** period of thought; he is a Marxist from the time he enters the theoretical scene. Thus, when Lenin's notes, thoughts, and commentaries written at different historical periods are indiscriminately thrown together, it is difficult for readers to realize that in his Marxist philosophical notebooks, there are many shallow, imprecise entries. This leads readers to miss the fact that in Lenin's philosophical thought, there may be a developmental progression that moves from shallow to profound, from correct notions in general to concrete, scientific, essential understanding. In other words, when we oversimplify matters, when we non-historically reorganize Lenin's texts from different historical periods according to topic, what results is a kind of non-scientific, **forced logical homogeneity. Second**, different versions of "Lenin's notebooks" were artificially arranged into a **hierarchical** structure. Non-excerpt notes, and especially reading commentaries, were given secondary placement, to the point that these important notes were not seriously examined or studied for many years, which ultimately produced a blind spot and textual rupture in the study of Lenin's *Philosophical Notebooks*. This is what causes scholars to unconsciously equate the *Bern Notes*, which focus on Hegel's philosophy, with the *Philosophical Notebooks*, while at the same time not according sufficient attention to the other notes and documents in these notebooks[10]. Through careful consideration of these questions, in this fourth study of Lenin's notes, his *Philosophical Notebooks* were, for the first time, historically "restored" to the concrete historical circumstances of the entire development of Lenin's thought. The historical meaning and profundity of thought in each document were carefully highlighted, paying special attention to the **relative comparison** among documents in a certain philosophical context. Furthermore, I assiduously delved into the internal connections between Lenin's philosophical situating and his practical construction. It can be said that this study constitutes the most complete "field work" on Lenin's *Philosophical Notebooks* and their related texts, both in China and abroad.

My **second** conclusion was that through historically differentiating the various periods in Lenin's research, through understanding the particular thought context and complex background of different texts focusing on real or theoretical issues, it is not difficult for us to **see** the basic

---

10   In October 2007, I engaged in conversation with the well-known American Leninologist Kevin Anderson on this topic. He also admitted that this is an issue that has not been accorded sufficient attention in the West

logical thread and theoretical situating space of the changes, development, and even important leaps in understanding undergone by Lenin's philosophical thought over the course of 20 years. This is what excites me the most. I have discovered that as early as the late 19th century, young Lenin, as a practical revolutionary Marxist, obviously focused on the **subjective dimension** of the historical dialectic in his arguments against Narodism. Much like Plekhanov and others, Lenin emphasized the necessity of the development of capitalism in Russia; such a practical disposition in the objectification of philosophical logic emphasized the fact that social historical development was a "natural historical process." In contrast, in the early 1900s, the Bolshevik Party centred around Lenin disagreed with the Mensheviks as to the future of the Russian Revolution; in this debate, Lenin clearly proposed to bring into play the revolutionary potential of the proletariat and revolutionary party. Thus he turned from focusing on the objective dimension to focusing on the **subjective dimension**, under the premise of objective, real conditions. However, at this time, Lenin was unable to find philosophical support for this new practical turn. Although in the debate against Russian *Machism* in 1908 Lenin correctly stood with Plekhanov, effectively using the important scholarly work *Materialism and Machism* to defend the theoretical basis of Marxist philosophy, yet philosophical materialism was unable to more profoundly support Lenin's revolutionary practical creativity at this time. It was evident that Lenin needed real historical dialectic guidance. This was his most important reason for resolving to studying Hegel's philosophy and understanding the dialectic theory in 1914, during the First World War. I have discovered that only in the process of Lenin's study of Hegel's philosophy – especially his *The Science of Logic* – was he able to gradually and profoundly understand Marx's practical dialectic views on changing reality and "destroying existence." Through this process, Lenin obtained the weapon of philosophical theory that he needed to guide the Russian October Revolution to victory. This was an extremely complex process of philosophical shifting.

My **third** conclusion was the proposition of a name for Lenin's *Bern Notebooks*. Though *Bern Notebooks* sounds like something new, it is actually made up of the notes that Lenin took on Hegelian philosophy while living in Bern, Switzerland between 1914 and 1915. Lenin's "Conspectus of Hegel's Book *The Science of Logic*" was the focal point of this group of documents. In actuality, *Bern Notebooks* comprise a group of important reading notes centred on Hegelian philosophy, especially the question of the dialectic (epistemology), filling eight notebooks in total. In this study of the Bern Notebooks, the important philosophical changes that I had already discovered in Lenin's process of learning and researching Hegel's philosophy were interpreted with greater specificity, rethought, concretized, and re-situated. I was able to make great progress in the areas of comparative analysis to the original context of Hegel's philosophy, Lenin's micro-proofs in the process of his philosophical shift, and Lenin's ultimate philosophical conclusions.

My **fourth** and final conclusion relates to the research methods of this book. Specifically, these represent a new attempt at methodological development, formed on the basis of my own independent philosophical thought: textual **situating** interpretation (also referred to as the philosophical situating theory or theoretical logical situating theory). Here I surpass the textual interpretive method used in my own *Marx Revisited*. In this book, I do not stop at the **modern** realm of textual discussion, *i.e.*, **the attempt to close in on the imagined original textual context** in a philosophical interpretive sense; in other words, I acknowledge, in a certain sense, the legitimate place of **post-modern** textology, in particular Barthes' idea that the essence of textual reading is not reductionist, but rather creative production. I will explicate this new method a little further.

First, the reason why I have decided to effectuate this change of method is my gradual realization that in our past research, we forced too much of our own understanding on the historical texts; when we insist on writing "Marx believed," "Lenin's dialectic," or "Heidegger asserted," etc., when we argue for our own understanding and perspective until we are red in the face, we have not realized that we are causing the text to speak for **us**, rather than speak for itself in an **objective textual context**[11]. Therefore, in my most recent study of Lenin's Philosophical Notes, I have consciously abandoned the practice of directly equating my own subjective understanding with Lenin's original ideas. From the beginning, my premise is that the author of the text is **not present**, acknowledging the **impossibility** of absolutely restoring the original

---

11   Most distressing is the practice, common in our Marxist-Leninist public classes, of teachers who never seriously studied the classic works of Marx, Lenin, or Mao mixing second-hand dogmas copied from textbooks with their own shallow understanding and insisting that it is the absolute truth (if students incorrectly memorize even one line, they are marked down for it). The baffling logic employed by these teachers is that "I am Marx," "What I say is the truth." Even more than teaching students a course in propaganda, this demeans Marxism, reducing the truth to a fallacy, reducing the essence to a phenomenon. I believe that the young students who do not believe this so-called "Marxism" cannot be faulted for it,

context of these texts. Thus, I am only able to re-create a mirror of Lenin's thought **that I understand**, according to texts which have already become history as well as their related details.

Second, my reason for employing this new method in this particular book is that the texts on which I base my analysis here are no longer **completed texts** (what I refer to in Marx Revisited as the third kind of texts, or published works). Even **generative texts** (what I refer to as the second kind of texts, or incomplete manuscripts and letters) are used sparingly in this book; instead, I employ **sub-texts** (what I refer to as the first kind of texts, or reading notes, outlines, and thoughts)[12] and **draft texts**. These "draft texts" refer to the large number of **reading commentaries** included in Lenin's *Philosophical Notes* (these notes were ignored by past researchers)[13]. Unlike independent reading notes, these commentaries were written directly on the documents that Lenin was reading, often in the form of symbols with very little writing[14]. The act of recording these markings and then selectively organizing them into a text already represents an **artificial** restructuring of the text. I believe that this fourth kind of "text" may, in a sense, more accurately reflect the basic reading framework and actual scholarly level of the original reader. However, because the markings and commentaries in these notes often do not indicate a clear direction or value judgment, they lead us to depart from clear and direct identification of the text, which in turn causes us to read and re-interpret the reading itself. This results in the appearance of the **guesses**, **assumptions**, and **subjective** identifications of the re-reader (the second reader) in the philosophical situating of the present. These reconstructed guesses and identifications are primarily

---

12   Refer to pages 13-20 of *Marx Revisited*.

13   It is worth remarking that Marx and Engels also left behind a large body of reading notes that spanned a large time period and are extremely profound in terms of content. This is what forms the last section of the fourth part of *MEGA 2*; in the original Soviet publishing plan, there were to be 30-40 volumes in this section. Unfortunately, this plan was discontinued because of special historical circumstances, so that these notes have never been published in their entirety. We also know that Mao Zedong left a great deal of philosophical, historical, and literary reading notes. The study of these draft texts will be a necessary but extremely difficult and complex project for us in our future study of Marxist texts. I hope that my own early research and naming of these draft texts will give my successors some necessary scholarly experience to build on.

14   This is not absolute either; some commentaries include a great deal of text. For instance, when I was a graduate student, Professor Sun Bokui told us that he had filled all the white space in one of his copies of Marx's *1844 Manuscript* with reading notes. He went on to tell us that he had already read innumerable manuscripts before this: on some of the earlier ones, he had read them until they fell apart. On every assignment that we handed in to him, almost every inch of white space would be filled with ideas and commentaries on ways we could improve.

based on the **seen** and **unseen** logical symptoms expressed by the commentator as he reads the textual discourse. Furthermore, these identifications are primarily not in the details of the marks or subtle words, but rather in a completely new philosophical **situating**, *i.e.*, attempting to simulate the mental activity of the original reader who is no longer present. This was an aspect that the past interpretive methods of which I have spoken were unable to directly attain. As such, I had no choice but to propose a new situating theory. Unlike my previous textual interpretation, I no longer suggest what the logic of Lenin's philosophy really **was**; rather, I carefully identify the thought situating, produced by myself in this time period, which is **essentially nothing more than an imitation**. Thus I am forced to be more honest with myself and more substantial in my scholarship; what is mine is mine, I should not insist that it is someone else's.

Finally, the development of this new thinking is the result of two aspects of criticism and questioning: **first**, the criticism of some of my teachers, especially Professor Sun Bokui, asking me why, if he had studied Marx for his entire life, did he not see the things I claimed were there in Marx's texts? **Second**, the questions of many of my students in classroom discussions: "Why can't we see what you are pointing out in the same text? Do the ideas in your book belong to the original author or to you?" In the past, I always avoided directly answering these questions, because I was afraid of appearing to be a "holy man" speaking new dogmas. In fact, for a long time Chinese philosophers have spoken on the authority of "holy men" (in the past we had the "Six Scriptures," and now we have Marx and Lenin)[15]. This is because in our theoretical discussions, "Marx" has become a synonym for "truth." On an unconscious level, as long as we can say that our own opinion was expressed by Marx, we are afforded a certain degree of political insurance. These are the residual effects left on the scholarly world by recent history. In reality, this is not a Marxist scientific attitude. Our inheritance and development of Marxism must not be realized through purposeful theoretical smuggling and logical murkiness.

---

15   There is another interesting phenomenon worthy of mention here: the issue of the underlying, unconscious grammatical structure of Stalinist dogmatism. In other non-Marxist fields of research, some theorists non-critically view their objects of research (whether it be a modern Western philosopher or a great artist) as objects of worship, never wondering if what they study contains mistakes. Although they do not study Marx, in the depths of their hearts their language is still Stalinist, and so they do not stop to think if they have offered anything independent or original in their repetitive commentaries. The other form of this Stalinist dogmatism is theoretical neo-fascism: this remnant of the Cultural Revolution often simply declares that something in the East or West has already died, and then invents an even more terrifying false narrative logic and declares that this great "other" is the absolute truth.

I will give further explanation of this "philosophical situating theory" in the introduction to this book. Beyond this, I am only able to provide an extremely brief introductory discussion of this concept. The theory of situating is my general, **Eastern** view of **man's** ontology. It does not touch on the question of the ultimate origin of the universe according to traditional ontology, but rather only discusses the highest constitutive level and pinnacle experiential state of man's historic existence[16]. I differentiate between **material ordering elements** in the space of social life and man's different levels of subsistence, in particular the different life circumstances that he is able to reach based on his different subsistence states and levels of consciousness. I define the highest level of existence attainable by the subject as **free existential situating**. In the metaphysical self-reflection and worry of our day, because people are worried that existence will become petrified and concepts will become dead logos essence, they crossed out "existence" and "concepts" (Heidegger's "deletion" and Derrida's "blotting out"). A situating existence refers to the simultaneous constructing and deconstructing that takes place within a single entity. The existence of a specific circumstance does not remain, but is rather constantly and painstakingly rebuilt. Of course, in actual history, situating existence often exists in conjunction with "other mirror image"[17] and **false situating** (illusion)[18]. I will explain this theory further later on in this book, using specific works to gradually give a comprehensive explanation. In this book, I only use the interpretive method of **philosophical situating** for the first time in the realm of textual research. It is closely related to the textual interpretive method that I have already proposed in my past textual research, but in comparison, the thinking represented by the theory of situating is much deeper.

---

16 In November 2007, at a symposium on academic paradigms and the unity of academic disciplines, an elderly history professor from Taiwan's Central University mistakenly referred to me as an "idealist" as I discussed the relation between my theory of situating and the study of history.

17 Other theoretical mirror image: "other" refers to a Lacanian dominant misunderstanding; this refers to the structured method of thinking developed by a thinking subject that relies on the ideas of others.

18 On the subject of false situating, Lacan's theory of big and small Others, Althusser's theory of ideology, and Baudrillard's theory of virtual reality all provide in-depth discussion. My concept of false situating, borrowed and re-structured from these three scholars, goes beyond the anti-identification ideological inquiry relations of Lacan, Althusser, and Baudrillard's. It refers to a historical philosophical historical link, i.e., something that is assumed to be true in one period of time is found to be a false situating phenomenon at a new level of existence and cognition. This is an extremely complex theoretical problem.

Unlike the logic of modern structuralism, the theory of situating that I propose no longer halts at the rule of a linear relation system or pre-existent thought framework. Rather, philosophical situating is the **emergence** of a complete conscious phenomenon, expressing the complex state and structural essence of the historical generation of a person or a movement[19]. The rational framework of Kant's scientific structuralism, as well as the symbol systems of Saussure's linguistics are merely simple manifestations of philosophical situating, because in similar rational frameworks and symbol systems, the conscious circumstantial generation of individual subjects and groups of subjects may be completely different. Of course, the most important real basis of the realization of consciousness and thought situating is historical social life; practical existential ordering is the true ontological basis for all psychological phenomenology, but as the philosophical theoretical logic itself is realized as understanding and consciousness under certain conditions, the situation becomes much more complex. Beliefs, emotions, value

---

19   The theory of pre-rational framework dominance is a cognitive structural theory that gradually formed in the 1950s and 60s under the discrete influence of neo-Kantianism. It is composed of several different threads of logic, pulled from divergent theoretical fields. **First**, it comprises the breakthroughs in the modern study of natural scientific history; expressed in a form unlike Gaston Bachelard's neo-epistemological scientific views, the school of scientific history accomplishes many of the same goals. Where Bachelard's school synthesized the heterogeneous historical progression of common knowledge and science using the concept of "epistemological rupture" – a concept expressed in part by Foucault's "knowledge forms" and Althusser's questioning theory – the school of scientific history described the structural "revolutions" in the development of scientific knowledge using Thomas Kuhn's abstract paradigm theory. **Second**, it comprises a logical thread from the structuralist school, evidenced by Saussure's linguistic structuralism and Piaget's scientific structuralism. The former emphasized the simultaneous dominant structure of the divergent systems of relationships between linguistic symbols themselves, while the latter proposed the functional cognitive psychological aligned structures that are constantly being constructed by cognitive subjects. Related to the structuralist school are Simon's generative symbols and Chomsky's underlying linguistic exchange systems. **Third**, it comprises the complex science of modern natural scientific methodology. On the basis of systemics, synergetics, and catastrophe theory, dissipative structure theory guides a functional variable structural existence state and systemic structure; this was also the earliest counteraction to the theory of rational framework dominance in modern natural scientific methodology. After the mid-1960s, the pre-rational framework theory was deconstructed in every scholarly field; through Lakatos' explanation, Kuhn's paradigm theory ultimately perished under Feyerabend's "anything goes" epistemological anarchy. Meanwhile, Foucault's knowledge forms were exploded by the "grenade" of his own new discourse unfolding logic, and Saussure's linguistic structures disappeared in the face of Derrida's deconstruction theory, Barthes' dual textuality, Lacan's big Other theory, and cynical ideology. Thus we can refer to the epistemological realm of today as a "post-paradigm" era. It is interesting to note that when I mentioned the "post-paradigm" era at the symposium which I attended, most of the literary historians in attendance seemed astonished and afraid.

standards, as well as the hidden psychological complexities of individuals and groups can all randomly become the **dominant** elements of situating. Consciousness and philosophical situating are the **emergence of the whole picture** of one's psychological life; it is only in writing, speaking, and expressing one's emotions that we express the rational structure, logical intentions, and emotional impulses that are **able to be manifested**. In this sense, philosophical situating often happens **unconsciously**. In this process, **logical threads** that cannot be clearly explained become crucial in situating.

In this book, I am not able to discuss my theory of situating in any great detail, only bringing it up in the context of textual interpretation. This book can thus be thought of as a small experiment in philosophical discovery. Of course, the whole of the development of social history proves that change in a broad sense is not always successful; in terms of philosophical history this is particularly true. Nevertheless, in an age that promotes creativity and originality, I am willing to take this first step.

The structure of this book is as follows. I begin with an introduction and divide the book into two parts. In the introduction, I primarily give an overview of the text of Lenin's *Philosophical Notebooks*, critique the traditional theories and problems with the research that has been previously conducted on the *Philosophical Notebooks*, and then focus on explaining my theory of philosophical situating, which I propose in this book, as well as the draft text interpretive method and philosophical historical model. Part One primarily traces the general thread of young Lenin's understanding of philosophical theory. Here I begin with his first philosophical text, "What the 'Friends of the People Are,'" and examine his process of philosophical change until about the time of the writing of *Materialism and Empirio-Criticism*. Of course, the two subjects here are the interpretation of various historical documents written by young Lenin in his early political practical struggles before 1908, and the interpretation of the many reading notes and sparse separate notes taken by Lenin as he learns and studies philosophy between 1908 and 1913. The new understanding that I bring here focuses on young Lenin's philosophical materialist **Other theoretical mirror image** in the context of Marxist philosophy, as well as the connections and de-linking in his stance of political practice. In the second part, I focus on the excerpted notes and small number of independent thoughts taken and written by Lenin as he studied Hegel's philosophy between 1914 and 1915. This is a topical study of the *Bern Notebooks*. The central line of thought in the second part of this book, after overthrowing the a priori framework established in the "planned conception theory" proposed by past Soviet scholars, discovers the profound philosophical shift that Lenin experienced as he moved closer to truly understanding Hegel's philosophy; this shift was from an Other theoretical framework to an **independent reading** situating space. The analysis and discussion of this shift constitutes the most important progress made by this book in terms of Lenin's philosophical thought. It completely changes the traditional notions that have been promulgated by Soviet scholars for years. Furthermore, the latest results of my research demonstrate that even in the final revolutionary thought context of the *Bern Notebooks*, Lenin's understanding did not come close to surpassing the depth of thought in Marx's **historical** dialectic. Finally, I include an article on the theoretical logic of the dialectic which I wrote 25 years ago as an appendix to this book, because it is related to Hegel's The Science of Logic and the practical dialectical concepts developed by Lenin in the *Bern Notebooks*.

It can be seen that just like Marx Revisited, the primary thinking of this book is aimed at overthrowing past interpretive models.

I am somewhat surprised to look back today and realize that I have been studying Lenin's *Philosophical Notebooks* for over 25 years. In this space of time, which has stretched for almost as long as my entire career, the space between myself and Lenin's thought seems to have shrunk, but has also retreated from an assumed truth to a subjective theory of situating.

In the autumn of 2002, early snowflakes already swirl above Moscow's Red Square. Standing before Lenin's Mausoleum and gazing at the great man who seems merely to sleep, I stare for a long while at that face, seemingly so full of life. I think, was it really from this brain that sprung those radical thoughts which inspired the backwards, oppressed peoples of the world to rise up in opposition to the tyranny of capitalism? Was it really from this brain that emerged the texts that have moved the left-wing parties in the Eastern World for the past century? Was it really this brain that concocted the complex philosophical logic and discourse on which I painstakingly ponder night and day? During all these years writing and thinking on the historical development of Lenin's thought, what comes again and again to my mind is the face of a man, filled with proud revolutionary passion, shrouded by the swirling fog of war; however, the Lenin I see in my dreams does not sleep, but rather tirelessly speaks, reads, writes, and struggles.

Perhaps as moved as I, a tourist next to me murmurs to himself, and a statue-like Russian soldier nearby quietly stands and extends his index finger over his lips, calling us to silence as if fearing that we would wake the sleeping giant in our presence.

Sleep peacefully Lenin. Even if your material existence is someday buried, your thoughts have already been understood once more by the world[20]; the road to liberation that you paved, now once more echoes with the steps of giants in that piece of yellow earth far in the east.

Returning to Lenin means stepping into the future.

Zhang Yibing

Fourth manuscript revised in Taipei, Taiwan, October 2007

---

20   Professor Zizek recently wrote a book which shares its Chinese title with mine (the English version is titled Repeating Lenin). In June 2007, I invited Professor Zizek to speak at Nanjing University, and we had the opportunity to discuss this issue. The title of his book, unlike mine, was a call to repeat the heroic acts of Lenin as a never-yielding radical revolutionary. He was very moved when I said this, because not everyone had understood the point of his book. Professor Zizek told me that he even had a falling out with his old friend Laclau over this issue.

INTRODUCTION

1 *The Heterogeneity of Lenin's Thought*
2 *What kind of a "book" is made up of
  Lenin's Philosophical Notebooks?*
3 *The Basic Layout of Philosophical Notebooks*
4 *The Textual Structure of the Bern Notebooks*
5 *Overview of Past Research on
  Lenin's Philosophical Notebooks*
6 *Reconsidering the Issue from
  another Perspective*
7 *Bern Notebooks: The Historical Process
  of Lenin's Philosophical Shift that took
  place in His Study of Hegel's Thought*

INTRODUCTION

Lenin's *Philosophical Notebooks* are an extremely important, unfinished collection of manuscripts in the developmental history of Marxist philosophy. For the better part of a century and especially after the 1960s, Marxist scholars in both China and elsewhere engaged themselves in the profound research of these documents, which have been referred to as Lenin's philosophical "laboratory." These scholars were able to produce numerous writings and analyses, which were, for that time, of quite impressive quality[1]. On the other hand, a few modern Western "Leninologists" and Western Marxist scholars have expressed a great deal of interest in this body of texts, and although they have attained a great deal of success in their study of these writings, many of them pursue their research with the goal of finding evidence that will lead to the **self-rupture** of the progression of Lenin's philosophical thought; this is a goal with which I cannot agree[2]. This is why a seri-

---

1   Refer to Kedrov's Study of Lenin's *"Philosophical Notebooks,"* Huang Nansen's *"Philosophical Notebooks" and the Dialectic*, and Wang Dong's The *"Conception of Lenin" in Dialectical Scientific Systems*.
2   The actual differences between Marxism and Western Marxologie, Western Leninology and Western Mao-studies have been once again muddled by those who do not understand Marxism. It is laughable that non-Marxist "Marxologie" should become

ous study of the true logical line of thought in Lenin's *Philosophical Notebooks*, and especially the *Bern Notebooks*, is so important in our Marxist theoretical construction and ideological struggle today. The new Chinese edition of the Collected Works of Lenin (second edition, 60 volumes) provides an essential textual basis for this research. Here I will do my best to avoid using the traditional interpretive framework to re-annotate Lenin's thought, nor will I use **an *a priori*, subjective logical analytical method in examining Lenin's text**s; rather, I will truly and sincerely begin by simulating Lenin's line of thought as he read in order to investigate the underlying significance of the important logical shifts and leaps of understanding in the philosophical progression of Lenin's understanding and development of the materialist dialectic. This research will be based primarily on a new interpretive method, the theory of **philosophical situating**. This is an experiment, as well as another breakthrough in terms of interpretive models.

1 THE HETEROGENEITY OF LENIN'S THOUGHT

It is first important for me to make clear that Lenin's *Philosophical Notebooks* do not constitute a readily existent philosophical work; it merely brings together the various **heterogeneous**, diverse sub-texts and draft texts in Lenin's process of philosophical **learning** and research over the course of 20 years (from the late 19th century to the early 20th century). These documents directly reflect the fact that Lenin's process of philosophical learning and research was a complex process of thought and cognition that spanned many years. I emphasize the fact that this was a process of "learning" for Lenin in order to highlight the historical fact, hidden for many years under the facade of ideology, that young Lenin was not an expert philosopher. I would especially like to point out that Lenin was always a staunch Marxist; young Lenin had developed a good foundation and concrete research in economics and political theory. When I say that Lenin was always a Marxist,

---

their new orientation in constructing Marxist philosophy. Professor Yao Shunliang has written extensively on this discussion. Recently, along with Nanjing University's Professor Zhang Chuanping, I have begun to organize a translated series of Western Leninology works, and we have already purchased the rights to a number of works. Of these, the translation of Kevin Anderson's *Lenin, Hegel, and Western Marxism* has already been completed, and will soon be published in my Modern Scholarly Translations series. Professor Anderson himself was able to visit the Nanjing University Marxist Philosophy Department in October 2007 and deliver a topical lecture on his study of Lenin; during that visit, we were able to exchange ideas on a deep level.

more specifically I mean from the time he entered the Russian social historical scene with his revolutionary texts. Of course, during his adolescence and youth, Lenin did have a period when he was not a Marxist. Although he had brothers who directly participated in the democratic revolutionary struggle, he was most influenced by Russian Narodnik ideas. Data suggests that in Lenin began reading Marx's Capital in the fall of 1888, a study that would last a year. Although the Lenin family moved to Samara and he was preparing to earn his law degree, Lenin still found time to complete his study of *Capital*[3]. The objects of his study at the time included *The Communist Manifesto, The Condition of the English Working Class, The Poverty of Philosophy, The French Civil War, Critique of the Erfurt Program, The French Class Struggle, and Anti-Dühring*[4]. However, in terms of the recognition and understanding of philosophical thought, Lenin's 20 years of philosophical development was not an **absolutely homogeneous**, smooth process of change.

My reason for bringing up these issues is that in the traditional research of scholars from the former Soviet Union and Eastern Europe, there is a distinct lack of a historical **sense of time** in their understanding of the development of Lenin's philosophical thought. In order to build and uphold the image of Lenin as absolutely correct and always correct in the history of Marxist philosophy, they have no qualms about glossing over the **concrete theoretical nature** of Lenin's thought process, producing instead a **falsely smooth, homogeneous, continuous logical entity** to non-historically usurp the true Lenin. *Later on in this book, we will discuss the reasons for this historical phenomenon.* Therefore, in the commentary on the development of Lenin's thought by Soviet scholars, we cannot find the concrete changes that took place in Lenin's thought process over the course of 20 years, neither do we see differences between the different texts or the concrete improvements that Lenin made in his own understanding of philosophy. I believe that this is a concrete manifestation of the "glorious history" framework, premised by subjective idealist logic, in the study of Lenin's philosophy[5].

---

3   Fisher does not agree with this view, instead arguing that Lenin began to read *Capital* while in Samara. He also contends that Lenin still held Narodnik sympathies while living in Samara. See *The Life of Lenin* by Louis Fischer.

4   According to Adoratsky, Lenin took notes on Anti-Dühring, but these were later lost. See How *Lenin Studied Marx* by Adoratsky.

5   Refer to my article in the October 2005 edition of *Scholar's Monthly*: "How Should we Truthfully Review the Philosophical History of Marxism?"

I must point out that this phenomenon has also appeared in the study of Leninist philosophy outside of China; for instance, Balibar (a student of Althusser's), viewed Lenin's philosophy as a homogeneous thought entity, writing that it approached Darwinism and Socialism, and lay between historical Marxism and determinist Marxism[6].

Here I propose the epistemology that Lenin's philosophical thought can be thought of as comprising several definite **non-continuous** time periods. It is my opinion that the origins of Lenin's philosophical thought can be traced to the late 19th century, and that his internally logically linked progression of thought can be divided into three periods:

The **first** time period was Lenin's early philosophical developmental period, which began with "What the 'Friends of the People' Are and How They Fight the Social Democrats" (abbreviated below as "What the 'Friends of the People' Are") and continued until 1906[7]. During this period of time, Lenin's philosophical thought was not expressed as research and progress in terms of theoretical scholarship, but rather a process by which he, as a practical Marxist involved in a real revolution, flexibly employed Marxist philosophy. *Young Lukacs observed that the reality of the revolution was the centre of Lenin's thought, as well as the determining link between him and Marx (see **On Lenin**, 1924).* This observation is correct. I am of the opinion that this was primarily expressed as Lenin's emphasis on addressing the objective premise of social historical development and the versatility of the revolutionary historical subject at different periods of the Russian Revolution according to actual needs. *The author of volume 5 of the Soviet work **Philosophical History** believes that the first Leninist period in the history of Marxist philosophy came between 1894 and 1907. According to this belief, this was a period of time in which the Leninist period emerged in dialectical*

---

6   See Balibar's *The Philosophy of Marx.*
7   Lenin's original name was Vladimir Ilyich Ulyanov. He was born in April 1870 in the town of Simbirks to a family of intellectuals. His maternal grandmother was a German. In August 1887, Lenin entered Kazan University to study law; in December of that same year, he was arrested while participating in a student movement and expelled from the university. At that time, Lenin had already begun to come into contact with Marxist thought, translating *The Communist Manifesto* and portions of *Capital* from German. In 1889, Lenin's family moved to Samara, where he completed the requirements for law school. In 1891, he took the St. Petersburg University law exam, passing with excellent marks and thus receiving his diploma. In 1892, Lenin became an attorney's assistant before becoming a defense lawyer in the local Samara courts in March of that year. Lenin wrote "New Economic Developments in Peasant Life" in 1893. In that same year, 23 year old young Lenin moved to St. Petersburg and joined the Russian political struggle, and from there entered the scene of Russian history.

materialism and historical materialism[8]. *Furthermore, in terms of dialectical materialism, Lenin struggled against neo-Kantism, Narodism, and subjective socialism, while in terms of historical materialism, he proved the use of subjective elements in social life.* I believe that this overall conclusion is too abstract, because in these over 10 years of revolutionary practice, Lenin emphasized different topics at different times and in analyzing different real problems. My evaluation of this period of time is different from the views espoused by traditional Marxist philosophical historians; I have discovered that during this period of time, young Lenin **attached** himself to his teacher Plekhanov and the theoreticians of the Second International. Adoratsky[9] wrote that by this time, Lenin was already familiar with all the works of Plekhanov[10]. Deborin also pointed out that Lenin was a student of Plekhanov when it came to philosophy, which Lenin himself made clear more than once[11]. Furthermore, when it came to understanding the **philosophical** theory of Marxism, many of young Lenin's views were not completely accurate; he had not yet formed his own independent philosophical context or theoretical paths. *Soviet scholar Adoratsky wrote that by this time, Lenin had already given a "glowing commentary" on dialectical materialism, which proved that from his youth, Lenin had already read, studied, and grasped all the major works of Marx and Engels*[12]. *Such an assessment is obviously exaggerated, and forms the starting point for the false situating ideology in the study of Lenin's thought in the former Soviet Union. Adoratsky also believed that Lenin had taken notes on Anti-Dühring and other philosophical works, but that these notes had been lost.*

---

8   Dynnik, ed. *History of Philosophy*, volume 5. 1975. Beijing Sanlian Press, page 34 (Chinese).

9   **Vladimir Viktorovic Adoratsky** (1878-1945) was a well-known Soviet philologist. Adoratsky was born in the Russian Kazan Mountains in 1878 and passed away in 1945. In 1897 he entered Kazan State University studying law; there he was a classmate of Lenin. In 1900 he began to participate in revolutionary activities, joining the Bolsheviks in 1904. He participated in the general strike of 1905, and was consequently exiled. That same year, he met with Lenin in Switzerland. Starting in 1905, Lenin charged him with important research on Marx's writings. Adoratsky served as the head of the USSR National Archives as well as the vice-head of the Central Archive Institute.

10   Refer to Adoratsky's "On Lenin's Study of Philosophy" in *Selected Works of Adoratsky*.

11   Refer to the appendix of Deborin's *Philosophy and Politics*. Of course, Deborin came suffered Stalin's criticism for saying this historical truth, and was forced to delete it from later editions of *Philosophy and Politics*.

12   Refer to Adoratsky's "On Lenin's Study of Philosophy" in *Selected Works of Adoratsky*.

In the fall of 1893, Lenin moved from Samara to St. Petersburg, where he wrote the famous "What the 'Friends of the People' Are." The central thread of this work was opposition to Narodism; like Plekhanov, Lenin at this time emphasized the objective necessity for capitalism to develop in Russia. In December of 1895, Lenin was arrested and confined to prison, where after 14 months of imprisonment, he was exiled to Siberia in 1897. He remained in the village of Shushenskoye in the Minusinsky District, Yenisei Gubernia until 1900. *The author of the fifth volume of the Soviet Philosophical History claims that while in exile, young Lenin engaged himself in the profound study of the philosophical works of Kant, Hegel, and French materialists, exchanging a great number of letters with Plehanov on questions of philosophy[13]. According to Wittle, among the books that Lenin sent to his mother when he left exile in 1900, there were selections from Spinoza, Kant, Fichte, Feuerbach, Plekhanov, etc.[14]. However, there is no first-hand direct evidence to support these views. There is, on the other hand, evidence to suggest that between 1894 and 1895, Lenin studied Engels'* **The Origin of the Family, Private Property, and the State** *and* **The Housing Question**, *as well as volume three of Marx's Capital. In terms of philosophy, he assiduously read and studied* **The Holy Family** *by Marx and Engels, and read Mehring's* **Selected Works of Marx**, *Engels, and Lassalle in 1901 before Plekhanov. He would make specific mention of young Marx's doctoral thesis[15].* Between 1900 and 1903, young Lenin left Russia with his teacher Plekhanov and the other members of the "Labour Liberation Society," living in Switzerland, Germany, France, and England. His relationship with Plekhanov was close during this time. Existing evidence indicates that around 1903, Lenin attempted to study and learn Western philosophical history while living in Geneva, but he did not complete the construction of a logic of philosophical history at this time[16]. Because of these circumstances, the philosophical shifts that took place in Lenin's thought at this time were primarily influenced by Plekhanov and the other thinkers of the Second

---

13   Dynnik, ed. *History of Philosophy*, volume 5. 1975. Beijing Sanlian Press, page 34 (Chinese). Nadya Krupskaya also expressed similar views. See Krupskaya's *Remembering Lenin* (1972). People's Press, page 28.

14   See Wittle's *Dialectical Materialism*.

15   See Plekhanov's letter to Lenin on September 21, 1901.

16   Adoratsky once wrote that when Lenin was exiled between 1898 and 1898, he studied pre-Marxist philosophical history, including Spinoza, Hume, Kant, Fichte, Schelling, Hegel, and Feuerbach. Refer to Adoratsky's "On Lenin's Study of Philosophy" in *Selected Works of Adoratsky*.

International, as well as the demands of actual political struggle. During this period of time, Lenin had very little independent philosophical thought; the philosophical views of classical authors such as Engels, combined with those of Plekhanov and others, formed his **Other mirror image**. *My use of this concept borrows from Lacan's mirror stage theory, in which he proposes that the formation of man's psychological ego first identifies itself by establishing its relation to an external mirror.* What I wish to explain here is that young Lenin's philosophical views at this time were primarily **identified** and **accepted** through the external, authoritative theoretical logic of Plekhanov and other outside sources.

The **second** time period came between 1906 and 1913; I believe that this was an important period of time during which Lenin **studied and grasped the theories of philosophical materialism**. In November 1907, Lenin left Russia, spending over nine years in foreign lands. *He did not return to Russia until April 1917. In early January, 1908, after living in Stockholm and Berlin for a time, he settled in Geneva. During this time he travelled widely between many cities throughout Europe.* During this historical time, Lenin spent his time participating in ever-more intense political struggles, as well as the systematic study of philosophical theory. He made great progress in his understanding of the basic theories of Marxist philosophical materialism and epistemology. The author of the fifth volume of the Soviet Philosophical History believed that the second Leninist period in the history of Marxist philosophy came between 1908 and 1917. He claimed that this was a creative developmental period for dialectical materialism and historical materialism[17]. The logical confusion which I mentioned earlier takes place in the analysis of this period of time. This is because the 1908 work Materialism and Empirio-Criticism and the 1914-15 Bern Notebooks were arbitrarily viewed as a **homogeneous** logical continuum. Here we must be careful to both oppose Western Leninology's artificial logical rupture between Lenin's *Materialism and Empirio-Criticism* and *Bern Notebooks* while at the same time defining the internal links and important differences between these two critical texts. In 1906, in response to Anatoly Bogdanov's incorrect Machist views in his Empirio-monism, Lenin wrote a long essay entitled "The Philosophical Understanding of Ordinary Marxism," which took up three notebooks. Unfortunately,

---

17   Dynnik, ed. *History of Philosophy*, volume 5. 1975. Beijing Sanlian Press, page 37 (Chinese).

these notebooks were later lost. In early 1908, in order to more effectively oppose Machism and its Russian adherents, Lenin twice systematically learned and studied many philosophical texts; besides Marx,
Engels, and Plekhanov, he even studied many historical Western philosophers and modern schools of philosophy. Of these, the most important
and those on which he focused the most were by the materialist philosophers Feuerbach and Dietzgen, as well as the Russian materialist
philosopher Chernyshevsky. Through the academic study and logical
identification of the logic of philosophical materialism, Lenin became,
for the first time, a Marxist thinker with **profound philosophical training.** Lenin's *Materialism and Empirio-Criticism*, which was written
during this period of time, was a glorious work of active philosophical
materialism. Arrayed against the newest advances of natural science,
Lenin courageously defended the materialist premise of Marxism on
the front lines of the complex theoretical debate of his day. However,
his thinking at this time lacked a deep understanding of Marx's theory of historical dialectics **based on practice**, so that in his critique
of *Machism* and other idealist philosophies, there are numerous places
where Lenin's thought could be **made more profound.** *In particular,
here we must consider the Russian Marxist and Bolshevik Bogdanov's
deliberate mixing of philosophical materialism with the bourgeois economic fetishisms that Marx criticized. This mixing caused Lenin's theoretical critique and struggle to become that much more difficult and
complex. On this point, the critiques of Plekhanov, Deborin, and others
against Bogdanov lacked true theoretical punch. For a more in-depth
discussion, please refer to the appendix to the second chapter.* More importantly, Lenin was unable to connect philosophical materialism with
the revolutionary intentions of the Bolshevik party.

The **third** time period began in 1914, and most importantly Lenin's
topical study of Hegel's dialectics and epistemology between 1914 and
1916, *i.e.*, Lenin's constantly changing and leaping forward philosophical thoughts in the *Bern Notebooks*. Lenin arrived in Bern, Switzerland
on September 5, 1914, beginning his third systematic study of philosophy in a relatively short space of time. Lenin decided to systematically
learn and study Hegel's philosophy first because he carefully read the
correspondence between Marx and Engels in 1913, discovering that
when Marx and Engels discussed the dialectic, they always pointed to
Hegel at the same time. Second, he studied Hegel to meet the practical needs of the revolutionary struggle. I believe that through this third
study of philosophy during this period of time, Lenin was able to break

through the Other philosophical mirror image established by the explanatory discourse of Plekhanov and others and more profoundly understand and grasp the **revolutionary essence of the practical dialectic** in Marxist philosophy within an independent philosophical situating space. Thus he became a truly great Marxist philosopher. *However, it is important to point out that there is still a definite theoretical distance between the context of Lenin's understanding of Marx's logic of practical dialectics in the* **Berlin Notebooks** *and the logic of Marx's historical materialism and historical dialectic. We must take care to not non-historically exaggerate Lenin's philosophical theoretical thinking, which is an important logical level on which this book focuses.* It was precisely during this period of important philosophical progress that Lenin, through a more profound understanding of Marx's practical dialectic, discovered a true scientific methodological manual for the practice of the Russian social revolution. In the later Russian proletariat revolution, Lenin's deep understanding and utilization of the materialist dialectic truly caused Marxist scientific methodology to become a powerful spiritual weapon in the proletariat revolution and in the struggle and liberation of the oppressed peoples of the East. After the victory in the October Revolution, Lenin continued to pursue philosophical research[18]. He even directly proposed that a systematic study of Hegel's dialectic from a materialist perspective be organized, *i.e.*, the dialectic which Marx actually used in his *Capital* and other historical and political works[19]. It is evident that Lenin planned on continuing the important theoretical thought he began in the *Bern Notebooks*, but unfortunately history prematurely brought an end to this possibility.

In these three developmental periods, the texts we see are all different. Of course, in order to thoroughly study this 20-year-long process of philosophical shifting, my research is not restricted to Lenin's *Philosophical Notebooks*, which make up the primary object of this book; rather, my interpretive objects also include the other works and documents written by Lenin during these years. In addition to the famous Materialism and Empirio-Criticism, I have also studied "What

---

18   According to Adoratsky, Lenin purchased *Historical Materialism* and *On Philosophy*, two books by the Italian Marxist philosopher Labriola. In June 1921, Lenin again studied Hegel's Spiritual Phenomenology and *The Science of Logic* as well as Eelin's *Hegel's Philosophy: A Theory on the Concreteness of God and Man*. Refer to Adoratsky's "On Lenin's Study of Philosophy" in *Selected Works of Adoratsky*.

19   Lenin, Vladimir. "On the Significance of Militant Materialism." *The Collected Works of Lenin* (Chin. 2. Ed.) volume 43, page 29 (Chinese).

the 'Friends of the People' Are," and some of the correspondence between Lenin and Gorky, "Conspectus of *Correspondence of Marx and
Engels*," and *Karl Marx*, etc. The complete historical interpretation of
these texts will provide a new situating context for the philosophical
thought development of Lenin's early and middle years.

Let us first examine the basic layout of Lenin's *Philosophical Notebooks*.

2 WHAT KIND OF A "BOOK" IS MADE UP OF LENIN'S *PHILOSOPHICAL NOTEBOOKS*?

It is my understanding that, unlike the what all past researchers have
asserted, Lenin's *Philosophical Notebooks* are actually not a "book,"
not a work that he consciously wrote, neither are they a scholarly document in a proper sense. To be accurate, these notebooks are actually a
collection of Lenin's qualitatively different reading notes, thoughts, and
commentaries over the course of 20 years (from 1895 to 1916) brought
together, organized, and edited by later scholars. We have already seen
that this was a body of academic texts that include **many heterogeneous elements**. Each text reflects a different level of philosophical
research at different periods of Lenin's life; there is certainly no philosophical homogeneity here. Therefore, the practice of traditional researchers, in which heterogeneous texts from different time periods are
imagined to be **homogeneous** is illegitimate in terms of methodological
premise, non-scientific in terms of textual research methods, and necessarily subjectively illusory in terms of cognitive results. I believe that
to attempt to establish a kind of unified dialectic or epistemological
logical system for Lenin's 20 years of philosophical notes is, from the
start, a non-historical, ideological illusion and false academic situating
phenomenon.

At the same time, I realized that Lenin took these notes completely
for his own philosophical learning and research, and as such, we find
very little **external ideological language restrictions or linguistic em-
bellishment**. Because of this, the Lenin that we find reflected in these
notes is truer. One of my important views is that in these documents,
not all of Lenin's ideas are **absolutely correct, without mistake**; particularly in his early readings, there are different degrees of misunderstandings in his understanding of Marx, Engels, and the works of other
philosophers. To put it even more directly, the ideas and views that
Lenin expresses in these notes and commentaries are not all true. This

is a point that requires our judicious differentiation, and is also where I differ from traditional Leninist philosophical research in terms of **basic identification methods**. *Predrag Vranicki, a Marxist philosopher from the former Yugoslavia made a very profound observation in his History of Marxism. He points out that in the later development of Marxism, every view of Lenin (as well as those of Marx and Engels) was idolized. Some of the weak points in the classical thinkers were even made out to be strong points, becoming "sacrosanct"[20]. This is a tragedy in terms of the research methods of philosophical history.*

In volume 38 of the Collected Works of Lenin, there are collected a vast body of excerpts, short writings, notes, and commentaries made by Lenin between 1895 and 1916 as he studied philosophy. These make up what people normally refer to as Lenin's *Philosophical Notebooks*. These documents were not published during Lenin's life, neither were they published all at once.

I will now briefly outline what I understand about the logic of the textual layout and publishing situation of the Philosophical Notebooks. The first documents to come to scholarly attention were the excerpts and notes written by Lenin on Hegel, Feuerbach, and others while he lived in Bern, Switzerland; these comprised eight notebooks, what I refer to as the *Bern Notebooks*. These notebooks were the primary object of traditional studies on Lenin's *Philosophical Notebooks*. These documents were first published in the famous Soviet publication *Under the Banner of Marxism* in 1925 (Deborin was the editor-in-chief at the time). In that same year, the Soviet *Bolshevik* magazine published a portion of the notes, including Lenin's "Discussion on Dialectics." Almost the entire text of these notes was published in the ninth volume of the 1930 Russian edition of the *Collected Works of Lenin*[21] (the first three notebooks) and then twelfth volume (last five notebooks)[22]. At the time, these texts

20   Refer to the second volume of Vranicki's *The History of Marxism*.
21   I read through this book at the Russian National Archives; its publication date is 1929. It is a small, deluxe edition book, with a hard red cover, and it includes the first three notebooks of the *Bern Notebooks*. The cover of the book has a picture of Lenin from 1914, and its table of contents is found at the end of the book. The book begins with an introduction written by Deborin, containing five sections and 21 pages. After this comes an explanatory note by the publisher. Lenin's notes begin on the 24th page.
22   This book is also a deluxe edition with a light blue cover. The publishing date is 1930, and it contains the latter five notebooks of the *Bern Notebooks*, as well as Lenin's excerpts from *The Holy Family* written in 1895 and other notes. The introduction to this book was written by Adoratsky, it is divided into four sections and takes up 20 pages,

were titled "Philosophical Notebooks: Hegel, Feuerbach, and Others." In the twelfth volume was published, for the first time, Lenin's outline of *The Holy Family* and other philosophical notes. Among these notes were included three notes written by Lenin and Bukharin on Nevsky's *Dialectical Materialism and Dead, Reactionary Philosophy*[23], as well as Lenin's notes and excerpts on Clausewitz's theory of war. This last document was not included in the final Philosophical Notebooks. In 1933, these philosophical notes from different time periods were edited and independently published, under the title Philosophical Notebooks. The editors at the time were Adoratsky and Sorin. Between 1934 and 1958, six editions of this book were published. Afterwards, many of Lenin's other reading notes and related materials were published. It is important to remark that while Stalin was alive, these important texts were not included in the *Collected Works of Lenin*, simply in order to protect the **ideological theoretical authority** of *Materialism and Empirio-Criticism, which Stalin had officially approved. It is also in this sense that Stalin qualified Lenin's **Philosophical Notebooks** as immature "thought experiments."* After Stalin passed away, the editor of the fourth edition of the Russian *Collected Works of Lenin* re-edited and added to these texts, publishing them for the first time in volume 38[24]. The editor of the fifth edition of the Collected Works of Lenin again edited the notes and added some of the most important texts (including Lenin's notes on *The Works of Dietzgen*), published in volume 29[25]. I have remarked that in the overview of Soviet scholarly research on Lenin's *Philosophical Notebooks* in the 1980s, the

---

after which comes an explanatory note from the publisher to the reader. On pages 26 and 27 there is a facsimile of two pages from Lenin's notes on *The Holy Family*. The main body of text begins on the 28th page. Between pages 288 and 289 tehre is a facsimile of Lenin's "Conspectus on Hegel's *Dialectics*."

23   These notes were first published in volume 12 of the *Collected Works of Lenin* in 1920. It is likely that Lenin and Bucharin exchanged notes on the same written page at the time. The content of the notes deals with Bogdanov's *Tectology: The General Science of Organization* (1912), a book which greatly influenced Buharin's *Theory of Historical Materialism*. In these notes, however, we can see that Bucharin had already realized that Bogdanov's "tectology" was nothing more than "*Empirio-monism.*" Lenin's sarcastic reply was that Bucharin had "fallen for it," though Bucharin denied this. Refer to volume twelve of the *Lenin Manuscripts*, Soviet National Press, 1930, pages 384-5.

24   I purchased this book at a used bookstore in the 1980s. The layout and content of the documents in the book are almost completely identical to volume 38 of the Chinese translation of the *Complete Works of Lenin*, right down to its brown, deluxe hard cover.

25   I found this book in the Russian National Archives. Its layout and content are identical to the Chin. 2. Ed. of volume 55 of the *Complete Works of Lenin*, though the color of its cover is different.

work of Chinese Professor Wang Dong is extremely systematized and complete[26].

The first Chinese translation of *Lenin's Notebooks* appeared in the 1930s. In March 1935, in *Critique of Hegelian Philosophy*, translated and edited by Liu Ruoshui and published by the Shanghai Xinken Bookstore, under the heading "Overview of Hegel's Historical Philosophical Lectures" there were three documents from Lenin's *Bern Notebooks*: "Conspectus of Hegel's Book Lectures on the History of Philosophy," "Georges Noel: Hegel's *Logic*," and "Notes on Reviews of Hegel's *Logic*." In January 1939, the Yan'an Liberation magazine published "Lenin's Notes on the Dialectical Method" in volumes 60 and 61, translated and edited by Ai Siqi. These documents included three documents from Lenin's *Bern Notebooks*, namely "On the Question of Dialectics," the third part of "Conspectus of Hegel's Book *The Science of Logic*," and "Notes on Reviews of Hegel's Logic." In August 1949, the Liberation Publishing Company published Lenin's "Conspectus of Hegel's Book *The Science of Logic*," translated by Cao Baohua and edited by Bo Gu. This edition included the Chinese translation of the entire introduction written by Adoratsky for the twelfth volume of the Collected Works of Lenin. In 1956, the Chinese Communist Party Central Publishing and Translation Bureau first published an independent book of Lenin's *Philosophical Notebooks*, based on the 1947 Russian text[27]. In 1959, the Central Publishing/Translation Bureau published the first edition of the Collected Works of Lenin, including Lenin's Philosophical Notebooks as volume 38. This work was based on the fourth edition of volume 38 of the Russian text of the *Collected Works of Lenin*. In 1962 a single book containing the Philosophical Notebooks, organized almost exactly the same as volume 38 of the Collected Works was published[28]. The 1990 edition of volume 55 of the *Collected Works of Lenin* contains a new version of the *Philosophical Notebooks*, translated from volume 29 of the fifth edition of the Russian *Collected Works*. There have been somewhat large changes made in terms of content and layout compared with the earlier Chinese edition. Additionally, beginning in the 1970s, there appeared a few editions of Lenin's *Philosophical Notes* translated into minor Chinese dialects[29]. I would now like to briefly introduce the basic layout of these different editions.

---

26 Refer to Wang Dong's The "Conception of Lenin" in *Dialectical Scientific Systems*.
27 Lenin, Vladimir Ilyich. *Philosophical Notebooks*. People's Press (1956) (Chinese).
28 *Ibid.*
29 In July 1976, Lenin's "On the Question of Dialectics" was translated into Mongolian in stand-alone book form by the Xinjiang People's Press; in November 1979, Lenin's "Conspectus of Hegel's Book *The Science of Logic*" was translated and published in Mongolian.

The 1956 Chinese stand-alone edition of *Philosophical Notebooks* included 28 documents, the fewest of any Chinese edition of *Philosophical Notebooks*. *Here, a section of notes recorded just after "Conspectus of Aristotle's Book* **Metaphysics**" *was included as an independent text. Later editions combined these notes with the "Conspectus of Aristotle's Book* **Metaphysics.**" The documents here are divided into two levels: first, the excerpted notes and thoughts from 10 notebooks organized into 13 documents, and second, lower level texts, including reading notes and commentary organized into 15 documents. *In later editions of Philosophical Notebooks, the notes exchanged by Lenin and Bukharin on Nevsky were all left out. This was for a very simple reason: Bukharin had become a target of the revolution. Another possibility is that of the three notes exchanged between the two men, Lenin only wrote one line of the second note while Bukharin wrote the first and third.* I believe that this is a line of thought in the editing that lacks structure, causing the organization of the texts to appear somewhat crude. This will not be the focus of our discussion here.

The primary line of thought in the editing of the main text in volume 38 of the first Chinese edition of the *Collected Works of Lenin* (volume 38 of the fourth Russian edition) is a **historical logical framework**. *I will discuss later on the fact that this is the only correct organizational arrangement. There were 46 documents included in this edition. This was the edition of Lenin's Philosophical Notes that included the most number of texts.* However, in the actual editing process, the structure of the texts became extremely complicated. In this edition, the documents were divided into three **hierarchical levels** of differing importance. First were excerpted notes and Lenin's recorded thoughts on his readings, as well as some reading notes; the main text here is composed of Lenin's 10 independent notebooks, plus three books of notes taken between 1903 and 1904, as well as a bibliography from 1909. There are 27 documents included in this part, which are organized completely according to chronological order. "Conspectus of Feuerbach's Book *Exposition, Analysis and Critique of the Philosophy of Leibnitz*," which was note dated, was included at the end of the notebooks. *I am basically in agreement with how these texts were arranged.* This was the first important level of text. However, following this first level of chronologically ordered texts, we find the second level of texts, which were the reading notes that Lenin took between 1913 and 1916, organized into 14 documents. These documents were artificially divided into two parts: book titles and extremely short commentaries written by Lenin between 1912 and 1916, followed by four notebooks of reading notes taken between 1913 and 1916. *Five documents from the first part were deleted from volume 55 of the second Chinese edition of the* **Collected Works of Lenin***. The last document in the second part, "Hilferding's Finance and Capital" was also deleted in the second Chinese edition.* This was the second level of documents. The third level of documents is comprised of five documents of reading commentaries that Lenin wrote between 1908 and 1911. The organizational layout of these texts also does not take chronology into account. It is evident that this was the least important level of text. These three sections were not labelled with headings. In this edition, there are five pages of facsimiles of Lenin's original manuscripts (there are also three other photographs, one a portrait of Lenin, one of the cover of Lenin's "Conspectus of *The Science of Logic,*" and one of the Bern Library). This edition was organized according to a haphazard logical structure, being based on **incomplete historical chronology** as well as on **hierarchy of importance**.

Volume 55 of the second Chinese edition of the *Collected Works of Lenin* (volume 29 of the fifth Russian edition) completely abandoned the chronological organizational structure used in volume 38 of the first edition, and instead strengthened the **non-historical hierarchical structure** of the texts. In terms of textual selection, six documents were omitted from the second edition that had been included in the first[30], and five documents of reading notes were combined into two. Furthermore, two larger documents of reading notes were also added. This caused the number of texts to drop from 46 independent documents to 39, though the content actually increased. I believe that the textual structure here is a typical example of the **logic of artificial understanding**; the three levels of text, which were not very clear in the first edition, were made more evident in the second edition. The first group of texts was composed of research excerpted notes and thoughts; this was the primary content of Lenin's 10 notebooks. This group contained 11 excerpted documents under the title "Excerpts and Short Essays." Here, in order to relate Lenin's two sections of excerpted notes on Feuerbach, the editor placed "Conspectus of Feuerbach's Book *Exposition, Analysis and Critique of the Philosophy of Leibnitz*" in front of the eight *Bern Notebooks. There is some room for discussion on this editing decision.*

---

30 Professor Wang Dong mistakenly believes that seven documents were removed from "Notes on Imperialism," when in fact only six were removed. See *The "Conception of Lenin"* in *Dialectical Scientific Systems.*

This is because in terms of the content of thought in this notebook, logically it should come after Lenin had basically completed his study of Hegel's philosophy. This group was determined to be the **first** level of text. It is interesting to note that the documents included in one of Lenin's eight notebooks on Hegel's philosophy (entitled *Philosophical Notebook*) were divided into two parts. Three documents of excerpts and two documents of thoughts were included in the first level of text, while the rest were sent to the **second** level. *This means that the notes and thoughts written by Lenin in the same notebook were artificially broken apart by later scholars.* The second level of text was titled "Reading Notes on Books, Essays, and Book Reviews," and it included 21 documents. In the first place, the four documents of reading notes written between 1903 and 1909, which had been included in the chronological section in the first edition, were placed on this level of text, a fate shared by the 11 documents of reading text from the *Philosophical Notebooks* which juts discussed. One of the documents even had its name changed. The five original documents of reading notes were combined into two, and six were deleted. *This was perhaps because they directly included Lenin's "Notes on Imperialism"*[31]. The sequence of the text was also modified. The **last** level of text, just as in the first edition, included reading commentaries; the editors of the second edition titled this section "Commentaries." In terms of content, two new documents were added to this section, increasing the number of documents from five to seven. Additionally, seven pages of photographs were added to the original five pages (the portrait of Lenin was removed). *In the Chinese translation, a few essential words were also changed. I will analyze this issue later on in this book.*

It is my opinion that neither of these editions is ideal in terms of layout and structure, because there is too much artificial interference in both. They were both examples of the **subjective intentions and ideological frameworks** of the textual experts from the former Soviet Union and Eastern Europe. This is because in this non-historical textual interpretive framework, only in the arrangement of texts into "important" and "unimportant" can **ideological domination** from outside the text become apparent. I am opposed to these theoretical attacks from outside the text. I believe that to allow "things to be things" (to use Heidegger's words), to allow texts to flow in their original chronology, is the most natural method of organization. The only non-controversial

---

31 *The Collected Works of Lenin* (Chin. ? Ed.), volume 54.

way to organize these 20 years of philosophical notes is to strictly follow chronological sequence, tear down the hierarchy of texts, and allow what Lenin wrote in each year naturally come to the surface. This will give readers the truest form of textual existence, rather than forcing them to look through the dead, illusory lens of some textual expert's historical understanding.

Therefore, I advocate using the **overall chronological sequence** of the texts to interpret and study the process of change in Lenin's philosophical thought. *This is the historical research line of thought on which this book is based.* I have discovered that the Soviet scholar Volodin proposed a new editing plan; he believes that because Lenin's philosophical notebooks do not constitute a "book," the excerpts, summaries, reading notes, and other materials in the present volume 29 should be organized sequentially and placed into the other corresponding volumes of the *Collected Works of Lenin*[32]. Although I agree with Volodin's basic line of thought, I cannot agree with a plan to disperse and dilute Lenin's notes, burying them in other texts; so doing would annul the generative group of texts in the historical study of Lenin's philosophy. I propose that we keep Lenin's philosophical notes together in one volume, but that we strictly organize them according to chronology; those texts that are not dated can be included as appendices. At times, the simplest method is the truest. Of course, this is only the recommendation of a philosophical researcher, not a textual expert.

3 THE BASIC LAYOUT OF *PHILOSOPHICAL NOTEBOOKS*

There are 48 documents of the *Philosophical Notebooks* that we have available to us (39 documents from volume 55 of the second Chinese edition of the *Collected Works of Lenin* and 46 from volume 38 of the first edition). According to the research of scholars in the former Soviet Union[33] we have the following information about these documents[34]:

---

32 Refer to Volodin's "Lenin and Philosohpy: Should We Bring up this Question Again?" on page 132 of *Lenin Studies*.
33 Because all the documents in the Chinese edition of the *Philosophical Notebooks* and the *Collected Works of Lenin* were translated from corresponding Russian texts, when I refer to "editors" in this book, I mean textual experts and original editors from the Soviet Union and Eastern Europe.
34 My research is based on the Chin. 2. Ed. of the *Collected Works of Lenin* and other Chinese-language published materials.

The first document is "Conspectus of the Book *The Holy Family* by Marx and Engels," written by young Lenin in 1895[35]. This is the earliest "philosophical notebook" left to us by Lenin. The version of *The Holy Family* which Lenin read was published in 1845 by the Frankfort-on-Main Literary Publishing House. The editors deduced that these notes were taken by Lenin during his first trip outside of Russia as he attempted to establish ties with the Emancipation of Labour Group. Lenin did not mark a specific date on this text, but it was likely written while he studied at the Berlin Royal Library in August 1895. These excerpts were taken in a single notebook, and the manuscript took up 45 pages. Lenin wrote in German. This document was first published in 1930, in volume 12 of the *Collected Works of Lenin*. I will delve more deeply into the analysis of this text in the first chapter of this book.

The second and third documents are Lenin's reading notes on Fr. Überweg's *Outline of the History of Philosophy* (published in Leibniz between 1876 and 1880) and Fr. Paulsen's *Introduction to Philosophy* (published in Moscow in 1899[36])[37]. These two documents were completed by Lenin while living in Geneva in 1903. These reading notes were written in a single notebook, both preceded and followed by economics notes. Both were published for the first time in 1930 in volume 12 of the Russian *Collected Works of Lenin*.

The fourth document was written by young Lenin in 1904: "Note on a Review of *The Wonders of Life* and *The Riddle of the Universe* by E. Haeckel"[38]. This book review was published in the November 15 edition of the *Frankfurter Zeitung*. These reading notes were written by Lenin on a single free page. Lenin took most of the page to discuss many foreign language books on the question of land. This document was published for the first time in volume 38 of the fourth edition of the Russian *Collected Works of Lenin* in 1958.

---

35 *The Collected Works of Lenin* (Chin. 1. Ed.), volume 38, pages 5-38; *The Collected Works of Lenin* (Chin. 2. Ed.), volume 55, pages 5-36.

36 The *Collected Works of Lenin* (Chin. 1. Ed.), volume 38; in the first edition, the pages in the original Russian version were included, though this information was deleted from volume 55 of the second Chinese version.

37 *The Collected Works of Lenin* (Chin. 1. Ed.), volume 38, pages 39-42; *The Collected Works of Lenin* (Chin. 2. Ed.), volume 55, pages 5-36.

38 *The Collected Works of Lenin* (Chin. 1. Ed.), volume 38 contains the publication date, name, and original author, but volume 55 of the second edition deletes this information. Refer to *The Collected Works of Lenin* (Chin. 1. Ed.), volume 38, pages 43-44 and *The Collected Works of Lenin* (Chin. 2. Ed.), volume 55 page 327.

These four documents represent some of the notes that young Lenin took as he learned and studied philosophy. These can be seen as the first group of text. At this point, we cannot say that Lenin **systematically** studied philosophy. Lenin's first systematic study of philosophical theory began in 1908, with the theoretical preparation he undertook in opposition to *Machism*. Documents five through seventeen reflect this process, and these thirteen documents make up the second group of texts.

The fifth document was written by Lenin in May 1908: commentaries on Plekhanov's *Fundamental Questions of Marxism*[39]. These notes recorded Lenin's understanding of his philosophy teacher Plekhanov's basic viewpoints as he began to write *Materialism and Empirio-Criticism*. Parts of this document were first published in volume 25 of the Russian *Collected Works of Lenin*, and the text in its entirety was published in 1958 in volume 38 of the fourth edition of the *Collected Works of Lenin*. I believe that this was an important guiding text in Lenin's systematic philosophical study; the place of Feuerbach, Dietzgen, and other philosophers in the annals of philosophical materialism was established here. We will discuss this document further in the second chapter of this book.

The sixth document includes the commentaries that Marx took on Joseph Dietzgen's *Collection of Brief Philosophical Works* (published in Stuttgart in 1903)[40]. This text was first published in volume 55 of the Chin. 2. Ed. of the *Collected Works of Lenin*. Lenin's commentaries on this book were not completed all at once, and his notes and markings were made with four different coloured pencils. Most of the commentaries were written as he was in the process of writing *Materialism and Empirio-Criticism*. As such, the time of this commentary was probably between February and October of 1908. In 1913, Lenin read this book again as he wrote an article commemorating the 25th anniversary of the death of Dietzgen. I should make it clear that these were two different groups of commentaries from different time periods **combined together**; it is fortunate that by 1913, Lenin had not yet experienced any great philosophical shift, and so these draft texts were, in general, **homogeneous**. This document was published for the first time in volume 29 of the fifth Russian edition of the *Collected Works of Lenin* in

---

39 *The Collected Works of Lenin* (Chin. 1. Ed.), volume 38, pages 457-461; *The Collected Works of Lenin* (Chin. 2. Ed.), volume 55, pages 445-448.
40 *The Collected Works of Lenin* (Chin. 2. Ed.), volume 55, pages 359-444.

1963. According to my newest research, this draft text has important significance in terms of the development of Lenin's Other mirror image in his philosophical materialism. We will discuss this important document further in the third chapter of this book. This is the first time a Chinese scholar has interpreted this text.

The seventh document consists of commentaries that Lenin took in October 1908 on V. Shulyatikov's *The Justification of Capitalism in West-European Philosophy* (published in Moscow in 1908)[41]. These were reading notes and commentaries that Lenin completed as he finished writing *Materialism and Empirio-Criticism*. This document was first published in 1937, in the Soviet magazine *Proletarskaya Revolyutsia*.

The eighth document consists of commentaries written by Lenin in 1909 on Abel Rey's Modern Philosophy (published in Paris in 1908)[42]. This was a continuation of Lenin's critique of another of Rey's books – *The Physics Theories of Modern Physicists* (1907) in Lenin's *Materialism and Empirio-Criticism*. This document was published independently in the Russian edition of *Philosophical Notebooks* in 1933. We will discuss the seventh and eighth documents in greater depth in the fourth chapter.

The ninth document consists of reading notes that Lenin took in the latter half of 1909 on the books on the natural sciences and philosophy in the Sorbonne Library. This was primarily an overview of recently published books and periodicals between 1908 and 1909[43]. Lenin mentions six books on physics, two periodicals that he read, and a number of books on modern European philosophy and science published between 1908 and 1909. Of these, the page numbers of the corresponding material of several books are recorded[44]. This document was published, in part, in volume 25 of the 1933 Russian edition of the *Collected Works of Lenin*.

---

41   This article of summaries was originally placed after Deborin's *Dialectical Materialism* in volume 38 of the first edition of *The Collected Works of Lenin*, but was moved before the Levine's commentaries of *Modern Philosophy* in volume 55 of the second edition. Refer to *The Collected Works of Lenin* (Chin. 1. Ed.), volume 38 pages 5-38; *The Collected Works of Lenin* (Chin. 2. Ed.), volume 55, pages 545-564.

42   *The Collected Works of Lenin* (Chin. 1. Ed.), volume 38, pages 462-536; *The Collected Works of Lenin* (Chin. 2. Ed.), volume 55, pages 465-515.

43   *The Collected Works of Lenin* (Chin. 1. Ed.), volume 38, pages 45-49: *The Collected Works of Lenin* (Chin. 2. Ed.), volume 55, pages 328-330.

44   Volume 38 of the first edition of *The Collected Works of Lenin* includes the name, author, and original Russian notes written by Lenin on this text; volume 55 of the second edition deletes this information.

The tenth document is a collection of important excerpted notes. We can assume that these are Lenin's "Conspectus of Feuerbach's Book *Lectures on the Essence of Religion*," which he wrote about the same time as *Materialism and Empirio-Criticism*[45]. We can only assume this because this document is not specifically dated, and there are two possible time frames in which it could have been written. The first possibility is that it was written between 1909 and 1912, specifically when he was researching at the Paris National Library between January and June 1909, though he remained in Paris until 1912. The second possibility was that he wrote it during his last visit to Paris in January 1914. As such, the editor labelled this document "Not earlier than 1909." The results of my textual research show that I tend to believe the first possibility that this text was written between January and June of 1909. This is because here, as with his *Materialism and Empirio-Criticism*, the focus of Lenin's thought was still **philosophical materialism**. This was the beginning of Lenin's second systematic study of philosophy. These notes were not taken in a separate notebook, but were rather written on leafs of free paper[46]. Of course, we know that around 1914 Lenin again looked at these notes, because on the first page he wrote "Feuerbach volume 8," using the blue pencil made famous in the *Bern Notebooks*. This document was published for the first time in volume 12 of the Russian *Collected Works of Lenin*, and we will analyze it in greater depth in chapter five of this book.

The eleventh document consists of commentaries that Lenin made on Deborin's *Dialectical Materialism*, published in the collection Na Rubezhe, St. Petersburg, 1909[47]. The full text of this document was published for the first time in volume 38 of the Russian fourth edition of the *Collected Works of Lenin*.

The twelfth document consists of commentaries made by Lenin between October 1909 and April 1911 on Plekhanov's book on *N. G.*

45 *The Collected Works of Lenin* (Chin. 1. Ed.), volume 38, pages 51-79; *The Collected Works of Lenin* (Chin. 2. Ed.), volume 55, pages 37-59.

46 Professor Wang Dong calls this a "separate notebook" without a cover. See Wang Dong's *The "Conception of Lenin" in Dialectical Scientific Systems*. Chinese Social Science Press (1989), page 28 (Chinese).

47 Volume 55 of the second edition of *The Collected Works of Lenin* incorrectly titles this text "Commentaries on A. Deborin's Dialectical Materialism." See *The Collected Works of Lenin* (Chin. 1. Ed.), volume 38 pages 537-545; *The Collected Works of Lenin* (Chin. 2. Ed.), volume 55, pages 516-522.

Chernyshevsky (St. Petersburg, 1910)[48]. The full text of this document was published in volume 38 of the Russian fourth edition of the *Collected Works of Lenin*.

The thirteenth document consists of commentaries on Yuri Steklov's *Chernyshevsky's Life and Activities (1828-1889)* (published in 1909 in St. Petersburg)[49]. This is a document that was added in the latest edition, and was first published in volume 67 of *Literary Heritage* magazine in 1959. We will discuss documents eleven through thirteen in chapter 6.

Documents fourteen through seventeen consist of reading notes taken by Lenin in 1913. These notes were disjointly taken in a book of notes on "Austrian Farming Statistics," obviously not Lenin's philosophy and research, but rather a continuation of his thoughts in his two forays into the study of philosophy. The fourteenth document contains two bibliographic articles on works of philosophy and science[50]; the fifteenth contains a book review and reading notes on Plenge's *Marx and Hegel*[51]; the sixteenth contains a review of Perry's *Present Philosophical Tendencies*[52]; the seventeenth contains reading notes on Aliotta's *The Idealist Reaction against Science*[53]. These documents were first published in volume 31 of the Russian *Collected Works of Lenin* in 1938. These documents do not contain qualitatively important content.

---

48   Plekhanov's work was first published as an essay in 1892; in 1894 he published a stand-alone German edition, and after corrections by Plekhanov himself in 1909, it was published as a book in St. Petersburg in 1910. See *The Collected Works of Lenin* (Chin. 1. Ed.), volume 38 pages 565-626; *The Collected Works of Lenin* (Chin. 2. Ed.), volume 55, pages 523-559.

49   *The Collected Works of Lenin* (Chin. 2. Ed.), volume 55, pages 560-610.

50   Lenin read this book in his second systematic study of philosophy.

51   *The Collected Works of Lenin* (Chin. 1. Ed.), volume 38, page 449; *The Collected Works of Lenin* (Chin. 2. Ed.), volume 55, page 331.

52   *The Collected Works of Lenin* (Chin. 1. Ed.), volume 38 pages 450-451; *The Collected Works of Lenin* (Chin. 2. Ed.), volume 55, page 332.

53   *Ibid.*, page 333.

4 THE TEXTUAL STRUCTURE OF THE *BERN NOTEBOOKS*

Beginning with the eighteenth document, we enter the third time period in Lenin's philosophical development, which was also his third systematic study of philosophy and Hegel's philosophy in particular. During this period of time, Lenin directed his thoughts towards the **dialectic**. It is important that we understand that here Lenin was not writing an already-"conceived" philosophical book of **research notes and topical materials**, but rather merely his general notes as he attempted to understand Hegel's philosophy and thereby more deeply grasp Marx's materialist dialectical thinking. This is the third group of materials. This group encompasses documents eighteen through twenty eight; spanning 1914 and 1915, it includes the important excerpted notes and thoughts that Lenin wrote while living in Bern, Switzerland and studying Hegel's philosophy. Of course, this is the focus of the discussion in the second part (six chapters) of this book. I believe that these documents can be referred to as Lenin's *Bern Notebooks*. *This is the primary content that I deal with when I refer to Lenin's **Philosophical Notebooks**.* We already know that Lenin read Hegel's philosophy around September 1914 as he moved from Poronin, Austria to Bern. According to the markings and library records found later, we can confirm that Lenin completed his entire process of reading and research in the Bern Library.

There are eight total notebooks in Lenin's *Bern Notebooks*. Beginning with the first notebook, Lenin expounds a framework from which he intends to comprehensively and systematically study Hegel's philosophy. Lenin, of course, dealt first with Hegel's The Science of Logic, producing the most important and valuable document of the Bern Notebooks. The version of Hegel's *The Science of Logic* that Lenin read was included in volumes three to six of the German *Collected Works of Hegel*; of these, "Logic" occupied volumes 3-5 and "Small Logic" volume 6. *Lenin's mother had German blood, and thus Lenin was able to master German.* Lenin also read in English and French. The eighteenth document, which includes the majority of the excerpted notes on The Science of Logic, was completed on December 17, 1914 according to his own notation on the notebook[54]. Lenin's excerpted notes were completed

---

54   *The Collected Works of Lenin* (Chin. 2. Ed.), volume 55, page 202. However, after this Lenin also read the ending portion of *The Shorter Logic* in volume 6 of *The Collected Works of Hegel.*

in three notebooks[55]. According to Lenin's own pagination, 48 pages were used in the first notebook. It included excerpted content from the preface to the first and second editions of *The Science of Logic*, the introduction, "The Doctrine of Being," and the first part of "Essence."

38 pages of the second notebook were used by Lenin as part of the *Bern Notebooks* (pages 49 to 88). Excerpted material in this part came from the second part of "Essence," as well as "The Doctrine of the Notion." 26 pages of the third notebook were used by Lenin (pages 89 to 115), and it includes the main text of "The Doctrine of the Notion." In addition, excerpts from Hegel's *Small Logic* (volume six of the *Collected Works of Hegel*) are interspersed through the second and third notebooks. The second part of the third notebook also includes two other documents of reading notes. The first of these is the nineteenth document, "On Hegel's Newest Documents"[56] while the second is the twentieth document, excerpts from Perrin's *Treatise on Physical Chemistry. Principles*[57]. Parts of these documents were published in the first and second editions of the 1925 *Under the Banner of Marxism* magazine, and their entire text was published in volume 9 of the Russian *Collected Works of Lenin*.

In another notebook labelled "Other + Hegel," Lenin wrote three documents of reading notes, including the twenty-first document (reading notes on Peter Genov's Feuerbach's *Epistemology and Metaphysics*)[58], the twenty-second document (reading notes on Paul Volkmann's *Epistemological Foundations of the Natural Sciences*)[59], and the twenty third document (reading notes on Max Verworn's *The Hypothesis of Biogenesis*)[60]. Following this, Lenin includes excerpts from Hegel's *Lectures on the History of Philosophy*; this twenty-fourth document was written in two separate notebooks[61]. Afterwards, Lenin began a new notebook, titling it "Hegel." This notebook primarily contains excerpts

---

55   *The Collected Works of Lenin* (Chin. 1. Ed.), volume 38, pages 81-257; *The Collected Works of Lenin* (Chin. 2. Ed.), volume 55, pages 71-206.

56   *The Collected Works of Lenin* (Chin. 1. Ed.), volume 38, pages 259-267; *The Collected Works of Lenin* (Chin. 2. Ed.), volume 55, pages 336-340.

57   *The Collected Works of Lenin* (Chin. 1. Ed.), volume 38, page 367; *The Collected Works of Lenin* (Chin. 2. Ed.), volume 55, page 340.

58   *The Collected Works of Lenin* (Chin. 1. Ed.), volume 38, pages 369-371; *The Collected Works of Lenin* (Chin. 2. Ed.), volume 55, pages 5-36.

59   *The Collected Works of Lenin* (Chin. 1. Ed.), volume 38, pages 372-373; *The Collected Works of Lenin* (Chin. 2. Ed.), volume 55, page 343.

60   *The Collected Works of Lenin* (Chin. 1. Ed.), volume 38, pages 374-375; *The Collected Works of Lenin* (Chin. 2. Ed.), volume 55, page 344.

61   *The Collected Works of Lenin* (Chin. 1. Ed.), volume 38, pages 369-339; *The Collected Works of Lenin* (Chin. 2. Ed.), volume 55, pages 207-268.

from Hegel's *Lectures on the History of Philosophy*[62], and is the twenty-fifth document. In this notebook, Lenin also recorded excerpts from "Hegel on Plato's Dialogues"; these are the last supplementary notes in the second volume of Hegel's *Lectures on the History of Philosophy* (volume 14 of the *Collected Works of Hegel*). As such, it is not an independent document[63]. All of these documents were first published in volume 12 of the Russian *Collected Works of Lenin* in 1930.

The last notebook was a record of the final reading and thought experiments the Lenin conducted with relation to Hegel. Lenin titled it "Philosophy." Here there are 10 separate documents. We find excerpts from Lenin's continued study of works on natural science, as well as research books on ancient Greek philosophy and dialectical thinking, including Aristotle's *Metaphysics*, Lassalle's *The Philosophy of Heraclitus the Obscure of Ephesus*, and Noel's *Hegel's Logic*. There are also two short self-summaries that Lenin writes on his study of Hegel's philosophy. In sequential order, these documents are: the twenty-sixth document (reading notes on Dannemann's *How did Our Picture of the World Arise?*)[64], the twenty-seventh document (reading notes on Darmstaedter's *Handbook on the History of the Natural Sciences and Technique*)[65], the twenty-eighth document (reading notes on Napoleon's *Pensées*)[66], the twenty-ninth document (reading notes on Noel's *Hegel's Logic*)[67], the thirtieth document ("Plan of Hegel's Dialectics (*Logic*)")[68], the thirty-first document (reading notes on Haas' *The Spirit of Hellenism*

---

62   *The Collected Works of Lenin* (Chin. 1. Ed.), volume 38, pages 341-353; *The Collected Works of Lenin* (Chin. 2. Ed.), volume 55, pages 269-278.

63   *The Collected Works of Lenin* (Chin. 1. Ed.), volume 38, page 339; *The Collected Works of Lenin* (Chin. 2. Ed.), volume 55, pages 267-268. Both editions place this text after Lenin's notes on Hegel's *Lectures on the History of Philosophy*.

64   *The Collected Works of Lenin* (Chin. 1. Ed.), vol. 38, p. 376-377; *The Collected Works of Lenin* (Chin. 2. Ed.), vol. 55, p. 347. Vol. 38 of the first edition of *The Collected Works of Lenin* include the original title and author of this text while vol. 55 of the second edition deletes this information.

65   *The Collected Works of Lenin* (Chin. 1. Ed.), volume 38, page 378; *The Collected Works of Lenin* (Chin. 2. Ed.), volume 55, page 348. Volume 38 of the first edition of *The Collected Works of Lenin* include the original title and author of this text while volume 55 of the second edition deletes this information.

66   *The Collected Works of Lenin* (Chin. 1. Ed.), volume 38, page 379; *The Collected Works of Lenin* (Chin. 2. Ed.), volume 55, page 349.

67   *The Collected Works of Lenin* (Chin. 1. Ed.), volume 38, pages 359-366; *The Collected Works of Lenin* (Chin. 2. Ed.), volume 55, pages 279-285. Volume 38 of the first edition of *The Collected Works of Lenin* include the original title and author of this text while volume 55 of the second edition translates this information into Chinese.

68   *The Collected Works of Lenin* (Chin. 1. Ed.), volume 38, pages 354-358; *The Collected Works of Lenin* (Chin. 2. Ed.), volume 55, pages 286-291.

in Modern Physics)[69], the thirty-second document (reading notes on Lipps' *Natural Science and World Outlook*)[70], the thirty-third document ("Conspectus of Lassalle's Book *The Philosophy of Heraclitus the Obscure of Ephesus*")[71], the thirty-fourth document (*On the Question of Dialectics*)[72] and the thirty-fifth document ("Conspectus of Aristotle's Book *Metaphysics*")[73]. Besides *On the Question of Dialectics*, which was published in 1925 in the Soviet magazine Bolshevik, the rest of the documents here were published for the first time in volume 12 of the Russian *Collected Works of Lenin*.

At the end of the *Bern Notebooks,* we find "Conspectus of Feuerbach's Book *Exposition, Analysis and Critique of the Philosophy of Leibnitz.*" I have reason to believe that Lenin's first impression of this book came when he read Feuerbach's *Lectures on the Essence of Religion* in 1909, because Feuerbach mentions this book in the last lecture. Furthermore, this piece may be a side-effect of his thought shift that came after reading the *Correspondence of Marx and Engels* in late 1913, because there he saw in a letter from Marx on January 11, 1868 that Feuerbach did not understand dialectics[74]; Lenin also saw that Marx wrote of his "admiration" for Leibnitz[75]. These factors contributed to Lenin's decision to read this book by Feuerbach after studying Hegel. Of course, here I am only hypothesizing. In addition, an examination of the specific content of this notebook reveals that the thoughts and views expressed by Lenin in these commentaries could not have come **before** his research on *The Science of Logic*. This thirty-sixth document was written in a separate notebook, title "Feuerbach": Lenin did not mark the date of its

69   *The Collected Works of Lenin* (Chin. 1. Ed.), volume 38, page 380; *The Collected Works of Lenin* (Chin. 2. Ed.), volume 55, page 349. Volume 38 of the first edition of *The Collected Works of Lenin* include the original title and author of this text while volume 55 of the second edition deletes this information.
70   *The Collected Works of Lenin* (Chin. 1. Ed.), volume 38, page 381; *The Collected Works of Lenin* (Chin. 2. Ed.), volume 55, page 350.
71   *The Collected Works of Lenin* (Chin. 1. Ed.), volume 38, pages 384-402; *The Collected Works of Lenin* (Chin. 2. Ed.), volume 55, pages 292-304.
72   *The Collected Works of Lenin* (Chin. 1. Ed.), volume 38, pages 403-412; *The Collected Works of Lenin* (Chin. 2. Ed.), volume 55, pages 305-311.
73   *The Collected Works of Lenin* (Chin. 1. Ed.), volume 38, pages 413-423; *The Collected Works of Lenin* (Chin. 2. Ed.), volume 55, pages 312-319.
74   Lenin, Vladimir. "The Correspondence of Marx and Engels." In *The Collected Works of Lenin*, volume 58, page 145 (Chin. 2. Ed.).
75   In the first edition of the Chinese Collected Works of Lenin, this notebook was placed after the *Bern Notebooks*; in the second edition it was placed in front. I agree with the latter method.

writing. This document was first published in volume 12 of the Russian *Collected Works of Lenin* in 1930.

Finally, both Chinese editions included portions of Lenin's "Notes on Imperialism," which he wrote between 1915 and 1916. Volume 38 of the first edition includes eleven documents (documents 37 through 48). First, nine documents of bibliographic information and a few commentaries were published, almost exactly in the same format as the original[76].Second, a few of Lenin's comments on Hilferding's *Finance Capital* were included, primarily focusing on Hilferding's discussion of *Machism*[77]. Finally is included Lenin's semi-independent notes on Johann Plenge's *Marx and Hegel* included in the second book of his "Notes on Imperialism"[78], a document that Lenin had read over in the past. Volume 55 of the second Chinese edition, on the other hand, deleted much of the bibliographic information, as well as Lenin's commentary on Hilferding's *Finance Capital*, leaving only some of the bibliographic information[79] and Plenge's *Marx and Engels*[80]. These documents were published between 1933 and 1936 in volumes 22, 27, and 29 of the Russian *Collected Works of Lenin*.

In these notes, Lenin used underlining to emphasize certain parts of the text. Parts of the text are underlined once to show importance, while others are underlined twice to show even greater importance. *In the Chinese translation, Lenin's single underlining is expressed using bolded characters, while his double underlining is expressed using bolded characters and emphasis marks.* In general, Lenin would often use big or small squares to encapsulate his more important independent ideas. There are roughly 170 such squares in the *Notebooks. Some Soviet scholars believe that the text in the squares represent Lenin's "mature viewpoints," his "ultimate conclusions"*[81]. *This is, of course, inaccurate.* Furthermore, there are many other markings in the notebooks, which were mostly related to Lenin's specific use in other textual contexts, they did not have any absolutely fixed meaning. I believe that we should not be too inflexible in our interpretation and identification

76   *The Collected Works of Lenin* (Chin. 1. Ed.), volume 38, pages 445-448.
77   *Ibid.*, page 454.
78   *Ibid.*, pages 440-443; The Collected Works of Lenin, volume 55, pages 353-356.
79   *Ibid.*, pages 351-352.
80   *Ibid.*, pages 353-356.
81   Refer to Kiselyov's *On Lenin's "Philosophical Notebooks."* People's Press (1956) pages 4 and 6 (Chinese).

of these symbols. I will give further explanation of this point when we come to concrete textual analysis.

5 OVERVIEW OF PAST RESEARCH ON LENIN'S *PHILOSOPHICAL NOTEBOOKS*

In the traditional research on the *Philosophical Notebooks* conducted by Soviet and Western "Leninology" scholars, Lenin's notes and reading notes taken as he studied and learned philosophy between 1895 and 1913 – and in particular the many reading commentaries that have already been published – have largely been ignored. In the scope of this research, these commentaries are seen as secondary material outside the realm of **excerpted** notes; save for a general mention in a few scholarly works, these documents have not become the object of in-depth study. Furthermore, researchers have not realized that these notes provide us with an important logical thread, one which ties together the whole evolution of Lenin's philosophical thought. Almost without exception, the main focus of the research on Lenin's *Philosophical Notebooks* has been on his *Bern Notebooks*, even non-scientifically using the appellation *Philosophical Notebooks* in reference to the *Bern Notebooks*. This is a truly bizarre logical replacement by which a single point is used in the attempt to cover an entire surface.

We can go so far as to say that in terms of the current research on the Philosophical Notebooks, the false image that continues to dominate the scholarly scene is this: the *Philosophical Notebooks* (which are really just the *Bern Notebooks*) were an incomplete work by which Lenin creatively **constructed a system of materialist dialectics** in his process of reconstructing Hegel's philosophy. *Of course this does not account for the views of Western Marxism and Western Leninology; according to the scholars of these schools, Lenin's Philosophical Notebooks (which are really just the **Bern Notebooks**[82]) are a **declaration of conversion to Hegel's idealism**. These scholars even believe that the Philosophical Notebooks annul the materialist conceptual framework established in **Materialism and Empirio-Criticism**. This is a myth established by Western Leninologists in the wake of the Western Marxologie theories of "Two Marxes" (the humanist young Marx and*

---

82   Both the French and English translations of Lenin's *Philosophical Notebooks* included only those research notes which Lenin took in his study of Hegel's philosophy between 1914 and 1915; thus for them, *Philosophical Notebooks* were what I call the Bern Noteooks.

*the scientific socialist old Marx) and "Marx-Engels Antagonism,"
that there are "Two Lenins" (the old materialist Lenin of **Materialism
and Empirio-Criticism** and the Hegelian idealist of the **Philosophical
Notebooks**).* I am firmly opposed to such theories. In these theories,
Lenin's Philosophical Notebooks are identified as a **homogeneous**,
scientific work of Marxist philosophy. In their examination of the
Philosophical Notebooks, scholars have imagined an ***absolute level of
maturity*** for this "work" of Lenin's; there are almost no researchers
who call into question the absolute correctness of the *Philosophical
Notebooks. "Lenin never made a mistake".* This was both an ideological legacy left by the Marxist research of the former Soviet Union, as
well as "common knowledge" developed over many years of Marxist
philosophical historical research in China. I cannot but say that this is a
false academic image and a **logical shadiness**[83].

We must make clear that the results of my research on Lenin's
Philosophical Notebooks directly refute these ideological theoretical
prejudices. In order to postulate these historical preconceptions, in order to create a situating space in which to "revisit" the development of
Lenin's philosophical thought, here let us first engage in a discussion
of **philosophical genealogy**[84] or **archaeology of academic logic**. To
accomplish this, we will review the historical process of the traditional
research methods.

After its victory in the October Revolution, although the new red government expulsed a good number of intellectuals[85], Lenin did not oppose
himself to Deborin and the other Mensheviks simply because of past
political divisions. The first scholar to write on Lenin's *Philosophical*

83   Here I use logical "shadiness," which appears to be a qualitative identification of
a thing or object; in fact I mean something quite different. The word shadiness, from
the French "louche," actually means something that appears to have one connotation
but actually connotes something quite different entirely. I borrow this concept from
Bourdieu.
84   Modern academic genealogical studies began with Nietzche's analysis of the latent logical framework in Christian culture; genealogical research means examining
the birth, development, and death of the underlying logical thread of a cultural philosophy or academic discourse through investigation of textual historical materials and
phenomena.
85   According to textual records, in August of 1922 the Soviet government arrested
over 100 bourgeois intellectuals, exiling them over the course of the next few months.
Among those exiled was Eelin; legend has it that after reading Eelin's *Hegelian
Philosophy's Concrete Explanation of Man and God*, Lenin tried to have him freed, but
he was exiled in spite of Lenin's efforts.

Notebooks was Deborin. *At this time, Bogdanov, Lunacharsky, and others who held incorrect Machist views were still working normally and engaging in scholarly research. Lunacharsky even served as a high-ranking official as the Commissar of Enlightenment (head of education).* In volume 9 of the *Lenin Manuscripts*, published in 1929, Deborin wrote a scholarly introduction for the first three *Bern Notebooks* (Conspectus of Hegel's Book *The Science of Logic*). Deborin wrote that from his examination of the notes, in 1914 Lenin appeared to be preparing to write a book on materialist dialectics. He continued:

> **I do not doubt that if Lenin were able to continue his research to the end, he would have revitalized and furthered the development of dialectical materialism, bringing this field to a whole new level. If anyone is able to find *differences* from within similarities, then they would be able to see that Lenin's understanding of materialist dialectics opened a new stage in the development of dialectical materialism. There are differences between Plekhanov and Lenin, differences which reflect the characteristics of different historical phases in the development of the proletariat struggle and revolutionary activities[86].**

In this commentary by Deborin, he consciously used the word "if" twice; in other words, he emphasized that the research of his day had not realized this "new stage." Furthermore, he specifically compared Lenin's thought with that of Plekhanov to represent different periods of revolutionary history. This was to protect his own teacher, not mentioning Lenin's supersession and critique of Plekhanov in the *Bern Notebooks*. I believe that in terms of the research on Lenin's *Bern Notebooks*, this introduction by Deborin may very well be the most important research achievement by the Soviet scholarly world before the 1960s. Although Deborin's research also comprised numerous problems, including a weak **homogeneous** situating logic[87] and a method of **isolated** textual proof (for instance, he overemphasized the uniformity of Lenin

---

86   Deborin, Abram. *Introduction to volume 9 of "The Lenin Papers"*. Soviet National Press (1929) page 3 (Chinese).

87   From Deborin's introduction we can see that his citations from the third section of Lenin's notes skip about without sequence; for instance, he cites the content of Lenin's final summary of his learning with the philosophical situating logical antecedent. For this reason, I believe that even Deborin was forced into a particular interpretive framework, he still unconsciously assumed the philosophical homoneity of Lenin's *Bern Notebooks*. Of course, his primary analysis still followed Lenin's process of reading. However, in spite of this, we find no evidence that Deborin deeply understood Lenins philosophical epistemology and restructuring of theoretical thought.

and Hegel's thought, downplaying Lenin's criticism of Hegel's idealist viewpoint). Nevertheless, because Deborin had not yet been forced into Stalin's ideological framework, his work was able to preserve some of its valuable originality. Here, in terms of the situating logic of methodological interpretation, what is most important is that the primary content of Deborin's interpretation was written according to the progression of Lenin's excerpted notes of Hegel's *The Science of Logic*. In other words, **historical chronology** was what moved his analysis. *In our discussion of the Bern Notebooks in the second part of this book we will examine more closely the detailed content and academic value of Deborin's introduction to Lenin's **Bern Notebooks**.* It is evident that Deborin's academic appraisal of Lenin was quite modest, and no fixed notion of Lenin's philosophical thought was formed from it. *In the 1930s, when Deborin and his followers came under the condemnation of Stalin, his appraisal of Lenin was criticized[88]. Because of this, Deborin was forced to publicly acknowledge his "mistakes," admitting that his evaluation of Lenin as a theorist was too low, and concede that Lenin's philosophical thought had already reached a "new level" in the development of Marxist philosophy[89]. **Though he was not wrong and knew he was not wrong, under the violent interrogation of ideological powers that be he was forced to distort his views and admit he was wrong**; this was the "road to survival" for many scholars and thinkers under the rule of Stalin's dogmatism, including such familiar scholars as Lukacs and Bloch. We will discuss Deborin's thought in greater detail in the second part of this book.*

---

88   Between 1929 and 1930, Deborin and his followers engaged in lively debate with a few young philosophers from the Red Teachers Institute on the relation between philosophy and reality. In the tradition of the ancients, Deborin denied any direct relation between academics and real life, emphasizing that the primary goal of theoretical work should be academic research. In August and October of 1930, the institute reached two separate decisions criticizing Deborin's school for its tendency to depart from reality. In the second decision, it specifically pointed out that Deborin had not sufficiently praised Lenin's philosophical thought and not realized that Lenin's work had already reached a "higher stage" of dialectical materialism. At the same time, it criticized Deborin's attitude towards Hegel and Feuerbach. As the debate reached its climax, Stalin gave a speech at the Institute on December 9, 1930, directly making his position clear in the conflict. He criticized Deborin's view as Menshevik, as well as Deborin's attitude towards Lenin's philosophy. Afterwards, the Institute called a meeting of all party members on December 29 and made a third decision, classifying the false views of Deborin's school as "anti-Leninist," "anti-dialectical materialism," and "anti-Marxist." On February 25, 1931, Deborin was removed as the editor-in-chief of *Under the Banner of Marxism*, replaced by his ideological opponents.

89   See Deborin's "Letter to the Editor" in *Pravda*, December 18, 1931.

I have found that the first scholar to theoretically summarize Lenin's philosophical thought was a Marxist philosopher who had worked together with Lenin: Adoratsky. Like Lenin, he graduated from Kazan University with a degree in law. *Lenin wrote that Adoratsky was "reliable," and that he was "a Marxist of fine upbringing"*[90]. According to Adoratsky's own memoir, he began to see Lenin frequently in 1904, and the two men maintained a close relationship. *He was one of the scholars personally assigned by Lenin to organize the documents of Marx and Engels after the October Revolution*[91]. In the 1930s, Adoratsky published the first group of documents on Lenin's philosophical notebooks[92]. His most important contribution to this research was the introduction he wrote to the volume twelve of the Lenin Manuscripts (1930), which later became a stand-alone piece entitled "On the Study of Lenin's Philosophy." In this essay, Adoratsky gave a fairly comprehensive overview of the historical developmental process and basic content of Lenin's philosophical thought. I have found that Adoratsky's appraisal of Lenin's philosophical research is actually quite objective. This is because in defending Lenin, Adoratsky did not move beyond such questions as "did Lenin focus on philosophy before 1908?" and "around 1906, did Lenin express his philosophical opinions as an ordinary Marxist?" *I believe that these were legitimate questions for that time.* Adoratsky believed that between 1894 and 1905, Lenin was already an "exceptional dialectical materialist." For Adoratsky at this time, Lenin had not yet been dressed up as a **philosopher**. In his analysis of the Bern Notebooks, Adoratsky believed that Lenin consistently maintained the position of Marxist dialectics; in order to meet the needs of the real life struggle, the "unparalleled proletariat leader and theorist Lenin continued to deepen his theoretical study of this revolutionary method on the eve of the socialist revolution." Of course, much like Deborin's expression, Adoratsky wrote that "**if** Lenin planned to write a book on the dialectic, then for this task he had accumulated a body of rich and comprehensive materials (especially on the question of Hegelian dialectics)"[93]. The use of the word "if" here is very important; at least Adoratsky does not directly affirm that the goal of Lenin's research at this point was to write a theoretical work on the dialectic. Rather, Adoratsky clearly points out that like Marx, Lenin could not "find time" to write a

---

90   From the *Collected Works of Adoratsky*. Translated by Shi Zhu, Beijing Sanlian Press (1964), page 559 (Chinese).
91   *Ibid.*, pages 548-549 (Chinese).
92   *Ibid.*
93   *Ibid.*, page 439 (Chinese). Emphasis added.

book on the dialectic[94]. Furthermore, Adortatsky's analysis and discussion of Lenin's philosophical thought cannot be thought of as professional scholarship, and so we can pass over it without too much worry. However, I must point out the fact that Adoratsky's research methods on Lenin's philosophical thought in the 1930s opened a non-historical precedent; in his many essays on Lenin, we find that he takes Lenin's works from **different time periods** (such as Materialism and Empirio-Criticism and the Bern Notebooks) and **non-chronologically** muddles them. He topically studies them, confirming their **homogeneity and absolute truth**. *A typical example of this is Adoratsky's* **The Philosophical Significance of Lenin's Works**, written in 1930[95]. This paved the way for a dangerous road, leading to logical shadiness. This theoretical tendency was elevated into an even more absolute method by the new generation of Stalinist philosophers such as Eugene and Mitin. They viewed the homogenized Leninist philosophical thought structure as the Leninist period in Marxist philosophical history. *In 1936, Mitin published an essay summarizing the philosophical battle lines and work of the revolution, calling Lenin's Philosophical Notebooks a "philosophical introduction to the great proletariat revolution"[96]. He did not specify whether or not he meant Lenin's entire 20 years of philosophical learning and research with his grandiose conclusion.*

It should be pointed out that when the 1930s made necessary a unified system of thought, Stalin established a new, forced ideological discourse system with his *History of the Soviet Communist Party*; in that book, the famous second section of the fourth chapter, Dialectical Materialism and Historical Materialism, expounded that traditional philosophical interpretive framework[97]. I believe that in that particular historical time period, there was an important historical logic to doing this. However, when every principle in this book is taken as a "bright, guiding light"[98],

---

94   *Ibid.*, page 439 (Chinese).

95   *Ibid.*, pages 446-466 (Chinese).

96   Refer to *Selected Works of the Deborin School*. Jilin People's Press (1982) page 117 (Chinese).

97   *The History of the Soviet Communist Party* was published in 1938. Though there were several authors, after 1948 Stalin was listed as the sole author. According to Pankratova's *25 Years of Soviet Historical Science*, the true author of this book was the Soviet historian Jaroslavsky. Refer to Pankratova's book for more information

98   On February 5, 1941, the editing department of *Under the Banner of Marxism*, along with the Philosophy Research Center of the Soviet Science Institute met in Moscow to celebrate the 10th anniversary of the decision of the Central Committee with regards to *Under the Banner of Marxism*, eventually writing their famous "Letter to Comrade Stalin." See *Selected Works of the Deborin School*. Jilin People's Press (1982) page 173.

a dogmatic, ideological **discourse tyranny** is formed. After this point, in all the Soviet Union – including Eastern Europe – only Stalin was able to think creative thoughts. Also for the demands of **homogeneity of thought**, Stalin chose the easily understood, easily propagandized *Materialism and Empirio-Criticism* as the basic viewpoint of Lenin's philosophical thought from among the heterogeneous, varied levels of Lenin's philosophical texts, confirming the statement that Lenin had brought dialectical materialism to a new level[99]. Furthermore, in 1946 Stalin directly identified Lenin's *Philosophical Notebooks* as an immature "thought laboratory"; this statement caused the study of Lenin's *Philosophical Notebooks* to enter a low point in the study of philosophical history in the former Soviet Union. The first three editions of the *Collected Works of Lenin* did not even include the Philosophical Notebooks; in the second edition of the 1955 *Brief Biography of Lenin*, published by the Central Marxist-Leninist Research Institute, there was not any mention of the *Philosophical Notebooks*[100]. After Stalin passed away, Lenin's Philosophical Notebooks were finally added to the fourth edition of *Collected Works of Lenin* as an addendum.

It was not until the 1950s and especially the death of Stalin that the study of Lenin's *Philosophical Notebooks* began to revive; the research on Lenin's Bern Notebooks, in particular, entered a new stage of development. Scholars began to criticize the incorrect Stalinist practice of viewing Lenin's *Bern Notebooks* as "self-excerpts" and thus refuting their place in the history of the development of Lenin's philosophical thought[101]. This was an extremely important improvement. However, I have found that from this point forward, the majority of Soviet scholars begin to develop a kind of theoretical situating logic that resulted in a **re-annotated topical understanding** and **expectation of homogeneity**. In *Marx Revisited* I discussed the practice of re-evaluating classical texts using the framework of external philosophical principles and non-historically homogenizing the classical authors. To use the words of Japanese scholar Kojin Karatani, this is the practice of reading classical texts through the lens of an "external ideology"[102]. Although Stalin was no longer there, his dogmatic interpretive framework had become profoundly embedded in the minds of Soviet scholars.

---

99   A decision of the Soviet Central Committee confirmed Leninism was confirmed as a new stage in the development of Marxist philosophy.

100   Refer to *Concise Biography of Lenin*. People's Press (1957) (Chinese).

101   Refer to *Study on Lenin's "Philosophical Notebooks."* Beijing Sanlian Press (1964) page 24.

102   Refer to Karatani's Marx: *The Center of Possibilities*. Central Translation Press (2006) page 2.

Here let us examine Kiselyov's *On Lenin's "Philosophical Notebooks,"* the work which has had the earliest and most profound influence on Chinese research of the *Philosophical Notebooks*. *In the 1950s, Kiselyov was the Soviet expert counsellor for the Chinese Communist Central Party School. As part of his guidance and training for Chinese translators of classical Marxist texts, and in particular as part of the translation and editing of Lenin's **Philosophical Notebooks**, he gave 25 systematic lectures in 1956 alone; his book **On Lenin's "Philosophical Notebooks"** was published in 1956 by the People's Press, based off of these lectures. This book has become an important reference for Chinese translators of classical Marxist texts.* I believe that this book is a **false-situating theoretical illusory construct**, typical of the framework of latent Stalinist dogmatism[103].

I believe this about Kiselyov's book for several reasons. **First**, it manifested a **non-historical, non-textual** topical framework. Kiselyov only gives a very brief history of Lenin's thought and textual description at the beginning of his book. *This section of his book is extremely crude and inaccurate,* full of arbitrary statements. Kiselyov next organizes Lenin's 20 years of philosophical learning and research into four broad topics: dialectics, epistemology, dialectical logic, and philosophical history (this history focused on Hegel and Feuerbach). What is most important here is that under the influence of this non-historical topical logical illusion, we are unable to see the **heterogeneity** of Lenin's reading and research notes in most of the sub-texts and draft texts. Furthermore, we are unable to see the **concrete context** of Lenin in each case, and thus are unable to see the **true progression and changes** in Lenin's experimental thinking. In short, Lenin's diversity of notes is non-historically reduced to a single corpus of text that can be cut and pasted at will. Kiselyov's work implied that individual scholars could study Lenin's *Philosophical Notebooks* according to however they themselves decided to divide up the topics of his notebooks, and that they could pick and choose textual fragments to fit their categories. In

---

103 A false-situating logic is the term which I use to designate the use of an *a priori* ideological illusion to replace real, concrete, historical theoretical research in the field of philosophical research. False-situating logic can be manifested in different historical forms in different eras and research fields. The metaphysical petrification opposed by Hegel and Heidegger, the economic fetishisms opposed by Marx, the sensuality and naturalness opposed by young Lukacs, the "guiltless" reading opposed by Althusser, and the notional imperialism opposed by Adorno and Lacan are all different aspects of what I call false-situating logic.

this topical false-situating logic, not only do we not truly examine the text, but we also fail to have any chance of entering the realm of Lenin's thought.

Second, my low opinion of Kiselyov's book comes from his **expectation of homogeneity**. This is the inevitable result of the theoretical illusion of this research model. In *Marx Revisited* I identified this "theory of anything" that exists in the traditional study of classical Marxist works: the belief that anything Marx and Engels said was absolutely true and accurate. This "accuracy" and "truth" was without any kind of historical, chronological basis: "This has given rise to the erroneous belief that researchers of Marxist philosophy are free to **uniformly** cite anything they desire from volume one to volume fifty of *The Complete Works of Marx and Engels*, without giving any special historical explanation"[104]. I have found that the research on Lenin suffers from this same malady. In this book by Kiselyov, he never considered whether or not Lenin's understanding of philosophical materialism or Hegelian philosophy ever changed, nor did he ever wonder whether or not Lenin's thoughts on the dialectic ever grew more profound. In short, Kiselyov's false-situating logic has no room for the dimension **of heterogeneous historical considerations**. As such, in the whole of his research on the *Philosophical Notebooks*, Kiselyov only gives an **oversimplified, uniform** treatment of Lenin's 20 years of philosophical study and thought. He groups texts based merely on the object of study (such as dialectics, epistemology, or Hegel). Kiselyov even mentions that famous statement by Stalin, that Lenin's *Philosophical Notebooks* were nothing more than a laboratory for philosophical thought[105].

I found that after the 1930s, in all the early research on Lenin's thought by Soviet scholars, it was impossible for anyone to admit that Lenin could have been **wrong**, that he may have progressed from **immature to mature**, that he could have progressed from **shallow to profound**. On the contrary, these were historical facts hidden by false-situating ideology. The laughable purpose of this practice was to maintain the image that Lenin was **always correct**. It is my opinion that the true historical admission that Lenin could have made mistakes does not, in the least, affect his image as a great Marxist thinker. However, in the false historical lens and logical illusions promulgated by scholars such as Kiselyov, how is it possible for us to truly see Lenin's philosophy?

---

104   Refer to the first page of my *Marx Revisited*.
105   Refer to Kiselyov's *On Lenin's "Philosophical Notebooks."* People's Press (1956) page 6 (Chinese).

It is unfortunate that we have seen this false situating research model become the basic research paradigm for the majority of Soviet and Eastern European scholars. Other representative works of this genre that have been translated into Chinese include *A Study of Lenin's "Philosophical Notes"*[106] and Suvorov's *The Question of Dialectics in Lenin's "Philosophical Notes"*[107]. However, scholars from the Soviet Union and Eastern Europe did not suggest that Lenin had written his notes in preparation for a book on the philosophy of the dialectic.

Following the printing of the newest version of the *Philosophical Notebooks* in volume 29 of the fifth edition of the *Collected Works of Lenin* in 1963, the study of Lenin's philosophical thought by Soviet scholars reached a new period of excitement. It is not hard to see that the ideological illusions of the research of this time period also began to gradually intensify. In many scholarly studies, **Leninism** began to be seen as an important stage in the history of Marxist philosophy; Lenin was said to have **"creatively investigated and solved"** the **"most important philosophical questions"** in Marxism[108]. It is my opinion that such conclusions grossly overstate Leninism's true worth. I believe that Lenin primarily united Marxism with the reality of the Russian revolution. As such, he truly did bring Marxism to a new Leninist stage in terms of political and economic theory. However, I have doubts as to the legitimacy of referring to his work as an **independent Leninist stage** in the **philosophical history of Marxism**. As a matter of fact, in the modern development of Marxist philosophical history, there was an irreplaceable period of **Leninist philosophical thought**; Lenin did make great efforts and contributions in opposing Machism, upholding materialism, and in profound understanding of the materialist dialectic. However, from a philosophical standpoint, I do not believe that there was ever a Leninist philosophy as **differentiated from Marxist philosophy**. Of course, this is a question that merits further discussion.

In their understanding of the development of Lenin's thought, these scholars clearly viewed the *Philosophical Notebooks* as a "direct

---

106 Refer to *Study on Lenin's "Philosophical Notebooks."* Beijing Sanlian Press (1964) (Chinese).
107 See The *Dialectical Problem in Lenin's "Philosophical Notebooks."* Qiushi Press (1981) (Chinese).
108 Dynnik, ed. *History of Philosophy*, volume 5. 1975. Beijing Sanlian Press, page 15 (Chinese).

continuation" of *Materialism and Empirio-Criticism*[109]. I believe that this is an inaccurate conclusion for two reasons. **First**, the Philosophical Notebooks include 20 years of Lenin's excerpted notes and commentaries, and as such, its content was quite varied. This being the case, how could it be called a continuation of *Materialism and Empirio-Criticism*, which was written in 1908? For instance, Lenin wrote his important "Conspectus on the Book *The Holy Family*" in 1895; this work cannot be reconciled with the notes he wrote around 1903. *The reason for this misunderstanding was that for Soviet scholars, Lenin's **Philosophical Notebooks** were the same thing as his **Bern Notebooks**.* **Second**, in these non-historical conclusions, the objective heterogeneity of thought between Lenin's *Materialism and Empirio-Criticism* and the *Bern Notebooks* is completely glossed over. Although I do not agree with the practice of Western Leninologists and some Western Marxist scholars of diametrically opposing these two texts, I believe that to ignore the theoretical differences between these two works and Lenin's own important philosophical progress flies in the face of historical fact.

I have also found that in the appraisals of Lenin's philosophical thought in the scholarly scene of the former Soviet Union, there gradually arose a subjective, non-historical false-situating element that came to exert dominating influence: the view that Lenin was **always correct**, that he was an ever-victorious theoretical hero of Russian Marxism. Thus Lenin began to be bizarrely deified. *Fisher pointed out the fact that for the sake of ideological correctness and to emphasize Lenin as a national hero, Soviet authorities consciously hid Lenin's German heritage on his mother's side*[110]. Let us turn to the actual views of Soviet scholars on the relation of Lenin to other Marxists to illustrate this point:

> **Plekhanov and the other Marxists of the Second International underestimated the materialist dialectic; they were not able to use it in the process of their epistemology. Unlike them, Lenin elucidated the significance of materialist dialectics as the scientific epistemology and logic of Marxism. He profoundly and comprehensively proved the laws and categories of materialist dialectics, enriching the epistemology of dialectical materialism with new historical experience and modern science[111].**

109   *Ibid.*, page 174 (Chinese).
110   Fisher wrote that in order to create a national image of Lenin, he was portrayed as a 100% pure-blood Russian. Refer to Fischer's *The Life of Lenin*.
111   Dynnik, ed. *History of Philosophy*, volume 5. 1975. Beijing Sanlian Press, p. 21.

Just looking at the words, this statement does not appear to have anything wrong with it. However, the essential point is that this general, qualitative analysis does not account for **chronology**. Whether purposeful or not, in this non-historical assertion, Lenin's important understanding of materialist dialectics gained after 1914 is muddled together with all of his philosophical thought. This creates the impression that Lenin was always different from Plekhanov, hiding the fact that from the late 19th century to the early 20th century, Lenin was a faithful student of Plekhanov, as well as the fact that before the *Bern Notebooks*, Lenin did not profoundly understand Marx's materialist dialectics. Hiding these important historical facts was what led to the creation of a false ideological myth. *Deborin was criticized for writing the simple fact that Lenin was a student of Plekhanov.* Such oversimplified and non-historical elevation of Lenin's logic was exactly what glossed over the significance of the important thought revolution that took place in Lenin's *Bern Notebooks*. I believe that this ideological false-situating notion and idealist methodological structure is antithetical to Marx's historical materialism.

By the late 1970s, there was little doubt that the most important research model in the traditional study of Marxist philosophical history was the results of the well-known Soviet scholar Kedrov's research. Before I continue, I must admit that out of all the research on Lenin's philosophical thought conducted in the former Soviet Union and Eastern Europe, Kedrov's research, and his topical study on the *Philosophical Notebooks* in particular, was the most systematic and most profound of all. I even believe that Kedrov's research begins to manifest elements of the internal deconstruction of the false-situating framework of Stalin's dogmatism. This is because it was in Kedrov's research that the practice of pigeon-holing classical texts using "philosophical principles" was gradually replaced by deep understanding of the text. Though the old ideological framework still existed, its controlling power over logical thought was beginning to **diminish**. However, it was Kedrov that brought an *a priori*, **deterministic**, illusory interpretive model to the study of Lenin's philosophical thought. This is the traditional model that continues to strongly influence our research of Lenin's *Philosophical Notebooks* (Bern Notebooks), *i.e.*, the **planned conception theory** that Lenin was preparing to write a scholarly work of materialist dialectics. *Kedrov himself wrote that Adoratsky and Yudin indirectly expressed*

that Lenin had plans to write a work of philosophy[112]. What finally ce-
mented this view was the viewpoint expressed by nine Soviet scholars in
their biography of Lenin[113]. According to my research, the birth of this
illusory model can be divided into two time periods.

In the **first** period, Kedrov wrote in his 1973 book *Study of Lenin's*
"Philosophical Notebooks" that Lenin's study of Hegel's philosophy in
the Bern Notebooks could be divided into three stages: in the first stage,
Lenin used excerpts to gather material for the book on dialectics that he
was planning to write. This basically referred to Lenin's entire process
of reading and studying Hegel. In the **second** stage, Lenin established
and explicated the general plan of dialectics. This basically referred to
Lenin's *Plan of Hegel's Dialectics (Logic)* and the field of knowledge of
epistemology and dialectics that should be formed from it. In the **third**
stage, Lenin's planned work on dialectics began to take shape. This referred to Lenin's text *On the Question of Dialectics.* It is interesting to
note that Kedrov believed that the third stage pointed towards a fourth
stage that had not yet happened. In this imaginary fourth stage, Lenin
would "systematically explicate the theory of materialist dialectics"[114].
Here Kedrov's assumption is that on the eve of the October Revolution,
Lenin read Hegel's philosophy with the goal of writing a scholarly work
on dialectics. In other words, the entire process of studying Hegel's philosophy was really Lenin's process of gathering materials, devising a
plan of writing, and beginning to realize his plan. I belief that this is a
subjective deduction based on *a priori* determinism. However, in the
research of Lenin's *Philosophical Notebooks* of the day, this conclusion
can truly be called an important theoretical "breakthrough."

In the **second** time period, with the 1983 publishing of *Narrative*
Methods of the Dialectic, Kedrov took this theoretical "breakthrough"
to a whole new level. In this book, Kedrov proposed that Lenin had,
from the **late 19ᵗʰ century,** already begun to establish a "grand plan"

---

112   See Kedrov's *Narrative Methods of the Dialectic.*,China Social Science Press
(1986) page 8 (Chinese).

113   See Kedrov's *Narrative Methods of the Dialectic.* China Social Science Press
(1986) page 8 (Chinese). In the second edition of this book, Kedrov wrote specifically
that Lenin planned to write a book on materialist dialectics, but was unfortunately unable to realize his plan. In the following three editions of his book, he did not alter
even one word of this declaration. This point was an important basis of his theoretical
structure.

114   See Kedrov's *Study of Lenin's "Philosophical Notebooks,"* Qiushi Pres (1984),
pages 377-378 (Chinese).

for a **systematized materialist dialectical** system. *This means that Kedrov generalized his a priori deterministic illusion from the **Bern Notebooks** to the whole developmental process of Lenin's philosophical thought. Thus a new false-situating logic was born and developed.* For Kedrov, this "plan" of Lenin's began in his actual revolutionary struggle between 1894 and 1913, actually taking place in 1913-1914 with two of Lenin's completed texts: his understanding of Lenin's plan to restructure the dialectic from reading *Correspondence of Marx and Engels* and his simple and systematized explication of dialectics in *Karl Marx*. *It is to Kedrov's credit that he was the first Soviet scholar to focus on and study Lenin's **Correspondence of Marx and Engels**.* Following this, Kedrov went even further, restructuring his original "three stages" theory of Lenin's materialist dialectic system into a complex **multiple planned** structure. To use his own words, this was his process of "beginning to realize his plan." This structure can be further divided into two levels. **First**, the four "plans" that Lenin himself developed in the latter stages of his research on Hegel's philosophy (1914-1915). These were the "first plan" (September to December 1914) during which Lenin wrote his "Sixteen Elements of the Dialectic" while studying Hegel's *The Science of Logic;* the "second plan" (December 1914 to 1915) during which Lenin wrote his "Plan of Hegel's Dialectics (Logic)" while studying Hegel's *Lectures on the Philosophy of History*; the "third plan" (1915) during which Lenin studied Lassalle's Heraclitus, which Kedrov later re-dubbed "the plan at the source of dialectics"; the final plan (late 1915), during which Lenin wrote *On the Question of Dialectics* after reading Aristotle's Metaphysics. Kedrov wrote that this fourth plan could be seen as an outline of a future work on dialectics, or the beginning of an explanation of dialectic methods, the first draft of an explanation of dialectics[115]. On the **second** level we find Kedrov's own plan to begin putting the "four plans" into action, for which he also had four "outlines"; this brought the total number of plans and outlines in his theory of planned conception to eight. In his final outline, what he called the overall plan combining Lenin's four plans on the study of dialectics, Kedrov directly proposed his own conception of the system of materialist dialectic theory[116].

---

115   See Kedrov's *Narrative Methods of the Dialectic.* China Social Science Press (1986) page 314 (Chinese).
116   *Ibid.*, pages 403-412 (Chinese).

I should point out that in the traditional interpretive framework of the time, for Kedrov to have proposed such a complex theoretical system of expression, to have constructed the historical simulacra of Lenin's creation of the system of materialist dialectics, was truly an exceptional work of scholarly research. If we had lived in that time, it is not certain that we could have surpassed him. However, with the progress of time and thought, we are now afforded a new thought premise, methodology, and textual resources by which we can see Kedrov's theoretical false-situating logic. This is because we can see that in Kedrov's logically shady, a priori planned conception theory, Lenin's true process of philosophical improvement was severely hidden. *To use the words of Kojin Karatani, external significance systems had drowned out the text*[117]. For the space of many years, this a priori theory of planned conception seemed incontrovertible within the scholarly circles of the former Soviet Union, Eastern Europe, and China. Badiou wrote that only in breaking down something that is "given" in man's understanding will we be able to approach the truth. *Here Badiou approaches Lacan, who wrote that **breaking apart is truth***. Thus we have no choice but to break down, and thus to advance.

20 years have already passed from Kedrov's last work on Lenin's *Philosophical Notebooks*. The readability of historical texts, as well as the quality, logical platform, and philosophical progression of scholarly research in our day all demand that we change our line of thought[118].

---

117   Refer to Karatani's *Marx: The Center of Possibilities*. Central Translation Press (2006) page 8(Chinese).

118   I should also mention that beginning in the 1920s and 1930s, there was a line of philosophical research that diverged from the orthodox Marxist ideological framework of the Stalinist system. This was the theoretical road opened by Western Marxists and Western Marxologists. The first to criticize Lenin's *Materialism and Empirio-Criticism* without having read the *Bern Notebooks* was Karl Korsch. In his 1930 article, On the Current Problems of the Study of Marxism and Philosophy, Korsch called Lenin's *Materialism and Empirio-Criticism* an **unconsciously** Hegelian work. when Lenin's Bern Notebooks were published, the majority of Western Marxists (neo-Marxists) and Western Marxologists approved of the basic views in Lenin's *Philosophical Notebooks* (actually the Bern Notebooks) while criticizing, to different degrees, the views in *Materialism and Empirio-Criticism*. *Here, the majority of Western scholars did not seriously study Lenin's process of philosophical learning between 1895 and 1913, and thus completely ignored many of Lenin's early philosophical notes and reading commentaries that were already published. This caused them to lack the process dimension in their study of Lenin's **Bern Notebooks**. This led, inevitably, to problems of historical misunderstanding.* In other words, this established a new model of theoretical logic, i.e., the simple antithesis of Lenin's *Materialism and Empirio-Criticism* and the *Bern*

In 1990, A.I. Volodin said that serious historical-philosophical research of the *Philosophical Notebooks* had not yet begun in Russia[119]. This statement has a certain level of truth. Therefore, let us start again. Let us start again in the innovative field of Chinese Marxist philosophical research.

6 RECONSIDERING THE ISSUE FROM ANOTHER PERSPECTIVE

From our discussion of the past section it is not difficult to see that in their study of Lenin's Philosophical Notebooks, Soviet scholars fell into a two-layered theoretical trap. At the first level, under the dominating ideological influence of the Stalinist framework, they gave into a variety of arbitrary, subjective pre-conceptions and logical postulates; at the second level, they viewed Lenin's 20 year process of gradual philosophical development and constantly changing thought as nothing more than the realization process of a pre-determined scholarly writing plan. From our perspective today, this line of thought is a linear, subjective, false situating logic. One of the important theoretical goals of this book is to disprove this latently idealist research methodology and way of thinking.

It is my opinion that as Lenin entered the scene of social history under the direction of Plekhanov and others, he was a steadfast Marxist; he successfully applied the basic views of Marxism to many of the political, economic, and real-life problems facing the Russian Revolution. This is a historical fact that cannot be denied. However, recognizing this point does not necessarily mean that Lenin was, from the beginning, a mature Marxist in terms of **all** of Marx's basic theories. I believe that

---

Notebooks. For instance, one neo-Marxist wrote that the views in *Materialism and Empirio-Criticism* did not represent the ultimate philosophical views of Lenin's, but rather that the *Philosophical Notebooks* were his most important work. In these notebooks, Lenin supposedly critically re-examined his prior philosophical views. Vranicki wrote that Lenin's creative philosophical legacy was included in these Philosophical Notebooks. Furthermore, the earliest translators of the Bern Notebooks into French and English had very particular views on his philosophical thought. Althusser, Leven, and Anderson all conducted systematic and profound research on Lenin's philosophy. However, when I asked the visiting Professor Anderson in October 2007 why his work did not mention the results of Leven's Lenin research, he replied that Leven's research cannot be called true scientific thought.

119 See Volodin's "Lenin and Philosohpy: Should We Not Bring up this Question Again?" In May 2007, during the China-Russia philosophy symposium, my expression on these thoughts caused something of an uproar among the assembled scholars.

because Lenin did not pay as much attention to philosophy before 1908 as he could have, his systematic understanding and grasp of Marxist philosophy was far inferior to his achievements in the fields of politics and economics. In a certain sense, the basic viewpoints and standpoints of Lenin towards Marxist philosophy in his early years primarily came from his teacher Plekhanov and others; at this stage, he did not even have the real motivation or scholarly basis from which to develop his scholarly research of the field of philosophy or engage in theoretical construction. Furthermore, he was unable to unify his philosophical standpoint with his practical intentions. Two pieces of evidence support my view. First, there is no historical proof or textual support to uphold Kedrov's assertion that Lenin began pondering on the creation of a materialist dialectical theoretical system in the late 19th century. Second, in order to criticize the errors of Russian Machism, beginning in 1908 Lenin twice engaged in the systematic, academic study of philosophy. However, even though his study was systematic and academic, this only allowed him to increase his knowledge of philosophical materialist theories; like Plekhanov and the other theorists of the Second International, Lenin at this time had not yet truly realized the essential place of practical **historical dialectical** theory in Marx's philosophy. In fact, Lenin's understanding would not begin to change until 1913, when he read the correspondence between Marx and Engels. Combined with the urgent demands of the actual struggle of the Russian proletariat revolution, Lenin resolved himself while in Bern to seriously study Hegelian philosophy with a special focus on his dialectical theory. The results of this study are what we know as the *Bern Notebooks*.

I believe that Kedrov's so-called theory of "planned conception" is nothing but **falsely complex simple addition**. He uses this theory to caricature Lenin's profound, difficult, and complex thought experiment in the *Bern Notebooks* into an external process of theoretical construction. In refuting Kedrov's planned conception theory, I am led to encounter a new question: in Lenin's 20 year process of philosophical study, were his theoretical goals and line of logic always the same? Or, as Kedrov put it, were these 20 years nothing but the realization and formation of a "conception" of the system of materialist dialectics? In particular, were Lenin's Bern Notebooks, in which he studied the philosophy of Hegel, a homogenized thought process? Was it a process by which Lenin repeatedly wrote and expanded his materialist dialectical logic system, as Kedrov suggests? Here the results of my research unequivocally answer a resounding "no."

Take the last question, for example. In my latest research, I have found that the *Bern Notebooks* manifest an **Other homogeneity** in Lenin's early reading and thought logic; however, this false homogeneity disappears as Lenin's reading and research grew deeper. As a matter of fact, Lenin's thought encountered multiple contradictions in its progression; it even experienced numerous breaks in logic. However, it was precisely this true – though twisted – path of thought progression that led him to realize his own important logical shift and leap in understanding. It is interesting to point out that as he completed his research, Lenin once again unconsciously established a kind of new **non-homogeneity** in his own theoretical summary. This was a living, variable theoretical thought situating space, one with profound significance.

The focus of Lenin's process of reading and study, core of his whole-hearted thought experiment in the Bern Notebooks of Hegel's philosophy was dialectics. Compared with Hegel, the master of speculative philosophy, and Marx the founder of Marxist philosophy, I believe that Lenin at this time did not manifest a sufficiently thorough accumulation of philosophical knowledge and ability. Although Lenin accepted and believed in Marxism early on, he had never received systematic or professional philosophical training. Therefore, as he began to encounter truly profound philosophical thinking and theoretical speculative frameworks, it was inevitable that he felt at least somewhat lost. This was one area of scholarship in which he differed greatly from young Marx. Thus at this time, Lenin had not yet penetrated to the deepest level of Marx and Engels' theory of historical materialism. Even after Lenin completed his research of Hegel's philosophy and reached a deeper level of philosophical understanding, we still cannot lightly say that he had, in general, **developed** Marxist philosophy. Objectively speaking, through his research of Hegel Lenin was able to more deeply understand some of Marx's important ideas and basic thought process; he was even able to surpass Marx's thought on **certain questions**. I am afraid that this is a conclusion based on the honest search for true facts.

In fact, this is apparent not only with the *Bern Notebooks*. It is inappropriate for us to make subjective, arbitrary, indiscriminate, linear, and homogeneous conclusions about any of Lenin's 20 year long process of reading and learning. It is based on the understanding of this fact that I will explore a new interpretive method in this book, *i.e.*, approaching the object of research in **re-simulated thought space** and with

re-constructed logical structures in textological research. I refer to this unique interpretive method as the **theory of philosophical situating**. Looking at the circumstances of research created by the theory of philosophical situating, Lenin's thought experiment appears as a true, complex, functionally shifting logical space; most importantly, this **logical space** did not originate directly from Lenin, but rather from the **simulated** theoretical thought context constructed by me – the reader. I must make it clear that here I imply an important change in terms of methodology: in past textological research, although we realized there was an unavoidable historical distance between the text and the reader, we, as interpreters, always viewed our own understanding and conclusions as the objective reflection of the meaning of the text. Unlike this method, in the theory of philosophical situating that I propose here, the **present textual context**, divorced from the original author of the text, is constructed by the textual researcher. In other words, at this present moment, the opening of the field of meaning of the text is always **this-sided**. There is no doubt that when faced with static historical texts, we cannot completely reproduce the original context of the text. *It is in this sense that I am opposed to the simple theory of reflection.* In textual research, scholars often make such identifications as "Marx believed...", "Confucius advocated...", "For Heidegger...", etc. In fact, all of these expressions are all re-constructed from our own, new "**Me**" thought context. While this reconstructed may be unconscious under the majority of circumstances, we nevertheless take our own re-constructed thought contexts to be the objective meaning of the text, without even realizing it. *For Althusser, this is called guiltless reading.*" Hence in this book I attempt to realize a methodological shift; from interpretation based on words and sentences to grasping the latent discourse logic of the text; from textual interpretation in an explanatory context to a re-situating of the true thought context. In doing so, my goal is to construct a completely new contextual framework of scholarly logic, thus surpassing traditional textual interpretive methods, or in other words, establish a **post-textological** line of thought[120].

---

120   From the time that I proposed my own textual interpretive methods in the research of Marxist philosophy in the 1990s, I have been delighted to find many of the younger generation of scholars participating in the continual evolution of this methodology; these scholars have conducted promising work in the profound textual interpretation of the classical texts of Marxist philosophy. It is unfortunate that a minority of scholars have illegitimately used the word "textology" to refer to metaphysical empty talk that lacks actual interpretive practice. Even worse, many have equated textual interpretation in a hermeneutic sense to the establishment of textual authenticity in the realm

This method is actually the application of the **theory of situating existence** to textual interpretation. *The theory of situating existence is a philosophical concept on which I have long pondered. Further discussion of this expansive idea will have to come later.* In this book, I am only able to illuminate this new method of thought in a general way. Here, I will refer to it as the **theory of textual situating**, for the time being.

I do not believe that the essence of any theoretical scholarly thought can be seen as a solidified logical construct, like Newton's substantive time-space theory; rather, it is a complex, chronologically changing, **situational** construct of scholarly thought. The essence of philosophical situating is its **non-paradigm** nature. It is not a synthetic image with any kind of dead or petrified (present) conceptual framework, but rather a process of functional questioning and thinking; it is often expressed as a **fragile ever-reconstructing set of questions** and the **support for a temporary standpoint**. Here, multiple **logic rays**[121] bearing different arrows of time are interwoven, as are different **theoretical loops**[122] and **discourse détournement** processes[123]. The construction of an academic thought context is usually undertaken by a thinking subject, when

---

of philology. Laughably, some who do not refer to the original documents (or even copies), who do not even understand the original language of the text, have the nerve to declare that their pieced-together analyses from secondary sources are "textological authentication." Strictly speaking, this is not textological interpretation or philology, but rather a kind of mutated scholarly plagiarism.

121 **Logic rays**: in the natural sciences, the word ray (or ray) refers to an electrical wave with a shorter wavelength that is only perceived naturally with great difficulty. These include infrared, x-rays, etc. Here, my use of the idea of a logic ray refers primarily to a latent intention that is not directly expressed in the thought space. This could include man's practical intentions, his moral or value orientations, as well as his emotions and metnal structure; in short, the various levels that are unconsciously, latently developed in the logical situation. Therefore, the discovery of specific logic rays in the research process will penetrate the outer level and enter the marrow, the hidden aspects of understanding.

122 **Theoretical loops:** The word loop refers to the path of electricity in a circuit, as it passes through different media and returns to where it began; it is also referred to as a closed circuit. In neuroscience, loops also explain the paths of consciousness that suddenly appear in networks of nerves. Here I use **closed theoretical loops** to express an Other line of thought that exists in theoretical confirmation, and **open theoretical loops** to identify the progress of independent thought.

123 The concept of **détournement** was proposed by the French situationalist Guy Debord. It originally referred to the artistic, extra-normal situations used to break down the domination of traditional perspectives. See Debord's *The Society of the Spectacle*.

specific **scholarly memory points**[124] are repeated or activated based on **Other theoretical mirror images** readily at hand or **theoretical production curves**[125], whether this process be conscious or not. The relation between the thinking subject and the specific theoretical construct or theoretical production curve is an asymmetrical, **bi-lateral construction**. In the generative process of thought situations, the theoretical construct or production curve develops a repetitive, structuralized influence on the thinking subject. The thinking subject, on the other hand, rejects these changes in thought space, to the point that a qualitative change takes place in the theoretical construct or production curve. *Later we will see that thought situations of different natures will be constructed in completely different ways.* Of course, the different unconscious logic rays and sceptical questions of the thinking subject itself are the true motivating force of situating changes in thought. At the same time, this non-linear situating logical loop is realized through a gestalt-shift of the whole, and a new situating logic forms a new thought situation in that moment. Certain thought situations, usually because of shifts to the theoretical production function in terms of time or space, devolve in the new thought space into **false-situating illusions.** *False situating images and illusions are always historically identified in historical logical shifts. In our discussion of past theories, we put this paradigm into practice.*

I believe that the basic theoretical logical situation constructed in the interpretation of classical texts can be divided into the different historical contexts of the **psychological-association situation**, which enters classical texts based on historical thought, as well as, in our interpretation of the text, the **original thought situation** that directly confronts the world. The former encompasses the scope of hermeneutics, or what we call textology. *To use the words of the Chinese professor Feng Youlan, this is the concept of "as he said." Because the reader can never reach the complete unification of his own situation with the original context of the text in his research, therefore "as he said" is necessarily always*

---

124   **Scholarly memory:** This term refers to the Other scholarly sources that remain in the knowledge structure of the thinker. Scholarly memory is usually expressed as point knowledge and thought fragments of **scholarly memory points**, complex knowledge forms that form **scholarly memory groups**, and mirror image **Other theoretical production curves**, etc.

125   **Theoretical production curves** are a concept borrowed from Marx. For Marx, they were used to designate a break from petrified conceptual frameworks. They primarily refer to the constructive, living layout of the production and reproduction of the thought of the subject in functional thought and questioning.

a historical reformation of the image and simulation of meaning. The latter is the original generation of the thoughts of the reader himself. *This situation approaches what Professor Feng referred to as the "next he said" thought situation, in which the philosopher, as a reader, speaks his own words after truthfully confronting the texts, thus generating an academic thought situation that belongs to himself.*

We will discuss this original (**productive**) situating theory a little bit later; here we will first turn our attention to the first aspect of textual meaning of the philosophical situating theory, the question of synthesizing different historical scopes in textual interpretation in the context of traditional hermeneutics. I now believe that there is no such thing as synthesizing of historical scopes: the overlap or intersection of two scopes or viewpoints is nothing but an illusion, because in the interpretive process of any text, there is no question of combining new and old. The truth is, so-called historical scopes (the original meaning field of the author and text) are always re-constructed by the reader through activating dead texts and words. The essence of these historical copies and invented replacements is based on our modern understanding of significance, because the events truly present in the interpretation of the text are understandings reconstructed from levels of textual significance that the reader can enter. Even if there did exist so-called historical synthesizing, it could only be the intersection between **two different thought situations**. Furthermore, in the intersection of the two, the thought situation of the reader necessarily occupies a **power discourse** position, while the writer, who is not present, and the text, which is silent, are weak.

Here we can look at a readily available example: the reception of my *Marx Revisited* among Chinese scholars. My thinking in this book originated in the late 1980s, and the writing of it was completed in 1998. After submitting it to the publisher, I discovered in the editing process that it began to become an **objective** text; for me, the basic framework and primary views of the book had become locked in and dead. In the first edit I was only able to make small modifications to some of its views; in the second edit I was only able to change certain words, and in the third edit even the words had become locked in. When I first received a copy of *Marx Revisited*, the first edition had already become a historical text. At that moment I suddenly realized that my relationship to this book had become very interesting. As the author of this book that took ten years of dedicated effort, that filled over 600 pages of text, although I still lived (I still existed), I began to become estranged to my own work. I felt near and yet distant at the same time. In many of the important chapters and sections, only through my serious and focused study was I able to truly re-activate those theories and views, which were made up of words and sentences. Only then was I able to re-construct my original thought context, and thus **dimly reach** my thought situation at the time I wrote. Even after all this effort, my examination of my original thought situation still deviated subtly from its original state; in other words, even I – the original author, in this case – had great difficulty in completely recreating the original context of the text, in returning the historical scope of this text. Thus it goes without saying that attempting to bridge enormous distances of time, space, and social historical background, not to mention the effects of the medium of different linguistic systems, is all but impossible[126]. *My thoughts here are beginning to be echoed in some modern European philological research*[127].

In the example of *Marx Revisited*, there are several other important reasons why the original writing context cannot be returned. First, there were important changes between the published version available to readers and the version that I wrote myself. I not only deleted some of my critical reflections towards Marx during the editing process, but I also pondered on and adjusted some of the more unfamiliar concepts in my original draft, including some of the concepts I defined myself. In the writing and editing process of this book, it is inevitable that many of these same things will occur. *This type of textual production and certain concealment of information is evident in many of Marx's early texts as well. When young Marx wrote **The Holy Family** and **The German Ideology**, it was during the period of book censorship in the kingdom of Prussia. One of the articles of the Prussian censorship law stated that any printed work under 21 pages would not have to be censored. Therefore, for the purposes of publishing, many of the texts by Marx and Engels included many sections that did not correspond to their original theoretical intentions. Furthermore, Marx*

---

126   When a translator friend of mine heard that what we call textual research is often based on translated Chinese texts, she remarked with some disdain the fact that we study translated works. I somewhat shamefully realized that I had truly been despised. However, in the situating theory that I propose here, this illegitimacy has some hope of being resolved. This is because the meaning of traditional modern foundationalist reduction is here replaced by re-structured productive creation.

127   One textual expert wrote that while the author is still alive, he becomes a conception that changes innumerably. When these conceptions appear again in manuscripts, they become even more complex.

and Engels deleted large portions of their own text as they edited their work. In many sections, their deletions did not come because they had discovered mistakes in terms of their writing, but rather because of political constraints or relationship constraints (for instance, Hess, the representative of the German "true socialism" that Marx and Engels criticized in **The German Ideology**, *participated in the writing of* **The German Ideology**). *Thus we can see that just because portions of text were deleted does not mean that the author believed them to be wrong or without value. On the other hand, Marx and Engels also left a large number of notes and manuscripts that they were either unable to publish or were abandoned part way through. These notes can be found in the well-known fourth section of MEGA 2. It is worth noting that the context of these texts often approach more closely the true context of the author. I have given a more detailed explanation of the three types of Marxist texts in* **Marx Revisited**, *and so I will not do so here*[128].

In addition, although I thoroughly understood post-modern textological concepts, I still insisted on using textual interpretive methods based on the context of **modern** philosophical hermeneutics. I felt at the time that the choice of this writing **strategy** was very important, because I hoped that my ideas and lines of thought would be understood by the majority of my Chinese colleagues and readers. In the second chapter of another of my books, *Problématique, Lecture Symptomale et Idéologie: A Textological Reading of Althusser,* because I had to use the textological method of "symptom reading" – another modern logical framework – in examining Althusser, who was the object of my research, I included an article that critiqued Barthes' post-modern textological thoughts in an appendix in order to introduce a new theoretical reference system[129]. Also because of this, in many of the expressions of Marx Revisited, I did not arrive at absolute conclusions, rather putting my theoretical effort to helping Marx's thought move towards modern openness. Unfortunately, if the theory is not thorough, the logical standpoint will be muddled and unclear. This naturally made the **reappearance** and **re-situation** of my thought scene all but impossible.

---

128   I recently read an article stating that it would be "illegitimate" to study the thought of Marx and Engels using portions of deleted text and things they did not wish to publish. This is an overly simplistic, unthinking arbitrary conculsion. The author of this article should study the meaning of textual research. Refer to the second issue of *Zhejiang Social Science* (2005).
129   Refer to my chapter two of my *Problématique, Lecture Symptomale et Idéologie: A Textological Reading of Althusser*. Central Translation Press (2003).

Given those my own feelings towards my work, it is hardly surprising that so many diverse and baffling things have been said by those others who read my *Marx Revisited*. In the **first** place, the old professors of my teachers' generation have strong views about what they read, expressing discontent with many of the concepts, methods, and even words that differed from the traditional framework. I remember one venerable scholar asking me in all seriousness, "Why do you use 'context' and not a word that everyone understands, such as 'background'?" *As a matter of fact, "context" and background" really do imply different things. My teacher,* Professor Sun Bokui also expressed sharp disagreement with some of my concepts in the book, such as "historical phenomenology" and "dual discourse." This kind of criticism is completely understandable. However, thinking about it from another perspective, our predecessors developed specific theoretical situations and conceptual/terminology systems, all of which are products of a certain time period. As time moves on and thought progresses, is it really necessary for us to **always use** the same unchanging logical standards and discourse systems? In fact, so doing would also be an unconscious re-situating process from the **past to the present**. **Second**, many modern theorists expressed doubt over my proposal that we "revisit" Marx, suggesting instead a modern Marx in opposition to the past Marx. They did not understand that by proposing that we "revisit" Marx, I was merely proposing a clearing-out of past logical positions that my goal was to allow Marx to step out of an ideological false-situation into a more open and tolerant today. It is evident that in their theoretical realm of discussion, my thought situation was not even basically simulated. A **third** group was made up of subjective, arbitrary, and rash scholars who violently placed what they supposed to be the framework of *Marx Revisited* in their critical sights before even understanding the general gist of the text. I believe that this is an underlying form of theoretical fascism[130]. A **fourth** group of scholars simply op-

---

130   After the publishing of *Marx Revisited*, someone in China went so far as to write *Back to the Whole Marx*, in an attempt to cartoonishly criticize my work. Besides making ignorant and arbitrary deductions about philosophical history, the author also touted the absolute veracity of his own ideas. I find it difficult to believe that there would still be a market for this kind of theoretical narcissism and thought imperialism in our modern day. In fact, the majority of younger scholars in China today understand that we can only come to relatively logical theoretical explanations in any scholarly realm; everyone is free to exchange and discuss on equal footing, contributing to a more tolerant and harmonious theoretical environment. Thus we can together create a tomorrow filled with national spirit and cultural resurgence. I believe that before engaging in prideful and egotistical criticism, such scholars should at least first understand the object of their criticism.

posed the textological research in *Marx Revisited* with philological proof, not understanding that philological **explanations** are only the premise and basis of textological **understanding**. A profound understanding of Marx's thought is the goal of scholarly research itself[131]. A **fifth** group of theorists engaged in profound interpretation and accurate criticism of *Marx Revisited*; they understood many of the basic points I made and extracted many of the important problems with my work[132]. However, it is not difficult for us to see that without exception, each of these interpretations of *Marx Revisited* wove its own views and discourse into the logic and discourse of the book; what they accomplished was, for the most part, re-construction and explanation of textual thought. However, I must say that they incited very interesting discussion.

For readers who share the same time period, historical background, cultural background, and language as the author of a text to have such diverse views on a text, it is easy to see how readers who are separated from authors by time and language have great difficulty in attempting to bridge the gulf between their thought situations. **Interpretation is the re-simulation and re-situating of thought, not a return to the original context of thought.** My views on textual interpretation here approach the post-modernism of Barthes' later years in that it is based on the reader's productive view of the text; however, I continually remind myself that I cannot fall into Barthes' relativist logical trap of intertextuality.

According to the theory of situating that I propose here, I specify the traditional textual interpretive progression into three different periods. First is **symbolic textual explanation**, then **understanding of interactive meaning fields**, and finally the **thought situation of productive**

---

131 At the beginning of the last century, there existed in European scholarly circles a metaphysical opposition between explanation and understanding in social scientific research methods. Comte's positivism favored fact-based explanations, while Dilthey emphasized spiritual theories in his "human historicism." Later, Winch suggested methodologically synthesizing the two viewpoints. Today, there exists in the study of Marxist philosophy the practice of setting textual explanations against textual understanding, and especially of deifying philology (to use Professor Xia Fan's words, this is the "MEGA fetishism," a very profound identification). This tendency is assuredly in opposition to the progression of history. Even more laughable, textological understanding becomes, for these scholars, a metaphysical "mystery" that they cannot understand.
132 Wang Jinfu's article can be found in issue 10 of *Nanjing Social Science* (1999), Yan Yan's article in Mongolia Social Science (2005) issue 2, and Hu Daping's in *Humanities Journal* (2005) issues 5 and 6.

textual reading. However, I have also found that my explanation of textological research methods in *Marx Revisited* was overly simple. This led readers to easily develop Other significant addenda, leading to breaks in understanding.

First, the explanation of symbols is the most basic level of textual explanation, a level that most readers will be able to reach through some effort of their own. On this level of reading, readers are limited by the understanding of the literal words and sentences on the page, they are unable to step beyond the surface level meaning of the connotations of the symbols and reach a deeper level of significance. The readers at this level are usually average readers, including the majority of students who read the text. In facing classical texts, they are limited by their own knowledge and backgrounds; they are unable to surpass this level and enter a deeper level of understanding. For this reason, I believe that the problems of traditional hermeneutics do not exist for **non-scholarly** readers.

Second, the next level of textual interpretation is an idealized interactive field of meaning. This is a process of reading and understanding that parallels traditional hermeneutics. This was the most important result of Western textology since Husserl. Views belonging to this level of understanding include Gadamer's philosophical hermeneutics, Althusser's pure structuralism and "guilty reading" in a Lacanian context. These textual interpretive models can be included among the ranks of **modern** textual interpretive methods, because they are based on a kind of dualistic epistemological framework. Under these models, dead texts and living readers exist in an unequal logical relationship. At the same time, the consciousness that **seeks to return** to the original text is still an important theoretical goal of this type of textual interpretation.

I believe that in addition to the two circumstances that I described above, there is a **third** level of textual interpretation: the philosophical situating theory of productive textual reading. In fact, the most important element of the philosophical situating theory rests on the understanding that **the purpose of reading is not the restoration of some original context, but rather creative production**. It is my opinion that the true basis of textology is "relational ontology"; to put it more clearly, I believe that **there is no such thing as a text divorced from the reader**. *Of course, to prevent misunderstanding, I should point out that this is not an "ontological" identification, but rather a simple* *realization that none of a reader's texts are **dead**.* As such, in textology, the dualistic division between the text and the reader is always false. In the reading of a text, the text in the scope of the reader is always re-activated by the reader: this is a **relational** existence. *In Spivak's explanation of Derrida's **Of Grammatology** she makes an interesting point, that this text does not have any firm homogeneity; a "book" is a "text" formed from similar and dissimilar structures, and therefore the "homogeneity" of the book cannot be reproduced. In each reading, we develop a false impression of the "original text"*[133]. In the process of explaining a text, the reader always has the advantage over the writer; what exists is always the particular theoretical mirror actively constructed by the reader's own theoretical logic, it is just that scholars have the tendency to idealistically identify their own explanations as the original context of the text. It is in this sense that Derrida compared the results of linguistic translation and textual interpretation to tracks or traces, thus explaining how the original meaning is no longer present; I believe that this is too negative a view. In other words, every kind of textual interpretation is actually "**Me**" speech conducted by the reader under the name of the text, not a true revelation of the **objective textual context**. Even for philological studies aimed at objectivity of historical materials, the situation is no different[134]. *Kojin Karatani wrote that true reading means not postulating any philosophical premise other than the "work" itself, not premising the intentions of any author*[135]. I believe that this is a goal that is impossible to attain. Such idealized "clean" reading is nothing but the illusion of literary scholars, because the any reading is only a kind of reading of the subject itself.

This books research on Lenin falls mainly into the second and third levels; at the same time, it is also "draft document" thought experiment.

133　Refer to Spivak's translator's note in Derrida's *Of Gramatology*. Beijing University Press (2007) page 4.

134　For instance in the organization of the texts of Marx and Engels by the German Marxist researcher Talbot, behind the so-called "value neutrality" there lurks a deconstruction of Marxism. I should go on to point out that the "Marxologie" turn of Talbot, who was a Marxist philologist from former East Germany, was forced by bourgeois ideology. In actuality, many of her important ideas have not yet stepped out of the shadow of the Stalinist framework. This is a more complex theoretical and actual problem. Some of my German friends who are familiar with what is going on pointed out that even with her turn to Marxologie, she has still been marginalized in recent MEGA research.

135　See Kojin Karatani's Marx: *The Center of Possibilities*. Central Translation Press (2006) page 2 (Chinese).

In *Marx Revisited*, I differentiated between the three basic types of Marxist text. First were the formal texts, or Marx's published essays, books, and other works; second were the generative texts, referring to Marx's manuscripts and unfinished works that were still in the production process; third were sub-texts, including excerpted notes and other theoretical outlines. As I have already given a more detailed differentiation of these texts in Marx Revisited, here I merely name them again. Because of this, the circumstances of my research become somewhat more complicated. Lenin's process of philosophical study is primarily made up of excerpted notes/written thoughts/outlines and a small amount of unpublished text. These fall into the categories of generative text and sub text. He even leaves a more obscure form of text, reading commentaries or what I call **draft text**.

At the same time, I now realize that for every original thinker, the generation of an original context of thought (the innovative (**productive**) theory of situating that we discussed earlier) is always an extremely complex process. However, I have also found that the theoretical generative process of nearly every thinker moves from an **Other mirror image space**, through an **independent thought situation**, and finally to an **innovative thought situation**.

What I refer to as **Other mirror image space** means the dominant discourse in one's academic thought construct depends on and borrows from, whether consciously or not, the academic thought logic (texts) of the **Other mirror image**[136]. In general, Other thought situating is supported and constructed, whether consciously or subconsciously, by various **inactive** theoretical resources (scholarly memory groups) and Other theoretical problematics, thus resulting in a kind of synthetic thought. *To borrow and re-write Julia Kristeva's words, this is a simplified intertextuality.* The relation between the theoretical production function and the thinking subject is usually expressed as structural influence and conceptual anchoring of the Other theoretical **framework** over the subject, while the subjects thought space is manifested as simple reproduction or a closed theoretical loop. This results in a certain amount of productivity and relative theoretical independence. The

---

136   This concept was proposed by Lacan, though his idea is divided into the small other (other) and the big other (Other); the former refers to the ontological misunderstanding towards the mirrored projection of self of the individual subject in the early stages of his self-establishment; the latter refers to the interrogatory construct of the individual subject by the entire linguistic symbolic system.

most evident thought context activated here is, in essence, a mirrored unconscious **agreement**. Rendering the situation even more complex, the scholarly memory in Other thought space often reappears under the form of **imagined** logical misunderstandings[137] and logical shadiness. Often, under this imagined conceptual misdirection, possible meanings and actual meanings are separated from one another. I have found that this kind of Other logical construction most often takes place in the early period of a thinker's academic development. This was true for Lenin's early work as well. Although young Lenin's thought and research in the fields of social economic development and actual political struggle makes him appear to be a mature Marxist from an early age, his early understanding of philosophy was primarily the product of Other cognitive structures. It can be said that what he relied on at the time were the philosophical notions of Plekhanov, Dietzgen, Feuerbach, and others. This same phenomenon arose in Lenin's early study of Hegelian philosophy. *Plekhanov's philosophical thought rested in Other cognitive structures for his entire life; the few innovative contributions he made were really misunderstandings of Marx, such as geographical determinism. We will discuss this point in greater detail later on.* To give another example, the development of German philosophy in the early 20th century primarily took Husserl's phenomenology as its Other mirror image; Heidegger, Scheler, Gadamer, and Marcuse all advanced their own philosophical innovations from this phenomenological mirror image. The development of French philosophy in the early 20th century, on the other hand, took Jean Hyppolite and Alexandre Kojeve interpretations of Hegelian philosophy as its Other mirror image; Barthes, Lacan, Sartre, Merleau-Ponty, Foucault, and others were either direct participants in Kojeve's discussion classes, or developed their own philosophical thought under the powerful influence of this French-style Hegelian mirror image. *Another even more complex question arises here: under the rule of medieval theology as under the domination of Stalinist ideology, oppressive Other mirror image structures became the only existential form of individual thought. Here, thought is stagnant and dead.*

In contrast, **independent thought situating** takes place as a thinker begins to move through a transitional developmental link towards his

---

137 **Imagined misunderstanding** or false understanding refers to a quickly dissolved transitional misunderstanding between the ideological false situation and the historical situation. False cognition is usually a logical element of Other thought space.

own mature theories. At this time, the thinker begins to escape the controlling influence of Other theoretical frameworks and establish his own independent thought. Though there is still corresponding intertextual thinking, under most circumstances what were once Other, external mirror image frameworks transition into the production of "Me" academic thought. In terms of the relationship between the theoretical production function and the thinking subject, the latter will begin to engage in more proactive construction activities, forcing the original theoretical academic resources to serve its new thought framework. The closed theoretical loop and simple reproduction in Other thought space begins to be challenged by new dimensions of thought, and the constructive change of theoretical logic into innovative theoretical **production functions** becomes inevitable. Thus "Me" theoretical production and open theoretical loops become the basic content and method of operation of the thought situation. For instance, young Marx's thought around 1844 was actually influenced by many Other thought resources, including Hegel and Feuerbach, both of whom were active in his underlying logic. These influences also include young Engels and Hess, who directly occupied the same discourse level as he, as well as English classical economics, which he was bent on refuting. It is not difficult for us to see that young Marx never simply succumbed to any Other framework, but rather continually attempted to convert the thought of others into his own theoretical logical elements. For instance, the theory of labour alienation in the *1844 Manuscript* was the result of these multiple intertextualities creating an independent thought situation. However, although young Marx's critique of the bourgeoisie was undertaken from the political standpoint of the proletariat, the theoretical problematics that he used were still Other constructs (the logic of Feuerbachian humanist alienation).

Innovative thought situating refers to the construction process of a thinker's own independent, complete theoretical logic and thought space through innovative theoretical production. Needless to say, this takes place almost exclusively in the mature stages of a thinker's theoretical creation. At that point in time, the thinker finally begins to critically surpass the entire Other thought framework that had dominated him in the past, sublating the false question-resolution lines of thought of his predecessors into the illusion of ultimate truth. Thus scholarly memory escapes from the original, unconscious mirror image acceptance and misunderstandings, often as intentionally transformed and altered meanings are activated. Thus the thought of his predecessors is deepened in a completely new discourse system or independent theoretical problematic, especially as he discovers areas in his predecessors question-resolution frameworks that they themselves had not considered. Thus the possible meanings and actual meanings of an academic concept are newly and systematically created, ultimately creating a new and unique innovative thought space. The moment where innovative thought situating takes place is the one at which great philosophical changes take place. These changes may even lead to a re-writing of the whole of philosophical history in a new theoretical loop. Of course, from the perspective of post-modernism, absolute philosophical innovation cannot exist; therefore, this so-called independent thought situation is essentially a more advanced synthesis of intertextual thought intertwining (Barthes' words). I have found that some of the greatest theoretical academic innovations in the history of philosophy take place in the theoretical situating of thought resurgence and logical integration. For instance, Plato's idealism came after Socrates, Kant's a priori epistemology came after Hume, Hegel's Absolute Idea came after Fichte and Schelling, Marx's historical materialism came after Hegel, Feuerbach, and Ricardo, and Heidegger's ontology came after Husserl, etc.

Of course, thinking of the entire developmental process of a philosopher's thought, at any of his productive periods he may experience whole shifts of thought situations; however, the most important shifts in thought space are still the gestalt shifts from Other mirror image space to independent thought situations. This shift is a process from quantitative change to qualitative change as Other thought continually concedes to independent thought, and as the thinking subject transitions from a passivity to active construction and independent thought. Of course, there are only a few truly innovative thinkers who are able to ultimately establish independent theoretical production functions. *At the same time, the majority of scholars who do not progress beyond Other frameworks should not be excluded. Of course, there is another exception here, that of a thinker who peculiarly regresses from independent or innovative philosophical situating to a state of Other mirror imaging. Such an occurrence is most often due to the external oppression of **ideological force**. For example, the Western Marxist thought of young Lukacs was forced into an Other mirror image of traditional philosophical explanatory frameworks under pressure from Stalinist ideological dogmatism. Bloch's situation was similar to this.* To take another example from the early thinking of Baudrillard, which I am studying right now, between 1969 and 1973 the surface level of his thought was expressed as theoretical borrowing from Lefebvre, Barthes, and others; later, he began to use Saussure's discourse in moving from affirming to refuting Marx's critical logic, which became an important logical reference for him. However, in the depths of Baudrillard's thought, he was heavily influenced by the Other discourse of the grass roots romanticism of Mauss and Bataille. Thus we can see that in Baudrillard's thought there was never a clearly defined period in which he was completely dominated by an Other thought framework – from the beginning his conceptual situating was independent. By the time he wrote *Symbolic Exchange and Death*, Baudrillard used the paradigm of simulacra and simulation to bring light to his own innovative thought situation. I will go into further discussion of Baudrillard in a book that will soon be published: *Baudrillard: A Deconstruction of the Post-Modern Academic Myth*[138].

This new viewpoint is also my newest **interpretive model of philosophical history**.

I believe that the independent, sincere attitude of this new method in re-evaluating the historical process of progression of Lenin's philosophical thought will inevitably lead to the demise of the oversimplification, linear determinism, subjective postulation, and false situating of past Soviet and Eastern European research. Thus a completely new historical logical thread in the study of the development of Lenin's philosophical thought will begin to appear.

7 *BERN NOTEBOOKS*: THE HISTORICAL PROCESS OF LENIN'S PHILOSOPHICAL SHIFT THAT TOOK PLACE IN HIS STUDY OF HEGEL'S THOUGHT

I have repeatedly explained how Lenin's work on the economic and political theory aspects of Marxism matured very early, standing at the pinnacle of the modern development of Marxism in his actual struggles against Russian Narodism, the theorists of the Second International, and Plekhanov and the Mensheviks. However, this was not the case in the field of philosophy. Lenin's theoretical starting point was not rooted in philosophical concepts, but rather the reality of the Russian Revolution. His attention to philosophy came as a result of his deep understanding

---

138   Refer to my *Contra Baudrillard: Déconstruction of a Post-modern Academic Myth*.

of real-life struggles and a scientific worldview. Between 1895 and 1913, these were the first and second time periods in Lenin's understanding of Marxist philosophical theory, and in these two periods, the development of his thought was manifested as a complex process of change and deepening. I have provided a basic explanation of this point previously, and in the main text of this book I will develop it further; here I will give a little more explanation of the third time period in the development of Lenin's philosophical thought, and especially to the internal logical progression in the *Bern Notebooks*.

From the perspective of the interpretive context of the philosophical situating theory proposed in this book, Lenin's study of Hegel's philosophy in the *Bern Notebooks* was not a smooth, homogeneous logical progression; in the entirety of this cognitive process, Lenin's understanding of Hegel's philosophy was not always correct. I believe that the *Bern Notebooks* were not **topical materials and research notes** prepared in order to write a scholarly book, but rather learning and reading notes in a general sense. *According to the understanding of textual phylogenetics, the pre-textual generative process of a work includes "outlines, material notes, drafts, and manuscripts" etc.*[139]. *We can be sure that the* **Bern Notebooks** *were not intended as topical research notes in preparation for a work on material dialectics, because before them, Lenin did not leave any writing or thought outlines for a book on dialectics. The facts in existing documents show that before writing any important scholarly work, Lenin would always write outlines of his thought or writing plans. I will explain later how the small summary of Lenin's thought at the end of the* **Bern Notebooks** *was not any kind of "writing plan" or systematic logical conception.* These important reading notes reflect for us the multiple shifts in philosophical understanding and major detournements of theoretical logic experienced by Lenin's thought during this time period. I believe that these notebooks can be divided into several heterogeneous stages. In the first stage, Lenin was still under the influence of the **Other mirror image context**, when he used refutational concepts in his understanding of Hegel. During the second stage, multiple logical cognitive frameworks came into violent conflict, resulting in philosophical contradictions. In the third stage, Lenin entered an **independent thought space**, one in which his thought experienced major shifts and where his understanding progressed in leaps and bounds. The fourth and final stage was where Lenin summarized his philosophical research.

---

139   See *Textual Phylogenetics*. Tianjin People's Press (2005), page 29 (Chinese).

I believe that before beginning our study of the *Bern Notebooks*, we must first consciously understand the following methodological problems. **First**, as he began to enter his study of Hegel's philosophy, Lenin consciously constructed an **Other** reading framework; using Lacan's big Other theory to analyze this, it is not difficult for us to see that this was a **mirror image Other** originating from Marx, Engels, Plekhanov, Feuerbach, and Dietzgen. *According to Lacan's discourse logic, the Other is an external image that is not myself; while the Other is not me, but in the process of losing myself, I come to reside within the Other[140]. However, my use of the concept of Other mirror images is not a simple pejorative; it is a neutral judgment, referring merely to the fact that as Lenin began studying Hegelian philosophy, he did so with an external theoretical authority as the thought reference system to his analysis and research.* In my opinion, Lenin's Other mirror image cognitive circumstances as he began to examine Hegel's philosophy were primarily formed from three scholarly memory groups. **First**, an incorrect understanding of Marx's abstract potential meaning of "inversion" in Hegel's dialectics; this was a **false** actual meaning in this Other mirror image. **Second**, the philosophical standpoint of general materialism established by Feuerbach and Dietzgen's concepts; here Lenin basically borrowed the original scholarly memory points, though his problem was that he misunderstood them as Marx's materialist notions. **Third**, a somewhat unenlightened explanation of Marxist philosophy as reconstructed and inherited from Plekhanov; objectively speaking, this included misunderstandings of correct content. We can see that the Other mirror image in Lenin's thought was extremely complex at this time. Its first theoretical component was a false actual meaning, its second component was a misunderstood essential actual meaning, and its third was formed from the addition and overlap of dual voices, including Marx as misunderstood by Plekhanov and views that truly belonged to Plekhanov. Furthermore, the second and third theoretical components formed the subsidiary awareness of the first abstract potential meaning. I believe that this is a crucial philosophical situating plot, namely that as Lenin began reading Hegel, his theoretical thinking subject was constructed by this **Other influence.** *Of course, Lenin at this time certainly believed that this was a correct reading reference system.* It was this external mirror image Other that constructed the whole of the theoretical circuit in Lenin's early reading. At that stage, Lenin's every qualitative

---

140   Refer to chapters 2, 7, and 8 of my *The Truth that could not be: Reflection of Lacan's Philosophy*. Commercial Press (2006).

judgment of textual restructuring originated from this **closed** line of thought, with its continually returning standpoint and basis of principle. Here, we can conclude that the subjective operation of Lenin's theoretical thought was in **Other thought space**[141].

The **second** methodological problem that we have to understand is Hegel's enormous system of speculative philosophical logic and the simple qualitative judgment that Lenin made of it at the beginning of his research, as well as his later understanding of this speculative logical system. Looking at Lenin's excerpted notes from the early part of this stage, his thought did contain some original Hegelian speculative logical situations, but these were in a **deactivated** stage; naturally Lenin was not able to reproduce or restructure Hegel's original logical situation. Although there was another kind of activation of this theoretical logic by Lenin in this stage, at the most this was merely a false theoretical image. We must point out the fact that the logic of Hegel's dialectic did not begin to be truly activated until after Lenin's own thought had experienced a great shift in understanding; this was a recognition and activation of Marx's philosophical context reached through the transformation and adjustment of **practical** materialism. Furthermore, I believe that even though this is true, we cannot simply decide that Lenin ultimately grasped Hegel's philosophy in its entirety. On this point we will see later that based on different cognitive frameworks, Lenin's understanding of Hegel's philosophy manifested two completely different **philosophical theoretical spaces**.

---

141   Here there is another example I can use to further explicate this so-called Other context. Recently, several theorists have written hundreds of pages, critically interpreting my *Marx Revisited*. Their sole **affirmative reference** were the "newest findings" of Western Marxist philology, and as such, their "criticism" could never escape from simple dependence on external textual data in their assertion that Back to Marx included many "obsolete" ideas. This is a typical example of the Other mirror image of the **unthinking subject**. Without independent thought, one cannot but rely on the theoretical logic of others in one's theorizing, succumbing to external authorities and becoming a pitiful tailist of Other ideas. At the same time, these scholars criticized and denigrated the innovative scholarly thought of *Marx Revisited* as speculative metaphsyics. In the autumn of 2006, in the first "International Symposium on Contemporary Capitalism," I met with the leader of these critics, the well-known English Marxist philologist Professor Carver. One evening, while exchanging ideas with English scholars at a reception, somebody mentioned these "criticisms" of *Marx Revisited*. After stating that he did not want to enter this "war," Professor Carver said to me in front of the other five English scholars: "You are an innovative scholar and they are not." It is evident that he also knew of the pitiful **Other** discourse of these critics.

The **third** methodological problem is the Marxist philosophy established by Marx and Engels, as well as Lenin's understanding and development of that philosophy. The new philosophical scope developed by the Marxism of Marx and Engels had already been accepted and understood as a basic standpoint, viewpoint, and methodology by young Lenin. There is little doubt that even before systematically reading Hegel's philosophy, Lenin was already a staunch Marxist. However, when Lenin later stated that not a single Marxist in the 20th century truly understood Marx, his viewpoint was very profound. We can easily see that Lenin's thought discourse was not static or homogeneous; rather his understanding of Marxist philosophy was developed through a process of deepening. In that process, Lenin's understanding of Marxist philosophy underwent a momentous leap in understanding. However, the leap in understanding here was not an "epistemological rupture" in a Bachelard-Althusser sense, but rather a rapid increase in understanding in the **same line of logic**. In my opinion, this increase in understanding was based on his activation of Hegel's philosophical logic and **re-situating** of Marx's philosophical thought more that it originated from his direct interpretation of the texts of Marx and Engels. Beginning at this point, Lenin was able to step onto a higher level of independent thought in terms of Marxist philosophy.

Fourth, we must consider the true practical motivation of Lenin's systematic philosophical research. In Lenin's entire progression of reading and study of Hegel's philosophy, this practical motivation was not a dominant theoretical directness, but rather an invisible **logic ray**, manifested in Lenin's philosophical situation. I believe that there are two lines of thought here: first, the actual subjective dynamism of the proletariat class, on which Lenin had begun to focus beginning in 1900, and second, flexibility used in the strategies of the actual revolutionary struggle. The essence of the former lay in opposing the economic determinism of the Second International and Plekhanov, thus scientifically evaluating the direction and future of the Russian Revolution; the emphasis of the latter lay in managing the diverse dialectical relations in the actual, complicated struggle, such as the different contradictory choices and strategies employed in the First World War, as well as the Treaty of Brest Litovsk which came soon after the victory of the October Revolution and the numerous policy adjustments that came in the period of "perestroika."

My most recent research findings show that in the whole writing process of the *Bern Notebooks*, Lenin's philosophical epistemological progression experienced four distinct stages.

In the **first stage**, Lenin constructed a reading space aimed at learning, in which existed two basic discourse threads.

The first thread was Hegel's philosophical logic as a historical textual form; it existed in *The Science of Logic, Small logic, Lectures on Philosophical History, and Historical Philosophical Lectures. More accurately put, this is not the entire field of Hegel's philosophical logic, because Lenin did not read the **Phenomenology of the Spirit**, **Natural Philosophy**, or **Spiritual Philosophy***. The second thread was composed of the basic Marxist notions that Lenin accepted into his own theoretical logic. *However, this was not complete either, because in the field of philosophy, Lenin had not yet read young Marx's **1844 Manuscript**, or **The German Ideology**, in which Marx and Engels truly generated the general theory of materialism, or **Letter to Annenkov, Grundrisse**, etc. This ensured that Lenin's understanding of the thought context of Marxist philosophy could not truly be called complete.*

This second discourse thread was expressed here as the "materialist inversion" of Hegel's dialectics by Marx and Engels; it is evident that Lenin viewed this as the primary theoretical reference system for his critical reading of Hegel's philosophy. Careful analysis reveals that Lenin's discourse thread here contains several logical thought points. **First**, Marx and Engels' inversion of Hegel's dialectics. Lenin's understanding of this was, at first, simply an external Other theoretical mirror image rather than his own independent thought. In addition, in Lenin's thought space at this time, the potential meaning and actual meaning of Marx's "inversion" theory were disparate at this time, primarily meaning that Lenin followed Feuerbach and Dietzgen in simply replacing Hegel's Idea with a material **concept**. **Second**, Lenin's understanding mirror image of philosophical materialism, including the scholarly memory of the philosophical textual constructs of Feuerbach and Dietzgen, as well as Plekhanov's misunderstood explanations. The essential logical point here was the objectively existing material and external natural world that was **not determined by the will of man.** **Third**, here there was also an important standard of logical differentiation, *i.e.*, the general differentiation between materialism and idealism. These were the correct logic proceeding from material to perception to the idea of materialism, and the **incorrect logic** proceeding from the idea to perception and then to material of idealism. This became an important window into Lenin's early "inversion" of Hegel in his reading.

As we read and as these two discourse threads come into hermeneutic contact, Lenin did not plan on **phenomenologically** entering Hegel's philosophy, i.e., he never attempted to recreate the thought context of the Absolute Idea from the theoretical logic components established by Hegel. It is evident that from its starting point, Lenin's understanding stood with materialist philosophers, premised on the refutation of the legitimacy of the whole of Hegel's philosophical logic. He never attempted to develop a more complete context of Hegel's philosophical logic. *Deborin wrote that Lenin believed that Hegel's system was basically correct[142], which may be a correct judgment. However, this understanding did not come until Lenin's final stage of reading **The Science of Logic**; it was the result of intense logical detournement philosophical re-situating. Lenin, who had just entered the study of Hegelian philosophy, could not have arrived at this conclusion. For this reason, Deborin's "correct" judgment lacks historical, concrete time reference.* In other words, Lenin's encounter with Hegel was built on the deconstructive activities of overall refutation; faced with Hegel's philosophy, he desired merely to extract elements of the dialectic that he would be able to use himself from the ruins of deconstructed idealism. *Later he referred to these elements as the essential elements of dialectics.* At this time, the first qualitative judgment that Lenin made of Hegel's philosophy was that Hegelian philosophy (idealism, the idea of God) was **nonsense**. Lenin did not understand the true secret of Hegel's philosophical logic. In this discourse that aimed at disproving Hegel, there was no theoretical possibility of activating and completely rebuilding Hegel's philosophical context in Lenin's early logical space. As such, as we see Hegel's philosophical views on which Lenin focuses and which he chooses to excerpt, as deactivated theoretical points obtained from certain fragments of logical context; furthermore, the original systematic nature of Lenin's philosophical notions, with the exception of his materialist "inversion," do not exist anymore. Even if part of the content existed in Lenin's logic, there is no way of confirming it today. I believe that Lenin's early reading and research of Hegel's philosophy was, overall, an unsuccessful thought experiment. In other words,

---

142   Deborin, Abram. *Introduction to volume 9 of "The Lenin Papers".* Soviet National Press (1929) page 3 (Chinese).

it was heavily influenced by an external, Other mirror image, a **false** reading in a closed, false theoretical circuit. Imagine that if the overall theoretical logic of Hegel's philosophy was not present, how could one say that he had obtained a true knowledge of Hegel's dialectical thought? In addition, it is possible for us to deduce that as Lenin began reading Hegel's *The Science of Logic*, it was very difficult for him. He often felt consternated by its abstruse content; the situation was not, as Kedrov would have us believe, one where Lenin effortlessly reconstructed Hegel's philosophy, establishing the great logical system of the materialist dialectical method.

However, this state of affairs went through an important change in Lenin's **second stage**. From the logical development of the text, this change, at the beginning, was not actively pursued by Lenin, but rather a **passive ingestion** in the reading process. As Lenin approached a truer understanding of Hegel, the new **theoretical thought context** developed from the overall logic of *The Science of Logic* and other texts caused him to approach a **previously unknown** Marxist materialist dialectic Logic. In Lenin's progression of reading, more and more non-Other thoughts began to challenge his previous reading framework and a new, independent line of thought in his reading began to emerge from the paradoxes of his thought and self-reflections. In his original line of thought, Lenin directly **opposed** Hegel to Marx, while in the new thought context that was gradually being generated , Lenin began to group Hegel's dialectical logic (not idealism!) with Marx's historical materialism and Darwin's theory of evolution. As his research delved deeper, this theoretical intention began to become more and more intense; however, his original reading framework still occupied a dominant position, and as such, from the texts written in his second period, we often see contradictions and uncertainty as Lenin vacillates between two very different reading frameworks. This is because in Lenin's **polyphonous** logical situation and reading scope at this time, an element of deconstruction already begins to work its way to the surface, though the original logic still occupies the dominant position for a time. Expressed in fashionable terminology, the former was a power discourse, and the latter a sprouting **refutational logic**. It is evident that the second period in Lenin's reading of Hegel's philosophy was one in which contradictory, dual logics unconsciously tangled together, forming a unique situating context in which the new and old logics waxed and waned but did not experience fundamental change.

In the third stage of Lenin's reading, the vague, new logic finally began to take shape as a completely new theoretical context. From Lenin's own theoretical logical detournement, Lenin was able to reconstruct the theoretical context of Hegelian and Marxist philosophy. This was concretely expressed as **two** important epistemological shifts.

I believe that Lenin's first epistemological shift at this stage took place during his reading and pondering on the "Doctrine of the Notion" section of Hegel's *The Science of Logic*. Through complex, revolutionary thought experimentation, Lenin was able to bring out a completely new line of reading logic: a thorough renewal of his overall understanding and appraisal of Hegelian philosophy. This leap in understanding founded on the basis of his original overall refutational interpretive framework. Thus the contradictions and paradoxes between his two lines of reading logic were finally resolved. *I must emphasize the fact that the original reading line of thought was not determined by Lenin to be **wrong**, but rather sublated as an **unconscious structure** that did not harmoniously fit into the new logical framework of his reading.* At this time, Lenin was still critically reading Hegel's philosophy, although these criticisms were much more profound than the simple refutations he made in his early studies. At the same time, Lenin finally realized that one of the **structural elements** of Marx's whole theory was **historical dialectical logic**, reconstructed from Hegel's philosophy by materialism. As Lenin's understanding began to change, his original philosophical logic space also began to experience an earth-shattering gestalt shift. What were once general materialist methods as an Other mirror image and the simple logic that materialism was correct and idealism **incorrect** were broken down, the results of this deconstruction the result was expressed as the utter division of the original scholarly memory groups. **First**, the newly more deeply understood philosophical logic of Marx and Engels appears for the first time here, thus correcting many of the false theoretical misunderstandings in Lenin's earlier reading; **Second**, Lenin utterly surpassed the **explanation** of Marxist philosophy that had been misunderstood by Plekhanov and others; **Third**, this explanation became the object of Lenin's criticism, the "old materialism" of philosophers who were not even as "smart" as Hegel (Feuerbach and Dietzgen). **Fourth**, Lenin found that there was a great need to proceed from the perspective of dialectics and expand the criticism of Kant and Machism. This was a restructuring and deepening of his own original "dialectical materialist" thought space. It is not difficult to see that when these important theoretical logic references began to experience important shifts, Lenin's philosophical theoretical situation would naturally be utterly restructured. A host of new views and lines of thought began to appear, and a completely new, open theoretical circuit began to coalesce. Most important in this process, Lenin realized that only through truly understanding Hegel's dialectical philosophy could he more deeply penetrate the new philosophical scope created by Marx and Engels.

It was also in this third stage that Lenin's thought experienced a second shift in understanding: this was the process by which he truly grasped the true meaning of materialist dialectics and creatively developed it in his new theory. This allowed his new theoretical situating logic to reach a new level of strength and stability. At this point, Lenin first begins to profoundly understand Marx's true scientific materialist dialectical thought, as well as Marx and Engels' **deeper** critique of idealism and agnosticism in their new **practical** materialist scope. Thus Lenin ultimately surpassed old materialism, using this scientific theory (logic) in his understanding of the world, in directing practice, recreating the world, and realizing the great meaning of the philosophical revolution. Also because his attitude towards Hegel's philosophy experienced such a thorough shift, Lenin's overall grasp of dialectics also shifted, thus manifesting a completely new vision of dialectics, or *objective, actual, practical dialectics*. From my textual analysis I deduce that this second shift was too far distant from the first; more directly, I believe that it took place as Lenin was studying the second section (Objectivity) of the third book of Hegel's *The Science of Logic*. Here, Lenin uses the method of **comparison** for the first time in examining the overall framework of the materialist dialectic that he understood and Hegel's idealist dialectic. This important discovery of Lenin's was based on the logical premise of **philosophically qualified subjective participation**; of course, this participation was not that of Hegel's subjective idea, but rather of objective practice. Furthermore, this "practice" appeared as the dialectical basis of **ontology**. I believe that this is the key to understanding the second detournement of theoretical logic in Lenin's *Bern Notebooks*. Evidently, when compared with the simple conceptual exchange of Lenin's prior "inversion" thinking, this materialist reconstruction of Hegel was truly thorough, expressed as the inversion and restructuring of the whole of Hegel's logic. Here Lenin began to appreciate the place and function of man's active, objective, **practical**

dialectics in his relations with objects and the outside world. Thus he was able to attain the underlying theoretical logic demonstrated by the new philosophical scope of Marx and Engels in *The Germany Ideology*, one that he had not been able to reach before. This was that the nature that **surrounds** us is the product of practice; objective practical dialectics is the true basis of the new worldview of Marxist philosophy, and all this was the most important foundational principle of historical materialism. In his second line of comparative thought undertaken not long after, Lenin went on to realize that it was practice that **drew** a diagram of the objective world; this was the ultimate confirmation of the important place of practical dialectics on the ontological level of philosophy. The objective diagram of the world in the minds of men was not a direct reflection of the outside world. The axes which weave this diagram are the dimension of practical function that changes external reality. In other words, the quantitative and qualitative progress made based on man's purposes (needs). Here Lenin finally realized his own **independent** theoretical thought situation. At this time, although he had not read *The German Ideology* or *Grundrisse* by Marx and Engels, he revealed his genius in reaching the theoretical scope of Marx and Engels, even realizing his own theoretical innovations in a few important aspects. Furthermore, this important new understanding reached by Lenin also included the new viewpoint of reconfirmed, synthesized dialectics, epistemology, and logic on the basis of practice.

The fourth stage in the *Bern Notebooks* is formed by Lenin's summary of his research and study of Hegel; it begins with the last chapter in *The Science of Logic* ("The Idea") and appears first in the form of "16 Elements of Dialectics," and then scattered throughout the various excerpted notes, reading notes, and thoughts.

Unlike Kedrov's view, I believe that the "16 Elements" were not the result of Lenin's conscious, active construction of a materialist dialectic theoretical **system**. Rather, they were merely a summary of his findings on materialist dialectics in his research, a short summary of **subjective** dialectical theory. To depart from this particular context and artificially and abstractly elevate it – especially to view that the "16 Elements" were a direct representation of an **objective** dialectical structure – does not conform to Lenin's original desires. Most interestingly, in these summarized elements, Lenin does not touch on some of his new findings from his research and thought experiments, namely the

practical logical situation. It is my view that Lenin wrote this small summary not as an outline or writing plan for the direct construction a materialist dialectical logical structure, but rather as a brief overview of some things that he uncovered in his study of Hegelian philosophy that left a deep impression on him, especially several dialectical and epistemological viewpoints. Therefore, in this summary he did not more deeply discuss the practical aspect of dialectics and epistemology. Not long after, Lenin again began to read Hegel's philosophical works. At this time, Lenin again confirmed the practical dialectical thought space that he had discovered previously. He discovered the logical structure of materialist dialectics, *i.e.*, the specific, concrete logical framework formed by the movement of man's subjective dialectics and objective dialectics through the medium of practical dialectics. Here, **subjective dialectics were not directly connected to objective dialectics but rather moved at the same pace as the practical dialectical structure; through concrete, real, historical** human practice, it conforms to one aspect of the innumerable aspects that appear simultaneously in things. Lenin profoundly realized that the subjective dialectic did not directly reflect the objective dialectic; only through continually developing practical dialectics ("technology, history, etc.") and under certain practical, functional conditions of history could people reflect certain qualifications of the objective dialectic in terms of "certain links" that they understand.

After completing his reading of Hegel's philosophy, Lenin wrote three summaries of his own thoughts: "Conspectus of Hegel's Book *The Science of Logic*," "Conspectus of Lassalle's Book *The Philosophy of Heraclitus the Obscure of Ephesus*," and *On the Question of Dialectics*. I believe that the first of these was a **summary of his reading**, the second was a **re-evaluation** of the formation of the dialectical theoretical logical structure, and the third included some of Lenin's **thoughts and reflections** on his own experience learning dialectics. Of these, I believe the most important was "Conspectus of Hegel's Book *The Science of Logic*," because this was a holistic, logical analysis of his reading of Hegel. In this text we find that Lenin already grasped the theoretical fact that Hegel's dialectical structure was the **logical reflection** of the epistemological structure of the human subject. Hegel's mistake was only in idealistically confirming this **subjective cognitive structure** of the subject as **foundational essence** that objectively exists. In critically restructuring Hegel, we cannot view this subjective cognitive structure as the objective structure itself, but must rather reconfirm the true foundation of the subjective cognitive structure from within the subject: that foundation is practice. The subjective cognitive structure of man (logic) is constrained by the structure and logic of man's objective practical progress. The logical, progressive increase in **degree of order** that Hegel describes is nothing more than the practical degree of digging down as the subject moves towards the object. Only through the intermediary of practice can objective structures be expressed historically. It is my opinion that as Lenin read Hegel's philosophical works, this was the **pinnacle** of his independent thought situation. It is in this sense that he profoundly grasped the whole of the essence of Marx's materialist dialectical method, thus making his thought much more profound.

There is one final point for me to explain. This gestalt shift that took place for Lenin's philosophical thought in the *Bern Notebooks* was not directly due to his study of the texts of Marx and Engels. 10 or more years earlier, Lenin had already seriously studied Marx's *Capital* and his other important published works; around 1913, he once again concentrated on studying the works of Marx and Engels, only without such profound thoughts and philosophical constructions. During this study, he approached the subject from the perspective of Hegelian philosophical logic that he had originally attempted to refute, actually activating his own deeper, holistic understanding of Marx's theoretical logic. This was truly a high quality logical situation of Marxist philosophy. I believe that there is another aspect that is important for us to understand: beginning from our discussion here, it seems as though Lenin profoundly understood Marx's historical dialectics and revolutionary critical spirit through reading and understanding Hegel's dialectics. The truth, however, is rather more complex, because the actual motivation for his philosophical shift was the **practice and struggle of the real revolution**. We know that for a long time before this, the Bolshevik Russian Revolution led by Lenin had been coming under the criticism and doubt of Lenin's teacher Plekhanov and the thinkers of the Second International; after all, Russia's capitalist development was still in its infancy, and its real foundation of productive forces were far from reaching the objective material preconditions set by Marx and Engels for the proletariat revolution. Lenin was unable to find a ready answer for this argument, no matter how he searched through the political economic, historical, and social political texts of Marx and Engels. However, after reaching the pinnacle of his independent philosophical situation in reading Hegel's philosophy, he was pleased to discover the assertion that **practice creates and changes existence** in Marx's practical dialectics of. We should point out that this was an **unconscious detournement of academic discourse**. When Lenin passionately declared that no 20th century Marxist understood Marx, this conclusion did not only refer to philosophical theory, but also to the scientific dialectical method of the real proletariat revolution.

Therefore, I believe that Lenin's study of Hegel's philosophy in the *Bern Notebooks* ultimately points not towards the writing of a **predetermined, systematic** work on materialist dialectics, but rather to the reality of the Russian proletariat practice and revolution. *Badiou said that Lenin always loved events and did not specially engage in theorizing; this is correct*[143]. The theories of Soviet scholars, especially Kedrov's "planned conception theory," do not inspire confidence. On the eve of the October Revolution, why would Lenin want to write a book on philosophy? Would he really ignore the winds of war sweeping over all of Europe, bury himself in the study of Hegelian philosophy and dialectical questions to write a book or to prepare for the real revolution? This is not a question that can be answered with subjective guesswork and arbitrary judgments; rather, it must be answered by scientifically examining textual truth, analyzing textual plots, dissipating ideological illusions, and re-simulating historical fact.

Therefore, let us revisit Lenin!

---

143   Refer to *Ontology and Politics: Conversations with Badiou*. Guangxi Normal University Press (2006) page 314.

PART II

LENIN ON THE PATH TO PHILOSOPHICAL ENLIGHTENMENT

In part one of this book, we will examine the first two periods in the development of Lenin's philosophical thought, *i.e.*, his philosophical shifts between the late 19th century and 1913.

The first time period lasted from 1894 until around 1906. During this time, the actual philosophical documents left by Lenin are extremely rare; we can only **symptomatically** investigate Lenin's philosophical context from the large number of political texts he wrote on real problems. As such, to be honest I must concede that my grasp of the significance of Lenin's philosophical discourse during this period of time is completely based on my own **subjective situation** and **theoretical deductions**. The texts upon which I base my conclusions include the 1894 *What the "Friends of the People Are,"* Lenin's 1895 notes on *The Holy Family,* and a few scattered reading notes and political texts.

The second time period lasted from 1907 to 1913. In addition to his published texts, Lenin conducted two systematic studies of philosophy during this time, leaving for us extensive reading notes and commentaries, including the famous *Materialism and Empirio-Criticism*[1], several articles propagandizing Marxism ("The Historical Destiny of the Doctrine of Karl Marx" and "The Three Origins and Three Components of Marxism"), as well as a large number of sub texts and draft texts. The latter include: letters exchanged between Lenin and the Russian author Gorky, commentaries on Plekhanov's 1908 work Fundamental Problems with Marxism, commentaries on the *Collected Works of Dietzgen*, a large number of commentaries on Western works of philosophy and science, commentaries on Deborin's philosophical articles, commentaries on Chernyshevsky's texts, and excerpted notes on Feuerbach's *Lectures on the Essence of Religion*. Of course, to this long list we should add the extremely important outlines and excerpted notes that he took on the *Correspondence of Marx and Engels* in 1913.

I believe that these sub texts and draft texts are the key to our understanding of Lenin's philosophical thought at different time periods, opening a truer window of textual analysis and philosophical research. Regrettably, these texts were largely ignored in the traditional research of Lenin's philosophy. The philosophical notes and reading commentaries left by Lenin during these two time periods have been severely ignored by both Soviet scholars as well as in the research of Western Marxists. In fact, I believe that these primary source notes and commentaries are essential to our **re-simulating** the **possible** "original" context of Lenin's thought and writing, to our understanding the essence of Lenin's philosophical thought.

---

1   In the research on Lenin's philosophical thought by our group of Chinese scholars, the topical research on this important work of Lenin's was conducted by Professor Liu Huaiyu. As such, this book will not examine this text in detail.

CHAPTER ONE

YOUNG LENIN IN REVOLUTIONARY PRACTICE AND THE SUBJECTIVE DIMENSION OF HISTORICAL REALITY

As early as the late 1880s, with Lenin's first emergence on the scholarly and revolutionary scene, he was already a Marxist. This was one aspect in which Lenin differed greatly from Marx and Lenin. In other words, although there was a period that we can refer to as young Lenin, his thought at that time still existed under a Marxist philosophical framework. However, although Lenin was a Marxist from the start, in terms of his understanding of Marxist philosophy, and especially his understanding of materialist dialectics, young Lenin's thought inevitably experienced a long process of continual learning, continual deepening. I believe that just within the decade of 1894 to 1905, Lenin's philosophical understanding experienced several major philosophical shifts, which were expressed as shifts in different examination dimensions of real social historical development; these changes in terms of perspective caused the real logic ray within his philosophical concepts to change correspondingly. Furthermore, this change in young Lenin's philosophical concepts was also linked to the philosophical development of his teacher Plekhanov in ways that cannot be ignored. I believe that compared to the studies of Lenin in traditional Marxist philosophical history, such an understanding is an important "discovery," coming after throwing off the explanatory framework of the former Soviet Union and Eastern Europe.

1 YOUNG LENIN AND THE OBJECTIVE DIMENSION OF HISTORICAL DIALECTICS

I have found that Lenin was a Marxist from his youth. However, the basic Marxist theories that young Lenin accepted were mostly economic principles and political theories related to the actual struggle of Russia. Purely academic philosophical research had not yet entered the scope of his research, because what **young** Lenin cared about here was the real development and fate of Russian society. *Maslow wrote specifically about this. Thinking about the primary characteristics of young Lenin's thought in the 1880s, he wrote that Lenin cared more about the pressing questions of Russia's destiny, not purely theoretical questions[1]. Krupskaya, Adoratsky, and young Lukacs all identify this fact.* As such, some of Lenin's early reading notes and commentaries reveal that he focused on Marx's Capital as well as texts on economics and scientific socialism during this period of time[2]. In texts such as his 1893 "On the So-Called Market Question," we can already see that he used Marx's economic views to analyze the question of Russia's economic development[3]. To give another example, in his preparatory research for The Development of Capitalism in Russia, Lenin embarked on another deeper and more serious study of Capital, though his focus here was on concrete questions of economic and social development, lacking further thought on the historical materialist principles and scientific methodology of Marx's study of economics[4]. *I believe that this was an important support for the theoretical situating of young Lenin.* I should also point out that in terms of Lenin's direction and emphasis at this time, his understanding was basically correct and not without depth; in particular, his application of some of the scientific methods and basic principles of

---

1   See Maslow's Remembering Lenin. Moscow (1989) volume 3 page 25.
2   See volume 57 of the second edition of the Chinese *Collected Works of Lenin*.
3   See volume 1 of the second edition of the Chinese *Collected Works of Lenin*.
4   See volume 57 of the second edition of the Chinese *Collected Works of Lenin*.

Marxism to the social reality of Russia displayed rare perspicacity and historical concreteness.

However, this does not mean that young Lenin's understanding of **all** Marxist theories was always absolutely correct and thorough. *This arbitrary logic and oversimplified examination existed in the conclusions of Soviet scholars under the influence of the Stalinist dogmatic ideological framework towards the thought of young Lenin.* Proceeding from the research perspective that I propose here, i.e., objective analysis based on the historical developmental process of Lenin's philosophical thought, it is not hard to see that young Lenin's scientific understanding of Marxist philosophical theories did not come all at once. It is common knowledge that, in terms of philosophical theory, Lenin was nourished by his mentor – Plekhanov – as well as the theorists of the Second International. *Korsch also identified this scholarly connection*[5]. It is evident that the theoretical situation of young Lenin's philosophical thought was inevitably a kind of **Other** context. Especially in his early theoretical investigations, we are unable to see that he engaged in numerous, profound, or systematic studies of philosophical theory. Analyzing the text, we even find that the philosophical thought of young Lenin at this time manifests an unstable, variable quality. This is especially true in his understanding of historical materialism and dialectics; in the understanding of young Lenin, there clearly existed multiple theoretical deviations. In this section we will specifically examine the developmental path of young Lenin's philosophical thought.

In 1894, the first published philosophical paper on philosophy (*What the "Friends of the People" Are*) by the 24-year-old young Lenin defined the materialist dialectic understood by Marx and Engels as "the rejection of the methods of idealism and subjectivism in sociology"[6]. This was a method that *proceeded from objective reality. If this was his basis and **theoretical starting point for understanding materialist dialectics**, then we must say that Lenin was correct.* However, in his opinion, materialist dialectics were "the scientific method in sociology, which consists in regarding society as a living organism in a state of constant development," and the substance of this dialectic was "social evolution as the natural historical process of development of social-economic

5   See Korsch's *Marxism and Philosophy*. Chongqing Press (1989) page 80.
6   Lenin, Vladimir. "What the 'Friends of the People' Are." *Collected Works of Lenin* (Chin. 2. Ed.) volume 1, page 153 (Chinese).

formations"[7]. There is little doubt that this understanding was really quite distant from the rich connotations of Marx and Engels' historical dialectics. Although the historical materialism and historical dialectics developed by Marx and Engels are of the same substance, they are obviously not the same thing. I should also point out that young Lenin here imprecisely identifies the central idea of historical materialism as viewing "the social movement as a process of natural history, governed by laws not only independent of human will, consciousness and intentions, but, rather, on the contrary, determining the will, consciousness and intentions of men"[8]. *Unfortunately, this not **entirely accurate view** was taken as a classical expression of the basic views of historical materialism in the philosophical systems of the Stalinist era*[9]. Why did Lenin believe this?

After carefully considering the other texts written by Lenin at this time, I have found that the real efforts of young Lenin at this time were directed to the work of struggling against Russian Narodism[10]. *As such, this was a **definite theoretical situation** produced to meet the important theoretical demands of an actual political struggle.* We know that the debate between Russian Marxists and Narodniks primarily revolved around the question of Russia's social developmental direction. At this time, Russia was obviously at a low level of capitalist development: according to 1881 statistics, there were only about 1 million industrial workers compared with 75 million peasants. *Later Lenin would write that this was a great sea of small producers.*

---

7   *Ibid.*, pages 135 and 159 (Chinese).
8   *Ibid.*, page 136 (Chinese).
9   This false explanatory position originated primarily from the theorists of the Second International, who incorrectly viewed the blind movements ("quasi-naturalness") that are similar to the natural world and that appear in the development of social history in Marx's special theory of historical materialism as a general law of historical materialism. Refer to my *The Subjective Dimension of Marxist Historical Dialectics.*
10   Russian Narodism appeared in the 1870s, formed after a group of leftist intellectuals came into contact with Marxism. It was a social school of thought that carried the emotion of nationalism. Mikhailovsky was a representative of this school. Seeing the cruel exploitation of workers and social inequality brought on by the European capitalist system, these thinkers attempted to skip over capitalism in the development of Russia's society. They wanted to reach agricultural socialism by avoiding class conflict and following the path of Russia's communes. To this end, they even wrote directly to Marx, which led to Marx's famous letter to Zasulich. It was in this particular historical context that the Narodnik thinkers would consider themselves "friends of the Russian people."

What did Lenin see as Narodism? According to his own later definition, Narodism can be understood as containing the following three characteristics.

First, they believed that **capitalism in Russia would mean weakness, regression**. Lenin believed that the Narodniks attempted to hinder the birth and development of capitalism in Russia. **Second**, they believed that the **whole Russian economic system was too unique, especially the peasants and their villages, labour groups, etc**. Lenin believed that the Narodniks viewed Russia's peasant village society (village commune) as something higher and better than capitalism. **Third**, they ignored the fact that explanation on any trend of social thoughts and of legal and political institutions must be sought in the material interest of the various classes. In short, Lenin believed that Narodism was a school of thought that did not give a "materialist" explanation of social phenomena[11]. In essence, Narodism denied the rule of capitalism in Russia, denied the place of factory workers as the soldiers of the proletariat revolution, denied the meaning of the revolution and the political freedom of the bourgeois class, and called for an immediate realization of socialist revolution proceeding from peasant villages[12]. *In the complex reality of political struggle, young Lenin's political mind was relatively clear; in analyzing questions, he was always able to quickly grasp the crux of matters.*

At this point in time, Lenin emphasized the objective necessity and universal meaning of the development of capitalism in Russia. He welcomed the coming of Russian capitalism, because capitalism was the objective precondition for socialist revolution. As such, he did not acknowledge the "special" Russian path as taught by the Narodniks; he believed that Russia could not stagnate at the level of village communes, that it must pass through capitalism as it developed towards communism. Lenin developed this attitude after reading Marx's letter to Zasulich[13], which

---

11   Vladimir. "The Heritage we Renounce." *The Collected Works of Lenin* (Chin. 2. Ed.), volume 2, pages 404-405.

12   Lenin, Vladimir. "How the Revolution Should Be Advanced." *The Collected Works of Lenin* (Chin. 2. Ed.), volume 11, pages 22-25.

13   **Vera Zasulich** was a well-known Russian Marxist. Though she once agreed with the views of the Narodniks, she was confronted with Marx's March 8 response to her February, 1881 letter, in which he suggested surpassing capitalism without passing through its "Caudine Forks." Marx wrote four drafts of his reply to Zasulich. He clearly proposes the "Caudine Forks" idea in the first draft of his letter, though this point is not directly confirmed in his last draft. However, in the preface of the 2. Russian Edition of the *The Communist Manifesto* which Marx wrote, he conditionally identified this possibility.

is enough to explain his firm beliefs. *Young Lukacs also remarked this point (see his On Lenin, 1924). Between November 1877 and January 1882, Marx formed a very mature view of Russian peasant communes. To put it briefly, if the Russian revolution was able to ignite successful Western European proletariat revolutions, then Russian agricultural communes may be able to directly become the developmental starting point of communism without passing through capitalism. This is* **first** *because in Marx's opinion, "the fatal crisis which capitalist production has undergone in the European and American countries where it has reached its highest peak, a crisis that will end in its destruction, in the return of modern society to a higher form of the most archaic type — collective production and appropriation." Furthermore, in terms of Russia's social economic circumstances, only through the development of agricultural communes can it escape from the desperate stage at which it finds itself[14]. This should give the non-capitalist development of Russia's agricultural communes legitimacy in terms of real economic operation.* **Second**, *Russia's agricultural communes possess powerful vitality, both when compared to primitive communes and in synthesizing Russia's particular social and natural environment. As such, even though Russia's agricultural communes were disappearing and transitioning to private ownership, under the historical conditions of capitalism's "battle both with science, with the popular masses, and with the very productive forces which it engenders"[15], as soon as it loses this battle and ends, then Russia's agricultural communes will be able to obtain all the material conditions necessary for them to engage in collective labour without passing through capitalism. In surpassing capitalism, this analysis of the special circumstances of Russian society was combined with the world historical analysis of capitalism. In other words, in dealing with the question of the future development of Russian society, Marx's underlying theoretical basis was still founded on the comprehensive understanding of capitalist modes of production[16]; in his concrete analysis on the Russian*

---

14   Refer to "Marx to Zasulich, March 8, 1881." *The Collected Works of Marx and Engels* (Chin. 1. Ed.), volume 19, People's Press (1963) pages 439 and 437.

15   Refer to "Marx to Zasulich, March 8, 1881." *The Collected Works of Marx and Engels* (Chin. 1. Ed.), volume 19, People's Press (1963) page 432.

16   In fact, for a long time before 1877 Marx's views on Russia's social development and revolutionary road were primarily rooted in the objective historical condition of total social revolution. Especially in his criticism of Bakunin's anarchist views, Marx based his ideas on his level of understanding of the historical meaning of Russia's agricultural communes, emphasizing that total social revolution is linked with certain historical conditions. These conditions are the precondition to social revolution. Refer to *The Collected Works of Marx and Engels*, volume 2, People's Press (1972) page 635.

Commune- in its historical context- and he combines the analysis on Russia's special social conditions with the internal contradictions of the highly developed capitalist system. Thus, Marx differed fundamentally from both the romantic views of the Russian Narodniks, as well as the liberal views of the Russian bourgeoisie. In the Russian introduction to the second edition of the Communist Manifesto, he gives a classical elucidation of the concrete form of the Russian Revolution: If the Russian Revolution becomes a clarion call to incite Western proletariat revolutions and the revolutions are able to complement one another, then the present Russian communal property system can become the starting point of the development of communism[17].

In fact, in Lenin's "On the So-Called Market Question" written the year before, he already counters Narodism using Marxist economics. Using Marx's economic views, he proved that capitalism was already the basic background of Russia's economic life[18], as well as the objective necessity for the development of capitalism in Russia. Here it seems as though Lenin desires to explain his point using philosophical methodology.

We can see that in the struggle against Narodism, the theoretical intentions of young Lenin primarily proceed from of his examination of the **objective dimension** of social historical development. He believed that the methodology of the Narodniks was essentially **subjectivist** sociology. *I have found that this view is shared by Nicolas Berdyaev, who once wrote that for the Russian Narodniks, external Marxism, through the reconstruction of Narodism, had its economic materialism transformed into a new form of subjective sociology[19].* Thus it was with the ultimate goal of countering Narodism's opposition to the development of capitalism in Russia that Lenin would emphasize the objectivity and "natural order" – **not determined by the will of man** – of social historical development. In other words, for young Lenin, no matter the opposition of the Narodniks, capitalism would have to **objectively grow** in Russia. Lenin would later give a more precise overview of this point: "full victory of this peasant movement will not abolish capitalism; on the contrary, it will create a broader foundation for its development, and will hasten and intensify purely capitalist development. Full victory of

---

17   *The Collected Works of Marx and Engels* (Chin. 1. Ed.), volume 19, People's Press (1963) page 326.
18   *The Collected Works of Lenin* (Chin. 2. Ed.), volume 1, page 88.
19   Berdyaev, Nikolai. 1999. *The Truth of Philosophy and the Reality of Knowledge Levels*. Yunnan People's Press, page 12.

the peasant uprising can only create a stronghold for a democratic bourgeois republic, within which a proletarian struggle against the bourgeoisie will for the first time develop in its purest form"[20].

On a deeper level of social understanding and in response to the grandiose, subjectivist claims of Mikhailovsky[21] and others that history was created by "individuals possessing all thought and emotion," young Lenin
emphasized the objective "social facts" formed by the so-called social
activity of these individuals. *This is a typical Durkheim-style sociology
term. At this time, one of the important philosophical backgrounds that
exerted the most influence on the Russian scholarly scene was the sociology of France and Germany. The greatest influence on Peter Struve[22]
was Georg Simmel[23]. This particular theoretical situation led Lenin to often discuss issues within the context of sociology, perhaps without really
realizing it. Ironically enough, under the rule of Stalin, Soviet scholars
declared sociology to be a bourgeois "false science."* Lenin seems to
identify the fact that the "thought and emotion" of these individuals was
expressed as actions, thus creating certain social relations. These social
relations, which cannot necessarily be observed directly, form the essence
of objective social fact. This view is basically correct.

In Lenin's opinion at this time, historical materialism could be understood at two levels. The central concept of the **first** level was made up
of "social economic forms." In other words:

**Taking as its starting-point a fact that is fundamental to all
human society, namely, the mode of procuring the means of
subsistence, it connected up with this the relations between
people formed under the influence of the given modes of procuring the means of subsistence, and showed that this system
of relations ("relations of production," to use Marx's terminology) is the *basis* of society, which clothes itself in political
and legal forms and in definite trends of social thought[24].**

20   See Lenin's "Petty-Bourgeois and Proletarian Socialism." *The Collected Works of
Lenin* (Chin. 2. Ed.), volume 12, page 38.
21   **Nikolay Mikhailovsky** (1842-1904) was a Russian Narodnik theorist, art critic,
and philosopher.
22   **Peter Struve** (1870-1944) was a Russian economist, philosopher, and the representative of Legal Marxism.
23   See *The Collected Works of Lenin* (Chin. 2. Ed.), volume 1, pages 373-374..
Berdyaev wrote that for a time, Simmel was almost taken to be a Marxist. See
Berdyaev's *The Truth of Philosophy and the Reality of Knowledge Levels.* Yunnan
People's Press (1999) page 13.
24   Lenin, Vladimir. "A Criticism of Narodnik Sociology," *The Collected Works of
Lenin* (Chin. 2. Ed.), volume 1, page 372.

We can easily see that Lenin's examination of society here proceeds from modes of production, in particular the **social relations** between men; he did not, like Marx and Engels, proceed from the **production and reproduction of material means of subsistence**. *Later, Mao Zedong would follow the same line of thought as Lenin.* Although young Lenin had not yet read The German Ideology by Marx and Engels, this important concept was described in detail in Marx's *Capital* as well as many of Engels' published texts. However, viewing this structure as merely the **outer clothing** of the economic basis is obviously inaccurate.

In terms of the **second** level, Lenin points out:

> **The actions of "living individuals" within the bounds of each such social-economic formation, actions infinitely varied and apparently not lending themselves to any systematization, were generalized and reduced to the actions of groups of individuals differing from each other in the part they played in the system of production relations, in the conditions of production, and, consequently, in their conditions of life, and in the interests determined by these conditions—in a word, to the actions of *classes*, the struggle between which determined the development of society[25].**

Lenin believed that through such a differentiation, the "subjectivism" of Narodism is replaced by the view that social processes are natural historical processes; without this viewpoint, there cannot be science.

I believe that it was correct for Lenin to fuse Marxist theory with revolutionary practice under particular social historical conditions. However, Lenin's overall concrete overview of Marx's concepts here is not precise.

According to Marx's understanding, the general theory of historical materialism established in 1845 revealed that the production and reproduction of material life was the basis of all human social existence. This level of objective existence, formed by the actions of man, is not determined by **individual** will, consciousness, or intentions; at the same time, social life determines all the ideas of man. These were the most important, most general, and most basic principles of historical materialism. However, this did not mean that Marx believed that human social movements were always "natural historical processes," never determined by **man's** will. The social historical process "not determined by

25 *Ibid.*, page 373.

the will of man," identified here by Lenin, was a situation that actually only appeared under certain historical conditions. *Furthermore, Marx's later special theory of historical materialism goes on to reveal that only in the commodity-market economy social form that appears after the emergence of industry is man unable to control the social history that he creates. He describes the abnormal situation of enslavement to economic forces as an abnormal social phenomenon similar to the blind movements of nature. For further discussion of this point, refer to my examination of quasi-naturalness in* **The Subjective Dimension of Marxist Historical Dialectics**[26]. I believe that young Lenin at this time was unable to deeply understand or appreciate the scientific connotations of Marx's important thought, and so in actually applying the views of historical materialism, it was inevitable that various small problems emerge. What is strange is that later Soviet traditional Marxist philosophical research mutated young Lenin's imprecise understandings into general views of historical materialism in philosophical principles. This was an incorrect understanding added onto Marxism. I have noticed that these imprecise theoretical placements began with the conclusions of Adoratsky. Because he was unable to differentiate between the general and special levels of Marx's historical materialism, he directly identified Marx's explanation of economic social forms – as misunderstood by Lenin – as being general laws of the "social process"[27]. Likewise, the author of volume 5 of the Soviet History of Philosophy not only does not differentiate the problems at this theoretical level, he even refers to Lenin's explanation as a "further development of historical materialism." There is no doubt that this was a significant logical mistake.

I have also found that young Lenin's philosophical thought at this time was significantly influenced by the thinkers of the Second International, especially the effects of what Kautsky called the "conception of the social organism" under the background of social Darwinism. Therefore we often see young Lenin declaring that economic laws are unlike the laws of physics and chemistry, but that "economic life constitutes a phenomenon analogous to the history of evolution in other branches of biology." Thus Marx's scientific study of capitalism reveals "the special (historical) laws that regulate the origin, existence, development, and death of a given social organism and its replacement by another and

---

26   Refer to chapter three of my *The Subjective Dimension of Marxist Historical Dialectics* (published by Canut International, English Version, November 2011)

27   From the *Collected Works of Adoratsky*. Translated by Shi Zhu, Beijing Sanlian Press (1964), page 429 (Chinese).

higher organism"[28]. *In reading Kautsky's On Historical Materialism, it is not hard to see the latent connections that this view has with Kautsky's interpretation of historical materialism. Hence, this is certainly a subsidiary context originating from* **Other mirror images**. In fact, human social existence and the laws of its historical movement are quite different from the laws that govern the existence and movement of organisms in general. Therefore, it is obviously non-scientific to simply compare social existence and its movements to the existence and movements of general living things. I must emphasize the fact that acknowledging a certain immaturity in certain areas of young Lenin's philosophical theories denigrates him; rather, I believe that this is the basis from which we can objectively and comprehensively examine the growth of young Lenin's thought, a sincere attitude that truthfully examines philosophical history. *Laughably, Lenin's imprecise understanding of historical materialism was later simply identified by Soviet scholars as a new development of Marxism.*

It is here, with Lenin's narrow understanding of Marx's dialectics to be social economic forms as "special social organism," viewing its movement and development as a "natural historical progression" that he naturally opposes the practice of linking Marx's dialectics with Hegel's dialectics. He especially opposes "triads," discussing the negation of the negation within the framework of dialectics.

In *What the "Friends of the People" Are*, in his rebuttal of Mikhailovsky's assertion that Marx constructed his social theoretical foundation on Hegel's triads, young Lenin simply categorizes the affirmative words of Engels on the law of the negation of the negation in Engels' *Anti-Dühring* as "nothing but a relic of the Hegelianism out of which scientific socialism has grown," or "a relic of its manner of expression." *This is a particular theoretical context constructed for the purpose of* **refutational debate**. Thus, triads and trichotomies are described as "nonsense," "the lid and the shell...in which only philistines could be interested"[29]. It is here that in order to refute Mikhailovsky, Lenin seems to view "affirmation – negation – negation of the negation" as Hegel's equation, separating it from Marx's dialectic and then criticizing Mikhailovsky's incorrect practice of confusing Hegel's triads with Marx's dialectics. I have found that Lenin never positively

28   Lenin, Vladimir. "What the 'Friends of the People' Are." *Collected Works of Lenin* (Chin. 2. Ed.) volume 1, page 136 (Chinese).
29   *Ibid.*, page 137 (Chinese).

affirms triads, much less explains the important historical connections between Hegel's philosophy and Marx's thought. However, we should not place too much blame on young Engels, because at this time he did not even know that the *1844 Manuscript, The German Ideology*, and *Grundrisse* even existed. Thus he could not have deeply understood or correctly grasped the true content and complex, changing process of the development of Marx's thought. Because of this, Lenin's understanding of Marx's philosophical historical context could only be theoretical imagination that was separate from the true logical progression of philosophical history; given this situation, it is not surprising that he did not grasp the internal connection between Marx's philosophical thought and that of Hegel. For this reason, young Lenin's thought at this period of time necessarily contained several imperfect elements.

First, because young Lenin had not conducted a profound, systematic study of Hegel's dialectical theory at this time, he could only criticize the idealist essence of Hegel's "triads" in a general, principled way. *Lenin gradually came to realize this himself later on, rapidly changing his attitude.* In his theoretical discussion at this stage, Lenin focused on refuting Hegel's philosophy, especially his dialectics.

Second, on the subject of Marxist material dialectics, and especially the relation between the dialectics in Marx's *Capital* and Hegel's idealist dialectics, young Lenin had not reached a level of complete understanding. He was only able to rest at the level of generally differentiating between the two. This made Lenin's process of criticizing Mikhailovsky more difficult, because although Marx and Engels thoroughly criticized Hegel's speculative triads, at the same time they acknowledged its logical elements, continually **revealing** the law of the negation of the negation in objective movements. Lenin obviously overlooked this point. However, this did not ultimately influence the debate of Lenin as a Marxist, because in Lenin's defense of Marxism in terms of the overall principles of historical materialism and dialectical theory, his efforts were proven to be extremely effective.

I have remarked that Althusser also realized this theoretical attitude manifested by the 24-year-old young Lenin. He refers to the 12 pages in Lenin's *What the "Friends of the People" Are* that criticize the dialectical "triads" as Lenin's clear statement of opposition to Hegel[30]. *Althusser also knew that before 1894, Lenin had not read any of Hegel's*

---

30   Refer to Althusser's "Lenin before Hegel," in *Lenin and Philosophy*. Yuanliu Press (Taiwan) (1990), page 135 (Chinese).

works. According to Althusser's view, Lenin "understood Hegel" after reading Marx's *Capital*, or, inverting the expression, Lenin did not have to directly read any of Hegel's work in order to understand Marx. After truly understanding Marx, Lenin also profoundly understood Hegel's philosophy. Althusser even goes on to write as if he were Lenin: "For the past 50 years nobody has understood Hegel, because without studying and understanding *Capital*, one cannot understand Hegel!"[31]. This is truly irresponsible scholarship!

Althusser was the first to propose, in the 1950s, that Lenin was already a "completely mature dialectical materialist" when he wrote *What the "Friends of the People" Are*[32]. This viewpoint was echoed by Kiselyov in the 1950s, when he asserted that as Lenin wrote What the "Friends of the People" Are, he was "theoretically completely mature"[33]. In that same time period, a work by Belorussian scholars on Lenin's Philosophical Notebooks reached a similar conclusion[34]. I believe that these statements exaggerate the truth. In analyzing their discourse, we find that these are typical examples of ideological Stalinist dogmatism, because if we conclude that young Lenin's first politic al text on philosophy was "completely mature," then we must go on to conclude that all of his later thought and ideas were equally correct and great[35]. This is a clear reflection of the influential "theory of anything" in the history of Marxist philosophy.

Readers should already be able to tell that my attitude here is fundamentally different from that found in past research. I do not simply laud the correctness of the philosophical views in young Lenin's *What the "Friends of the People" Are*; rather, using the original theoretical logic of Marx and Engels' historical materialism as a reference, I minutely

---

31 *Ibid.*, page 137 (Chinese).
32 See Althusser's On Lenin's *Study of Philosophy* from the *Collected Works of Althusser*. Beijing Sanlian Press (1964) page 428.
33 See Kiselyov's *On Lenin's "Philosophical Notebooks."* People's Press (1956) page 1 (Chinese).
34 See Althusser's On Lenin's *Study of Philosophy* from the *Collected Works of Althusser*. Beijing Sanlian Press (1964) page 20.
35 In the *Brief Biography of Lenin* published by the Central Marxist-Leninist Research Institute of the Soviet Union, the 23-year-old Lenin who has just arrived in St. Petersburg is referred to as a "Marxist revolutionary who is completely mature, full of scholarly learning, and possessing limitless loyalty to the worker class." The biography goes on to claim that by the time Lenin was 24, "like Marx and Engels, he possessed the many qualities of a great scholar, researcher, and revolutionary leader with close ties to the masses." See *Brief Biography of Lenin*, People's Press (1957), page 12.

analyze the **possible** theoretical conditions and logic rays that emerged from the complex mental struggle through which young Lenin's philosophical thought passed at that time. This is signifies a fundamental difference in terms of methodological context from the interpretive models that take each of Lenin's words as the absolute truth.

2 YOUNG LENIN AND HIS PHILOSOPHY TEACHER, PLEKHANOV

The textual fact that Althusser ignores is that young Lenin's attitude towards materialist dialectics, in particular towards the negation of the negation and even Hegel himself, would change not long after. *I have already pointed out that Althusser's analysis of Marx is often imprecise with details; when it comes to the study of Lenin's texts, the situation becomes even worse.* I believe that these changes were brought about by the publishing of *The Development of the Monist View of History* (abbreviated as *Monist View of History* below) by Lenin's teacher, Plekhanov. I am able to make this deduction because through careful examination of historical texts, there is no evidence that young Lenin engaged in independent philosophical research during this period of time. Furthermore, the shift in young Lenin's thought took place not long after the publishing of Plekhanov's work. However, this is nothing more than a **subjective** deduction.

As we know, Ziber was the first thinker to introduce Marxist philosophy to Russia[36], but Plekhanov was one of the Russian Marxists whom Engels felt most worthy of praise[37]. *When Engels was alive,*

---

36   **Nikolai Ziber** (1844-1888) was a Russian economist and a professor of economics at Kiev University. As early as the 1870s, Ziber began to introduce Marx's economics views in his own economics research. Marx mentions him in the introduction to the second edition of *Capital.*

37   Georg Plekhanov (1856-1918) was a well-known Russian Marxist theorist. He was born on December 11, 1856 in the Russian village of Gudalovka in the Tambov Province. His father was a member of the hereditary nobility and a retired officer in the military. His mother, Maria Feodorovna, was a distant cousin of Vissarion Belinsky. In 1866 Plekhanov entered the Konstantinov Military Academy where he studied until his graduation in 1873, whereupon he enrolled in the St. Petersburg Metallurgical Institute. He served as the chairman of the general committee of the Russian Social Democratic Worker's Party, and was one of the founders and leaders of the Russian Marxist Party. He was one of the first thinkers to propagate Marxism in Russian and Europe, and a famous activist in the Russian and International worker's movement. Plekhanov was always well-respected by Lenin. In his early years, Plekhanov was a Narodnik before coming into contact with Marxism in 1882. He was the first to translate *The Communist*

Vera Zasulich wrote that he believed only two people truly understood Marxism, namely Mehring and Plekhanov. In 1889, after Plekhanov met with Engels in London, the two scholars continued to correspond through letters, including 14 letters from Plekhanov to Engels and 5 letters from Engels to Plekhanov. It could be said that the large number of Marxist books that Plekhanov wrote "reared an entire generation of Russian Marxists"[38]. Lenin himself wrote that he knew almost all of Plekhanov's work, and that the Monist View of History in particular left a lasting impression on him. Of course, Plekhanov was the philosophical mentor for the scholars of Lenin's generation. In 1900, as the political differences between Lenin and Plekhanov began to worsen, Lenin wrote: "Blinded by our love, we had actually behaved like **slaves**, and it is humiliating to be a slave. Our sense of having been wronged was magnified a hundredfold by the fact that "he" [Plekhanov] himself had opened our eyes to our humiliation"[39]. Thus we can see that young Lenin believed deeply in Plekhanov, in every aspect of scholarship. *Even later, as Plekhanov began walking towards political ruin and Lenin was forced to utterly cut himself off from his teacher, Lenin's basic philosophical views were still basically the same as Plekhanov's. This would not change until 1914.* It would not be an exaggeration to say that Plekhanov's explanation of Marxism was the false **identity mirror image** and **theoretical circuit** of all leftist Russian intellectuals.

The majority of Plekhanov's work focuses on introducing Marxism; though these texts reveal that he **understood** Marxism, unfortunately Plekhanov very rarely actually put Marxism into revolutionary practice

---

Manifesto into Russian. In 1883, Plekhanov formed the Emancipation of Labor Group in Geneva with Lev Deutsch, Vasily Ignatov, and others. This group translated into Russian and published many of the works of Marx and Engels, including *Hired Labor and Capital, The Philosophy of Poverty, On Feuerbach, On the Change of Free Trade, Engels on Russia,* and others. Plekhanov was one of the first Russian Marxists to openly criticize Narodism; like Lenin, he emphasized the necessity of capitalism in Russia. He spent his life writing revolutionary articles and books. He first criticized the alterations and distortions of Marxism by Bernstein and Struve, then later the empiricist mistakes of Bogdanov. After 1900, Plekhanov worked together with Lenin in editing *The Spark* and *The Dawn,* two Russian Marxist newspapers. However, after the second congress of the Russian Social-Democratic Labor party in 1903, Plekhanov gradually parted ways with Lenin's Bolshevik faction, later opposing the October Revolution. Plekhanov passed away in Finland on May 30, 1918. His primary works include: *The Development of the Monist View of History* (1895) and *Fundamental Problems of Marxism* (1908).

38   See Lenin's "The Vperyod Faction," *Collected Works of Lenin* (Chin. 2. Ed.) volume 16, page 267 (Chinese).

39   See Lenin's "How the 'Spark' was Nearly Extinguished" *Collected Works of Lenin* (Chin. 2. Ed.) volume 4, page 304 (Chinese).

concretely or correctly. *This was an important difference between him and Lenin.* Furthermore, there were two major weaknesses with his introduction of Marxist theory and criticizing the revisionists: **first**, there were obvious elements of mechanical materialism mixed into his understanding of Marxism, which were primarily based on the incorrect thinking of **geographical environmental determinism**. **Second**, he was unable to truly, scientifically understand Marx's historical dialectic; in other words, he only grasped a passive, abstract, idea dialectic. *These ideas were not only expressed in Plekhanov's philosophical thought, but also in his political activities.* I bring up this point in order to reemphasize the fact that for a relatively long time, Lenin was heavily influenced by Plekhanov's philosophical thought; thus in a certain sense, Plekhanov's understanding of Marxist philosophy became the **Other mirror image** that Lenin noncritically accepted. Although Lenin firmly opposed Plekhanov's incorrect political activities, it was not until later that he realized Plekhanov's **philosophical** theoretical weaknesses. *For instance, in some of his post-1908 works criticizing Machism and Kantism, Lenin began to mention Plekhanov's philosophical "vagueness," though he was unable to fundamentally account for the origin of those mistakes. Therefore, although Lenin began to consciously separate his philosophical ideas from those of Plekhanov, at this time these differences were not heterogeneous. His true shift took place after 1914, in the latter half of "Conspectus of Hegel's Book The Science of Logic" in his* **Bern Notebooks**. *This was where Lenin's own philosophical thought experienced a revolutionary leap in understanding, allowing him to more profoundly realize the origins of Plekhanov's mistaken thinking. In spite of this, Lenin would always believe that Plekhanov was an extraordinary Marxist philosopher, referring to "all of his philosophical works" as "excellent additions to the texts of international Marxism," and suggesting that they be read as communist textbooks. Lenin believed that if one did not study and learn his philosophical work, then could not be a truly conscious and enlightened communist. From this we can see that Lenin always maintained an attitude of respect for his teacher.*

Now let us first briefly examine Plekhanov's *The Monist View of History*, which directly influenced young Lenin's philosophical thought. This was an important scholarly work, written by Plekhanov specifically to criticize Mikhailovsky's Russian Narodism[40]. *This book echoed many of Lenin's anti-Narodnik articles written in the same time period. These articles represent Lenin's efforts to move in the same direction as his teacher in the philosophical debate of the time; in terms of both political standpoint and philosophical ideas, both teacher and student were basically analogous at this time.*

First, in this book we find that while, like Lenin, Plekhanov refutes Mikhailovsky's attacks on Marx's materialist dialectics, he does not simply refute "triads" as young Lenin did. Rather, he first reveals the essential "negation of the negation" laws that lie beneath the surface level of the "triads." It is important to note that unlike young Lenin's abstract refutation of Hegel, Plekhanov actually makes an objective, historical evaluation of Hegel's dialectics. In Plekhanov's theoretical situating, the old materialism of the 18th century was unable to deal with the "great problem" of "the complex and variegated chain of concrete phenomena," a problem that was "grasped" and completed by Hegel's dialectics[41]. Unlike Lenin, who described Marxist dialectics merely as the **objectivity** ("natural historical processes") of social historical progress, Plekhanov defined dialectics as the method of **examining the world in terms of the connections and developments of phenomena** on the level of metaphilosophy. Plekhanov accurately observes: "To this metaphysics Hegel opposed his **dialectical philosophy**, which examines all phenomena in their development and in their interconnection, not as ready-made and separated from one another by a veritable gulf"[42]. Plekhanov's understanding of the dialectic here is correct. *It is evident that Plekhanov's thought space here approaches that of Engels as he wrote **Anti-Dühring**.*

Second, Plekhanov accurately begins with the contradictions that form the essential structures of things (the inevitability of transforming into the opposite), and views contradiction as the internal motivating force of the development and movement of things. Beginning with quantitative changes, he captures the essential changes (revolutionary negation)

40　This book was written by Plekhanov in 1892, and was to be secretly published under the title *Our Opinions Differ: Book Two*. Later, when the time for public publishing was ripe, its title was changed to *The Development of the Monist View of History*. When it was published in January 1895, Plekhanov used the pen name "Beltov."
41　Plekhanov, Georg. *The Monist View of History*. Beijing Sanlian Press (1965), page 60 (Chinese).
42　*Ibid.*, appendix 2, part 2 (Chinese).

that are the fundamental links of development, finally commenting on the developmental process of antagonism from the perspective of history, or in other words, the law of the negation of negation. In his opinion, the so-called "triads" were nothing more than the **external** characteristics of the affirmation-negation (new affirmation)-negation of the negation (new negation). I have found that Plekhanov's analysis of the theoretical logic of dialectics was one of the most profound and clear expressions of dialectics in all of Marxist philosophical theory. Thus Plekhanov concluded that Mikhailovsky's simple categorization of Hegel's philosophy into external "triads" was fallacious, because "Not once in the eighteen volumes of Hegel's works does the "**triad**" play the part of an "**argument**"[43]. Plekhanov points out that the negation of the negation was not a "main principle" of Hegel, but was rather rooted in the principle that "every phenomenon is transformed into its own opposite"[44]. *Contradiction is the basis of the negation of the negation.* Furthermore, Plekhanov profoundly concludes that "every phenomenon, developing to its conclusion, be-comes transformed into its opposite; but as the new phenomenon, being opposite to the first, also is transformed in its turn into its own opposite, the third phase of development bears a **formal resemblance to the first**"[45]. Thus Plekhanov is able to avoid the mistake of only looking at the great number of external "triads" created to meet the needs of Hegel's speculative idealism, successfully revealing the internal structure and essence of the negation of the negation (triad). This theoretical point is both profound and powerful, and the theoretical prowess that Plekhanov demonstrates here is far above that of young Lenin at this time. *For a discussion of the internal logical structure of materialist dialectics and the negation of the negation in particular, refer to my last appendix.*

Third, it is also in this book that Plekhanov counters Mikhailovsky's criticism of some of Engels' examples used to explain the law of the negation of the negation, in particular the "triad" of **growing oats**. Proceeding from Mikhailovsky's conclusion that "it is about time we ceased to believe that oats grow according to Hegel," Plekhanov methodically counters his malicious attack on Engels' correct explanation of the negation of the negation. At the same time, Plekhanov historically and more profoundly explains Hegel's views on the genesis and

---

43   *Ibid.*, page 66 (Chinese).
44   *Ibid.*, pages 66-67 (Chinese).
45   *Ibid.*, page 66 (Chinese).

development of dialectical thought. Plekhanov attempts to identify the fundamental differences between Hegel's idealist dialectics and Marx's materialist dialectics, beginning from ancient antithesis-synthesis philosophy to contemporary metaphysical ideas that oppose dialectical thought, as well as from Leibnitz to classical German philosophy. Thus he fully proves the objectivity premise of material dialectics. Finally, Plekhanov sardonically concludes that "oats" will continue to grow according to Hegel. *Obviously, Plekhanov's important conclusion here left a deep impression on young Lenin, spurring a subtle change in him towards this same viewpoint. It is my view that this was a closed theoretical circuit and parallel shift originating from an **Other mirror image** (Plekhanov's discourse) in the thought of young Lenin.*

I must specifically point out here that Plekhanov's discussion of the dialectic here was predicated on Engels' logic in *Anti-Dühring*; thus his dialectics belonged to the logical level of **metaphilosophy**. As such, he was not able to understand that Marx derived the legitimacy of historical dialectics from the **modern production** of social historical development. *Young Lenin correctly derived dialectics from Marx's examination of social history, though he mistakenly viewed particular qualifications of historical development (natural historical processes that do not depend on the will of men) as the dialectical method itself. This is an extremely complex and intertwined situating relationship.* However, Plekhanov did not know of the existence of *The German Ideology* or *Grundrisse*, and as such did not know of Marx's more profound and more complex theories of historical materialism and historical dialectics. As such, we cannot fault him for not having achieved perfection here.

Fourth, we can see that Plekhanov also discusses Marx's historical materialism in his book. *This can even be called the primary argument of Plekhanov's work. Lenin read his other book on historical materialism, **Fundamental Problems of Marxism**, in 1908. We will discuss the effect of this other book on Lenin later on in our investigation.* However, in discussing historical materialism, Plekhanov never mentions dialectics or even Marx's historical dialectics. It is in his process of attempting to explain the Marxist conception of history that we find the critical problem with his interpretive logical situation: **the theory of geographical environmental determinism** which lay at the foundation of his argument. Actually, before attempting to explain the Marxist scientific conception of history, Plekhanov makes a correct observation: "In order to understand the historical views of Marx, we must recall the conclusions at which philosophy and social and historical science had arrived in the period immediately preceding his appearance"[46]. *This is a critical viewpoint; because only in attaining such an understanding can we distinguish Marx's true theoretical contributions. This was also one aspect of my efforts in **Marx Revisited**.* Plekhanov correctly grasped the fact that French historians had already understood that "'civil conditions,' 'property relations,' constitute the basic foundation of the entire social order." Hegel, in his idealist jurisprudence, had also fully realized this problem. Plekhanov believed that Marx stood on the shoulders of his philosophical predecessors, recognizing the foundational place of "civil society" in the structure of society, and thus concluding that "the anatomy of civil society is to be sought in political economy." Plekhanov argued that Marx would go on to propose what determines certain economies of society, and here his analysis of Marx is very interesting:

> **The great scientific service rendered by Marx lies in this, that he approached the question from the diametrically opposite side, and that he regarded man's nature itself as the eternally changing result of historical progress, the cause of which lies *outside* man. In order to exist, man must support his organism, borrowing the substances he requires from the *external nature surrounding him*. This borrowing presupposes a certain action of man on *that* external nature. But, "acting on the external world, he changes his own nature." In these few words is contained the essence of the whole historical theory of Marx**[47].

It is not wrong to say that Marx believed man's nature constantly changed in the movement of history. However, the critical mistake that Plekhanov makes here is his assertion that the cause of historical progress lies **outside** of man. Plekhanov recognizes the fundamental position of material production in social existence. Unlike young Lenin, whose explanation proceeded from relations of production and economic forms, Plekhanov more correctly grasped the importance of **forces of production**. He concisely points out that "economic structures" are **"determined by the state of their forces of production"**[48]. *This was a point to which young Lenin did not pay attention at the time.*

---

46 *Ibid.*, page 106 (Chinese).
47 *Ibid.*, page 106 (Chinese).
48 *Ibid.*, pages 163, 178, and 183 (Chinese).

In a 1902 article criticizing Struve, Plekhanov again clearly brings up this important Marxist view[49]. However, because of the influence of the **substantive factor theory**[50], Plekhanov's understanding of productive forces began to deviate from the truth, as he falsely identified the essential elements of material production as **material labour tools.** *In his 1902 article criticizing Struve, Plekhanov also emphasizes this point, using the example that the nature of weapons determines the structure of the military*[51]. Even more deadly to Plekhanov's argument, in his refutation of critiques against historical materialism and in order to defend the objective foundational place of labour tools, Plekhanov goes so far as to bring in the argument that natural geographical environments are foundational conditions that determine labour tools and forces of production. He believed that human subsistence, engaged in productive labour, always resides in a particular geographical environment, and thus the environment affects subsistence in three ways. First, it provides "necessary materials" for the improvement of labour implements. Second, it is "the object the working up of which would presuppose perfected implements." Third, he emphasizes the crucial role of "natural communication" in geographical environments[52]. Thus Plekhanov believes that "in the historical process of the development of productive forces, the capacity of man for. "toolmaking" must be regarded first of all as a **constant magnitude**, while the surrounding external conditions for the use of this capacity in practice have to be regarded as **a constantly varying magnitude**"[53]. The place of these two different magnitudes is obviously intentional, because constantly varying magnitudes cause changes to constant magnitudes. Thus geographical environment is the **ultimate determinant**. I believe that it was precisely Plekhanov's mechanical deterministic views that led him to ultimately adopt a mistaken position in terms of the actual revolution. Lenin would understand this point in his later *Bern Notebooks*.

---

49 Plekhanov, Georg. *Against Revisionism in History.* People's Press (1957), pages 184 and 220(Chinese).

50 It is my understanding that traditional textbooks give a *substantive* factor understanding of the forces of production, focusing on workers, labor tools, and objects of labor, etc. This is a false misunderstanding of Marx's expression of the labor process in *Capital*. For Marx, productive forces merely expressed the functional qualifications of a certain level and capability of a society's productive development; they were not three substantive things.

51 See Plekhanov's "On the So-called Crisis in the Marxist School" in *Against Revisionism in Philosophy*.

52 Plekhanov, Georg. *The Monist View of History.* Beijing Sanlian Press (1965), page 11 (Chinese).

53 *Ibid.*, pages 112-113 (Chinese).

Plekhanov correctly observed that the legal and political superstructure of a society was determined by **modes of production and the inter-human relations created by these modes of production**[54]. He even correctly criticizes the old materialism, in that it causes man to completely obey blind material, identifying the historical subjectivity composed by social practice in the developmental of history[55]. However, at the end, Plekhanov views geographical environment as the ultimate basis of social existence, which led to his downfall. He believed that the development of the productive forces is itself determined by the qualities of the geographical environment surrounding man:

> **The characteristics of social man are determined at every given time by the degree of development of the productive forces, because on the degree of the development of those forces depends the entire structure of the social union. Thus, this structure is determined in the long run by the characteristics of the geographical environment, which affords men a greater or lesser possibility of developing their productive forces**[56].

It is true that Plekhanov conceded that as productive forces develop, "the dependence of man on his geographical environment is transformed from **direct to indirect**," and that now, "the **geographical** environment influences man through the **social** environment"[57]. However, this does not change his emphasis on geographical environment on the level of his ontological logic[58]. *Plekhanov's mistakes here have already been pointed out in past research. In fact, to this mistake we should add the related mistake of social Darwinism[59]. I will not delve further into this mistake at this time.* I should point out here that this grave theoretical error by Plekhanov was never consciously identified by Lenin; it was actually Stalin who correctly pointed it out in the 1930s[60].

---

54   *Ibid.*, page 132 (Chinese).
55   *Ibid.*, pages 176-177 (Chinese).
56   *Ibid.*, page 195 (Chinese).
57   *Ibid.*, page 195 (Chinese).
58   This incorrect view also appears in other works by Plekhanov that introduced Marxism, such as his 1908 *Fundamental Problems of Marxism* (Plekhanov, Georg. 1957. *Fundamental Problems of Marxism*. People's Press (Chinese).). Lenin read this book the same year it was published, noting a few short commentaries on it.
59   Plekhanov directly links Marx with Darwin. He believed that Marx's research picked up at the conclusion of Darwin's research. He goes so far as to mistakenly refer to Marxism as the sociological application of Darwinism. This was a mistake made by many of the theorists of the Second International.
60   See Stalin's *Conversations with the committee of the Philosophical and Natural Science Red Teachers' Institute*. In *Translated Philosophical Works* (1999) vol. 2 (Chin).

Finally, one aspect of Plekhanov's book that has often been ignored is that Plekhanov discovered a critical principle in Marx's historical materialism: **supersession of economic necessity**. This may also be an instance in which he surpasses the theorists of the Second International. I believe that Plekhanov correctly grasped the **critical dimension** of historical materialism from Marx's economics research; Plekhanov profoundly pointed out that a new form of slavery – economic necessity – had appeared in capitalist modes of production.

> **The greater grows man's authority over nature, the more his productive forces develop, the more stable becomes this new slavery:** *with the development of the productive forces the mutual relations of men in the social process of production become more complex*; **the course of that process completely slips from under their control,** *the producer proves to be the slave of his own creation* **(as an example, the capitalist anarchy of production)[61].**

Plekhanov passionately claims that it is Marxism that first indicated how to deal with economic necessity. *This so-called economic necessity was really the "natural historical process" that Lenin identified as the economic-social form central to Marx's dialectics.* As soon as man realizes the reasons for his enslavement to economic necessity, there appears "the opportunity for a new and final triumph of **consciousness** over **necessity**, of **reason** over **blind law**." This is not precise! For Marx, it is not consciousness and reason that triumph over economic necessity, but rather conscious proletariat revolution. *In fact, in terms of philosophical logic, Plekhanov's views here are similar to those of the later Western Marxists. Unfortunately, he did not proceed from this point and scientifically counter Bogdanov's malicious attacks on materialism, which proceeded from the theory of fetishisms. As for Lenin, he was never able to more profoundly understand this point[62].* It is in this

---

61   Plekhanov, Georg. *The Monist View of History*. Beijing Sanlian Press (1965), page 195 (Chinese).

62   In *The Development of Russian Capitalism*, Lenin mentions Marx's theory of fetishisms; relative to the savages in primitive society, he clearly understands his own relations of production, pointing out that the fetishisms of capitalist society express man's social relations as commodity relations, because each commodity is produced for an unknown consumer and realized in an unknown market. For Lenin here, fetishisms are merely understood vaguely. However, Lenin obviously does not understand the deep critical implications of Marx's theory of fetishisms, causing him to ignore a deeper logical level of Bogdanov's mistakes: the transition from the critique of the fetishism of objectified relations in capitalism to the fundamental misunderstanding of philosophical materialism.

context that Plekhanov opposed viewing Marxist philosophy as "economic materialism," insisting that it be called **dialectical materialism**, identifying it as a "practical," "active" philosophy. Chronologically speaking, Plekhanov's views here preceded the similar conclusions of young Lukacs, Gramsci, and Korsch by nearly 30 years. *Even more interesting, the reason why Bogdanov accepted and peddled Machism based first on* **opposition to the idea of fetishisms** *and criticism of economic materialism. Though their logical starting point was correct, they walked a deviant path; in opposing a material god and the world of idols, they fell into the logical trap of idealism[63]. Lenin did not directly treat this question in his* **Materialism and Empiro-Criticism***.*

We can see here that Lenin was unable to completely grasp or understand the majority of Plekhanov's philosophical views in this important work; a few of Plekhanov's theoretical ideas, however, exerted a significant influence on his thought.

3 YOUNG LENIN READS *THE HOLY FAMILY*

As we have already discussed, young Lenin's thought undoubtedly experienced a process of historical change. As a warrior in the struggle against Narodism, his theoretical centre and actual logic ray was naturally the **objectivity** of the movement towards capitalism of Russian social historical development; as such, he had no choice but to direct most of his energy towards the study of politics and economics. As such, it was all but impossible for him to completely and comprehensively grasp Marxist philosophical theory, like his teacher Plekhanov. As soon as he realized this deficiency in his scholarship, he concentrated on studying philosophy.

In my research, I found that Lenin was a revolutionary thinker who possessed an incredible talent for learning and research. The year after completing *What the "Friends of the People" Are*, in early 1895, young Lenin read Plekhanov's *The Monist View of History* (this book was published in January of that year). *However, Lenin did not leave commentaries or other reading notes. I conclude that Lenin must have*

---

63   This viewpoint was first proposed in Bogdanov's 1908 article "The Idol State and Marxist Philosophy." I believe that even though Bogdanov was mistaken, his theory still attains a certain level of theoretical depth. I will provide more specific analysis of this point in our later discussion of Lenin's first systematic study of philosophy around 1908.

read this book based on the fact that his thought experienced shift to parallel Plekhanov at this time. This is, of course, merely a deduction. Apparently in order to investigate his past understanding of Marxism and distinguish between his thought and the theoretical circuit of his teacher, Lenin seriously studied Marx and Engels' *The Holy Family* between April and September of that year. It was at this time that 25-year-old young Lenin recorded his first somewhat more complete "philosophical notebook"[64]. *According to my textual analysis and categorization, this notebook belongs to the category of* **sub text**.

From this notebook we can clearly see that Lenin's reading process was very meticulous. His line of thought in taking excerpts was very clear, displaying a strong ability to grasp the overall thrust of the text. He was able to quickly identify the basic scholarly points of the text, manifesting rare perspicacity and precision in his grasp of concepts. It was only because his philosophical theoretical foundation was weak, because his subsidiary awareness was thin, that he was unable to truly capture some of the most important **theoretical symptoms** in the Marx and Engels' thought process. *Of course, these limitations were also caused by the particular historical circumstances of his time, and so we should not use our scholarly standards of today to demand too much from the young Lenin.* Regardless, this sub-text is a crucial historical text in our study of the development of Lenin's early philosophical thought. Here we will begin with this notebook in our examination of Lenin's basic understanding of the thought of Marx and Engels in *The Holy Family*.

The **first** aspect is that this notebook clearly demonstrates that at the time, Lenin already accurately realized that *The Holy Family* was a transitional work; with great perceptiveness he historically noticed that Marx and Engels were at a point of important **philosophical shift** in *The Holy Family*.

The **first** evidence for this understanding comes when Lenin writes: "Marx here advances from Hegelian philosophy to socialism: the

---

64   This notebook was written by Lenin in Germany. At the time, Lenin was traveling outside Russia, trying to establish the Labor Emancipation Group. An analysis of existing documents reveals that around August of 1908, Lenin studied and wrote in the Berlin Royal Library; he read the original German version of *The Holy Family*. These excerpted notes were written in a separate notebook, occupying 45 pages in total. Because Lenin did not record the date of his writing, we can only deduce the probably dates by looking at the dates of his stay in Germany.

transition is clearly observable—it is evident what Marx has already mastered and how he goes over to the new sphere of ideas"[65]. *However, Lenin does not know that Marx's transition to socialism took place a little earlier than **The Holy Family** (it actually took place as Marx wrote* **Critique of Hegel's "Philosophy of Right"**). *These immature socialist ideas were more evident in the 1844 Manuscript, to which Lenin did not have access.* The transition to which Lenin refers here is the criticism of Marx and Engels against classical political economy with the help of Proudhon, the expression of indignation towards bourgeois society. *Lenin correctly observes that "Marx's tone in relation to Proudhon is very laudatory"[66].* This critique primarily focused on the self-contradictions produced as classical economics affirmed the **system of bourgeois private property**[67]. Though Proudhon conducted all the criticism he could of national economics from the perspective of national economics, there was nowhere else for him to go.

The **second** evidence for this understanding came when Lenin wrote: "Marx's view—already almost fully developed—concerning the revolutionary role of the proletariat." From the content of Lenin's excerpts we can see that Lenin here referred to Marx's view that the bourgeoisie and the proletariat were the thesis-antithesis of "man's self-alienation." More importantly, Marx had already confirmed the revolutionary historical mission of the proletariat. *Interestingly enough, young Lenin was never able to understand the remnants of humanism in Marx's thought. Such concepts as "alienation," "the essence of man," and "species-consciousness" were completely ignored in Lenin's summary, not inciting his interest at all.* I believe that this was the result of the closed theoretical circuit brainwashing conducted by the economic determinist thinkers of the Second International by using positivism. In fact, I believe that Lenin never entered the theoretical scope of humanism. We can also observe this in Lenin's study of Feuerbach's philosophy. Vranicki also observed this point, writing that man's problems basically

---

65   Lenin, Vladimir. "Conspectus of the Book *The Holy Family*." *The Collected Works of Lenin* (Chin. 2. Ed.), volume 55, page 6.

66   *Ibid.*, page 6.

67   In fact, before 1858 Marx had not yet developed a scientific understanding of the basic structure of "capitalism." He did not even use the word "capitalism," using instead "bourgeois society." This understanding was gained in the progression of his research on economics. I am in the process of conducting further topical research on this subject.

lay outside the scope of Lenin's philosophy[68]. I believe that man and his essence are philosophical qualifications that seem to be missing from Lenin's theoretical situating, but I cannot be sure whether this is related to the "humanist absence" in the traditional philosophical explanatory framework.

The **third** evidence came when Lenin wrote that "Marx approached the basic idea of his entire "system," sit venia verbo, namely the concept of the social relations of production"[69]. Analyzing the content of the notes, we find that Lenin primarily referred to the following expression of Marx: "the **object as being for man**, as the **objective being of man**, is at the same time the **existence of man for other men**, his human relation to other men, the **social behaviour of man to man**"[70]. Lenin refers to this expression as "highly characteristic," because Marx's thought here begins to approach objective social relations of production that are not determined by the will of individuals. I believe that this is one of the most important thoughts written by Lenin in these notes. I have also noticed that at the end of these notes, Lenin also pays careful attention to one of the most important passages in *The Holy Family*: the importance, in one's "knowledge of historical reality…[of] the theoretical and practical relation of man to nature, natural science and industry," as well as the importance of "the industry of that period, the immediate mode of production of life itself" to a correct understanding of any historical period[71]. To the side of this passage of excerpts, Lenin draws a vertical line and writes "Notabene" (pay attention).

The **fourth** evidence is that because Lenin was more familiar with political economy at this time, he was able to astutely remark that in Marx's process of criticizing Proudhon, he had already begun to "**approach the labour theory of value**"[72]. *This conclusion is correct, because in the **Paris Notebooks** and the **1844 Economic and Philosophical Manuscripts**, written not long before, young Marx – like young Engels – employed the logic of philosophical humanism to counter the labour*

---

68   Vranicki, Predrag. *History of Marxism* (volume 2), People's Press: 1988, page 32 (Chinese).

69   Lenin, Vladimir. "Conspectus of the Book *The Holy Family*." *The Collected Works of Lenin* (Chin. 2. Ed.), volume 55, page 6.

70   See *The Collected Works of Marx and Engels* (Chin. 1. Ed.), volume 2, People's Press (1957), page 52 (Chinese).

71   Lenin, Vladimir. "Conspectus of the Book *The Holy Family*." *The Collected Works of Lenin* (Chin. 2. Ed.), volume 55, page 30.

72   *Ibid.*, page 13.

theory of value[73]. However, Lenin was not aware of the existence of these texts. This conclusion primarily referred to Marx's discussion of the relation between production and labour time in "Critical Comment 4."

There is a special theoretical situation that merits our attention here: Lenin's apparent **lack of feeling** towards the content of the fifth chapter of *The Holy Family*. As we know, the second section of the fifth chapter of *The Holy Family* contained Marx's brilliant analysis of the "secret of the speculative structure" in Hegel's idealist philosophy. In that section, Marx begins with the dialectical relationship between the general concept of "fruit," which is then separated into the concretely existing individual fruits, such as "apples" and "pears." He then materialistically dissects how speculative philosophy engages in the collective essential abstraction of material, moving towards ontological inversion. This was an extremely profound **dialectical** viewpoint. However, I have found that Lenin does not take comprehensive notes on this important discussion on dialectics; he merely indicates that this criticism of Hegel is "very interesting." I believe that this particular textual phenomenon explains Lenin's **insufficiently profound** research in terms of his basic philosophical theoretical situating, and especially with regards to the dialectic. Although Lenin writes, "Hegel 'very often' gives a real presentation, embracing the thing itself—die Sache selbst—within the speculative presentation"[74], I still believe that at this time, he was not very clear what Marx actually meant with this passage.

The **second** aspect of Lenin's text was that he paid great attention to Marx and Engels' discussion of the **role of the masses in the development of social history**. As we all know, in the sixth chapter of *The Holy Family*, Marx and Engels criticize the "absolute criticism" of Bauer and others because it degrades the masses. Marx and Engels point out that the essence of this theoretical standpoint is the betrayal of history itself by "ideas," and that "The '**idea**' always exposed itself to ridicule insofar as it differed from '**interest**.'" Young Lenin focuses on this passage by Marx and Engels, taking many lines of excerpts. He especially notes how Marx and Engels explain the creative role that the masses play in the development of social history, because this was a pressing question that he was facing in the real revolutionary struggle of the time. One

---

73   See chapters 2 and 3 of my *Marx Revisited.*
74   Lenin, Vladimir. "Conspectus of the Book The *Holy Family.*" *The Collected Works of Lenin (Chin. 2. Ed.), volume 55, page 13.*

passage by Engels was particularly exciting to the young Lenin:

> *History* does *nothing*, it "possesses no immense wealth", it "wages *no* battles". It is *man*, real, living man who does all that, who possesses and fights; "history" is not, as it were, a person apart, using man as a means to achieve *its own* aims; history is *nothing but* the activity of man pursuing his aims[75].

As a matter of fact, Lenin had similar thoughts as to the social histori-cal development of Russia. He wished to prove that the masses were the true force for creating and changing history. *I believe that this also influenced his emphasis of the objective aspect of social historical pro-gress that "is not determined by the will of man." In the process of his philosophical shift at this time, Lenin's theoretical logic ray that focused on reality began to transition from the objective dimension of social history to the subjective dimension, emphasizing the creative role of the masses in history. What's more, this was not merely a theoreti-cal goal for him: in the not distant future, he would actually realize his goals through the great October Revolution. In Lukacs 1924 **On Lenin**, he discusses this point in greater detail.*

The **third** aspect of Lenin's "Conspectus of the Book *The Holy Family*" was Lenin's assertion that the "most valuable" part of *The Holy Family* was the "short sketch of the history of French materialism," the fourth subsection of the third section of the sixth chapter of *The Holy Family*, entitled "The Critical Battle Against French Materialism." Lenin me-ticulously records almost all the important points under this heading. I have found that as Lenin read *The Holy Family*, he began to develop a new interest in **philosophical materialism**. In fact, as Lenin read the second section of the sixth chapter, he discovered that Engels "warmly praised" Feuerbach[76]. In addition, Lenin's excerpts from the different sections of chapter six that are labelled "notable" are Marx and Engels' critique of Hegel's speculative idealism and affirmation of Feuerbach's materialism[77]. Also, Lenin accords particular attention to "the connec-tion of the **materialism** of the eighteenth century with **English** and **French communism** of the nineteenth century." As Marx and Engels

---

75 See *The Collected Works of Marx and Engels* (Chin. 1. Ed.), volume 2, People's Press (1957), page 118 (Chinese).

76 Lenin, Vladimir. "Conspectus of the Book *The Holy Family*." *The Collected Works of Lenin* (Chin. 2. Ed.), volume 55, page 18.

77 *Ibid.*, page 29.

repeatedly emphasized, "nothing is easier than to derive socialism from the premises of materialism"[78]. Lenin found that Marx and Engels discussed the relation between the utopian socialists such as Fourier and Owen, Babouvism, and even a few "communists" and materialism. Lenin summarizes thus:

> **Fourier proceeds immediately from the teachings of the French materialists. The *Babouvists* were crude, immature materialists. Bentham based his system on the morality of Helvétius, while Owen takes Bentham's system as his starting-point for founding English communism. *Cabet* brought communist ideas from England into France. The "more scientific" are *Dézamy, Gay,* etc., who developed the teaching of materialism *as real humanism*[79].**

I believe that it is completely possible that after reading this passage, Lenin developed the idea of partisanship in philosophical materialism. From Marx and Engels' discussion he found that in recent Western history, materialist theories seemed to always give birth to socialist and communist revolutionary schools of thought. Unfortunately, Lenin did not immediately develop this idea; for a relatively long time, he tended to separate the **philosophical worldview and real political standpoints** of individuals. This was how he viewed Plekhanov and even Bogdanov. In his opinion, Plekhanov was correct in his worldview but incorrect in his political position, while Bogdanov was correct in his political position but incorrect in his worldview. Thus Lenin at this time was unable to see the inseparable internal connection between one's worldview and his political position. *Lenin's mistaken understanding here would not be overcome until around 1908. It is interesting to note that his theoretical realization of this point came as he read Dietzgen's philosophical texts.*

The Soviet scholar Adoratsky concluded that from Lenin's "Conspectus of the Book *The Holy Family*," we were able to see how meticulously Lenin studied Marx's dialectical materialism, how he developed a Marxist materialist worldview, how profoundly he grasped every detail of Marx's method[80]. I believe that such a conclusion is certainly exaggerated. First, *The Holy Family* did not contain "dialectical

---

78   *Ibid.*, page 28.
79   *Ibid.*, pages 28-29.
80   From the *Collected Works of Adoratsky*. Translated by Shi Zhu, Beijing Sanlian Press (1964), page 506 (Chinese).

materialism", as has been suggested; second, there was nothing in Lenin's notes to suggest that he "profoundly grasped" Marx's method. As such, Adoratsky's statement here is nothing but purely abstract exaggerated praise. *Kedrov also mentions this book in his **Study on Lenin's "Philosophical Notebooks,"** though he only regurgitates what Lenin wrote, not leaving any worthwhile understandings*[81].

4 THE SUBJECTIVE DIMENSION: THE EARLIEST CHANGES IN YOUNG LENIN'S THOUGHT

In Lenin's "Frederick Engels Obituary," written in September 1895, we discover some subtle changes in his thought. In this text, Lenin first mentions Marx and Engels' The Holy Family, asserting that this text "contains the foundations of revolutionary materialist socialism"[82]. This document was published about six months after the publishing of Plekhanov's *The Monist View of History*.

At the beginning of the obituary, Lenin correctly points out that "socialism is not the invention of dreamers, but the final aim and necessary result of the development of the productive forces in modern society"[83]. This is an extremely important theoretical premise. Young Lenin's thought did not merely proceed from social relations, but rather focused on more **foundational** material productive forces; from Plekhanov he realized that "development of human society is conditioned by the development of material forces, the productive forces"[84]. *I assert that Lenin's view here was a mirror image understanding acquired from Plekhanov rather than a result of his own research because in **The Holy Family** (what he was reading at the time), Marx and Engels do not directly discuss the foundational, determining role of material productive forces, there they approached objective economic relations.* Furthermore, Lenin realized that Hegel's theories included revolutionary elements, because Hegel recognized "the law of the eternal development of the world." In an 1899 book review of Kautsky's *Bernstein und das sozialdemokratische Programm. Eine Antikritik*, Lenin discusses the laws and necessity of the negation of the negation[85].

---

81   See Kedrov's *Study on Lenin's "Philosophical Notebooks,"* Qiushi Press (1984), pages 80-90 (Chinese).

82   Lenin, Vladimir. "Frederick Engels Obituary" *The Collected Works of Lenin* (Chin. 2. Ed.), volume 2, page 7.

83   *Ibid.*, page 1.

84   *Ibid.*, page 230.

85   *See* Lenin's "Book Review-Kautsky",*The Collected Works of Lenin*, vol. 4, p. 176.

A more important change in this text is that young Lenin at this time shifts the focus of his theoretical struggle from **opposing Narodism** to **"awakening class-consciousness in the Russian workers.**" *In the party platform of the Russian Social Democratic Party, which was formed later that year, Lenin draws attention to the "class-consciousness" of the Russian working class*[86]. *However, it is my understanding that this was not a **philosophical Other mirror image** from Plekhanov or anyone else, but rather necessitated by the development of Lenin's actual political struggles of the time. This was an **independent** change in Lenin's real, revolutionary, practical logic. It was precisely this change in terms of real logic ray that caused him to diverge from his teacher Plekhanov.* This was a shift from emphasizing the examination of the **objective dimension** of social history to examining the **subjective dimension**. The original emphasis was the attempt to explain the objective necessity of capitalism in Russia to the Narodniks; by this time, Lenin's primary goal was to awaken a **subjective critical consciousness** in the Russian working class against capitalism. Lenin would later summarize this goal, calling it "The degree of economic development of Russia (an objective condition) and the degree of class consciousness and organization of the broad masses of the proletariat (a subjective condition inseparably connected with the objective condition)[87]. If I am correct, this was the preliminary thought logic of young Lukacs' later History and Class Consciousness.

In 1900, Lenin clearly expressed that he "defended Plekhanov"[88], and under the direct support of Plekhanov's Labour Emancipation Group, young Lenin established *The Spark*[89]. From December of 1900 to October of 1903, *The Spark* published 51 editions. In 1901, in a response to a letter to the editor from the readers of *The Spark*, Lenin gave further clarification to this new theoretical direction. To their accusations that *The Spark* "rarely considers the material elements and

---

86   See Lenin's "Draft and Explanation of a Programme for the Social-Democratic Party" *The Collected Works of Lenin* (Chin. 2. Ed.), volume 2, page 85.
87   See Lenin's "Resolution of the Third Congress of the R.S.D.L.P. on a Provisional Revolutionary Government" *The Collected Works of Lenin* (Chin. 2. Ed.), volume 11, page 12.
88   See Lenin's Letter"To Krupskaya" (September 1900).
89   *The Spark* (Iskra) was the first all-Russian political paper founded by Lenin. On December 24, 1900, the first edition of *The Spark* was published in Leipzig, Germany. It was soon moved to Munich, then again to London in April 1902. In the spring of 1903 it was moved to Geneva. Lenin was both the editor-in-chief and the leader of *The Spark*.

material environment of movements," that it "over-emphasizes the influence of thinkers who participate in movements on the direction of those movements," Lenin replied that they were followers of "economism." He no longer simple emphasizes "social economic forms" or "natural historical processes," but rather focuses on explaining that in truly considering material elements, one must deal with them critically, point out the dangers and weaknesses of spontaneous movements, and elevate spontaneity to consciousness. The Lenin we see here is obviously very different from the young Lenin of the past. The logic ray and **understanding dimension** with which Lenin examined reality had both changed. He now believed:

> **The "ideologist" is worthy of the name only when he** *precedes*
> **the spontaneous movement, points out the road, and is able**
> **ahead of all others to solve all the theoretical, political, tac-**
> **tical, and organizational questions which the "material ele-**
> **ments" of the movement spontaneously encounter.**[90]

Here we find that Lenin's thinking point gradually shifted towards the mutual effects of the revolutionary party and the material environment of the development of Russian society. He was most interested in the **active role of man** in affecting his social environment. I believe that Marx and Engels' idea in *The Holy Family* that "history does nothing," that man is the one who creates all ideas, had already deeply influenced Lenin. This point greatly surpassed Plekhanov's idea of deep-rooted external determinism. Here, Lenin's divergence from Plekhanov in terms of political stance and philosophical views had already become clear. Soon he would begin to surpass his teacher in terms of political ideas. There is little doubt that this thought shift in terms of political theory also implied the emergence of division and fresh debate within the Social Democratic Party: conflict was inevitable.

In Lenin's *What is to be Done*, written between Autumn 1901 and 1902, Lenin describes the origin and basic process of this debate. He writes that in the 1880s and 1890s, at the beginning of the spontaneous Russian workers' movement, different groups united under the banner of Marxism in opposing their collective enemies: the Narodniks. Lenin

---

90   See Lenin's "A Talk with Defenders of Economism" *The Collected Works of Lenin* (Chin. 2. Ed.), volume 2, pages 326-327.

refers to this as a "honeymoon period" with "Legal Marxism"[91]. During this period, Russian Marxists attempted to explain to people the **objective necessity** of developing a capitalist economy in Russia; however, after Marxism obtained decisive victory in Russia, the task was no longer to emphasize the necessity of a particular economic law, but rather to elevate the spontaneous struggle of the workers' movement into a **conscious** political struggle. This was a direct explanation and identification of the important shift in actual logic ray by Lenin himself.

I have found that this is the philosophical essence of the divergence between Lenin's Bolsheviks and Plekhanov's Mensheviks. Here we can see the determining influence of the critical shift in Lenin's philosophical thought on his political stance. Given the rapid development of the Russian Revolution and in opposition to Plekhanov's insistence on maintaining the objectivist standpoint with the "Legal Marxists" (emphasizing the necessity of attaining certain capitalist economic conditions), Lenin had already begun to ponder how to unleash the **subjective dynamism of the proletariat class** under existing objective conditions. This was a new theoretical logic ray that focused on reality. This was also the basis for the Menshevik criticism of the Bolsheviks as being "idealists." *Here, the authors of volume five of the Soviet **Philosophical History** confuse these two diametrically opposed thought tendencies of Lenin. They only remark that Lenin's thought at this time primarily "philosophically proves the role of subjective elements in social life," and that he opposes the objectivism of "Legal Marxism." They do not see that Lenin's thought here had already experienced an important shift. Furthermore, we also find that Lenin here strongly emphasized the central place of political class struggle in the theoretical system of Marxism[92]. This thought would later directly influence Mao Zedong. In Lenin's opinion, whether or not to recognize the leading place of political class struggle is the basic criterion by which to measure a socialist political party. Thus, in the Socialist International Conference*

---

91   "Legal Marxism" refers to a group of leftist intellectuals in Russia in the late 1800s and early 1900s, represented primarily by Struve. In the theoretical battle against Narodism, they allied with the Russian Social Democratic Party; however, in 1900, they parted ways with Marxism, turning to Kantianism and religious mystical speculation. Because they often published articles in *Herald of Life* and other legal publications, they were sardonically referred to by Lenin as "Legal Marxists."

92   See *The Collected Works of Lenin* (Chin. 1. Ed.), volume 1, pages 262-263; volume 2 pages 85-91 and 432; volume 6 pages 251-252; volume 7 page 168; volume 10 page 339.

of October 1908, when Kautsky and Adler refused to recognize English workers' parties engaging in the class struggle as part of the conference, Lenin expressed his extreme indignation[93]. Also in this text, Lenin clearly points out that "the **spontaneous** development of the working-class movement leads to its subordination to bourgeois ideology." He even goes on to suggest that if leaders "fail to divert the working-class movement from the path that is determined by the interaction of the material elements and the material environment is therefore **tantamount to renouncing socialism**"[94]. This is because it is impossible for the working class to spontaneously develop socialist thinking: "[this consciousness] would have to be brought to them from without."[95] It is evident that Lenin's goal here is no longer to explain the objective necessity of the development of capitalism in Russia; now his new desire is to transform modern society into socialist society. *We have sufficient reason to believe that in his later* **Bern Notebooks**, *Lenin was ecstatic to find that the essence of Marx's practical dialectics was the transformation and "abolition" of existence by the objective revolutionary activities of man.* Thus, Marx necessarily focused more on the **class consciousness** of the working class, the "true political consciousness."

> **The consciousness of the working masses cannot be genuine class-consciousness, unless the workers learn, from concrete, and above all from topical, political facts and events to observe *every* other social class in *all* the manifestations of its intellectual, ethical, and political life; unless they learn to apply in practice the materialist analysis and the materialist estimate of *all* aspects of the life and activity of *all* classes, strata, and groups of the population**[96].

Lenin acerbically criticizes the "economists" who believe that workers' movements should not go beyond the level of spontaneous economic struggles. In Lenin's opinion, "From the correct Marxist premise concerning the deep economic roots of the class struggle in general and of the political struggle in particular, the Economists have drawn the singular conclusion that we must turn our backs to the political struggle

93   Lenin, Vladimir. "International Bureau of Socialist Parties." *The Collected Works of Lenin* (Chin. 2. Ed.), volume 17, pages 212-213.
94   Lenin, Vladimir. "What is to be Done." *The Collected Works of Lenin* (Chin. 2. Ed.), volume 6, page 38.
95   *Ibid.*, page 29.
96   Lenin, Vladimir. "What is to be Done." *The Collected Works of Lenin* (Chin. 2. Ed.), volume 6, pages 66-67.

and retard its development, narrow its scope, and reduce its aims"[97]. Lenin's own view is clear: he believes that the workers' dissatisfaction with the capitalist system should be transformed into conscious political struggle, and that this transformation "should be done by **us**"[98]. If not, what is the point in establishing the Social Democrat Party? He goes so far as to directly criticize Plekhanov, writing that his teacher it was not enough that his teacher merely conceded the fact that capitalism **was becoming** the primary mode of production in Russia; the correct expression should have been "capitalism **has already become** the primary mode of production"[99]. *The later "Draft and Explanation of a Programme for the Social-Democratic Party," directly used Lenin's corrected ideas when it employed the phrase, "...in Russia, where capitalism is the ruling mode of production..."[100]. I have also found that not long before this, Lenin privately exchanged ideas with Plekhanov. Lenin wrote that the "**overemphasis** of " economic" agitation...was the legitimate and inevitable companion of **any step forward** in the conditions of our movement which existed in Russia at the end of the 1880s or the beginning of the 1890s[101]. He believed that in his day, however, there were new tasks and goals for the Russian Social Democratic Party. Looking back from our perspective today, Lenin's views here are worthy of discussion.*

However, between 1901 and early 1902 Lenin still enjoyed a good relationship with Plekhanov; in the correspondence between the two thinkers, we see that Lenin often asked for theoretical help from his teacher and exchanged ideas with him[102]. *According to Plekhanov's own words, Lenin reminded Plekhanov of Struve's **On Freedom and Necessity** in 1900, while they were both opposing Struve's "Legal Marxism"[103].*

97   Lenin, Vladimir. ""Abolition of the Monarch and the Republic." *The Collected Works of Lenin* (Chin. 2. Ed.), volume 11, pages 22-23.
98   Lenin, Vladimir. "What is to be Done." *The Collected Works of Lenin* (Chin. 2. Ed.), volume 6, page 187. This sentence was written as part of Lenin's correction of Plekhanov's draft for the Russian Social Democrat party.
99   *Ibid.*, page 219. This sentence was written as part of Lenin's correction of Plekhanov's draft for the Russian Social Democrat party.
100   Lenin, Vladimir. ""Draft and Explanation of a Programme for the Social-Democratic Party." *The Collected Works of Lenin* (Chin. 2. Ed.), volume 7, page 426.
101   Lenin, Vladimir. "Letter to Plekhanov, November 9, 1900." *The Collected Works of Lenin* (Chin. 2. Ed.), volume 44, pages 72-73.
102   *Ibid.*, pages 147-149, 183-184, and 205-207.
103   Plekhanov, Georg. *Against Revisionism in History*. People's Press (1957), page 334 (Chinese).

The relationship between the two began to become tense in May 1902. After reading Lenin's "Draft and Explanation of a Programme for the Social-Democratic Party," Plekhanov rather caustically commented on Lenin's work, using some insulting language. In response, Lenin wrote directly to Plekhanov, stating that their personal relationship had been damaged, that it had been "ended"[104]. However, in spite of this, for another relatively long period of time the two men continued to exchange work-related correspondence. It was not until the summer of 1903 at the second congress of the Russian Social Democrat Party in London that the political stances of Lenin and Plekhanov began to become "very clear"[105]. Although The Spark was determined to be a central party newspaper, in the wake of increasingly severe questions of principle in the party, as the party split into Bolsheviks (meaning majority) and Mensheviks (meaning minority), *The Spark* also began to break into different camps, and Lenin resigned as editor-in-chief[106]. *At first, Lenin fired Axelrod, Trotsky, and Potresov from the editorial staff of **The Spark**, but Plekhanov later asked them to return, forcing Lenin to resign. On December 22, 1904, Lenin's new paper, **The Forward**, published its first article from Geneva. At this point, direct conflict and struggle became inevitable; beginning with its 52 edition, **The Spark** became a tool of the Mensheviks. Lenin would later refer to it as **The New Spark**[107]. Another important point to bring up is that within Lenin's Bolshevik camp, there were two thinkers who had already succumbed to Machism: Bogdanov and Bazarov. At this particular time, Lenin naturally did not directly criticize their philosophical worldview, though Plekhanov refused to desist in criticizing Bogdanov.* I have realized that Plekhanov's criticism of Bogdanov is sometimes directed at Lenin. Plekhanov clearly indicates that he and Bogdanov "**represent two directly opposed world-outlooks**"[108]. Plekhanov accuses Bogdanov of "advancing under the false banner of Marxism," and then peddling his own "idealism." Furthermore, Plekhanov sharply points out that "materialism became the basis of socialism and communism," that Marxists

104   May 14 letter, not included in English volume 43.
105   See "The Second Congress of the League of Russian Revolutionary Social-Democracy Abroad." *The Collected Works of Lenin* (Chin. 2. Ed.), volume 7, page 389.
106   Lenin, Vladimir. "Letter to Plekhanov, November 6, 1903." *The Collected Works of Lenin* (Chin. 2. Ed.), volume 44, page 386.
107   Lenin believed that The Spark began to turn to Menshevism with its 51st edition, so he refers to editions 1-50 as the "old *Spark*".
108   See Plekhanov's "Materialismus Militans: Reply to Mr Bogdanov" People's Press (1957), page 336.

could not refer to idealist Machists as "comrades"[109]. When Kautsky entered the fray, Plekhanov attacked him with equal fervour, claiming that he did not understand Russia's situation, that he had overlooked the "theoretical bourgeois reaction [Machism] which is now causing real havoc in the ranks of our advanced intellectuals"[110]. However, Lenin did not believe this way at the time, separating political stance from worldview. He did not yet know the philosophical foundation on which the shift in his political stance and practical logic ray would be based.

It is very interesting to note that in Lenin's 1904 text "One Step Forward, Two Steps Back," we are still able to find a continuation of Plekhanov's views in *The Monist View of History*, which we have already examined in previous sections. As Lenin analyzed the struggle of the Russian Social Democrats, he began to realize that "that development does indeed proceed dialectically, by way of contradictions." Before, Lenin did not have this dialectical view, and certainly did not have a view of contradictions. Lenin wrote that in this struggle, the minority become the majority and the majority become the minority, "each side passes from the defensive to the offensive." The object of struggle becomes the negation of the negation in continual squabble. Lenin concludes: "In a word, not only do oats grow according to Hegel, but the Russian Social-Democrats war among themselves according to Hegel"[111]. Lenin's last line was also a continuation of similar views expressed by Plekhanov. More importantly, Lenin refers to the dialectic thus, "...the great Hegelian dialectics which Marxism made its own, having first turned it right side up..." This can be thought of as a new historical appraisal of Hegel. This confirms what we have already seen, that Lenin depended on Plekhanov in terms of his theoretical logic; even after they parted ways politically, Lenin continues to believe in his teacher's philosophical reliability. In other words, up to this point Lenin's philosophical ideas were still **externally composed of logical mirror images from Other theoretical authority**. Lenin's thought circuit in terms of philosophical theory originated with Plekhanov, although they had already broken off ties politically.

I must also point out that between 1903 and 1904, Lenin read two books on basic philosophical theory while living in Geneva, Switzerland. These

---

109   *Ibid.*, page 337.
110   *Ibid.*, page 446.
111   Lenin, Vladimir. "One Step Forward, Two Steps Back" *The Collected Works of Lenin* (Chin. 2. Ed.), volume 8, page 411-412.

were Friedrich Überweg's *Outline of the History of Philosophy* (the 1876-1880 Leibnitz edition) and Paulsen's *Introduction to Philosophy* (1899 edition). However, the results of this study were evidently not ideal. From our existing notes, Lenin's opinion of the first book was not high, feeling that its content was outdated and that "three-fourths of its content is made up of the names of people and books"[112] without any substantive content. As such, there are only a few lines of notes on this book. Lenin seems to have had more interest in the second book. His interest focused on the question of philosophical materialism; because the author was an idealist, Lenin was able to gain an understanding of basic philosophical issues from his critique of materialism[113]. Besides this, Lenin also read a review of Haeckel's *The Wonders of Life and The Riddle of the Universe* in 1904[114]. I deduce that this was Lenin's first non-systematic study of basic philosophical theory outside his own grasp of Marxist philosophy. This could very well have been because pompous philosophers had begun to crop up among the activists in the Social Democrat party, including Plekhanov, Bogdanov, and Bazarov. Lenin realized at this time that his own philosophical background was not profound enough, that he was unable to clearly and precisely distinguish between important, basic philosophical concepts. Several researchers have pointed out that when Bogdanov published his first book, *Basic Elements of the Natural View of History* in 1899, Lenin thought it was a new work by Plekhanov. He was unable to see the errors in Bogdanov's scholarly standpoint[115]. Of course, his study of philosophy at this time was not systematic. On the other hand, I believe that perhaps it was precisely because of the intensifying political division between Lenin and Plekhanov that young Lenin began to realize the need to independently face unfamiliar philosophical theory, thus setting himself to work. However, objectively speaking, I also believe that his study at this time did not significantly alter his philosophical standpoint. In terms of philosophical ideas, he had not yet escaped from Plekhanov, whom he had already begun to oppose politically. Lenin did not know that Plekhanov's incorrect political standpoint was closely

---

112   Lenin, Vladimir. "Fr. Überweg. Outline of the History of Philosophy" *The Collected Works of Lenin* (Chin. 2. Ed.), volume 55, page 323.

113   Lenin, Vladimir. "Fr. Paulsen. Introduction to Philosophy" *The Collected Works of Lenin* (Chin. 2. Ed.), volume 55, pages 324-326.

114   Lenin, Vladimir "Note on a Review of The Wonders of Life and The Riddle of the Universe" *The Collected Works of Lenin* (Chin. 2. Ed.), volume 55, page 327.

115   See "Materialism and Empirio-criticism and its Critics" in *Lenin Studies* (1995) volume 5 page 51.

correlated to his views on philosophical materialism. This is a different, profound contradiction of logical situations.

5 CLASS CONSCIOUSNESS AND THE DYNAMISM OF THE REVOLUTION

In 1905, the debate over the present and future of the Russian Revolution between the Lenin-led Bolsheviks and the Mensheviks became even more heated. *Lenin summarized this debate, writing: "The two big splits which occurred in the ranks of Social-Democracy—the split between the "Economists" and the old Iskrists in 1900-03, and the split between the "Mensheviks" and "Bolsheviks" in 1903-06"[116]. Lenin wrote that these two splits were both caused by the debate between opportunists and revolutionaries within the party.* The substance of the debate centred on the question of the leadership of the Russian bourgeois democratic revolution. Lenin wrote: "In the view of the Bolsheviks the proletariat has had laid upon it the active task of pursuing the bourgeois-democratic revolution to its consummation and of being its leader...The Mensheviks were inclined to the view that the bourgeoisie are the motive force and that they determine the scope of the bourgeois revolution." The Mensheviks believed that the proletariat class was incapably of leading a bourgeois revolution, much less see it through to the end and the establishment of a "revolutionary democratic dictatorship of the proletariat and the peasantry"[117]. These two outlooks were separated by a gulf of fundamentally divergent political thought.

In the early stages of the conflict, the division was primarily expressed as debate between Plekhanov's new version of *The Spark* and Lenin's *The Forward*, as well as debate surrounding the third conference of the Social Democrat Party. At this point, Lenin's opinion of his teacher Plekhanov seems to have shifted: "He makes no mention of the real situation in Russia; he employs all of his learning in manipulating a few unrelated quotations"[118]. Lenin points out that when confronted with the development of Russian society, the new-*Iskra* (new *Spark*) group

---

116   Lenin, Vladimir Ilyich. "Socialist Revolutionary Mensheviks." *The Collected Works of Lenin*, volume 13, page 391 (Chin. 2. Ed.).

117   Lenin, Vladimir Ilyich. "The Attitude Towards Bourgeois Parties." *The Collected Works of Lenin*, volume 14, pages 367-368.

118   Lenin, Vladimir Ilyich. "A Report on the Social Democrats' Participation in a Provisional Revolutionary Government." *The Collected Works of Lenin*, volume 10, 128 (Chin. 2. Ed.).

merely generally describes the process without discussing actual tasks. This method "reminds one of Marx's opinion (in his famous "theses" on Feuerbach) of the old materialism, which was alien to the ideas of dialectics." Lenin's observations here are extremely profound. He accuses the new-*Iskra* group of "[belittling] the materialist conception of history by ignoring the active, leading and guiding part in history which can and must be played by parties that understand the material prerequisites of a revolution and that have placed themselves at the head of the progressive classes"[119]. *Lenin often made mention of the 11th thesis in Marx's **Theses on Feuerbach**: "The philosophers have only interpreted the world, in various ways; the point is to change it." However, he wrote that Marx criticized old materialism with this thesis[120]. Precisely speaking, Marx was criticizing all past philosophy. It was in this sense that Marx's practical materialism surpassed Plekhanov's Feuerbachian philosophical materialism.* Reflecting on the "economists," Lenin wrote:

The Economists had learned by rote that politics are based on economics and "understood" this to mean that the political struggle should be reduced to the level of the economic struggle. The new-Iskraists have learned by rote that the economic basis of the democratic revolution is the bourgeois revolution, and "understood" this to mean that the democratic aims of the proletariat should be degraded to the level of bourgeois moderation[121].

At this time, Lenin's thoughts turned to the class-consciousness of the proletariat and the dynamism of revolutionary practice. He criticizes the "realism" of the so-called *Osvobozhdeniye* (emancipation group): "The *Osvobozhdeniye* League members know only pedestrian realism; the revolutionary dialectics of Marxist realism, which emphasises the urgent tasks of the advanced class, and discovers in the existing state of things those elements that will lead to its overthrow, are absolutely alien to them"[122]. Lenin wrote that "the **historical initiative** of the masses was what Marx prized above everything else." He "regarded world history

---

119   Lenin, Vladimir Ilyich. "How should The Revolution be Advanced." *The Collected Works of Lenin*, volume 11, page 25 (Chin. 2. Ed.).
120   *Ibid.*, page 25 (Chin. 2. Ed.).
121   Lenin, Vladimir Ilyich. "Two Tactics of Social Democracy in the Democratic Revolution.'" *The Collected Works of Lenin*, volume 11, page 93 (Chin. 2. Ed.).
122   Lenin, Vladimir Ilyich. "Revolution Teaches.'" *The Collected Works of Lenin*, volume 11, page 130 (Chin. 2. Ed.).

from the standpoint of those who **make** it without being in a position to calculate the chances **infallibly** beforehand"[123]. *Lenin's viewpoint here corresponds to that of Marx as expressed in **The Holy Family**.* It is evident that Lenin's understanding had already diverged greatly from that of Plekhanov, because as early as December 1905 Plekhanov proposed "to put the brakes on"[124]. *It is interesting to note that in late October 1905, Lenin wrote a sincere letter to Plekhanov, inviting him to "work together" with the Bolsheviks. Lenin believed that the division between the Bolsheviks and Plekhanov was "temporary," that it was brought about by special circumstances. In this letter, Lenin clearly writes that Plekhanov was "the best force among Russian Social-Democrats," expressing "the entire movement's extreme need of your guiding, close and immediate participation"[125]. Also in the letter, Lenin proposes meeting with Plekhanov and resolving misunderstandings between them. Of course, Lenin proposed doing so not to compromise with Plekhanov's mistakes, but rather in the hopes that he could bring Plekhanov onto the correct path of Bolshevism. Unfortunately Plekhanov rejected Lenin's offer. In the third edition of the 1905 Social Democrats Daily Journal, Plekhanov published a short comment accusing Lenin of being without principle for mixing himself with "Empirio-monism"[126]. Though this was truly a mistake of Lenin's at the time, it did not damage his correct political position.* Of course, Lenin also realized that the fundamental difference between Marxism and all other forms of socialist theory was that it combined "complete scientific sobriety in the analysis of the objective state of affairs and the objective course of evolution with the most emphatic recognition of the importance of the revolutionary energy, revolutionary creative genius, and revolutionary initiative of the masses"[127]. I believe that this was Lenin's effort to combine the objective dimension of social historical development with the subjective dimension of the dialectic. *Bochenski irresponsibly claims that Lenin gives special emphasis to the meaning of human will*

---

123   Lenin, Vladimir Ilyich. "Preface to the Russian Translation of Karl Marx's Letters to Dr. Kugelmann." *The Collected Works of Lenin*, volume 14, pages 379-381 (Chin. 2. Ed.).
124   *Ibid.,* , page 377 (Chin. 2. Ed.).
125   Lenin, Vladimir Ilyich. "Letter to G. V. Plekhanov 160." *The Collected Works of Lenin*, volume 45, page 129 (Chin. 2. Ed.).
126   See endnote 124 on page 418 of volume 45 of *The Collected Works of Lenin* (Chin. 2. Ed.).
127   Lenin, Vladimir Ilyich. "Against Boycott." *The Collected Works of Lenin*, volume 16, page 20 (Chin. 2. Ed.).

in social development; thus he abandons Marx's classical economic determinism"[128]. According to Wittle, Lenin transformed Marxism into something different from Plekhanov's evolutionary determinism, giving it a saving spirit that vitalized men's hearts[129]. This is obviously nonsense. First, Marx's historical materialism was not economic determinism, he only emphasized the foundational, determining role of material production and reproduction; second, Lenin's emphasis on the active role of class will in the progression of social history was founded on historical materialism. However, the question of how to bring this practical logic ray, which originated from actual political struggle, into line with a philosophical worldview had not yet entered into Lenin's thought space at this time.

Another important dialectical viewpoint that Lenin emphasized in the practice of the Russian Revolution was **concrete analysis of concrete problems.** He clearly understood the importance of this method from the beginning, maintaining that Marxism was not made up of "abstract formulae" or "pedantic methods." Rather, only through uniting Marxism with "the concrete environment of history" could the practical orientation of scientific socialism be upheld[130]. A true revolutionary, socialist party could only be one that united socialism with the Russian workers' movement[131]. "Concrete political aims must be set in concrete circumstances. All things are relative, all things flow and all things change"[132].

Here it would not help to bring up a concrete example. In a 1909 letter, Lenin discussed the debate on the future of Russian historical progress that took place in the late 19th and early 20th centuries, focusing primarily on the problems with capitalism. He wrote that in the early debate between the Russian Social Democratic Party and the Narodniks, the focus of the debate was whether the future of Russia would be

---

128   Bochenski, Jozef. 1965. *Soviet-Russian Dialectical Materialism.* The Commercial Press, page 32 (Chinese Edition).
129   Wittle. 1963. *Dialectical Materialism.* The Commercial Press, page 133 (Chinese Edition).
130   Lenin, Vladimir Ilyich. "Guerrilla Warfare." *The Collected Works of Lenin,* volume 14, pages 1-2 (Chin. 2. Ed.).
131   Lenin, Vladimir Ilyich. "Why the Social-Democrats Must Declare a Determined and Relentless War on the Socialist-Revolutionaries." *The Collected Works of Lenin,* volume 6, page 362 (Chin. 2. Ed.).
132   Lenin, Vladimir Ilyich. "'Revolutionary Communes' and the Revolutionary-Democratic Dictatorship." *The Collected Works of Lenin,* volume 11, page 69 (Chin. 2. Ed.).

capitalism or "the production for the people." At this point in time, history had already proven and confirmed the true birth of capitalism in Russia; however, after the "question has been settled both in theory and in reality," what ought to appear on the agenda is a "higher question": capitalism of type α or capitalism of type β. This question was the focus of the debate between the Bolsheviks and Mensheviks. Criticizing the Mensheviks, Lenin writes that Menshevism was "a doctrinaire simplification, vulgarisation and distortion of the herald of Marxism, and a betrayal of its spirit" because:

While fighting Narodism as a wrong doctrine of *socialism*, the Mensheviks, in a doctrinaire fashion, overlooked the historically real and progressive historical content of Narodism as a theory of the mass *petty-bourgeois* struggle of democratic capitalism against liberal-landlord capitalism, of "American" capitalism against "Prussian" capitalism[133].

This is why the Mensheviks would mistakenly believe that "peasant movements are reactionary," and then pitifully stand with the constitutional democrats in opposing the peasantry. This is why the Mensheviks mistakenly followed the bourgeoisie in emphasizing the "overall progress of economic development," rejecting the revolutionary dictatorship of the proletariat and peasant, and thus going against the progress of history. We can see that at important historical moments, Lenin was able to clearly defend the viewpoint of the dialectic, analyzing the circumstances of the revolutionary concretely, historically, and truthfully, and uniting the scientific theory of Marxism with reality. I should also point out that when we say young Lenin did not have a firm theoretical base, that he had not undergone systematic research training, this does not prevent us from asserting that he was a brilliant practitioner of the dialectic in the actual revolutionary struggle. *Here, Dunayevskaya proposes an interesting idea, that while insufficiently precise, still contains elements of truth. She wrote, "before 1914, Lenin was in a state of contradiction between practical dialectics in practice and Kautsky in thought"[134].* I believe that Dunayevskaya was referring to Lenin's correct application of dialectics to political struggle, but adherence to Kautsky's economic determinism in terms of theoretical thought.

---

133 Lenin, Vladimir Ilyich. "Letter to I. I. Skvortsov-Stepanov." *The Collected Works of Lenin*, volume 45, page 296 (Chin. 2. Ed.).
134 Dunayevskaya, Raya. 1998. *Marxism and Freedom*. Liaoning Education Press, page 174 (Chinese Edition).

However, the facts support the conclusions we have reached in this chapter, that in terms of both philosophical theory and general methodology, young Lenin affirmed the Kautsky of the Second International through following Plekhanov. At this time, he was not aware of the contradiction between his philosophical theory and the logic ray of his actual practice.

In Lenin's view, "the Marxist is the **first** to foresee the approach of a revolutionary period, and already begins to rouse the people and to sound the tocsin while the philistines are still wrapt in the slavish slumber of loyal subjects"[135]. He passionately declares, "we shall make the utmost use of **all** revolutionary possibilities"[136].

In 1906, only one year after the success of the bourgeois revolution, Lenin wrote that, "The people are now on the eve of another great struggle!"[137]. Quoting Maxim Gorky's *Song of the Stormy Petrel*, Lenin expresses his own revolutionary passion; "Let the storm rage louder!"[138]

135　Lenin, Vladimir Ilyich. "The Crisis of Menshevism." *The Collected Works of Lenin*, volume 14, page 157 (Chin. 2. Ed.).

136　*Ibid.*, page 176 (Chin. 2. Ed.).

137　Lenin, Vladimir Ilyich. "Declaration of our Group in the Duma." *The Collected Works of Lenin*, volume 13, page 224 (Chin. 2. Ed.).

138　Lenin, Vladimir Ilyich. "Before the Storm." *The Collected Works of Lenin*, volume 13, page 335 (Chin. 2. Ed.).

CHAPTER TWO

LENIN, PLEKHANOV AND
PHILOSOPHICAL MATERIALISM

As we have already made clear, at the end of the 19th and beginning of the 20th century, Lenin was an outstanding young Marxist but not a fully mature thinker in all areas of theoretical research. In fact, his most exceptional contributions were in political economy and politics, fields more closely related to social reality; when it came to philosophy, even he would not have referred to himself as an "expert." As such, in order to oppose the rise of *Machism* both within and without Russia around 1908, Lenin dedicated himself to his first serious and systematic study of **philosophical theory**. Based on particular theoretical circumstances and under the influence of Plekhanov, the topic with which Lenin began was philosophical materialism. I believe that his philosophical research at this time was extremely fruitful; because it laid the most important philosophical theoretical foundation for the later development of Lenin's thought, also providing the vital philosophical conditions for his more profound elaboration of Marxist research and leadership of modern philosophical debate. In this chapter we will see the actual background of Lenin's thought as he began this study of philosophy, as well as the commentaries that he wrote after reading Plekhanov's *Fundamental Problems of Marxism*.

1 THE BACKGROUND OF LENIN'S FIRST SYSTEMATIC STUDY OF PHILOSOPHICAL THEORY

In overcoming the stagnant ideas of the traditional research of Marxist philosophical history, in sincerely examining the large quantity of first-hand letters and documents left by Lenin from this period of time, it is not difficult for us to find a completely new, more real Lenin. In fact, in terms of philosophical theory, Lenin was always very humble, never thinking of himself as an expert in the field of philosophy, much less a master capable of creating his own independent philosophical system. As early as 1898, when Lenin read a discussion of philosophy in *The Wealth of Russia*, and especially in reading the scholarly discussion between Struve and Bulgakov, he refers to himself as "not competent" in a letter to a friend[1]. Although Lenin had written a few articles criticizing Struve, the subjective views throughout these articles still emanated from Plekhanov. The following year, Lenin staunchly opposed the then-popular neo-Kantism in a letter to a friend. He cautiously wrote: "I am very clear of my deficiencies in philosophical learning; until I study this more, I do not plan on writing articles on this subject"[2]. *Here we can bring up again that often-cited detail, that Lenin took Bogdanov's **Basic Elements of the Natural Conception of History** (published in 1899) to be a new book published by Plekhanov under a pen name. This error was committed because Bogdanov at that time was still a materialist. Later, under the influence of Ostwald's **Understanding from the Perspective of History** (1901), Bogdanov began to shift to Machism. This story is sufficient to demonstrate that Lenin's philosophical recognition abilities were insufficient. By this time, many years had already passed since the publishing of What the "Friends of the People" Are.* This portrays an enormously different picture from the philosophically and theoretically invincible, miraculous Lenin depicted by Soviet scholars. *There is another supplemental proof here: for Berdyaev, the most active Marxist philosophers at the time were Plekhanov, Bogdanov, and Lunacharsky. He makes no mention of Lenin[3].*

---

1   Lenin, Vladimir Ilyich. "Letter to A. N. Potresov." *The Collected Works of Lenin*, volume 44, pages 16-17 (Chin. 2. Ed.).
2   *Ibid.*, pages 31-32 (Chin. 2. Ed.).
3   Berdyaev, Nikolai. 1999. *The Truth of Philosophy and the Reality of Knowledge Levels.* Yunnan People's Press.

In 1901, Bogdanov published *Knowledge from a Historical Viewpoint*[4]. In 1902, Plekhanov wrote to Lenin, clearly pointing out that Bogdanov's philosophy was aimed at refuting materialism and stating his own plans to oppose Bogdanov[5]. In 1904, the Menshevik Axelrod published an article entitled "New Change in Revisionism" in the *New Spark*. In 1907, Plekhanov, Deborin, and other Mensheviks held a debate with Bogdanov and Lunacharsky in Geneva. Deborin submitted an article entitled "*Machism* and Marxism" at that conference. In 1907, Bogdanov published "An Open Letter to Comrade Plekhanov" in *Herald of Life*. In 1908, Plekhanov and Deborin published three open letters in response to Bogdanov, criticizing his erroneous philosophical ideas[6]. I have found that in this 1908 struggle between Bogdanov and Plekhanov, Bogdanov does merely promote Machism using findings from natural science, but resorts to even more cunning theoretical debate logic: he uses Marx's critique of bourgeois ideology (critical theory of fetishisms) to distort and refute philosophical materialism. Bogdanov's cunning tricks put Plekhanov, who did not have a deep understanding of historical materialist theories, at a disadvantage. I will go into greater depth on the context of this philosophical debate in the addendum to this chapter. This was the immediate background of Lenin's *Materialism and Empirio-Criticism*. Before this, Lenin had not publicly criticized his Bolshevik ally Bogdanov. *It is laughable to note that the authors of the fifth volume of the Soviet History of Philosophy*

4 **Alexander Bogdanov** (real name Malinouski) (1873-1928) was a well-known Russian thinker. He graduated from the University of Kharkiv in 1899 with a degree in medicine, which was also his original profession. He joined the Russian Social Democratic Party in 1896. In 1903 Bogdanov became a Bolshevik, and was elected as a permanent member on the Bolshevik Committee. He was elected as a central committee member at the third, fourth, and fifth congresses of the Russian Social Democratic Party. He served as editor for the Bolshevik papers *The Forward, The Proletariat, and The Herald of Life*. In 1909 he was expelled from the Bolsheviks. After the October Revolution, Bogdanov became the director of the Socialist Academy of Social Sciences and a professor at the University of Moscow. In 1921, he was named the director of the Moscow Institute for Haemotology and Blood Transfusions. He passed away in 1928 after a failed blood transfusion experiment. His primary works include, *Economics Curricula* (1897), *Fundamental Principles of the Natural Conception of History* (1899), *Empirio-monism* (1904-1906) *Social Psychology* (1906), *Introduction to Political Economy* (1914), *Science and the Working Class* (1918), *On The Culture of the Proletariat* (1924), and *Tektology* (three volumes, 1912-1929).
5 See Plekhanov's letters to Lenin, November 17-19, 1901. *Marxist-Leninist Research Material*, volume 1. 1982. The People's Press, page 78 (Chin. Ed.).
6 These three letters were published as a pamphlet under the name "Materialismus Militans." See Plekhanov's *Against Revisionism in Philosophy* (1957), People's Press.

*completely ignored historical fact in trying to create an ideological im-
age of Lenin, writing that "the Mensheviks were always opposed to
struggling against Machism, believing it 'unnecessary' and 'pointless.'
It was Lenin who explained the necessity and responsibility of opposing
Machism"[7]. In the* **Brief Biography of Lenin**, *published by the Soviet
Central Marxist-Leninist Research Institute, it records that Plekhanov
only published a few short essays opposing Machism[8]. This is certainly
nothing more than an ideological obfuscation.*

At around 1908, Lenin wrote a plan for lectures on Marxism. In this
outline, Lenin intended to demonstate Marxism in four subtitles: the
theory of surplus value, economic development (economic- industrial-
development in Russia and the world), class struggle, and philosophical
materialism. Under the title of philosophical materialism, Lenin makes
six points:

1. Marx'a theory=integrated world outlook.

2. Two main world outlooks and philosophical starting-points: religious
obscurantism and materialism.

3. Engels (Ludwig Feuerbach).

4. 1789 France—Hegel and Feuerbach in Germany (before 1848).

5. Dialectical materialism.

6. Russia: Chernyshevsky, Narodniks, present-day opportunists
(Bogdanov)[9].

The first thing to which I would like to direct the reader's attention is
that here Lenin has already categorized Bogdanov as an "opportunist."
*This is because Bogdanov had joined the "recall" party and the "ul-
timatum" party (the former had advocated that the Social Democratic
Party be recalled from the Duma, and the latter advocated that an ul-
timatum be sent to the Social Democrat Party forcing its expulsion). At
this point there were already serious political differences between Lenin
and Bogdanov[10].* However, it is my opinion that Lenin's understanding of the essence of Marxist philosophy was still not very precise or

---

7   Dynnik, ed. *History of Philosophy*, volume 5. 1975. Beijing Sanlian Press, page 81.

8   Brief *Biography of Lenin*. 1957. People's Press, page 78.

9   Lenin, Vladimir Ilyich. "Plan for Lectures on Marxism." *The Collected Works of
Lenin*, volume 17, 312 (Chin. 2. Ed.).

10   According to Krupskaya's memoirs, L*enin's falling apart with Bogdanov took
place around February 13, 1908. See Krupskaya, Nadya. Reminiscences of Lenin.*
People's Press (1972), page 159.

complete. This can primarily be seen in his continuation of Plekhanov's (Dietzgen's) identification of Marxist philosophy as mere dialectical materialism and immediately equating it with **philosophical material- ism**. More importantly, Lenin incorrectly **viewed historical material- ism as the application of philosophical materialism in the field of history**. In his opinion at the time, "the dialectical materialism of Marx and Engels goes further than the Encyclopaedists and Feuerbach, for it applies the materialist philosophy to the domain of history, to the domain of the social sciences"[11]. Therefore, when discussing histori- cal materialism, he often refers to it as the **materialist conception of history**[12]. This viewpoint is imprecise, because this would mean that the dialectical materialism of Marx and Engels was nothing but a gen- eralization and application of materialism in the field of history. It is my opinion that this was the result of the philosophical influence of Plekhanov (Dietzgen). This mistaken opinion directly became an im- portant point in the Stalinist dogmatic philosophical interpretive frame- work, continuing to influence generations of scholars to this day.

In 1908, Lenin wrote "Marxism and Revisionism." This was an ex- tremely important text, because during this time, because it was here that a new split began to emerge in the theoretical situating of Lenin's thought. The overall content of the article was a historical review of the struggles between Marxism and various inimical schools of thought, with an emphasis on reformism within the ranks of Marxism itself. In addition to the international reformist movement led by Bernstein, Lenin also points out in this text that events had taken place near to him that made him indignant. *This was, in fact, not something that Lenin had just discovered. We have already discussed Plekhanov's criticism of him for separating political stance from philosophical thought.* Lenin wrote that even in Russia, some scholars were attempting to use the chance of criticizing Plekhanov's political opportunism to propagate a kind of "reactionary philosophical garbage." These scholars were Bogdanov, Bazarov, Lunacharsky, who were political allies of Lenin at this time. In the blink of an eye, they had become Russia's "neo-Humeists and

---

11   Lenin, Vladimir Ilyich. "The Attitude of the Workers' Party to Religion." *The Collected Works of Lenin*, volume 17, page 391 (Chin. 2. Ed.).

12   For a long time, historical materialism was also identified as the materialist con- ception of history. This is actually a serious misunderstanding. It debases the historical science that Marx and Engels established as a scientific worldview – historical materi- alism – into a department of philosophy in the field of social history. I will discuss this issue in greater depth later on.

neo-Berkeleyist revisionists." *Here Lenin referred to An Outline of the Philosophy of Marxism, which was written by Bogdanov, Bazarov, Lunacharsky, and others*[13].

> **In the sphere of philosophy revisionism followed in the wake of bourgeois professorial "science". The professors went "back to Kant"—and revisionism dragged along after the neo-Kantians. The professors repeated the platitudes that priests have uttered a thousand times against philosophical materialism—and the revisionists, smiling indulgently, mumbled (word for word after the latest *Handbuch*) that materialism had been "refuted" long ago. The professors treated Hegel as a "dead dog", and while themselves preaching idealism, only an idealism a thousand times more petty and banal than Hegel's, contemptuously shrugged their shoulders at dialectics—and the revisionists floundered after them into the swamp of philosophical vulgarisation of science, replacing "artful" (and revolutionary) dialectics by "simple" (and tranquil) "evolution"**[14].

It is evident that the "bourgeois professors" of whom Lenin spoke were the foreign physicists who believed in *Machism*: "*Machism* takes materialism for metaphysics! There is now a group of famous, modern natural scientists, who suggest with electrons and rays and other "miracles" the existence of god – a very crude god, but also a very cunning god, idealism"[15]. Here, Lenin's position was very clear: remain steadfast in criticism and struggle. It is interesting to note that Lenin at this time also believed "the only Marxist in the international Social-Democratic movement to criticise the incredible platitudes of the revisionists from the standpoint of consistent dialectical materialism was Plekhanov"[16]. However, at almost the same period of time, Lenin accuses Plekhanov of defending political revisionism[17]. Here, the two men share an ex-

---

13   *An Outline of the Philosophy of Marxism* (St. Petersburg, 1908). This collection of essays included Bogdanov's famous "An Idolatrous Country and Marxist Philosophy," among others. In fact, the authors of this work were a philosophical group that had congregated around Bogdanov. They also published Collection of Texts on the Realist Worldview (1904) and *Collection of Texts on Collectivist Philosophy* (1909).

14   Lenin, Vladimir Ilyich. "Marxism and Revisionism." *The Collected Works of Lenin*, volume 17, page 13 (Chin. 2. Ed.).

15   Lenin, Vladimir Ilyich. "Letter to Maxim Gorky." *The Collected Works of Lenin*, volume 46, pages 242-243 (Chin. 2. Ed.).

16   Lenin, Vladimir Ilyich. "Marxism and Revisionism." *The Collected Works of Lenin*, volume 17, page 16 (Chin. 2. Ed.).

17   Lenin, Vladimir Ilyich. "How Plekhanov and Co. Defend Revisionism." *The Collected Works of Lenin*, volume 17, page 260 (Chin. 2. Ed.).

tremely complex relationship, one that is difficult to accurately examine from without. Politically, Lenin is clearly at odds with his past teacher; philosophically, however, Lenin still steadfastly stands with Plekhanov. This was a unique theoretical situating that appeared in Lenin's thought at this time. Lenin at this time was not aware that on a deeper level of thought situating space, Plekhanov's political "surrenderism" was the inevitable result of his demotion of Marxism to the philosophical materialism of Feuerbach (Dietzgen). Philosophical materialism could not support Lenin's political stance. The philosophical basis of the October Revolution could only be the **practical dialectic** in historical materialism. This was an understanding that Lenin was only able to reach after the *Bern Notebooks*. Understanding this point is vital to our deeper comprehension of the underlying shift in Lenin's philosophical thought at this time. This theoretical circumstance once again proves the conclusion we reached earlier, that for a long period of time, Lenin depended on the **Other situating** of Plekhanov for his philosophical logic. In Deborin's *Lenin the Thinker*, written in the 1920s, he very tactfully dissected the relationship between Plekhanov and Lenin. He wrote that Plekhanov was first a theorist, while Lenin was first a practitioner, politician, and leader." This sentence was deleted from the 1961 edition, published in Philosophy and Politics[18]. Later we will look specifically at this textual event.

However, faced with an increasingly complex philosophical conflict, Lenin still felt that he was not versed enough in basic theory. In a letter to Gorky, Lenin once again conceded his lack of training in philosophy, which made it impossible for him to publish his views. I have noticed that Lenin began to develop a close friendship with Gorky after 1907. In the letters which Lenin wrote to this great Russian poet, he more truthfully and frequently discusses his true level of philosophical knowledge. I believe that the ten years of correspondence with Gorky reflect one aspect of Lenin's philosophical study and thought transformation. This was a truth that Soviet scholars did not see and did not want to see. As Lenin read the writings of his political allies Bogdanov and Bazarov, he grew even angrier. Lenin conceded that Plekhanov was politically wrong, but maintained that his critiques of Machism and Russian empiricism were nevertheless correct. It is also because Lenin agreed with what Plekhanov defended in terms of philosophical thought that he

---

18 Deborin, Abram. 1965. *Philosophy and Politics*. Beijing Joing Publishing Company. Book Two, appendix, page 817.

unambiguously wrote: "I give **all** my sympathy **to Plekhanov**"[19]. At the same time, he painfully discovered that "Plekhanov does harm to this philosophy by linking the struggle **here** with the factional struggle"[20]. *Lenin did not know that Plekhanov's political and philosophical views were in line with one another.* I have already pointed out previously that this was not a recent event; in the beginning, when Plekhanov and his cohorts stood up to criticize the Machism in the Russian party, Lenin did not publicly express his own standpoint. It was only **after** 1907 that Lenin began to realize the seriousness of the problem. *In fact, after Bogdanov published his first book promoting Machism, Plekhanov, Axelrod, Deborin, and others began to immediately criticize its incorrect thought[21]. In the beginning, although Lenin did not really agree with the philosophical views of Bogdanov, he did not understand that they were related to Bogdanov's correct political stance (Bolshevism). Of course, Lenin **never directly praised** Bogdanov's philosophical views. In the opinion of some other scholars, empiricism did not only become the philosophy of the social democrats at this time, but it even became the philosophy of the Bolshevik social democrats[22]. It is not hard to imagine the extent of the damage caused by Bogdanov and his followers.* This paradox between political views and scholarly ideas placed Lenin in a quandary. Fortunately Lenin understood that in order to publicly enter the philosophical debate, he would have to correct his own mistaken thinking and **reunite his worldview with his practice**. To do this he would need a powerful weapon of theoretical thought: philosophy.

In another letter written by Lenin to Gorky, he carefully reviewed his own relationship with Bogdanov. According to Lenin's memory, he first met Bogdanov in 1904. At the time, Bogdanov was a little-known theorist, and his *Concise Economics Curriculum* (1897) met with Lenin's approval[23]. The two exchanged books, with Lenin sending Bogdanov a

---

19   Lenin, Vladimir Ilyich. "Letter to Maxim Gorky (February 7, 1908)." *The Collected Works of Lenin*, volume 45, page 171 (Chin. 2. Ed.).
20   Lenin, Vladimir Ilyich. "Letter to Maxim Gorky." *The Collected Works of Lenin*, volume 45, page 176 (Chin. 2. Ed.).
21   See Axelrod's article in the 77th edition of The Spark, entitled "New Change in Revisionism." In 1908, Plekhanov, Deborin, and others published numerous articles in the Menshevik *Golos Sotsial-Democrata* criticizing the philosophical mistakes of Bogdanov, Bazarov, and Lunacharsky.
22   Berdyaev, Nikolai. 1999. *The Truth of Philosophy and the Reality of Knowledge Levels.* Yunnan People's Press, page 14.
23   Lenin, Vladimir Ilyich. *The Collected Works of Lenin*, volume 4, pages 32-39 (Chin. 1. Ed.).

copy of his "One Step Forward, Two Steps Back," and Bogdanov returning with *Empirio-monism*. Lenin wrote that he was unable to accept Bogdanov's views at the time. In his later work and in order to meet the needs of the political struggle, Lenin promised Bogdanov and his followers that he would "not discuss philosophy." *According to Trotsky's memoirs, in the autumn of 1902 Lenin had already discussed his opinion of Bogdanov with Trotsky in London. He believed that at the beginning, Lenin approved of Bogdanov's combination of Marxism with Machism. I believe that this could have been a misunderstanding by Trotsky, because he knew next to nothing about philosophy. He also wrote that Lenin told him "I am not a philosopher...but Plekhanov believes that Bogdanov's philosophy is an utterly transformed form of idealism"[24]. Trotsky's chronological recollection may also have some problems. This is because Bogdanov's Empirio-monism was not published until 1904, and this was the year that he met Lenin.* Therefore, the divisions and contradictions between the two did not immediately erupt. It was only in early 1906, when Bogdanov sent a copy of the third volume of Empirio-monism to Lenin that Lenin immediately replied with a letter on philosophical questions that filled three notebooks. Lenin wrote that "I explained to him that I was just **an ordinary Marxist** in philosophy, but that it was precisely his lucid, popular, and splendidly written works that had finally convinced me that he was essentially wrong and that Plekhanov was right"[25]. *Unfortunately, this "long letter" that Lenin mentions was never published and the notebooks have been lost.* At this point, as Lenin read *An Outline of the Philosophy of Marxism* by Bogdanov and others, he was unable to be still any longer. He believed that every article in this book drove him mad with anger. In March 1908, Lenin wrote to Gorky:

> **Their book is ridiculous, harmful, philistine, fideist—the whole of it, from beginning to end, from branch to root, to Mach and Avenarius. Plekhanov, at bottom, is *entirely* right in being against them, only he is unable or unwilling or too lazy to say so *concretely*, in detail, simply, without unnecessarily frightening his readers with philosophical nuances. And at all costs I shall say it *in my own way*[26].**

---

24   See Trotsky's *Autobiography*. China Social Science Press, 2003, page 152.
25   Lenin, Vladimir Ilyich. "Letter to Maxim Gorky." *The Collected Works of Lenin*, volume 45, page 182 (Chin. 2. Ed.).
26   *Ibid.*, page 192 (Chin. 2. Ed.).

Lenin had discovered that he did not walk "the same road" as these political comrades. *One year later, Lenin profoundly reflected to himself that in terms of philosophy, there were definite differences between himself and Bogdanov*[27]. *Also because of this, Lenin had to admit that this philosophy was **distant from the worldview of the proletariat**[28]. At this time, Lenin also understood that worldview could not be separated from actual political practice. It was only here that Lenin's surface-level split in thought and contradictory theoretical logic situating were reunited. However, as Lenin began to return to the philosophical materialist views of Plekhanov, a more profound contradiction was born. This was because he could not understand the fundamental heterogeneity between Plekhanov's Feuerbachian-Dieztgen philosophical materialism and the revolutionary stance of the Bolshevik party. Although he criticized Bogdanov's idealism, he was unable to resolve the false unity between the logic ray of his own political practice and his philosophical stance.* At this point in time, Lenin had no choice but to resolve himself to struggle against this false school of thought. In April of that year, he told Gorky "the time for notebooks is past." He then proceeded to write an inflammatory article, "Marxism and Revisionism." He refers to this article as a "most formal declaration of war"[29]. At this time, Gorky invited Lenin to the Italian island of Capri, where he lived; Lenin was hesitant because Bogdanov, Bazarov, and Lunacharsky were also invited, but in the end decided to go. *In 1909, Gorky founded a school to publicize the ideas of Bolshevism with Bogdanov, Lunacharsky, and others.* Just before leaving, Lenin wrote to Gorky, maintaining that he would not discuss philosophical or religious questions with Bogdanov and co. However, he not only went on to discuss philosophical issues, he even asked Bogdanov to his face questions such as "why is Machism more revolutionary than Marxism"[30]. Krupskaya wrote that Lenin told Bogdanov "we must separate for two or three years." She also wrote that Lenin at this time was "diligently studying philosophy"[31]. This preparation was certainly for the coming theoretical battle.

---

27   *Ibid.*, page 253 (Chin. 2. Ed.).
28   Lenin, Vladimir Ilyich. "To Pupils of the Capri School." *The Collected Works of Lenin*, volume 45, page 257 (Chin. 2. Ed.).
29   Vladimir Ilyich. "Letter to Maxim Gorky." *The Collected Works of Lenin,* volume 45, page 199 (Chin. 2. Ed.).
30   See page 103 of Fischer's *The Great Man, Lenin* (China Social Science Press, 1989). Fischer includes a few photographs of Lenin playing chess with Bogdanov at Gorky's house in Capri. Fortunately I was able to find one of these photos at the Russian Archives.
31   Krupskaya, Nadya. 1972. *Remembering Lenin*. People's Press, volume 1, page 413 (Chinese Edition).

Because Lenin was unable to find the necessary materials in Geneva, Lenin was forced to return to London, where he began his important systematic study of philosophy in the British Museum, the same place where Marx himself had once studied. During this time, Lenin completed his well-known Materialism and Empirio-criticism, which he had already begun earlier.

2 DRAFT TEXT: READING NOTES AND THEIR INTERPRETATION

Observing the philosophical battle that had already begun to rage around him, Lenin realized that in order to comprehensively critique Machism he would have to systematically study philosophy and improve his "incompetent" abilities in terms of philosophical theory. I have found that Lenin began his serious theoretical preparation in 1908 in order to effectively participate in the debate with the erudite "philosophers." We can see that Lenin focused on studying a body of important, modern **materialist** philosophical works and related documents. This is primarily because Plekhanov always opposed Machism from the perspective of philosophical materialism. *For Plekhanov, the basic philosophical stance of Marx and Engels was French Materialism, as well as a philosophical materialism approved by Feuerbach and Dietzgen. He even believed that the critiques levelled against Feuerbach by Marx and Engels did not touch on his basic materialist views*[32]. *This view is utterly wrong. Marx and Engels' critique of Feuerbach proceeded precisely from their criticism of the non-historical nature of* **old materialism**. *Interestingly, Plekhanov claimed that he personally asked Engels, who supposedly responded that the philosophy of Marx and Engels ran parallel to Spinoza's materialism*[33]. *This is a fallacious claim. Looking a little bit further, Plekhanov opposed Bernstein, Struve, and others from the stance of general philosophical materialism*[34]. *At this time, Lenin did not recognize this shadiness of theoretical logic.* The most important representatives of philosophical materialism here were Feuerbach and Dietzgen. For Plekhanov, Feuerbach was most certainly **higher** than Dietzgen, and his thinking directly influenced Lenin. The most important evidence of this influence is the brief commentaries written by Lenin as he read Plekhanov's ***Fundamental Problems of Marxism***

---

32 Plekhanov, Georg. "Bernstein and Materialism" in *Against Philosophical Revisionism*. 1957. People's Press, page 22 (Chinese edition).

33 *Ibid.*, page 23 (Chinese edition).

34 See the various texts in *Against Philosophical Revisionism*.

around May of 1908. The editors of volume 29 of the fifth Russian edition of the Collected Works of Lenin organized these commentaries after Short Philosophical Works of Dietzgen; I believe that the order here should have been reversed. It is obvious that Lenin began to read the works of the two important representatives of philosophical materialism, Feuerbach and Dietzgen, after reading Plekhanov's **Fundamental Problems of Marxism.** *Of course, this is only my logical deduction.* However, before interpreting these important notes, let us first briefly discuss the unique type of text that they represent: draft text.

Draft texts, or reading commentaries, are the latest form of document to enter the scope of my research. This is obviously different from the three categories of text that I analyzed in *Marx Revisited*, which were completed **formal texts**, **generative texts** that were still in the process of theoretical construction (also including notes with clearly expressed views or thought intentions), and **sub texts**, made up of thoughts, feelings, and reading notes. Reading commentaries are the first impressions left by the reader in his first contact with a document; often, reading commentaries are the precursor to excerpted notes and recorded reflections. Generally speaking, reading commentaries are recorded in the margins of the document being read, and often include various symbols (place markers, arrows, underlines, etc.) and a small quantity of written words. I refer to these as pre-texts because they do not manifest logic structures, complete discourse systems, or patterns of expression in a general textual-structural sense. Therefore, in terms of the original meaning of the text, this type of text actually **does not exist**. Usually, the process of editing, formatting, and printing draft texts into a viewable form is a re-situating of reading space and an **objectified** restructuring of words. However, as we read these special meaning-symbols that have a certain material carrying capacity, we can basically rediscover the original thought context of the reader and simulate our qualitative judgment through careful and active situating,

First, based on the philosophical goals of the commentator at the time of his reading, we can determine the nature of his basic logic structure at that time. This is because a reader's approach to any text is determined by his cognitive framework. *According to cognitive psychology, the transmission of knowledge messages is not a linear process of simple sending and receiving; rather, it is a* **structuralized**, **synthetic**, *process in which the reader is only able to* **see** *what he understands and* *eliminates or **refuses to see** information that does not fit into his own cognitive logical structure. This information that is unable to be processed is what Piaget refers to as the "mysterious remainder" ("E")*[35]. In these commentary notes, the focal point of the reader will provide us with an important clue in our simulation of his line of thought, pointing the way for our philosophical reconstruction.

Also, another more important, direct from of commentated notes are the various symbols and words recorded by the commentator. Using the basic affirmative or refutational marks and symbols left on the original text, we can determine the basic theoretical stance of the reader; from emphasis marks (underlines, exclamation points, and words such as "notable," "important," etc.) we can determine the focus of the reader's thought; from uncertainty symbols (such as question marks) we can determine the level of his logical maturity, etc. Naturally, the small amount of actual written comments is even more important. Although they are often extremely short, the viewpoints of the commentator are often clear and unmistakable. Regardless, the interpretation of draft texts is a difficult task.

Of course, the interpretation of draft texts only takes place in another re-situated aspect of **our thought**. This is a completely new textual interpretive experiment: interpretation in a **"me" logic situating**. The interpretation of draft texts cannot be used as direct proof of a thought context, but only as a supplementary proof of what the interpretation of other texts already reveals; nothing more.

Now that we have gone over the basic elements of draft texts, we are ready to examine Lenin's reading commentaries of Plekhanov's *Fundamental Problems of Marxism*.

---

35   Refer to page 146 of *Selected Works of Zhang Yibing*. Guangxi Normal University Press, 1999.

3 ANNOTATIONS TO PLEKHANOV'S
FUNDAMENTAL PROBLEMS OF MARXISM

Plekhanov's *Fundamental Problems of Marxism* was an important extended essay on the basic viewpoints of Marxism that he wrote in opposition to Machism[36]. This text was written between November and December of 1907, and then published in May 1908 as a separate pamphlet by the Russian publishing house Our Life. It is evident that Lenin read this book soon after it was published. Plekhanov's Fundamental Problems of Marxism is composed of a short introduction and sixteen sections; at the end of the text is an addendum entitled "Dialectics and Logic." The first three sections discuss fundamental philosophical questions, reiterating the materialist base of Marxist philosophy; the fourth section explains Marx's relation to Feuerbach; the fifth section discusses dialectics; sections six to sixteen elucidate important views of the materialist conception of history. The appendix is a supplement to the fifth section.

We can see that Lenin's commentaries on Plekhanov's *Fundamental Problems of Marxism* were very simple and few. I have two hypotheses as to why this is the case. **First**, he only read Plekhanov's book in a simple sense, and thus selectively choose portions of the content in his rapid perusal to commentate on. **Second**, Lenin read this text very carefully, but was unable to more deeply understand these deeper philosophical questions. As such, he was only able to see those things with which he was already familiar and that he felt were interesting. The content that he was **able to see** and that **activated his thought** was proportionately very small. Both of these reading circumstances are possible explanations for Lenin's small number of notations. Here I will assume that Lenin's reading followed the second possibility.

I have found that Lenin's reading commentaries begin from page 23. The first question for our consideration is: why did Lenin not leave any notations before page 23? Let us first look at what Plekhanov had to discuss in the first 23 pages, which include the majority of the content of the first three sections. Here Plekhanov primarily discussed the relationship between the German philosophers of the early 19th century (Hegel and Feuerbach) and the new world view of Marx and Engels.

---

36   Plekhanov, Georg. 1957. *Fundamental Problems of Marxism*. People's Press(Ch.)

In the introduction, Plekhanov asserts that Marxism is "an integral world-outlook…[it is] **contemporary materialism**, at present the highest stage in the development of that **view upon the world**"[37]. This is correct. Plekhanov goes on to correctly point out that the basis of Marxist philosophy cannot be separated from "philosophical materialism." This is an overview of the entire book. *He makes special mention here of Dietzgen, who had imprecisely "vulgarized" Marxist philosophy.*

In the first section, Plekhanov primarily discusses the evolutionary process of Marxist philosophy, correctly distinguishing between several stages of progression. First, he identifies young Marx at the time of his doctoral thesis as a "complete Hegelian idealist." Second, during the time of the *Deutsch-französische Jahrbücher*, Marx and Engels were "firm adherents of Feuerbachian 'humanism.'" According to his own definition later on, the basis of this humanism was philosophical materialism, and so this was young Marx's **first shift** in philosophical thought. Third, as Marx and Engels wrote *The Holy Family*, they "made several important steps in the **further development** of Feuerbach's philosophy." Fourth, the "direction" of these improvements "can be seen" in Marx's 1845 Theses on Feuerbach. This, of course, refers to the establishment of Marxism, the **second shift** in Marx's thought[38]. I have found for the first time that Plekhanov's analysis of the philosophical development of Marxism was also a theory of two shifts. I believe that this was the result of a fairly profound understanding of philosophical history, and it was different from the views of Soviet and Eastern European scholars. This being said, Plekhanov's understanding of Marxist philosophy was filled with numerous misunderstandings.

Plekhanov believed that it was difficult to truly understand this period of philosophical history for two reasons. **First**, researchers were not adept at using materials relating to philosophical history, lacking also the theoretical "training" necessary to profoundly understand these materials. This resulted in their inability to grasp Marx's complex process of shift. Having written this point, I find myself on the verge of laughing, as I recall a group of Chinese theorists who recently dedicated themselves to disproving the "dual shift" in the development of Marx's thought. There are other scholars who take young Marx's Feuerbachian "humanism" as Marxist philosophy. Compared with

---

37   *Ibid.*, page 1 (Ch.).
38   *Ibid.*, pages 3-4 (Ch.).

Plekhanov's research abilities, is this not a reversal of 100 years of re-search on Marxist philosophical thought? On the other hand, Plekhanov believed that "there is, in the first place, **little knowledge of Hegelian philosophy**, without which it is difficult to learn Marx's method"[39]. *This is an extremely important view, which Lenin would come to understand more profoundly in his **Bern Notebooks**, and then deepen into the internal logical relation between Hegel's **The Science of Logic** and Marx's **Capital**.* **Second**, Plekhanov also believed that this situation was also brought about by researchers' "little **knowledge of the history of materialism**." Without understanding historical materialism, it is impossible to see that Feuerbach was the "immediate precursor" to Marx and Engels. Feuerbach "in considerable measure worked out the philosophical foundation of what can be called the world-outlook of Marx and Engels." As such, Plekhanov's primary goal in his book was to explain the relation between Feuerbach's philosophical materialism and the Marxist philosophical worldview, emphasizing the fact that the basis of historical materialism **was still** philosophical materialism. It is obvious that this view has problems with itself.

In the first half of the second section, Plekhanov primarily explains the basic views of Feuerbachian philosophy, beginning with his humanist thought. It is apparent that Plekhanov attempts to explain Feuerbach's humanism as "materialist theory," though his expression of such Feuerbachian views as "man takes for God that which is his own essence, his own spirit," left Lenin, for whom contemporary German philosophy was still foreign, bewildered. Next, even though Plekhanov explains Feuerbach's critique of the idealist essence of Hegel's philosophy, when he repeats such concepts as Kant's "the external world receives its laws from Reason instead of Reason receiving them from the external world, is closely akin to the theological concept that the world's laws were dictated to it by divine Reason," or Feuerbach's "I am 'I' to myself, and at the same time I am '**you**' to others. The 'I' is the **subject**, and at the same time the **object**," it was impossible for this information to fit into Lenin's "cognitive structure." *As such, most of these concepts would have been, as Piaget wrote, "mysterious remainders" in Lenin's reading at the time.* The second half of the second section would also have been unfamiliar and abstruse for Lenin, because Plekhanov goes on to discuss the relation between Feuerbachian humanism and Spinoza's philosophy. He writes: "Thus, Feuerbach's 'humanism' proved to be

---

39   *Ibid.*, page 4 (Ch.).

nothing else but Spinozism disencumbered of its theological pendant. And it was the standpoint of this kind of Spinozism, which Feuerbach had freed of its theological pendant that Marx and Engels adopted when they broke with idealism." Here, Plekhanov's discussion is overly simplified. He asserts that the substance of Spinoza's argument is material, and so **"the Spinozism of Marx and Engels was indeed materialism brought up to date"**[40]. I believe that Lenin did not understand the true significance of this assertion. Not directly recording notes on the pages one reads is a **symptom of reading/understanding difficulties**.

However, at the end of Plekhanov's discussion of the second section, he makes a point that greatly surprised me. As he explained how Marx's *Theses on Feuerbach* were a development of Feuerbachian materialist thought, he mentions the difference between Marxist practice view and Feuerbachian materialism:

> **According to Feuerbach, our *I* cognizes the *object by coming under its action*. Marx, however, objects by saying: our *I* cognizes the object, *while at the same time acting upon that object*... The striving to examine the interaction between object and subject precisely from the point of view in which the subject appears in an active role, derived from the public mood of the period in which the world-outlook of Marx and Engels was taking shape[41].**

Plekhanov's view here is extremely profound. Interestingly enough, this view seems to fly in the face of his geographical determinism. However, he never correctly combined this important thought with the **practical** views proposed by Marx in the *Theses*. This view was different from Plekhanov's philosophical materialist logic situating, but conformed to Lenin's practical logic ray at this time. *In his later **Bern Notebooks**, as Lenin's thought experienced its second important detournement of theoretical logic and leap of understanding, he came to understand this point at a deeper level. At that point, Lenin understood Marx's **practical dialectic logic** more profoundly than Plekhanov, ultimately deriving the philosophical basis for the October Revolution.* Here in *Bern Notebooks*, Lenin did not highlight this important view in any way.

---

40   *Ibid.*, page 9 (Ch.).
41   *Ibid.*, pages 10-11 (Ch.).

The primary content of the third section continued Plekhanov's philosophical historical discussion of philosophical materialism. Here, Plekhanov moves from Germany to the other "outstanding materialists of the seventeenth and eighteenth centuries." He successively depicts La Mettrie, Diderot, Hobbes, Huxley, and Forel in their respective philosophical struggles against idealism. Apparently none of these were sufficient to excite Lenin's interest. However, on page 23 of this book, in the second half of the third section, we finally see Lenin's first commentary. Lenin drew three horizontal lines and wrote the word "notable" under Plekhanov's assertion that the premise of philosophical materialism did not depend on the existence of thought, in the author's summary of how Feuerbach's materialism resolved **basic philosophical problems**. This was Lenin's first point of focus. *This was one of two times that Lenin wrote "notable," and the only time in his commentaries on this book that he drew three lines to indicate emphasis.* What left the deepest impression on Lenin was that the basis of philosophical materialism did not depend on the material existence of thought. *This was what Bogdanov and his ilk were attempting to disprove.* Lenin also remarked on Plekhanov's assertion on the next page that "Feuerbach's philosophy is far clearer than that of J. Dietzgen." *At the end of his study, Lenin repeated this view, which he felt was very important.* Under this sentence Lenin drew another horizontal line and added parentheses on the margins to indicate its importance[42]. This let Lenin know that the works of Dietzgen and Feuerbach formed the most important basic views of philosophical materialism. I have found that here, Plekhanov makes the incorrect interpretation that the philosophical materialism of Dietzgen and Feuerbach was the immediate foundation for Marxist philosophy. This misunderstanding was internalized by Lenin into an *Other mirror image logical support point and dominant theoretical circuit*.

In the fourth section, Plekhanov explained the relationship between Marx/Engels and Feuerbach by using Marx's Theses on Feuerbach. He opposed the viewpoint that Marx and Engels had once been followers of Feuerbach; rather, after the development of their new world view, they utterly refuted Feuerbach and especially his philosophical materialism. Plekhanov believed that from Marx's 1845 Theses on Feuerbach we can see that "The Theses in no way eliminate the fundamental propositions in Feuerbach's philosophy, but only correct them, and – what is most

---

42   See *The Collected Works of Lenin*, volume 55, page 445 (Chin. 2. Ed.).

important – call for an application more consistent (than Feuerbach's) in explaining the reality that surrounds man, and in particular his own activity"[43]. *This conclusion is not entirely incorrect. Plekhanov is correct in stating that the foundation of the new world view of Marx and Engels was still materialism; however, Marx and Engels' new world view was certainly not a development of Feuerbach's philosophy, but rather ended all old philosophy, including philosophical materialism. Plekhanov was never able to grasp the revolutionary significance of Marx's new materialism[44].* In this section, Plekhanov concretely discusses some of the important views in *Theses on Feuerbach* as well as how they continue Feuerbach's philosophy. For instance, he mentions Feuerbach's description of the relation between subject and object and its connection to the third thesis, as well as Feuerbach's assertion that "Man's essence is only in community, in Man's unity with Man" and its similarity to Marx's assertion that "human essence is the ensemble of the social relations." These explanations are mostly imprecise, and Lenin does not make any notations here. It is not until the last line of this section, when Plekhanov asserts that "an understanding of the **methodological significance of historical materialism** is necessary," that Lenin draws a vertical line to indicate importance.

The fifth section contains Plekhanov's discussion of Marxist dialectics, and from the notations we can see that Lenin expressed a certain degree of excitement here. Plekhanov again focuses on the view that Plekhanov expressed in the previous section, "one of the greatest services rendered to materialism by Marx and Engels lies in their elaboration of a **correct method**"[45]. It is also at the beginning of this section (page 31) that Plekhanov brings forth his first critique of Feuerbach: "had little appreciation of [Hegelian philosophy's] **dialectical element**, and made little use of it"[46]. *Although Lenin does not immediately notate this viewpoint, in the small summary at the end of Bern notes he directly borrows the phrase "dialectical elements" and related concepts.* It is apparent that Plekhanov's views on this point left a deep impression on Lenin. One particular viewpoint in this discussion of the dialectic by

---

43   Plekhanov, Georg. 1957. *Fundamental Problems of Marxism*. People's Press, pages 10-11 (Ch.).

44   Refer to the fourth chapter of my *Marx Revisited*.

45   Plekhanov, Georg. 1957. *Fundamental Problems of Marxism*. People's Press, 21 (Ch.). See also *The Collected Works of Lenin*, volume 55, page 446 (Chin. 2. Ed.).

46   Plekhanov, Georg. 1957. *Fundamental Problems of Marxism*. People's Press, page 21 (Ch.).

Plekhanov was especially noted by Lenin:

Many people confuse dialectic with the doctrine of development; dialectic is, in fact, such a doctrine. However, it differs substantially from the vulgar 'theory of evolution', which is completely based on the principle that *neither Nature nor history proceeds in leaps and that all changes in the world take place by degrees*[47].

In examining the notations we find that this was the content to which Lenin paid the most attention in Plekhanov's book, drawing multiple horizontal lines under many of the sentences in this passage. Some of the sentences even received three horizontal underlines, and three vertical lines in the margin. Lenin also wrote "notable" and underlined Plekhanov's words "leaps" and "by degrees." Evidently Lenin agreed with this viewpoint of Plekhanov's. *In our later analysis of the **Bern Notebooks**, we will see that Lenin focused on a similar viewpoint of Hegel's.*

Beginning from the sixth section Plekhanov begins to discuss the materialist conception of history in Marxism. In order to highlight the materialist character of the conception of history of Marx and Engels, Plekhanov repeatedly emphasizes his mistaken **theory of geographical determinism**. From Lenin's notations we find that he draws two horizontal lines under Plekhanov's expressions of this theory. First, on page 39, Lenin highlights the phrase "the properties of the geographical environment determine the development of the productive forces." Next, on pages 46-47 in the seventh section he highlights the phrase: "According to Marx, the geographic environment affects man **through the medium of relations of production, which arise in a given area on the basis of definite productive forces, whose primary condition of development lies in the properties of that environment**"[48]. However, we find no evidence that Lenin doubted these false expressions. *I have already pointed out that in the development of Lenin's philosophical thought, even though he repeatedly criticized Plekhanov's philosophical mistakes, he never directly opposed the theory of geographical determination.*

---

47   Plekhanov, Georg. 1957. *Fundamental Problems of Marxism*. People's Press, 22 (Chinese). See also *The Collected Works of Lenin*, volume 55, page 446 (Chin. 2. Ed.).
48   Plekhanov, Georg. 1957. *Fundamental Problems of Marxism*. People's Press, 28, 32 (Chinese). See also *The Collected Works of Lenin*, volume 55, pages 446-447 (Chin. 2. Ed.).

In reading the rest of the text, Lenin seems to not have discovered anything else worthy of his attention. He only makes a few notations next to a few of Plekhanov's views on the basic elements of the materialist conception of history.

At the end of his commentaries, Lenin writes one line of his reflections: "Feuerbach and Dietzgen. 24"[49]. *"24" most likely refers to page 24, in the third section, where Plekhanov discusses Feuerbach and Dietzgen.* This indicated that Lenin understood that the two most important figures in philosophical materialism were Feuerbach and Dietzgen: he now had a goal for his next reading project.

49　*The Collected Works of Lenin*, volume 55, page 448 (Chin. 2. Ed.).

ADDENDUM 1

THE FETISHISM OF MATERIAL RELATIONS: A FORGOTTEN PHILOSOPHICAL CONTEST

A COMMENTARY ON THE 1908 PHILOSOPHICAL DEBATE BETWEEN PLEKHANOV AND BOGDANOV

To the knowledge of those who lived in socialist countries steeped in Stalinist thought, it was Lenin and his *Materialism and Empirio-criticism* who effectively countered the Machism and Idealist schools of thought that had begun to creep into the ranks of Russian Marxism during the "crisis" caused by the revolution of the natural sciences at the beginning of the last century. However, as we truthfully study philosophical history and dust off the layers of ideology blocking our understanding, an important historical fact leaps into focus: the politically misguided Mensheviks were the first to openly oppose Machism, even before Lenin. Here, what is most important for us to focus on was the philosophical debate between Plekhanov and Bogdanov. However, in our day, our purpose in exploring this ideologically hidden historical incident is not merely the search for historical truth, but also to highlight the complexity of this philosophical struggle and its modern significance.

In order to explain the true logical baseline of this philosophical battle, it would be best to first begin with an examination of what Bogdanov was trying to promulgate with his *An Outline of the Philosophy of Marxism* that made Lenin so angry in 1908. After, we will take a detailed look at the philosophical contest between Plekhanov and Bogdanov.

We have already become familiar with the brainless, Machist Bogdanov who Lenin criticizes in *Materialism and Empirio-criticism*. However, very seldom have we looked at how Bogdanov as a Bolshevik grafted Machism to Marxism. For Lenin and Plekhanov, who were Bogdanov's primary philosophical opponents, this was also a question that received little attention. Through my study and analysis of historical documents, I have found that Bogdanov had two methods of dealing with this issue: first, he began with the relation between natural science and philosophy, emphasizing the relationships between Marxist philosophy and natural science. Second, he proceeded from Marx's theory of social criticism, emphasizing that the refutational object of Marxist philosophy was philosophical materialism, which emerged as a fetishism.

The **first** method was expressed most clearly in Bogdanov's introduction to the 1907 Russian edition of Ernst Mach's *Analysis of Sensation*. In that introduction, Bogdanov emphasizes the fact that the foundation of Marxist philosophy is natural science, and that the newest findings of natural science were contained in Machism. Thus Machism logically becomes the newest scientific foundation of Marxist philosophy. Lenin rightfully accused Bogdanov of having a simple mind; Bogdanov's laughable theoretical logic goes thus: **"A philosophy that provides our era with a complete and true worldview should be based on natural science."** Marx's philosophical foundation was natural science: **"Marxism is nothing but a philosophy of natural science in social life"**[1]. Meanwhile, Mach was the greatest thinker in natural scientific philosophy. Thus although Mach's thought was a bourgeois thing, this did not prevent Marxism from being based on his thought. *Here Bogdanov goes so far as to use what Marx learned from Hegel, Ricardo, and Darwin as evidence in support of his position as a Machist*[2]. Responding to the critiques of Plekhanov and others, Bogdanov even believed that the 19th century bourgeois philosophy of d'Holbach, on which Plekhanov relied, was not as good as Mach's 20th century moderate socialism. What I understand now is that Bogdanov's theoretical mistake was primarily due to his inability to grasp the fact that although Marx and Engels learned much from many bourgeois thinkers, they did so in a **critical, surpassing** way, while Mach merely bowed down at the feet of Mach, becoming the philosophical slave of the bourgeoisie without question or thought. Nikolai Berdyaev wrote that Bogdanov called Mach and Avenarius the "saviors of proletariat philosophy"[3]. Under the

---

1   Bogdanov, Alexandr. "What can Russian Readers learn from Ernst Mach?" In *Selected Readings of Marxist Philosophical History*, Beijing University Press, 1984, page 730 (Chinese).

2   Bogdanov, Alexandr. "What can Russian Readers learn from Ernst Mach?" In *Selected Readings of Marxist Philosophical History*, Beijing University Press, 1984, page 734 (Chinese).

3   Berdyaev, Nikolai. 1999. *The Truth of Philosophy and the Reality of Knowledge Levels*. Yunnan People's Press, page 5 (Chinese).

contemptuous gaze of this Russian theological philosopher, Bogdanov excitedly passed out his crude writings on metaphysics. Even constantly mentioning such authoritative names as Avenarius and Mach could not help him. Lunacharsky went so far as to create a new form of proletarian religion based on Avenarius' philosophy[4]. I believe that this was truly a shameful thing to do.

Bogdanov's second method is what we will focus our discussion on at this point. After 1906, Bogdanov's mistaken practice of peddling Machism in Russia came under the sharp criticism of Plekhanov and others, and so naturally Bogdanov was forced to constantly defend his own actions. In 1908, Bogdanov led a group of Russian Machists in writing the famous An Outline of the Philosophy of Marxism. In the article entitled "The Idol State and Marxist Philosophy," the theoretical logic used in Bogdanov's defense of Machism shifts dramatically. Here, he begins his tactical counterattack using Marx's critique of economic **fetishisms**. Please note that this is a drastically different theoretical starting point from the one used in his interpretation of the **foundation of natural science** of Mach and Avenarius. In Bogdanov's opinion at this time, the primary contradiction in modern scholarly thought was the struggle between science and fetishisms. This was a completely new perspective. I believe that this was a strategy that Bogdanov had to rack his brains in order to devise. Its purpose was to use the **immediate links between Mach and Marx in terms of social historical theory** in order to crush his opponent.

At the beginning of that article, Bogdanov writes:

> **The increase in social productive forces and the development of society's control over nature is immediately reflected in scientific understanding. On the other hand, the idol of understanding and the material god express society's weakness and productive insufficiency in the struggle against nature. Thus is brought to pass the conflict between science and fetishism[5].**

At first glance it is not easy to see exactly what Bogdanov is trying to say in this passage, though connecting it to the textual context makes his meaning much clearer. What he means by "scientific understanding" here is actually Machism, which originated from the revolution in natural sciences. By "idols and material gods," on the other hand,

---

4   *Ibid.*, page 14 (Chinese).
5   Bogdanov, Alexandr. 1981. "The Idol State and Marxist Philosophy," In *Translated Marxist-Leninist Works*, volume 14, page 158.

he refers to philosophical materialism, the stance upheld by both Plekhanov and Lenin. This is a truly cunning theoretical identification. Bogdanov believed that material gods filled our life, that idols were everywhere, and that the root cause of this phenomenon was not philosophy, but rather the dominant role of **modern capitalist economic relations.** *Compared to his prior views, based on the combination of natural science with philosophy, this was an even more malicious theoretical logical link.* Bogdanov believed that the foundation of fetishism philosophy was based on the fact that the fetishism of exchange value had permeated every aspect of modern life, and that this fetishism understood man's relations of labour to be attributes of things[6]. *Marx's actual argument here makes two theoretical points. First, he criticizes classical economics for not understanding capital as a social relation, but rather as a thing; second, he critically identified how inter-human labour relations in capitalist market exchange had been inverted into inter-thing relations. In the three great fetishisms (commodity fetishism, money fetishism, and capital fetishism), people took this inverted material phenomenon to be material reality (wealth).* In fact, Bogdanov's statement itself is not incorrect; it is a decent summary of Marx's critique of bourgeois ideology (fetishism) as expressed in *Capital*. This was an important theoretical viewpoint at the time. *One of the founders of Western Marxism, young Lukacs, only arrived at this understanding 20 years after Bogdanov.*

However, for Bogdanov, it was precisely under the influence of this fetishism-thinking that all laws and moral restraints in capitalist society were not taken as reflections of their own real relations, but rather as forces that put pressure on man and demand his absolute obedience[7]. In fact, from the perspective of Marx's historical phenomenology, Bogdanov's analysis here is also not completely mistaken. In the bourgeois kingdom, the social relations created by man become an external material force, expressed in an inverted form. This force rules and enslaves man himself; this was the essence of capitalist ideology that Marx attempted to reveal. I have found that after the Second International, Marx's important views on historical phenomenology here have been completely ignored by an "orthodox Marxism" which has become saturated by positivism. This ignorance applies to Russian Marxists Plekhanov and Lenin as well. Besides Bogdanov and Deborin

---

6   *Ibid.*, page 158 (Chinese).
7   *Ibid.*, page 158 (Chinese).

in 1924, the critical logic of Marx's historical phenomenology did not reappear until later, when Western Marxism reintroduced a distorted form of it.

It is interesting to note that Bogdanov was able to see the continuity between the idol worship of natural economic forms to the abstract fetishism of highly advanced commodity economic forms. He noted that Marxism was a "historical-philosophical critique" or "social-interpretive critique" that was able to penetrate fetishisms. I must say that here Bogdanov truly does proceed from Marx's theory. As we have already pointed out, the theoretical starting point of Bogdanov and his cohorts was the attempt to **unite Marxism to Machism**. Where they originally emphasized the link between natural science and philosophy, here they bring out the logical link between social historical theory and philosophy. *This was a common goal of the Russian Machists in 1908. In that year, a Russian Machist wrote directly to Mach, asking him if the views of the founder of "scientific socialism" (referring to Marxism) could be united with the principles of Mach's theory[8]. Another important aspect to mention here is that the tendency in theoretical logic to **graft Marxism with a particular school of Western philosophy** began with the Machists.*

However, Bogdanov's theoretical intention was not to explain Marx's scientific social critical theory; his discussion had an ulterior purpose. He suddenly changes course, writing that in most people's understanding, the laws of the natural world are not understood as the actual existence of things, but rather as an independent existence that controls the world, a substance to which both things and men must be obedient[9]. In the counterattack against Bogdanov's mistaken thinking by Plekhanov and others, the substantive differences between the theoretical problems that he proposes were crudely overlooked. I believe that we can admit that Bogdanov's views here, there was included a certain degree of important, new content from the modern revolution in natural science. This was his profound realization that the substance of the "laws" of the natural world were composed of certain real relationships (more precisely, this substance was based on a natural scientific image at a certain level of practical relations). Historically, what men have seen as objectively existing things and external laws (such as Newton's "universal"

---

8 Dynnik, ed. *History of Philosophy*, vol. 5. 1975. Beijing Sanlian Press, page 146.

9 Bogdanov, Alexandr. 1981. "The Idol State and Marxist Philosophy," In *Translated Marxist-Leninist Works*, volume 14, page 158 (Chinese).

objective laws) are really the result of a subjectively reflected outside world created by certain practical relations (science and technological structure) under specific historical conditions. Thus Bogdanov was able to correctly assert that scientific knowledge is produced where in to what degree in accordance with where and to what degree man conquers nature. *This was a correct viewpoint that Lenin later expressed himself. It is evident that the significance of Bogdanov's philosophical shift in 1908 cannot be underestimated. It is my opinion that Lenin came to this correct understanding in his **Bern Notebooks**.*

However, even though Bogdanov introduced new facts in scientific understanding, his mistake lay in his refutation of **objective material existence**, viewing it as a "fetishism" in the conception of nature. I have also remarked that the theoretical situating of this refutation itself is also extremely complex. Bogdanov asserted that the sphere of social labour was also that of social experience. All systems of understanding are produced here, and the kingdom of fetishisms also emerges from this place[10]. This assertion is also profound and correct. For Marx, there was no such thing as consciousness, understanding, or ideas devoid of concrete social historical life; all of man's ideas (including his understanding of nature) could only be the products of the **social existence of a certain time period**. Unfortunately, what Bogdanov attempts to prove using Marx's correct theoretical discourse was a mistaken idealist view. *Later we will see that Plekhanov and Lenin, who maintained correct materialist views, were not aware of this correct basis in Bogdanov's mistaken thought.*

Next, Plekhanov employs this same logic in attempting to explain the historical appearance of philosophical materialism as the "thing-in-itself" of the foundation of the world. According to Bogdanov himself, in the primitive thinking of the ancient past, the world was an active compound; it was not until later that this compound was crystallized into a **thing**[11]. It is clear that Bogdanov made this declaration in hopes of quietly transitioning from Marx's **practical relational ontology** to Mach's **relational ontology**. This is because he was unable to realize that these two ontologies were fundamentally opposed in their philosophical essences. Neither was he able to realize that if the "world" referred to the external natural material faced by primitive man, then it could not be

---

10   *Ibid.*, page 160 (Chinese).
11   *Ibid.*, page 163 (Chinese).

an "active compound." At the same time, if the "world" referred only to human social life existence (Husserl and Heidegger's "live world") then the concept of an "active compound" has some merit. I believe that Bogdanov's major problem was his mixing of different, fundamentally heterogeneous theoretical logics, *i.e.*, viewing the external natural material world and the **historical understanding** of that world as the product of man's activity and relations. His foundation of philosophical idealism was produced from the false logical situating of this thought confusion. Hence his attempt to graft Marxism to Machism was mistaken. *This was the essential problem with Bogdanov's philosophy that Plekhanov and his followers were unable to grasp in 1908.*

In Bogdanov's opinion, "things" only appear as men become more dependent to complex material tools in their labour.

> **As implements become more complex and varied, the process of producing them not only begins to play an important role in life, but also begins to gradually become independent from the process of using them. At this point, implements become the stable crystal of a series of complex and chaotic labour activities, and we begin to have the category of "things"[12].**

In Bogdanov's opinion, "things" were crystallized in reference to the appearance of tools. He argued that in every concept of a thing, much of it was composed of the syntheses and links between a series of actions, both of individuals themselves, as well as actions that they experience and that exist in the natural world. *It is surprising to me that Bogdanov is able to directly explain the relation between linguistic forms and human labour, much as Marx did in his "Notes on Wagner's 'Lehrbuch der politischen Ökonomie'"[13]. Although his expression is vague, Bogdanov's ideas are extremely profound.* Bogdanov believed that where the view of a "compound" world of active relations was "primitive dialectics," the material world view related to the complex structure of tools was a "static" idea. For Bogdanov, "primitive dialectics" approached Marx and Mach, while "statics" belonged to the philosophical materialism of Plekhanov and others. It is interesting to note that in the process of opposing Plekhanov's "statics," Bogdanov directly linked what he called constructive tectology with Marx's eleventh thesis in *Theses on Feuerbach*. He proposed that constructive tectology

---

12   *Ibid.*, page 163 (Chinese).
13   *Ibid.*, page 163 (Chinese).

did not try to "explain the world," but rather constructed the world by organizing various empirical elements into nature, labour, or thought.

I believe that Bogdanov's "thing" here is a muddled concept. **First**, the "material" or "thing" in the philosophical materialism of Plekhanov and Lenin was not the concept of "thing" that existed in an idea sense, but rather referred to objective things and material phenomena that existed outside of man. However, the "thing" that Bogdanov describes here approaches the **Kantian phenomenological world**, the **subjective views** of men towards the objective existence of the external world. If Bogdanov's starting point proved that man's view of the external world depended on social historical practice (and especially on labour production and historically changing implements) through this definition of "thing," then he would not have been incorrect, but would rather have conformed to Marx's historical materialism. However, his purpose was the refutation of the premise of philosophical materialism, and the result was pitifully ridiculous. **Second**, Bogdanov did not realize that Marx had already investigated social existence, as different from natural material existence, using similar logic. This **social existence** referred to **social relational being** in historical materialism. This being did not exist in the form of a substance in natural material; rather, it was constructed and deconstructed by man's social historical activity and relationships. This depth was unattainable by the superficial Bogdanov. Regardless, I believe that some of Bogdanov's thoughts here should not be scoffed at.

In Bogdanov's system, there was distance between the notion of the "thing" and the "thing-in-itself." He begins with the Kantian dualistic world, inevitably produced by underdeveloped, manual labour societies. The first aspect of this world is the visible empirical world, and the second is the hypothetical, invisible world behind the empirical one; this is the objectively existing world. Next, Bogdanov falsely links the invisible "stuff" of the second aspect of the dualistic world with ancient, primitive animism. He writes that this second, invisible world, is seen to be more important, essential, and ruling, whether by the "spirit" of the animists, the "being" of Kant, or the "material" of Plekhanov[14]. Furthermore, Bogdanov connects this essentialist view to the emergence of theodicy. I have found that here, Bogdanov correctly explains how religious theology constantly enters into man's thoughts based on his social links, his "understanding." Ideas about spirits and gods are

---

14   *Ibid.*, page 164 (Chinese).

only replacements made by the common emotions and wishes of men in their species-relations. Until Kant and philosophical materialism, the invisible thing-in-itself, which had always hid behind experience within a shell of material, actually originated from man's **mutual understanding**, and was **replaced** by idolization. We must admit that Bogdanov can be quite profound.

Here it is not difficult for us to see how cunning Bogdanov's refutational logic really is. His opposition to the dualistic world was derived from his need to affirm the "empirical monism" of Mach and Avenarius; his opposition to essentialism was aimed at destroying objective material existence. In order to do this, he had no qualms with non-historically muddling the essentially heterogeneous theories of ancient animism, German classical philosophy (Kant), and all the contemporary philosophical materialists. In the process, his proof actually produced a few truly profound (and a few seemingly profound) views. It can be said that Bogdanov's idealist logical construct was an extremely complex false logical situating project.

In Bogdanov's opinion, improvements in technology and understanding, as well as the broadening of new labour relations, have begun to bring about the demise of dualistic animism; however, the dualistic thought pattern has persisted, especially in the understanding of materialism, which persisted in the form of the idolized thing-in-itself. More importantly, the most important social existence foundation of the "thing-in-itself" can be found in the **spontaneity** in the economic life of capitalist society. *Bogdanov is really quite wily, hiding his distorted points under many seemingly reasonable layers.* Bogdanov writes:

Anarchic or unorganized division of labour, expressed in exchange systems, has created a new form of rule by spontaneity over consciousness, or in other words, the rule of man by social relations. This has also created new forms of fetishisms, namely, the fetishism towards "commodity" value and towards the abstract metaphysics of the "substance" and "effectiveness" of all material[15].

Bogdanov believed that materialist philosophy of Lenin and Plehanov was nothing more than the expression of fetishisms in philosophy. At the same time, the fetishisms of capitalist society had generalized the type of thought forcibly formed in the sphere of commodity exchange

---

15   *Ibid.*, page 166 (Chinese).

to all "things"[16]. Where primitive fetishisms replaced actual material with "a living and concrete material god," the fetishisms of capitalist commodity exchange replace actual material with an "abstract material god." Here, Bogdanov soberly states that exchange value produced by labor is seen as determining the "effectiveness" of the movement of commodities on the market. Human labour, trapped within the material god of exchange value, is seen as the internal essence of material (commodities), while the results of human understanding (the summary of experience), trapped within the dual material gods of substance and effectiveness, are seen as the veiled essence of material and process. Bogdanov concludes that this is also a fetishism[17]. Here, Bogdanov cunningly hides a linkage point of theoretical logic: capitalist objectified **relational existence**, which had already been revealed by Marx, is again deified into a **material** force. Bogdanov meant that Plekhanov and Lenin did not understand that in Marx's critical theory of fetishisms, **the criticism of the fetishism of objectified relations was materialistic criticism**. It is obvious that this is Bogdanov's gross logical mutation of Marx's scientific socialist critical theory. However, it is unfortunate that Plekhanov and others did not remark this important theoretical clue. Bogdanov did not understand economics, but he did know how to write on the **historical phenomenological critique** of capitalist economic relations in Marx's political economic theory. Though Plekhanov and Lenin understood political economic theory much better than Bogdanov, their critical logic was unable to combine economics with philosophy. This is a regrettable logical contrast.

I believe that Bogdanov was discussing a theoretical problem that he was incapable of profoundly mastering. For Marx, the idea of economic fetishisms in bourgeois society was not a philosophical abstract, but rather an **objective historical abstract** of objective exchange relations formed in commodity production and the market. This historical abstract emerged from the equivalent reference systems in commodity exchange, moving from equivalents to general equivalents, to money, and finally to the pinnacle: the rule of capital which can generate money. Here, **abstract capital relations** are not a subjective idea, but rather the ruling and dominating relations in actual capitalist production. In revealing the historical fact that abstract had becoming ruling, in criticizing the inversion of inter-human relations into inter-thing relations in the exchange market, and in opposing the enslavement of man by market spontaneity and man-made material

---

16   *Ibid.*, page 166 (Chinese).
17   *Ibid.*, pages 166-167 (Chinese).

economic forces, Marx was not refuting materialism but rather proving the scientific nature of historical materialism[18]. Marx's profound historical phenomenology was transformed by Bogdanov into a weapon to oppose philosophical materialism. This is an incredible theoretical irony. Unfortunately, the Russian Marxists of the time, led by Plekhanov, were unable to penetrate this thick mist of confusing logic. *Later, scholars under framework of Stalinist dogmatic ideology further confused things, saying that Bogdanov affirmed the idea of bourgeois fetishisms; they were always passionately engaged in futile, ridiculous theoretical hand-waving*[19].

In Bogdanov's discussion in the latter half of "The Idol State and Marxist Philosophy," there is little worth seriously to discuss. He spends a lot of time explaining how the empirical criticism of Mach and Avenarius proposed empirical monism based on the revelation of fetishisms and idols. The logical linkage point here is the supposed homogeneity between Mach's relational ontology and Marx's relational ontology. His final conclusion was that Marxist social philosophy was currently the most monist world view completely based on experience. He therefore refers to this world view as "empirio-monism"[20].

In fact, Bogdanov's opposition to fetishisms was sincere, but he stood with Mach, looking at the world from the perspective of idealism. For Bogdanov, a non-fetishistic scientific understanding should follow Mach's empirical monism; it would view everything as different organizations of empirical elements, thus, the existential foundation of the entire world would be composed of empirical relations. Furthermore, if experience belongs to the sphere of subjective consciousness, then consciousness is the basis of existence. Thus he reached the fallacious conclusion that Lenin criticized:

In their struggle for existence men can unite only with the help of consciousness: without *consciousness* there can be no intercourse. Hence, *social life in all its manifestations is a consciously psychical life...* Society is inseparable from consciousness. *Social being and social consciousness are, in the exact meaning of these terms, identical*"[21].

---

18   Refer to chapter nine of my *Marx Revisited*.

19   ee page 276 of the Soviet *Philosophical Encyclopedia* (volume 1), Shanghai Translated Works Press, 1984 (Chinese).

20   Bogdanov, Alexandr. 1981. "The Idol State and Marxist Philosophy," In *Translated Marxist-Leninist Works*, volume 14, page 181 (Chinese).

21   Bogdanov, Alexandr. "The Development of Life in Nature and Society," cited in "Materialism and Empirio-criticism." *The Collected Works of Lenin*, vol. 18, p. 337.

Lenin gives an effective and clear retort to this unintelligent historical idealist error in his *Materialism and Empirio-criticism*, so I will not tarry any longer on this subject.

I have not seriously read any of Bogdanov's other works, but judging from the thought and philosophical depth demonstrated in this work, I find that I cannot underestimate him. His mistakes, rooted in correct historical phenomenology, are not easy to refute with general philosophical materialism.

What important theoretical work did the Russian Marxists of the early 20th century do to combat Bogdanov's cunning philosophical errors? In 1907, at the debate in Geneva mentioned earlier, Deborin submitted an article titled "Machism and Marxism," giving the following expression of the basis of the Marxist world view:

1. Only the natural world actually exists.
2. The existence of the natural does not depend on the subject.
3. The subject is a part of the natural world.
4. All understanding is produced from experience, from perception obtained from the outside world by the subject.
5. Therefore, the outside world (existence) determines our consciousness.
6. Given that reality is the sole object of understanding, our understanding can only conform to the truth, be objective, when it is in line with reality, with existence[22].

Deborin wrote himself that these two points were the materialist philosophical principles upon which the scientific socialism of Marx and Engels depended. Although he is correct in this assertion, I believe that Deborin's explanation here merely **demotes** Marxist philosophy into the premise and foundation of general philosophical materialism. The biggest problem with his logic is that it is abstract and non-historical. In 1908, Deborin was unable to publish anything more authoritative in the wake of Bogdanov's new fallacies. In *Dialectical Materialism* (1909), Deborin explains at length the similarities between historical "dialectical materialism" and general philosophical materialism. However, in differentiating between the two materialist world views, he only explains such characteristics of Marx's dialectical materialism as its emphasis on material change and its view of the world as

---

22   Deborin, Abram. 1965. "Machism and Marxism," in *Philosophy and Politics*, book 1. Beijing Sanlian Press, pages 43-44 (Chinese).

a process and consequent transcendence of the contradiction between existence and non-existence, etc. He hoped to use this to disprove the "material disappearance" theory of Machist idealism[23]. Giving such a roundabout explanation against Bogdanov's complex distortions and fallacies (Bogdanov tried to base himself on Marx's social critical theory) was utterly weak and powerless. *Of course, when the manuscript of* **The German Ideology** *was published in 1924, Deborin quickly wrote "Marxism and History"; in that article, his understanding of Marxist historical materialism had taken an obvious step forward[24].*

Between 1908 and 1909, Plekhanov declared theoretical war on Bogdanov's empirical monism, a struggle that would last over three years. During that time, Plekhanov published three open letters to Bogdanov. These three letters were likely his most authoritative texts in this theoretical battle.

The first open letter was published in 1908, in editions 6 and 7 (May and June) of *Golos Sotsial-Demokrata*. This letter was written in response to an open letter by Bogdanov to him in the July 1907edition of *Herald of Life*. In this letter, Plekhanov profoundly points out an important phenomenon in the Russian theoretical sphere:

> **Idealism of all varieties and shades, under the impact of reaction and the pretext of revising theoretical values, is holding veritable orgies in our literature, and when some idealists, probably for the sake of spreading their own ideas, proclaim their views to be Marxism of the very latest model[25].**

It is evident that Plekhanov's thinking is very clear at this point in time. He writes that he firmly opposes those who falsely march under the banner of Marxism, attempting to peddle their own brand of idealism. Here Plekhanov clearly states that he does not believe Bogdanov is a Marxist, and that the two could not be "comrades." Unfortunately, in the concrete discussion of the letter Plekhanov entangles himself in some of the minor details of his relationship with Bogdanov, arguing endlessly against Bogdanov's calling him a pupil of Holbach. It is not

---

23   Deborin, Abram. 1965. "Dialectical Materialism," in *Philosophy and Politics*, book 1. Beijing Sanlian Press, pages 88-116. This text was originally published in 1909, and Lenin took excerpted notes of it at that time.

24   Refer to the research addendum following chapter 10 of this book.

25   Plekhanov, Georg. 1957. "Materialismus Militans," In *Against Revisionism in Philosophy*. People's Press, page 331.

until the end of the letter that he cites *The Holy Family* in explaining the inevitable link between general philosophical materialism and socialism[26]. Plekhanov goes on to point out that historically speaking, materialism has represented the class and power of revolution; thus it is the bourgeois class that "detests materialism," because "the bourgeoisie, ruling in a society based upon bitter mutual competition among the commodity producers (capitalist enterprises), is naturally inclined to a complacency in which there is no trace of altruism." This causes the mental structures and moral inclinations of the bourgeoisie to tend towards egoism, whether consciously or unconsciously. Plekhanov's expression here is profound; it can be thought of as an effective delineation between political stance and philosophical party principles. However, in terms of responding to Bogdanov's wily, mistaken thinking, Plekhanov's retort is less than effective.

In his second open letter, published in editions 8-9 (July-September) of the same magazine, Plekhanov criticizes Bogdanov's explanation on the relation between things and the thing-in-itself. His line of thought still maintains the basic limits of materialism and idealism, with a special emphasis on the foundational nature of material (bodies):

> **We call material objects (bodies) those objects that exist independently of our consciousness and, acting on our senses, arouse in us certain *sensations* which in turn underlie our notions of the external world, that is, of those same material objects as well as of their relationships[27].**

Astute readers will find that in refuting Bogdanov, Plekhanov continues to emphasize the premises of philosophical materialism, that natural material exists **before** the human subject; this is what Marx called the eternal precedence of the natural world over the human race. As such, Plekhanov always maintained that if there were no men on earth, there would obviously be no **human experience;** however, this material planet would continue to exist, hence, this proves that it exists "**outside** of human experience." Thus Plekhanov concludes that the assertion that "there can be no object without a subject" is untenable, because "the existence of the subject presupposes that the object has reached a certain stage of development"[28]. Furthermore, this historically pro-

---

26   *Ibid.*, page 344.
27   *Ibid.*, page 359.
28   *Ibid.*, page 379.

duced subject is, itself, a part of objective existence. I believe that the use of philosophical materialism to oppose the idealist turn in Mach's relational ontology (as well as Heidegger's later existential relational ontology and Whitehead's process philosophy) is correct in terms of surface level logic. However, because the thought points of these two theories are not on the same level, the effectiveness of this theoretical debate becomes very limited. Based on the primary analysis in the second letter, Plekhanov returns to the general discussion of Mach's empirical monism.

Plekhanov's third letter to Bogdanov was written 1909, published, of course, after Bogdanov's "The Idol State and Marxist Philosophy." In this letter, Plekhanov denies Bogdanov's desire to "become a good Marxist." He concisely points out that Bogdanov is one of those who, "while claiming the title of Marxist, want to adapt their outlook to suit the palate of our contemporary little bourgeois supermen"[29]. However, in terms of substantive discussion, Plekhanov's retort of Bogdanov remains at the level of general objective confirmation. Plekhanov writes that Bogdanov understands "the objectivity of external things" thus:

The objectivity of external objects is always reduced to the exchange of utterances *in the last analysis*, but is by far not *always* directly founded on it. In the process of social experience certain general relationships are created, general law-regulated relationships (abstract space and time are among these), which characterise the physical world which they embrace. These general relationships, socially formed and consolidated, are for the most part connected by the social coordination of experience, and are for the most part objective[30].

Summarizing Bogdanov's ideas, Plekhanov quotes, "In general, the physical world is socially-coordinated, socially harmonised, in a word, **socially organized experience**"[31]. *This is one of Bogdanov's important logical support points.* For instance, the abstract forms of time and space are not objective forms, but rather "**the social organization of human experience... Coordinating his experiences with**

---

29   Plekhanov, Georg. 1957. "Materialismus Militans," In *Against Revisionism in Philosophy*. People's Press, page 403.
30   Bogdanov, Alexandr. *Empiriomonism*, volume 1. Quoted in Plekhanov, Georg. 1957. "Materialismus Militans," In *Against Revisionism in Philosophy*. People's Press, page 406.
31   *Ibid.*, page 411.

the experiences of other people, man created the abstract forms of time"[32]. In Plekhanov's opinion, Bogdanov viewed the material world as the result of social organized experience, believing that it "is more able than any other to make deductions in the spirit of Marxism"[33]. This is because Bogdanov asserted that "where Mach outlines the connection between cognition and the social-labour process, the coincidence of his views with Marx's ideas occasionally becomes really striking"[34]. Compared to the critical assertions discussed earlier, Bogdanov's argument here is affirmative. Plekhanov laughs at Bogdanov's inference here, humorously writing that according to Bogdanov's understanding, "the existence of men preceded the existence of our planet: first came men; men began to give 'utterance', while socially organising their experience; out of this happy circumstance came the physical world in general and our own planet in particular"[35]. After this joke, Plekhanov goes on to point out that Bogdanov's views seem to touch on Marx's "economic materialism"; however, economic materialism only recognizes that "on the basis of the economic relationships and the social existence of men which they determine, corresponding ideologies arise." Bogdanov, on the other hand, tries to develop the "physical world" as well from this basis. Plekhanov believes that it was here that Bogdanov took an important step towards idealism. Here, Plekhanov's retort finally carries some weight. However, I must add that Marx's "economic materialism," to which Plekhanov alludes here, does not actually exist; this was merely a product of the mistaken interpretation of the theorists of the Second International.

It is unfortunate that in his later discussion, Plekhanov merely repeats himself, again using the views of general philosophical materialism to oppose and disprove Bogdanov. It is certain that his method had little to add. I should also add that while the direction of Plekhanov's criticism against Bogdanov was correct, he makes no mention of Bogdanov's subtle attack on philosophical materialism from the perspective of Marx's critique of fetishisms. Why was this? Had the philosophical debate really ended? I doubt it.

---

32   *Ibid.*, page 414.
33   Plekhanov, Georg. 1957. "Materialismus Militans," In *Against Revisionism in Philosophy.* People's Press, page 412.
34   Bogdanov, Alexandr. Empiriomonism, volume 1. Quoted in Plekhanov, Georg. 1957. "Materialismus Militans," In *Against Revisionism in Philosophy*. People's Press, page 413.
35   Plekhanov, Georg. 1957. "Materialismus Militans," In *Against Revisionism in Philosophy.* People's Press, page 411.

CHAPTER THREE

READINGS ON DIETZGEN'S PHILOSOPHICAL MATERIALISM

I have deduced that in 1908, after reading Plekhanov's *Fundamental Problems of Marxism* and understanding the importance of studying Feuerbach and Dietzgen, Lenin chose to study the latter. Thus Lenin began seriously to study on Dietzgen's *Philosophical Essays*[1]. I believe that Lenin chose to study Dietzgen first for two reasons: first, Lenin was proficient in German, and second, Dietzgen was a worker-philosopher praised by Marx and Engels, and third, Bogdanov and co. often criticized Dietzgen in their discussion of so-called positivism[2]. From this we can see that Dietzgen's philosophical materialism exerted an important influence on Lenin. As such, let us begin our analysis in this chapter with Lenin's study of Dietzgen.

---

1   The edition of Dietzgen's *Philosophical Essays* that Lenin studied was printed in Stuggart in 1903.
2   In the 1908 *An Outline of the Philosophy of Marxism*, one of the articles was titled "The Philosophy of Dietzgen and Modern Positivism."

1 LENIN STUDIES DIETZGEN'S PHILOSOPHICAL MATERIALISM

In 1908, Lenin studied the *Philosophical Essays* of Joseph Dietzgen, a philosopher from the working class who had been praised both by Marx and Lenin. Although Lenin did not leave any notes from his reading on this book, he did leave commentaries. Of course, these are what I refer to as **draft texts**, and they have been re-structured in their printing. *Lenin's commentaries on this book were only just recently translated into Chinese, and were included in the content of volume 55 of the new edition of the* **Collected Works of Lenin**. *This content was not included in the 1963 edition of the* **Collected Works of Lenin***, and as such, did not receive its due attention in past research of Lenin's philosophical thought. The Soviet scholar Kedrov was the first to study these commentaries in his Study of Lenin's* "**Philosophical Notebooks**." *However, I believe that his study was insufficiently profound.*

From the texts we have available to us, we can see that whenever Lenin agreed with Dietzgen, he marked an "α," (or "α α" for emphasis). Where Lenin disagreed with Dietzgen, he marked a "β" (or "β β" for emphasis). In these commentaries we also find a small amount of written commentary. This allows us to more clearly **judge and guess** Lenin's basic theoretical orientation and possible logic.

This collection of Dietzgen's work includes seven articles that he wrote for the German papers *Volksstaat* and *Vorwärts* between 1870 and 1878, as well as "Excursions of a Socialist into the Domain of Epistemology" (1887). In first studying Dietzgen's manuscript as a **complete theoretical image** and then examining the textual details revealed by Lenin's notations, we will be able to derive a fairly clear picture of Lenin's basic theoretical circumstance at the time of his study.

The first essay included in this collection was Dietzgen's "Scientific Socialism" (1873). In that text, Dietzgen points out that Marx's socialist theory is scientific because it was not an artificial design, but rather "generalizations drawn from economic facts." This is correct. As a materialist philosopher, Dietzgen was opposed to the theological idealism which argued that ideas create material; he argued that "the world is not the attribute of spirit, but, on the contrary, that spirit, thought, idea is only one of the attributes of matter." He proposed that Hegel's two students, Marx and Feuerbach, had climbed to the "pinnacle" of materialism. We should point out that though Dietzgen's identification here was not incorrect, he did not realize that there was a fundamental **heterogeneity** between Marx and Feuerbach, both of whom were materialists. This is what caused him to conclude: "Marx, the leader of scientific socialism, has achieved splendid success by applying inductive logic to branches of knowledge which have hitherto been maltreated by speculation"[3]. I assert that he was incorrect because Marx did not apply traditional philosophical materialism (empirical, inductive positivism) to social life, but rather first established the "historical science" of historical materialism in the **practice of social life**; it was this that caused him to experience a fundamental revolution in his philosophical world view. Dietzgen's mistake was that he confused Marx's new materialism with Feuerbach's old materialism. He **mistakenly believed** that Marx's new philosophy applied the inductive method of philosophical materialism to abstract spiritual conclusions from material facts. More importantly, he **directly links** this old materialism **with socialism**. In this first article, although Lenin does not use α to indicate his affirmation on Dietzgen's views, we do find that he underlined and made vertical notations next to the passages that we have cited here. In Lenin's **possible thought space**, this could have been the start of a misunderstanding that existed from the beginning.

I should add here that this misunderstanding was identical to Plekhanov's views. At the end of the 19th century and beginning of the 20th, Plekhanov correctly opposed the mistakes of Bernstein and others, though an extremely complex theoretical context began to appear during this time. When Bernstein wrote that the most critical foundation of Marxism, the law that ran through the whole Marxist system was the unique historical theory of historical materialism, he was only partly correct, eventually going on to completely revise Marxism. When Plekhanov correctly criticized Bernstein's mistakes, he used general materialism as his philosophical weapon, consigning Marx's new world view to old materialism, which included Spinoza, 18th century French materialism, and Feuerbach's philosophical materialism. Plekhanov even stubbornly maintained this view in the theoretical struggle against Machism[4]. Although he mentioned Marx's *Theses on Feuerbach*, he obviously did not truly understand the profound significance of Marx's philosophical

---

3   Dietzgen, Joseph. "Scientific Socialism," cited in *The Collected Works of Lenin*, volume 55, page 360 (Chin. 2. Ed.).
4   Refer to the various articles in *Against Revisionism in Philosophy*, People's Press, 1957 (Chinese).

revolution. Thus, in his **correct** opposition to idealism, Plekhanov was still superficial. Lenin did not begin to gradually understand this until his later systematic study of Hegelian philosophy. As Lenin studied Dietzgen, however, he did so under the influence of Plekhanov's mistaken understanding. This is also a complex thought circumstance. *We can see that this would certainly have strengthened and stabilized the related theoretical misunderstanding in Lenin's Other mirror image.*

The second article was Dietzgen's "The Religion of Social-Democracy," written between 1870 and 1875. I have found that Lenin begins to notate his affirmations and refutations in this article. There are six lectures in this text. In the first, Lenin continues to use the underlines and margin lines that he employed in the previous article; this may have been related to the fact that Dietzgen continues to discuss general problems with religion, as he had in his first article. However, beginning with the second lecture of "The Religion of Social-Democracy," Dietzgen proposed that a new form of religion had appeared with social democracy. Here, Lenin notes his first refutational "β"; he obviously did not agree that the Social Democratic Party should also have a religion. However, Lenin did agree with Dietzgen that "the materialistic social-democrat has made it his special duty, to judge people not by their flashes of thought, but by their palpable actions." Dietzgen also proposes labour that appears as a sensuous object. I agree with Marx and Engels that though Dietzgen lacked systematic philosophical training, he was often able to bring up profound thoughts. For instance, he realized that "the power of our material production, in the productivity of modern industry" was what truly formed the objective basis of modern democracy[5]. Lenin marked this statement with an "α" to express his agreement. However, I believe that here Dietzgen had not yet united this correct thinking with his old philosophical materialism in terms of ontological logic. Looking at the logical whole of Lenin's philosophical thought at this time, I also believe that Lenin had not fully understood the complex relation between the two. *This is an extremely important question in terms of micro-discourse structure.*

---

5   Dietzgen, Joseph. "The Religion of Social-Democracy," cited in *The Collected Works of Lenin*, volume 55, page 365 (Chin. 2. Ed.).

As Lenin continued his reading, he noted an "α" and a "β" next to Dietzgen's statement that "in the place of religion, social-democracy puts **humanity**," to express his partial agreement. In the third lecture, in Dietzgen's discussion of religious ideas and the essence of spirit, Lenin seems to agree with the majority of Dietzgen's views. He especially agrees with Dietzgen's continuation of Feuerbach's line of thought, linking religious theology with idealist philosophy, an idea that profoundly influenced Lenin. *At the beginning of Lenin's study of Hegel's The Science of Logic, Lenin basically equates the "ideas" of idealism with God. This is an instance of an Other logical mirror image.*

I believe that Lenin's most important understanding in terms of the basic philosophical ideas in this text are concentrated in the second part of the fourth lecture and in the fifth lecture. *Looking at the details of the text, we find that beginning in the fourth lecture Lenin begins to add a box around his affirmative alphas to express emphasized agreement. At the same time, Lenin begins to write the word "notable" more often to emphasize certain parts of the content. I have also seen that in the entire first lecture, there was only one "notable," and in the second and third lectures there were no "notable"s.* In the second part of the fourth lecture, Dietzgen primarily discusses the scientific spirit, which is incompatible with religion. For Dietzgen, the essence of this anti-religious scientific spirit was the "materialist world view," and that philosophy was "a subject which closely concerns the working class." Dietzgen believed that religion, and especially Christianity, was a spirit that **enslaved man**, while science was an emancipation of thought. Dietzgen powerfully asserts: "The emancipation of the working classes requires that they should lay hold on the science of the century. The mere sentiment of indignation against the unjust conditions under which we suffer does not meet the case of freeing the working class"[6]. Thus we must grasp the scientific method of thinking and epistemology in order to break the bonds of idealism and truly stand on material reality. *In this passage of Dietzgen's thought, Lenin almost completely fills the margins with double underlined alphas and the word "notable."* In order to do this, in the fifth lecture, Dietzgen specifically proposes a theory of "democratic materialism," which is related to reality[7].

---

6   *Ibid.*, page 372.
7   *Ibid.*, page 374.

In the fifth lecture, Lenin reads Dietzgen's direct explanation of philosophical materialism for the first time:

> **Philosophic materialists, on the other hand, are those think-ers who put the real world at the beginning, at the head of their investigation, and the idea or spirit as the sequel and outcome, as the product, while their opponents follow the op-posite method: they decree, after the religious method, the rise of reality from the logos (God spoke and it was), the ma-terial world from the idea[8].**

Lenin underlines many of the sentences in this passage and draws three vertical lines in the margins of this paragraph. He even writes a boxed "α" at the end of the paragraph. We can see that Lenin thought deeply on Dietzgen's theoretical overview of philosophical materialism. He most likely emphasized this expression so much because Plekhanov never gave such a clear summary himself. *In Lenin's **Materialism and Empirio-criticism** it is not difficult to see the re-structuring of this view in Lenin's logical circuit.*

According to Dietzgen's explanation of the sixth lecture, the theoretical logic of philosophical materialism is divided into three points. **First**, Dietzgen discusses the foundational concept of philosophical material-ism, the conception of matter that contained all materials of the world[9]. *Lenin places parentheses around this passage and then writes four al-phas. We can see that this expresses absolute agreement. This makes me think of that famous definition of material given in Lenin's **Materialism and Empirio-criticism**.* **Second**, Dietzgen discusses **induction**, as dif-ferentiated from the spiritual deduction of idealism. Dietzgen goes so far as to assert that social-democrats can prove everything using **in-duction**. It was through this change in methodology that the social-democrats were able to "put a systematic conception of the universe" in place of religion[10]. This is likely the historical origin of the definition of philosophy in our traditional textbooks: "philosophy is a systematic, theoretical view of the world." **Third**, Dietzgen asserts that unlike the conceptual deductive logic that proceeds from god to man to material in religious theology, the induction of philosophical materialism proceeds from **experience** to reason. Thus Dietzgen concludes that empirical

---

8   *Ibid.*, page 374.
9   *Ibid.*, page 376.
10   *Ibid.*, page 377.

phenomena are the most important starting point of philosophical materialism. However, Lenin is clearly opposed to Dietzgen's conclusion. *Lenin often uses betas to mark related expressions of Dietzgen, sometimes even using double betas.*

2 DIETZGEN: "COMRADE" OF MARX AND LENIN

There was not much content in the third article, "Ethics of Social-Democracy" (1875), that excited Lenin's interest. However, he did remark Dietzgen's use of the concept of "economic materialism." *Dietzgen's use of different concepts is often quite loose; many concepts do not have concrete connotations for him. However, Plekhanov also used this concept.*

The title of the fourth article was "Social-Democratic Philosophy" (1876). I believe that this was a critical text in Lenin's study of Dietzgen's philosophical thought. According to my analysis, of all of Dietzgen's articles this one had the deepest influence on Lenin. Of course, its substance was still the **basic principles of philosophical materialism**.

It is not difficult for us to see that here Dietzgen begins to connect his own views to those of Marx. *From Lenin's notations we see that he was very much aware of this situation.* Dietzgen refers to Marx and Engels as his "comrades," pointing out a general principle of Marx's historical materialism: "the world is not governed by Ideas, but, on the contrary, the Ideas by the material world." *This is an imprecise re-expression of Marx and Engels' assertion that **social existence and social life determine consciousness**.* It is interesting to note that Dietzgen remarked that the basis of Marx's philosophical methodology and socialist ideas was "the productivity of social labour." He goes on to note that "Science or education cannot bring it [human happiness]; productive labour must do it, which, through science and education, can be made more productive"[11]. I believe that viewing labour productivity as the basis of Ideas is already largely superior to the scope of general philosophical materialism; however, this was still an imprecise expression. The foundation of Marx's new world view is **historical** material practice, not **labour as subjective activity.** What brings true emancipation to man is not abstract labour (productivity), but rather the developmental

---

11 *Ibid.*, page 381.

capacity for producing and reproducing material means of subsistence; in other words, the **material productive forces** of society as a whole. Therefore, although Dietzgen proudly believed that his philosophical ideas were the same as those of Marx and Engels, I do not believe that Dietzgen truly understood their historical materialism at this time. *Dietzgen would often humbly admit, "I am not an academician, but a simple tanner who learned Philosophy by himself"*[12]. This false, surface-level "similarity" would soon be disproven. I have found that Lenin did not pay much attention to this extremely important content in the process of his own reading.

As Lenin continued his reading, a few aspects of Dietzgen's thought came to directly influence his thought. The **first** aspect focused on **basic philosophical problems**, an emphasis in Dietzgen's work. Dietzgen clearly delineates his "basic philosophical problems": "which takes the precedence: thought or being, speculative theology or inductive science." Or in other words, is matter or reason primary? Dietzgen clearly points out, "the question as to which is primary, mind or matter, contains also the problem as to the right way to justice and truth"[13]. *I have found that Dietzgen proposes "basic philosophical problems" of philosophy much earlier than Engels, who resummarized these problems in his 1886* **On Feuerbach***, 10 years after Dietzgen.* Of course, Dietzgen's answer is that "it is the material world which forms the substance of our conceptions." He writes: "Where there is intellect, thinking, consciousness and knowledge, there must be an object, too, a matter which is perceived, and that is the **main** thing"[14]. He is correct with both of these statements, this is the general basis of philosophical materialism. However, what Dietzgen does not realize is that this idea of general philosophical materialism is different from Marx's new outlook that he had just cited. For Dietzgen this is not an isolated phenomenon: when he reads Marx and Engels he is influenced by them, but when he attempts to think independently, the **old problematics** begin to resurface. This means that Dietzgen's basic stance and theoretical logic circuit are still mired in philosophical materialism.

Even more ridiculous, Dietzgen refers to his philosophy as a theory of mechanics! "We don't look for salvation in subjective schemes, but we see it growing as a sort of organic product out of the inevitable course

---

12   *Ibid.*, page 383.
13   *Ibid.*, page 382.
14   *Ibid.*, page 400.

of actual development." Thus he sees the principles of philosophical materialism as **mechanical**[15]. I have found that Lenin did not directly refute this mistaken expression of Dietzgen's. *From Lenin's textual commentaries we can see that Lenin began with reading this portion of text before leaving his own conclusions. In the previous text, he wrote the word "notable" several times and also made some underlining and drew a few symbols. It was not until "Ethics of Social-Democracy" that he wrote text in two places that do not have direct qualitative semantic meaning*[16]. *This is very similar to Marx's situation as he began to study economics, a field with which he was unfamiliar. At the beginning, he was silent, but as he read and learned, he gradually developed the ability to express himself with professional language*[17]. However, Lenin's reading at this time was still very distant from this level of depth; he still had a long process of thought development to undergo. It is my understanding that Lenin did not truly reach the true philosophical context until the latter stages of his research of Hegel's philosophy; it was then that he truly understood Marxist philosophy.

The **second** aspect of Dietzgen's work that influenced Lenin's thought was the **delineation of basic schools of philosophy and the Lenin's partizan principle in philosophy**. For Dietzgen, the different answers to the major philosophical questions led to the formation of different schools of thought, namely materialism and idealism. *Here, Lenin writes the words "two philosophical factions" in the margins. The movement from a materialist answer to basic philosophical questions to the delineation of two basic philosophical factions was certainly the most important logical support point of the theoretical mirror image and logic circuit in Lenin's philosophical materialism.* Dietzgen clearly opposes dualism in philosophy, proposing a "monistic conception of the world"[18]. Lenin also wrote commentary on this passage. For Dietzgen, idealism had "made mysterious" existing material forces; the idealists did not understand that reason and material came from the same source. Materialism, on the other hand, "assumes matter as the premise, as the cause of the idea"[19]. *This is the first theoretical level. Lenin is obviously in agreement here.* Dietzgen quickly links this differentiation of

15   *Ibid.*, page 382-383.
16   See *The Collected Works of Lenin*, volume 55, page 379-380 (Chin. 2. Ed.).
17   Refer to the second chapter of my *Marx Revisited*.
18   Dietzgen, Joseph. "The Philosophy of Social-Democracy," cited in *The Collected Works of Lenin*, volume 55, page 399 (Chin. 2. Ed.).
19   *Ibid.*, page 400.

philosophical factions with the development of actual history. He asserts that philosophical idealism, which advocated the primacy of spirit, was always developed by the aristocracy, while philosophical materialism, which respected sensuous existence, necessarily belonged to "ordinary people." For Dietzgen, the former is the "reactionary group" that defends actually existing religions, states, families, and morals, while the latter is made up of revolutionary social-democrats. Furthermore, he clearly criticizes the "intermediate members and conciliating quacks"[20]. Lenin writes "very good" at two points in this passage. Looking at all of Lenin's commentaries, these purely affirmative assessments are very rare. I believe that this was the origin of Lenin's philosophical party principle. We have already seen how in 1895, as young Lenin read *The Holy Family*, he also read Marx and Engels' description of the link between materialism and socialism. However, Lenin was unable to grasp the importance of that issue at the time. Aron wrote that Lenin began to link his political and philosophical tendencies together after 1917[21]. This assessment places Lenin's shift chronologically much too late. In Lenin's famous 1908 *Materialism and Empirio-criticism*, he already publicly declared the party principle in philosophy. I believe that Dietzgen's discussion here reminded Lenin that it was impossible to simply separate philosophical theory from political stance. This may have been one of the foundations for Lenin's decision to resolve to criticize his own political comrades. In Dietzgen's later "Limits of Cognition," he again directly criticizes the practice of viewing philosophy and social democracy as two unrelated, unconnected things. He argues that epistemology is the most important aspect of socialism[22]. However, Lenin himself was under this mistaken understanding at the time; it is not difficult to see the impact that this critique of Dietzgen's would have on Lenin.

The **third** and most important aspect that influenced Lenin was Dietzgen's **conception of matter**. In this article, Dietzgen introduces an important heterogeneity, between his materialism and "old materialism" in terms of the understanding of the concept of matter. This is a very interesting point that he brings up. Dietzgen believes that traditional, old materialism proceeds from perceivable material, and has "misled

20   *Ibid.*, page 395.
21   Aron, Raymond. 2007. *D'une sainte famille à l'autre. Essai sur le marxisme imaginaire*. Shanghai Translated Works Press, 101.
22   Dietzgen, Joseph. "The Philosophy of Social-Democracy," cited in *The Collected Works of Lenin*, volume 55, page 400-405 (Chin. 2. Ed.)

the old materialists to their atomistic speculations, misled them to make the ponderable the final cause of things." Dietzgen proposes that "**the conception of matter must be given a more comprehensive meaning**. To it belong all phenomena of reality, also our force of thinking"[23]. The first sentence is correct, but there are problems with the second. How can our subjective force of thinking **be included** in material? Nonsense! In fact, Dietzgen's original intent may have been to oppose idealism by putting thinking within the concept of material, but this is obviously in vain. *Gelfand's analysis of Dietzgen's views here is interesting. He asserts that Dietzgen attempted to prove the empirical nature of the content of thinking, thus disproving a priori idealism; however, Dietzgen was never able to really accomplish this*[24]. Nevertheless, this conception of matter was still influential for Lenin in his philosophical struggle, because matter was not only something that could be touched, but also included all reality.

I should make clear that in this article, Dietzgen also emphasized that philosophy was an independent field of study, different from natural science: "some call [it] Logic, or Epistemology or Dialectics"[25]. Lenin underlined this passage, marked it with three vertical lines, and wrote "notable." *Later, while studying Hegel's philosophy, Lenin would again come across this proposition. At that time, Lenin developed the view that the logic, epistemology, and dialectics in Hegel's philosophy were united.*

The next three articles in Dietzgen's *Philosophical Essays* were all **attacks on agnosticism**. Dietzgen clearly opposed Kant's thing-in-itself, believing that the opaqueness of the thing-in-itself was nothing more than exaggeration of reason. He agreed that whether in the natural sciences or in the general knowledge of man, there were some things that man did not yet understand; however, this did not mean that they could never be known. Dietzgen actively pointed out that in the limited knowledge of individuals and the limitless development of general knowledge, the world could be understood.

---

23 *Ibid.*, page 400.
24 Gelfand. 1984. "Dietzgen's Philosophy and Modern Positivism," in *Marxist-Leninist Research Materials*, volume 5, page 108 (Chinese).
25 Dietzgen, Joseph. "The Philosophy of Social-Democracy," cited in *The Collected Works of Lenin*, volume 55, page 399 (Chin. 2. Ed.).

3 ON "DIALECTICAL MATERIALISM" AND EPISTEMOLOGY

After the seven articles discussed above, the last article in Dietzgen's *Philosophical Essays* was an 1887 work on epistemology, titled "Excursions of a Socialist into the Domain of Epistemology." In this text, we can see that after 10 years of studying the philosophy of Marx and Engels, Dietzgen's thought had changed considerably. He even directly identifies the critical influence that Marx and Engels had exerted on him.

According to Dietzgen himself, his quest for truth and justice began during the tumultuous European revolutions of 1848. He began by studying Feuerbach's materialist philosophy, which formed an important theoretical foundation for him. However, true enlightenment came to him when he discovered the socialist thought of Marx and Engels. He identifies Marx and Engels as the "acknowledged founders" of this social science. *Lenin emphasizes this point in a marginal note.*

> **Of still greater help in my thirst for knowledge was the *Communist Manifesto*. Most of all, however, I owe to the work of Marx which appeared in 1859 under the title: *A Contribution to the Critique of Political Economy*. There it is stated in the preface that the way in which man earns his daily bread, that the level of civilisation on which a generation physically works, determines the mental standpoint or the way in which it conceives and must conceive the True, the Good and Right, God, Freedom and Immortality, Philosophy, Politics and Law[26].**

Because it is really quite amazing that Dietzgen was able, as a simple worker, to teach himself philosophy, we cannot fault him too much for his slight distortions of Marx's scientific thought in his transmission of it. *We know that Dietzgen sent a copy of the manuscript for his **Nature of Human Brain Work** to Marx in September of 1868. After reading it, Marx sent it to Engels and asked him for specific opinions. Marx and Engels were very moved by Dietzgen's work, lauding him highly and claiming that his thought displayed a dialectical spark. They asserted that Dietzgen independently discovered materialist dialectics without relying on them or Hegel. In 1868, Engels directly praised Dietzgen in his **On Feuerbach**.* Dietzgen persisted in emphasizing the intimate

26   *Ibid.*, page 451.

connection between one's progressive, revolutionary political stance and one's philosophical world view. This assertion is easily found throughout his epistemological theory.

We can see that many of the basic views of philosophical materialism, which we were able to dimly glimpse before Dietzgen's article, are collected and systematized here.

First is the premise of materialism. Dietzgen is the first to clearly propose the important concept of **dialectical materialism** at this point. *This concept, after meeting the approval of Plekhanov, Lenin, and Stalin, would later come to refer to the ontology and epistemology of all of Marxist philosophy for more than a century. Dialectical materialism, by simply adding the theoretical logical situating of materialism to the dialectical method, is actually Dietzgenism.* Dietzgen wrote that the entire foundation of his epistemology "derives all its ideas, conceptions and thoughts from the monistic world which science calls the "physical world"[27]. Therefore, without things that can be understood in the outside world, our brains would not have understanding; this is actually a principle of general philosophical materialism. But Dietzgen goes farther, remarking on Engels' critique of old materialism. In the third section of his text, Dietzgen uses an attention-grabbing title: "Materialism **versus** Materialism." *From the discussion of this book we can see that Dietzgen was already very familiar with Engels' Anti-Dühring. Lenin was also aware of this.* This is because he realized that Engels was identifying a "new materialism," something that Dietzgen had not grasped before. Furthermore, Engels uses a specific qualification in reference to old 18th century materialism: **metaphysical, mechanical** materialism. Did Dietzgen not just use "mechanical" to describe his own materialism in an article not long before this one? This was a painful discovery for him. However, he still carefully analyzed Engels' views, focusing, of course, on Engels' discussion of "metaphysical" rather than "mechanical." In fact, looking through Dietzgen's articles we find a gradual process of thought change. Interestingly enough, the development of his thought was completely **opposite** from the interpretive logical sequence that I described in the preface to this book: Dietzgen began with his own independent, creative philosophical thought, *i.e.*, what Marx and Engels called his independent discoveries, before incorporating the thought of Marx and Engels as his Other logic base and primary theoretical circuit. There is no evidence to suggest that Lenin was aware of this.

---

27   *Ibid.*, page 413.

Dietzgen realized that Engels did not use metaphysics in the traditional sense (Kant said that metaphysics could be separated into God, freedom, and immortality); rather, Engels had already turned to a new, restructured logical context, *i.e.*, the idea of "concrete dialectical nature" in German philosophy. This was an identification of the opposition between dialectics and metaphysics. He found that this new philosophical cognition produced out of the perversion of German idealist philosophy was materialism combined with dialectical thought, or "dialectical materialism"[28]. Here Lenin uses two long diagonal lines to highlight "dialectical materialism." *Because Dietzgen used "dialectical materialism" to explain the philosophy of Engels (Marx), it is very easy to develop a false misunderstanding of theoretical logical situating at this point.* However, in his understanding, idealism and metaphysical old materialism both absolutely emphasized one aspect of spirit and matter; this is because they did not understand the unity, singleness, generality, and universality of the natural world, because they had not considered the "achievements" of dialectics in German philosophy.

With this premise, Dietzgen was able to further discuss the differences between dialectical materialism and mechanical materialism in terms of the conception of matter. Relative to the understanding of old materialism that matter was merely perceivable objects, Dietzgen again proposed that the conception of matter needed to be expanded to include all existing matter. Importantly, Dietzgen understood "social materialism," produced after the perversion of German idealism.

[This materialism] is called "Socialist" because it was the Socialists Marx and Engels who first enunciated clearly and distinctly that the material, that is, the economic conditions of human society form the basis from which the entire superstructure of the juridical and political institutions as well as the religious, philosophical and other modes of thought are at each historical epoch in the last instance explained. Instead of explaining, as hitherto, the existence of man out of his consciousness, it is now, on the contrary, the consciousness which is to be explained out of his existence, that is, from the economic position, from the way and manner of bread-winning[29].

---

28   *Ibid.*, page 422.
29   *Ibid.*, page 426.

I believe that this was the most important expression of the basic views of Marx's historical materialism in Dietzgen's text. He does not proceed from matter to explain consciousness, but rather uses man's economic position and the way and manner of his bread-winning." Here, Dietzgen unconsciously highlights the fundamental differences between Marx's new philosophical world view and his own general philosophical materialism. Unfortunately, Dietzgen was unable to consciously understand this theoretical logical situating heterogeneity; he wishes to enter Marx's revolutionary thought space, but his theoretical logical circuit is insufficient here. *Unfortunately, these complex logical circumstances and contradictions did not spark Lenin's interest.*

Dietzgen wrote that socialist materialism "understands matter not only as the ponderable and tangible, but the whole real existence. Everything that is contained in the Universe – and in it is contained everything." However, he repeatedly and mistakenly believes that spirit is also material, because spirit is also a part of the epistemological material of man[30]. "The thoughts, too, their origin and nature, are just as real matters and materials worthy of study as any"[31]. Dietzgen, the self-taught worker-philosopher, seems to be unable to move beyond this point. *Lenin did not directly approve of Dietzgen's views here, merely drawing three arcs in the margin.*

The primary views in this text were still those of Dietzgen on epistemology, and these can be seen in the following examples.

First, man's organ of cognition was produced in the natural world, and man's spiritual phenomena are the result of the eternal movement and development of the natural material world. In this sense, Dietzgen asserted that man's understanding is essentially a reflection of one part of nature by another[32]. This is a simple empirical deduction, a crude materialism. This passage is quite different from his understanding on Marx's historical materialist views expressed earlier. *Here, Lenin wrote in the margin "a reflection of other parts of nature," though he did not express opposition to this point. This reveals the baseline of his thought situating.*

---

30   *Ibid.*, page 425.
31   *Ibid.*, page 427.
32   *Ibid.*, page 430.

Second, Dietzgen discusses the limitlessness of man's cognition. In the fourth section of his text, under the heading "Darwin and Hegel," Dietzgen discusses the relation between a world in constant motion and change and the understanding of man. *This direct link between Darwin and Hegel directly influenced Lenin; in his later study of Hegelian philosophy, this would become an important element of scholarly memory in Lenin's thought.* Dietzgen believed that Darwin and Hegel had both proposed theories of development in different scholarly fields (the origin of species on the one hand and human thought processes on the other); according to this idea, the natural world was in constant motion and development, and so understanding it would naturally also have to be limitless: "Nature, both as a whole and in its parts, is inexhaustible, not knowable to its last particle, – consequently without beginning and end...The recognition of this everyday **Infinitude** is the **result** of science"[33]. Here, Dietzgen uses the example of the limitlessness of the atom. *Lenin paid special attention to this point; on the same page, under the word "notable," he uses two lines to write "the atom cannot be measured, limitless," and "the atom is infinite." This scholarly memory point would resurface in his **Bern Notebooks**.*

Third, Dietzgen discusses the question of essence and phenomena in epistemology. Dietzgen understood that Kant's division of the world into an unknowable "thing-in-itself" and a phenomenological world was a mistake of separating the essence from the appearance. Dietzgen proposed using a dialectical method to resolve the contradiction between essence and phenomena: "The essence of the Universe consists of phenomena and its phenomena are essential"[34]. According to Dietzgen, it was a scientific impulse to constantly go beyond the appearance and attain truth, to obtain an essential understanding of things through the relative truth of phenomena. *Lenin would discuss the relation between essence and appearance in greater depth in his later study of Hegelian philosophy.*

At this point, Lenin terminated his serious and systematic reading of Dietzgen's philosophy. I myself believe that Dietzgen's important philosophical ideas directly composed the immediate foundation and theoretical logical circuit of Lenin's **philosophical materialism** at this time. They effectively supported his response to the mistakes of

---

33   *Ibid.*, page 433.
34   *Ibid.*, page 443.

Machism, and provided a Marxist basis of from which he could launch a correct counterattack.

In 1913, Lenin wrote an article to commemorate the 25th anniversary of Dietzgen's death. In it, Lenin praised Dietzgen's philosophical thought, calling him "a worker who arrived at dialectical materialism, i.e., Marx's philosophy, independently." Of course, Lenin also pointed out that Dietzgen's understanding of the philosophy of Marx and Engels was not entirely correct[35]. Lenin wrote:

> **Dietzgen, therefore, laid his greatest stress on the historical changes that had taken place in materialism, on the *dialectical* character of materialism, that is, on the need to support the point of view of development, to understand that all human knowledge is relative, to understand the multilateral connections between, and interdependence of, all phenomena in the universe, and to develop the materialism of natural history to a materialist conception of history[36].**

This was a relatively high appraisal of Dietzgen's theoretical thought.

---

35 Lenin, Vladimir Ilyich. "Twenty-FifthAnniversary of the Death of Joseph Dietzgen." *The Collected Works of Lenin*, volume 23, 151-152 (Chin. 2. Ed.).
36 *Ibid.*, page 152.

CHAPTER FOUR

LENIN BEGINS TO UNDERSTAND MODERN WESTERN PHILOSOPHY

From February to October, 1908, Lenin completed his famous *Materialism and Empirio-criticism* while living in Paris; the book was published in May 1909 in St. Petersburg. However, with the publishing of this book Lenin did not stop his learning and investigation in the field of philosophy. This is most likely because after Lenin published *Materialism and Empirio-criticism*, both Plekhanov and Bogdanov published articles criticizing his lack of philosophical training[1], which hurt Lenin deeply. As such, from late 1908 to 1909, Lenin continued to read numerous philosophical texts, beginning his **second** systematic study of philosophy. *In 1913, as Lenin turned to topical research in other subjects, he still paid attention to the newest developments in philosophy and science.* From the reading notes and commentaries that Lenin left from this time, we can see that Lenin had a strong desire to comprehensively understand contemporary schools of philosophical thought, including the developmental state of Western philosophy and science. It is evident that he studied many introductory works on

---

1 After Lenin published *Materialism and Empirio-criticism*, Plekhanov's student Axelrod published an article criticizing Lenin's critique of Machism for its lack of professionalism and for not building on Plekhanov's scholarly views in the seventh edition of the 1909 *Modern Life*. Axelrod goes so far as to say that Lenin's work has no independent reason to exist. In 1909, Bogdanov also published an article titled "Belief and Science," in which he claimed that Lenin did not understand the thinking of the object of his criticism, much less Western philosophical history. This article was later included in his book *The Demise of the Great Fetishism: Belief and Science*, which was published in Russia in 1910.

Western philosophy, as well as several works on natural science[2]. I have found that Lenin's interest in Western philosophy and scientific knowledge was an important part of his third venture in philosophical research (1914-1916). However, the focus of Lenin's study at this point was naturally a deeper understanding of materialist philosophy; he still based his research on materialist philosophers. I have found that in Lenin's second systematic study, he consciously realizes that he has a certain degree of authority to speak on philosophical matters, and so he appears to be much more calm and collected when dealing with important philosophical questions. At the same time, he continued his tireless struggle against all mistaken thinking.

1 A STRANGE ABERRATION IN LENIN'S READING

Lenin's reading commentaries on modern philosophy primarily concentrated on two books: Vladimir Shulyatikov's *Justification of Capitalism in Western Philosophy*[3] and Abel Rey's *Modern Philosophy*. Textual evidence suggests that both of these notes were completed after Lenin wrote *Materialism and Empirio-criticism*. I believe that Lenin read both of these works in order to further confirm the basic views he laid out in *Materialism and Empirio-criticism*. I have also found that Lenin's attitude towards these two books is completely different from that shown in his commentaries on Dietzgen's work. In terms of his tone, he seems to be doubtful and refutational throughout the notes. In fact, in specifically examining Lenin's critical opinions of these two works, I have found that **not all** of his critiques are correct; in several places, the thought and theoretical logical situating that Lenin demonstrates in his commentaries are **not even as profound as the object of his criticism!** This may be a phenomenon that past researchers have overlooked, or in other words, a truth that we saw but refused to acknowledge because of ideological reasons.

Shulyatikov's *Justification of Capitalism in Western Philosophy* has an important characteristic: **it links the development of Western philosophy with the real development of social history**, what Shulyatikov

---

2   According to Fischer, Lenin spent this time studying Hume, Hegel, Huxley, Diderot, Fichte, and others; he also studied and commented on the works of other second rate philosophers. However, we do not have any of Lenin's notes to support such an assertion. See Fischer's *The Great Man, Lenin* (China Social Science Press, 1989), page 108.
3   **Vladimir Shulyatikov** (1872-1912): A Russian literary critic and Bolshevik. His book *Justification of Capitalism in Western Philosophy* was published in Moscow in 1908.

calls a "social and genetic analysis of philosophical concepts and systems"[4]. This basic logic is certainly correct and profound. As Marx first expressed the principles of historical materialism, he pointed out that all ideas belong to a certain historical age. *Lukacs understood this logic and applied it to the explanation of the logical origins of Hegelian philosophy using the French Revolution and industrial revolution; Adorno, on the other hand, profoundly expresses this logic using the link between musical theory and social historical reality (such as the relation between the musical mode of Beethoven's symphonies and the structural system and laws of movement in industry).* Here I must point out that this correct line of thought had actually **originated with Marx**, a fact that Shulyatikov clearly pointed out in his book: "Marx in Vol. I of *Capital* and K. Kautsky had noted the dependence between abstract religious views and the development of commodity production"[5]. However, Lenin strangely opposes this view, an attitude which is truly bewildering. *It is somewhat amusing that the Soviet scholar Kedrov referred to Shulyatikov as a "vulgar socialist and shallow materialist"; he wrote that Shulyatikov's study of the linkages between the development of philosophical thought and social history was akin to searching out the class, even the economic equivalent of a philosophy[6]. This attempt to justify the illusory image of an invincible, all-powerful Lenin went to any lengths to hide the truth, even sacrificing the scientific method of Marxism; this is yet another example of how scholars of that time **non-historically constructed history.***

In Shulyatikov's introduction, he criticizes the dualistic separation of politics and philosophy by some Marxists. He firmly criticizes the idea that the thinkers of the vanguard proletariat could simultaneously believe in neo-Kantianism or Machism. Shulyatikov clearly points out that philosophical ideas are used to denote "social classes, groups, sections and their mutual relations." He even writes that when we concretely analyze the philosophical logic of a bourgeois thinker, "dealing with a picture of the class structure of society, depicted by means of conventional symbols"[7]. *This logic is obviously over-simplified.* However,

4   Shulyatikov, Vladimir. Justification of Capitalism in Western Philosophy, cited in *The Collected Works of Lenin*, volume 55, page 450 (Chin. 2. Ed.).

5   *Ibid.*, page 452.

6   See Kedrov's *Study of Lenin's "Philosophical Notebooks,"* Qiushi Press (1984), page 127 (Chinese).

7   Shulyatikov, Vladimir. Justification of Capitalism in Western Philosophy, cited in *The Collected Works of Lenin*, volume 55, page 449-450 (Chin. 2. Ed.).

I believe that although Shulyatikov's analysis is over-simplified and too direct, his basic view itself is completely correct. However, Lenin writes in the margin of this passage: "incorrect." I believe that this may have been because the mistaken practice of separating political stance from philosophical outlook **was something that Lenin himself had long been doing**. Although by this time he had already begun to realize that one's philosophical ideas could not be simply separated from his political stance and had begun to criticize the mistaken philosophical world view of his Bolshevik ally Bogdanov, he was unwilling to admit his mistake under the criticism of another. This was most unfortunate, because this attitude caused him to commit some errors in the commentaries on this text. I have noticed that Kedrov's research evades this important textual detail.

It is interesting to note that many of Shulyatikov's passages in this book are extremely confused. At the beginning, in his explanation of his own views, Shulyatikov uses some of the arguments in Bogdanov's "Authoritarian Thought," even asserting that this Machist "had opened a new era in the history of philosophy." His basic argument here was that the mind and body are both confirmed in certain social relations, and that these two philosophical concepts reflected the antithesis between the organizing "top strata" and the executive "lower strata." I must also point out that Shulyatikov not only did not understand Bogdanov's original meaning, but he was also unable to justify his own extension of Bogdanov's thought. Hence his views are necessarily incorrect, and naturally deviated from Marx's correct theoretical logic which we identified earlier. Lenin writes "what nonsense" next to this passage, a criticism that Shulyatikov deserved.

Next, Shulyatikov uses his equation of the interdependence of philosophical logic and social reality to explain the **simultaneous** development of Western social history and philosophical history. Defining **organizers**, who appeared in late primitive society, Shulyatikov writes: "the organizers were gradually transformed into the owners of the instruments of production, which had once belonged to society." *In fact, this was an identification of what Marx referred to as the appropriators and owners of private property. "Organizer" is an imprecise expression of this concept.* Shulyatikov believes that with the emergence of these organizers, the concept of the mind became more and more **abstract**. *Lenin writes in the margin, "nothing but idealism."* The logical connection here seems to be that as "organizers" gradually departed from concrete labour, the "organization" began to gain on "metaphysical" qualities, thus causing ideas themselves to become more and more abstract. I do not believe that this is a deduction which can be substantiated using the real development of social history. In fact, the abstraction of ideas is more related to the structure of man's social intercourse and production; it is not directly related to the existential form of the subject. Lenin's reaction to this was, "Fiction and empty phrases. Indeed, very "general" words. The savage and primitive communism is slurred over. Materialism and idealism in Greece as well"[8]. *It is obvious here that the Plekhanov-Dietzgen Other mirror image that dominated Lenin's thought at this point – the basic problems and factions of philosophy– had already become the closed theoretical circuit of the conceptual standard of his critique.* Next, as the social divisions between the upper and lower strata in the Greek cities gradually deepened, the antithesis between mental phenomena and substance began to be solidified, and thus "essence and the world of phenomena are declared to be incommensurable magnitudes." This means that the ruling class began to monopolize cultural thought, and the labouring class devolved to the point that it merely engaged in material, manual labour, a real change that directly influenced the antithesis between "substance" and the "world of phenomena" in philosophy. In fact, though this analysis makes some good points, Lenin still had a low opinion of it. He believed that Shulyatikov was unable to derive the antithesis between materialism and idealism, while at the same time muddling many of the questions in the history of philosophy that had already been made clear in the past. *This returns Lenin to the idea of the fundamental factions in philosophy.* Overall, this appraisal is correct, but I believe that Shulyatikov's original intent in analyzing the shifts in philosophical history using the development of social history and the division in social structure is basically correct.

Shulyatikov's important thought logic is primarily expressed in his discussion on the period of manufacturing production. *His direct reference to the similar ideas of Marx and Kautsky comes at this point in his book.* However, in terms of his writing, he still awkwardly uses the ridiculous, external equation of "organizer" and "organized." In his view, the medieval artisan worked together with his apprentices, and so fulfilled the dual role of organizer and organized; this veiled the real antithesis

---

8   *Ibid.*, page 451.

between these two groups, making it so that the "antithesis of mental and corporeal, active and passive, principles, in the sphere of ideology, could not take a sharp form"[9]. This analysis has basically no basis. Looking at the history of the medieval ages, the power of the church symbolized the spiritual while secular life was looked down on because it was material. This may have been the most pointed antithesis formed between the spiritual and material in an inverted form. Even for the early manufacturers, just because creativity and manual work were combined in the work of manufacturers, this would not directly lead to some kind of philosophical parity theory. I believe that this is nothing but a subjective, false situating put forth by Shulyatikov. In Shulyatikov's opinion, this situation changed remarkedly during the period of manufacture production, as the division between organizer and organized became much clearer. First there appeared workers (purely "organized") at the lower stratum who only engaged in material production, as well as "groups of administrators and manufacture site owners" Shulyatikov asserted that "manufacturing owners are purely organizers"; the unwritten implication here is that **bourgeois philosophy** is the result of the development of this industrial production and structural division. My analysis is that this thought logic may be correct overall, but in Shulyatikov's specific expression of it, he is a hopelessly muddled the issues. We can see that Lenin still does not affirm Shulyatikov's correct overall line of thought, simply criticizing his "nonsense," and thus refuting the similar ideas of Marx and Kautsky. *Lenin notes next to this passage, "not in the same sense as yours"*[10].

Next, Shulyatikov explains the thought of a few representatives of contemporary Western philosophy. In his explanation of Cartesian philosophy, in order to "translate" Descartes' philosophy into "the language of class relations," Shulyatikov accuses the world of Descartes' system of being organized along the lines of a manufacturing enterprise, which caused philosophy to be enslaved to capital. *This expression was a continuation of the traditional philosophical historical assertion that philosophy became the slave of theology in the middle ages.* Shulyatikov believed that a new evaluation on philosophy would have to be easily determined by the recent shifts in the relations between organizers and organized in the manufacturing industry. For instance, the division of labour had caused "the concept of the worker as merely a saddler

9   *Ibid.*, page 452.
10   *Ibid.*, page 452.

or merely a paper-hanger gives way to the concept of the worker in general." According to his earlier assertion that labourers (organized) represented perceptual substance, then the modern proletariat would naturally become a more **abstract** general material. *Here Shulyatikov profoundly proposes the concept of a "generic concept"*[11]. I believe that although this analysis is not accurate enough, it does possess a certain depth of situating logical thought. This is because Marx also trod this road, when profoundly revealing Ricardo's scientific abstract method. Categories such as labour in general and production in general could only be developed on the basis of the division of labour in industrialized production and advanced market exchange by **the objective abstract in relations of economic intercourse**; only after this can the idea of economy in general emerges[12]. I believe that Shulyatikov's line of thought and logical situating orientation here were absolutely the same as Marx's, but his concrete analysis and conclusions were insufficiently precise. *However, Lenin only gives an extremely simple appraisal of Shulyatikov's thought: "Notable. What nonsense!* **The proletariat = matter**"[13]. I have found that Kedrov's related research did not even reach the depth of the philosophical situating that we have identified here. In addition, Shulyatikov directly identifies the generative foundation of mechanical materialism as the 17th century English bourgeoisie, because "the English bourgeoisie were laying the foundations for large-scale capitalist economy... They imagined the whole world in the form of an organization of material particles united in accordance with immanent laws"[14]. Furthermore, he incorporated the materialist thought of "man is a machine" (the French enlightenment philosophers into his framework of "organizer" and "organized.") However, the overall thought logic here is still correct. *Lenin, though, is still opposed to it.*

In Shulyatikov's later discussion on Spinoza, Leibnitz, Beckley, Hume, and others, Lenin did not make many more notations. However, when Shulyatikov writes, "Spinoza's conception of the world is the song of triumphant capital, of all-consuming, all-centralizing capital," Lenin remarks in the margin, "infantile." In fact, Shulyatikov's view here has a certain degree of deep philosophical perspicacity. And when Shulyatikov writes, "Leibnitz's God is the owner of an exemplarily

---

11 *Ibid.*, page 455.
12 See my *Marx Revisited*.
13 Shulyatikov, Vladimir. Justification of Capitalism in Western Philosophy, cited in *The Collected Works of Lenin*, volume 55, page 454-455 (Chin. 2. Ed.).
14 *Ibid.*, page 455.

organized enterprise and is himself the supreme organizer," Lenin's only comment is "phrase-mongering." Here we can see that Lenin's attitude throughout his reading of the entire book was refutational.

Shulyatikov's analysis of German classical philosophy seems to be even more muddled. At one point, his original intention seems to be the assertion that Hegel's dialectics were the "real background" of the manufacturing industry, reflecting the greatest division between the various functions and roles in manufacturing industry. However, Shulyatikov writes, "the ideologist of the manufacturers considers this breaking-up process to be the process of the **internal development** of this or that 'principle'"[15]. As I have already pointed out, the basic logic of Hegel's philosophy was actually a profound theoretical reflection on capitalist modes of production; its essence was the idea that "abstract becomes ruling" in the space of actual commodity-market exchange. In his *Grundrisse*, Marx had also noted this point[16]. The direction of Shulyatikov's analysis here is correct, but his specific line of thought is, as always, muddled. *Lenin's only comment here was his usual "what nonsense."*

In Shulyatikov's section entitled "The Revival of the 'Manufacturing Philosophy,'" he proposes that neo-Kantianism is a new form of the bourgeois world view; in his discussion of empirio-criticism, he clearly points out, "The socio-economic background of the philosophical contest in question was, in this case, the comparatively insignificant difference between the most advanced and the somewhat less advanced types of modern capitalist organizations"[17]. These were evidently correct conclusions. This is also the first point at which Lenin concedes that Shulyatikov makes some "true" points; he uses affirmative notations such as "true" and "correct" in this passage.

At the end of the book, Lenin records the following concluding assessment:

> **The entire book is an example of extreme vulgarization of materialism. Instead of a concrete analysis of periods, formations, ideologies—*empty phrases* about "organizers" and ridiculously strained, absurdly false comparisons. A caricature of materialism in *history*. And it is a pity, for there is an attempt made in the direction of materialism[18].**

---

15   *Ibid.*, page 455.
16   See chapters 1 and 8 of my *Marx Revisited*.
17   Shulyatikov, Vladimir. Justification of Capitalism in Western Philosophy, cited in *The Collected Works of Lenin*, volume 55, page 461 (Chin. 2. Ed.).
18   *Ibid.*, page 464.

I presume that as Lenin read this book, his basic emotional attitude was mistaken. Shulyatikov's basic scholarly position on many important principles was correct, such as his examination of the history of Western philosophy from the perspective of the actual historical progression in the development of social practice, and his opposition to Machism and empirio-criticism (especially his criticism on separating world view from political stance). However, I believe that what we find in Lenin's reading commentaries was not an attitude insisting to find the truth. In addition, Lenin's own philosophical ideas, as well as his Other mirror image from Plekhanov and Dietzgen, were not necessarily any more intelligent than Shulyatikov, the object of his criticism. This is something to which we must pay careful attention. *Kedrov's research of this text is extremely superficial, his examination was over simplified; apart from reproducing Lenin's commentary, it is impossible to see any independent thought in his work.*

2 COMMENTARY ON REY'S *MODERN PHILOSOPHY*

The second book in Lenin's study of Western philosophy was Abel Rey's Modern Philosophy (1908)[19]. In contrast to the critical tone of the last text, Rey claims that he maintains a so-called objective, unbiased neutral stance. In fact, I have found that Rey's stance is based on Machist **relational ontology**. *Of course, Lenin concluded that Rey did have certain elements of materialism; to use Lenin's words, this was "shamefaced materialism."* Interestingly, we can see that here Lenin did not have the same intense refutational impulses that he had towards the previous text; his commentaries are actually quite few. *I believe that this may have been because he had already completed his critique against Machism in Materialism and Empirio-criticism; there he critiqued another book written by Rey: **The Physical Theories of Modern Physicists**. As such, he read this book merely as a supplementary proof of his own theories.* As with Shulyatikov's work, we will descriptively re-create and philosophically situate the thought space of Lenin's reading at this point.

According to Rey, his primary goal in writing this book was to "contrast two points of view: the positive, 'scientific' and the 'pragmatic'"[20].

---

19   **Abel Rey** (1873-1940) was a French positivist philosopher. He was the author of Modern Philosophy (Paris, 1908).
20   Lenin, Vladimir Ilyich. "Remarks on Abel Rey's Modern Philosophy." In *The Collected Works of Lenin*, volume 55, page 465 (Chin. 2. Ed.).

My impression is that Lenin would not have been familiar with this delineation of philosophical factions **outside** of "idealism" and "materialism." As he read the fifth section of the first chapter of this book, Lenin began to remark the author's basis for making this delineation of factions; he separates the factions by their relations to **knowledge** and **action**: in positivism ("dogmatism of science"), "one has to know in order to act: cognition produces action." In pragmatism, on the other hand, "knowledge follows the requirements of action: action produces cognition"[21]. *Lenin wrote "notable" next to this passage. In the second chapter, Lenin comments on the two scientists whom he had dealt with in Materialism and Empirio-criticism: Poincaré and Mach. He referred to these two men as "great scientists" and "pitiful philosophers."* We can see that he was very interested in the attitude of the author towards these two scientists. Two points incited his interest: the author suggesting a relation between Poincaré and Kantianism, and the relation between Machism and rationalism.

The third chapter is primarily a discussion on the problem of matter. Lenin's commentaries show that he thought especially hard on the content of this chapter. We can see that because Rey himself was an idealist, so his discussion on the concept of matter would naturally oppose the materialist conception. As such, in the first section when Rey historically summarizes the problem of matter, he writes "disputes about the reality of the external world…increasingly appear to be an outdated and sterile game which must be left to classic philosophy"22. *This was a kind of theoretical accord reached by modern Western philosophy under the name of rejecting metaphysics.* In the second section, Rey simply and directly justifies the views of Mach, believing that the work of modern physicists had already moved away from the idea of material phenomena and forms in classical mechanics. Rather, new physics surpasses the abstract language of perceptual mathematics in confirming existence itself. As such, this new physics can also be called "**conceptual** physics"[23]. *Lenin underlined these expressions, and in some places double-underlined them.* He also wrote "notable" in the margins. It is interesting to note that here Lenin did not write "nonsense" and other refutational commentaries as he had in the previous text; rather, we do not find any negative commentaries until the fifth and sixth sections of this

21   *Ibid.*, page 466.
22   *Ibid.*, page 476.
23   *Ibid.*, page 479.

chapter: he twice writes the sarcastic comment "ha ha." The first comes when Rey writes, "a natural classification, hence one which reproduces the order of nature"; the other in Rey's "general review" of the problem of matter, when Rey suggests that scientific laws "tell us why and how the given thing is what it is, by what it was conditioned and created, because they analyse the relations on which it depends," concluding that physics studies those relationships[24]. This is an ontological definition. *This relational ontology is the logical basis of Machist philosophy, only this time expressed idealistically by Rey. Another modern idealist master advocating relational ontological logical situating was Heidegger.* Thus Rey believes that because when knowledge is present it depends on these historical relations, therefore the knowledge that we obtain through science is necessarily "relative." I believe that Mach's essential argument, which is based on the relational ontology of perceptual experience, is idealist and incorrect; however, this relational ontology includes extremely important philosophical thought. If it could be linked to Marx's historical practical relations, it would produce extremely deep thought. Lenin does not express clear opposition to this, only writing the underlined marginal note, **"the essence of Rey's agnosticism"**[25]. According to my analysis, Lenin did not understand Marx's complex thought situating circumstance with regards to the practical, historical essence of the problem of consciousness; of course, he would not have known Marx's important definition of consciousness given in *The German Ideology* (consciousness is my relationship with my environment), and thus was certainly unable to see the logical elements of the mistaken **theory of ontological relations** espoused by Rey and Mach. Because the scientific knowledge of a given time period can only be the result of the externally existing, limiting understanding reached by a certain level of social practice, it **cannot** be a **direct reflection** of objective material substance. Thus, the recognition that the object of scientific knowledge is formed by certain theoretical "relation systems" has correct and truthful connotations. Interestingly, when Lenin read of the debate between energetics and mechanics in the seventh section, he noted his agreement in terms of **epistemological logic** next to the assertion by mechanics that the "laws" of energetic could be taken further: "[these laws are] reducible to other, more profound, laws." *In Lenin's later **Bern Notebooks**, he uses Hegelian philosophy to discover this progression of understanding based on practical history in Marxist philosophy thoroughly.*

---

24   *Ibid.*, page 483.
25   *Ibid.*, page 483.

The fourth chapter concerns the problem of life. In this chapter, Rey primarily discusses mechanics and its relation to his theory of "neo-vitalism." At one point, when Rey writes that "nature is of itself one whole," Lenin expresses his wholehearted approval. According to Rey's analysis:

> **Science cannot resolve to consider as isolated for all time the various orders of facts for whose sake it is divided into particular sciences. This division has entirely subjective and anthropomorphic causes. It proceeds solely from the requirements of research which compel the serialization of questions, the concentration of attention on each of them separately, starting with the particular in order to arrive at the general[26].**

This is an extremely profound viewpoint; it is also an understanding space that general philosophical materialist epistemology is unable to attain. In fact, in the context of Marx's thought, this was a problem of **practical logic**. The "anthropomorphic" essence divided by science is the **orderliness** of man in terms of the **progress of historical practice**. In the process of Lenin's later study of Hegelian philosophy, he understood this point through the "practical equation." At this point, Lenin actually draws three vertical lines in the margin of this paragraph, writing the words, "An approach to dialectical materialism"[27]. What was Lenin's true thought process at this point in his theoretical situating? This is a question that has no easy answer.

In the fifth chapter, Rey discusses the problem of mind; in fact, he examines phenomena of the mind from the scope of physiology and psychology. However, Lenin was able to find a few familiar elements in Rey's discussion, including, in the second section, the different views on the foundational nature of the mind in idealism and materialism. *However, in my reading, I have been able to detect subtle indications that Lenin's overall understanding of the new science of psychology was not yet practiced enough. Rey, on the other hand, bases his discussion on a firmer understanding of psychological research. In his examination of a few important theoretical questions, his views very possibly had touched Lenin deeply, to the point that in Lenin's later* **Bern Notebooks**, *he makes frequent mention to psychology when he discusses epistemology and mental phenomena.* In the fourth section

---

26   *Ibid.*, page 493.
27   *Ibid.*, page 493.

of this chapter, Rey focuses on explaining the general characteristics of mental activity. Proceeding from Mach's views, Rey discusses the two relations that men face in empirical activity: the first is an **objective relationship** "independent of our organism and biological activity." This relation is the research object of the natural science. The second type of relation depends intimately on our organism and biological activity; the sum of this type of relations forms "psychological activity." Rey writes that scientists idealistically believe that in studying objective relations, they can eliminate subjective human elements; however, they forget that the foundation of scientific understanding is also human experience. It is this experience that man assumes to be "existing" which may be determined by **some kind of existent relationship**[28]. Because different people have different relations, it is possible for them to develop completely different and even distorted experiences. These expressions include a good deal of very profound thought. *Nearly fifty years later, the British scientist-philosopher Polyani in his* **Personal Knowledge** *analyzed this problem on an ontological level.* At this point in his reading, Lenin suddenly writes in the margin, "experience of socially organized individuals"[29]. Rey did not originally intend to make this point, but rather tended to be more like Bogdanov, whom Lenin criticized. Of course, this could very well have been a new problem that Lenin began to understand at this time. I hypothesize that this new, so-called socially organized individual experience is not a **direct reflection** by man onto external natural material, but rather refers to the different understandings of men determined by different social lives towards external, objective existence. This is certainly a profound understanding. *In Marx's historical materialism, when he writes that "social existence determines consciousness" and social life determines man's ideas, he does not only refer to how external material substance that exists independently apart from man determines his ideas, but rather he expounds how the various historical social relations in men's social existence structurally constrain his ideas.* At the same time, this understanding brings in elements of epistemological value judgment. The fifth section of this chapter examines the important problem of the **unconscious**. However, this section does not spark a great deal of interest in Lenin. This lack of interest continues through the sixth chapter.

---

28   *Ibid.,* page 497.
29   *Ibid.,* page 497.

The seventh chapter discusses problems with which Lenin was familiar: cognition and truth. It is easy for us to see that in the discussion of this sphere of knowledge, Lenin's thought process very noticeably becomes more active. The first point that sparks Lenin's interest is Rey's affirmative discussion on scientific methods in the first section of chapter seven: "Experimental verification...is the criterion of truth"[30]. This is because this view begins to approach the criterion of practice sought in Marxist philosophy. However, as Rey criticizes the so-called pragmatists in the second section, Lenin expresses his own doubt. Rey writes by mind: "Certainly the theory by mind as a mirror of things, and of truth as a copy, is **crudely** superficial. The evolution of scientific truths through all the mistakes which strew the path of science **proves** this"[31]. Here, Lenin first draws three vertical lines, then writes "sic!" and "Ha!". These notations indicate that he doubted the accuracy of the views expressed in this paragraph. However, it is my understanding that Rey's views here are correct. Therefore, I believe that perhaps Lenin's notations indicate another meaning, namely his surprise at seeing such correct views expressed by someone such as Rey. However, what is most difficult to understand is Lenin's commentary in the fourth section. After reading Rey's discussion of "absolute realism," he first uses inverted parantheses to highlight this portion of text, then writes, "absolute realism (=historical materialism)." *These inverted parentheses were an affirmative symbol; in his commentaries on this book, Lenin uses these symbols three times*[32]. Lenin's intentions here are difficult to understand; in particular, what were the connotations of the historical materialism that he brings up here? The equals sign here is obviously inaccurate.

I have found that the most important content of this commentary included Lenin's qualitative judgment of Rey's epistemology in this section: "shamefaced materialism." Rey believed that "truth is the objective," and that the "objective" was made up of the objective relations that exist independent of the cognitive entity. Thus Rey writes that "The objective is the sum-total of the relations which are independent from the observer"[33]. Lenin is obviously in agreement with this expression, because, as we are able to see, he uses the inverted parentheses to make an affirmative notation in the margin. However, when Rey writes, "In

---

30   *Ibid.*, page 502.
31   *Ibid.*, page 503.
32   *Ibid.*, page 478.
33   *Ibid.*, page 502.

practice, it is that which everyone admits, that which is the subject of universal experience, universal agreement, using these words in a scientific sense," Lenin draws four vertical lines in the margin, and he would certainly not agree with such a statement. Lenin writes in the margin, "Rey's theory of cognition = shamefaced materialism"[34]. *This use of the term "shamefaced materialism" is evidently a reference to Lenin's Other mirror-image, in which Engels criticizes agnosticism[35]. In the commentaries of this book, Lenin uses this expression in two other places[36].* Also in this section, I have found that Lenin begins to gradually agree more frequently with Rey; for instance, when Rey writes that the abstraction of scientific truth "aims at discovering the given as it really is, independent from the individuals and circumstances which change it; it aims at **discovering the objective**, the concrete par excellence, the real"; under the words "the objective," Lenin draws three horizontal lines to demonstrate the importance of this concept[37]. Later, as Rey discusses the relation between truth and error, he proposes an "important conclusion": "error is not the absolute antithesis of truth." Rey's argument proceeds thus: error is a "lesser truth," because truth is approached through revealing the subjective aspects of error. Whole truth is always approached through a process of development. "The history of science, moreover, shows us the truth in the **progress** of development; **the truth is not yet formed, but is rather in the process of formation. |Perhaps|** it never will be formed, but it will always be more and more formed."[38] Lenin boxed the word "perhaps" to indicate its importance. In addition, he writes next to this passage: "truth and error (approach to dialectical materialism)"[39]. I believe that this may have been Lenin's highest praise of Rey in his commentaries on this text.

In the eighth (concluding) chapter of this book, Rey did not bring up any views that attracted Lenin's special interest, but rather more clearly demonstrated his idealist essence. In addition, as Lenin read this book, he attempted to make an index of the major problems in the book, including the page numbers where corresponding problems appeared, in

---

34 *Ibid.*, page 505.
35 See Engels' "Ludwig Feuerbach and the End of Classical German Philosophy," in *The Collected Works of Marx and Lenin*, volume 21, page 318.
36 Lenin, Vladimir Ilyich. "Remarks on Abel Rey's Modern Philosophy." In *The Collected Works of Lenin*, volume 55, page 509 (Chin. 2. Ed.).
37 *Ibid.*, page 505.
38 *Ibid.*, page 506.
39 *Ibid.*, page 506.

the margins of an advertisement. However, this index never went beyond page 113[40].

I have noticed that although the Soviet scholar Kedrov studied these commentaries, unfortunately we are unable to find any of Kedrov's own independent cognition or conclusions: he merely regurgitates the points that Lenin makes in his commentaries[41]. According to Kedrov, Lenin's commentaries here were components of creative research, and his reading touched on materialist dialectics and its application in the fields of philosophy and history, as well as in the fields of natural science, religious criticism, and others[42]. I believe that such an appraisal of Lenin's commentaries is quite exaggerated.

3 A BROAD PHILOSOPHICAL RESEARCH SCOPE: READING NOTES ON WESTERN PHILOSOPHY AND SCIENCE

Lenin's study of modern Western philosophy and science began at the end of 1908 and continued until the first half of 1909. In addition to his direct notes on the two major works discussed above, he also left a few other textual reading notes. Most important of these notes was a two-page reading record of his studies in the Sorbonne Library. From these reading notes we can understand that the primary thrust of Lenin's research at this time was on the newest discoveries of modern physics, as well as the newest conclusions of modern philosophy. We arrive at this conclusion because the reading record shows that the texts that Lenin read and borrowed were all new books and periodical essays published around 1908. This demonstrates that Lenin wished to use primary source documents to confirm the basic stances and scientific data he employed in *Materialism and Empirio-criticism*.

The first words of Lenin's reading notes on natural science and philosophy are: "Sorbonne. New books." He then divides his notes into three parts. The first two parts include the books that entered the Sorbonne Library vaults in 1908 on natural science and philosophy; the third part includes new books that entered the vaults in 1909. However, because Lenin was studying at the Sorbonne Library in the first half

---

40   *Ibid.*, page 506.
41   See Kedrov's *Study of Lenin's "Philosophical Notebooks,"* Qiushi Press (1984), pages 137-149 (Chinese).
42   *Ibid.*, page 148-149.

of the year, there were not that many new 1909 books. The first part includes a work by Richard Lucas on radioactivity, Mach's *Grundriss der Physik*, Planck's *Das Prinzip der Erhaltung der Energie*, Riecke's *Handbuch der Physik*, Salignac's *Questions de Physique générale et d'Astronomie*, and Thomson's *Die Korpuskulartheorie der Materie*. All of these books were published in 1908, and the majority of them were in the original German. The second part is made up of philosophical works, including *Vierteiljahrsschrift für wissenschaftliche Philosophie and Archiv für Philosophie* (2te Abteilung). As Lenin read the 1909 edition of *Vierteiljahrsschrift für wissenschaftliche Philosophie*, he noticed a review of Stein's *Philosophische Strömungen der Gegenwart* by Richter. The review motivated him to find Stein's book, which he must have read at least perfunctorily because he writes: "Pages 1-293: Philosophical Trends...Pages 294-445: Philosophical Problems." He then goes into depth on 10 philosophical trends:

Ten trends in philosophy :

1) neo-idealism (voluntarist metaphysics)

2) neo-positivism (pragmatism) of W. James

3) "new movement in natural philosophy" (Ostwald

and the "triumph" of energetics over materialism)

4) "neo-romanticism" (H. St. Chamberlain, etc.)

5) neo-vitalism

6) evolutionism

7) individualism

8) geisteswissenschaftliche Bewegung (Dilthey)

9) philosophiegeschichtliche

10) neo-realism (Eduard von Hartmann!!!)[43].

From this detailed list, I believe that Lenin did not only flip through this book, but rather read it carefully. From this book Lenin began to understand some of the most important philosophical schools of thought that were beginning to gain prominence in the early 20th century, including those of such leading early 20th century philosophers as James, Spencer, Nietzsche, Dilthey, and others. However, I believe that Lenin did not

---

43   Lenin, Vladimir Ilyich. "Remarks on Books on the Natural Sciences and Philosophy in the Sorbonne Library." In *The Collected Works of Lenin*, volume 55, page 329 (Chin. 2. Ed.).

carefully read or study the works of all these various new philosophical trends; rather, he was taken aback by "neo-realism," writing three exclamation points behind Hartmann's name. Next, Lenin lists the titles of a few new books, including Schinz's *Die Wahrheit der Religion nach den neuesten Vertretern der Religionsphilosophie*, Guenther's *Vom Urtier zum Menschen* (an illustrated atlas), Pelazza's **R. Avenarius e l'empiriocriticismo**, and Spaventa's *La filosofia italiana nelle sue relazioni con la filosofia europea*.

In the last part of his notes, Lenin lists a few new books published in 1909, including Boltzman's *Wiener wissenschaftliche Abhandlungen* and Strache's *Die Einheit der Materie, des Weltäthers und der Naturkräfte*. At the very end of his notes, Lenin records a 1908 essay critiquing Mach in the second volume of *Archiv für Philosophie*. Because this was apparently the author's second essay on Mach, Lenin wondered "where is the first?"[44]. We can see that Lenin was still unable to put down Mach.

Lenin's attention to Western philosophy and science was not only evident in his second systematic philosophical study, but also in his third. By that time, although his principal object of study had shifted to Hegel, we are still able to see that he was concerned with the newest developments in Western philosophy and science.

To cite another example, we are also able to find reading notes on research material in Lenin's *1913 Notebook on "Austrian Agricultural Statistics," Etc.* I believe that these books were philosophical texts that Lenin came across in his studies at the Sorbonne Library and which he could not help but pick up and read. My hypothesis is based on the fact that his reading notes are scattered throughout this notebook, including a simple bibliographic list as well as a couple of excerpts. The first two books we find are Raab's *Die Philosophie von R. Avenarius*, and Perrin's *Les atoms*. It is apparent here that Lenin's thinking in *Materialism and Empirio-criticism* continues to influence his research here, because he is unable to forget the mistakes of Mach and his ilk in philosophy and science. Next is a critical book review by Bauer on Plenge's *Marx and Engels*, which introduced Lenin to this work. In his later systematic study of Hegelian philosophy, Lenin carefully studied this book. *In our later discussion, we will examine the excerpts that*

44   *Ibid.*, page 330.

Lenin took from this book. Third, Lenin cites a book review by Sculler published in the April 1913 edition of *Thought* magazine on Perry's book *Present Philosphical Tendencies* (London, 1912). I believe that because positivism approaches materialism in a general sense, Lenin was eager to better understand this school of thought. Perry's book undertakes a comparative analysis of naturalism, idealism, pragmatism, and realism. In his excerpts from this book, Lenin is obviously against Perry, because Perry's stance is idealist. However, Lenin did express interest in one of the views expressed in this book, namely a passage in which Schiller criticizes Perry's view on the relation between the organism and the environment. Here Lenin remarks that the author is opposed to an independently existing environment, rather proposing "the correlation of the mind and its 'environment.'" Lenin's marginal note: "interesting"[45]. Fourth, Lenin notes another book review, this one by Segond on Aliotta's book *The Idealist Reaction against Science.* What interested Lenin in this book was, once again, the evaluation of the thought of Mach and Avenarius. Of course, the book also discusses many new philosophical schools, including neo-Hegelianism, Bergson's intuitionism, Dewey's pragmatism, and the philosophy of values and the historicism of Rickert, Croce, Münsterberg and Royce. It is not difficult to see that by this time, the scope of Lenin's philosophical thought had already broadened immensely.

For a revolutionary philosopher, faced with a complex and challenging real-life struggle, to take the time to systematically study philosophy in this way demonstrates great foresight and courage. These were traits sorely lacking in the great majority of later Marxist practitioners.

---

45   Lenin, Vladimir Ilyich. "Remarks on R. B. Perry's Book Present Philosophical Tendencies." In *The Collected Works of Lenin*, volume 55, page 332 (Chin. 2. Ed.).

CHAPTER FIVE

LENIN'S EXCERPTED NOTES ON FEUERBACHIAN PHILOSOPHY

Around 1909, in Lenin's second systematic study of philosophy, he not only gained an understanding of Western philosophy and science, but also refocused his study of philosophical materialism, because this was the true supporting point of his philosophical theoretical logic situating. The most important object of this research was, of course, the man held by Plekhanov to be an incomparably great materialist philosopher: Feuerbach. Unlike his reading of Dietzgen, in which Lenin only made general commentaries, here Lenin takes careful and comprehensive excerpted notes. An examination of the surviving texts reveals that Lenin primarily recorded two sets of reading excerpts in his study of Feuerbachian philosophy: the excerpted notes on Feuerbach's *Lectures on the Essence of Religion*[1], which we shall examine in this chapter, and his notes on Feuerbach's *Exposition, Analysis, and Critique of the Philosophy of Leibnitz*, which he recorded after his study of Hegelian philosophy during his third systematic study of philosophy. Here, we will first look at the excerpted notes on the first book. Why did Lenin decide to study *Lectures on the Essence of Religion*, volume 8 of *The Collected Works of Feuerbach* at this time? I believe that Lenin most likely read through Feuerbach's other works, and as this book was a

---

1 This book contained the lectures given by Feuerbach in Heidelberg between December 1, 1848, and March 2, 1849. He was forced to speak in the municipal hall because the authorities would not permit him to speak at the university. The basis for Feuerbach's lectures came from his well-known 1845 work *The Essence of Religion*. This text was published in Leipzig in 1851; it was later included in *The Collected Works of Feuerbach*, as volume 8. The version that Lenin read was borrowed from the French Paris National Library, in the original German.

collection of Feuerbach's later, more easily understood discourses, it made sense that Lenin made it the object of his textual research. Past research on Lenin has not paid this important collection of excerpted notes enough attention; though the Soviet scholar Kedrov did touch on the content of this text in his *Study on Lenin's "Philosophical Notebooks,"* his discussion again simply regurgitates Lenin's views with almost no profound conclusions[2]. In this notebook, Lenin used Feuerbach's philosophy to strengthen the important general notions in his own understanding of philosophical materialism. This thinking did not lead to any important changes to the logic structure in Lenin's long held thought space.

1 NATURE AND RELIGION

The first and second lectures in Feuerbach's book primarily explain the background of his lectures, as well as some of his basic thoughts on religious criticism that had already been published in other works. At the beginning of the first lecture, Lenin gives a remark on Feuerbach's slogan of the 1848 Revolution: *"We now want to be political materialists."* *This phrase seemed strange to Lenin, who wrote "sic!" in the margin next to it. We know that Feuerbach's declaration here was targeted at responding to the critique of Marx and Engels that he did not understand the essence of social history, that he did not care for politics. This time, he had already realized that reading and writing were not enough: "we demand that the word become flesh, the spirit matter"[3]. Lenin did not know to what Feuerbach was referring with this statement.* In this lecture, Feuerbach expresses another view that impressed Lenin deeply, *i.e.*, that he fled to the countryside in order to "live with nature," to escape the "god-believing world," and abandon "all extravagant ideas." In the margin here, Lenin writes "down with Überspanntes [extravagant things]"[4]. At the end of this lecture, Feuerbach summarizes his own work, and Lenin noticed that he included one of his books on Leibnitz. *This book would become an object of his reading in his later systematic study of dialectics.*

---

2   See Kedrov's *Study of Lenin's "Philosophical Notebooks,"* Qiushi Press (1984), pages 91-103 (Chinese).
3   Feuerbach, Ludwig. "Lectures on the Essence of Religion," in *Selected Philosophical Works of Feuerbach*, volume 2, The Commercial Press (1984 edition), page 503.
4   Lenin, Vladimir Ilyich. "Conspectus of Feuerbach's Book The Essence of Religion." In *The Collected Works of Lenin*, volume 55, page 38 (Chin. 2. Ed.).

In Lenin's reading through the second lecture, he only focuses on Feuerbach's definition of "sensuousness." Feuerbach describes sensuousness as the unity of material and spiritual; the sensuous is the real. This confuses Lenin, writing "'sensuousness' in Feuerbach" to express his confusion[5]. I feel that Lenin was unable to understand that this so-called sensuousness, this "unity," was actually **practical materialism**, which Marx took as the logical starting point for his new philosophy. Expressed using Marx's words, this is the revolutionary perceptual **activity** that unifies subjective dynamism with the objective object. *Lenin did not profoundly understand practice until he had **read** and **understood** Hegel, and truly grasped the secret of practical dialectics through sensuous practical activity.* We can see that in his process of reading Feuerbachian philosophy, Lenin had always focused on the basic principles and views of **general** materialism. *This focal consciousness in his reading was directly correlated to Plekhanov's philosophical interpretation of Feuerbachian philosophy. Of course, this continually strengthened the philosophical materialist notions in Lenin's own Other mirror image, constructing a continuously returning theoretical logic circuit.*

In the third and fourth lectures, Feuerbach primarily analyzed the historical reason and actual basis of the founding of religion; here Lenin only takes brief excerpts and does not express his own views. I have found that Lenin had little interest for many of the important questions of classical German philosophy. For instance, he skimmed over the question of man and alienation, as well as the question of man's essence, including all ideas related to Feuerbach's humanist philosophical logic. In fact, this was an extremely important part of Feuerbach's philosophy, and especially his religious critical theory. These ideas were also the most important theoretical discourse and theoretical problematics in young Marx's philosophical theoretical situating around 1844. However, Lenin passed right over these concepts, perhaps not understanding them. In fact, these notions were so important for Feuerbach that he directly opened his third lecture with the famous statement: **"theology is humanism"**[6]. For Feuerbach, so-called god is nothing but the deification and inverted alienation of man's essence. In this book, Feuerbach profoundly points out that the secret of theology is

---

5   *Ibid.*, page 38.
6   Feuerbach, Ludwig. "Lectures on the Essence of Religion," in *Selected Philosophical Works of Feuerbach*, volume 2, The Commercial Press (1984 edition), page 518.

in humanism. Whether in terms of its subjective or objective views, what the essence of religion reveals and expresses is always man's essence[7]. In this sense, Feuerbach points out that the history of religion (or godly history) **was** human history; it deceived us in that it was an inverted, idolized history. In fact, this was the central argument of the philosophical thought situating of the entire book. Because he was unable to penetrate Feuerbach's theoretical views here, Lenin was unable to see the significance of this deeper historical philosophy, neither was he able to engage in new thought situating on a higher level of logic in his later opposition to idealism and godly discourse.

It is evident that because of Lenin's **Other mirror image, which came from Plekhanov,** he was unable to see **anything** beyond the philosophical notions of materialism. This was also the result of being latently restricted by a closed theoretical circuit. Here Lenin excerpts one of Feuerbach's phrases: "The being, whom man presupposes ...is **nothing other than nature,** not your God"[8]. Feuerbach clearly points out that his philosophy could be summarized in two words: "nature and man." Of these two, Lenin **only notices** nature. *Perhaps this is one of the historical reasons for why the problem of man was always ignored in the traditional Marxist philosophical interpretive framework.* Feuerbach goes on to write an extremely important expression, that nature is physically and chronologically first but not **morally** first; conscious, rational man is second chronologically but first in terms of rank. It is very clear that Feuerbach's philosophy is humanism, with man as the centre of its logic and nature as merely the foundation. However, Lenin only excerpts the first layer of meaning here. *By now, it is now impossible to miss the logical gaps in Lenin's Other theoretical mirror image.* I believe that here we can already see that Lenin's reading of Feuerbach was **logically selective**; based on his Other mirror image of philosophical materialism, Lenin searched for similar materialist expressions without truly, **phenomenologically** entering the whole of Feuerbach's philosophical logic. This inevitably damaged his research and understanding of Feuerbach. *A similar Other reading logic also appears in the first half of Lenin's **Bern Notebooks**; the difference, however, is that Lenin searched for dialectical "elements" in Hegel's **The Science of Logic** based on his mirror image of philosophical materialism.*

---

7 *Ibid.*, page 520.
8 Lenin, Vladimir Ilyich. "Conspectus of Feuerbach's Book The Essence of Religion." In *The Collected Works of Lenin*, volume 55, page 38 (Chin. 2. Ed.).

In the fourth lecture, Feuerbach opens by stating that the basis of religion is man's "feeling of dependence"[9]. According to Feuerbach, Friedrich Schleiermacher was the first to propose this idea, but that it was attacked by speculative, Hegelian philosophers. Feuerbach concludes that those speculative philosophers "do not construct their notions in accordance with things, but rather construct things according to their notions"[10]. Out of this lecture, Lenin only records this one passage, emphasizing Feuerbach's critique of speculative philosophers. Furthermore, Lenin specifically writes next to this passage, "refer to Marx and Engels." I believe that this context most likely reminded Lenin of Marx and Engels' critique of Hegelian speculative philosophy in *The Holy Family*. In the main text of this lecture, Feuerbach spends a good deal of time discussing the problem of fear, though this did not arouse Lenin's interest.

In the fifth lecture, Feuerbach proposes that it is the fear of death that arouses in man the notions of immortality and deity. He goes on to discuss man's early worship and deification of nature, as well as the "super-naturalism" of monistic religion (Christianity) that denigrates nature. The sixth lecture extends this discussion to animal worship and the worship of other objects. Feuerbach's concluding view is that the substance of man's worship of objects is actually the worship of himself. This was a logical step towards his theory of the **species-essence alienation of god**. Obviously, there was little in these two readings that aroused much interest in Lenin.

Lenin's reading of the seventh lecture seems to have become the **first** high point in his thought on Feuerbach's philosophy. In this lecture, Feuerbach proposes the relation between **egoism** and religion. This was very interesting to Lenin. Feuerbach explains that his egoism was not the selfish, harmful, philistine and bourgeois egoism in a moral sense, but rather **love for oneself in an ontological sense**. U*sing the discourse of psychoanalysis, this is Freud's concept of self-love.* Feuerbach writes that man's love for himself, his love for the essence of humanity, is the motivating force that satisfies and develops all instincts and talents. Without this satisfaction and development, he is not and cannot be a truly complete man[11]. Lenin's reaction to this expression of Feuerbach's

9   Feuerbach, Ludwig. "Lectures on the Essence of Religion," in *Selected Philosophical Works of Feuerbach*, volume 2, The Commercial Press (1984 edition), page 526.
10   *Ibid.*, page 526.
11   *Ibid.*, page 526.

is to write "very important"[12]. Feuerbach also makes another interesting analysis, writing that the love of a specific person or a specific object is always indirect love of oneself. This is because I can only love something that conforms to my thought, to my emotions, and to my essence. *This notion, expressed differently, is similar to Freud's mental image self-love*[13]. Of course, Lenin wrote that this passage was "very important" not because of any interest in Feuerbach's psychoanalysis, but rather as a recognition that this egoism was opposed to "theological hypocrisy, religious and speculative fantasy, political despotism." This was political criticism level of thought.

I have found that beginning with the seventh lecture, Lenin stops marking the divisions between lectures, rather focusing on excerpting the issues he finds important. I believe that this represents an important shift in the circumstances of his reading. Looking at the text of the notebooks, with the exception of a passage on the concept of "energy," Lenin directly skipped the eighth and ninth lectures, only beginning to take excerpts again at the end of the ninth lecture. Lenin's discussion of Feuerbach's concept of "energy" was his first longer discussion in these notes. He writes:

> **Incidentally, on p. 78 Feuerbach uses the expression: Energie, d. h. Thätigkeit [energy is activity]. This is worth noting. There is, indeed, a subjective moment in the concept of energy, which is absent, for example, in the concept of movement. Or, more correctly, in the concept or usage in speech of the concept of energy there is something that excludes objectivity. The energy of the moon (cf.) versus the movement of the moon[14].**

This passage of Lenin's thoughts leaves me extremely confused. For Feuerbach, "energy" primarily refers to dynamism, but Lenin writes that it possesses subjective elements. The concept of movement, however, has no subjectivity; in other words, the concept of energy includes something that excludes objectivity, which seems to suggest that energy is a subjective concept. However, later on, Lenin goes on to mention the "energy of the moon." It does not seem possible to reconcile these two

---

12   Lenin, Vladimir Ilyich. "Conspectus of Feuerbach's Book The Essence of Religion." In *The Collected Works of Lenin*, volume 55, page 40 (Chin. 2. Ed.).

13   Refer to page 311 of my *The Truth (the Impossible): Reflection of Lacan's Philosophy,* Commercial Press (2006).

14   Lenin, Vladimir Ilyich. "Conspectus of Feuerbach's Book The Essence of Religion." In *The Collected Works of Lenin*, volume 55, page 40 (Chin. 2. Ed.).

ideas. Nevertheless, this energy that excludes subjectivity may have share some similarities with his Practical Idea that "destroys existence" in the latter stages of Lenin's study of Hegelian philosophy.

2 MATERIALISM, OR MATERIALISM

We have already seen that Lenin's ultimate motive in studying Feuerbach was still philosophical materialism. Hence, in his excerpts from Feuerbach's *Lectures on the Essence of Religion*, we see that Lenin continues to focus on Feuerbach's excellent expressions on materialism. *Feuerbach's materialist notions, combined with Dietzgen's thought, formed the most important philosophical materialist foundation of Lenin's thought at this time. They also formed the foundational Other mirror image of all of his philosophical thought at this time.*

First, Lenin accorded a great deal of attention to Feuerbach's exposition of the primary nature of **natural material** existence, the philosophical precondition. On page 107 of the original text, Lenin excerpted this line from Feuerbach: "...Nature is a primordial, primary and final being..." Later, after flipping through a few more pages, Lenin recorded Feuerbach's argument that sensuousness is primary, emphasizing in a marginal note: "the sensuousness =the primary, the self-existing and true"[15]. It is evident that Lenin was especially interested in the **general principles of philosophical materialism** that Feuerbach introduced in his discussion of the problem of religion. Lenin reminded himself that Feuerbach was taking sensuousness to be the "philosophical starting point." On page 114 of the original text, Lenin excerpts another expression from Feuerbach that contains the same meaning: "Nature= the primary, underivable primordial being." Thus we can see that the primary focal point of Lenin's reading at this time was his search for Feuerbach's general materialist premise; Lenin still attempted to use this premise to fashion his own basic critique of Machism.

Of course, Lenin was also aware that although Feuerbach's materialism was directly perceivable and moving, it was not truly scientific thought. *His Other reference system here was Engels.* On page 116, in the 11th lecture, Lenin wrote as he read Feuerbach's definition of the natural world: "It turns out that nature=everything except the supernatural. Feuerbach is brilliant but not profound. Engels defines more

---

15 *Ibid.*, page 40.

profoundly the distinction between materialism and idealism"[16]. In fact, Feuerbach's explanation of nature was designed to illustrate the differences heterogeneity between his approach to nature and that of Spinoza. Feuerbach's attitude was clear refutation of nature as a deified, supernatural, abstract thing. Later, he went on to list a large number of concrete, sensuous things. For Lenin, this was not a comprehensive analysis. *The mirror image reflected in Lenin's theoretical thought space at this time came from the concise basic philosophical questions and answers in Engels' **On Feuerbach**.* In the latter half of the eleventh lecture, Feuerbach primarily discusses deity and theology, polytheism and monotheism, etc.

Second, Lenin confirmed Feuerbach's philosophical qualification of **objectivity**. At the very end of the eleventh lecture, Lenin read Feuerbach's discussion of abstract concepts. In response to Hegel's practice of objectifying ideas, Feuerbach retorts that "no objective validity and existence, no existence outside ourselves" can be accorded to abstractions[17]. Lenin astutely seizes upon Feuerbach's refutational explanation here, writing in the margin, "objective = outside ourselves"[18]. Entering the twelfth lecture, Feuerbach continues to discuss the foundational character of nature, going so far as to criticize the godly world as inverted because it departs from nature; he proposes that god is abstracted nature. We know that this view complimented his earlier lecture on the theory that **man is god**. For Feuerbach, godliness was nothing but the abstract result of diverse objectively existing attributes. He writes that all godly attributes those that are not borrowed from man, are derived from nature. For instance, power, eternity, limitlessness, and generality all originate from abstractions of man and natural existence. Thus godliness is nothing more than the abstract collection of all the essential, the perfect[19]. Feuerbach's view here is quite profound. However, Lenin did not focus on Feuerbach's critique of religion at this time, rather devoting all his energy to comprehending materialist views.

---

16   *Ibid.*, page 42.
17   Feuerbach, Ludwig. "Lectures on the Essence of Religion," in *Selected Philosophical Works of Feuerbach*, volume 2, The Commercial Press (1984 edition), page 599.
18   Lenin, Vladimir Ilyich. "Conspectus of Feuerbach's Book The Essence of Religion." In *The Collected Works of Lenin*, volume 55, page 42 (Chin. 2. Ed.).
19   Feuerbach, Ludwig. "Lectures on the Essence of Religion," in *Selected Philosophical Works of Feuerbach*, volume 2, The Commercial Press (1984 edition), page 605.

This continued until the thirteenth lecture, where Feuerbach begins to discuss the evil god in theology and proposes the new view that the spirit of god was nothing but a world in **thought**. The world should be the existential sum of man and nature, and when men suppose god to have an existence outside of themselves, in fact they rebut the objectivity of the natural existence that **does not depend on our thought**. After reading this point, Lenin writes: "being outside ourselves = independent of thought"[20]. Lenin continues to focus on objectivity. Lenin realizes here that a qualification of objective existence is a characteristic that is **independent of human thought**. Looking at the matter more deeply, this objective qualification of philosophical materialism was a qualification that had not passed through historical materialist reflection. I say this because, objectivity in social historical existence and development is objective matter independent of human thought, not objective social relationship structures and practical laws of activity that depend on the will of individuals. After the Second International, this point, originally made by Marx, was mistakenly interpreted as natural process that is independent of **human** will. This is a more complex theoretical problem[21]. Lenin goes on to excerpt Feuerbach's exposition of time and space premised on objective existence.

Third, Lenin recognizes Feuerbach's materialist **epistemology**. At the beginning of the fourteenth lecture, Feuerbach discusses the relation between the concept of species and individual existence. He profoundly points out that many general concepts, arbitrarily deified by Plato and Hegel, were certainly not essence unto themselves, but rather expressions or qualifications of individuality. Abstract **species** concepts were premised on the sensuous existence of **individual** human subsistence, not the other way around[22]. In fact, the connotations of this argument begin to approach historical dialectical thought; however, in Lenin's Other mirror image at this time, it was difficult to develop enough logical understanding to astutely grasp new and more profound things outside the realm of philosophical materialist concepts, and thus Lenin only excerpted one small fragment of Feuerbach's exposition. After excerpting

20   Lenin, Vladimir Ilyich. "Conspectus of Feuerbach's Book The Essence of Religion." In *The Collected Works of Lenin*, volume 55, page 44 (Chin. 2. Ed.).

21   Refer to the introduction and third chapter of my work *The Subjective Dimension of Marxist Historical Dialectics*, Nanjing University Press (2002).

22   Feuerbach, Ludwig. "Lectures on the Essence of Religion," in *Selected Philosophical Works of Feuerbach*, volume 2, The Commercial Press (1984 edition), page 626.

a passage by Feuerbach on the determinism of nature, Lenin's interest was aroused in another of Feuerbach's epistemological views. In discussing the intimate relation between inorganic and organic things in the natural world, Feuerbach points out that man's existence was mutually dependent on the outside world: the existence of man comes about because of the influence of all of nature. Here Feuerbach poses a question: "If man had more senses, would he discover more things in the world?" Feuerbach's own answer was certainly negative. He writes that "Man has just as many senses as are necessary for him to conceive the world in its totality, in its entirety"[23]. It is evident that Lenin was in agreement with Feuerbach's view here, first repeating Feuerbach's question and answer, and then boxing in the words, "important against agnosticism"[24]. Lenin even underlined these words three times. It is obvious that Lenin thoroughly enjoyed Feuerbach's intelligent expression of this concept.

Furthermore, in the fifteenth lecture, Feuerbach uses some of the chemistry knowledge that he was able to understand at the time to criticize Liebig. Lenin writes in the margin: "Feuerbach and natural science!! NB. Cf. Mach and Co. today"[25]. Lenin's thinking point here was the fact that Mach, Bogdanov, and others had developed natural science into the foundation of a new mutation of idealism, while Feuerbach had intimately linked natural scientific progress with materialism. Lenin obviously believes that Feuerbach's path is the correct one. However, Lenin was unable to see at this time that man's deeper understanding of the character of nature would only come as the **level of historical practice** grew deeper and more developed as well. He would, however, come to profoundly understand this point later on.

Finally, Lenin remarked Feuerbach's materialist views on the essence of psychological phenomena. In the sixteenth lecture, Feuerbach primarily discusses the question of how religion exerts influence; Lenin did not excerpt from this lecture. It was in the seventeenth lecture, where Feuerbach discussed psychological phenomena, that Lenin did become interested. Feuerbach concedes that psychological phenomena are not simply produced by natural matter. He writes that a professor, a "state councillor," cannot be explained directly by natural existence. *Here Lenin writes that Feuerbach's expression is "witty."* The spirit or

---

23   *Ibid.*, page 630.
24   Lenin, Vladimir Ilyich. "Conspectus of Feuerbach's Book The Essence of Religion." In *The Collected Works of Lenin*, volume 55, page 46 (Chin. 2. Ed.).
25   *Ibid.*, page 46.

psyche developed relatively late in the process of man's social histori-cal development. It is a human activity, the highest activity of man, a mark of the difference between man and animal. Nevertheless, spirit does not thus become the primary thing in nature[26]. Feuerbach argues that though spiritual phenomena are higher, they develop in accordance with man's body and senses. Furthermore, its activity is dependent on the human brain, this material organ: "Mental activity is also a bod-ily activity." Ultimately, the human brain is a product of nature. Lenin obviously agrees with Feuerbach here, writing in the margin: "Refer to Dietzgen"[27]. *Feuerbach plus Dietzgen formed the most important logi-cal support for Lenin's philosophical materialism.*

3 "A GERM OF HISTORICAL MATERIALISM"

By the eighteenth lecture, Feuerbach's discussion extended into social life. He transfers the debate between nature and god into the compara-tive context of despotism vs. constitutional monarchy, of Eastern man vs. Western man. *This may have been a shift in Feuerbach's thought process after Marx criticized him for not focusing enough on political issues.*

Feuerbach writes that in the past, all good things in man's life and exist-ence were attributed to god, while all the bad things were attributed to the devil. In contrast, he argues that the life of any individual is only the product of a **certain** social environment. The good things done by a man cannot come completely from his own will, but are a function of the social and natural conditions that form him and educate him. He is the result of relationships and environment[28]. *This is very profound thought.* Feuerbach even goes on to point out that god is nothing but a personification of the relations in which man is born, lives, and acts. This is also a very profound theoretical insight. Feuerbach has already seen that man can only be the **product of a certain epoch**. He even includes himself in this assessment, writing that he is a "nineteenth

---

26 Feuerbach, Ludwig. "Lectures on the Essence of Religion," in *Selected Philosophical Works of Feuerbach*, volume 2, The Commercial Press (1984 edition), page 657.
27 Lenin, Vladimir Ilyich. "Conspectus of Feuerbach's Book The Essence of Religion." In *The Collected Works of Lenin*, volume 55, page 47 (Chin. 2. Ed.).
28 Feuerbach, Ludwig. "Lectures on the Essence of Religion," in *Selected Philosophical Works of Feuerbach*, volume 2, The Commercial Press (1984 edition), page 665.

century man," and that man essentially belongs to a certain time period:

> **Thus we see that through my self-activity, my work, and the effort of my will, no matter what kind of man I become, I become that man through my relationships with this nation, this region, this world, and this nature. I will always exist within these environments, these relations, these circumstances, and the events that constitute the contents of my biography[29].**

Feuerbach even goes on to use the term "social relations." Though in 1848 Feuerbach was not aware of Marx's Theses on Feuerbach and The German Ideology, his arguments here are already quite similar to those of historical materialism. *In fact, as early as his 1841 **The Essence of Christianity**, Feuerbach had already proposed that man's consciousness is the product of culture, writing that it was the product of human society[30]. Likewise, in the text on which Feuerbach's lectures was based, **The Essence of Religion** (1845), he writes a surprising expression: "That on which on certain man, a certain nation, or a certain tribe relies is not general nature, not the land in general, but rather the land in this place; it is not water in general, but rather the water at this place, this river, this well"[31]. The essence of man lies in his "national character," for instance, an Indian person who leaves India is no longer Indian. Here his view is even more profound.*

The ever-observant Lenin remarks that Feuerbach's thought here contains "a germ of historical materialism." In his comments on the eighteenth lecture, Lenin first uses six vertical lines in the margin to indicate importance, then boxes the words: "*213* in the middle and *215* in the middle 'natural' und 'civil' world." He then writes in the margin "a germ of historical materialism"[32]. This was an extremely important commentary.

In the second part of the nineteenth lecture, Feuerbach declares that he has terminated the first part of his discussion, demonstrating that nature

---

29   *Ibid.*, page 667.
30   Feuerbach, Ludwig. "The Essence of Christianity," in *Selected Philosophical Works of Feuerbach*, volume 2, The Commercial Press (1984 edition), page 437 (Chinese).
31   Feuerbach, Ludwig. "Lectures on the Essence of Religion," in *Selected Philosophical Works of Feuerbach*, volume 2, The Commercial Press (1984 edition), page 437.
32   Lenin, Vladimir Ilyich. "Conspectus of Feuerbach's Book The Essence of Religion." In *The Collected Works of Lenin*, volume 55, page 48 (Chin. 2. Ed.).

is the foundation of religion. He also writes that it is his intention to explain "man's spirit" as expressed in the spirit of religion. In other words, Feuerbach's intention here was to shift his study from nature to the question of human existence. In this domain, Lenin's thought was, of course, much deeper than Feuerbach's, and so it is not surprising that Lenin was not interested in this portion of Feuerbach's discussion.

Beginning with the twentieth lecture, Feuerbach begins to discuss fetishisms, a topic which did not spark Lenin's interest. *We all know that Marx's famous critical theory of the three great economic fetishisms in capitalism was actually influenced and inspired by Feuerbach's critical views on religion. As we have already discussed, Lenin did not focus on this important theory in his study of Marx's economic works. Thus is not surprising that he would not remark a similar version of this fetishism theory put forth by Feuerbach in his critique of theology.* Lenin goes on to excerpt Feuerbach's assertion that "religion is poetry." In this lecture, Feuerbach makes two other important points, namely his critical analyses of idol worship and icon worship[33], neither of which interested Lenin. The reason for this lack of interest is simple: Lenin's Other mirror image theoretical circuit did not contain any corresponding elements.

In the twenty-first lecture, Feuerbach continues his explanation that in addition to idol worship, another important source of god is man's imagination. The twenty-second lecture focuses on man's pursuit of emotion and the basis of theology. The twenty-third lecture begins to touch on "practical purpose." For Feuerbach, human society was still in its youth, mired in ignorance and helplessness. Under the pressure of life's necessities, man kneels before god, demanding that god complete those things that he himself is unable to do in real life. Therefore, "what later became the object of man's self-activity, all of culture, was, at the beginning, the object of religion."[34] Lenin did not excerpt these elements of Feuerbach's discussion, simply giving an overview of Feuerbach's viewpoints in these lectures.

In several of his later lectures, Feuerbach goes on to discuss topics such as man's special organs, miracles, resurrection, ideals, and immortality.

---

33 Feuerbach, Ludwig. "Lectures on the Essence of Religion," in *Selected Philosophical Works of Feuerbach*, volume 2, The Commercial Press (1984 edition), page 690-691.

34 *Ibid.*, page 711.

In the last lecture (the thirtieth) he writes that God "is the fulfiller, or the reality, of the human desires for happiness, perfection, and immortality." The essence of godliness is not man's actual desires, but rather "imaginary desires"[35]. This desire is the true meaning of god, and as such, if god is taken away from man, he loses his carnal heart. This is also a very profound view. However, we can see that Lenin did not care at all for Feuerbach's theoretical analysis of the essence of religion, rather continuing his search for materialist views. Interestingly enough, what Lenin finds in Feuerbach's last lecture is socialism! Lenin writes that the last lecture, "could be put forward almost in its entirety as a typical example of an enlightening atheism with a socialist tint (concerning the mass that suffers want, etc., p. 365 middle), etc."[36].

In Lenin's "Additions and Notes" section after the main body of text, he again mentions Feuerbach's "germ of historical materialism," mainly in a long explanatory note on the fifth lecture. Lenin writes, "Here there are many details, quotations, which contain repetitions. I pass over all that. I note only the most important of that which affords some interest: the basis of morality is egoism"[37]. Interestingly enough, at the end of all his excerpts, Lenin once again notices the social historical thought in Feuerbach's philosophy, and especially its historical materialist connotations. Next to Feuerbach's concrete discussion of egoism, Lenin writes, "a bud (Зацаток) of historical materialism." He had previously used "germ" (Зародыш). When Lenin came across another important passage of Feuerbach's in the "Notes" section, he was extremely moved. He first excerpted Feuerbach's words:

> **One has only to cast a glance at history! Where does a new epoch in history begin? Only wherever an oppressed mass or majority makes its well-justified egoism effective against the exclusive egoism of a nation or caste, wherever classes of men (sic![38]) or whole nations, by gaining victory over the arrogant self-conceit of a patrician minority, emerge into the light of historical glory out of the miserable obscurity of the proletariat. So, too, the egoism of the now oppressed majority of mankind must and will obtain its rights and found a new epoch in history[39].**

---

35 *Ibid.*, page 777.
36 Lenin, Vladimir Ilyich. "Conspectus of Feuerbach's Book The Essence of Religion." In *The Collected Works of Lenin*, volume 55, page 51 (Chin. 2. Ed.).
37 *Ibid.*, page 52.
38 This was written by Lenin.
39 Lenin, Vladimir Ilyich. "Conspectus of Feuerbach's Book The Essence of Religion." In *The Collected Works of Lenin*, volume 55, page 55 (Chin. 2. Ed.).

Next to this line of text, Lenin wrote "NB" twice, and then the words, "A bud of historical materialism, see Chernyshevsky." A little farther down he writes: "NB, Feuerbach's 'socialism.'"[40] At the end of this passage, "These lectures were delivered from 1.XII.1848 to 2.III.1849 (Preface, p. V), and the preface to the book is dated 1.I.1851. How far, **even** at **this time** (1848-1851), **had** Feuerbach **lagged behind Marx** (*The Communist Manifesto* 1847, *Neue Rheinische Zeitung*, etc.) and **Engels** (1845: *Lage*)"[41].

At the end of his reading, Lenin reaches the conclusion that "the term 'the anthropological principle' in philosophy, used by Feuerbach and Chernyshevsky, is **narrow**. Both the anthropological principle and naturalism are only inexact, weak descriptions of **materialism**"[42]. This was the object of his theoretical research. Of course, though it is not incorrect to refer to humanism (anthropology) as an inexact expression of materialism, so doing is nothing but an expression of the old materialist conception of history. This is because its underlying logic is still a **latently idealist conception of history**. Lenin was naturally unable to understand this point at this time.

At the end of the notes, Lenin touches on the ninth volume of the Collected Works of Feuerbach, which includes Feuerbach's 1857 *Theology*. According to Lenin, there is nothing of interest in that work besides parts 34 and 36[43]. With this statement Lenin concluded his study of Feuerbach's philosophy. *We should point out that in his third systematic study of philosophy, Lenin once again considered and read the works of Feuerbach. However, Feuerbach and his philosophical materialism were not the focus of Lenin's attention during that study.*

---

40   *Ibid.*, page 52.
41   *Ibid.*, page 53.
42   *Ibid.*, page 58.
43   *Ibid.*, page 59.

CHAPTER SIX

RUSSIAN THINKERS: STILL MATERIALISM

As we have previously indicated, at around 1909 the emphasis of Lenin's second philosophical study was still philosophical materialism. In addition to his focus on Feuerbach, he also examined two Russian philosophers, Deborin and Chernyshevsky. Lenin's understanding of Deborin was realized through reading and interpreting one of his philosophical treatises. As for Chernyshevsky, Lenin read two works about him by other philosophers. During this systematic materialist philosophical study, Lenin also leaves a rich collection of reading notes. In this chapter we will turn our attention to these commentaries as we attempt to understand the important progress of Lenin's grasp of materialist philosophy.

1 MATERIAL SUBSTANTIVE ONTOLOGY: COMMENTARY ON DEBORIN'S DIALECTICAL MATERIALISM

I have found that Lenin's attitude must have appeared extremely serious and intolerant to people who shared similar views, because at this time he had already begun to think of himself as somebody who more deeply understood the basic viewpoints of Marxist philosophy. As such, when he came across scholars who discussed Marxist philosophy, he would criticize them unmercifully. This was the case in his reading of Deborin's Dialectical Materialism around 1909. *We already know that Deborin was a fairly influential Marxist philosopher in Russia at the time, but that in terms of politics, he was a* **Menshevik**. Deborin's article Dialectical Materialism was published in St. Petersburg, in the collection Na Rubezhe. I believe that in this article, Deborin's understanding of Marxist philosophy does not surpass the basic logic of old materialism. As Lenin read this text, his most common reaction to Deborin's analysis is negative and sarcastic.

At the beginning of the article, Deborin first discusses the pessimism of Schopenhauer's death philosophy, attempting to point out that his was an optimistic life philosophy. He then goes on to provide philosophical explanations of cognition, arguing that cognition is one of the tools by which man rules nature[1]. Lenin makes no comment on these views.

Deborin writes that dialectical materialism as a world view "provides an answer of to the question of the structure of matter of the world." This is, of course, a non-scientific explanation. Lenin writes in the margin, "inexact"[2]. I have found that later, when this article was included in Deborin's collection Philosophy and Politics, this passage, which had been criticized by Lenin, was not there. Deborin remarked that Lenin's commentaries primarily touched on the inexactness of the terminology of individual problems, as well as the obtuseness of philosophical language. Essentially Lenin did not see that I had already departed from Marxism. As I edited this book, I of course considered Lenin's opinions[3]. In other words, Deborin deleted some of the passages that Lenin

---

1 Deborin, Abram. "Dialectical Materialism," in *Philosophy and Politics*, Beijing Sanlian Press (volume I), page 88 (Chinese).

2 Lenin, Vladimir Ilyich. "Remarks on Books: A Deborin, Dialectical Materialism." In *The Collected Works of Lenin*, volume 55, page 516 (Chin. 2. Ed.).

3 Deborin, Abram. "Dialectical Materialism," in *Philosophy and Politics,* Beijing Sanlian Press (volume I), page 4 of the introduction (Chinese).

criticized. It is not difficult for us to see that the majority of Russian Marxists at the time still had an inexact understanding of Marxist philosophy. This situation was related to Plekhanov's imprecise explanation of Marxist philosophy. In a certain sense, Plekhanov constructed the Other mirror image that influenced all Russian Marxists. Deborin himself wrote that the purpose of his article was to discuss the "epistemological problems" of dialectical materialism. *This was likely the reason behind Lenin's careful reading of this article. Cognition and epistemology were philosophical questions to which Lenin accorded a great deal of attention at this point in time.* Deborin first summarizes the general developmental track of human cognition from prehistoric times until modern philosophy. I believe that even in his basic expressions Deborin was insufficiently professional and precise. We can see that at that time, empiricism had a great influence on the realm of Russian philosophical research, because Deborin's argument revolves around the question of **a priori-experience-sensation**.

It is interesting that in this narration of the history of philosophy, Hegelian philosophy, and in particular his dialectic, became the focus of Deborin's discussion. This study of Hegel took up nearly three pages of Deborin's text. In this discussion of Hegelian dialectics, Deborin primarily elucidated the essential differences between Hegel's dialectic and the materialist dialectic, as well as the basic logic structures of these two dialectics: the alternation of internal contradiction, and historical self-movement. Here, Deborin specifically introduces Engels' expression of Hegel's dialectics, the question of inversion. *This was a question in which Lenin was keenly interested in his **Bern Notebooks**. At the beginning, it was only one of the Other mirror image support points for Lenin's reading, but it was later deepened into an extremely profound understanding of the practical dialectics of Hegel and Marx.* However, Lenin did not seem to be particularly interested in this point, making only one small mark in the margin next to this passage. At the same time, Lenin underlined one of the phrases in this passage, but it did not concern Hegel, but rather Deborin's summary of the philosophies of Hume, Kant, and Fichte.

I have found that the worst thing about this article was Deborin's explanation of the epistemology of dialectical materialism. Deborin believed that dialectical materialism viewed nature as a directly observable whole, while mathematics and geometry were the observable results of universal, actual existence. This is certainly not Marx's philosophical language. Deborin writes:

> **Man *cognizes* to the extent that he *acts* on, and he himself is subject to *the action of, the external world.* Dialectical materialism teaches that man is impelled to reflect chiefly by the sensations he experiences as he acts on the external world... Proceeding from the consideration that it is possible to dominate nature only by submitting to her, dialectical materialism calls upon us to coordinate our activity with the universal laws of nature, with the necessary order of things, with the universal laws of development of the world[4].**

This critically important passage is reflective of his central argument, demonstrating that Deborin and Plekhanov were in the same, homogeneous theoretical circuit of philosophical materialism; in essence, the dialectical materialism that they understood was old materialism. At this time, Deborin was still unable to see the **practical historical essence** of the epistemology of Marxist philosophy. For this reason, Deborin necessarily joins with Dietzgen and Plekhanov in interpreting Marxist philosophy as a **theory of epistemological passivity**. This is evidenced in his assertion that the depth of a person's cognition is determined by the influence of the external world on the thinking subject. On the other hand, we know that for Marx and Engels, "it is precisely **the alteration of nature** by men, not solely nature as such, which is most essential and immediate basis of human thought"[5]. However, once this historical, practical relationship enters Deborin's scope of understanding, it becomes an external relationship in which nature acts on man and man acts on nature. Furthermore, when Deborin discusses man's influence on the world, he simplifies the epistemological basis into feeling. I do not believe that Lenin at this time would have directly refuted this fundamental error of Deborin's. Next to this passage, Lenin actually draws three vertical lines to indicate that it was important. *Objectively speaking, Lenin did not truly understand Deborin's underlying epistemological errors until his later study of Hegelian philosophy. In Plekhanov's Fundamental Problems of Marxism, which Lenin had just read, he came across the following expression: "According to Feuerbach, our 'I' cognizes the **object by coming under its action**. Marx, however,*

---

4   *Ibid.*, page 98.
5   See Engels, Frederick. Dialectics of Nature, "Notes and Fragments." *Collected Works of Marx and Engels*, volume 20, page 573-574 (Chin. 1. Ed.).

objects by saying: our 'I' cognizes the object, while at the same time acting upon that object[6]. Looking at the whole of Plekhanov's theoretical logic at this time, this was an expression that just happened to be correct, because it did not change his ultimate theory of geographical determination.

After discussing the dialectical views of such ancient Greek philosophers as Parmenides and Heraclitus, Deborin summarizes all of Western philosophical history using the historical, logical thread of rationalism, empiricism, and perceptualism. Next, Deborin concentrates on the discussion of 17th and 18th century French materialist philosophy. In summary, his understanding was still imprecise. On the one hand, Deborin classifies French materialism as "metaphysical materialism," identifying the mistake of their philosophy in its being a substantively unchanging theory (metaphysical elements) and a theory of incognisability (incognisable elements). Marx and Engels, on the other hand, as well as the "outstanding" dialectical materialist Plekhanov, all revealed the "superficiality" of this metaphysical materialism[7]. Deborin goes on to directly cite a lengthy passage from Plekhanov. *In this text, Deborin cites Plekhanov as an authoritative source on the level of Marx and Engels; Feuerbach also gets this treatment. All of this was derived from the Other mirror images and inevitable theoretical circuits in Deborin's own thought space.* Thus, according to Plekhanov, Deborin identified the mistake of French materialism as the antithesis between Kant's thing-in-itself and the phenomenological world; in other words, "the metaphysically absolute antithesis of the 'immanent' to the 'transcendental'"[8]. *Plekhanov's original expression was "the being of matter is not divorced from its essence"[9].* Lenin was very dissatisfied with Deborin's explanation, writing in the margin: "rot!" and "this is a muddle." I believe that Lenin's commentary here does no injustice to Deborin's views.

It is not difficult to see that whenever Deborin tries to explain Marxist philosophy in a holistic way, he invariably made mistakes. For instance, when he discusses the ontological basis of dialectical materialism, he

---

6 Plekhanov, Georg. 1957. *Fundamental Problems of Marxism*. People's Press, pages 10-11 (Chinese).
7 Deborin, Abram. "Dialectical Materialism," in *Philosophy and Politics*, Beijing Sanlian Press (volume I), page 104 (Chinese).
8 *Ibid.*, page 102.
9 *Ibid.*, page 104.

writes, "Dialectical materialism puts material substance, the real substratum, at the basis of being"[10]. It is well known that taking material substance as the basis of existence is a general premise of philosophical materialism; however, this view was precisely what Marx's philosophical revolution **directly aimed at refuting**. For instance, in the first thesis in Marx's *Theses on Feuerbach*, Marx criticizes Feuerbach's old materialist philosophy for understanding the world as sensuous substance. In fact, though the *Theses on Feuerbach* had already been published by this time, they did not arouse the interest of Russian Marxist philosophers; on the contrary, in Deborin's text, Feuerbach's philosophical materialist views are taken positively and cited throughout. *We can see that although Lenin was very hard on Deborin, he did not make any commentaries refuting this passage of text. Rather, he used a series of criss-crossing diagonal lines and the letters "NB" to indicate his attention. This is a revelatory detail; we can deduce that Lenin's views at this time did not exceed Deborin's understanding. It is actually quite likely that some of Deborin's thoughts may have latently strengthened Lenin's Other mirror image.* Thus Deborin agrees with Plekhanov's definition of matter "as the totality of things-in-themselves, since these things are the source of our sensations"[11]. Much like Plekhanov at this time, Deborin did not realize that the starting point of Marx's philosophical revolution was *historical practice*; after recognizing the basic stance of general materialism, Marx went on to assert that man's cognition did not directly originate from external matter divorced from man, but was rather based on the **sensory actions and relations by which men change the external world.**

Furthermore, Lenin was very much opposed to Deborin's constant use of the expressions and terminology of Western bourgeois philosophy in his explanation of dialectical materialism. Next to a passage by Deborin including such terms as "immanent," "transcendental," and "subjective other-sidedness," Lenin writes in the margin, "Correct truths are outlined in a diabolically pretentious, abstruse form. Why did Engels not write such gibberish?"[12]. Lenin's criticism is certainly germane.

---

10   *Ibid.*, page 105.
11   From Lenin's "Remarks on Books: A Deborin, Dialectical Materialism." In *The Collected Works of Lenin*, volume 55, page 521 (Chin. 2. Ed.).
12   *Ibid.*, page 521.

The conclusion of Deborin's text reads thus:

> **Dialectical materialism proceeds from the *recognition of things-in-themselves* or the external world or *matter*. 'Things-in-themselves' are cognizable. The unconditional and absolute is rejected by dialectical materialism. Everything in nature is in the process of change and motion, which are based on definite combinations of matter. According to dialectics, one "form" of being changes into another through leaps. Modern theories of physics, far from disproving, fully confirm the correctness of dialectical materialism[13].**

It is my opinion that this was likely the basis for the fundamental logic in later Soviet textbooks. However, although Lenin did not seem to think much of Deborin, he did not oppose these empty dogmatic expressions, because they were basically identical to his views in *Materialism and Empirio-criticism*. *In October 1930, when **Mitin** engaged Deborin in philosophical debate, he directly cited Lenin's commentaries of this text; however, his assessment carried an overly heavy ideological emphasis[14].*

2 UNDERSTANDING CHERNYSHEVSKY

Lenin was likely very familiar with the philosophical materialism of his compatriot, Chernyshevsky. *According to relevant records, Lenin once said that he first came into contact with philosophical materialism, Hegelian philosophy, and dialectical thought through Chernyshevsky[15].* After writing *Materialism and Empirio-criticism*, Lenin went on to write a supplemental text, "From What Angle did N.G. Chernyshevsky Criticize Kantianism," including it as a supplement to section one of the fourth chapter of his book. In late 1909, Lenin sent to A.I. Ulyanova-Yelizarova, who was in charge of the publication of *Materialism and Empirio-criticism*. She decided to include the text at the very end of Lenin's book. In this text, Lenin primarily analyzes the introduction to the third edition of Chernyshevsky's 1888 text *The Aesthetic Relation of Art to Reality* (this edition was released in 1906). Lenin refers to Chernyshevsky as a

---

13   Deborin, Abram. "Dialectical Materialism," in *Philosophy and Politics,* Beijing Sanlian Press (volume I), page 116 (Chinese).

14   See Mitin's Our Philosophical Differences, in *Selected Works of the Deborin School*, Jilin People's Press (1982), pages 242-268 (Chinese).

15   Refer to volume 17 of *Translated Marxist-Leninist Works,* People's Press (1981), page 119 (Chinese).

"great Hegelian and materialist," fully affirming his materialist stance as well as his correct attitude in criticizing Kantianism and Machism. At the same time, Lenin correctly observes that "owing to the backwardness of Russian life, [Chernyshevsky] was unable to rise to the level of the dialectical materialism of Marx and Engels"[16].

Examining the commentaries that we currently have available to us, between 1909 and 1911 Lenin read two works on Chernyshevsky, one by his teacher Plekhanov (*N.G. Chernyshevsky*)[17], and the other by Yuri Steklov (*Herald of Life and Activities of N.G. Chernyshevsky*)[18]. *Like Lenin's commentaries on Dietzgen's works, which we have already discussed, this is the first time that Yuri Steklov's book has been translated into Chinese.* Neither of these books are works of topical research, but rather provide an overall assessment and introduction to Chernyshevsky's thought. There is no evidence to indicate that Lenin was particularly moved as he read these two works. I believe that he was merely attempting to further his understanding of this Russian materialist philosopher through reading about him. As such, in our discussion I will forego the content that is unrelated to philosophy and primarily focus on the background and circumstances of Lenin's reading of Chernyshevsky's philosophical thought.

Let us begin with Lenin's commentaries on the first book. Lenin read a revised edition of Plekhanov's older book, which included four articles on Chernyshevsky published in the *Sotsial-Demokrat*[19]. Where these articles were later published together in German, N.G. Chernyshevsky was published in Russian fifteen years later, after Plekhanov's revisions. Kedrov asserted that these commentaries indicate that Lenin was focusing on how Plekhanov used Menshevism to "obliterate" Chernyshevsky's revolutionary democratic theory[20]. Kedrov does make a good point: Lenin really had discovered many of Plekhanov's new changes, a fact which Kedrov studies in minute detail. Interestingly, out of all the analysis of Lenin's commentaries in Kedrov's *Study of Lenin's 'Philosophical Notebooks,'* this section was the best-written

---

16   Lenin, Vladimir. *Materialism and Empirio-criticism*. In *The Collected Works of Lenin*, volume 18, page 376-379 (Chin. 2. Ed.).
17   This book was published in October 1909 by the Russian publication *Wild Rose*.
18   This book was published in St. Petersburg in 1909.
19   The *Sotsial-Demokrat* was a collection of four volumes of Russian literary critique, published in Geneva between 1890 and 1892 by the Labor Emancipation Group.
20   See Kedrov's *Study of Lenin's "Philosophical Notebooks,"* Qiushi Press (1984), page 154 (Chinese).

and most profound. I believe that precisely because Lenin was criticizing Plekhanov here, the context conformed well to the discourse oppression of Stalinist ideology. Thus I am led to guess that Kedrov's understanding must have been relatively profound, but in the face of Lenin's obvious errors, he preferred to purposefully make himself seem "unintelligent" in order to avoid the refutational doubt of those who controlled the ideological party line. This is truly phenomenon that would be funny if it were not so true.

In the first section of his book, Plekhanov discusses the relation between Chernyshevsky and Feuerbach, concluding that Chernyshevsky was "a follower of Feuerbach"[21]. *From the text we can see that much of Lenin's critical commentary was not directed at Chernyshevsky,* but rather at Plekhanov's assessment of Chernyshevsky. In the third section, Lenin remarks on Plekhanov's views on the relation between matter and the sensation. The second part of Plekhanov's work concerns Chernyshevsky's conception of history, and in the third section of this part, Plekhanov analyzes the historical idealism in Chernyshevsky's view of history. According to Plekhanov, Chernyshevsky asserted that "progress is based on intellectual development," not realizing that "the successes and development of knowledge may depend on social relations"[22]. Plekhanov affirms that "social views are determined by social interests; and social thought, by social life," not the other way around. Lenin highlights Plekhanov's expressions here. In the fifth and sixth sections of the second part, Plekhanov points out the distance between Chernyshevsky and Marxism, stressing that since Chernyshevsky had applied Feuerbachian thought to other domains, many of his weaknesses "resulted from the insufficient elaboration of Feuerbach's materialism." Thus, when Chernyshevsky proudly proclaims himself to be a materialist, he actually does so with an idealist conception of history. In order to make this point, Plekhanov brings in Marx's criticism of Feuerbach from his Theses on Feuerbach, that Feuerbach takes theoretical activity to be "true human activity." Here, Lenin writes in the margin: "This is also the shortcoming of Plekhanov's book on Chernyshevsky"[23]. This is a very profound viewpoint.

21   See Plekhanov's G.V. Chernyshevsky, as cited in *The Collected Works of Lenin*, volume 55, page 532 (Chin. 2. Ed.).

22   See Plekhanov's G.V. Chernyshevsky, as cited in *The Collected Works of Lenin*, volume 55, page 537 (Chin. 2. Ed.).

23   Lenin, Vladimir. "Remarks on Books: G.V. Plekhanov's N.G. Chernyshevsky." In *The Collected Works of Lenin*, volume 55, page 537 (Chin. 2. Ed.).

In the third part of Plekhanov's book, he discusses Chernyshevsky's literary viewpoints, focusing on the analysis of Chernyshevsky's concept of "reality." In his opinion, Chernyshevsky's concept of reality came from Feuerbach; it was Feuerbach who confirmed the foundational place of sensuous reality after opposing the pre-eminence of pure thought in speculative philosophy. I believe that Plekhanov's analysis of this section is worthy of discussion, because Feuerbach's sensation and Chernyshevsky's reality as the basis of literary art were not the same thing; the senses of the first were **natural** relations, while the reality of the latter referred to activity in **social life**. Plekhanov directly explains this point as he cites a lengthy passage from Chernyshevsky on social intercourse[24]. In the text Lenin merely marks this passage without giving his own conclusions on Plekhanov's analysis. It is evident that Lenin was not sufficiently sensitive to this discussion of underlying theoretical questions.

The second half of the book concerns Chernyshevsky's views on politics and economics. In terms of the entire book, there was not much content here that could fundamentally influence Lenin's philosophical ideas, though Lenin did highlight some views that differed from Plekhanov's in the discussion of individual problems.

Next, from Lenin's commentaries on Yuri Steklov's book we can see that Lenin was hoping to get a better idea of Chernyshevsky's basic circumstances by reading this book. The content of Lenin's commentaries does show that he gained much more here than he did from Plekhanov's book. *In a letter to Gorky in this same time period, Lenin wrote that this was a good book on Chernyshevsky[25]. Kedrov asserts that where Plekhanov attempted to obliterate Chernyshevsky's revolutionary democratic ideas, this book attempts to approach Chernyshevsky's views to Marxism[26].*

In the third chapter of this book, the author cites the following passage by Chernyshevsky:

> **With the emergence of Feuerbach, the development of German philosophy was complete. It had obtained positive results, throwing off the pedantic philosophical forms of metaphysical, a priori philosophy; recognizing that its results**

---

24   Refer to *The Collected Works of Lenin*, volume 55, pages 542-543 (Chin. 2. Ed.).

25   See Lenin's "Letter to Gorky (early May, 1911)," *The Collected Works of Lenin*, volume 46, page 45 (Chin. 2. Ed.).

26   See Kedrov's *Study of Lenin's "Philosophical Notebooks,"* Qiushi Press (1984), p. 158.

conformed to natural scientific theory, it joined with the general theory of natural science, even humanism[27].

After reading this passage, Lenin was reminded of Engels' words, first underlining the text and then writing "See Engels." He goes on to write, "The relation between Feuerbach and general conclusions"[28]. *According to the editor of volume 55 of* **The Collected Works of Lenin***, Lenin was thinking here of Engels' views on philosophy and general science and relations in* **Anti-Dühring***. I am not of the same opinion.* I believe that here, Yuri Steklov was identifying Chernyshevsky's approach towards Feuerbach's **humanist logic**. Moreover, Chernyshevsky's expression was basically correct, Feuerbach's thought truly was the combination of natural materialism and humanism, and the basis of natural materialism was the "general conclusion" of natural science at the time. Marx and Engels both criticized Feuerbach for lacking the dimension of social history, because even if he did enter history, he did not do so as a **materialist**. The mistake of Feuerbach's Russian student Chernyshevsky was that was exactly the same of as his teacher. I believe that Lenin did not disagree with Chernyshevsky's overview of Feuerbach, but that he thought of Engels' assessment of Feuerbach, which most likely was Engels' critique of Feuerbach's natural materialism in his *On Feuerbach*. Of course, this is only a deduction on my part.

Continuing on, Lenin's interest was sparked by two different discussions in this book. **First**, Yuri Steklov's summary of basic philosophical problems, because according to Chernyshevsky, idealism held that spirit came before the natural world, while materialism argued that nature or matter came before spirit. Next to this sentence Lenin writes, "Inexact! Refer to Feuerbach"[29]. *The editors of volume 55 of* **The Collected Works of Lenin** *seem to believe that Lenin's marginal note meant that he believed that the author's expression of basic philosophical problems did not conform to the definitions given by Engels in* **On Feuerbach***; this conclusion is most likely correct.* **Second**, next to Yuri Steklov's citation of a long passage from Chernyshevsky on humanism, Lenin writes "NB." However, I have found that Lenin at this time did

---

27   See Chernyshevsky's *Overview of the Gogol Period in Russian Literature*, as cited in *The Collected Works of Lenin*, volume 55, page 158 (Chin. 2. Ed.).

28   Lenin, Vladimir. "Remarks on Books: Yuri Sterlov's Herald of Life and *Activity of N.G. Chernyshevsky*." In *The Collected Works of Lenin*, volume 55, page 564 (Chin. 2. Ed.).

29   *Ibid.*, page 564.

not completely understand the context of **philosophical humanism**, and so was certainly unable to appreciate the supersession and refutation of Feuerbach's humanism by Marx and Engels. As I have already pointed out, the issue of alienation in the context of humanism was never an element to which Lenin accorded special attention. This was a very regrettable logical gap in Lenin's philosophical thought situating at this time.

At another point, the author points out that the essence of idealism is "directly observable," and that materialism does an active system possess revolutionary emotion in which various classes integrate with one another, made up of different stages of social progress. He goes on to unabashedly assert that Chernyshevsky links a philosophical world view with practical pursuits, understanding that modern materialism is the philosophy of the working class[30]. Next to the words "directly observable," Lenin writes a question mark. However, he seems to agree with the author's views on the party principle in philosophy.

In the fifth chapter as Yuri Steklov begins to discuss the historical philosophy of Chernyshevsky, several viewpoints drew Lenin's attention: **first**, the author believed that Chernyshevsky had already seen that industrial trends are the primary moving force of the historical development of our era[31]. Lenin marks vertical lines and the letters "NB" next to this passage. **Second**, the author writes that Chernyshevsky clearly understood that class struggle was the basis of ancient historical development, while the various classes of modern society were all formed in the process of production. This was especially true for the three elements of modern production (land, capital, and labour), which had created the corresponding "three basic classes": landlords, bourgeois, and workers. Next to this passage, Lenin first writes a question mark, then writes, "See volume 3 part 7 of Marx's *Capital*"[32]. The first question mark expressed doubt as to the author's assertion that Chernyshevsky "clearly" saw the relation between modern production and the three basic classes; Lenin did not agree with this view. Lenin believed that Marx provided a more scientific explanation of this argument in the third volume of *Capital*.

---

30   See Yuri Steklov's Herald of Life and Activity of N.G. Chernyshevsky, as cited in *The Collected Works of Lenin*, volume 55, page 565 (Chin. 2. Ed.).

31   *Ibid.*, page 568.

32   Lenin, Vladimir. "Remarks on Books: Yuri Steklov's Herald of Life and Activity of N.G. Chernyshevsky." In *The Collected Works of Lenin*, volume 55, page 569 (Chin. 2. Ed.).

Also in this chapter, Yuri Steklov's overall assessment of Chernyshevsky aroused Lenin's opposition. Yuri Steklov wrote:

Chernyshevsky examines human history from a strictly objective point of view. He sees that human history is a dialectical process by which progress comes from contradiction, from leaps that are, themselves, the result of gradual quantitative changes. The result of this unceasing dialectical process is the transition from a base form to a higher form. Man acting in history is made up of various social classes, his struggle is controlled by economic factors. Economic relations that determine the social and legal relations in society, as well as ideology, form the basis of historical progress[33].

After this passage, the author continues to summarize, writing, "can we doubt that this view approaches the historical materialism of Marx and Engels? The only difference between Chernyshevsky's world view and the system of the founders of modern scientific socialism is the former's lack of systematic expression and precision of terminology." Chernyshevsky's only shortcoming was his failure to clearly point out the determining effect of forces of production on social historical progress. Lenin's response to this declaration was that it was improper. He first boxed the word "only," then wrote a question mark next to this paragraph, and finally wrote "exaggerated" in the margin[34].

In general, I have found that Lenin believed Yuri Steklov's opinion of Chernyshevsky to be overly high, exaggerating many points. For instance, in Yuri Steklov's discussion of Chernyshevsky's political economic and socialist thought, he compares Chernyshevsky to Proudhon, concluding that Proudhon's starting point was the petty bourgeoisie while Chernyshevsky's was socialism. Lenin writes a question mark in the margin here to indicate his doubt[35]. When Steklov wrote that Chernyshevsky's thought was completely unrelated to the socialism of the petty bourgeoisie because he refuted the vitality of the petty bourgeoisie and did not idealize the "barbaric state of the clan system," Lenin again expresses doubt[36]. The majority of the rest of the content of this book concerned Chernyshevsky's socialist views; we will not proceed with a detailed discussion of these views at this time.

---

33   *Ibid.*, page 571.
34   *Ibid.*, page 571.
35   *Ibid.*, page 574.
36   *Ibid.*, page 575.

CHAPTER SEVEN

COMPREHENSIVE UNDERSTANDING AND PROPAGATION OF MARXISM

After the publishing of Materialism and Empirio-criticism, Lenin focused on strengthening his overall study and grasp of basic Marxist theory. Between 1909 and 1913, Lenin published a series of important articles propagating basic Marxist views; these articles included "The Historical Destiny of the Doctrine of Karl Marx," "The Three Sources and Three Component Parts of Marxism," and especially "Karl Marx." From this series of articles we are able to see the quality of Lenin's philosophy has already greatly improved, and his thought on Marxist philosophy has become much more profound. This chapter will primarily analyze and discuss some of the important philosophical views expressed in "Karl Marx."

1 MARXISM AS A GUIDE TO ACTION

In 1909, after Lenin's *Materialism and Empirio-criticism* was published but the intra-party struggle was still ongoing, as we have seen, a
host of documents reflecting the complex political struggle of the time
were published. However, by this time Lenin had already progressed
far beyond his earlier level; here he asserts that there is can no longer
be divergence between one's political stance and one's philosophical,
academic world views. He even states that Bolshevism must become
strictly Marxist Bolshevism[1]. *This was obviously a targeted statement,
because Bogdanov and his ilk were non-Marxist Bolsheviks.* Of course,
the philosophical debate at this time was still ongoing. Although some
people disagreed with publishing philosophical articles in the central
party publications, Lenin expressed his support for this practice[2]. At
this time, Lenin already understood that philosophy was vitally important as both a **world view and a methodology**. He began to emphasize
that Marxists must hold fast to their "world view established by Marx
and Engels"[3]. As such, around 1910, when some Russian thinkers began to argue that this Russian philosophical debate was nothing but a
"mirage," citing a letter by Kautsky in 1908 that supposedly claimed
Machism to be a "private affair," Lenin immediately and publicly criticized this erroneous view. Lenin pointed out that when Kautsky wrote
this letter, he did not truly understand Russia's Machism; rather, Kautsky
merely hoped to encourage reconciliation between Russian Marxists.
According to Lenin, Kautsky himself was always opposed to idealism
and supportive of materialism. *However, this does not mean that we can
conclude that Lenin already understood the underlying problems with
Kautsky's philosophical theories by this time.* Therefore, to cite this letter in an attempt to refute the significance of the theoretical debate had
no persuasive power. Lenin strongly believed that the philosophical debate was actually linked to the different factions in Marxism[4].

---

1   Lenin, Vladimir. "Discussion on the Question of Otzovism and Ultimatums." In
The Collected Works of Lenin, volume 19, page 13 (Chin. 2. Ed.).
2   Lenin, Vladimir. "Discussion on the Question of Printing Philosophical Articles in
Central Newspapers." In *The Collected Works of Lenin*, volume 19, page 27 (Chin. 2.
Ed.).
3   Lenin, Vladimir. "The Faction of Supporters of Otzovism and God-Building." In
The Collected Works of Lenin, volume 19, page 129 (Chin. 2. Ed.).
4   Lenin, Vladimir. "Our Recallists." In *The Collected Works of Lenin*, volume 20,
page 105 (Chin. 2. Ed.).

However, at this time, Lenin was beset by another important challenge: his philosophy teacher, the famous Marxist theoretician Plekhanov, was taking every opportunity to maliciously attack the Marxism of Lenin and the Bolsheviks as a "narrow, shallow Marxism"[5]. *In fact, Plekhanov and his followers had already repeatedly criticized Lenin for being "unprofessional" in his philosophical research. The same year as **Materialism and Empirio-criticism** was published, the Menshevik philosopher Axelrod published an article in the July edition of **Modern World** in which she directly questioned the quality of Lenin's research, arguing that Lenin only **shallowly opposed Machism**.* However, Lenin's riposte to Plekhanov and his followers would come in the struggle of political practice. I have found that Lenin never directly counter-attacked Plekhanov in terms of philosophical theory. In response to the Menshevik Marxist theoreticians, Lenin's most common response was "You have **memorized** fragments of Bolshevik phrases and slogans but your understanding of them is precisely nil"[6]. In other words, "The special feature of Russian opportunism in Marxism, *i.e.*, of Menshevism in our time, is that it is associated with a doctrinaire simplification, vulgarization and distortion of the letter of Marxism, and a betrayal of its spirit"[7]. It is evident that here Lenin stresses Marxism not as a dead doctrine, but rather a living guide to action. If this is ignored, then:

We turn Marxism into something one-sided, distorted and lifeless; we deprive it of its life blood; we undermine its basic theoretical foundations—dialectics, the doctrine of historical development, all-embracing and full of contradictions; we undermine its connection with the definite practical tasks of the epoch, which may change with every new turn of history[8].

Lenin began to develop the understanding at this time of dialectics as the "living spirit" of Marxism, a deeper view of Marxist philosophy and especially dialectical theory. It is my understanding that this was a theoretical summary of Lenin's own flexible application of dialectics to revolutionary practice. In fact, precisely because Lenin viewed dialectics

---

5   Lenin, Vladimir. "The Liquidation of Liquidationism." In *The Collected Works of Lenin*, volume 19, page 64 (Chin. 2. Ed.).

6   Lenin, Vladimir. "The Faction of Supporters of Otzovism and God-Building." In *The Collected Works of Lenin*, volume 19, page 75 (Chin. 2. Ed.).

7   Lenin, Vladimir. "Letter to I.I. Skvortsov-Stepanov." In *The Collected Works of Lenin*, volume 45, page 296 (Chin. 2. Ed.).

8   Lenin, Vladimir. "Certain Features of the Historical Development of Marxism." In *The Collected Works of Lenin*, volume 20, page 84 (Chin. 2. Ed.).

as a guide to revolutionary action, there arose a more pressing internal need for him to profoundly study dialectical theory. I have found that around 1910, another intense debate took place in the Russian scholarly circle around Marxist dialectical theory. First, Berman's *Seeing the Dialectic from the Perspective of Modern Epistemology* viewed dialectics as a remnant of Hegel's idealist philosophy. In response to this book, Deborin wrote "The Destroyer of the Dialectic"[9], explaining the historical relation between Hegelian philosophy and Marxist materialist dialectics. However, it was his emphasis of this point that would later, in 1930, become one of Deborin's theoretical "sins."

On the other hand, Lenin had to deal with the enormous pressure of the so-called orthodox Marxists of the Second International. As early as 1903 when divisions began to appear with the Social-Democrat party, the majority of the thinkers of the Second International were already criticizing Lenin's Bolsheviks, both in terms of the political practice of the Russian Revolution as well as philosophical theory. In order to consolidate his support, Lenin tried everything he could think of to gain the backing of these philosophers; by 1909, he believed that his efforts had begun to bear fruit. He even believed that Rosa Luxemburg and Karl Kautsky had been won over by him: "[they] are in our Party—have been won over to our point of view"[10]. As we will see later on, Lenin was overly optimistic here. At the same time, in response to domestic and foreign criticism, Lenin began to publicly emphasize that in addition to **subjective** proletariat elements, the revolutionary practical road of Bolshevism would be established according to "**objective**, economic conditions, which would **allow** the possibility of an 'American' line of capitalist development in Russia"[11]. *In comparison to Lenin's differing emphasis on the objective and subjective dimensions in the past, this represents his first attempt, in terms of theoretical logic, to **unify the objective and subjective dimensions of historical dialectics**. He hoped to thus emphasize that the social economic development of capitalism in Russia (the objective dimension) was an important, real basis of the proletariat revolution (subjective dimension).* In a 1911 letter to Gorky, Lenin responded to Gorky's assertion that the Bolshevik international

---

9   Refer to Deborin's "The Destroyer of the Dialectic," in the June 1910 edition of *Modern World*.

10   Lenin, Vladimir. "The Faction of Supporters of Otzovism and God-Building." In *The Collected Works of Lenin*, volume 19, page 105 (Chin. 2. Ed.).

11   Lenin, Vladimir. "Some Sources of the Present Ideological Discord." In *The Collected Works of Lenin*, volume 19, page 137 (Chin. 2. Ed.).

policies contained quixotic elements, writing that "without the development of capitalism, there is no guarantee of defeating capitalism"[12]. *This was an important supplementary proof of his thought.*

In early 1913, in commemoration of the thirtieth anniversary of Marx's passing, Lenin wrote two introductory articles on Marxist theory. The first of these was "The Historical Destiny of the Doctrine of Karl Marx," which was published in the March 1, 1913 edition of *Pravda*[13]. The other article, "The Three Sources and Three Component Parts of Marxism," was also published in March 1913 in the Prosveshcheniye magazine. These two articles clearly show that Lenin had already begun to increasingly emphasize the grasp and understanding of all the theories and systems of basic Marxist theory; this was unlike his earlier attitude, in which he primarily focused on the political and economic content of Marxism. I believe that this was the result of Lenin's first and second systematic studies of philosophical theory, as well as his participation in the philosophical theoretical battle of his day. In these two articles we see that Lenin's basic overview of the different historical eras and developmental paths, as well as his explanation of the basic theoretical principles and background of Marxism, were all very clear. One of the more important views that he expresses here is his first clear elucidation of the **historical** essence of Marxist theory:

> **The history of philosophy and the history of social science show with perfect clarity that there is nothing resembling "sectarianism" in Marxism, in the sense of its being a hidebound, petrified doctrine, a doctrine which arose *away from* the high road of the development of world civilization. On the contrary, the genius of Marx consists precisely in his having furnished answers to questions already raised by the foremost minds of mankind. His doctrine emerged as the direct and immediate *continuation* of the teachings of the greatest representatives of philosophy, political economy and socialism[14].**

This statement is extremely important. *It is unfortunate that this correct understanding of Lenin's did not continue under the Stalinist system.* In

---

12 Lenin, Vladimir. "Letter to A.M. Gorky (January 3, 1911)." In *The Collected Works of Lenin*, volume 46, page 16 (Chin. 2. Ed.).

13 Lenin, Vladimir. "The Historical Destiny of the Doctrine of Karl Marx." In *The Collected Works of Lenin*, volume 23, pages 1-4 (Chin. 2. Ed.).

14 Lenin, Vladimir. "The Three Sources and Three Component Parts of Marxism." In *The Collected Works of Lenin*, volume 23, page 41 (Chin. 2. Ed.).

his expression of Marxist philosophy, Lenin emphasized the stance of philosophical materialism. He also began to explain how Marx applied Hegel's dialectic to "enriching" materialism. In this article, he summarizes dialectics as "the doctrine of development in its fullest, deepest and most comprehensive form"[15]. It is this theory that allows Marxist philosophers to promote "the doctrine of the relativity of the human knowledge that provides us with a reflection of eternally developing matter." However, we are also able to see that Lenin here persists in mistakenly believing that historical materialism was Marx's application of philosophical materialism to "to include the cognition of **human society**"[16].

Also in 1913, as he discussed his struggle against Machism with Gorky, Lenin resolutely declared, "friendship is friendship, business is business," stressing that if Bogdanov and his followers did not learn their lesson from the events of 1908-1911, if they continued to stubbornly believe in Machism, then Lenin would have no choice but to tirelessly struggle against them[17]. *Of course, Bogdanov and his followers did not abandon their mistaken views, though it seems as though Lenin does not make any more public statements against them, even if he did engage in another systematic study of philosophical theory.*

2 THE PHILOSOPHICAL VIEWS IN *KARL MARX*

In early 1914, Lenin committed to write an entry in the *Granat Encyclopedia* on Marx, and the result was "Karl Marx." Lenin began to write in spring of that year, but a heavy load of party commitments and his work for the *Pravda* hindered his progress, preventing him from finishing his work on time. As such, he was forced to write to the editor on July 8, 1914 to apologize for being unable to complete his work and suggested finding another person to write the article. The editor wrote back the same day, maintaining that he wanted Lenin to write the article and agreeing to push back the manuscript due date. Lenin accepted this invitation. Not long after, the First World War broke out and Lenin was arrested by Austrian authorities. He was unable to continue his work until he moved to Bern in September, 1914. On November 4, 1914, Lenin sent the completed text of "Karl Marx" to the editorial

---

15 *Ibid.*, page 42.
16 *Ibid.*, page 45.
17 Lenin, Vladimir. "Letter to A.M. Gorky (January 8, 1913)." In *The Collected Works of Lenin*, volume 46, page 215 (Chin. 2. Ed.).

department of the Granat Encyclopedia. Volume 28 of the seventh edition of the *Russian Granat Encyclopedia*, published the next year, contained the article written by Lenin, with the name V. Ilyich. *When this text was published, the articles on "socialism" and "strategy of the proletariat struggle" were not included.*

It is commonly known that Lenin began his study of Hegelian philosophy during this same period of time. According to his notes in the *Bern Notebooks*, he finished reading *The Science of Logic* on December 17 of that year. Thus I deduce that the main text of "Karl Marx was most likely completed as Lenin was studying Hegel. However, looking at the content of the article, we find that when Lenin finished writing the piece in November, his thought theoretical situating had not experienced any great change. Here let us first give a simple overview of the basic views of Marxist philosophy expressed in this article.

Lenin believed that Marxism was the system of Marx's views and teachings; its primary content was economics theory, while a philosophical worldview formed the premise of Marxism. Lenin's understanding of these points was precise.

First, Lenin still views philosophical materialism as the fundamental basis of Marxist philosophy. Because he was not able to read such important documents as the *1844 Manuscript* or *The German Ideology*, he still relied on Engels' interpretive or argumentative texts to identify materialism. In this text, Lenin's citations from Marx primarily come from *The Holy Family*, *Capital*, and *Theses on Feuerbach*; his citations from Engels primarily come from *Anti-Dühring* and *On Feuerbach*. In the article, the primary basis of Lenin's argument can be traced to Engels' views on the basic problems of philosophy and the material unity of the world. However, the level of understanding of Marx's new materialist world view was obviously still not complete enough, because he still classified Marx's philosophical revolution after 1845 as general **philosophical materialism**[18].

Of course, Lenin had already accurately highlighted the differences between Marx's materialism and old materialism. **First**, he identified the

---

18   In the writing outline for this text, Lenin still begins with philosophical materialism. See Lenin's Plan for the article "Karl Marx," in *The Collected Works of Lenin*, volume 26, page 373. See also his "The Three Sources and Three Component Parts of Marxism." In *The Collected Works of Lenin*, volume 23, page 42, 45.

mechanical nature of the old materialism. This was correct, but Lenin simply understands this mechanical materialism as "failing to take into account the latest developments in biology and chemistry (and the electrical theory of matter)"; this was imprecise. Marx and Engels used the term "mechanical" to describe a general characteristic of old materialism in order to explain how it shared the same features as Newton's mechanical theory of gravity (1686). This was not a problem due to lack of scientific development. **Second**, Lenin pointed out the "non-historical, non-dialectical" metaphysical characteristics of old materialism. Lenin writes that old materialism "did not adhere consistently and comprehensively to the standpoint of development." Though this was not incorrect, though when Marx criticized the non-historical nature of Feuerbach's old materialism, he primarily wanted to explain how Feuerbach could not **historically** deal with nature and human existence because he did not understand the **historical nature of material practice**. *In his later study of Hegel's theories, Lenin would come to profoundly understand this point.* **Third**, Lenin saw old materialism as having abstractly understood the human essence rather than viewing it as the sum of certain social relations[19]. This understanding is also somewhat correct, but those who understand this part of philosophical history all know that Marx's critique of Feuerbach's abstract idea of human essence in *Theses on Feuerbach* was primarily to refute the logic of Feuerbach's **abstract humanist** alienation conception of history. Proceeding from actual social existence, this is a basic principle of **historical** materialism. However, at this time Lenin was still unable to see the entire expression of historical materialism in *The German Ideology*, by Marx and Engels. I have also found that in the writing outline for this text which was prepared earlier, Lenin confirmed Marx's philosophy as "dialectical materialism, materialist conception of history"[20]. This meant that Lenin was still under the inexact belief that historical materialism was the application of dialectical materialism into the field of history.

Next, in this text Lenin first fully expresses his understanding of Marx's dialectical philosophy. Although Lenin had not yet completed his comprehensive study of Hegelian philosophy, he was already able to say: "As the most comprehensive and profound doctrine of development,

---

19   Lenin, Vladimir. "Karl Marx." In *The Collected Works of Lenin*, volume 26, page 55 (Chin. 2. Ed.).
20   See Lenin's Plan for the article "Karl Marx," in *The Collected Works of Lenin*, volume 26, page 372 (Chin. 2. Ed.).

and the richest in content, Hegelian dialectics was considered by Marx and Engels the greatest achievement of classical German philosophy"[21]. I should point out that Lenin's theoretical discourse here already includes some of the characteristics of later Stalinist dogmatism. For instance, he uses **absolute statements**, such as the "most comprehensive," "most profound," and "greatest achievement." Another example is his use of the phrase "the doctrine of development in its fullest, deepest and most comprehensive form" in his "The Three Sources and Three Component Parts of Marxism"[22]. Here, Lenin goes on to cite some of Engels' general expressions of the dialectic as found in *Anti-Dühring* and *On Feuerbach*. Of these, the most well-known is his expression on dialectics as "the science of the general laws of motion, both of the external world and of human thought." The substance of dialectics was its idea of development. *At this time, Lenin did not remark the holistic concept of linkages in the dialectic; links only appear as an aspect of development for him.* Thus:

> **A development that repeats, as it were, stages that have already been passed, but repeats them in a different way, on a higher basis ("the negation of the negation"), a development, so to speak, that proceeds in spirals, not in a straight line; a development by leaps, catastrophes, and revolutions; "breaks in continuity"; the transformation of quantity into quality; inner impulses towards development, imparted by the contradiction and conflict of the various forces and tendencies acting on a given body, or within a given phenomenon, or within a given society; the interdependence and the closest and indissoluble connection between *all* aspects of any phenomenon (history constantly revealing ever new aspects), a connection that provides a uniform, and universal process of motion, one that follows definite laws—these are some of the features of dialectics as a doctrine of development that is richer than the conventional one[23].**

Examining Lenin's expression here, he was not yet able to add the new insights he gained during his study of Hegelian philosophy into his explanation of the dialectic.

---

21   Lenin, Vladimir. "Karl Marx." In *The Collected Works of Lenin*, volume 26, page 55 (Chin. 2. Ed.).

22   Lenin, Vladimir. "The Three Sources and Three Component Parts of Marxism." In *The Collected Works of Lenin*, volume 23, page 42, (Chin. 2. Ed.).

23   Lenin, Vladimir. "Karl Marx." In *The Collected Works of Lenin*, volume 26, page 57 (Chin. 2. Ed.).

Third, Lenin argues that the materialist conception of history had elimi-nated the mistakes of past conceptions of history. These mistakes be-longed to the idealist conception of history, which believed that thought motivations formed the basis of history and ignored the role of the mass-es of people. Although both of these points may have been correct, they could only be complete inasmuch as they were established on the basis of the essence of historical practice of historical materialism. I believe that Lenin's explanation of the materialist conception of history demon-strates that he did not fully understand Marx's **historical** materialism, because he still sees historical materialism as the **application** of philo-sophical materialism to the realm of "human social life." Rather, the first textual explanation that Lenin cites actually conveys an opposite logic. This passage was taken from the first volume of Marx's *Capital*: "Technology discloses man's mode of dealing with Nature, the immedi-ate process of production by which he sustains his life, and thereby also lays bare the mode of formation of his social relations, and of the mental conceptions that flow from them"[24]. This passage profoundly explains the essence of Marx's new materialist theoretical situating while cor-recting some of the fatal errors of traditional philosophical materialism. Marx's new materialism argued that matter does not produce ideas; only the historical progression of mankind – and especially human life itself – can form the true foundation of the spiritual ideas of a given period of history. Technology is the most basic productive structure in material productive practice, immediately reflecting man's **dealing** with nature in a given period of time. In other words, it reflects in human notions **the material existence that is changed in man's historical practical activ-ity.** This material existence primarily referred not to material substance but rather to man's social life itself. As such, Marx believed that there was no such thing as an abstract relation between matter and conscious-ness. Rather, he argued for a concrete relation between social existence and consciousness **based on historical practice**: all consciousness was merely **historical, social** consciousness. At this point, Lenin was not able to see this underlying truth. In the next line that Lenin cites from the preface to Marx's *Contribution to the Critique of Political Economy*, we find: "It is not the consciousness of men that determines their being, but, on the contrary, their social being that determines their consciousness"[25]. In fact, Marx was not applying philosophical materialism to the realm of

---

24   Cited in Lenin, Vladimir. "Karl Marx." In *The Collected Works of Lenin*, volume 26, page 58-59 (Chin. 2. Ed.).
25   *Ibid.*, page 58.

social history, but was rather examining the true basis of a new materialism in the changes to the practice of social practice; his generative logic was reversed. With **Dietzgen**, Lenin was in a closed theoretical loop and thus explained things invertedly.

In his later explanations of class struggle, economic teachings, and socialist theories, Lenin's discussion is basically correct. However, Lenin completely overlooks Marx's criticism of the three great fetishisms, a theory with profound philosophical significance, in his explanation of Marxist economic theory. *It is certainly regrettable that Lenin did not realize was that Bogdanov had distorted this exact theory into a weapon to use against philosophical materialism. It was not until young Lukac's* **History and Class Consciousness** *that Marx's teachings on this point would again be brought forth, though in a non-scientific form.*

At the end of this passage, Lenin includes another passage entitled "Tactics of the Class Struggle of the Proletariat." In this passage it is not hard for us to see that Lenin's motive was to find a **subjectively active** theoretical basis for the revolutionary practice of his Bolshevik party. This is why he begins with the words, "as early as 1844-45, one of the main shortcomings in the earlier materialism—namely, its inability to understand the conditions or appreciate the importance of practical revolutionary activity…without **this** aspect, materialism is incomplete, one-sided, and lifeless"[26]. In fact, what Marx was criticizing was not Feuerbach's old materialism; rather, he **simultaneously** criticized Feuerbach and Hegel, indicating that the former could not proceed from active revolutionary practice and understand material existence from the perspective of sensuous, world-changing activity, while the latter erroneously mutated active subjectivity into mental activity. Lenin immediately proceeds from Marx's critique to analysis of the actual proletariat revolution; although he seems to be explaining Marx's basic teachings, his true object was to find legitimate theoretical support for the Russian proletarian revolution within Marx's notion of dynamism. More importantly, Lenin was not able to acquire direct legitimacy from the philosophical materialism to which he and Plekhanov adhered. *This important theoretical foundation was not ultimately, logically proven until Lenin's study of Hegelian philosophy in the* **Bern Notebooks**, *through his deeper understanding of the revolutionary dynamism inherent in Marx's philosophy using practical dialectics.*

---

26   *Ibid.*, page 77.

3 MARXIST PHILOSOPHICAL HISTORICAL THREAD

As an encyclopaedic entry, Lenin's article "Karl Marx" included a detailed bibliography at the end. From this bibliographic information we can see that Lenin's research was serious and comprehensive, already taking on the form of a professional scholar. In this bibliography we find the Marxist philosophical historical thread that Lenin understood at this time. *In the writing outline for this text, Lenin wrote that he would give an overview discussion of the developmental process of Marxism"[27].*

Lenin's understanding of young Marx's process of philosophical change can evidently be summed up as a "**single change theory.**" Lenin already understood that Marx's 1841 doctoral thesis on the epicurean philosophy of nature still held fast to the viewpoint of Hegelian idealism. This was correct. *In the preface to this article in the encyclopaedia, Lenin also correctly identified this point.* However, examining the articles that Marx published in 1842 as he worked for the Rheinische Zeitung, Lenin believed that "we see signs of Marx's transition from idealism to materialism and from revolutionary democracy to communism." Lenin goes on to assert that "this transition was finally made" when Marx worked with Ruge as editors-in-chief of the *Deutsche-Französische Jahrbücher*[28]. This conclusion is obviously imprecise. Even if we only look at the texts available to Lenin at the time, we can still deduce that young Marx's thought was still idealist before 1843. In the articles he wrote for the *Rheinische Zeitung*, Marx's basic philosophical logic was still a Hegelian idealized theory of idea-pre-eminence; he used such phrases as "base materialism" and "theories that one can buy with three coppers" to describe materialism. Therefore, at the most we could say about young Marx at this time was that he had a feeling that material interest always "had the upper hand" in social life. Beyond this, it is impossible to say that any shift in the philosophical or political stance of young Marx had occurred by this point in his life. It is evident that there were serious problems with Lenin's qualitative conclusions at this point in his text. *I cannot say whether Lenin's conclusions were based on first-hand documents, or whether he was citing the views of others. Looking at the overall context of this text, I believe that the latter*

---

27   Lenin, Vladimir. "Outline to the text 'Karl Marx.'" In *The Collected Works of Lenin*, volume 26, page 375 (Chin. 2. Ed.).
28   Lenin, Vladimir. "Karl Marx." In *The Collected Works of Lenin*, volume 26, page 83 (Chin. 2. Ed.).

possibility is somewhat more likely. However, we cannot fault Lenin for his mistakes here, because he could not have read Marx's 1843 *Kreuznach Notebooks*, and thus could not have known that in Marx's historical research based on the French Revolution, he **understood himself** that social structures in social history were based on relations of property. This is what led Marx to accept the views of Feuerbach's philosophical materialism. Here, Lenin is actually merely citing a conclusion that Engels reached, that Engels and young Marx had both come under the influence of Feuerbach, becoming Feuerbachians for a time[29]. Actually, Marx's shift in thought was not as simple or externalized as Engels believed. Young Marx's transition to materialism was primarily realized internally, through his historical research; it was not until later that he identified with Feuerbach's viewpoint[30]. Furthermore, young Marx's political stance while he worked for the *Rheinische Zeitung* was still democratic, not communist in the least. As such, the dual philosophical-political shift that young Marx experienced did not take place in 1842, but rather at the end of 1843, as he began writing *Critique of Hegel's 'Philosophy of Right,'* and commenced his research in the *Kreuznach Notebooks* (May-October 1843). This shift was completed by 1844, though because Lenin did not know the important influence of young Engels and Hess on Marx or know of the existence of the *Paris Notebooks* and the *1844 Manuscript*, he could not have realized that young Marx's shift at this time did not establish Marxist theory per se, but was rather simply the **first** shift in Marx's philosophical thought. The essence of this shift was **general philosophical materialism and philosophical communism**. Lenin could not even have discovered the intermediate stage through which young Marx passed. This was a stage defined by the **humanist-alienation conception of history**, in which labour forms man's species-essence, and **ethical** communist thought that results from the sublation of alienation. *Furthermore, as Lenin's 1913 text "The Historical Destiny of the Doctrine of Karl Marx" points out, Marx's views on the historical mission of the proletariat class were formed in 1844, with the publishing of* **The Holy Family** *with Engels*[31].

Along with Professor Sun Bokui, I believe that Marx's **second philosophical shift** took place in 1845. In a host of texts which Lenin would not have been able to access (including what I refer to as the February

29 *Ibid.*, page 48.
30 Refer to the first section of the second chapter of my *Marx Revisited.*
31 Lenin, Vladimir. "The Historical Destiny of the Doctrine of Karl Marx." In *The Collected Works of Lenin,* volume 23, page 1 (Chin. 2. Ed.).

1845 Brussels Notebooks A, the March 1845 *On List*, the May-July 1845 *Brussels Notebooks* B, and *The German Ideology*), as well as in *Theses on Feuerbach*, in which "germs of a new world view" could be found, Marx realized his second revolutionary philosophical shift. It was not until this shift that the basic establishment of Marxist doctrine took place. It was also in this shift that the basic framework of the general theory of historical materialism and the doctrine of scientific socialism, which was directed towards social historical reality, were first established.

We can see that in the overview of post-1846 texts written by Marx and Engels, Lenin very accurately summarized the textual history of Marx and Engels, as well as the actual history of the creative practice of the proletariat revolution. This summary included the publishing information for the texts of Marx and Engels after their deaths, with special emphasis accorded to the Russian translations of the classical texts of Marx and Engels. This accurate summary of the historical circumstances of these texts demonstrates the comprehensiveness and profundity of Lenin's grasp of historical materials.

The most important index here is Lenin's topical summary of modern Western scholarly work as it relates to Marxist research. Lenin believed that the many authors who studied Marxism could be divided into three categories: "Marxists who, in important matters, adhere to Marx's point of view; bourgeois writers, in essence hostile to Marxism; and revisionists, who, while claiming to accept certain fundamentals of Marxism, in fact replace it with bourgeois conceptions"[32]. In addition, Lenin provides detailed categorization of the texts themselves. He begins with biographies of Marx, then continues to cite texts concerning Marxist philosophy and historical materialism, then books on Marx's economic theories, and finally texts relating to the Second International and Russia. It is worth pointing out that from this categorized review of texts, we can observe the philosophical ideas and standpoints which formed Lenin's thought situating at this time.

In these biographical texts, we find such names as Engels, Liebknecht, Lafargue, Mehring, Kautsky, Zetkin, Annenkov, Schurz, and Kovalevsky. The majority of these people came into direct contact with

---

32   Lenin, Vladimir. "Karl Marx." In *The Collected Works of Lenin*, volume 26, page 88 (Chin. 2. Ed.).

Marx while he was alive. As such, their recollections, for the most part, give a sense of actually being there, a truthful timeliness.

Of the many authors who studied Marxist philosophy, Lenin still placed his own teacher, Plekhanov, at the forefront. The majority of the 20th century texts introducing and interpreting Marxist philosophy discussed here were all written by him. Lenin refers to these works as the "best exposition" of Marxist philosophy[33]. *I have found that regardless of the political divisions between Lenin and Plekhanov, Lenin still viewed his teacher as the most important basis for his learning of Marxist philosophy. This philosophical dependence would not change until Lenin reached the latter stages of his study of Hegelian philosophy. At that point, through his own arduous philosophical research, Lenin found that the majority of Marxists, including Plekhanov, did not really understand Marx.* The second scholar that Lenin cites here is the Italian Antonio Labriola, whose *Historical Materialism* occupies a prominent place in Lenin's text. It is impossible for us to guess as to whether or not Lenin had read Labriola's book. *According to Adoratsky, Lenin ordered two books by the Italian Marxist philosopher Labriola in 1920:* **Historical Materialism** *and* **On Philosophy**. In this book, Labriola interprets Marxist philosophy differently from the interpretive logic that traced its roots back to Dietzgen and Plekhanov. Labriola uses historical materialism as his logical basis in interpreting Marx's line of thought. Mehring's *On Historical Materialism* approached this issue from basically the same perspective. In addition, Lenin also cited a large number of works that discussed or criticized Marxism, giving brief reviews of each of these.

In studying the texts of Marxist economics, the works of Kautsky and Bernstein head the list, while Hilferding's *Finance Capital* is praised as "the further development of Marx's economic views as applied to recent phenomena in economic life"[34]. *Such an assessment is obviously exaggerated; in his later notes on imperialism, Lenin would reach an important new understanding regarding Hilferding.* Lenin also asserts that Hilferding's outstanding errors in the theory of value were corrected by Kautsky. Lenin refers to Rosa Luxemburg's Die *Accumulation des Kapitals* as a new work on the Marxist theory of the accumulation of capital, though his appraisal of it is clearly lower than his opinion of

33   *Ibid.*, page 89.
34   *Ibid.*, page 92.

Hilferding's work, citing three essays which criticize Luxemburg's text. *At this time, there had not yet been direct theoretical debate between Luxemburg and Lenin on the questions of proletarian political parties and the dictatorship of the proletariat.*

At the very end of this textual overview, there were two major foci of Lenin's thought. **First**, he wished to identify the problems of revisionism from within Marxism, referring primarily to Bernstein's works and Kautsky's critique of them. **Second**, he wished to discuss and rectify the texts of the Russian Narodniks with regards to Marxism.

Lenin's conclusion to this text reads, "For a correct appraisal of Marx's views, an acquaintance is essential with the works of Frederick Engels, his closest fellow-thinker and collaborator. It is impossible to understand Marxism and to propound it fully without taking into account all the works of Engels"[35]. *This is a declaratory sentence form of which Lenin was kind fond. However, Lenin would soon realize that without understanding Hegel's **The Science of Logic**, it is impossible to correctly understand Marx's **Capital**. Of course, this was Lenin's ultimate conclusion after studying Hegel's philosophy.*

---

35   *Ibid.*, page 94-5.

CHAPTER EIGHT

LENIN'S OUTLINE ON THE CORRESPONDENCE BETWEEN MARX AND ENGELS

The Marx-Engels Correspondence (1844-1883) (Abbreviated below as *Correspondence*) was an extremely important document of notes, written by Lenin in late 1913[1]. *Chronologically speaking, this text was obviously completed before Lenin wrote "Karl Marx."* In this document we are able to see an important reason for Lenin's changing understanding of Marx's materialist dialectics. This reason was Lenin's recognition of Hegel's essential role in the theoretical establishment of Marxist dialectics. In *Correspondence*, Lenin discovered that each time Marx and Engels discussed dialectics, they unfailingly mentioned Hegel; it seemed to Lenin that whether or not one understood Hegel's philosophy became an external sign of whether or not one understood dialectics. This was a thought situating point that grew ever stronger and clearer as Lenin read *The Marx-Engels Correspondence*. Of course, Lenin's

---

1 *The Marx-Engels Correspondence* was edited and published by Bebel and Bernstein as requested by Engels. This book was published in September 1913 in Stuttgart by the Dietz Publishing Company. It appears that Lenin obtained this book soon after its publishing.

Correspondence touches on a wide variety of scholarly fields, but the focus of our analysis and interpretation will primarily be on Lenin's philosophical thought space; as such, our study inevitably is characterized by purposefulness and selectivity.

1 DIALECTICS: WHY HEGEL?

In my basic categorization of texts in textual interpretation, letters belong to the second category of text: **generative texts**. By examining correspondence texts, especially the correspondence between two close friends, we are more able to find the genuine essence of the exchange of thought, as the writers are free of the direct supervision of ideological Others. Because of this, as Lenin read the exchange of letters between Marx and Engels, it was as if he was able to directly observe the true dialogue between the two men. This dialogue composed the most true of thought circumstances, and Lenin's reading of this dialogue would have been **a reconsideration of the thought situating of Marx and Engels**. At the same time, this would naturally have inspired self-reflection and self-examination in Lenin, leading to a more complex recognition of **multi-dimensional thought space**. It is obvious that Lenin's thought situating at this time could not directly "integrate" with the situating revealed in the correspondence of Marx and Lenin; Lenin's situating was rather expressed as **an "upward looking" logical dimension**.

Lenin seemed very cognizant of the aforementioned significance of this correspondence, and so focused seriously on his study of the correspondence of Marx and Engels. As early as 1907, he himself edited a volume of correspondence from Marx to Dr. Kugelmann, also writing a Russian preface to the letters written by Marx, Engels. *Not long after reading The Marx-Engels Correspondence, Lenin wrote a review of it, which was to be published in a 1914 edition of Prosveshcheniye magazine. However, after writing the beginning of the article, Lenin stopped working on it. In November 1920, in commemoration of Engels' 100th birthday, Lenin published this unfinished article in Pravda*[2]. Lenin was not pleased with Bernstein's editing, writing that "After his notorious 'evolution' to extreme opportunist views, Bernstein should never have undertaken to edit letters which are impregnated through and through

---

2   This text merely completed an overall appraisal, as well as a general overview of the background of Engels' early letters. Refer to Lenin, Vladimir. "The Correspondence of Marx and Engels." *In The Collected Works of Lenin*, volume 24, pages 274-281 (Chin. 2. Ed.).

with the revolutionary spirit"[3]. *This was why Lenin charged Adoratsky with re-editing The Marx-Engels Correspondence in 1922. This reader-friendly edition was published in late 1922. Lenin highly praised the scholarly and political value of The Marx-Engels Correspondence:*

> **Not only do Marx and Engels stand out before the reader in clear relief in all their greatness, but the extremely rich theoretical content of Marxism is graphically revealed, because in their letters Marx and Engels return again and again to the most diverse aspects of their doctrine, emphasising and explaining—at times discussing and debating—what is newest (in relation to earlier views), most important and most difficult[4].**

It is not hard to feel that Lenin's assessment here was heartfelt. I believe that he was able to see the true directness and sense of presence that the correspondence revealed of Marx and Engels.

Examining the documents we have available to us, Lenin's "outline" of *The Marx-Engels Correspondence* was written on 76 pages of notebooks. On the cover of the notebook, Lenin wrote the words "Marx-Engels Correspondence." *On the upper left-hand corner of the cover, we find the editorial mark left by Nadya Krupskaya*: XVI. Lenin read the September 1913 (Stuttgart) German edition of *The Marx-Engels Correspondence*, which included 1386 letters written between Marx and Engels. Lenin carefully pored over these four thick volumes, highlighting the content of about 300 letters. Looking at the actual writing of the notebook, we find that Lenin used four different coloured pencils in this outline (light black, dark black, red, and light blue). From this we can see that he read, reflected on, and studied these letters multiple times. Looking at the facsimiles of this text, it is evident that Lenin first used a light black pencil to make his first outline, which already including some early markings (underlinings and parentheses). In Lenin's second reading he used a dark black pencil, with which he **retraced** some of the earlier markings made with the light pencil and made other markings (underlinings, marginal lines, and page numbers corresponding to his notebook, etc.). Lenin's third reading was made with a red pencil in hand, which he used to **add** commentaries and a few markings; in

---

3   Lenin, Vladimir. "The Correspondence of Marx and Engels." In *The Collected Works of Lenin*, volume 24, page 274 (Chin. 2. Ed.).

4   *Ibid.*, page 275.

addition, we can also find a few underlinings, markings, and numbers recorded with a blue pencil. Just looking at the text, it is evident that Lenin took his reading and study of this text very seriously.

Of the 76 pages of notes, Lenin used 61 pages to record his notes on the four volumes of correspondence. Beginning on page 62, Lenin takes excerpts from 19 letters between Marx and Engels. I have found that the edition currently printed was not a direct publication of Lenin's original notes, but was rather a **restructured compound text**. When the first 61 pages of Lenin's notes were edited and published, Soviet scholars structurally included corresponding content from the original letters in printed text, going so far as to mark Lenin's reading comments (such as underlinings, marginal lines, and the letters "NB," etc.) in certain parts of the text. As such, to more precisely identify this text we should say that it is a compound of Lenin's outlines, excerpts, and reading commentaries on *The Marx-Engels Correspondence;* this text is truly a typical situating draft text. The editors evidently attempted to use this method to recreate the complex circumstances of Lenin's thought at the time, an attitude which is worthy of our praise.

Existing notebooks indicate that Lenin's reading did not begin with the first volume of the *Correspondence*; rather he began with the second, then the fourth, the first, and finally concluded with the third volume. Looking at Lenin's notebooks, we find that the first 10 pages were reading outlines of the second volume, pages 11-31 were outlines of the fourth volume, pages 33-43 outlined the first volume, and finally pages 44-61 outlined the third volume. Beginning on page 62, Lenin begins to record excerpted passages from 19 letters. At the very end of the notebooks Lenin includes an index of names. Our interpretation here will proceed according to the sequence of Lenin's reading. Therefore, let us begin with volume two of *The Marx-Engels Correspondence*.

The second volume of *The Marx-Engels Correspondence* includes the letters exchanged between Marx and Engels beginning in January 1854. During this period of time, the focal point of the discussions of Marx and Engels included the military engagements of various countries throughout the world, including Russia; the primary content focused on the review of different military struggles by Engels. These discussions were not very interesting to Lenin. The first outline that he writes concerns a May 3 letter from Marx to Engels. I believe that what aroused Lenin's interest here was Marx's discussion of the religious problems between different nations. An analysis of later outlines reveals that Lenin did not read with any **clear purpose** in mind, but based on the discourse system with which Lenin was already familiar, he tended to focus more on social struggle, the details of historical facts, and the discussion of economics. As such, the content he includes at the beginning of **Correspondence** tends to be related to these topics.

In an August 15, 1857 letter from Marx to Engels, Marx jokingly declared that in order to act as a military man in Lenin's "forum," in assessing the hostilities in Delhi, he would use dialectics to dissimulate his non-professional in some of the discussion on military matters. Lenin was obviously interested by this, but he was somewhat disappointed. Lenin writes in his outline, "dialectics=eclecticism (joke), perhaps I (K. Marx) was wrong (about the British in Delhi – 1856), but I can use 'some dialectics' to escape." Lenin's angry conclusion was, "written ambiguously"[5]. Not long after this joke, Marx again discusses the dialectic; however, this instance of dialectics as a methodology pointed directly towards the **idealist** Hegel.

On January 14, 1858, Marx excitedly wrote to Engels to inform him that his economics research had made great progress, for instance overthrowing the doctrine of profits in traditional economics research. Also in this letter, Marx also happened to mention several of Hegel's books that someone had given to him. Marx wrote that he perused *The Science of Logic*, and that this book "helped me greatly in the method of refining my materials." Marx continued, stating that "if I have time later to do more of this kind of work, I would take a couple of pages to explain the logical elements of Hegel's method that he discovered and then mystified, making them accessible to ordinary people"[6]. This passage of Marx's no doubt surprised Lenin. He first wrote "Logical elements in Hegel's *The Science of Logic* in his method," going on to box a reminder to himself: "Marx 1858: Marx peruses Hegel's *The Science of Logic* and plans to use one or two pages to explain its logical elements." Finally, he boxes the words, "His (Hegel's) shortcoming is 'mystification'"[7].

I believe that Marx's comment here was something that Lenin did not expect. This is **first** because Lenin did not understand how Marx could

---

5   *Ibid.*, page 29.
6   *Ibid.*, page 35-6.
7   *Ibid.*

accord such importance to Hegel's philosophy in his own Marxist **economics research**, which was why he wrote "1858." *He was confused because in his own economics research, he did not think of this methodological situating thought point; furthermore, his basic attitude towards all philosophical idealism was utter refutation and criticism.* **Second**, here Lenin saw, for the first time, Marx identify that the dialectical method was primarily elucidated in Hegel's *The Science of Logic*, but that this was still dialectics in a mysterious form. This evidently left a deep impression on him. Third, Marx wrote that he himself planned to express the dialectic in a more accessible, scientific way. I believe that this was the first important philosophical gain that Lenin made in his study of *The Marx-Engels Correspondence*, even if it came by accident for Lenin. A.İ Volodin also comments on this point[8].

Another reason why I call this an important gain is that in Lenin's later outlines, he immediately notices another instance where Marx discusses the dialectic, in the primary content of another letter written from Marx to Engels about two weeks later. In that letter, Marx tells Engels that he is reading Lasalle's *The Philosophy of Heraclitus the Obscure of Ephesus*. Marx's conclusion is that it is "an extremely boring work." However, in his discussion of this book, Marx again brings up dialectics, criticizing Lasalle for trying to explain Hegel's *The Science of Logic* using Heraclitus. Marx believes that such an attempt had obviously failed, because Lasalle "did not add anything new," and "did not provide any critical thought about the dialectic itself." Marx points out: "It is one thing to use criticism to first bring a science to a point where it can be dialectically explained; it is quite another to apply an abstract, ready logical system to the muddled notions of that system"[9]. Lenin noted Marx's assessment here, writing that "Lassalle's Heraclitus is the homework of a grammar student. No criticism of the concept of dialectics"[10]. We can see that Lenin began to pay close attention to Marx's understanding of dialectics. He began to gradually realize that in Marx's scientific research, the dialectic occupied **an even more important methodological place**. Furthermore, he noticed that each time Marx mentioned the dialectic, **he always mentioned Hegel**, and especially *The Science of Logic*. In fact, *I have found that in a January 29*

---

8   Refer to Volodin's article "Lenin's Philosophy: Should we not Discuss it?" 1990, no. 5. Also see page 133 of the first volume of *Lenin Studies* (1993).

9   Lenin, Vladimir. "The Correspondence of Marx and Engels." In *The Collected Works of Lenin*, volume 58, pages 38-39 (Chin. 2. Ed.).

10   *Ibid.*, page 36.

letter from Marx to Engels, Marx already mentions Lassalle's book, though Lenin did not "see" this book at the time.

Between 1857 and 1858, Marx's economics research experienced a climax of creative thought; as such, in the correspondence between him and Engels of this time period, we are able to see the sparks of important thought cascading out of Marx's theoretical works. On April 2, 1858, Marx wrote to Engels, introducing a "brief outline" of his own economics research. In addition to listing the six books of his work (1. On Capital. 2. Landed Property. 3. Wage Labour. 4. State. 5. International Trade. 6. World Market.), Marx gives the basic line of thought for the first of four parts of the book (capital in general, completion, credit, and share capital). He also provides a more detailed logical structure for the study of capital in general, discussing the ideas of value, money, and capital. In this letter, Marx explains some of the important progress he had made in the study of the first two questions. Lenin's outlines show that he accorded a great deal of attention to this letter. He first highlights the historical relation between rent and capital under conditions of capitalism. Lenin accurately summarizes: "modern form of landownership = the product of the influence of capital on feudal land ownership etc." Lenin, who had already accumulated a great deal of knowledge and experience in terms of economics research, is next interested in Marx's discussion of value. In the context of Marx's thought, he first goes through an overview of classical economics theories from William Petty to the teachings of Ricardo on value; for Marx, this is "the most abstract form of bourgeois wealth."

It already presupposes 1. the transcending of indigenous communism (India, etc.), 2. of all undeveloped, pre-bourgeois modes of production which are not in every respect governed by exchange. Although an abstraction, it is an historical abstraction and hence feasible only when grounded on a specific economic development of society[11].

Looking at the text, Lenin immediately grasped this philosophically significant thinking of Marx's. Lenin writes: "Value. Abstract, but **historically** abstract, can only emerge on the basis of a definite level of economic development"[12]. In the latter part of the notebook beginning with the excerpted notes on page 62, the first passage to be excerpted

11   *Ibid.*, page 38-9.
12   *Ibid.*, page 40-1.

was this one[13]. Of course, although Lenin was conscious of the basic importance and significance of Marx's words here, I believe that Lenin at this time neither really understood nor re-structured the profound meaning of Marx's ideas. In other words, I believe that Lenin here was still unable to truly enter Marx's **original thought situating**.

This is **first** because Lenin did not understand that Marx was discussing the **objective** abstract of social economic activity in relations of exchange, *i.e.*, the relations of value that men objectively form in exchange; Marx was not referring to the formation of the **notion** of value. Furthermore, this **abstract** value relationship **objectively exists** independent of the will of man (to use the discourse of philosophical materialism), because in the philosophical materialism that Lenin understood, abstraction was a **subjective** mental activity. **Second**, Lenin was not able to understand what was meant by historical abstract, because he supported a kind of non-historical philosophical materialism, not deeply understanding the practical, historical social epistemology of Hegel-Marx. **Third**, I have remarked another important piece of evidence: when Lenin read the February 25, 1859 letter from Marx to Engels, which also discusses this important problem, he did not take additional notes on it.

In our reading of this text, there are two other outlines that deserve to be analyzed: the first is of a July 4, 1858 letter by Engels, in which he discusses the relation between Hegel and natural science. Here Lenin writes the words, "**Hegel and modern natural science**"[14]. This is the last mention of Hegel in the second volume of correspondence. The second outline is of Marx's assessment of Darwin at the very end of this volume. Lenin writes, "Darwin and Marx," going on to record two sentences separated from the main text by two vertical lines: "**Darwin – provides a natural historic basis for 'our point of view'**" Lenin then underlines this sentence, drawing further attention to it. He next writes: "October 9, 1860. Marx: Darwin's *Natural Selection*. 'Although this book is written in crude English, it provides a natural historic basis for our point of view'"[15]. Looking at these outlines, it is evident that Lenin accorded a great deal of importance to Marx's views here, emphasizing them in three different ways. However, he did not go on to investigate what Marx really meant by "our point of view." *In his earlier reading of*

---

13   *Ibid.*, page 464.
14   *Ibid.*, page 43.
15   *Ibid.*, page 464.

Dietzgen, Lenin had touched on the relation between Darwin and philosophy. This Other mirror image caused Lenin to immediately acquire a kind of refracted scholarly memory as he read Marx's words. In his later study of Hegel's The Science of Logic, Lenin again makes mention of this viewpoint.

2 IT IS A MISTAKE TO NOT UNDERSTAND HEGEL'S DIALECTIC

Lenin next studied the fourth volume of correspondence. At the beginning of his research, Lenin again encounters Hegel, who always seems to be tangled up in discussions of dialectics. I presume that a subconscious idea is beginning to take shape for Lenin: in the methodological space of Marx and Engels, Hegel is always present. The fourth volume includes the third letter that Marx wrote to Engels on January 8, 1868. In this letter, Marx discusses how Dühring equated him with Stein, a viewpoint with which Marx was not in agreement. Marx asserted that he himself "worked with dialectics," while Stein merely piled up the shells of the Hegelian category: the triads. This allowed Lenin to understand Marx's judgment of traids as the "shell" of Hegel's speculative philosophy. Lenin writes, "NB, dialectics." He then goes on to make a differentiation based on Marx's viewpoint: **"Dialectics are correct? 'Dead tricotomies' (Stein's)"**[16]. It is evident that Lenin was not very clear as to what Marx really meant by tricotomies, and so uses a question mark to link these two concepts. *This is because in the early philosophical situating of Lenin's memory, he had already provided a simple refutation of Engels' use of Hegelian triads in his discussion of the negation of the negation. However, he here finds that in front of "tricotomies," Marx had added the qualifier "dead." As such the question becomes: what are "not-dead" tricotomies? In his later excerpted notes, Lenin directly records this passage of text*[17]. *He even goes on to cite this point in his article "Karl Marx"*[18].

Three days later, on January 11, 1868, Marx encounters another of Dühring's books in the British Museum: Natürliche Dialektik. In this book, Dühring is opposed to Hegel's "unnatural dialectics." Marx's assessment of this viewpoint is that Dühring does not understand

---

16   *Ibid.*, page 464.
17   *Ibid.*, page 464.
18   Lenin, Vladimir. "Karl Marx." In *The Collected Works of Lenin*, volume 26, page 57 (Chin. 2. Ed.).

Hegel's dialectics at all. Like the other German thinkers of the time, he sees Hegel's dialectics as a "dead dog"[19]. Marx wrote at the time that Feuerbach had to take a good deal of responsibility for this mistaken understanding, because it was Feuerbach who ignored the dialectical thought in Hegel's philosophy in his criticism of Hegel. Lenin must have been very surprised at this point in his reading: not only was Marx criticizing a **materialist philosophy**, but he was unabashedly criticizing Feuerbach for **not understanding** Hegel's dialectics. In his outline, Lenin draws two vertical lines, on the left writing "Feuerbach was wrong to not understand Hegel's dialectics," and on the right "**NB, Feuerbach and dialectics**"[20]. Lenin even underlines the right hand sentence to emphasize its importance. *In the thought logic and theoretical circuit that Lenin originally inherited from Plekhanov, philosophical materialism was seen as **correct**, and Hegel thus very logically was **wrong**. However, the important support for this logical situating was actually deconstructed by Marx, as he identifies a seemingly inevitably right materialist philosopher as being wrong for not understanding Hegel. For Lenin and his Other mirror image Plekhanov, this was a completely inverted standard. As such, Lenin's surprise would have been great. In his excerpted notes, Lenin specifically records this passage of text*[21].

On March 25 of that year, Marx writes to tell Engels that he is reading the works of the palaeontologist Maurer. Marx writes that Maurer did not merely study the class struggles of primitive society, but also provided a new basis to the analysis of the class struggles of human society at different stages of development. Marx compares the study of palaeontology to human social development, writing that "Owing to a **certain judicial blindness**, even the best minds fail to see, on principle, what lies in front of their noses. Later, when the time has come, we are surprised that there are traces everywhere of what we failed to see"[22]. Marx cites the historical reaction of philosophers to the French Revolution and the Enlightenment, how everything was viewed

---

19   Marx's sarcastic use of the words "dead dog" here is actually taken from a passage in the preface to the second edition of the works of Hegel. There he cites another discussion, in which the following analogy is used: "When people discuss Spinoza, it is like they are discussing a dead dog."

20   Lenin, Vladimir. "The Correspondence of Marx and Engels." In *The Collected Works of Lenin*, volume 58, page 61 (Chin. 2. Ed.).

21   *Ibid.*, page 58.

22   *Ibid.*, page 58.

as medieval and romantic. Marx goes on to mention communists who run to ancient primitive societies to find egalitarian relations of modern socialism. Lenin highlights Marx's views here. However, an even more important view expressed in this letter was Marx's discovery of a surprising notion, that human language was actually the result of the **social relations** formed as humans interact with one another.

> **But what would *Old* Hegel say, were he to learn in the hereafter that the *general* [das Allgemeine] in German and Nordic means only the communal land, and that the particular, the *special* [das Sondre, Besondere] means only private property divided off from the communal land? Here are the logical categories coming damn well out of 'our intercourse' after all[23].**

Marx is here explaining an extremely important viewpoint of historical materialism, that man's notion of language does not emerge from Hegel's absolute logic, nor is it, as the old materialists argued, the reflection of speculation on matter; rather, the essence of ideas comes from man's real **life**. Unlike all the other scholars, Marx directly finds some important archaeological evidence from Maurer's historical biological study, concluding that certain logical notions come from man's **economic intercourse**. Marx found that the word for "general" that Hegel loved to use actually carried the connotations of communal land in German and Nordic, while the word for "special" originated from the word for private property divided off from the communal land. As such, Marx realized that the concrete connotations of language are derived from the **relations** of economic intercourse. This is ironic, given Hegel's idealist logic. *We know that the relation of possible meanings and actual meanings in Saussure's linguistics was opposed to the direct meanings of actual objects in linguistic symbology (alphabetic writing). Saussure proposed the relationship between the divergent systems of generative symbols of linguistic meaning. Such an assertion was a refutation of the reflectionism of traditional materialism. However, Marx's view here brings up an important epistemological problem, that although linguistic concepts do not directly refer to material objects, they are still dependent on social relations, and this actual relationship is the real basis for the relations of symbol systems. Later, as Marx took notes on a textbook on political economy, he provided a more profound explanation of this idea.* I have found that Lenin outlined this

---

23   *Ibid.*, page 67.

viewpoint, writing: "**Hegel's shortcoming**." To the right of a dividing line, he goes on to note: "Hegel did not see that abstract notions are produced by our intercourse"[24]. I believe that Lenin at this time did not yet truly understand the underlying connotations of this passage by Marx, because this was not only Hegel's mistake but also the mistake of all past philosophy. Of course, this was also the mistake of Lenin's Other mirror image of the philosophical materialism of Feuerbach and Dietzgen.

In the first half of 1868, Marx's economics research entered a new and even more important period. He and Engels often exchanged the important findings of their economics research, and it is this content that makes up much of the first half of the fourth volume. However, Lenin did not seem to be interested in this section of correspondence, because his outlines reveal that he was still focusing on the areas of social reality and political struggle, in addition to philosophy. An important area of interest to him was Marx and Engels' discussion of the workers' philosopher Dietzgen. I have found that Lenin accorded a great deal of attention to this.

In an October 4, 1868 letter, Marx tells Engels that he is sending a package containing numerous letters from other people, including a manuscript and letter from Dietzgen. Marx believed that it would be best if the redundant portions of the book could be eliminated and if it could be published as the work of a tanner – a worker. Lenin immediately highlighted this passage[25]. Lenin was naturally interested in Marx's attitude towards Dietzgen. It would be a month until Engels responded to Marx on these questions. On November 6, Engels wrote to Marx to give his own opinions on Dietzgen's manuscript. Generally speaking, Engels did not believe that Dietzgen was a born philosopher, because although he had absorbed the teachings of Feuerbach, Marx, and natural science, his terminology was disorganized; although there were some preliminary signs of dialectics in his discourse, dialectics had not become an internal methodology. Lenin remarked Engels' views, writing, "Engels on Dietzgen (very **confused**)." At the same time, Lenin also noticed that Engels doubted the originality of some of Dietzgen's ideas, such as his expression of the thing-in-itself. Lenin was so focused on Dietzgen because this worker-philosopher was one of the philosophical foundations

---

24   *Ibid.*, page 66.
25   *Ibid.*, page 83.

of his own materialist ideas. The next day, Marx immediately replied to Engels, writing a letter in which he agreed with most of what Engels had expressed, but expressing that with the exception of being based on the thought of Feuerbach and others, Dietzgen's thought was "entirely his own independent achievement." Most importantly, Marx observed that "it is his bad luck that it was precisely Hegel that he did **not** study"[26]. This remark must have been astonishing again for Lenin: it is bad luck for a materialist philosopher to not have studied Hegel? If so, then what about Lenin himself? Of course, he had not studied Hegel either! Lenin wrote in his outline: "**Marx on Dietzgen...primarily, Dietzgen had not studied Hegel...**"[27]. I suspect that Lenin's reason for not writing "it is his bad luck," was that he was unwilling to see this assessment again; it was a "shadow" over his heart. *I believe that here Dietzgen began to lose respect in Lenin's eyes; after reading Marx's later comment that Dietzgen had regressed, Lenin began to believe that there was no hope for Dietzgen[28]. In his later excerpted notes, Lenin consecutively excerpted from the three letters between Marx and Engels from October 4 to November 7, 1868[29]. This was a rare occurrence in his excerpts, which demonstrates the influence of these letters on Lenin's thought at the time.*

In the remainder of his reading, Lenin's anxiety over this problem not only did not reduce, but actually increased, because he saw several more of Marx's references to Hegel. In an April 14, 1870 letter to Engels, Marx discusses a pamphlet he recently read, written by the Scottish Hegelian philosopher Stirling, in which he specifically criticizes Huxley. Marx writes that it is "[Stirling's] knowledge of Hegel's dialectic allows him to demonstrate Huxley's weaknesses — where he indulges in philosophizing"[30]. Marx's unspoken meaning was that an understanding of Hegel's dialectic would allow one to see the weaknesses of a materialist philosopher. It is evident that for Marx and Engels, not only are dialectics inextricably tied up with Hegel, but also a proper understanding of dialectics would allow one to see the problems with materialist philosophers (previously it was Feuerbach and Dietzgen). This could not but have led to the enlargement of the shadow in Lenin's heart. Lenin comments in his outline: "Stirling's dialectics

---

26 *Ibid.*, page 90.
27 *Ibid.*, page 90.
28 *Ibid.*, page 182.
29 *Ibid.*, page 469.
30 *Ibid.*, page 142.

and Huxley," which was the title of his outline. He next goes on to write in greater detail: "Stirling (British Hegelian – **idealist**) understood Hegel's dialectics, correctly points out **Huxley's weakness**." It is interesting to note that after writing "correctly," Lenin suddenly breaks up the sentence, draws four vertical lines, and writes the letters "NB"[31]. It is evident that he was very interested in the view that understanding Hegel's dialectics would allow one to correctly see the **weaknesses of materialist philosophers**. *In his later excerpted notes, Lenin records this expression of Marx's*[32].

As he continued his reading, Lenin leaves several more outlines on philosophy. For instance, he records Marx's famous statement that "practice surpasses all theory," a view which he expands and explains in his later study of Hegel[33]. To cite another example, Lenin records the discussion of Marx and Engels on the subject of Huxley's materialism; in this discussion, the phrase of greatest interest to Lenin was, "when we truly observe and think, we will never depart from materialism"[34]. He also observed that Marx "admired Leibnitz"[35], as well as Engels' thoughts on natural dialectics[36]. Lenin had the sense that no matter what Marx and Engels discussed, Hegel was always present. Hegel not only appeared in Marx's discussion of philosophical dialectics and study of economic problems, but also in Engels' study of natural dialectics and even in Marx's discussion of calculus[37].

It is now possible for us to conclude that in Lenin's process of understanding the thought exchange space of the correspondence between Marx and Engels, he came upon these unquestionable facts: Hegel's philosophy (especially Hegel's *The Science of Logic*) is the most important foundation of dialectical theory. An understanding of Hegel's philosophy (dialectics) will allow one to see the theoretical weaknesses of some philosophical materialists. I deduce that this was one of the most important thought motivations that pushed Lenin to resolve to study Hegel's philosophy.

---

31 *Ibid.*, page 142.
32 *Ibid.*, page 471-2.
33 *Ibid.*, page 92.
34 *Ibid.*, page 94. In his article "Karl Marx," Lenin would go on to borrow this phrase directly. See Lenin, Vladimir. "Karl Marx." In *The Collected Works of Lenin*, volume 26, page 54 (Chin. 2. Ed.).
35 Lenin, Vladimir. "The Correspondence of Marx and Engels." In *The Collected Works of Lenin*, volume 58, page 145 (Chin. 2. Ed.).
36 *Ibid.*, page 160-2.
37 *Ibid.*, page 179-80.

3 DIALECTICS: THE SPIRIT OF MARXIST PHILOSOPHY

Lenin continued with the first volume of the *Marx-Engels Correspondence*, which included the letters exchanged between Marx and Engels between 1844 and 1853. In this volume of correspondence, only letters from Engels to Marx were included for the years 1844-1846, and the majority of the letters in which Marx and Engels discussed philosophical problems were not included; this is most unfortunate.

The first few letters in the first volume were written by young Engels to Marx. In these letters, Engels discusses a few extremely important theoretical problems. I call them important because this time period was the eve of the founding of historical materialism, and many critical **symptoms of change** begin to appear in the theoretical logic of these letters. For instance, in the first letter Engels suggests that Marx write a few books to clear up past prejudices and conceptions of history, and to provide theoretical "backup" to the proletariat struggle. The second letter was more important, mentioning several important figures who directly influenced the philosophical changes of Marx and Engels. The first of these was the German economist List, the founder of the theory of productive force; the second was Hess, a German thinker who became a communist before Marx and Engels, and whose focus on economic alienation theory formed the logical premise of Marx's *1844 Manuscript*; the third person was Stirner, the first German scholar to attack the idea of "species," thoroughly refuting Feuerbach's (young Marx's) humanist logic. These three men all came to play important roles in Marx's process of establishing historical materialism[38].

It is especially important to note that young Engels discussed the theoretical significance of Stirner's egoism. He believed that Stirner's egoism was "more important" than Hess' thought, and that he and Marx "while inverting it, [could] continue to build on it." Engels' profound analysis finds that Stirner's critique of Feuerbach's humanism is correct, but that he should not have stopped at the individual as "the ego"; rather, he should materialistically proceed from empirical individuals, and then ascend to "man" as a whole[39]. *This viewpoint would later be-*

---

38   Refer to section three of chapter one and section three of chapter five of my *Marx Revisited*.

39   Engels, Frederick. *Marx-Engels Correspondence*, Beijing Sanlian Press (1957), volume 1, pages 8-9 (Chinese).

come an important part of historical materialism: the relation between actual individuals and social life. However, we find that Lenin did not note Engels' discussion here at all, only drawing four vertical lines in the margin of this letter. It seems as though the several passages of important content that we have just introduced did not arouse Lenin's interest. Logically speaking, Lenin's thought at this time should have been more very active, because young Marx and young Engels were already professional masters of philosophy, discussing the most important philosophers and philosophical questions of the time. However, what we find is that Lenin was never able to rouse any interest in himself towards the philosophical questions that Marx and Engels discussed in this "prehistoric" time period. The reason for this is simple: the background of this historical context was unfamiliar to him. Evidently, Lenin's philosophical thought framework and theoretical circuit was inevitably unable to understand what Engels was writing about here.

It is not difficult to see from the outlines that Lenin was unusually silent as he read the first volume of correspondence. Because he did not encounter any content or philosophical problems that corresponded to his philosophical thought framework at the time, after leaving a very few reading notations and commentaries on socialism and real-life problems, he quickly ended his reading of the first volume.

Lenin's last reading was of the third volume in *Correspondence*, which included the letters exchanged between Marx and Engels between 1861 and 1867. The time frame of these letters corresponded to Marx's focused study of economics. As we know, Marx was very cognizant of dialectics in his own study of economics, a phenomenon that certainly aroused Lenin's interest. As such, Lenin's logical thought began to be active again as he read and notated the third volume.

The first signs of mental activity that we can see from Lenin's outlines came as he read a letter from Marx to Engels dated December 9, 1861. In this letter, Marx informs Engels that he agrees with his strictures on Lassalle, which Engels had expressed in a December 2 letter to Marx. Marx goes on to write that "ideologism permeates everything, and the dialectical method is **wrongly** applied." Lassalle's mistake is that he treats dialectics as the summation of individual cases; "Hegel never described as dialectics the subsumption of vast numbers of **cases under**

a general principle"[40]. Lenin accords special attention to two elements of Marx's discussion. First, Marx's mention of dialectics, and second, Marx's **positive** citation of Hegel's thought. This is why Lenin records, on the second half of page 45 in his notes, "Lassalle is an 'ideologue,' wrongly applies dialectics: 'takes cases to be a general principle.'" This last phrase is Lenin's own summary, which he emphasizes with double-lined parentheses. Next, Lenin records Marx's expression completely: "December 9, 1861. Marx: 'the second volume is more interesting, if only by reason of the Latin quotations. Ideologism permeates everything, and the dialectical method is wrongly applied. Hegel never described as dialectics the subsumption of vast numbers of cases under a general principle'"[41]. *Later, Lenin would again make mention of this viewpoint in his "On the Question of Dialectics."*

What next piqued Lenin's interest was a letter from Engels to Marx, written on June 16, 1867. In this letter, Engels reviews the method that Marx used in the first chapter of the first volume of *Capital*. As we know, in that chapter, Marx used the dialectic that proceeded from abstract to concrete, as introduced in Hegel's *The Science of Logic*, to explain his revolutionary economics findings. Engels proposes that Marx "could provide rather more extensive historical evidence for the conclusions you have here reached dialectically," also suggesting that Marx use the method of Hegel's *Encyclopaedia*, *i.e.*, "each dialectical transition emphasized by means of a special heading." *This refers to The Small Logic.* Engels goes on to assert that "those who are capable of thinking dialectically will understand [*Capital*]"; here he primarily refers to Marx's direct use of Hegel's dialectical logic in the first chapter of the first volume of *Capital*[42]. Of course, Lenin noted this assessment by Engels. In his outline he writes: "Engels on first chapter of Capital: more historical, concrete..."[43]. *In his later study of Hegel's philosophy, Lenin finally understood the significance of this viewpoint. This passage by Engels was re-written by Lenin to read: without understanding Hegel's The Science of Logic, one cannot understand Marx's **Capital**, especially its first chapter.*

---

40   *Ibid.*, page 56.
41   *Ibid.*, page 56.
42   *Ibid.*, page 56.
43   *Ibid.*, page 442.

Next, Lenin read Marx's true thoughts on his own Capital, included in a June 22, 1867 letter from Marx to Engels. In this letter, Marx tells Engels that he partially accepted Engels' suggestions, including an appendix to *Capital* which he divided into small paragraphs, each with its own heading. We know that in the first chapter of *Capital*, Marx proceeded from abstract to concrete much like Hegel in *The Science of Logic*; in other words, he began with the simplest, most abstract commodity phenomena in capitalist economic relations and proceeded through the complex historical changes in relations of money before finally reaching the truly puzzling capital relations. Marx writes:

> The *simplest form of a commodity*, in which its value is not yet expressed in its relation to all other commodities but only as something *differentiated* from its own natural form, embodies the *whole secret of the money form* and thereby, *in nuce* [in embryo], *of all bourgeois forms of the product of labour*[44].

At the same time, Marx explains how, at the end of the third chapter of *Capital*, he "quote[s] Hegel's discovery of the **law of the transformation of a merely quantitative change into a qualitative one** as being attested by history and natural science alike"[45]. Lenin highlights this important explanation in his outlines.

Finally, Lenin read one of Marx's own explanations, that Capital was the first application of the **dialectical method** to political economy. Lenin highlights this viewpoint, double-underlining the words "dialectical method"[46].

I have found that these three important theoretical views were all theoretical thinking points that prompted Lenin to experience an important shift in understanding in the latter stages of his study of Hegelian philosophy. From Hegel's *The Science of Logic* to Marx's *Capital*, and from Hegel's idea dialectics to Marx's practical dialectics, Lenin ultimately realized an extremely profound, revolutionary shift in cognition and logical détournement in terms of Marx's philosophical thought. This very well may be the most basic theoretical significance of Lenin's notes on *Marx-Engels' Correspondence*.

---

44   *Ibid.*, page 445.
45   *Ibid.*, page 446.
46   *Ibid.*, page 450.

On October 30, 1913, Lenin wrote to his sister, mentioning that he had recently read the *Marx-Engels Correspondence*, and concluding that "there are many interesting things in this collection of letters." He expressed his desire to write a review of the collection for the *Prosveshcheniye* magazine. *The Proletariat Truth* published an advertisement for this in its December 14, 1913 edition, though Lenin would never finish this article, only completing the very first part. It was not until 1920 that this text was published in *Pravda*, and because Lenin only finished his section on the early thought of young Engels, it was appropriately published on the commemoration of Engels' 100th birthday. When the article was published, Lenin specifically added a subheading that read, "Engels was one of the founders of communism." However, we also see Lenin's following important viewpoint:

If one were to attempt to define in a single word the focus, so to speak, of the whole correspondence, the central point at which the whole body of ideas expressed and discussed converges—that word would be *dialectics*. The application of materialist dialectics to the reshaping of all political economy from its foundations up, its application to history, natural science, philosophy and to the policy and tactics of the working class—that was what interested Marx and Engels most of all, that was where they contributed what was most essential and new, and that was what constituted the masterly advance they made in the history of revolutionary thought[47].

It is evident that Lenin already understood that for Marx and Engels, dialectics was not some general scholarly viewpoint that one could do without; rather, dialectics constituted the spirit of all of Marxist philosophy. Furthermore, in order to understand dialectics, one must inevitably go through Hegelian philosophy, and especially Hegel's *The Science of Logic*. This was the most important of Lenin's discoveries after reading *The Marx-Engels Correspondence*.

---

47   *Ibid.*, page 276.

PART II

BERN NOTEBOOKS: LENIN ON THE SHOULDERS OF PHILOSOPHICAL GIANTS

The third stage of the development of Lenin's philosophical thought began in 1914; the central text during this period were the *Bern Notebooks*, with which we are familiar. These were a collection of extremely important excerpted notes and recorded thoughts, written by Lenin as he studied Hegelian philosophy in Bern, Switzerland between 1914 and 1915. The analysis of these notes will take place in the second part of this book, forming the main body of the content of the final six chapters. Objectively speaking, relative to prior studies of Lenin's thought, there are no new texts to analyze here; rather, the crucial interpretive problem for us to solve is **which thought framework** will be used to re-examine these texts. This part of the book constitutes the emphasis of the research and thought in *Lenin Revisited*. The theoretical situating method that I propose in this book is also **activated** primarily in relation to the context of the *Bern Notebooks*.

Under the influence of the Stalinist dogmatic ideological framework in the 1930s, the crude practice of non-historically forcing Lenin's philosophical thought into a homogenized interpretive context gradually became popular among Soviet scholarly circles. This practice was especially evident in the "planned conception theory," developed by the Soviet scholar Kedrov in his study of Lenin's *Philosophical Notebooks*, which became the most influential and most important theoretical reference model in this field of research for quite a long time. However, as we engage in profound examination, analysis, and investigation of Lenin's 20-year process of philosophical learning and study, we find that Kedrov's "planned conception theory" is a **false-situating, heavily biased by ideology**. Using a non-historical simulacrum, this false-situating created a fictional, theoretical thought historical situating in which Lenin's third systematic study of philosophy in the *Bern Notebooks* was seen as preparation for a work on dialectics. I believe that such an assertion does not stand up to serious philological or theoretical scholarly scrutiny. Using the new situating interpretive context that I simulate in this book, Lenin's study of Hegelian philosophy in the *Bern Notebooks* was certainly not a smooth, homogeneous logical progression. Furthermore, considering the whole of this study, Lenin's understanding of Hegelian philosophy is not always completely correct. I believe that the *Bern Notebooks* reflect the multiple important logical détournements and leaps in understanding that Lenin's thought experienced during this period in time. Through careful analysis, we are able to divide this process into the following heterogeneous stages: **first**, Lenin's understanding of Hegel is based on refutational notions. **Second**, various logical cognition frameworks come into intense conflict, a period of contradictory thought. **Third**, Lenin's philosophical thought shifts greatly, and his theoretical logic experiences major détournement. **Fourth**, Lenin summarizes his own philosophical research in a short overview. Following the thread of Lenin's logic, the thought logic of his early reading in the *Bern Notebooks* was an **Other unity**; not long after, as his reading and research grew more profound, this false unity and Other theoretical circuit naturally disappeared. In Lenin's own thinking logic, contradictory understandings led to the repeated emergence of logical ruptures. However, it was precisely in the self-reflection and pondering brought on by these contradictions and ruptures that Lenin stepped towards a new and important theoretical logical détournement. When his research finally came to an end, Lenin unconsciously constructed a new **non-unity** in his short theoretical overview.

The research in the second part of this book will use subtle, textual simulation-situating to support my theoretical conclusions.

I should also point out that in my following study of the *Bern Notebooks*, I will cite the views of a few Western Leninologists and Western Marxist researchers, in addition to those of Soviet and Eastern European scholars. Such scholars include Korsch, Althusser, Levinee, Dunayevskaya, and others; I include these important figures because the focus of their attention on Lenin's philosophical thought was concentrated on the *Bern Notebooks*. This research has become increasingly important in Western scholarly circles since Lefebvre's 1938 translation of the Bern Notebooks into French and Dunayevskaya's 1953 translation of the *Notebooks* into English. This increased the special intertextual perspective on this book, as well as differentiated their own views from Western Leninology.

Gadamer once said that texts are not independent, heterogeneous things, but rather relationships[1]. As we examine texts, a relationship has already occurred, and what we see can never be an independent text, but rather the relation of that text to us. The historical context of reading and study inevitably seeps into our understanding of the text. As such, I believe that Kedrov was unable to truly enter the philosophical, textual context of Lenin's *Bern Notebooks*, hampered as he was by doctrinaire constraints. Furthermore, when we admit to ourselves that the theoretical conclusions reached by Kedrov and his followers in a particular historical period cannot explain the possible space of closed text and enter the 21st century, when we sincerely re-examine this important body of texts, we will find that they are re-opened before our eyes. I truly hope that my study in this book will independently find and open a completely new reading and research vision, as Chinese Marxist scholars throw off the bonds of the ideological framework of former Soviet-Eastern European ideology.

---

1   Gadamer, Hans-Georg: *Hermeneutik-Ästhetik-Praktische Philosophie: Gadamer im Gespräch*, Commercial Press (2005), page 44 (Chinese).

CHAPTER NINE

LENIN'S PERSPECTIVE AS HE BEGINS
TO READ HEGEL'S PHILOSOPHY

In Lenin's early reading of Hegelian philosophy as part of his research for the *Bern Notebooks*, what we find is a fairly unsuccessful thought experiment, which took place under the influence of an external Other mirror image. It was also a **false** reading from within a closed theoretical loop. Concretely speaking, Lenin examined Hegel's complex speculative philosophical logic from the external **mirrored Others** of imprecisely understood Marx-Engels, Plekhanov, Feuerbach, and Dietzgen. It was under these circumstances that Lenin reached his earliest, simple refutational conclusions about Hegel's philosophy. As his reading and thinking began to deepen, Lenin's attitude towards Hegel's philosophy also began to change. The nearer he drew to Hegel, to the new theoretical **thought arena** produced by the internal, fixed overall logic of *The Science of Logic* and other texts, the nearer he drew to Marx. In other words, in the progression of Lenin's reading, a new line of reading thought began to emerge, which came into sharp conflict with his original reading framework. In this chapter, we will re-simulate the circumstances of Lenin's early reading.

1 WHY DID LENIN READ HEGEL?

According to my research, Lenin's post-1914 *Bern Notebooks* were written with the following important philosophical backgrounds. *First*, in early 1914, Lenin agreed to write an entry on Marx for the *Russian Granat Encyclopaedia*, which is now known as the famous text "Karl Marx." In this text, Lenin had to specifically introduce Marxist materialist dialectics. *Lenin's wife Nadya Krupskaya gave a direct explanation of this in her* **Reminiscences of Lenin**. *She writes, "In connection with the chapters on philosophic materialism and dialectics, Ilyich began diligently to reread Hegel and other philosophers, and kept up this study even after he had finished the article"[1]. However, Kedrov strangely takes this as direct evidence that Lenin was writing a work on dialectics; this is obviously an illegitimate use of history.*

The **second** background came at nearly the same time. After the First World War broke out, the social-democrats of the Second International (such as the German Kautsky and the Russian Plekhanov, among others) all devolved into chauvinism or social imperialism[2]. They exert themselves to justify opportunism and to justify imperialist wars "with a learned mien and with a stock of false quotations from Marx"[3] asserting in all honesty that their theoretical basis was "dialectics." This was also an important background to Lenin's research. Referring to the call for war by bourgeois governments, Lenin writes: "Plekhanov embellishes even this threadbare piece of vulgarity with his inevitable Jesuitical reference to 'dialectics'"[4], then turns around and insults Lenin and other leftist leaders for not understanding dialectics. On October 11, 1914, Plekhanov gave a lecture in Lausanne, Switzerland, which he titled "On the Attitude of the Socialists to the War." During his

---

1   Krupskaya, Nadya. *Reminiscences of Lenin*. People's Press (1972), p. 261.
2   After the beginning of the First World War, the German Social-Democrat Party actually voted to support the Kaiser's participation in the war; not long after, the various socialist parties and Marxists across Europe all declared their loyalty to their own countries. This caused the collapse of the Second International. At first, Lenin did not believe that the actions of the German Social-Democrat Party were true, thinking that they were some trick of the German Kaiser. Thus when their support for the war was confirmed as true, Lenin was very astonished.
3   Lenin, Vladimir. "The Collapse of the Second International." In *The Collected Works of Lenin*, volume 26, p. 226.
4   *Ibid.*, page 234.

remarks, Plekhanov accused Lenin of "metaphysics," asserting that "all of Lenin's words lack dialectics"[5]. It is important to note that Lenin did not directly rebut Plekhanov's critique that he "lacked dialectics"[6]. This incident made Lenin very angry, leading him to exclaim, "Plekhanov has set a new record in the noble sport of substituting sophistry for dialectics"[7]. He believed that with Kautsky and Plekhanov, "Dialectic is turned into the meanest and basest sophistry!"[8]. After this incident, Lenin began publishing a series of political editorials, directly struggling against the incorrect school of thought; at the same time, he resolved within himself to comprehensively understand dialectics.

Third, at this time, Lenin's theoretical examination of actual revolutionary practice was afflicted by his acceptance of Plekhanov's interpretation of Marxist philosophy (philosophical materialism); however, this notion that emphasized the determination of consciousness by matter could not provide legitimate support for the Bolsheviks' push for the practice of Russian proletarian revolution. Lenin's philosophical theoretical situating at this time was in dire need of a scientific standpoint, viewpoint, and method that would recognize the active, creative role of the revolutionary subject. This was a vital missing link in Lenin's theoretical logic. *However, he did not immediately realize that in his later learning and study of Hegelian philosophy, he would break through Plekhanov's false simulacra and closed theoretical circuit towards the essence of Marxist philosophy, truly acquiring historical, practical dialectics in Marxist historical materialism. This would be an important philosophical weapon that he wielded in the great Russian "October Revolution."* Interestingly enough, Lenin locked in Hegel's philosophy as the primary object of his learning and study of dialectics, in particular Hegel's *The Science of Logic*. Logically speaking, it seems as

---

5 Lenin, Vladimir. "Speech at G.V. Plekhanov's Lecture 'On the Attitude of the Socialists to the War'" In *The Collected Works of Lenin*, volume 26, page 60 (Chin. 2. Ed.).
6 See Lenin, Vladimir. "Speech at G.V. Plekhanov's Lecture 'On the Attitude of the Socialists to the War'" In *The Collected Works of Lenin*, volume 26, pages 20-22 (Chin. 2. Ed.). According to Krupskaya's memoirs, Ilyich had only ten minutes. He could only deal with the bare essentials. Plekhanov retorted with his usual display of wit. The Mensheviks, who were an overwhelming majority, wildly applauded him. The impression was that Plekhanov had won the day. See Krupskaya, Nadya. Reminiscences of Lenin. People's Press (1972), 261.
7 Lenin, Vladimir. "The Collapse of the Second International." In *The Collected Works of Lenin*, volume 26, page 234 (Chin. 2. Ed., 1990 edition).
8 *Ibid.*, page 252.

though since Lenin desired to more deeply understand Marxist materialist dialectics, he should have re-read Marx and Engels' *Capital* (and other philosophical texts); however, he did not do this. The question for us is, why not? The first reason was that in reading *The Marx-Engels Correspondence*, Lenin discovered that **Hegel was present** each time Marx and Engels discussed dialectics. From these letters, it seemed as though understanding Hegel's philosophy was the standard by which one could measure one's real understanding of dialectics as a whole. *I believe that when Lenin read and studied the philosophy Dietzgen and Feuerbach, he got a taste for reading first-hand works; as such, he had faith in his ability to understand dialectical theory from Hegel's own writings.* The second reason was that the theorists of the reformist faction and revolutionary faction in socialism all borrowed Hegel's "dialectics" in debating each other[9]. Here, Dunayevskaya's analysis is quite profound[10]. *In fact, Lenin had not yet conducted any kind of systematic study of Hegelian philosophy before this point, much less acquired a deep understanding of the dialectical thinking in Hegelian philosophy.*

In fact, as we have already pointed out, in the spring of 1914, Lenin had already begun to work on "Karl Marx"; however, because he was very busy at the time, he wrote in July to tell the editor that he would not be able to complete the work. The editor responded by insisting that it be Lenin who write the piece. Not long later, the First World War broke out on August 4, 1914 and Lenin was arrested by Austrian authorities. In September of 1914, Lenin reached Bern, Switzerland. Once there, he quickly buried himself in his work at the library, resolving to begin his own philosophical studies. Imagine that strange historical scene: the flames of war rise into the sky from all over the European continent, the first world-wide war, in which mankind slaughters itself at an unprecedented scale, grows ever more intense, the socialist workers' movement founded by Marx and Engels themselves is on the verge of its first great rupture, the leaders of the socialist political parties in various European countries were busy mobilizing their forces to participate in the fighting, and through it all, Lenin begins his year-long systematic study of Hegelian philosophy. This was truly great resolve on the part of Lenin! Dunayevskaya writes:

---

9   Dunayevskaya, Raya. *Marxism and Freedom*. Liaoning Educational Press (1998), page 158 (Chinese).
10   Dunayevskaya, Raya. *Philosophy and Revolution*. Liaoning Educational Press (2000), pages 86-88 (Chinese).

The simultaneous beginning of the First World War and vote of the German Social-Democrats in favour of the Kaiser fundamentally shook the philosophical foundation on which Lenin had always based himself, which he had always believed was firm and unbreakable. On August 4, 1914, he smashed to pieces those concepts in which all the different factions of the Marxist movement believed[11].

What are these "concepts" of which Dunayevskaya wrote? She points out that before August 4, all Marxists believed that material conditions prepared the foundation for the creation of a new society; as material conditions progressed, the proletariat became more and more ready to seize the ruling authority." For Dunayevskaya, the break out of the First World War and the reaction of the socialists of the various European countries to this event thoroughly smashed the basis of this idea. Examining the chaos and confusion, Lenin calmly grasped the irreversible destruction of the situation. Thus he attempted to find a new philosophical foundation for his thought and restructure his rationality through systematically studying Hegelian philosophy. It is evident that Dunayevskaya was very sensitive to these developments; we shall soon see the new philosophical foundation of which she spoke.

Another historical detail even more deserving of our attention is this: Lenin finished writing "Karl Marx" in November 1914, sending it to be published at that time. However, in early 1915, in a letter to the editors of the encyclopaedia, he wrote:

I would like to ask if there is time to make some revisions of the section on dialectics. What is the latest date by which I need to send the revisions? I have been studying this problem for the past half-month. I believe that if time permits, I will be able to make some additions[12].

What was the content that Lenin desired to revise and add to? What caused him to want to revise what he had already written? This is a question to which we must pay careful attention. Interestingly, Dunayevskaya's answer is that Hegel's logic constituted the philosophical basis for the internal division in Marxism[13]. She believed that

11 *Ibid.*, page 86.
12 Lenin, Vladimir. "To the Editorial Board of the Granat Bros. Encyclopaedic Dictionary." In *The Collected Works of Lenin*, volume 47, page 66 (Chin. 2. Ed.).
13 Dunayevskaya, Raya. *Marxism and Freedom.* Liaoning Educational Press (1998), page 158 (Chinese).

Lenin had crossed the bridge of Hegelian philosophy towards the ideal-ist belief that ideas create the world, thus fundamentally departing from philosophical materialism. I cannot agree at all with Dunayevskaya's explanation. In my opinion, this is a mistaken attempt to **Hegelianize** Lenin's thought at the time of the *Bern Notebooks*. This mistaken expla-nation, added to Kedrov's "planned conception theory" which has been dominant among Soviet-Eastern European scholarly circles for many years, are two opposing, erroneous logical identifications, both veil-ing historical truth, both rendering the complex threads of thought in the theoretical philosophical situating of Lenin's *Bern Notebooks* even more vague.

If both of these views are wrong, then what were the actual historical facts? Here we can return to a few important questions that we have already raised earlier: was the theoretical logic in the course of Lenin's Bern Notebooks a homogenized process? Was it the simple process of realization that Kedrov proposes in his "planned conception theory?" Furthermore, if we refute this proposition, *i.e.*, if we recognize the great changes that took place in Lenin's philosophical thought as he wrote the *Bern Notebooks*, then were these changes as great as Dunayevskaya's description? In other words, did Lenin move towards Hegelian ideal-ist idea dialectics and end there? This is a difficult research question and a critical component of our re-simulation of Lenin's thought space. Here we will first examine the circumstances of Lenin's early reading of Hegelian philosophy.

2 THREE FOUNDATIONAL ELEMENTS OF LENIN'S EARLY READING FRAMEWORK

As soon as Lenin opened the third volume of the *Collected Works of Hegel*, he was immediately taken by the introduction that Hegel wrote to the first edition of *The Science of Logic*[14]. As we all know, *The Science of Logic* was a continuation of *The Phenomenology of Spirit* in Hegel's overall philosophical progression. *Hegel referred to The Phenomenology of Spirit as the "introduction" to The Science of Logic*[15]. In The Phenomenology of Spirit, the Idea is raised out of

---

14   Hegel's *The Science of Logic* was divided into three volumes in the 1883 edition of The Collected Works of Hegel. The first part, *Objective Logic*, was divided between the third ("The Doctrine of Being") and fourth ("Essence"), while the second part, *Subjective Doctrine of the Notion*, was placed in the fifth volume.
15   Hegel, Georg Wilhelm Friedrich. *The Science of Logic*. Commercial Press (1977), volume 1, pages 103-104 (Chinese).

sensuous material phenomena and the self-consciousness that composes apperception using a critical refutational logical framework. To use Hegel's own words to express this, "I have exhibited consciousness in its movement onwards from the first immediate opposition of itself and the object to absolute knowing."[16] In *The Science of Logic,* the spirit proceeds from its own most simple, most immediate idea qualifications, passing through the progression of complex conceptual contradiction until it finally transitions to the pinnacle of the spirit: the Absolute Idea. As such, in this introduction Hegel first summarizes the pre-history of consciousness (from metaphysics, common knowledge-science, and knowledge-reason to spirit). I have found that the general exposition of metaphysics given by Hegel in this introduction, as well as his explanation of the relation between scientific and spiritual life, did not spark Lenin's interest.

In fact, through his study and learning of professional philosophical texts by Dietzgen and Feuerbach, by this time Lenin was already very familiar with **philosophical cognition**. Thus, although his motivation for reading Hegel came from a real need of revolutionary practice, in order to truly, **deeply understand and correctly apply dialectics to revolutionary practice**, each time Hegel brings up interesting cognitive theories, Lenin immediately remarks it in his notes. *Levine writes that in 1914, Lenin's primary interest was in applying dialectics to epistemology; he still focused on epistemological problems[17]. This is obviously not completely correct. Lenin did not study Hegel in order to study epistemology. In fact, dialectics were the focus of his study, and epistemology was only a field with which Lenin felt more comfortable. It was not until the philosophical situating of Lenin's later reading and study that the two logical lines of thought became unified.* As such, the excerpts in the notebooks reveal that Lenin approached his research with two points of interest: first, "the **movement** of scientific cognition – that is the essential thing." Second, "The 'path of self-construction' = the **path** (this is the crux, in my opinion) of real cognition, of the process of cognizing, of movement from ignorance to knowledge"[18]. Interestingly, "movement" and "path of self-construction" were both

---

16   *Ibid.*, page 29.
17   Levine, Norman. *Dialogue within the Dialectic*. Yunnan People's Press (1997), page 361 (Chinese).
18   Refer to *The Collected Works of Lenin* (Chin. 2. Ed.), volume 55, page 73. Let us emphasize again that in the text of the Bern Notebooks, Lenin primarily highlighted passages of text by underlining the words.

dialectical elements in epistemology. I have found that from the beginning, Lenin focused on dialectics from within the **theoretical circuit of the epistemological framework** with which he was familiar: this was an important **theoretical unconsciousness**. *Here, Kedrov's conclusion is that "Lenin immediately grasped the characteristics and centre of Hegel's The Science of Logic itself"[19]*. I believe that this conclusion was premature and exaggerated.

Here Lenin leaves the first of his boxes in these notes, in which he clearly proposes a reminder for the rest of his reading logic: Hegel's idealist dialectics must be **materialistically turned around**[20]. This was an important thinking principle of Lenin's early learning of philosophical materialism, which was also the deepest and most direct impression left to him about **materialist** dialectics as he read the *Marx-Engels Correspondence*[21]. For Lenin at this time, the relation between Marx and Hegel was one in which Marx *inverted* Hegel's idealist dialectics into materialist dialectics. Therefore, "Logic and the theory of knowledge must be derived from 'the development of all natural and spiritual life,'" and not from Hegel's idealistically backwards expression[22].

I must remind my readers that it is critical for us to understand this point, because this was a critical premise of Lenin's logical philosophical situating as he began his reading. This is a relatively important **logical entry** into our correct discussion of the true progression of Lenin's line of thought as he read.

In the early stages of Lenin's study of Hegel's *The Science of Logic*, his primary interpretive framework was composed of the following important **Other mirror image support points**:

19   Refer to Kedrov's *Study of Lenin's "Philosophical Notebooks,"* Qiushi Press (1984), page 127 (Chinese).
20   As we have already pointed out, in the notes, Lenin used differing sizes of boxes to emphasize his own important viewpoints. A rough estimate indicates that there are approximately 170 such boxes in these notes.
21   There, Lenin discovered that whenever Marx and Engels discussed dialectics, they almost always brought up Hegel. At the same time, their criticisms of Feuerbach, Dietzgen, and other old materialists were all based on their misunderstanding of Hegel's dialectics. This touched Lenin greatly; it was also one of the important theoretical reasons for Lenin's decision to ultimately resolve to profoundly study Hegel's philosophy. We have already specifically discussed this issue earlier in this book. Refer to pages 35, 43, 61, 89, 162-163, and 318 of volume 58 of *The Collected Works of Lenin* (Chin. 2. Ed.).
22   Refer to *The Collected Works of Lenin* (Chin. 2. Ed.), volume 55, page 73.

First, as we have already discussed, Lenin's central mirror-imaged theoretical support point was brought up by Marx himself: he wrote that his dialectics were "inverted" from Hegel, **changed from idealist dialectics to materialist dialectics**. However, I do believe that Lenin was capable of profoundly understanding this "inversion" from the beginning of his study; therefore, the "inversion" to which Lenin refers at this stage in his research was simply to **exchange** Hegel's concepts of spirit and consciousness as the essence of the world for concepts of a material and natural world. This is obviously a false situating of Marx's "inversion." Kedrov believes that Lenin's restructuring of Hegel's dialectics were completely in line with the work of Marx and Engels[23]. I, on the other hand, believe that such a generalized assessment of the different stages and changes in Lenin's reading progress is imprecise. Below, I will go on to explain how only after Lenin experienced an important détournement of theoretical logic could he truly attain and reconstruct Marx's thought context. On the other hand, some Chinese scholars, such as Professor Cong Dachuan, astutely points out that Lenin's "materialist inversion" was not a Marxist inversion of Hegelian philosophy[24]; however, he does not distinguish between the early and late periods of Lenin's study in the *Bern Notebooks* either, and so does not remark the fundamental changes that took place in Lenin's thought at the time. Lenin's viewpoint here is expressed very clearly in the text. In fact, in the early stages of his reading, he used different methods to continually remind himself of this; to use Lacan's words, this was **redundant** Other questioning coming from a theoretical Other.

The second mirror image theoretical support point was composed of the ready results of the critiques by Marx, Engels, and Plekhanov of Hegelian philosophy. In Lenin's **first stage of reading** (from the beginning of *The Science of Logic* to the end of the "general conclusion" of the second part, pages 72-146 of the Chinese edition of Lenin's *Philosophical Notebooks*) Lenin carefully referred to these classical authors from within a closed theoretical loop, placing and interpreting Hegel using the **readily available standpoints and conclusions** from **theoretical Other reflections**. *This is a non-reflective "as you read" reading method reading. In his early reading, Lenin cites Marx three times, Engels seven times, Plekhanov once, and Feuerbach twice; in his*

23 Refer to Kedrov's *Study of Lenin's "Philosophical Notebooks,"* Qiushi Press (1984), page 169 (Chinese).
24 Refer to Cong Dachuan's The Dialectical System: Marx and Lenin. *Yunnan Social Science*, volume 2 (1995).

later reading, this kind of focused citation stops almost completely; on the contrary, Plekhanov actually becomes the object of Lenin's criticism and reflection. This method of reading also immediately reflects the fact that as he began reading Hegelian philosophy, Lenin was not very confident, still incapable of constructing his own sovereign thought space. As such, he was in need of background support from Other mirror images. When a researcher is incapable of independently examining the object of his interpretation, his most common practice is to naturally reveal the **theoretical Others** who identify with him, and to continually borrow ready-made conclusions and statements from outside, authoritative figures within a closed theoretical circuit. This allows him to fill the logical gaps in his own situating space. This phenomenon generally takes place during a thinker's early logical situating period, or in the earliest stage of a researcher's turn to a new area of thought. However, even though this may have been the case, Lenin's reading scope was not wrong. Though some Western Leninologists have said that before Lenin understood Hegelian philosophy, he practiced "mechanical materialism" (or "vulgar materialism," to use Anderson's words), in fact, that **was actually** "dialectical materialism," only a **half-read** "dialectical materialism" in an Other scope. This "dialectical materialism" was not Lenin's sovereign, independent scope of understanding Hegelian philosophy, which only formed later[25].

The **third** mirror image theoretical support point was Lenin's basic judgment of Hegel's philosophical theoretical logic. We can see that Lenin's overall attitude was **general and fundamental refutation**; when commenting on the most important theoretical principles of Hegel's philosophy, he most often uses such words as "nonsense," "mysticism," and "unclear." It is evident that Lenin, for the time, did

---

25   For more on the distortions of Lenin's attitude here by Western "Leninologists," refer to Levine's *Dialogue within the Dialectic*; Leszek Kolakowski's *Main Currents of Marxism*; and Robert Payne's *The Life and Death of Lenin*. Of these, I believe that Levine's study of Lenin is the most profound. After grasping a few basic textual facts, Levine's interpretation reaches a higher scholarly level. However, his primary conclusions on the developments of Lenin's philosophical thought are not correct, because he is set on portraying Lenin as a laughable Hegelian. However, when I met with Kevin Anderson in October of 2007, he believed that Levine's research was insufficient. Among Western Marxists, Althusser and Dunayevskaya present more systematic studies. Refer to Althusser's Lenin and Philosophy, and Dunayevskaya's *Marxism and Freedom*, and *Philosophy and Revolution*. Dunayevskaya is more profound and more systematic, and even quite deep in some areas. However, her basic conclusions on Lenin's Bern Notebooks are as arbitrary and simple as Levine's.

not immediately realize the **comprehensive rationality** of Hegel's philosophy. This inability to understand was in line with Lenin's early philosophical thought logic. *This even though Lenin had already read of the great theoretical respect paid to Hegel by Marx and Engels in the* **Marx-Engels Correspondence.** *In the introduction to Deborin's translation of the Bern Notebooks, he vaguely points out that Lenin basically agrees with Hegel's system; such a view is obviously imprecise. This is because this "agreement" only takes place in the thought space of Lenin's* **Bern Notebooks** *after his theoretical logical détournement.* I have also found that Deborin focuses too much on Lenin's approbation of Hegel; this was likely the one of the reasons why he was later criticized for "Hegelizing" Lenin's thought.

It was precisely this important, special logical interpretive framework and line of thought that latently constrained Lenin as he **first entered** Hegelian philosophy. Althusser believes that Lenin's notes on Hegel's works maintained the standpoint he kept from "What the 'Friends of the People' Are," and *Materialism and Empirio-criticism,* which was the standpoint he had before he ever began reading Hegel's works[26]. If Althusser was describing Lenin's early reading framework, then he would have been correct; unfortunately, Althusser tries to apply this conclusion to Lenin's theoretical standpoints over the entire progression of his study of Hegelian philosophy, and so is ultimately incorrect. Dunayevskaya, on the other hand, remarks the different attitudes that Lenin had towards Hegel at different points in time, but does not go any further. She does not provide more profound textual analysis, especially her vague identification that Lenin did not simply accept Hegel in his *Bern Notebooks,* but rather "continued forward, attaining **new things**"[27]. Unfortunately, the "new things" of which she speaks here are idealist notions. I am resolutely opposed to this conclusion.

It is not difficult to see that from the second edition preface of *The Science of Logic* to the second chapter of the first part of "The Doctrine of Being," Lenin's reading progression in terms of his Other mirror images is peaceful. Maintaining a **refutational** attitude, he methodically flipped through over 170 pages of *The Science of Logic,* searching for "pearls" in the "manure heap" of Hegel's philosophy (to borrow Engels'

---

26   Refer to Althusser's "Lenin before Hegel," in *Lenin and Philosophy.* Yuanliu Press (Taiwan) (1990), page 137 (Chinese).

27   Dunayevskaya, Raya. *Marxism and Freedom.* Liaoning Educational Press (1998), page 157 (Chinese).

words). It is at this point that Lenin recorded reading commentaries that corresponded to the three Other subsidiary awareness references we have already discussed.

First, Lenin criticized and rejected the idealist basis of Hegelian philosophy. This was a different mass point from the Hegelian dialectics on which Lenin was focused and also from Marx's dialectics; I have found that Lenin demands almost constant "objectivism" from himself[28]. *This was the theoretical circuit formed by the basic starting point of the philosophical materialist teachings of Dietzgen and Feuerbach.* Soon after beginning "The Doctrine of Being" Lenin writes: "Heaven away: materialism." This expresses Lenin's desire to replace Hegel's Spirit with nature. Lenin goes on to write, "away with heaven – law-governed connection of the whole (**process**) of the world," by which he referred to the replacement of Hegel's idea structure with the objective connections of the objective material world[29]. Lenin emphasizes that he must do away with Hegel's "nonsense about the absolute (pages 68-69)." *Analyzing this from the perspective of mirror image projections, this conclusion is evidently related to Lenin's reading memory of Dietzgen and Feuerbach. Feuerbach, in particular, discussed the homogeneity – in certain respects – of materialism and theology. In **The Science of Logic**, these pages contained Hegel's discussion of "being" and "nothing." I have also found that later, when Deborin wrote on Hegel as the philosophical source of Marxist philosophy, he purposefully discussed "being" and "nothing" in order to make things more confusing. Could this have been to explain this theoretical missing-link in Lenin's **Bern Notebooks** by Deborin, the first editor of this collection of notes? It is impossible for us to tell[30].* At this point, Lenin draws a big box to remind himself that "I am in general trying to read Hegel materialistically: Hegel is materialism which has been stood on its head (according to Engels)—that is to say, I cast aside for the most part God, the Absolute, the Pure Idea, etc."[31]. *This was a clear self-identification of his own Other theoretical Other mirror image.* However, Lenin did not yet realize that by doing so, he was not emulating Marx's critical logical inversion of Hegelian philosophy, but rather merely replacing Hegel's concept of Spirit with his own concept of matter. Evidently,

---

28   Refer to *The Collected Works of Lenin* (Chin. 2. Ed.), volume 55, page 75.
29   *Ibid.*, page 77.
30   Refer to Deborin's "Hegel and Dialectical Materialism," in the second volume of *Philosophy and Politics*. Beijing Sanlian Press (1975), pages 609-613 (Chinese).
31   Refer to *The Collected Works of Lenin* (Chin. 2. Ed.), volume 55, page 86.

Lenin did not truly enter Marx's complex logical situating level, in which he "inverted" Hegel in terms of his own historical materialism and practical historical dialectics; rather, he was stuck at the surface level of this thought space. He did not realize that to use Marx's materialism to invert Hegel's dialectic, he did not simply need to externally replace Hegel's concepts of "Absolute Idea" and "God" with essentially homogeneous, **subjective** terms such as "matter" and "nature." In 1845-1846, and again in 1858, Marx twice discovered the historical secret of Hegelian philosophy. By penetrating the historical essence of industrial productive practice and the slave-like estranged relations inherent to the notion of "abstract becomes ruling" in the capitalist economic structure, Marx profoundly understood the **overall legitimacy** of Hegel's objective, idealist world view and logical situating. This was the revelation of the notion of the modern reign of capitalism, as well as the dominating essence of this modern practical structure over natural material existence. It is precisely the actual **ordering situation** of industrial practice that constructs the order and structure of the "world around us," constructing at the same time our subjective cognitive order and structure. Hegel merely historically used Idea logic to profoundly reflect this historical dialectic; for Marx, this was an idealist **structural inversion** in terms of logical situating, not an inversion of individual words. Lenin did not come to profoundly penetrate or comprehensively understand the underlying logical situating of Marx's inversion of Hegel's idealist dialectics until his later epistemological shift. Heidegger once said that when one inverts a metaphysical idea, one still ends up with a metaphysical idea. Here, I must admit that what Korsch said in 1930 is correct. He asserted that at most, this "materialist inversion" that Lenin attempted to bring to bear on Hegel's idealism was a change of terminology. He used the absolute existence of so-called "matter" to replace the absolute existence of so-called "Spirit"[32]. However, Korsch's later specific analysis was incorrect, something that we will discuss later in this book. In fact, Althusser also remarked this point, writing that if we interpret the Idea as matter, the result will only be a new materialist metaphysics (a mutation of classical philosophical materialism). What is impossible to understand, however, is his insistence that Lenin did not do this, because in interpreting Hegel, Lenin adopted a class viewpoint of the proletariat (a viewpoint of dialectical

---

32   Korsch, Karl. "On the Current State of 'Marxist and Philosophical' Problems." In *Marxism and Philosophy*. Chongqing Press (1989), page 81 (Chinese).

materialism)[33]. Althusser does not even believe that Lenin consciously tried to invert Hegel's idealism into materialism; he believes that Lenin used a so-called "revelatory method" in his reading of Hegel, i.e., he rejected completely useless propositions and arguments and retained a few select things, carefully removing their shells or freeing their cores from the thick shells with which they had become entangled through true re-structuring[34]. He continues, asserting that Lenin extracted those things in which he was interested from Hegel's completely different viewpoints. He refers to this as a revelatory process of peeling away, a purification process[35]. Althusser believes that there was no reason to use an "inverted" process on these "cores." Though Althusser always supported his views with profound textual hermeneutics in the past, his attitude here is really quite surprising. In his actual reading, each time Lenin came across Hegel's discussion of the interchangeability of finite and infinite, he would always write and box the words: "the dialectics of things themselves, of nature itself, of the course of events themselves"[36]. This was not Hegel's conceptual logical derivation at this point in the text. Furthermore, when Lenin read Hegel's further analysis of the continuous transcending change from finite to infinite of knowing and conceptual relations, he suddenly thinks of his own critique in *Materialism and Empirio-criticism* of Machism for having committed idealist errors in terms of matter. Here, he notes in the margin: "to be applied to atoms versus electrons. In general the infiniteness of matter deep within…"[37]. *In fact, an even deeper mirror image reflection here is likely Lenin's scholarly memory of Dietzgen.*

Second, Lenin attempted to materialistically "invert" the valuable portions of Hegelian thought, thus shining light on the "pearls" hidden behind idealist thinking. For instance, in his reading of the preface to the second edition, Lenin stands with the materialists when he comes upon Hegel's criticism of formal logic for only focusing on the external forms and instruments of human thought. Lenin clearly points out that the viewpoint of the traditional science of logics incorrect, because "Logic is the science not of external forms of thought, but of the laws

---

33   Althusser, Louis. "Lenin before Hegel," in *Lenin and Philosophy*. Yuanliu Press (Taiwan) (1990), page 139 (Chinese).

34   *Ibid.*, page 141.

35   *Ibid.*, page 144.

36   Refer to The Collected Works of Lenin (Chin. 2. Ed.), volume 55, page 92.

37   *Ibid.*, page 95.

of development 'of all material, natural and spiritual things'"[38]. When Lenin read Hegel's discussion of the relation between finite and infinite, he grasped the "comprehensive, universal flexibility of the concept." He affirms that this is "shrewd and clever" dialectical thought; at the same time, he reminds himself that "This flexibility, applied subjectively = eclecticism and sophistry. Flexibility, applied **objectively**, *i.e.* reflecting the all-sidedness of the material process and its unity, is dialectics, is the correct reflection of the eternal development of the world"[39]. We can see that what Hegel expresses as the dialectic between notions, becomes for Lenin the objective dialectics of the material world. Here, Lenin delves deeper into Hegel's underlying speculative logic situating.

Analysis of the text reveals that in addition to the two points I have discussed here, there are a few other important circumstances for us to understand at this point. First, Lenin directly agrees with some of Hegel's discourse **fragments** on the dialectic. For instance, form is form rich in content, living, form with living, substantive content, form with inseparably connected content[40]. Not only essence is objective, but semblance is also objective[41]. *We will engage in deeper theoretical discussion of these questions later on in this book.* **Second**, Lenin finds that some of Hegel's expressions "sound very materialistic!"[42]. *This was an assessment of Hegel's assertion that "What is first in science has had to show itself first, too, historically."* Lenin makes quite a few affirmative commentaries in these two categories of interpretive attitudes, including "excellent," "very important," and "subtle and profound." Third, and immensely important to our analysis here, Lenin often felt that Hegel was very difficult to understand, calling his words "obscure" and "unclear." For instance, when he came to Hegel's section on the objectivity of appearances, Lenin boxes the words: "NB: Unclear, return to this!" he writes a question mark. It seems as though Lenin is hesitating and questioning himself in his marginal notes. I believe that when Lenin read Hegel's dialectic of "Being—Nothing—Becoming" at the beginning of the "Doctrine of Being," he was not very comfortable. Furthermore, when he read Hegel's earliest expression of the negation of the negation, Lenin merely cites Engels' words:

---

38   *Ibid.*, page 77.
39   *Ibid.*, page 77.
40   *Ibid.*, page 91.
41   *Ibid.*, page 82.
42   *Ibid.*, page 81.

"abstract and abstruse Hegelianism"[43]. *I have noticed that in pages 72-149 of the* **Philosophical Noteboks**, *Lenin uses words such as "abstruse" and "obscure" seven or eight times. This shows that Lenin had great difficulty as he began reading* **The Science of Logic**; *unlike what Kedrov and others would have us believe, he did not easily recreate Hegel's philosophy and construct a system of materialist dialectics. Deborin, on the other hand, in his 1929 preface to the translation of* **Bern Notebooks**, *does remark Lenin's use of these words in his early reading of Hegel.*

3 WAS LENIN REALLY ABLE TO EASILY READ HEGEL?

"Hegel is obscure!"

In Hegel's idealist philosophy, were there really things that Lenin found obscure and difficult to understand? For many Soviet scholars of the *Philosophical Notebooks*, Lenin's process of learning and studying Hegel's philosophy always seems to be easy and without obstacle. For these scholars, from the beginning of his research to the end, Lenin was able to completely and profoundly understand and grasp the essence of the dialectics in *The Science of Logic*, thus painlessly constructing a complete system of materialist dialectics. *Dunayevskaya also seems to believe that Lenin's study of Hegel was easily carried out, that he was, from the beginning, able to "struggle against vulgar materialism." This is certainly a kind of false situating.* Proceeding from the textual context with a sincere desire to find the truth and seriously examining the thought space of the notes that Lenin took at this time, we find that the actual circumstances were actually very different. In reality, at the beginning of his study, Lenin was not able to easily or simply understand and grasp Hegel's philosophy; even when dealing with familiar epistemological problems and the dialectical thought on which he focused so much attention, Lenin still had to expend a great deal of effort to understand Hegel.

Those who have read Hegel's *The Science of Logic* all know that in the first section, "The Doctrine of Being," of the first volume of this book – and especially the first chapter of this section – Hegel insightfully discusses many views on the dialectic, such as the definition of

---

43   *Ibid.*, page 89.

determinateness in the general categories of the doctrine of being[44]. To other examples, there is Hegel's famous analysis of Kant's "hundred" in reality and possibility[45], as well as his analysis of sublation, the most important concept in dialectics and becoming, at the end of the first chapter[46]. However, from the notes that Lenin takes at this point, we see that he did not have any particular interest in these excellent passages by Hegel; we can see this because here Lenin makes very few evaluations of Hegel, rather simply making a few notations without passing judgment. Furthermore, he skips completely over some content that is seen as very important today. The substance of the problem was that in Lenin's reading space at this time, he lacked a cognitive structure that **corresponded** to Hegel's speculative logical situating. As such, though Hegel's dialectics anchored the development of the historical logic of dialectics in European philosophical history, Lenin was unable to recreate this situation in the situating of his own thought. The reason for this was simple: his theoretical circuit at the time did not contain any related thinking points. *These circumstances were very similar to Marx's "voiceless" state as he began to read classical economics[47]. Althusser also phenomenologically discovered this point, pointing out with a certain amount of confusion that Lenin "seems to have ignored the book on being"[48].* By the time Lenin reaches the discussion in the second chapter on "determinate being"[49], his silence not only does not ameliorate, it actually worsens. Lenin's notes show that he had no reaction at all to Hegel's discussion of immediate, pure determinateness (quality) that emerges as refutation of other matter[50], nor to his discussion of Spinoza's famous qualification of "affirmatively constructed negation"[51]. However, when Lenin comes to Hegel's first mention of the negation of the negation in *The Science of Logic*, the situation begins to change. Lenin begins to complain that Hegel is "fragmentary and highly obscure," boxing the quote from Engels: "abstract and

---

44 Hegel, Georg Wilhelm Friedrich. *The Science of Logic*. Commercial Press (1977), volume 1, pages 66-67 (Chinese).

45 *Ibid.*, page 75-8.

46 *Ibid.*, page 96-9.

47 Refer to chapter two of my *Marx Revisited*.

48 Althusser, Louis. "Lenin before Hegel," in *Lenin and Philosophy*. Yuanliu Press (Taiwan) (1990), page 139 (Chinese).

49 Hegel's "being" of "determinate being" is the same concept that rose to prominence in Heidegger's philosophy.

50 Hegel, Georg Wilhelm Friedrich. *The Science of Logic*. Commercial Press (1977), volume 1, pages 102-103 (Chinese).

51 *Ibid.*, page 105-7.

abstruse Hegelianism." I believe that Lenin **did not really understand** Hegel as he began his study of *The Science of Logic*; this is a truth that has perhaps been hidden for many years under an ideological facade.

Here, it is important for us to conduct a more detailed discussion. In *The Science of Logic*, "being" passed through Hegel's logical deduction, proceeding from an abstract qualification to "something," then from "something" to the second triad of "being-nothing-becoming." Much like the active sublative relation of "becoming" in the first chapter, the "something" here is the sublation of immediate qualitative qualification as a refutation of the differentiation between the differences of other things. Compared with the immediate qualification of quality (affirmation) and the limits of differentiation, this "something" that sublated differentiated refutation is the negation of the negation, which concludes the triad[52]. It is my opinion that Hegel's expressions here were not confused or particularly hard to understand; if, as Soviet scholars assert, Lenin already had a firm grasp of the basic framework of dialectics before writing the *Philosophical Notebooks*, then it should have been simple for him when reading Hegel's words at this point in *The Science of Logic*. However, in reality Lenin writes in the margin here: "incomprehensible." Where was the problem?

It is my opinion that Lenin, who had just begun to study Hegelian philosophy, could not have easily grasped Hegel's philosophical speculative situating. In fact, Lenin lacked even Marx and Engels' German cultural background as well as the philosophical historical context that their particular historical period allowed them to accept. This was an additional factor in rendering Lenin's process of systematically learning and studying Hegelian philosophy that much more difficult. Furthermore, even though Lenin had engaged in two prior systematic studies of the basic theories of philosophy, there he merely focused on the thought context of philosophical materialism; the dialectical discourse of Hegelian speculative philosophers in an idealist logical situating was still very foreign to him. As such, I believe that in this period of early study, Lenin was not able to accurately grasp Lenin's thinking logic on many levels of thought. It was unthinkable for him to have "restructured Hegelian dialectics," much less have developed a preconceived system of thought. *In **Dialogue within the Dialectic**, Levine concludes that there were fundamental "misunderstandings" in Lenin's*

---

52   *Ibid.*, page 108-9.

*general reading of Hegelian philosophy in **The Science of Logic**. First, he writes that Lenin did not correctly understand the intention and purpose of Hegelian philosophy. Second, he believes that Lenin did proposed imprecise definitions and uses of Hegel's special terms[53]. Levine accuses Lenin of changing **The Science of Logic**, which only studied spirit and not consciousness, into a "description of cognition." Levine believes that epistemology and consciousness are the objects of Hegel's **The Phenomenology of Spirit**[54]. I must concede that Levine's analysis has its accurate and profound elements, but there are also quite a few overly arbitrary conclusions. For instance, Levine insists that that the conceptual categories and logical structures of Hegel's idealism are the only standard by which understanding of Hegel can be measured; the results of one's reading must be in perfect accord with this standard in order to be acknowledged as legitimate. If they do not meet this standard, then they are said to lack understanding of the original text. This is obviously a laughably exigent theoretical stipulation. In fact, if we remove Hegel's idealistic trappings and look from the perspective of ordinary people, it is not difficult to see **The Phenomenology of Spirit** is a prehistory of species-consciousness – the formation of rational spirit. Marx, Engels, and later Lenin were all able to see this fact; this book can even be referred to as the "embryonic history" of the Spirit. In this phylogenetic pre-history of the Spirit, Hegel provides a condensed discussion of self-conscious structures related to the individual subject; his goal was to disprove the false-substance implied by sensuousness, then explain its inherent, subjectively composite nature. The pinnacle of self-consciousness is the notion of spirit of species-consciousness, and **The Science of Logic**, on the other hand, studies the logical phylogenetic structures of the ideas of this species-consciousness. According to Levine's summary, Hegel's **The Science of Logic** is the long, self-cognizing historical process of the Spirit. In order to reflect on history and understand its own power and world, it must arrive at the level of cognition[55]. In this view, in **The Science of Logic**, the idea moves from abstract to concrete, from being to doing, from finite to infinite, from general to absolute universal with internal speciality, and finally reaching absolute idea freedom. As a materialist philosopher, Lenin was able to phenomenologically enter **The Science of Logic**, identifying with the*

53   Levine, Norman. *Dialogue within the Dialectic.* Yunnan People's Press (1997), page 363 (Chinese).
54   *Ibid.*, page 364.
55   *Ibid.*, page 372.

determinist laws of Hegel's speculative games (just as Levine proves); this is a kind of research situating. However, Lenin was also able to maintain his own standpoint, and after demystifying Hegelian philosophy, reduce it to thought notions that could be understood by ordinary people, thus forming a second understanding situating. Thus, reading Hegel's **The Science of Logic** *epistemologically and correcting Hegel's mistaken self-reflection of* **impersonal** *Ideas to correct human consciousness or mankind's cognitive activity, is also a perfectly legitimate interpretation of Hegel. I should point out to readers that I believe that Lenin had difficulties in his early reading based on the problems with the philosophical situating of the second kind of thought that I have described here.*

In his early reading, I have found that although Lenin did understand some of Hegel's philosophical views in his original interpretive space, this cannot be thought of as a very accurate or profound grasp. It would be helpful for us to introduce a few examples to better illustrate this point.

The first example comes in the "introduction" to *The Science of Logic*. Here, Hegel reviews Kant's contributions to the dialectic. In reading this portion of text, Lenin comes across Hegel's analysis of Kant's refutation of arbitrariness in dialectics: "[Kant] exhibited [dialectics] as a **necessary function of reason**." Hegel fully affirmed this view, especially Kant's proposition of "the **objectivity of the illusion** and the **necessity of the contradiction**" when discussing the relation between the subject and the thing-in-itself[56]. Hegel's appraisal of this idea was also very high. I believe that when he came across these words, Lenin did not understand them at first, but that after careful consideration, he demonstrates his grasp of the subject matter by boxing the following statement after Hegel's paragraph:

> **Is not the thought here that semblance also is objective, for it contains** *one of the aspects* **of the** *objective* **world? Not only essence, but semblance, too, is objective. There is a difference between the subjective and the objective, BUT IT, TOO, HAS ITS LIMITS**[57].

---

56   Hegel, Georg Wilhelm Friedrich. *The Science of Logic*. Commercial Press (1977), volume 1, pages 108-109 (Chinese).

57   Refer to *The Collected Works of Lenin* (Chin. 2. Ed.), volume 55, page 89.

*At this point, the new Chinese version of the **Bern Notebooks** translates "semblance" (Schein) as "externality" – I believe that this is an improper modification[58]. I have seen that as Hegel discusses Kant here, he already saw that Kant "freed it from seeming arbitrariness...and exhibited it as a **necessary function of reason.**" For Hegel, Kant had overcome the practice of viewing the dialectic as merely "the art of practicing deceptions and producing illusions...that it is only a spurious game, the whole of its power resting solely on concealment of the deceit and that its results are obtained only surreptitiously and are a subjective illusion"[59]. Furthermore, Hegel later gives a specific explanation of the differences between semblance (Schein) and appearance (Erscheinung); thus it conforms to the original intent of the author to translate "Schein" as semblance, while translating it as "externality" will merely lead to controversy. In Professor Yang Yizhi's translation of The Science of Logic, he also uses the term "semblance"[60].* As we know, in Kant's "epistemological revolution," nature is exhibited to us in a particular form. Appearances (semblances) that take place in certain a priori apperception are not all subjective errors. For Hegel, semblances become expressions of essence. Semblance, like essence, is one aspect of objective Spirit. Evidently, if Lenin attempted to invertedly grasp this qualification proceeding from **materialist** dialectics in an ontological sense, he would have said that semblance is objective; but how can objective things be divided into **true** (appearance) and **false** (semblance)? This is likely why he wrote "unclear." *In Deborin's translator's introduction to the **Bern Notebooks**, he arbitrarily transforms Lenin's expressions of self-doubt into affirmative sentences.* However, When Lenin takes a step back, and considers the situation from the perspective of familiar epistemology, he gives the self-hypothesis that perhaps the reflection (content) of man is, itself objective; as such, false reflections (semblances) will also be objective, and the differences between subjective errors (semblance) and objective cognition (truth) will also be finite. It is my belief that Lenin's thought at this point still contained elements of doubt. He was not able to easily understand Hegel. Even after materialistically "inverting" Hegel, the issues still do not become very clear. It was not until Lenin progressed in his reading that things began to become clearer to him.

---

58   For more on the old version of the Bern Notebooks, see *The Collected Works of Lenin* (Chin. 1. Ed.), volume 38, page 137.

59   Hegel, Georg Wilhelm Friedrich. *The Science of Logic.* Commercial Press (1977), volume 1, pages 39 (Chinese).

60   *Ibid.*, page 39.

The second example comes when Lenin read the section on being-for-self in the third section of "The Doctrine of Being." When he saw Hegel's statement that "being-for-self is one," Lenin was confused. He writes: "Why being-for-self is one is not clear to me. Here Hegel is extremely obscure in my opinion"[61]. *Deborin also remarks this point in his introduction to the **Bern Notebooks**, but he does not identify the actual difficulties that Lenin faced in his study of Hegel's philosophy. He merely states that Lenin was strongly opposed to Hegel's concept of "being-for-self"*[62]. In fact, generally speaking Hegel's intention here is to oppose the idealist thing-in-itself proposed by Kant and Fichte (Fichte's "not-self") – the other-sided world – and a for-self phenomenological world, *i.e.*, what he called the dualism of determinateness and being-for-itself[63]. Hegel proposed that being-for-itself is "One" (monistic), because while Kant's this-sided empirical phenomena represented the "Many," a phenomenological "Many" represents the abundant characteristics of "One" (essence). Hence, "Many" can be thought of as the "Many of the One." More importantly, approaching the matter from Hegel's level of logic at this point, Hegel's tedious exposition of "One" and "Many" was precisely to shift the discussion from quality to quantity. Hegel's being-for-self "One" is immediately in accord with the **unity** of things themselves, as such, this "One" narrowly refers to the only essence as differentiated from others. However, because Lenin's ideas at this time were temporarily unable to move beyond the simple epistemological logic of philosophical materialism, he still awaited the "**transition** of the thing-in-itself to the appearance? Of the object to the subject?" within his own fixed theoretical circuit[64]. Thus he was, for the time being, unable to understand the "monistic" logic of Hegel's idealist speculative ontological situating. *However, we will soon see how not long later, Lenin correctly grasped Hegel's theoretical context here, which seemed so "obscure" to him at the beginning*[65].

---

61   Refer to *The Collected Works of Lenin* (Chin. 2. Ed.), volume 55, page 96.

62   Deborin, Abram. *Introduction to volume 9 of "The Lenin Papers"*. Soviet National Press (1929) page 3 (Chinese).

63   Hegel, Georg Wilhelm Friedrich. *The Science of Logic*. Commercial Press (1977), volume 1, pages 165 (Chinese).

64   Refer to *The Collected Works of Lenin* (Chin. 2. Ed.), volume 55, page 96.

65   When Lenin came to page 199, he wrote in a box: "In general, all this being-for-self was, probably, in part required by Hegel to deduce "the transition of *quality* into *quantity*" (199)—quality is determi-nateness, determinateness for self, posited-for-self, it is the One—this gives the impression of being very far fetched and empty." Refer to *The Collected Works of Lenin* (Chin. 2. Ed.), volume 55, page 97.

4 FROM "INCOMPREHENSIBLE" TO THE FIRST SIGNS OF MENTAL ACTIVITY

I have found that Hegel's definition of being-for-self as "One," caused a good deal of theoretical confusion for Lenin. From the text of the notebooks we can clearly see that on page 181 of *The Science of Logic* (volume three of the *Collected Works of Hegel*), Lenin first cites this passage, then boxes the words "very obscure." Looking at the details of the text, after reading page 186, he suddenly stops reading and returns to page 183, underlining the page number of that page. After excerpting Hegel's views on being-for-self, Lenin boxes the words "Dark Waters..." We can see that in his reading, Lenin returned to the theoretical enigma that he had been unable to solve previously. However, even on his second reading he was still unable to achieve a breakthrough of understanding. *This is a failed thought experiment that we should seriously revisit.*

However, it was precisely in the midst of this dark confusion that the first signs of **profound mental activity** began to appear from the underlying logic situating of Lenin's thought. *This activity, however, evidently did not come by digging through Hegel's "dung heap" to find "pearls," but was rather a **new logical refutation that did not really conform** to Lenin's original interpretive framework. It is my view that these are the possible sprouts of a heterogeneous thought situating; it constituted the basis of Lenin's own independent, sovereign thought situating. Expressed in traditional discourse, these were the possible roots of a new research paradigm or gestalt shift.* I deduce that it was precisely Hegel's afore-mentioned views, which led Lenin to write "Dark Waters...," that deeply touched his thought logic. However, this thought orientation ran **counter** to the Other mirror image support points in Lenin's original theoretical circuit; for the first time, Lenin's critical attack was **directed at materialism**! Of course, his attack was on "vulgar materialism." *It is in this sense that Anderson refers to Lenin's pre-1914 philosophical ideas as "vulgar materialism," which is an imprecise qualitative judgment.* In the box immediately following, Lenin writes:

> **The thought of the ideal passing into the real is *profound*: very important for history. But also in the personal life of man it is clear that this contains much truth. Against vulgar materialism. NB. The difference of the ideal from the material is also not unconditional, not inordinate[66].**

---

66 Refer to *The Collected Works of Lenin* (Chin. 2. Ed.), volume 55, page 97.

I believe that there are two theoretical points deserving of our attention here. **First**, Lenin underlines the word "profound," which can be thought of as a "clearing up" of his earlier "dark waters." Lenin is now able to see that beneath Hegel's **obscure** words, there was something truly **profound**. **Second**, this point impelled Lenin to independently reconsider his own original framework of knowledge. As he began his research, Lenin was aware that there was a limit to the differences between subjective things and objective things, though at that time he was unable to elevate this thought orientation to direct opposition against vulgar materialism[67]. Interestingly, after reading a few more pages, Lenin suddenly comes upon another important idea **not encapsulated by one of his original Other support points:** "Obviously, Hegel takes his self-development of concepts, of categories, in connection with the entire history of philosophy. This gives still a **new** aspect to the whole **Logic**"[68]. Another important new viewpoint! *This comment relates to his own prior discussion of logic as not only the external form of thinking, but also the reflection of objective laws.* It is evident that Lenin has already begun to unconsciously move into Hegel's logical framework using a **non-mirror image logical door.** I am certain of this because from his discussion here it is not difficult to see that Lenin's affirmation of Hegel is no longer based on the isolated approval of one of Hegel's specific dialectical views or reasonable epistemological fragments, but was rather an **overall** affirmation. Such an understanding is completely different from Lenin's earlier simple refutational reading logic. However, in the rest of his reading of the second section (quantity) and third section (measure), the amount of notes that Lenin makes decrease noticeably, neither did he make any worthwhile comments. I believe that this section was an inevitable low point in Lenin's reading of Hegelian philosophy.

Fortunately, this "silent" state did not last very long. As Lenin began reading "Essence" (volume four of the *Collected Works of Hegel*), Lenin's line of thought began to exhibit much more frequent bursts of heterogeneous thought situating. Compared with the low point at the end of the previous book, this round of excitement was evidently rooted in epistemology. Faced with Hegel's thoroughly idealist notions, Lenin finds himself **approving** of Hegel's words more and more frequently, at least in epistemological theoretical relations. For instance, Lenin agrees

---

67   *Ibid.*, page 82.
68   *Ibid.*, page 97.

with Hegel's differentiation of essence: "Semblance or Show (Schein), Appearance (Erscheinung), Actuality (Wirklichkeit). In particular, when Lenin comes upon Hegel's explanation that semblance is also an expression of essence, he writes:

> **I.e., the unessential, seeming, superficial, vanishes more often, does not hold so "tightly," does not "sit so firmly" as "Essence." Approximately: the movement of a river—the foam above and the deep currents below. *But even the foam* is an expression of essence![69]**

Lenin's tone here shows that he undoubtedly agrees with Hegel. Lenin begins to approve more frequently of Hegel's philosophical expressions.

It is also in this section that several new understandings begin to show in Lenin's thought. Primarily these focused on the profound significance of applying Hegelian thought to the critique of Kant, Hume, and Machism – the refutation of agnosticism **using dialectics**:

> **Thus here too, Hegel charges Kant with *subjectivism*. This *NB*. Hegel is for the "objective validity" (If it may be called that) of Semblance, "of that which is immediately given" [the expression "*that which is given*" is generally used by Hegel, and here see p. 21 i.f.; p. 22]. The more petty philosophers dispute whether essence *or* that which is immediately given should be taken as basis (Kant, Hume, all the Machists). Instead of *or*, Hegel puts *and*[70].**

A very important textual detail is at play here. In this passage of notes, Hegel is suddenly transformed into a **great philosopher**, because Kant and Hume are transformed, relatively, into "lesser philosophers." Furthermore, it is precisely because this conclusion was a *theoretically unconscious* debasement of these other philosophers that it is so incredibly important. *Althusser believes that in the process of reading Hegel's **The Science of Logic**, Lenin always agreed with Hegel in his critiques of Kant[71]. This expression is somewhat over-simplified.* At the same time, please note that this thinking point was already very different from Lenin's early understanding of Hegel's Kantian critique,

---

69   *Ibid.*, page 97.
70   *Ibid.*, page 111.
71   Althusser, Louis. "Lenin before Hegel," in *Lenin and Philosophy.* Yuanliu Press (Taiwan) (1990), page 141 (Chinese).

which was based on the perspective of general epistemology. At this point, Lenin's mind was certainly restructured with his former philosophical materialist critiques of Machism. I believe that Lenin had already thought of a different question at this time: would it be possible to deepen the criticism of Machism from the perspective of dialectics (as Hegel did)?[72]. This is, without a doubt, a completely new dimension of philosophical situating.

It is here that we find the first evidence of self-doubt, stemming from the level of logical thought, in Lenin's entire reading process. It is my belief that this was the first moment when Lenin began to break from the influence of his early Other mirror images. When Lenin came across the self-movement of contradiction in the "Essence" section, Lenin begins to question himself:

Who would believe that this is the core of "Hegelianism," of abstract and abstruse (ponderous, absurd?) Hegelianism?? This core had to be discovered, understood, rescued, laid bare, refined, which is precisely what Marx and Engels did[73].

It is my opinion that the thought symptoms revealed by the text here are evidence of Lenin's self-reflection and doubt towards his whole previous interpretive framework. We already know that in his original line of thought, he positioned Hegel **opposite** from Marx; here, on the other hand, the two threads of dialectical logic which had once been so entirely separate seem to gradually approach one another. A possible space for a new logical situating begins to expand.

Lenin quickly expresses a sentiment that **extends far beyond his reading logic**: "The idea of universal movement and change (1813 *Logic*) was conjectured before its application to life and society. In regard to society it was proclaimed earlier (1847) than it was demonstrated in application to man (1859)"[74]. I deduce that the first year (1813) referred to Hegel's ideal dialectics, while the second two years referred

---

72   On this point, the views of some Western scholars are incorrect. In the *Bern Notebooks* Lenin truly did understand that dialectics could be used to deepen his critique of Machism, but this does not prove that Lenin's standpoint in *Materialism and Empirio-criticism* is "mechanical materialism." In fact, Lenin was always a "dialectical materialist," it was merely that his understanding of materialist dialectics was more profound at this point.

73   Refer to *The Collected Works of Lenin* (Chin. 2. Ed.), volume 55, pages 117-118.

74   *Ibid.*, page 118.

respectively to Marx's historical dialectics (*The Poverty of Philosophy*, 1847) and Darwin's theory of evolution (*The Origin of Species*, 1859)[75]. *Dunayevskaya believes that here, Lenin was shocked to learn that Hegel's revolutionary dialectic preceded Marx's application of dialectics in* **The Communist Manifesto**[76]. *In fact, she is mistaken here, because the 1847 work which proposed historical dialectics was* **The Poverty of Philosophy**, *not* **The Communist Manifesto**. I must emphasize that at this time, in the context of Lenin's reading, the logic of Hegel's dialectic (not idealism!) had already been placed on the same level as Marx's historical materialism and Darwin's theory of evolution. I have found that as his reading progressed, this unconscious theoretical orientation of Lenin's continued to deepen. At the very end of this book, Lenin again questions himself:

> **If I am not mistaken, there is much mysticism and empty pedantry in these conclusions of Hegel, but the basic idea is one of genius: that of the universal, all-sided *vital* connection of everything with everything and the reflection of this connection— Hegel materialistically turned upside down human concepts, which must likewise be hewn, treated, flexible, mobile, relative, mutually connected, united inopposites, in order to embrace the world. Continuation of the work of Hegel and Marx must consist in the *dialectical* elaboration of the history of human thought, science and technique[77].**

Please note that this is the first time in Lenin's own expressions that he clearly indicates that Hegel and Marx **share a mutual** "work"! Another line of reading thought and theoretical logic can already be dimly seen, and the logic space of Lenin's thought situating seems as though it will be thoroughly restructured. Of course, here we only see the sprouts of this change. *I have noticed that Levine also astutely pointed out that Lenin's process of learning from Hegel began with 'Essence.' He also believes that the first book of* **The Science of Logic** *– "Doctrine of*

---

75 In The Marx-Engels Correspondence, Lenin read of Marx's statement about Darwin's *The Origin of Species* (1859), that it gave a natural historical basis to Marx's viewpoint. Refer to *The Collected Works of Lenin* (Chin. 2. Ed.), volume 58, page 58.

76 Dunayevskaya, Raya. *Philosophy and Revolution*. Liaoning Educational Press (2000), page 88 (Chinese).

77 Refer to *The Collected Works of Lenin* (Chin. 2. Ed.), volume 55, page 122. Lenin's reference to Hegel's philosophy as "mystic," borrows from Marx's words in *The Marx-Engels Correspondence*. See *The Collected Works of Lenin* (Chin. 2. Ed.), volume 58, page 36.

being" – did not leave any "impression" on Lenin's thought[78]. Levine's conclusions have a certain degree of merit. However, a few Western Marxists and Leninologists have gone too far in this direction, asserting that here Lenin begins to become "Hegelian." For instance, Dunayevskaya argues that beginning at this point in his research, Lenin "returns to Hegel"[79].

At the same time, I have also seen that Lenin is still encumbered by his old, narrow interpretive framework, which continues to play an overall role. Lenin continually tries to grasp the "wretched God"[80] who is worshipped in Hegel's logic, at the same time "consigning God, and the philosophical rabble that defends God, to the rubbish heap"[81]. As such, Lenin still attempts to immediately "turn around" Hegel in his reading: "concepts are the highest product of the brain, the highest product of matter"[82]. Lenin is disgusted by "constitutive things," which Hegel discusses as an idealist[83]. Lenin even asserts that "nine-tenths" of Hegel's thought is "chaff, rubbish," and that one must "**extract** the materialist dialectics from it"[84]. *However, Althusser arbitrarily takes this single expression as Lenin's overall qualitative judgment of Hegelian philosophy over the entire course of his reading; this is completely erroneous.* Of course, in a direct sense Lenin's critiques here are **completely correct**; but considering the underlying logic of Lenin's reading, this line of logic was at a completely different level of logical situating understanding from the nascent line of thought just beginning to sprout in Lenin's research. I believe that at this time, Lenin's reading scope had already begun to **encompass the conflict between two different logics**. However, Lenin's original logic was still dominant; to use popular terminology, it was a **power discourse**, while the new logic was nothing more than a **new refutational** logic. *This situation is very similar to the internal logical conflicts in young Marx's **1844 Manuscript**[85].*

---

78   Levine, Norman. *Dialogue within the Dialectic*. Yunnan People's Press (1997), page 361 (Chinese).

79   Dunayevskaya, Raya. 1998. *Marxism and Freedom*. Liaoning Education Press, 174 (Chinese Edition).

80   Refer to *The Collected Works of Lenin* (Chin. 2. Ed.), volume 55, page 124.

81   *Ibid.*, page 143.

82   *Ibid.*, page 139.

83   *Ibid.*, page 144.

84   *Ibid.*, page 129.

85   Refer to chapter three of my *Marx Revisited*.

In fact, in this same process of reading, several of Lenin's important understandings of Hegel's thought had already begun to deviate from the path of his original interpretation. First, in the first chapter ("Existence") of this section, Hegel gives a long exposition of the relation between things and matter, basically lowering the position of things constituted of matter to the level of material phenomena. He argues that compared with non-matter spirit, "things are appearances"[86]. This was an idealist game that Hegel had already played in The Phenomenology of Spirit. However, it is surprising that in his notes, Lenin did not express the level of criticism and indignation that one would expect from a "materialist" at Hegel's arbitrary debasement of matter. This is certainly a very obvious departure from his original reading logic. It is also in this section that Lenin comes upon Hegel's argument that "laws are the unity of appearances"; on the one hand, Lenin writes that he is "very confused," while on the other hand, he feels that this expression contains some vital thought. Lenin writes:

> **The concept of *law* is *one* of the stages of cognition by man of *unity* and *connection*, of the reciprocal dependence and totality of the world process. The 'treatment' and 'twisting' of words and concepts to which Hegel devotes himself here is a struggle against making the concept of *law* absolute, against simplifying it, against making a fetish of it. *NB* for modern physics!!![87].**

In a nearby marginal note (with vertical lines on both sides), Lenin affirmed this phrase of Hegel's: "Law is the enduring (the persisting) in appearances (Law is the identical in appearances)...Law = the quiescent reflection of appearances"[88]. I believe that these views originated with the Greek Eleatic School, and that generations of idealist philosophers had long supported them. However, Lenin does not simply refute these views at this time, but rather boxes the following assessment: "This is remarkably materialistic and remarkably appropriate (with the word "quiescent") determination. Law takes the quiescent—and therefore law, every law, is narrow, incomplete, approximate"[89]. Please note that if we were to use the simple logic of Lenin's original philosophical-materialist "inversion," then what we should find here is that "laws"

---

86   Hegel, Georg Wilhelm Friedrich. *The Science of Logic.* Commercial Press (1977), volume 1, pages 103-104 (Chinese).
87   Refer to *The Collected Works of Lenin* (Chin. 2. Ed.), volume 55, page 126.
88   *Ibid.*, page 126.
89   *Ibid.*, page 127.

are first the reflection of external laws, not stages in **human** cognition. **Laws as cognitive stages is Hegelian idealist logic.** However, Lenin not only approves of this expression here, but he also writes that modern physics should **take note of this**. *Why does he say this? Because something that physicists determine to be an objective law, may very well be sublated and shown to be a **transitional, limited** scientific cognitive result as new research comes to pass. For instance, consider the relation between Einstein's theory of relativity/quantum mechanics and Newton's mechanics; what Newton determined to be absolute, universal, and eternal, was shown by modern physics to be laws that govern only slow-moving, macro-movements.* Assuming we approach the issue from Lenin's original line of thought, laws would certainly have been a part of the external, objective world. How can objective things be **narrowly defined**? In fact, this was actually the logic of Hegel's objective idealism. For Hegel, any law can only be a **transitional**, notional link. *In Deborin's introduction to the **Bern Notebooks**, he points out that Lenin greatly appreciated Hegel's struggle against the practice of blindly worshipping laws and making them absolute; hence he began to focus on the importance of bringing this question to the forefront of modern physics. What laws reflect is merely the continual rapprochement to fact, not anything absolute[90]. Though Deborin's level of philosophical situating is overly simple, his views are fundamentally correct.*

I have found that here, Lenin was already able to derive ever deeper conclusions from the theoretical logic of Hegel's philosophy. This is certainly a good sign of Lenin's later development. Lenin no longer stands outside of Hegel's philosophy, bringing simple refutational assumptions in his rejection of Hegel's thought; rather, he has stepped inside Hegel's logical framework, finding those treasures of thought (and not pearls in the refuse) that Marx and Engels had discovered years before. *Here, allow me to mention the arrogant Levine once again. In **Dialogue within the Dialectic**, after citing Lenin's conclusions mentioned above, he asserts that Lenin fundamentally misunderstood Hegel's essential qualification, because the essential qualification in **The Science of Logic** was equal to persisting and being-in-self: "as persisting, it established unity and difference; as being-in-self, it is the introduction to substance"[91]. As I have already pointed out, Levine's standard is Hegel's speculative*

---

90   Refer to the appendix of Deborin's introduction to volume 9 of the *Lenin Manuscripts* (Soviet National Press, 1929, page 5).

91   Levine, Norman. *Dialogue within the Dialectic*. Yunnan People's Press (1997), page 368 (Chinese).

*philosophical logical structure. Using Hegel's eyes to measure, any-thing that is orthodox or fundamentalist obedience is "correct," any-thing else is a misunderstanding. On the other hand, what we find is that Lenin **never planned to be follower of Hegelianism**; he devoted himself to taking the notions of Hegel's thought and making them available for use. This is why he did not simply limit himself to an understanding of the transitional placements of "persisting" and "being-in-self," rather searching for a non-speculative explanation of the relation between es-sence and laws from within general epistemology. I believe that there is nothing to fault in his actions here. On the contrary, it is Levine him-self, a scholar who is busy misrepresenting Lenin's reading of Hegelian philosophy as "Hegelized Leninism" while at the same time deviously searching for signs of Lenin's disobedience to Hegel's theoretical logic, thus he contradicts himself.*

I have observed that in the third section ("Actuality") of "Essence," Lenin does not focus on the "Absolute" of the first chapter, but rather on the "actuality" discussed in the second chapter. However, at this time, he opened volume 6 of *The Collected Works of Hegel*, taking the content on "actuality" in Hegel's Shorter Logic to use as a reading ref-erence. *Perhaps he was thinking of Engels' comment that **Shorter Logic** was easier to understand*[92]. In the process of this comparative reading, we once again see signs of new, developing thought. When Lenin came upon the exposition of the category of "possibility" in the Shorter Logic, he first excerpted it, and then boxed the comment: "**The sum-total, the entirety of the moments of Actuality**, which, in its **unfolding** disclos-es itself to be Necessity. The unfolding of the sum-total of the moments of actuality $N B$ = the essence of dialectical cognition"[93]. Of course, the first sentence of the box was an excerpt, but he did add underlining to a few of the words that were not emphasized in the original text[94]. This is a detail of the commentary that deserves our consideration. The un-folding of actual moments is a movement of objective things; how can it all of a sudden equal the essence of dialectical cognition? However, this is a legitimate conclusion from within Hegel's idealist logic. *It is*

92 Refer to *The Collected Works of Lenin* (Chin. 2. Ed.), volume 55, page 132. In the *Marx-Engels Correspondence*, Lenin remarked Engels' comment that the *Shorter Logic* was more "popular." Refer to *The Collected Works of Lenin* (Chin. 2. Ed.), vol-ume 58, page 163.
93 *The Collected Works of Lenin* (Chin. 2. Ed.), volume 55, page 132.
94 Hegel, Georg Wilhelm Friedrich. *The Shorter Logic*. Commercial Press (1980), page 300 (Chinese).

evident that at this time, Lenin is already unconsciously standing on Hegel's logical measuring stick in terms of his latent interpretive logic. An unconscious change is beginning to develop in Lenin's theoretical thought space.

A similar example appears in a later passage. On page 301 of Hegel's Shorter Logic, Lenin read the words: "substance is an essential stage in the process of development of the idea"[95]. He immediately boxes the words: "Read: an important stage in the process of development of **human knowledge** of nature and **matter**[96]. What I must stress again is the fact that if we approach this using Lenin's original Other philosophical materialist interpretive framework, then Hegel's proposition is certainly wrong and even **impossible to turn around**. "Substance" should be something that exists in the external world, while man's notion of substance is a reflection of external, objective structures. Therefore, the words "substance is a stage in human cognition" is another example of **logic within Hegel's philosophical situating**! *Later, we will see that as Lenin approaches this interpretation from a new, conscious theoretical logical basis, he arrives at truly profound conclusions.*

To cite another example, when Lenin came upon Hegel's discussion of cause and effect in the third chapter ("Absolute Relation") of this section, he leaves another affirmative comment. He believes that although the explanation of historical reasons by Hegel's notions is idealist and mystic, at the same time he also refers to it as a "profound indication": "Hegel subsumes history **completely** under causality and understands causality a thousand times more profoundly and richly than the multitude of 'savants' nowadays"[97]. This is the first time that Lenin gives such exaggerated praise of Hegel's philosophy in his reading and study at this point in time. It is not hard for us to see how in Lenin's affirmation here, he reveals his own pleasure at having moved to a new, deeper level of understanding of Hegel's dialectics. *However, Lenin still uses the vague term "multitude of savants" here; we will soon see exactly which people Lenin meant by this statement.* I believe that this passage of textual details shows presages the emergence of a new theoretical situating line of thinking in Lenin's philosophical thought! The coming **détournement** of theoretical logic is inevitable.

---

95   *Ibid.*, page 313-4.
96   *The Collected Works of Lenin* (Chin. 2. Ed.), volume 55, page 133.
97   *Ibid.*, page 135.

CHAPTER TEN

THE SUDDEN EMERGENCE OF A NEW INTERPRETIVE FRAMEWORK AND DÉTOURNEMENT OF THEORETICAL LOGIC

In the *Berlin Noteboooks*, specifically in the second half of the first stage of Lenin's study of Hegel and the first half of the second stage, his theoretical thought space was made up of the movement and progression of the unconscious interweaving of two contradictory logics. At this point, his early Other mirror image framework collided violently with the independent, sovereign thought orientation that he had gradually developed over the course of his reading and thought. Of course, this conflict of thought was also an active process in which the old and the new repeatedly waxed and waned. After going through a time of profound thought, new sparks of thought in Lenin's theoretical logical situating that had recently begun to spring to life finally ignited into a new theoretical scene. Put another way, a completely new line of thought and research in Lenin's reading – a comprehensive understanding and evaluation of Hegel's philosophy – finally came into being. I believe that this was Lenin's first important theoretical logical détournement in the *Bern Notebooks*; through this shift, Lenin was able to construct his own independent theoretical context in the face of Hegelian philosophy and Marxist philosophy.

1 CRITICISM AND AFFIRMATION WITHIN LENIN'S CONSTERNATION: LOGICAL CONTRADICTIONS IN HIS READING

As Lenin began to read the second volume of *The Science of Logic*, entitled "Subjective Logic or the Doctrine of the Notion," (volume 5 of the *Collected Works of Hegel*), the conflict between Lenin's old interpretive framework and his new line of thought grew ever more heated in Lenin's thought. In the process of Lenin's reading, there existed two heterogeneous evaluation points. First, Lenin's general evaluation was a refutation of Hegel's basic principles, correcting the mistake of spiritual primacy into a materialist proposition. At the very beginning of this text, when Lenin read the introductory section entitled "On the Notion in General," he boxes a reminder to himself: "Should be inverted: concepts are the highest product of the brain, the highest product of matter"[1]. Soon after, as he simultaneously criticized the idealist errors of Kant and Hegel, he wrote: "Kant disparages knowledge in order to make way for faith: Hegel exalts knowledge, asserting that knowledge is knowledge of God. The materialist exalts knowledge of matter, of nature, consigning God, and the philosophical rabble that defends God, to the rubbish heap"[2]. It is evident that when it came to important questions of principle, Lenin was not very aware or clear. When Lenin read Hegel's criticism of Kant's exposition on the role of reason, he was unable to understand how the categories that Hegel identified were "constitutive things"[3]. Categories are notions; if they have a constitutive nature, then does this not become a theory of subjective creation? This is why Lenin criticizes these "**constitutive things**" as being "nonsense."

However, at the same time, in another box Lenin identifies the profundity of Hegel's explanation of the relation between sensuous experience and rational concepts. He even uses a specific example here, which may have come from Marx's *Capital*: Here, too, Hegel is essentially **right**:

---

1   *The Collected Works of Lenin* (Chin. 2. Ed.), volume 55, page 139.
2   *Ibid.*, page 143.
3   Hegel, Georg Wilhelm Friedrich. *The Science of Logic*. Commercial Press (1977), volume 1, page 145 (Chinese).

value is a category which dispenses with the material of sensuousness but it is **truer** than the law of supply and demand"[4]. *This is an extremely important orientation in Lenin's thought. Later we will see that the fruits of Lenin's new cognition were derived precisely from breakthroughs in this kind of thinking. In the realm of Lenin's theoretical unconsciousness, the subsidiary element of his philosophical situating was made up of thinking points similar to Marx's in the **Marx-Engels Correspondence.*** I would like to remind the reader to pay particular attention to this example.

First, Lenin's affirmation of Hegel's correctness did not proceed from philosophical materialism's general matter and nature; rather, it was elucidated using an example from Marx's study of the movements of capitalist market economies. I do not believe that Lenin sagaciously selected this example after a long period of careful thought; this is because the **category** of value of which he speaks here, as well as the "laws of supply and demand" do not come from nature or abstract matter **external** to man, but are rather reflections constituted by man himself of a certain social existence and movement. For Smith and Marx, value no longer was **natural** wealth, but rather **social** wealth, *i.e.*, created by man's labour activity. *This was an issue that Petty first pointed out in the realm of economics research. Marx's new materialism was established on the basis of this new, modern labour (industrial material production), though Lenin obviously has yet to understand this point.* What is important is that this marks the emergence of a new philosophical situating point, the first time in Lenin's interpretation of Hegel's philosophy that he links philosophical thought with the **economics research** with which he was the most familiar. In Lenin's past struggle against Mach and Bogdanov, the basis of philosophical materialism was always a natural matter divorced from man. Here, however, Lenin became conscious of the internal connection between philosophy and social life itself; this was the secret of the genesis of Marx's historical materialism. I believe that this new orientation in Lenin's theoretical situating caused him to reset the separation between his own active logic ray and his philosophical thought in the theoretical circuit of philosophical materialism. *Soon, Lenin will acquire a completely new basis to his logic ray, the practical, revolutionary historical dialectic of Hegel-Marx.*

---

4   *The Collected Works of Lenin* (Chin. 2. Ed.), volume 55, page 144.

Second, visible laws of supply and demand and the **invisible** value (law) of "sensuous matter" are all the results of man's objective economic activity. In contrast, the law of value is an essential law while laws of supply and demand are the expression of its movement. When Lenin uses this example to affirm Hegel, value is taken as a non-sensuous **category** and more profound than "laws of supply and demand" (more precisely, relations of supply and demand), which are **supported by sensuous phenomena**. However, Lenin overlooks the issue of the "inverted" reading of Hegel's "correctness" at this point. If it is not inverted, does that not mean that the truth of the non-sensuous value category is idealist? I believe that Lenin here finds himself **in the midst of an unconscious logical contradiction**.

As we continue our analysis, we begin to see signs of this contradiction seemingly everywhere. For instance, when Lenin read of Hegel's opposition to Kant's external form theory of logic, specifically his assertion that logic should not merely give a "**natural-historical description of the empirical phenomena of thought**," but should also "correspond to truth"[5], Lenin boxes the following sentiment:

> **Thus, not only a description of the *forms* of thought and not only a *natural-historical description of the phenomena* of thought (wherein does that differ from a description of *forms*??) but also correspondence with truth, *i.e.*??, the quintessence or, more simply, the results and outcome of the history of thought?? Here Hegel is idealistically unclear, and fails to speak out fully. *Mysticism*[6].**

In this passage, the uncertainty and hesitation in Lenin's thought experiment become clear. In these few short lines, he uses no fewer than six question marks. Immediately following, Lenin makes another smaller box, in which he writes: "**Not** psychology, **not** the phenomenology of mind, **but** logic = the question of truth." *In fact, Hegel's words here were not mystic; Lenin's conclusion depended on which line of thought he used to approach the question!* The problem was, Lenin did not understand that Hegel's science of logic was actually his ontology of the Notion. Hegel arbitrarily inverted human thought structures and their historical logic into the essence of the world. In Hegel's

---

5   Hegel, Georg Wilhelm Friedrich. *The Science of Logic*. Commercial Press (1977), volume 2, page 261 (Chinese).

6   *The Collected Works of Lenin* (Chin. 2. Ed.), volume 55, page 146.

objective idealist situating logic, his science of logic was a mutation of speculative theodicy, his dialectics described the historical process of the change and development of the Notion, and his epistemology was simply the historical process by which the Idea comes to know itself. Thus, these three things coincide in terms of the Absolute Idea. Of course, this is also an **idealist deductive history** of the history of human thought within actuality. Expressions such as "corresponds to truth" and "description of natural history" were not mystic in Hegel's speculative logic. It is simply that Lenin, standing on the outside of Hegel's philosophy, was naturally unable to penetrate these speculative games.

However, we soon see that Lenin includes another comment in a boxed note in the left margin: "In this conception, logic coincides with the **theory of knowledge**. This is in general a very important question"[7]. Please note that if two different logics are melded, then they become one thing. Lenin does not continue on this line of thought to consider if the coincidence of Hegel's notional, idealist logic as his ontology and his theory of knowledge could not be of the same structure as the line of thought of inverted general philosophical materialism. *That year, as Lenin read the works of Dietzgen, he unexpectedly came across this viewpoint, while this time, his understanding was his own. It is worth mentioning that this activation point of logical situating would later lead to another leap in thought, forming Lenin's views on the unity of epistemology, dialectics, and logic.*

At this point in his study, whenever Lenin read a passage of text, he would almost always form two different understandings and evaluations. Thus, as Lenin read in Hegel's "Division," and came across Hegel's assertion that "notion in its objectivity is the object which is in and for itself"[8], he wrote "NB" on both sides of the paragraph and then wrote in a box at the bottom of the page: "= objectivism + mysticism and betrayal of development." I believe that Lenin was likely completely confused by Hegel at this time. His "objectivism" referred to the fact that Hegel always based his philosophical discussions on true philosophical historical progression, often mentioning objectivity and things themselves; this is why Lenin believed that Hegel **appeared** to respect materialism of objective reality. However, all of this was expressed in

7 *Ibid.*, page 146.
8 Hegel, Georg Wilhelm Friedrich. *The Science of Logic*. Commercial Press (1977), volume 2, page 263 (Chinese).

a mysterious way, which made it difficult for Lenin, as a materialist philosopher, to understand. It is evident that this was a thread of understanding that lay in two completely different logical thought spaces.

2 THE REVOLUTIONARY LEAP IN LENIN'S RESEARCH LINE OF THOUGHT

As Lenin began to read the beginning of the first section ("Subjectivity") of "The Doctrine of the Notion," Lenin writes that he felt like he had a headache. In a marginal note, Lenin writes: "En lisant...These parts of the work should be called: a best means for getting a headache"[9]. I believe that the transition from "incomprehensible" to "headache" actually exhibited the most violent thought contradictions of Lenin's gradual deepening of reading and thought. This was also the eve of the emergence of Lenin's new thought logic.

It is commonly known that in this section of *The Science of Logic*, Hegel primarily describes the dialectic of the movement of the Notion; the centre of this philosophical theory was the relationship of the **general** and **individual** at the centre of Lenin's creative elucidation of the theory of materialist dialectics. However, at this time, if Lenin continued to be mired in his original Other interpretive framework, it would be impossible for him to continue moving forward. *Thus, Lenin specifically stopped for a time, and turned to read Kuno Fischer's* **Contemporary History of Philosophy**, *trying to find his views on this "obscure theory." However, Lenin was disappointed in the end, because this book did not, according to him, show "the reader* **how** *to look for the key to the difficult transitions, nuances, ebbs and flows of Hegel's abstract concepts."* Even more interestingly, there is a large portion of text, after pages 34 and 35 of the fifth volume of the *Collected Works of Hegel* where Lenin **does not make any reading excerpts**; this white space lasts for nearly one hundred pages. This was truly a rare occurrence in the *Bern Notebooks. This is also a textual detail that perhaps all previous researchers have ignored.* I have found that in these 100 blank pages of Lenin's notes from the "Doctrine of the Notion," Hegel discusses in the first chapter the "Notion's" universal, special, and individual characteristics. In the second chapter, he discusses "Judgement's" existence, negative, infinite, reflective, necessary, and notional forms; Hegel's first section of the third chapter, "The Syllogism of Existence," is also

---

9   *The Collected Works of Lenin* (Chin. 2. Ed.), volume 55, page 147.

included here[10]. Lenin makes no citation of any of this content. It is impossible for us to whether this is because of his "headache," or if there is some other factor leading to this abnormal silence. If we compare this with Lenin's later important philosophical shift, I believe that this was a process of painful pondering as Lenin read and slipped further into his logical contradictions. This is because it was precisely in the midst of this "dark water," and "extreme obscurity" that Lenin woke up from his "headache" and experienced a great shift in his thought.

Here we see that after this long white space in Lenin's notes, (from page 32 to page 125 of the fifth volume of the *Collected Works of Hegel*), Lenin again begins to take excerpts on page 125. He first cites Hegel's argument on syllogisms, and then writes in a marginal box: "The most common logical figures…are the most common relations of things." He notes: Irrelevant sentence[11]. XXXXX. After this point, Lenin's reading continued as it had, citing Hegel's evaluation of Kant's antinomies under the heading "On Kant" (pages 128-129 of the *Collected Works of Hegel*). We must pay close attention here! A strange new occurrence takes place here in Lenin's notes: he suddenly divides his notebook into **vertical** columns, adding a new box to the one on the inner margin[12]. What's more, the content of the new box did not discuss Lenin's thoughts on Kant's antinomies, but rather returned to a previous comment (on Hegel's analysis of syllogisms). This was a **returning** thought experiment, but this time, Lenin would not come back empty handed. He had come upon a new, important thought: "Hegel's analysis of syllogisms (E.— B.—A., *Eins* (individual); *Besonderes* (particular); *Allgemeines*, (universal) B.—E.—A., etc.) recalls Marx's imitation of Hegel in Chapter I"[13]. This certainly reflects a significant shift, a **logical**

---

10 Hegel, Georg Wilhelm Friedrich. *The Science of Logic*. Commercial Press (1977), volume 2, pages 267-347 (Chinese).

11 This footnote is on the Chinese translation of "figure".

12 *The Collected Works of Lenin* (Chin. 2. Ed.), volume 55, page 148. In addition to including facsimiles of pages from Lenin's important "Sixteen Essential Elements" and "On the Question of Dialectics," the new edition of *Philosophical Notebooks* also includes facsimiles of three pages from Lenin's "Conspectus" (pages 17, 65, and 100), two from Lenin's "Lectures on the History of Philosophy," and one from "Plan of Hegel's *Dialectics (Logic)*." This provides invaluable textological support for a correct, accurate understanding of Lenin's reading logic. Of course, I now possess copies of the entire manuscript of Lenin's *Bern Notebooks* and other major manuscripts from the *Philosophical Notebooks*.

13 *The Collected Works of Lenin* (Chin. 2. Ed.), volume 55, page 148; refer also to the facsimile of page 65 of the original text included on the next page of this book.

turning that figuratively turned on the light bulb for Lenin. *This shift is obviously related to the economics example that Lenin used as he read the introduction to this volume. In that example, Lenin was merely attempting to use formal relations of economic activity to compare Hegel's sensuous phenomena and essential laws; here, however, Lenin thinks of Marx's mention in his letters with Engels that the entire logical framework of the first chapter of **Capital** depends on Hegel's dialectical logic. This is an important indicator of non-Other judgement and heterogeneous thought.* I believe that there is another, even more profound level to this. Lenin's ability to discover this line of thought was related to Bogdanov's errors. This is because before Bogdanov became mired in the errors of Machism, he approached philosophy from the perspective of Marxist economics. This allowed Lenin to see where Plekhanov and Bogdanov had gone wrong! It also allowed him to suddenly realize that he had a way to surpass the theories of others. This marks the emergence of a completely new thought situating logic.

We can see immediately that after the emergence of these important indicators of Lenin's changing thought, the first great **détournement of philosophical logic** appears: Lenin's overall cognition of Hegel's philosophy experiences an extremely important shift. With this shift, Lenin's study of Hegel's philosophy entered its **third** important stage.

It is evident that Lenin was very excited about this turn of events. Looking at his original document, we can clearly see that he first drew a box that covered one third of the page. However, before writing his famous remarks in the box, Lenin first divides the two sides of the box into smaller boxes. In the left one he wrote: "**NB**: to be inverted: Marx **applied** Hegel's dialectics in its rational form to political economy"[14]. This is obviously a further understanding based on his earlier thought, but Lenin uses a more precise term in the place of "imitates": "applies." At the same time, although he does write "to be inverted" here, he specifically points out that Marx restructured and applied the (entire) **form** of Hegel's dialectics. *Later in our analysis we will see that this point is extremely important.* In the right box he writes: "NB: concerning the question of the true significance of Hegel's *Logic*." This is an **important breakthrough**! What does he mean by "true significance"? In his original interpretive framework based on the theoretical circuit of philosophical materialism, the significance of Lenin's understanding

---

14   Lenin's evaluation here refers back to a comment by Marx in the *Marx-Lenin Correspondence*. See the *Collected Works of Lenin*, volume 58, page 29 (Chin. 2. Ed.).

of Hegel was clear; to materialistically "invert" Hegel's thought and shift through the dung pile of Hegel's philosophy to find pearls. What had changed? Lenin is ready to engage in new theoretical situating and pondering. Returning to the larger box, Lenin writes in a long commentary that the formation and application of abstract concepts "already includes the idea, conviction, consciousness of the law-governed character to the world... To deny the objectivity of notions, the objectivity of the universal in the individual and in the particular, is impossible." Evidently, Lenin once again discovers that Hegel is "much more profound" than Hegel in terms of **philosophical theoretical logic**, directly transitioning from Hegel to the theoretical logic of Marx's analysis of commodities in Capital. This is a further confirmation of the content of Lenin's earlier box.

Lenin demonstrates his profound understanding:

> **The individual act of exchange of one given commodity for another, already includes in an underdeveloped form** *all* **the main contradictions of capitalism, so the simpler** *generalization*, **the first and simplest formation of notions (judgements, syllogisms, etc.) already denotes man's ever deeper cognition of the** *objective* **connection of the world**[15].

Here Lenin directly combines the logic of Hegel's dialectics and Marx's dialectics into the **same structure**. Lenin gives a comparison of Marx and Hegel. First, the simple value forms of commodity exchange already included all the contradictions of capitalist economic structures; second, Hegel's Notion was actually a profound reflection of the objective connection of the world. This is correct. However, I believe that by this time, Lenin had not realized that the emergence of value forms were objective abstractions that exist in man's objective economic behaviour; economic categories are not reflections of external matter, but rather historical reflection of social practice. This was something that he would not understand until later. It is in this sense that Lenin again emphasizes: "Here is where one should look for the true meaning, significance and role of Hegel's *Logic*. This NB[16]. After writing this passage, we find that Lenin added another, smaller box to the left side of his original one using a very thick line, as well as another box. In these three boxes, Lenin writes: "One would have to return to Hegel for a step-by-step analysis of any current logic and **theory of knowledge** of

---

15   *The Collected Works of Lenin* (Chin. 2. Ed.), volume 55, page 149.
16   *Ibid.*, page 150.

a Kantian, etc."[17]. *I believe that this is an expression of Lenin's desires and theoretical orientation for the next step of his thought experiment.*

I believe that the notes on this page are the most important thought experiment and logical restructuring up to this point in Lenin's reading of Hegel's *The Science of Logic*. It is also in this sense that Lenin's **original** reading line of thought experienced an **important logical détournement**. A new reading logic – an overall understanding and evaluation of Hegel's philosophy – suddenly appears, which is a leap in thought that is built on the overall refutation of Lenin's former interpretive framework. However, although the contradictions and conflicts between these two reading logics were completely resolved by Lenin, he did not simply judge his earlier line of thought to be **wrong**; rather, he absorbed it into the framework of his new reading logic as a discordant, **unconscious sub-structure**. Lenin continued to read Hegel critically, but the effectiveness and situating level of this criticism had already become much more profound. It is starting here that Lenin was truly able to theoretically grasp Hegel. Of course, it is also here that Lenin's original Other mirror image framework begins to **disintegrate**. The first relation to dissolve was the false "inversion theory" refutation by Marx and Engels of Hegel. At this point, Lenin is able to connect to Marx's logical situating level through his own profound thought, internally, through Hegel. Lenin was ready to construct his own sovereign theoretical thought space, realizing that grasping Hegel's philosophy would allow him to attain the depths of Marx's philosophy. We will soon see this important theoretical progression.

Here, one of Levine's conclusions is actually correct. He asserts that in September and December of 1914, the influence of Hegel's *The Science of Logic* on Lenin continually grew[18]. Of course, this influence was not, as Levine argues, the "Hegelianization of Lenin," but rather Lenin's deeper understanding and scientific cognition of materialist dialectics. Althusser also remarks this change, writing about it more subtly:

> **If readers were to compare the text of Hegel's Longer Logic with Lenin's notes, they would find that Lenin almost completely ignores the book on *existence*; with the exception of summary notes, he does not leave any commentary. This is**

---

17   *Ibid.*, page 149.
18   Levine, Norman. *Dialogue within the Dialectic.* Yunnan People's Press (1997), page 373 (Chinese).

strange, and it is symptomatic. When Lenin read the book on *essence*, readers will certainly find that his notes increase markedly (not only summary notes but also evaluator ones, most in favour, some not). Clearly, Lenin had a great deal of interest in this book. When Lenin came to the book on *subjective logic*, on the other hand, his notes become very frequent, and his evaluation of the Absolute Idea is very positive. Although this may be surprising to readers, Lenin read this chapter *materialistically*[19].

McLellan writes that here Lenin "turns away from criticizing Hegel to enthusiastically accepting the dialectical elements of Hegel's thought"[20]. This is obviously an oversimplified and incorrect expression. Dunayevskaya put it more precisely when she wrote: "when Lenin read 'The Doctrine of the Notion,' he broke away from his own philosophical past"[21]. This is a correct qualitative dividing point. However, Dunayevskaya's judgment also seems to be somewhat exaggerated, because she not only believes that Lenin immediately shifted to Hegel's position, but also claims that here, Lenin had comprehensively restructured his notion of the relation between materialistic or economic forces and man's subjective force, between science and human activity[22]. In fact, Lenin did not simply break from his past; in other words, he did not, as Dunayevskaya argues, become a Hegelian. The substance of Lenin's thought revolution here was a change in his **own** interpretive framework. I must concede that Dunayevskaya makes a profound point in her realization of the deep contradictions in Lenin's logical situating here, *i.e.*, the disconnect between Lenin's philosophical materialism that focuses on material beings that exist apart from man and his own active, practical ray, as well as the contradiction between the objective dimension of determinant, preconditional economic forces and the subjective dimension that emphasized the revolutionary, practical, creative power of the proletariat class. She cleverly points out that Lenin, who had just acquired a new level of theoretical situating, would be able to **synthesize** this contradiction! However, her new mistake lay in her identification of Lenin's shift in philosophical notions and basis in

---

19   Refer to Althusser's "Lenin before Hegel," in *Lenin and Philosophy*. Yuanliu Press (Taiwan) (1990), page 138 (Chinese).
20   McLellan, David: *Marxism after Marx*. Oriental Press (1986), page 135 (Chinese).
21   Dunayevskaya, Raya. *Philosophy and Revolution*. Liaoning Educational Press (2000), page 90 (Chinese).
22   Dunayevskaya, Raya. *Marxism and Freedom*. Liaoning Educational Press (1998), page 156 (Chinese).

practice as idealism. Later we will disprove her profound theoretical shadiness.

I believe that the first leap that emerged in the new logical situating of Lenin's thought as he read Hegel's philosophy was internally constituted of three new logical theoretical points. First, a new understanding of the value of Hegel's philosophy. Second, a profound understanding of the relation between Hegel's philosophy and the new vision of Marx's philosophy. Third, a realization of the necessity of deepening criticism of Kant-Machism using dialectics. It is evident that relative to the Other framework of his earlier reading, Lenin's philosophical theoretical logical space here was comprehensively restructured in terms of his overall understanding of Hegel's philosophy.

It is not difficult to see that the shift in Lenin's line of thought represented in the notes and additions in the boxes on this page collectively and directly point towards **the significance of Hegelian philosophy**. Here, Lenin suddenly reconsiders this significance (in his original interpretive framework, this was a preconditional understanding that he had thought was already clear), which represents a change in thought that was by no means small or narrow in scope. Rather, it was a breakthrough, out of the closed theoretical circuit of Lenin's old, thoughtless, Other mirror image framework, *i.e.*, a redefinition and replacement of Hegel's philosophical logic. Lenin seems to have acquired a completely new understanding: although Hegel's philosophical idealism is incorrect, the structures (forms) of his philosophical thought logic are not complete "nonsense." By this time, Lenin had already understood that in essence, Hegel invertedly and profoundly reflected the essence of the development and movements of the objective world. The significance of Marxism's rescue of Hegel's *The Science of Logic* was not a simple replacement of "God" and the "Absolute Idea" with "matter," nor was it an external "dressing-up" of Hegel into a materialist; rather, it was a serious investigation of the underlying significance of the logical structures of Hegel's philosophy (dialectics). This constructed a completely new, open theoretical circuit. As such, Lenin finally discovered that the restructuring of Hegel's idealist dialectics by Marx and Engels was not some kind of **inversion of terminology**, but rather an **inversion of the entire logic**[23]. As we know, for Marx, Feuerbach was the one who accomplished the move from Hegel's idealism to materialism; under Feuerbach's framework, the Absolute Idea

---

23   *The Collected Works of Lenin* (Chin. 2. Ed.), volume 55, page 202.

had already been changed into "sensuousness," "man," and "nature." More precisely, Marx's critical restructuring of Hegelian philosophy essentially implied the **deconstruction of all metaphysical methods of thought**. Heidegger noticed this point. *After he completed reading all of The Science of Logic, Lenin was already able to use the words "inversion of Hegel's system" with precision.* Thus, truly scientific dialectical thought was able to form in Lenin's philosophical thought, which he was then able to use in understanding the world, in leading the practical restructuring of the world, in **more profoundly** criticizing all idealism and agnosticism from within a new, **dialectical, historical** materialist scope, and ultimately in surpassing old materialism, thus realizing a great philosophical revolution. It was precisely through understanding Hegel's dialectical thought that Lenin was able to more profoundly step into the philosophical scope of Marx and Engels.

Concretely speaking, the immediate scope of understanding revealed by Lenin's passage of commentaries here was also based on his reflections on the three chapters in "Subjectivity" ("Notion," "Judgement," and "Syllogism"). As we have already discussed, these were the sections that had seemed so "obscure" to Lenin before. In this section of *The Science of Logic* that discusses subjectivity, Hegel's exposition primarily explains the universality, particularity, and individuality of the Notion. This kind of thinking seems to echo Aristotle's three major components of logic, but the substantive content has undergone a good deal of restructuring. For Hegel, the Notion is universal; however, this universality is not empty or abstract, but rather the "existence" and "essential unity" of logical progression[24]. Thus, this is not a commonality of individuals, but rather the unification of the individual (existence) into its own concrete self. In other words, this universality is already an abstraction of the concrete. In fact, in an earlier box, Lenin had already approached this vision of Hegel's. He wrote:

> **Obviously, here too the chief thing for Hegel is to *trace* the *transitions*. From a certain point of view, under certain conditions, the universal is the individual, the individual is the universal. Not only (1) *connection*, and inseparable connection, of all concepts and judgements, but (2) *transitions* from one into the other, and not only transitions, but also (3) *identity of opposites*—that is the chief thing for Hegel[25].**

24   Hegel, Georg Wilhelm Friedrich. *The Science of Logic.* Commercial Press (1977), volume 2, page 239 (Chinese).
25   *The Collected Works of Lenin* (Chin. 2. Ed.), volume 55, pages 147-148.

Lenin confirms: "The history of thought from the standpoint of the de-velopment and application of the general concepts and categories of the Logic—this is what we need!" It is not hard to see that this thinking is similar to some of the thought indications that Lenin had exhibited ear-lier, *i.e.*, the new orientation that combined dialectics, theory of knowl-edge, and the history of thought. In other words, Hegel's philosophy reflects the law-governed cognition of man's search for the essence of the outside world. *Kedrov incorrectly moves the point of Lenin's cor-rect acquisition of this understanding forward to his notes in "Doctrine of Being"*[26]. Of course, this evaluation refers not to some specific view of Hegel, but rather to the logical structure of the whole of Hegel's conceptual system (epistemology). Also because of this, Lenin writes: "The formation of (abstract) notions and operations with them **already** includes the idea, conviction, **consciousness** of the law-governed char-acter to the world. *Lenin underlined the word "consciousness" twice; here this word implies "awareness."* In Lenin's view at this time, the significance of Hegel's philosophy lay in the fact that he "is much more profound than Kant, and others, in tracing the reflection of the move-ment of the objective world in the movement of notions"[27]. The "move-ment of the objective world" refers here to the connections, transitions, and contradictions between things that Lenin had mentioned before. Hence, Lenin realized that it was in this important sense that Marx, based on a new materialist foundation, applied the whole of Hegel's dialectical logic (not individual words or views!) to his study of capi-talist economic relations. This is what allowed him to reach his overall logic that commodity exchange behaviour guides "**all** the major contra-dictions of capitalism."

I believe that the most important point of logic that Lenin makes in this comment is the last phrase, after he understands Marx's application of the logical forms of Hegel's dialectic, he writes a hyphen and then summarizes: "the simpler **generalization**, the first and simplest forma-tion of **notions** (judgements, syllogisms, etc.) already denotes man's ever deeper cognition of the **objective** connection of the world"[28]. The

---

26   Kedrov believes that as early as Lenin's reading of "The Docrine of Being," he had already understood that the transition from quality to quantity and then to the category of measure was a logical summary (representation) of the stages experienced by hu-man cognition. This is obviously an overly high opinion of Lenin's early reading. See Kedrov's *Study of Lenin's "Philosophical Notebooks,"* Qiushi Press (1984), page 179 (Chinese).

27   *The Collected Works of Lenin* (Chin. 2. Ed.), volume 55, pages 147-148.

28   *Ibid.*, page 149-150.

significance of this phrase is very profound. It is commonly known that Kant and others like him came to agnostic conclusions because although Kant saw the dynamism of subjective cognitive structures, he transformed this dynamism into an a priori, frozen, this-sided framework constraint. He was not able to see the continual transition of phenomena towards essence (the other-sided thing-in-itself), neither could he see the unified cognition (being-for-self) formed by essence through phenomenologically established man. Unlike these philosophers, Hegel profoundly understood that human cognition continually deepens through the active connection between phenomena and essence; this realizes the dialectical synthesis of cognitive contradiction. Thus we can say that the significance of Hegel's philosophy was an **active, revolutionary** epistemology. Thus, when Marx inverted Hegel in 1845, establishing historical materialism and historical dialectics, he no longer directly observed capitalist social phenomena, but rather proceeded from a revolutionary viewpoint that **sought to recreate the world**, critically revealing the internal contradictions in capitalist modes of production. In this sense, Lenin was able to more deeply understand the profound significance of Marxist revolutionary, active materialist dialectics by understanding Hegel's *The Science of Logic* (dialectics). Only thus was he able to discover the true errors of Bogdanov and his cohorts; only thus was he able to see that Plekhanov's critique of Machism was misguided. Finally, it was thus that his Bolshevik logic of revolutionary practice received logical support from Marxist historical dialectics.

3 THE THREE "APHORISMS" OF LENIN'S COGNITIVE BREAKTHROUGH

I believe that the thought experiment that we have reconstructed from the text exhibits the first theoretical logical pinnacle of Lenin's thought in the *Bern Notebooks*, and especially in the whole process of his reading of Hegelian philosophy. After acquiring this breakthrough in understanding, Lenin was understandably very excited. Immediately after his large box, he drew four smaller boxes, naming three of them "aphorisms." *These are the only three "aphorisms" in Lenin's reading of Hegel's philosophical works*[29]. It is my understanding that he called them "aphorisms" because Lenin was aware of the theoretical situating

---

29 The Russian term "афоризм" was originally translated into Chinese as "warning" – the current translation is "aphorism." Lenin uses this term once more in the *Bern Notebooks*, at the very end of his "On the Question of Dialectics." Refer to *The Collected Works of Lenin* (Chin. 2. Ed.), volume 55, page 309.

support points of his leap in thought. For instance, early in his process of reading and study, Lenin's thought had briefly shone with the light of new thinking; nevertheless, it was after this point that he continually acquired and perfected his own cognitive vision in a new theoretical logical situating space. This comprehensive shift in logical thought space was formed by three theoretical levels.

Specific analysis shows three crucial new thinking points. **First**, the **deepening** of the critique of Kantianism, second, the **internal** relation between Hegel's philosophy and Marx's philosophical vision, and **third**, the **secret** of Hegel's philosophy. I have found that this is the inverse of the thought logic in earlier, larger box. This first aphorism follows in the same vein as the logical thinking point at the very end of the left-hand smaller box.

The first aphorism is Lenin's **reflection** on criticism of Kant and Machism. As we have already seen, in the smaller, left-hand box above this one, Lenin had already expressed his desire to study Hegel in order to progressively analyze the epistemology and logic of Kantianism; this is actually a very important topic that Lenin proposes. However, although Lenin continues to consider how best to criticize Kant and Machism in this first aphorism, his approach shifts greatly; **he directs his critique against the Marxists who themselves criticize Kant and Machism**! Though apparently unthinkable, this shift essentially demonstrates a renewal of Lenin's cognitive situating at this time of great change. We must concede that Lenin here has become even more profound, the inevitable result of having delved deeper into Hegel's dialectics. This is evidently the first crack in Lenin's original Other mirror image framework, as he truly surpasses the philosophical false image of Plekhanov and others.

In this box, Lenin writes "two aphorisms." Both deal with the contemporary Marxists who criticize Kant and Machism. *Lenin first thinks of his "comrades-in-arms" who are already criticizing Kant and Machism. He first draws a dividing line, delineating the fundamental, theoretical heterogeneity of the new vision he has just acquired from their critiques. I believe that it is here that the Other mirror image which had, for so long, dominated Lenin's philosophical thought is ultimately shattered.* The first of these is Plekhanov, who was the most important Marxist in the Russian ideological battle against Kant and Machism. At the same time, he was the Marxist philosopher with the greatest influence on the development of Lenin's philosophical thought. Lenin writes:

> **1. Plekhanov criticizes Kantianism (and agnosticism in gen-**
> **eral) more from a vulgar-materialistic standpoint than from**
> **a dialectical-materialistic standpoint,** *insofar* **as he merely**
> *rejects* **their views from the threshold, but does not correct**
> **them (as Hegel corrected Kant), deepening, generalizing and**
> **extending them, showing the** *connection* **and** *transitions* **of**
> **each and every concept**[30].

Please note that that an important theoretical support point of Lenin's early reading was criticism of idealism **proceeding from materialism**. Here, however, the focus of his thought suddenly shifts to the relation between Marxist dialectical materialist theory and general philosophical materialism. Lenin found that Plekhanov's mistake was the he merely stood with the old materialists in "rejecting" idealism and agnosticism, but did not correct them as Hegel corrected Kant. Plekhanov did not adopt a dialectical position, and was thus unable to truly stand on the scientific position of Marx's materialist dialectics in explaining **what the correct viewpoint should be**! An interesting textual detail to note here is that Hegel here becomes the representative of the "correct view." Adoratsky argues that Lenin's critique of Plekhanov here coincided with his 1904 criticism of Plekhanov; I believe that this is a purposeful false-homogeneity[31].

The second level of situating thought is even more profound: "2. Marxists criticized (at the beginning of the twentieth century) the Kantians and Humists more in the manner of Feuerbach (and Büchner) than of Hegel"[32]. Here, Lenin has found that all Marxists who are opposed to Machism, and not only Plekhanov, primarily base their struggle on the **basic arguments of philosophical materialism**; they did not **simultaneously** address dialectical ("in the manner of Hegel"). I believe that at this time there was also a good of *self-reflection* on the part of Lenin here, because among the "Marxists (at the beginning of the twentieth century)" who opposed Machism, he must also include himself. However, we must be clear that from Lenin's reflections here, we reach many of the simple conclusions proposed by some Western

---

30   *The Collected Works of Lenin* (Chin. 2. Ed.), volume 55, page 150.
31   For Adoratsky's views refer to *Selected Works of Adoratsky*, Beijing Sanlian Press (1964), page 442.
32   *The Collected Works of Lenin* (Chin. 2. Ed.), volume 55, page 150.

Marxists and "Leninologists." These views portray Lenin at the writing of Materialism and Empirio-criticism as a "mechanical, vulgar materialist." *Dunayevskaya argues that in 1914, Lenin philosophically departed from the vulgar materialist philosophical theories that he advocated in his 1908 Materialism and Empirio-criticism, turning towards the new starting point of self-movement of thought*[33]. Such accusations are irresponsible and have ulterior motives. Here, Lenin consciously realized that Machist-style idealism could not only be criticized from the perspective of materialism, but that this criticism could be **deepened** using dialectics. More importantly, this idealism could be "corrected" using Marx's materialist dialectics. From Lenin's reflections, it is obvious that he had no intention of refuting materialism. Taking a broader look at the *Bern Notebooks*, and reading the entire process of his reading of Hegelian philosophy, we find that Lenin never attempted to change his materialist standpoint. *On this point Levine makes a correct argument. He writes that in the* **Philosophical Notebooks***, Lenin never completely abandoned his philosophical materialism*[34]. *In other words, it was not that he never completely abandoned materialist views, but that these views were never shaken. In this sense Lenin never changed, though his overall view of Hegelian philosophy may have shifted. On this point, Dunayevskaya believes that Lenin never changed his Marxist, materialist foundation, nor did he change his revolutionary views on class consciousness. What Lenin acquired from Hegel was a new theory, of the unity between materialism and idealism*[35]. *She even goes so far as to argue that the central thought of Lenin's* **Philosophical Notebooks** **(Bern Notebooks)** *was the revival of idealist truth*[36]. *This is a false view, characterized by self-contradiction and confusion.*

Furthermore, I believe that it was here that Lenin first truly realized how to more profoundly counter Bogdanov's errors, which were not simple fallacies. It was only at this time, after Lenin had entered a completely new level of philosophical thought situating through the profound logical relationship between the dialectics of Hegel and Marx

---

33   Dunayevskaya, Raya. 2000. *Philosophy and Revolution*. Liaoning Education Press, 90 (Chinese Edition).
34   Levine, Norman. *Dialogue within the Dialectic*. Yunnan People's Press (1997), page 361 (Chinese).
35   Dunayevskaya, Raya. 2000. *Philosophy and Revolution*. Liaoning Education Press, 91 (Chinese Edition).
36   Dunayevskaya, Raya. 1998. *Marxism and Freedom*. Liaoning Education Press, 159 (Chinese Edition).

that his vision truly surpassed that of Plekhanov for the first time. It was not until here that he understood how to concisely and powerfully criticize Bogdanov. This was what made him so excited.

After writing a passage of notes entitled "induction," Lenin suddenly pauses his reading, because of a surge in new thinking. In another box, Lenin writes another "aphorism" which further demonstrates his leap in thought. At the beginning of this passage, Lenin underlines the word "aphorism" with a thick horizontal line. *Neither of the other "aphorisms" had any emphasizing marks; Lenin seems to want to stress the important place of this "aphorism in his shifting thought.* It is not hard for us to experience Lenin's extreme excitement as he writes: "It is impossible completely to understand Marx's *Capital*, and especially its first chapter, without having thoroughly studied and understood the **whole** of Hegel's *Logic*. Consequently, half a century later none of the Marxists understood Marx!!"[37]. This is an extremely important and famous statement. According to my interpretation, there are two levels of meaning in this "aphorism." **First**, an explanation of the internal connection between Hegelian philosophy and Marxist thought: "It is impossible completely to understand Marx's *Capital*, and especially its first chapter, without having thoroughly studied and understood the whole of Hegel's *Logic*." At first glance, it seems as though Lenin is viewing Hegelian philosophy as the premise of Marx's *Capital*, because he emphasizes the word "whole." However, Lenin actually only wanted to explain the inevitable connection between the **logical structures** of Hegel's dialectics (this is the meaning of "whole") and the scientific dialectics employed by Marx in *Capital*; he certainly had no intention of making the gross generalization that Hegel's whole philosophy was the premise of Marxism[38]. This was an explanation specifically made of the substance of how to scientifically understand materialist dialectics.

Thus we are able to derive the second level of Lenin's meaning: in terms of scientifically grasping the meaning of Marx's dialectical thought through reading and understanding Hegel, "half a century later

---

37   *The Collected Works of Lenin* (Chin. 2. Ed.), volume 55, page 151.
38   For some Western Marxologists, Lenin's passage here is taken as proof that Lenin, at the time he wrote the *Philosophical Notebooks* (*Bern Notebooks*), Lenin had already become a "Hegelian." This is obviously confused in terms of theoretical logic, because these scholars were never able to completely grasp Lenin's reading logic in its entirety, nor its significance. Refer to Hook's *Political Power and Individual Freedom* (1959), page 404.

none of the Marxists understood Marx!!" As we have already pointed out, this reference to "Marxists" also included Lenin himself. *McLellan has correctly pointed out that this textual passage includes elements of "self-criticism"*[39]. Of course, Lenin was fundamentally different from Plekhanov and his cohorts, because Lenin understood Marx's material-ist dialectic at a deeper level. *Interestingly enough, Althusser arrived at a different conclusion after reading this passage. He asserts that* **nobody understood Hegel after half a century because without studying and understanding Capital, it is impossible to understand Hegel!**[40]. *I do not believe that Althusser's view is correct in terms of its intended theoretical meaning. However, insofar as he refers to Marx's unveiling of the secrets of industry and market logic hidden deep within Hegelian philosophy, Althusser's point is correct and profound.* At the same time, unlike past evaluations of Hegelian philosophy from within his origi-nal theoretical circuit, Lenin discovered here that Hegelian philosophy (*Logic*), was not a **dung heap** containing a few isolated "pearls," but rather concluded that its **entire** logical structure contained a holistic reasonableness; it was a caricatured expression of the whole human cognitive structure. We can conclude that Lenin's shift in his basic as-sessment of Hegelian philosophy was crucial to his first leap in under-standing and logical détournement in his reading logic.

Lenin's three "aphorisms" summarize his discoveries as he read the por-tion of Hegel's book on syllogisms. These aphorisms all concerned the meaning and significance of Hegel's philosophy (*Logic*). After summa-rizing these three important points on the transition between syllogisms in Hegelian philosophy, Lenin writes: "The exposition of connection and transitions (connection is transition), that is Hegel's task. Hegel actually **proved** that logical forms and laws are not an empty shell, but the reflections of the objective world. More correctly, he did not prove, but **made a brilliant guess**"[41]. At first glance, it seems as those this aphorism returns to an argument that Lenin made at the beginning, in the section on subjectivity[42]. However, we must consider the fact that after this shift in thought, Lenin had already discovered the meaning of Hegel's philosophy on a deeper level. As such, although the "con-nections" and "transitions," which Lenin takes to be Hegel's primary

39   McLellan, David: *Marxism after Marx*. Oriental Press (1986), page 135 (Chinese).
40   Althusser, Louis. "Lenin before Hegel," in *Lenin and Philosophy*. Yuanliu Press (Taiwan) (1990), page 137, 148 (Chinese).
41   *The Collected Works of Lenin* (Chin. 2. Ed.), volume 55, page 151.
42   *Ibid.*, page 147.

task, are called the "**reflection**" of the objective world, they are still not **direct reflections** of the essential structure of the objective world. Rather, this refers to man's **overall** reflection of external objects in his own cognitive structure ("forms and laws of logic"). However, this was not employing the simple direct observation of old materialism. Lenin expands this thought in another large box on the next page in his notes:

> **Knowledge is the reflection of nature by man. But this is not simple, not an immediate, not a complete reflection, but the process of a series of abstractions, the formation and development of concepts, laws, etc., and these concepts, laws, etc., (thought, science = "the logical Idea")** *embrace* **conditionally, approximately, the universal, law-governed character of eternally moving and developing nature...Man cannot comprehend = reflect = mirror nature** *as a whole*, **in its completeness, its "immediate totality," he can only** *eternally* **come closer to this**[43].

Here we see that Lenin was already able to consciously oppose old materialism. By understanding and surpassing the mysterious forms of Hegelian philosophy, Lenin grasped that the whole of human cognition was an eternal cognitive movement without end ("abstract process"), and that Hegel's *The Science of Logic* was the epitome of a great dialectical cognitive project, though it was turned around backwards. Thus Lenin was already able to accurately determine that "Hegel 'only' deifies this 'logical idea,' obedience to law, universality"[44].

Here we are finally able to complete the reconstruction of the theoretical circumstances of the first great logical détournement in Lenin's *Bern Notebooks*. I believe that in comparison to past research, which absolutely homogenized the early and late periods of Lenin's thought and engaged in non-historical topical analysis, the theoretical model which we have utilized here is closer to the original circumstances of the text, and thus can have a more profound effect on us. Continuing on, we come across more important thinking in Lenin's process of learning and studying Hegelian philosophy.

---

43   *Ibid.*, page 152-3.
44   *Ibid.*, page 152-3.

CHAPTER ELEVEN

ESSENTIALLY PRACTICAL MATERIALIST DIALECTICS

From the perspective of traditional research, through his understanding and reconstruction of Hegel's dialectical thought in the *Bern Notebooks*, Lenin arrived at a scientific understanding and grasp of the essence and basic theoretical structures of Marx's materialist dialectics. This conclusion has become theoretical "common knowledge," to the point that it is taken for granted. On the contrary, if we base our analysis on the context of the simulated thought situating that we have presented here, Lenin's important philosophical achievements can be reconfirmed in a historical phylogenetic sense. Most importantly, Lenin's development of dialectical materialist notions was certainly not a pre-meditated "conception" or "plan"; rather, in the actual process of reading, this development exhibited another leap in profound thought on the basis of the first important theoretical logical détournement. Where the first shift in Lenin's philosophical thought in the *Bern Notebooks* demonstrated a change to his entire framework of understanding in his reading, the second leap in understanding was a true acquisition and creative unfolding of Marx's essentially practical materialist dialectical truth in a new, sovereign philosophical situating. In my "simulation" of Lenin's thought, this second important logical détournement took place in three comparative thought situating experiments.

1 LENIN'S EARLY UNDERSTANDING OF DIALECTICAL THOUGHT IN THE PROCESS OF HIS READING

We already know that after his first important détournement of theoretical logic, the entire thinking framework of Lenin's reading changed significantly; the old theoretical logical circuit was replaced by a new, open circuit, and the logical ray of practice obtained a new logical basis. Following this, his theoretical thought situating and logical thought space both began to grow richer and more complex. **First**, in thinking on the question of dialectics, Lenin's attitude towards Hegel's philosophy shifted. He no longer sought after discourse fragments on dialectics after **simply** turning Hegel "upside-down," rather seeking to penetrate deeply into Hegel's philosophy in order to discover the basic logic that expresses dialectical thought. *Of course, this does not imply that Lenin's critical attitude towards Hegel's idealism changed, as the effort to cast off idealism was a thread that ran through the entirety of Lenin's reading process. In other words, the substance of Lenin's first shift in thought was certainly not, as some western Marxist theorists have suggested, a regression from materialism to idealism as Lenin became a Hegelian. This viewpoint is evidence of the extreme one-sidedness of these Western scholars. In fact, they must never have seriously studied Lenin's underlying reading line of thought here.* **Second**, Lenin ceases to frequently refer to theoretical Others such as Marx, Engels, and Plekhanov, but rather truly establishes his own independent vision and understanding, pursuing deeper theoretical knowledge of Hegel's philosophy through his own **sovereign** approach. It was only thus that Lenin was able to truly unfold his independent, systematic understanding of the essence of materialist dialectics.

At the same time I would like to specifically point out that the logical shift that took place as Lenin read Hegel appears at first to be an Althusser-style shift in question-form. However, I do not believe that there is evidence of a fundamental "rupture," because the theoretical framework of scientific Marxism consistently played a dominant role in Lenin's philosophical thought. *This is a basic difference between my understanding of this question and that of Western Leninologists.* Taking a broader look at the entire process of Lenin's reading and study, what we find is actually a continual deepening of Lenin's vision and understanding of one particular "question-form" (at the most this is only a shift of sub question-form), thus ultimately forming the logically constructive line of thought of his own independent materialist dialectical thought. This gave Lenin the ability to truly embrace and develop this scientific theory.

At the same time, I have found that even in the latter part of Lenin's reading of *The Science of Logic*, after his first important détournement of theoretical logic, he did not gain an understanding of materialist dialectics all at once; this was also a **continually deepening process**. We have already seen that at the beginning of his reading, it was Lenin's conscious goal to find the dialectical elements of Hegel's philosophy; thus, in the process of his reading, he devotes himself to uncovering all of Hegel's positive expressions of dialectics that are possible to find. In the early stages of his *Bern Notebooks* (meaning the first and second stages of his first shift in thought), Lenin's understanding of Hegel's dialectics was concentrated on two points. First was Hegel's micro-construction of the specific content of the dialectic. Notes on this topic took up the majority of the space in Lenin's notes (this was also the focus of past research on the *Bern Notebooks*). The **second** aspect of Lenin's thought **took place unconsciously**, as it was stifled under Lenin's refutational Other mirror-image reading framework. Nevertheless, as Lenin's thinking in these two aspects grew ever more profound, his understanding of Marxist materialist dialectics surpassed old bounds. Here we will simulate and reconstruct the important thought circumstances of Lenin's process of reading.

At the beginning of the *Bern Notebooks,* Lenin's overall understanding of Hegel's dialectics was not entirely coherent. Under the dominating influence of his past Other reading framework, one of his points of understanding was the constant quest for the **objective basis** of dialectics. As we have already seen, at first Lenin attempted to rewrite Hegel's dialectic of notions into a dialectic of matter. For instance, when Lenin came upon Hegel's proposition of the two basic demands of the dialectic in the introduction to *The Science of Logic* (the "necessity of connections" and the "the *immanent coming-to-be of the distinctions"*), he *immediately boxes the words: "This is what it means, in my* opinion: 1.

Necessary connection, the objective connection of all the aspects, forces, tendencies, etc., of the given sphere of phenomena; 2. The 'immanent **emergence** of distinctions'–the inner objective logic of evolution and of the struggle of the differences, polarity."[1] It is evident that what Lenin wanted then was an objective dialectic, and so he put all of his energy to escaping from subjectivity and epistemological connotations that fill Hegel's philosophy. However, looking at this more closely, we can see that there is a deeper theoretical paradox in Lenin's "rewriting" here. Please note that here Lenin is attempting to confirm the objectivity of connections, but **phenomena** themesleves are a **subjective** logical qualification. *In our later discussion we will see that there is no distinction between appearance and essence among objective objects; such a distinction is only valid relative to the subject (Lacan and Husserl's "for us").* I believe that Lenin was not conscious of the fact that Hegel's dialectics were precisely **objective** (notional) dialectics. His mistake was not in postulating the subjectivity of the **Idea**, but rather in **seeing man's subjective cognitive logic as objective dialectics**. Thus, simply exchanging gone concept for another (from "Idea" to "matter") is not sufficient to change the substance of Hegel's mistake. *Korsch and others noticed this point; we will engage in a more specific discussion of Korsch's views later on in this work.* Of course, Lenin's sovereign philosophical thought situating was still unable to clearly demonstrate this underlying logical paradox.

Lenin's second point of understanding concerns subjective dialectics. Though, in a sense, this is an affirmation of Hegel's notional dialectics, Lenin of course inverted the subjective dialectics of the self-cognition of the Absolute Idea into a reflection of external, objective dialectics. In this aspect Lenin was very sensitive, for instance in his praise for Hegel's "not abstract, dead and immobile, but concrete" description of dialectics, calling it "the spirit and essence of dialectics"[2]. This obviously refers to the characteristics of the subjective dialectical method, *i.e.*, a projection from the perspective of epistemology.

As we read Lenin's notes, we find that these two points of understanding intertwine in Lenin's early study of Hegel. "Away with heaven – law-governed connection of the **whole** (process) of the world"[3]. This is an **ontological** dialectic of **matter**. Soon after, Lenin writes:

1   *The Collected Works of Lenin* (Chin. 2. Ed.), volume 55, page 82.
2   *Ibid.*, page 84.
3   *Ibid.*, page 85.

Dialectics is the teaching which shows how *Opposites* can be and how they happen to be (how they become) identical,—under what conditions they are *identical*, becoming transformed into one another,—why the human mind should grasp these opposites not as dead, rigid, but as living, conditional, mobile, becoming transformed into one another[4].

This refers to **subjective** dialectics from a **cognitive perspective**. Continuing, Lenin writes: "Flexibility, applied objectively, i.e. reflecting the all-sidedness of the material process and its unity, is dialectics, is the correct reflection of the eternal development of the world"[5]. It is evident that Lenin's understanding of subjective dialectics is deepening. On the very next page, Lenin writes in a small box: "The dialectics of things themselves, of Nature itself, of the course of events itself"[6]. All of a sudden Lenin returns back to the first point. *This habitual thinking, in which Lenin repeatedly identifies theoretical points, is the logical circuit of theoretical thought which we have already discussed. Only through the closed identification of a viewpoint in a theoretical logical circuit will the viewpoint become firm and stable; logical circuits are important support points of certain thought situatings. It is not difficult to see how in Lenin's same theoretical logical situating space, a diversity of logical circuits unconsciously co-existed and interweaved. As soon as they are regarded simultaneously, the construction of their identical thought circumstances immediately changes. It is in this sense that Lacan and others argued that truth can only be glimpsed.*

This thinking point, which implies two different points of understanding, did not begin to change until the latter part of Lenin's reading of the first section of "The Doctrine of Essence." At that time, Lenin began to focus on the **holistic relationship** between Hegel's notional dialectics and materialist dialectics. *In other words, Lenin regards en face two qualitatively different logical circuits and directly links them to one another.* Put simply, Lenin finally begins to understand that the essence of Hegel's dialectics actually profound reflects ("brilliantly guesses") materialist dialectics, only under the form of mutated, inverted notional dialectics. Lenin believed that Hegel's notional dialectics was brilliant, considering its overall logic: "The universal, all-sided **vital** connection of everything with everything and the reflection of this

4   *Ibid.*, page 90.
5   *Ibid.*, page 91.
6   *Ibid.*, page 92.

connection— Hegel materialistically turned upside down"[7]. Materialist dialectics are identical to subjective dialectics. Lenin goes on to explain:

A river and the *drops* in this river. The position of *every* drop, its relation to the others; its connection with the others; the direction of its movement; its speed; the line of the movement—straight, curved, circular, etc.—upwards, downwards. The sum of the movement. Concepts, as *registration* of individual aspects of the movement, of individual drops (="things"), of individual "*streams*," etc.[8].

This is the reflection of material dialectics in notional dialectics. Lenin understood that this was the "scene of the world" of the whole of materialist dialectics as reflected by Hegel's *The Science of Logic*. It is my view that this was a notable jump in cognition for Lenin in his original Other framework.

We can see that as Lenin's reading grows more profound, his theoretical attention to the dialectics of matter increases. This is especially true in the subtle changes to the second important dimension of the overall logic of his understanding of dialectics, *i.e.*, his understanding of **objective dialectics in a philosophical, ontological sense**. These changes are concentrated in Lenin's understanding of laws and essential qualifications. According to the philosophical materialist interpretive circuit that made up Lenin's original Other mirror image, laws are the necessary trend and internal connections of the development of the **external**, objective world; this is an ontological category. In Hegel's philosophical system, on the other hand, laws and essence are merely a stage of realization in the historical self-progression of the Absolute Idea, as well as a transitional moment of the self-**cognition** of the ideal subject. As such, laws and essence are both rules that govern the objective movement of things, as well as a stage of logical subjective cognition. In short, laws and essence represent the coincidence of ontology and epistemology. This is why Hegel asserted that "Law is the Reflection of Appearance into identity with itself." Although Lenin was confused by Hegel's expressions, he was able to vaguely sense the reasonable nature of these arguments. As we have already pointed out, Lenin claimed laws are man's overall understanding of the unity and connections of the external world. He saw that Hegel "struggle[ed] against making the

---

7   *Ibid.*, page 122.
8   *Ibid.*, page 122-3.

concept of **law** absolute, against simplifying it, against making a fetish of it," even advising that modern physics take note of this[9].

I must point out that Lenin is not simply agreeing with Hegel here, but rather has begun to discover a logical thread that must be developed further: **the "objective laws" which philosophical materialism takes as ontological categories are not absolute.** An interesting detail is that in Lenin's past Other framework, laws were naturally external, objective rules, while Hegel's was that these objective rules were **related** to the ideal subject. It is evident that in Lenin's theoretical logical circuit at this time, it was **impossible to enclose** Hegel's views. *Unlike Marx, Lenin was not yet able to clearly understand that the external objects (things) and laws of movement which appear in our subjective vision cannot be directly equated to objective existence, because this "essence" and these "laws" are merely our **certain** reflection of external objects (essence and laws) at a **certain** stage of history through practice.* When Lenin writes "**law** and essence are concepts of the same kind (of the same order), or rather, of the same degree, expressing the deepening of man's knowledge of phenomena, the world, etc."[10], these two concepts constitute the subjective result of man's cognition of the external world (not merely in an ontological sense). Lenin goes on to point out: "The essence here is that both the world of appearances and the world in itself are **moments** of man's knowledge of nature, stages, **alterations** or deepenings (of knowledge)." I believe that Lenin at this time had not yet realized that the objective dialectics in his own original Other interpretive framework were about to be **split apart**, and that one part of this was related (objectively linked) to man (the subject)! In other words, the most important theoretical logical circuit and thought tendency in his prior **philosophical materialist** theoretical situating were about to be explosively torn apart.

We find that at this important moment in Lenin's thought, as he is deepening his understanding of the overall structure of dialectics, he experienced, as we have already discussed, the first leap in thought in his reading of Hegel. The situating of this new, sovereign thought logic led to a change in Lenin's attitude towards Hegel's philosophy, leading also to a sudden change in his overall grasp of the structure of dialectics. A completely new background of dialectical logical thought was brought

9   *Ibid.*, page 126.
10   *Ibid.*, page 127.

to the forefront and constructed, which was the appearance of **objective, real, practical dialectics**. This was the content of Lenin's second great leap in understanding, as well as the most important theoretical fruits of Lenin's study of Hegelian philosophy.

2 PRACTICAL DIALECTICS: LENIN'S NEW UNDERSTANDING ON MATERIALIST DIALECTICS

Lenin's new understanding of practical dialectics was primarily expressed as the first time in his notes that he used a **comparative** method to regard his own materialist dialectics and Hegel's idealist dialectics. In other words, the new logical construction of practical dialectics is exhibited in a comparative thought situating. It is my view that it is here that Lenin first consciously enriches and deepens his understanding and cognition of materialist dialectics through restructuring Hegel's idealist dialectics. This was a definite, important moment in Lenin's study.

In the excerpted text I have found that the logical precursor to Lenin's important creative theoretical thought situating was precisely the idea of **subjective participation in the qualification of philosophical ontology**. In the third chapter ("Teleology") of the second section ("Objectivity") of "Subjective Logic" in *The Science of Logic*, Lenin read Hegel's exposition on the relation between mechanism, chemism, and end: "End has shown itself to be the **third** to mechanism and chemism it is their truth"[11]. Of course, in Hegel's idealist logic, the purpose of this expression was to exhibit the dynamism of the Idea and the intent of the subject; as such, the first sub-heading of this chapter is entitled "Subjective End"[12]. However, this concept of "end" immediately led Lenin to materialistically think of **man's purposeful activity**, or **material practice**. I*n Lenin's early reading notes, the concept of practice only appeared once; furthermore, it emerged as an **epistemological moment** in the theoretical circuit of philosophical materialism[13]. As such, scholarly memory was certainly important in the formation of his philosophical situating, but the question of what important scholarly memory plays a constructive role under what circumstances is the complex result of accumulated thought.* Here, practice emerges as

---

11   Hegel, Georg Wilhelm Friedrich. *The Science of Logic*. Commercial Press (1977), volume 2, page 429 (Chinese).

12   *Ibid.*, page 430.

13   *The Collected Works of Lenin* (Chin. 2. Ed.), volume 55, page 142.

the dialectical basis of ontology – this is the key to understanding the second theoretical logical détournement in Lenin's study of Hegelian philosophy.

Let us return to the text itself. After citing a passage in which Hegel discusses the relation between "mechanism," "chemism," and "end," Lenin uses two lines to indicate separation into two columns, giving the right-hand column the title "Materialist Dialectics" and the left-hand column the heading "Hegel." The left side of the column contains excerpts from Hegel's The Science of Logic, while the right side contains Lenin's new understanding of materialist dialectics. *This is a written indication of the dual discourse in the text of the notes; I believe that this is Lenin's new **thought situating experiment**. New qualitative changes and logical **détournements** in the circumstances of Lenin's thought have finally resulted in the construction of thought activated by this textual expression. This is the "thought workshop" of Lenin's second important theoretical logical détournement that we can directly observe here.* Here we see the following new beliefs expressed by Lenin: "The laws of the external world, of nature, which are divided into **mechanical** and **chemical** (this is very important) are the bases of man's **purposive** activity"[14]. *Soon Lenin will discover that the division of mechanical and chemical laws was, itself, **devised by man**.* Nature is the premise and foundation of man's activity; this is materialism. Next, Lenin writes: "In his practical activity, man is confronted with the objective world, is dependent on it, and determines his activity by it... From this aspect, from the aspect of the practical (purposive) activity of man, the mechanical (and chemical) causality of the world (of nature) appears as though something **external**, as though something secondary, as though something hidden"[15]. The most critical point of this thought situating is this: Lenin had realized that the relation between human practice and nature was not, as Hegel argued, the relation between spirit and matter, but was rather **all part of the process of actual, objective existence**. *This was also the starting point of Marx's thinking on the problem of practice, an important aspect that was ignored by all of old materialism. Please note that beginning here, the logic of Lenin's understanding of materialist dialectics begins to approach Marx's corresponding context. It is precisely through practical logic that Marx reunited the one-sidedness of idealism on the one hand and old materialism on the other in traditional philosophy on a new foundation.*

---

14 *Ibid.*, page 157.
15 *Ibid.*, page 157-8.

Lenin creatively points out: "Two forms of the **objective** process: nature (mechanical and chemical) and the **purposive** activity of man"[16]. Interestingly, Hegel's original text mentions two forms of "objective processes," mechanism and chemism[17]. He asserts that "the end is the Notion that is posited as in its own self relating itself to objectivity"[18], or in other words that the end is a **subjective Notion** that is obtained **objectively**. The subjective side of the end faces an "**objective**, mechanical, and chemical **world**[19]. Here, the opposition between Hegel's subjective and objective worlds is very clear. If Lenin were to approach this idea using his original philosophical materialist logic circuit, if he materialistically turned Hegel upside down, then he could have merely recreated the "end" here as consciousness which **reflects** the objective world. Another important situating detail is that in Lenin's own definition of matter, subjective "matter" was unable to enter his fixed logic circuit of **objective existence**. However, in Lenin's new, restructured thought space, the form of Hegel's first two objective processes become, for Lenin, the material, objective "natural world." He even specifically indicates the form of another new objective process: "the **purposive** activity of man." This is an objective existence that his original material definition was unable to accept; Lenin's view of the objective world is obviously new. Man's purpose, in the form of his objective activity, enters the objective existence of our actual lives. *Please note that in Lenin's "recreation" of Hegel's dialectics here, he does not use matter to simply replace the spirit, which plays a dominant role for Hegel. Rather, he utilizes man's purposive practice, which possesses* **active material power.** *This is a very different method from the "recreation" (conceptual replacement) that he engaged in during his early Other reading of Hegel. Though his theoretical focal point was similar, the thought situating that evolved from it was very different.* In the new worldview that Marx and Engels began to establish in 1845, nature was the immediate basis for the survival of animals; men, on the other hand, change nature through their purposeful practice, forming a new basis of social existence[20].

---

16 *Ibid.*, page 158.
17 Hegel, Georg Wilhelm Friedrich. *The Science of Logic.* Commercial Press (1977), volume 2, page 429 (Chinese).
18 *Ibid.*, page 431.
19 *Ibid.*, page 432.
20 Marx, Karl and Friedrich Engels. *The German Ideology*, in The Collected Works of Marx and Engels, volume 3, page 24 (Chinese).

Therefore, Lenin points out:

At the beginning, man's ends appear foreign ('other') in relation to nature. Human consciousness, science ('the concept'), reflects the essence, the substance of nature, but at the same time this consciousness is something external in relation to nature (not immediately, not simply, coinciding with it)[21].

How did Lenin arrive at this conclusion? Lenin already understood that man's cognition and reflection of the external natural world was not the result of direct observation, as postulated in philosophical materialism, but necessarily **historically** projected external, objective objects in practice. *This was a deeper level of understanding that Dietzgen, Feuerbach, Plekhanov, and even Lenin as he wrote Materialism and Empirio-criticism were all unable to reach.*

Here, Lenin provides further confirmation using the example of the movement forms of objective mechanism and chemism (this is **human** technology – constructed by human social practical forces). Lenin points out that, on the one hand, technology is man's objective activity of recreating external objects; it is "determined by external conditions (the laws of nature). On the other hand, technology is man's purposive activity, and only at a certain depth of practical perspective can man understand and recreate the world. At the very end of this passage, Lenin stresses two important points with double parentheses: "((**TECHNIQUE** and the **OBJECTIVE** world. **TECHNIQUE** and **ENDS**)"[22]. In a later, large passage of excerpts, he underlines Hegel's following expression: "**IN HIS TOOLS MAN POSSESSES POWER OVER EXTERNAL NATURE. ALTHOUGH AS REGARDS HIS ENDS, HE FREQUENTLY IS SUBJECTED TO IT.**" In the margin of the page next to this passage, Lenin draws three vertical lines, writing: "Hegel and historical materialism." We can see that Lenin believed that this thinking already exhibited the "germ of historical materialism"[23]. *Evidently, in this comparative thought situating experiment, Lenin's profound understanding has allowed him to uncover more and more of Hegel's important thoughts, especially in terms of the logical similarities between Hegel and Marx.*

---

21 *The Collected Works of Lenin* (Chin. 2. Ed.), volume 55, page 158.
22 *Ibid.*, page 158.
23 *Ibid.*, page 159.

Why did Lenin write this? It would be most useful for us to return to Hegel's original text for the answer to this question. In Hegel's discussion under the heading "The Realized End" in the chapter "Teleology," he maintains the standpoint of the Absolute Idea, viewing the human subject as merely a purposeful possessor; man uses (objects as means) in interacting with natural objects. Furthermore, Hegel does not affirmatively explain man's active practice, but merely identifies it as the "cunning of reason," which realizes its own purpose through the mutual abrasion of two kinds of objects[24]. *This is the origin of Hegel's famous expression the "cunning of reason."* At this time, post-theoretical logical détournement Lenin was able to immediately pierce Hegel's veil of speculative idealism, realizing that this so-called "cunning of reason," which exists in social historical activity, were **precisely** the objective laws of social history which Marx and Engels had revealed. In addition, the essential point here is that these social historical laws, which are not determined by **individual** will, are constituted of man's active activity. *Here there are two situating activation points that merit our further consideration. **First**, in Lenin's "What the 'Friends of the People' Are," he over-generalized his definition of the progress of human social development as a "natural historical process" not determined by the will of man. The notions in his thought situating at that time cannot be equated in the least with his beliefs by this point in his study of Hegel. This is because the progress of social historical development, which is constructed by man's practical activity, is only invertedly expressed as a blind "natural historical process" under certain conditions of history. In Marx's vision of the "free kingdom" of communism, this "external necessity" (economic laws that emerge as the "invisible hand") **which is not determined by man's will** must be surpassed. However, Lenin does not directly compare these two heterogeneous thought situations at this time. **Second**, the facts of thought history that Lenin discovers here demonstrate that the historical materialism that Marx established was not the expansion and application of so-called dialectical materialism to the realm of history, rather, the worldview of historical materialism which begins with the logic of practice is the "ontology" of Marx's new worldview. Lenin did not investigate this point further.* This was a truly surprising discovery. Lenin originally planned to search for dialectics within Hegel's philosophy, but rather discovered "the germ of historical materialism" in his philosophy. Not

---

24   Hegel, Georg Wilhelm Friedrich. *The Science of Logic.* Commercial Press (1977), volume 2, pages 437-438 (Chinese).

without excitement, Lenin looks back at the publication date and location of this book: "Nuremberg, 21.VII.1816... This is in the §: 'The Realized End'"[25]. *What Lenin wanted to confirm was just how much before the establishment of Marx and Engels' historical materialism it was that Hegel proposed these views.* Continuing on, Lenin writes in the next box: "**HISTORICAL MATERIALISM AS ONE OF THE APPLICATIONS AND DEVELOPMENTS OF THE IDEAS OF GENIUS—SEEDS EXISTING IN EMBRYO IN HEGEL.**" He double-underlined all the text of this box to show its importance.

It is my personal opinion that though Lenin's conclusion here was correct, it was not precise enough. I believe that it somewhat correct because Lenin was able to rediscover the underlying relation between Hegel and historical materialism in the early 20th century. *In traditional research, scholars had only focused on the link between the dialectical theories of Hegel and Marx.* However, I also say that Lenin's expression was imprecise because its description of the scholarly background of historical materialism was incomplete; Lenin had evidently not yet seen the influence of classical economics (including the French Revolution) on Hegel, nor the direct role that classical economics, which was founded on the basis of modern industrial production, played in historical materialism[26]. *Later, in the 1930s, Lukacs was the first to propose and deepen this view, in his book **Young Hegel**.* At the same time, historical materialism was not the application and development of some kind of reasonable "seed" of Hegel's notional dialectics; the thought situating process of Marx's establishment of historical materialism was a more complex theoretical project, reaching a depth of thought space that Hegel's philosophy simply could not have tolerated. Regardless, Lenin's view here was progress reached after he realized his détournement of theoretical logic and formed a new thought situating. Considering the entire process of his reading of Hegelian philosophy, here Lenin begins to realize the role and place of man's active, objective, **practical dialectics** in his relation with objects and in the external world. In Lenin's context of thought, he had already reached the deep level of theoretical of logic exhibited in the new philosophical worldview of Marx and Engels' *The German Ideology.* This worldview asserted that the nature **around** us today is the result of practice (industrial production). Objective dialectics was the true basis of the

---

25   *The Collected Works of Lenin* (Chin. 2. Ed.), volume 55, page 159.
26   Refer to chapters 1-4 of *Marx Revisited.*

new Marxist philosophical worldview, and all of this formed the most important foundational principle of historical materialism. *This was a level of understanding that other 20ᵗʰ century Russian Marxists were unable to reach of Marx's thought.* Of course, these are only my guesses and reconstructions of theoretical thought.

Here we must address some of Korsch's critiques of Lenin. In Korsch's 1930 "On the Current State of 'Marxist and Philosophical' Problems," he accuses Lenin of not understanding Marx and Engels' scientific criticism of Hegel. He writes: "Marx and Engels' materialist inversion of Hegel's idealist dialectic merely released this dialectics from its ultimate mysterious shell. They discovered the **actual movement of history** under the idea of the 'self-movement' of 'idea' dialectics, declaring this historical, revolutionary movement as the sole 'absolute' existence"[27]. The primary analysis of Korsch's declaration here is correct. Unfortunately, the last sentence is where problems emerge. I believe that this returns to the **ontology of social historical existence** as confirmed by young Lukacs. This is the correct idea that Marx and Engels discovered the true basis of Hegel's Idea logic structure to be the movement of historical practice; however, Marx and Engels certainly never attempted to re-establish any kind of existential ontology; Marx's historical materialism of course recognized the **eternal pre-eminence** of natural matter, but he merely scientifically explained how man can only face the objective world under a certain framework of historical practice, developing certain historical notions. However, he did not, nor would he ever, try to postulate any kind of philosophical **absolute existence**. I believe that Lenin's recreation of Hegel here corresponds to Marx's historical materialism. He directly differentiates between two different realities, *i.e.*, natural existence premised by the matter of human social existence and the completely new social life that man creates through his purposeful, practical activity.

It is also here that we can see a new and important thinking point in the context of Lenin's thought: the question of Marx's **historical** dialectics. I would like to explain that although Lenin's understanding of practical dialectics had already reached a very profound dimension, his context still lacked an important qualification, i.e., the ontological dimension that highlights Marx's new worldview, or in other words, it

---

27   Korsch, Karl. "On the Current State of 'Marxist and Philosophical' Problems." In *Marxism and Philosophy*. Chongqing Press (1989), page 81 (Chinese).

lacked **actuality, concreteness,** and **historicalness. The fundamental basis of practical dialectics is historical materialism and historical dialectics.** This is a very important issue. If materialism, dialectics, and even the notion of practice are not coincided with the actual process of social history, then they cannot truly form the context of the "historical science" that Marx and Engels identified. Of course, here we must not be overly exigent, because Lenin was not able to read the important documents of Marx and Engels' establishment and development of this science (*The German Ideology* and *Grundrisse*).

It is interesting to note that in all Soviet scholarship, there is a sore lack of study of this important qualification of Marx's historical materialism. There is only one exception to this rule: the "reactionary scholar" Deborin. In a 1924 article titled "Lenin and Modernity," in the magazine *Under the Banner of Marxism*, the second section is called "Marxism and History." *This article was later deleted in its entirety from Deborin's later Philosophy and Politics.* This article demonstrates that Deborin already understood that the characteristic of the new worldview established by Marx and Engels was that it was primarily directed towards **history**[28]. Unfortunately, this discovery was later covered over again completely. *For more on this issue, please refer to the addendum to this chapter.*

It is plain that Lenin's important understanding of the problem of practice immediately led to a whole set of new beliefs. As Lenin read Hegel's discussion of practice as merely a transitional moment in the logic of the Idea, Lenin writes a new and important viewpoint in a large box, including the words, **"The categories of logic and human practice"** next to the box. He writes:

THAT IS NOT MERELY STRETCHING A POINT, A MERE GAME. THIS HAS A VERY PROFOUND, PURELY MATERIALISTIC CONTENT. IT HAS TO BE INVERTED: THE PRACTICAL ACTIVITY OF MAN HAD TO LEAD HIS CONSCIOUSNESS TO THE REPETITION OF THE VARIOUS LOGICAL FIGURES THOUSANDS OF MILLIONS OF TIMES IN ORDER THAT THESE FIGURES COULD OBTAIN THE SIGNIFICANCE OF AXIOMS. THIS NOTA BENE[29].

---

28   Deborin, Abram. "Philosophy and Politics," in *Philosophy and Politics*, Beijing Sanlian Press (volume II), 1965, page 835 (Chinese).

29   *The Collected Works of Lenin* (Chin. 2. Ed.), volume 55, page 160. A little later on, Lenin goes on to explain this view. See page 186 of the same book.

It is worth noting that under the words of this box, Lenin draws thick double underlines to indicate that they are particularly important. *This is the only time that we see such markings in all of Lenin's notes.* I believe that this textual detail reveals a new breakthrough in Lenin's understanding and grasp of the relation between cognition (logic structures) and external, objective structures. I believe this because based on Lenin's original Other interpretive framework, he would have "invertedly" written that man's cognitive structures (logic) were the reflection of external objective laws; however, here Lenin **sublates external objective laws into man's objective practical structures.** External laws are the premise; man's cognition of external laws, especially logical structures ("figures"), do not **directly correspond** to external objective structures, but rather through the "figures" of objective practical structures. There is no doubt that Lenin already clearly saw that Hegel began to approach "the concept of **truth**" **through** the "practical, purposeful activity of man." However, he also tries to include man's purposeful activity in the category of logic, turning practice into a subjective "syllogism." This is a trick of idealism. Lenin by this time was already able to perceive that the practical activity of man had to lead consciousness to the repetition of the various logical figures (the structure of practice), which is what gives these cognitive structures the significance of axioms. *The deeper level of thought situating that Lenin did not realize here was that the role of practice in cognition and truth was not simply "axiomatic significance" on a cognitive level, but also exhibits the historical functional relation of the value standard of for-self "upperhandedness" (to use Heidegger's words).* Lenin's cognitive results here are very important. Lenin's theoretical orientation here corresponds completely to Marx's understanding of the underlying connection between man's cognitive structures and practical (labour) activities in his critique of Wagner's textbook on political economy[30]. It seems that Lenin by this time was already standing with Marx on the same standard of logic. *Levine also correctly perceived this point[31]. Vranicki also arrives at a basically correct conclusion: "In constituting, establishing, and forming the laws and axioms of our thought, Lenin sees practice as the basis that can form the chain of our thought[32].*

30   See volume 19 of *The Collected Works of Marx and Engels*, page 405.

31   Levine, Norman. *Dialogue within the Dialectic.* Yunnan People's Press (1997), page 383 (Chinese).

32   Vranicki, Predrag. *History of Marxism* (volume 2), People's Press: 1988, page 32 (Chinese).

It is my conclusion that the most important foundation of the second great theoretical logical détournement in Lenin's *Bern Notebooks* was constructed here, because it was at this point in time that he finally developed his own unique, sovereign philosophical theoretical logical situating. As such, this can also be seen as the starting point of Lenin's great contributions to Marxist philosophical logic (especially materialist dialectics and epistemology).

3 PRACTICE: DRAWING A DIAGRAM OF THE OBJECTIVE WORLD

Not long after Lenin read the introduction to section three ("The Idea") of "The Doctrine of Notion," we first see that he directly approved of Hegel's philosophical thought, especially paragraphs 213-215 of the introduction to this section **"ARE PERHAPS THE BEST EXPOSITION OF DIALECTICS"**[33]. *At this moment, it is certain that Lenin already fully understood why Marx and Engels always mentioned Hegel when they discussed dialectics. The confusion that Lenin felt in reading the **Marx-Engels Correspondence** appears to have already disappeared.* In his later notes, Lenin bases himself on the logical thread that he had acquired earlier, recording important excerpts and his personal commentaries. Furthermore, here we see that Lenin wrote down his second **comparative** logical situating experiment. I understand that this was Lenin's new **epistemological** consideration after he confirmed the ontological place of objective practical dialectics. In other words, this was the essence of the supersession of Marx's active, revolutionary, reflection-theory based on practice over the direct-observational epistemology of general philosophical materialism.

As we know, "The Idea" was the last section of "The Doctrine of the Notion," and was also the pinnacle of Hegel's purely theoretical, logical, scientific construction, formed by the three chapters "Life," "The Idea of Cognition," and "The Absolute Idea." "Life" is the first moment of the Idea. Life is the highest developmental stage of natural laws, the preliminary coincidence of the Absolute Spirit with itself (spiritual essence) after it escapes external objectivity (nature)[34].

---

33 *The Collected Works of Lenin* (Chin. 2. Ed.), volume 55, page 162.
34 Hegel, Georg Wilhelm Friedrich. *The Science of Logic*. Commercial Press (1977), volume 2, page 475 (Chinese).

When Lenin first came across Hegel's use of the word "Life" in the footnote to paragraph 215 of *Shorter Logic*, he merely views life as man's natural living body[35]. However, as soon as Lenin actually read the content of Hegel's chapter "Life," he develops a new view. He found that from the perspective of the **relation** between cognition and practice, Hegel's "idea of including **Life** in logic is comprehensible— and brilliant..."[36]. Lenin goes on to cite Hegel's definition of life: "Life = individual subject separates itself from the objective." Though this is almost a word-for-word citation, Lenin did not add quotation marks[37]. This is a thought-symptom of identification. *Marx later restructured this idea, arguing that as soon as man engages in labour production through the use of tools, he separates himself from animals.* Lenin realizes: "If one considers the relation of subject to object in logic, one must take into account also the general premises of Being of the **concrete** subject (= **life of man**) in the objective surroundings"[38]. Here, life no longer refers to general, natural organisms, but is understood to mean man's actual social existence ("concrete subject"). Furthermore, this leads to Lenin's attention to the premise of social existence. As we know, for Hegel, "Life is the impulse of the Spirit"[39]. In other words, the essence of life is the subjective impulse to unify the subject and the object; this, in fact, is **practice**. Actually, this is merely the orientation of what Hegel calls the category of "Spiritual Life." Hegel merely puts a different facade on this word, and Lenin is able to immediately penetrate this speculation and see through to Hegel's true meaning. This shows Lenin's astute grasp of materialist practical dialectics.

In the next chapter, "The Idea of Cognition," subjective cognition comes onto the scene, implying practice as its own moment. However, in Hegel's logic, practice merely continues the impulse of "Life" as a moment of the Idea. After this point, Lenin's reading notes become even more active as he comes upon fresh thought activation points. In my opinion, Lenin begins to walk gradually towards the overall emergence of his own **sovereign philosophical thought situating**[40].

---

35   *The Collected Works of Lenin* (Chin. 2. Ed.), volume 55, page 170.

36   *Ibid.*, page 171.

37   Hegel, Georg Wilhelm Friedrich. *The Science of Logic*. Commercial Press (1977), volume 2, page 459 (Chinese).

38   *The Collected Works of Lenin* (Chin. 2. Ed.), volume 55, page 172.

39   Hegel, Georg Wilhelm Friedrich. *The Science of Logic*. Commercial Press (1977), volume 2, page 467 (Chinese).

40   *The Collected Works of Lenin* (Chin. 2. Ed.), volume 55, page 175.

At the beginning of the second chapter of the third section of *The Science of Logic,* Hegel begins immediately by criticizing Kant's metaphysical ideas, accusing him of "[having] generally in mind only the state of the metaphysics of his time, which in the main adhered to these abstract, one-sided determinations wholly devoid of dialectic"[41]. Hegel believed that it was because of these problems that Kant would follow Hume to agnosticism, breaking the link between appearance and the "thing-in-itself." Lenin seems to approve of Hegel's viewpoint here. In a marginal box, Lenin writes: "Hume and Kant do not see the appearing Thing-in-itself in "phenomena," divorce phenomena from objective truth, doubt the objectivity of cognition, remove anything empirical from the thing-in-itself..."[42]. *Althusser writes that in reading* **The Science of Logic**, *Lenin heartily agrees with all of Hegel's critiques of Kant's thing-in-itself agnosticism[43]. Broadly speaking, this conclusion is correct. However, when Althusser goes on to identify this attitude of Lenin's as proceeding from the views of philosophical materialism and scientific objectivity on the position of* **Materialism and Empiriocriticism**, *he becomes overly arbitrary and imprecise. For instance, in the textual context here, Lenin's affirmation of Hegel's critique of Kant did not stem from the reasons that Althusser lists.* However, unlike Hegel's line of thought in his resolution of Kantian problems, unified phenomena and objective truth were not impulses of the idea, but rather objective impulses of practice.

Lenin writes that if one wishes to swim, one must first get in the water[44]. Objects cannot automatically enter our minds; only by "getting into the water," by entering practice, can we capture objects. *Please note that Lenin's development of this important understand was already completely divorced from the philosophical materialist epistemology of Plekhanov, Dietzgen, and Feuerbach.* Because practice is a medium, understanding does not correspond perfectly to phenomena. External objects (nature) in practice and cognition "[are] **both** concrete **and** abstract, **phenomenon and** essence, **both** moment **and** relation"[45]. Hegel had already realized that Kant did not knowingly ignore the limits of

---

41   Hegel, Georg Wilhelm Friedrich. *The Science of Logic.* Commercial Press (1977), volume 2, page 475 (Chinese).

42   Althusser, Louis. "Lenin before Hegel," in *Lenin and Philosophy.* Yuanliu Press (Taiwan) (1990), page 141 (Chinese).

43   *Ibid.,* page 143.

44   *The Collected Works of Lenin* (Chin. 2. Ed.), volume 55, page 175.

45   *Ibid.,* page 143.

the results of human cognition. Kant had clearly indicated that the form "exhibited" to us of the "thing-in-itself" was a structure of the phenomenological world. Relative to the other-sided truthfulness of the thing-in-itself, "thought determinations in general, the categories, reflective determinations, as well as the Notion and its moments" become "objective things"[46]. *The "subjective" here obviously does not refer to absolute subjectivity in a Hegelian sense, but rather to debased, empirical subjectivity belonging to man.* Hegel, of course, does not agree with this expression. For him, it is necessary to use a contradictory view to analyze the limited nature of cognition. To use his words, "he contradiction of a truth that at the same time is supposed not to be truth"[47]. *Later, Heidegger expands this into the assertion that in revealing existence, the truth simultaneously obscures existence.* Cognition is a historical progression. It resolves its own contradictions in the course of its self-development. Lenin also approves of Hegel's views here, writing that "The **process** of cognition leads it to objective truth"[48]. Furthermore, the "abstract and divorced" nature of man's cognition of the reflections of external objects is subjective, while the "objective as a whole, in the process, in the sum-total, in the tendency, in the source." More importantly, "practice" is the means of eliminating one-sided subjectivity and objectivity[49]. Also, "the human notion 'definitively' catches this objective truth of cognition, seizes and masters it, only when the notion becomes "being-for-itself" in the sense of practice"[50]. It is evident that Lenin's attention is focused on Hegel's expression of the determination of practice.[51]

From Lenin's notes, we see that Lenin is able to accurately judge the true position of practice in Hegel's progression towards the "Absolute Idea." Although it seems as though practice is nothing more than a transitional movement in the process of cognition, it is actually the most important transition towards "objective truth." Lenin profoundly understands: "Marx, consequently, clearly sides with Hegel in introducing the criterion of practice into the theory of knowledge: see the *Theses on Feuerbach*" XXXXXXX. This is another coincidence

---

46   Hegel, Georg Wilhelm Friedrich. *The Science of Logic.* Commercial Press (1977), volume 2, page 485 (Chinese).
47   *Ibid.*, page 485.
48   *The Collected Works of Lenin* (Chin. 2. Ed.), volume 55, page 177.
49   *Ibid.*, page 177.
50   *Ibid.*, page 181.
51   *Ibid.*, page 181.

of Marx and Hegel that Lenin discovers in his research. Please note that this is another important progression in Lenin's study and thought. *However, because these new realizations conformed to his interpretive line of thought at this time, he does not appear to be particularly excited at this point. In Deborin's introduction to the translation of the **Bern Notebooks**, he accurately points out this point.*

However, temporary stillness was only a sign of coming revolution. Next we see that Lenin again uses vertical lines to separate another column in his notes, writing his **third** comparative thought situating experiment. In the left margin, under the heading "Practice in the Theory of Knowledge," he cites a long passage of Hegel's. Above this passage, he boxes the words: "Alias: Man's consciousness not only reflects the objective world, but creates it"[52]. His use of the word "alias" here referred to his earlier box, where he mentioned Marx's *Theses on Feuerbach*; it was also the heading of his comparative thought situating experiment here.

Looking closely at the textual details, if this proposition had appeared in the early stages of Lenin's reading (150 pages earlier), then it would have done so as **the object of Lenin's contemptuous criticism**. Of course, the true meaning of this proposition was not that man's thought can create the world; rather, it confirms that **actual** (not determined by the will of man) nature is still the precondition of man's subsistence, but that through **conscious**, objective, material practice (man's **actual** useful things), man can create for himself a new basis of objective subsistence, thus realizing the impulse for the subjective purpose ("its self"). Here, Lenin took direct inspiration from Hegel's qualification of practice. Hegel writes: "But in the Practical Idea it stands opposed as actual to the actual"[53]. Here there appear two "real things": external objective objects, and man's objective practical activity. The former is an internal premise, while the latter provides a new foundation. Lenin's famous words appear in his thought situating at this point: "**Practice is higher than (theoretical) knowledge**, for it has not only the dignity of universality, but also of immediate actuality"[54]. *This expression is directly related to Lenin's scholarly memory of a passage from Marx that he cited in his reading of the Marx-Engels' Correspondence. There,*

---

52 *Ibid.*, page 182.
53 Hegel, Georg Wilhelm Friedrich. *The Science of Logic*. Commercial Press (1977), volume 2, page 523 (Chinese).
54 *The Collected Works of Lenin* (Chin. 2. Ed.), volume 55, page 183.

Marx wrote that "practice surpasses all theory"[55]. Lenin underlines this excerpted sentence to highlight its importance.

When Hegel uses "good" to refer to something, Lenin draws upon the idea of the unity of "human practice" and "external reality" in his new thought situating to understand that Good refers to the actual demands on the external world. *Here we must make an important distinction. Lenin's understanding of practical active cognition did not imply that he directly identified with Hegel's idealist point of view. For instance, Levine argues that when Lenin believed in the greater dynamism and creativity of the spirit, he was no longer first a philosophical materialist[56]. This is certainly a mistake. Levine simply cannot understand that Lenin's dynamism here does not refer to Hegel's spiritual dynamism, but rather to Marx's **objective**, practical dynamism. Furthermore, Levine's view here is not in line with his repeated argument that Lenin never abandoned materialism ("philosophical theory of existence"). Here, Dunayevskaya makes a similar mistake. She continually repeats Lenin's statement that "man's consciousness not only reflects the objective world but creates it," citing it as a highlight of Lenin's thought at this time. However, in her theoretical situating, the central thought in Lenin's **Philosophical Notebooks (Bern Notebooks)** was the revival of idealist truth against vulgar materialism, where in Lenin's past **Materialism and Empirio-criticism**, he supported vulgar materialism[57]. This is an utterly unbelievable false interpretation.*

In a large box, Lenin rewords Hegel's "syllogism of action" as "**action**, practice, is a **logical 'syllogism'**...a figure of logic." *Please note that this figure of logic is the structure of human cognition. In this thought situating, it is Hegel's idealistically inverted theoretical logical structure.* At this time, Lenin no longer uses terms such as "matter" and "nature" to banish Hegel's idealistic "spirit," but rather emphasizes the arrival of the objective practice of the "active aspect" (Marx's words). I believe that here we can say that Lenin truly penetrates the secret of Hegel's philosophy, seeing that the true essence of this mysterious speculative logical structure is precisely the **logic of practice**! Lenin recognizes that Hegel's line of thought is correct, but concludes that:

---

55   *Ibid.*, page 92.
56   Levine, Norman. *Dialogue within the Dialectic.* Yunnan People's Press (1997), page 374 (Chinese).
57   Dunayevskaya, Raya. 1998. *Marxism and Freedom.* Liaoning Education Press, 159 (Chinese Edition).

Not of course, in the sense that the figure of logic has its other being in the practice of man (=absolute idealism), but vice versa: man's practice, repeating itself a thousand million times, becomes consolidated in man's consciousness by figures of logic. Precisely (and only) on account of this thousand-million-fold repetition, these figures have the stability of a prejudice, an axiomatic character[58].

We can immediately see that Lenin's views here are actually the repetition of some of his earlier comments[59]. Although he does not give any new material, his views here are actually much more profound in a new thought situating. Furthermore, Lenin continues to oppose Kant's idealist *a priori-ism* and Hegel's idealist ontologicalization of logical structures. Lenin discovers that the fallacies of Kant and Hegel were not caused because of the **inversion of matter into notions**, but rather by their transformation of man's practical activity into subjective syllogisms, by transforming objective behaviour structures (practical logic) into speculative, *a priori*, idea logic. It seems as though this is the idea framework (Kant's "integrated judgment" and Hegel's "Logic") characterized by the "stability of a prejudice, an axiomatic character". In fact, this prejudice comes from the **practical structure** or objective practical logic formed through the "thousand-million" repetition of practical activity. This is a very important progression of understanding; it was also a level of theory that Marx and Engels never reached in their philosophical research. On this point Lenin seems to surpass the thought context of Marx and Engels.

It is also in this box that Lenin gives further explanation of the three levels of meaning implied by the relation between the subject and object. First, "The **good end** (subjective end) versus **actuality** ("external actuality"); second, the external **means** (instrument), (objective); third, the coincidence of subjective and objective"[60]. In other words, man's demands of objective actuality can only come into play and be satisfied through practice (the use of instruments). Furthermore, in this relation, man's practice meets the objective world and has difficulty realizing the end. "The world does not satisfy man and man decides to change it by his activity"[61]. "The activity of the end is not directed against

---

58 *The Collected Works of Lenin* (Chin. 2. Ed.), volume 55, page 186.
59 *Ibid.*, page 160.
60 *Ibid.*, page 186.
61 *Ibid.*, page 182-3.

it-self....but aims, by destroying definite (sides, features, phenomena) of the **external** world, at **giving itself reality in the form of external actuality....**"[62].

At this point, Lenin profoundly elaborates his ideas:

> **The activity of man, who has constructed an objective picture of the world for himself, *changes* external actuality, abolishes its determinateness (= alters some sides or other, qualities, of it), and thus removes from it the features of Semblance, externality and nullity, and makes it as being in and for itself (= objectively true)**[63].

In this passage, Lenin first clearly determines that it is practice that **constructs** an objective picture of the world. This is the ultimate confirmation of the important role of practical dialectics on the level of philosophical ontology. Man's objective picture of the world is not a direct reflection of man onto the external objective world; rather, its lines of latitude and longitude change external reality, *i.e.*, according to man's purpose (needs), this or that aspects or matter that change the object. *For instance, consider the process of recreating natural conditions by constraining or lessening those aspects of the objective environment which are harmful to man (natural disasters), while at the same time preserving, prioritizing, and expanding those aspects of nature which are beneficial to man's subsistence (the concentrated optimization and utilization of agricultural goods, energy resources, and ecological habits). This causes those undesirable elements of the external world to be continually "removed" from nature, then become "for-self" (serving human subsistence) existence in terms of man's practical utilization.*

At this point, Lenin had already completed all of his confirmation of materialist practical dialectics. On the scientific basis of Hegel and Marx, he had truly moved forward the logical structure (not, as Kedrov says, the theoretical logical **system**) of dialectical theory. *On this point, Vranicki argues that after Engels, there was never a Marxist who was as able to grasp dialectical problems as Lenin*[64]. *This is an accurate assessment.* Lenin attained a truly profound theoretical level when he proposed objective qualification by which practice **abolishes** the

---

62   *Ibid.*, page 183.
63   *Ibid.*, page 187.
64   Vranicki, Predrag. *History of Marxism* (volume 2), People's Press: 1988, page 27 (Chinese).

external world and then **remakes** a picture of the objective world. As early as 1908, for Plekhanov and others who were still operating within the framework of philosophical materialism, this was a problem they dared not even think of. More importantly, it was in Lenin's profound understanding of the revolutionary, active nature of practical dialectics that he found the most crucial local support point of Marx's philosophical thought, thus providing **actual proof for the legitimacy of the October Revolution**: Russia's Bolsheviks and proletariats "resolved to change the world through their actions." I believe that this was the cognitive fruit of Lenin's *Bern Notebooks* with the most actual significance. This is because this was an important breakthrough for Lenin in terms of his theoretical logic of practice, having found the practical, active, dialectical manual for the October Revolution in the thought of Hegel and Marx. It was also here that the long divided actual practical logical ray and philosophical standpoint of Lenin's thought finally escaped from the **false homogeneity** of philosophical materialism, truly unifying with the practical dialectics of Marx's **historical materialism**. This was Lenin's greatest accomplishment in his study of Hegelian philosophy. *In Bochenski's **Soviet-Russian Dialectical Materialism**, he argues that the centre of Lenin's philosophy is a theory of will, not historical materialism. For him, this is why Lenin "ignored the standards of Marxism and called for then actualized revolution in Russia," when Russia was a country sorely lacking the necessary conditions for revolution, because its industry was not developed[65]. This is an extremely superficial declaration. Bochenski is unable to understand that the Marxism which Lenin used to guide the October Revolution was not a theory of will, but was rather practical dialectics that originated from Marx's historical materialism! This was the practical, active power of the proletariat founded on respect for objective material conditions.*

---

65   Bochenski, Jozef. 1965. *Soviet-Russian Dialectical Materialism*. The Commercial Press, 32.

ADDENDUM

A DELETED TEXT: THE CONCEPT OF HISTORY IN THE CONTEXT OF MARXIST PHILOSOPHY

DEBORIN'S INTERPRETATION ON MARXISM AND HISTORY

Deborin was a Marxist philosopher who lived at the same time as Lenin[1]. He was a loyal student of Plekhanov, and in the complex political struggle that took place in Russia in the early 20th century, he mistakenly stood with the Mensheviks. However, in the "Physics Crisis" that took place in the late 19th and early 20th centuries, he stood with Plekhanov and Lenin in criticizing the Machist and Empirio-critical movements that had begun to fester within Russia's Marxists. During that time, he wrote many articles defending materialism. After the

---

1   Abram Deborin (1881-1963) was a well-known Russian and Soviet Marxist philosopher. He was born in Lithuania in 1881 to a Jewish family. In 1897, he studied to be a locksmith and later supplied the Ukrainian government. Because of his association with "secretive social groups," he was arrested in 1902. The following year, Deborin fled Russia, studying philosophy and history at the Bern University in Switzerland. He joined the Bolsheviks that same year. In 1908 Deborin graduated with a degree in philosophy. In his early years, Deborin studied Plekhanov, becoming an important Marxist philosopher before the October Revolution and making substantial contributions in propagating Marxist philosophy. His 1909 article "Dialectical Materialism" was excerpted by Lenin. However, Deborin's political stance was always that of the Mensheviks. After the victory of the October Revolution, Deborin mainly worked in social science theoretical research and editing, becoming the representative of the "Deborin School," which published the magazine Under the Banner of Marxism and engaged in theoretical debate against the "mechanical theory." In 1929, Deborin joined the Soviet Communist Party, becoming a fellow at the Soviet Scientific Academy. In 1930, the "Deborin School" began to be criticized by Stalin. In 1935, Deborin began working in the Soviet Scientific Academy, serving as the head of the philosophy department, then the director of the history and philosophy department. His representative works include *Lenin the Thinker* (1925), *The Philosophy of Dialectical Materialism* (1931), *Feuerbaach* (1929), *History of 17th and 18th Century Materialism* (1930), *Dialectics and Natural Science* (1930), and *Philosophy and Politics* (collection of his works, published 1961).

victory of the October Revolution, Lenin did not strip Deborin or oth-
ers with politically incorrect views of their right to live and to speak[2].
Deborin served as the editor in chief of the magazine Under the Banner
of Marxism (founded in 1922) from 1926 to 1930[3]. In the 1930s, after
Lenin passed away, Deborin was criticized under Stalinist ideology;
he was still able to complete a large number of essays and scholarly
works, ultimately becoming an authoritative Marxist theoretician and
scholar in early Soviet scholarly circles[4]. Most of his essays have been

---

2   In 1921, after founding the Red Teachers' Academy, Lenin agreed to accept Deborin as a professor, though he clearly pointed out that if Deborin tried to preach Menshevism, he would be arrested.

3   Lenin accorded a great deal of attention to this publication. His essay "On the Significance of Militant Materialism" was published in the 1922 edition of this magazine. The publication of this journal ceased in 1944.

4   I have found that the assessment of Deborin among Chinese scholarly circles is still very much based on the views of former Soviet scholars. For instance, many Chinese dictionaries and websites give the following explanation of the "Deborin School": "A school of philosophical thought in the Soviet Union headed by the philosopher Deborin. It was formed during the theoretical debate against the Mechanists in the 1920s and blossomed during the debate against the orthodox school of thought in the late 1920s. In the 1930s, it disbanded under the criticism of Stalin and the central committee. Its theoretical publication was *Under the Banner of Marxism*. Its primary viewpoints included the emphasis on the universal significance of Marxist philosophy as a world-view and a methodology, and the criticism of the Mechanist view that 'science itself is philosophy.' It emphasized the connection between Marxist philosophy and the classical philosophical traditions of England, France, Germany, and others, even to the point of Hegelianizing Marxist philosophy. The "Deborin School" advocated a basis of practice and theory, as opposed to the orthodox call for a philosophy based on national industrialization and agricultural collectivization. It rejected and distorted the party principle of Lenin's philosophy. It underestimated the role of Lenin's works in the development of Marxist philosophy, denying the Leninist stage of philosophical development, and elevates Plekhanov's place in philosophical history. Stalin believed that the "Deborin School" was characterized by theory divorced from reality, that it had abandoned socialist construction, and that it had ceased to allow Marxist philosophy to serve socialism. The leadership of the party was stubborn, arrogant, and boastful, lacking the scholarly humility that they should have had. In 1931, this school of thought came under the criticism of the central committee as well as Soviet scholars. On January 25 of that year, the central committee decided to reorganize the editorial staff of *Under the Banner of Marxism*, removing the members of the "Deborin School" from their leadership positions in the various philosophical party organs. The philosophical views of this school of thought, as well as the Soviet criticism of these views, exerted considerable influence on the Soviet, Chinese, and Eastern European philosophical community. I believe that there are problems with the assessment of the philosophical views of the "Deborin School" by Soviet scholars. The scholarly criticism of Deborin was focused on three points: that he emphasized the connection between Marxist philosophy and classical philosophy, "Hegelianizing Marxism," that it elevated Plekhanov and reduced Lenin, and that it asserted that Lenin was a student of Plekhanov. I believe that besides

*collected in the 1961 work **Philosophy and Politics**[5]. I believe that the research on Deborin's thought was an important moment in Russian and soviet philosophical history. However, for many years we have seriously neglected this realm of research. Here we will merely focus on discussing the textual deletion of many of Deborin's articles written after 1924.*

*1924 was a year of unusual scholarly activity for Deborin. It is commonly known that many important events took place during that year. First, Lenin passed away, and second, the first section of the first volume of **Germany Ideology**, titled "Feuerbach," was published in the first volume of the Russian edition of **The Works of Marx and Engels**[6].*

*It was also in this year that Deborin published an article titled "Militant Materialist Lenin" in the first and second volumes of **Under the Banner of Marxism**. This text later became the first section of Deborin's **Lenin the Thinker**[7]. In this article, Deborin's thought is still homogeneous with his philosophical materialist viewpoint of 10 years before. Not long later, he published another article in the same journal titled "Lenin and the Modern Age," which was also included as the third article in Lenin the Thinker. I have noticed that in the second sub-section of "Lenin and the Modern Age" (titled "Marxism and History"), we find that here Deborin had already come upon a new understanding, that the new*

Deborin's so-called "Hegelianization," he was fundamentally correct in terms of the other two criticisms. This relates to the issues that I analyze in this text. The scholarly assessment of Deborin in the Soviet Union basically follows the views expressed by Stalin and the party committee of the Red Teachers' Academy in 1930, that Deborin's "Formalist" errors should be elevated to "Menshevik idealism" and "anti-Marxism." Stalin's views were primarily political in nature, and were completely untenable philosophically. This political qualification of the "Deborin School" continued until 1985 with the publication of *History of Soviet Philosophy*, when it finally changes tone and writes, "unfortunately, the philosophical position of the "Deborin School" was referred to by some philosophers as thoroughly idealistic, Hegelian, and anti-Marxist." I have also found that Zhou Guoping also wrote a few articles on Deborin in his early years; a few of his conclusions deserve affirmation, though his research is still overly simplistic and superficial.

5 Deborin, Abram. 1965. *Philosophy and Politics*. Beijing Joing Publishing Company, two volumes (Chinese).

6 Marx, Karl, and Friedrich Engels. *The German Ideology: Feuerbach, in The Works of Marx and Engels* volume 1, Moscow (1924), pages 211-256.

7 Deborin, Abram. *Lenin the Thinker*. Moscow: 1925. There are three articles included in this book: "Militant Materialist Lenin" (1924), "Dialectician Lenin" (1925), and "Lenin and the Modern Age" (1924).

*worldview established by Marx and Engels was turned towards **history**[8]. This was a completely new viewpoint. Deborin most likely arrived at this understanding because as an important theorist, Deborin had already read the manuscript of Marx and Engels' **The German Ideology**, astutely grasping from this text the true revolutionary character of the new worldview of Marx and Engels. There is a great difference between this new understanding of the essence of Marxist philosophy and the traditional explanation offered by the Second International Marxists. I believe that it is essential to review Deborin's philosophical thought. It is evident that Deborin himself consciously realized this, but because of specific ideological constraints, he had no choice but to veil his own great discovery. The textual deletion conducted against Deborin's 1961 Philosophy and Politics is a direct result of this **ideological oppression**.*

In Deborin's important collection of scholarly works *Philosophy and Politics* (1961), only the second and third articles in his *Lenin the Thinker* were included, and even these were heavily censored; the second article, "Lenin and the Modern Age," was completely deleted[9]. I believe that although this deletion seems to merely be a textual event, it actually was an attempt to gloss over the historical existence of important Marxist philosophical scholarly thought that had **previously been present**. This ideological deletion consciously covered up the true essence of the scientific worldview established by Marx and Engels in *The German Ideology* that had once been understood by Soviet scholars. This inevitably led to the overall lowering of the level of understanding of all Soviet Marxist philosophers, also providing necessary philosophical conditions to the ideological unfolding of Stalinist dogmatism. Here we hope to be able to recreate this particular ideological textual incident. Thus we will restore the textual existence of a period of understanding in the history of Marxist philosophy, historically and comprehensively reaffirming the scholarly place in the history of thought of Lenin's *Bern Notebooks*.

---

8   Deborin, Abram. 1965. *Philosophy and Politics*. Beijing Joing Publishing Company, volume 2, page 835 (Chinese).

9   *Ibid.*, pages 835-840 (Chinese). The Chinese edition of this work re-translated and published many of Deborin's deleted works as addenda. This has allowed the Chinese edition to possess important historical philological significance.

1 THE IDEOLOGICAL DELETION OF TEXT AND THE CREATION OF FALSE TEXT

First, it would useful for us to examine the deletion of content from two of the articles in Lenin the Thinker when it appeared in *Philosophy and Politics*. The **first** of these was titled "Militant Materialist Lenin," which had deletions in two areas. The first deletion was of a foot-note, which assessed Lenin and Plekhanov, explaining their views on Feuerbach. This footnote brought up two points. First, it pointed out the fact that **Lenin was a student of Plekhanov:**

> **In terms of philosophy, Lenin was Plekhanov's 'student,' a fact which he himself stated at more than one occasion. However, the fact that Lenin studied from Plekhanov did not prevent him from independently resolving problems, even correcting Plekhanov's views in several important areas. In a certain sense, these two thinkers can be thought of as mutually complementary[10].**

It is most unfortunate that this paragraph of fundamentally factual de-scription was completely deleted. The reason was very simple: in an ideological discourse situating, how could Lenin the Bolshevik be a student of Plekhanov the Menshevik?[11]. How can the truth be "mutu-ally complementary" with fallacy? In Stalin's 1930 criticism of the "Deborin School," the elevation of Plekhanov's philosophy and the denigration of Lenin's thought were cited as two of Deborin's main crimes. *In Stalin's discourse at the Red Teachers' Academy, Stalin clearly pointed out that Plekhanov should be exposed, his philosophi-cal ideas should be exposed, his arrogant attitude towards Lenin should be exposed. In particular, Stalin targeted Plekhanov's attitude towards Lenin's Materialism and Empirio-criticism[12].* It is obvious that it was important to create ideological homogeneity and protect Lenin's image

---

10 *Ibid.*, page 817 (Chinese).

11 In the debate between Deborin and Mitin, Mitin argued that it should cease to be said that Lenin was a student of Plekhanov. He asserted that from his earliest days, Lenin was already a singular, complete, absolutely orthodox, independent Marxist. The true history of the development of Marxism continued from Marx and Engels to Lenin; it certainly did not pass through Plekhanov. See Mitin's *A Summary of post-Philosophi-cal Debate, in Selected Works of the Deborin School*, Jilin People's Press (1982), pages 242-268 (Chinese).

12 See *Stalin's Conversations with the committee of the Philosophical and Natural Science Red Teachers' Institute.* In Translated Philosophical Works (1999) volume 2 (Chinese).

of **superiority**, and so it was no longer possible to mention the actual fact that Lenin was a student of Plekhanov. *Not respecting history or arbitrarily altering history was one of the major ways by which Stalin's dogmatic, oppressive, ideological discourse glossed over facts. I should also point out that Deborin's assertion that Lenin "corrected" Plekhanov was actually imprecise. What actually happened was that in Plekhanov's 1908* **Fundamental Problems of Marxism**, *he criticized Feuerbach for not understanding the vitality of Marx's practical critique. In Lenin's 1909* **Materialism and Empirio-criticism**, *on the other hand, he argued that like Marx and Engels, Feuerbach epistemologically took note of practice, "taking the summation of human practice as the basis of epistemology." Later, in Plekhanov's 1915* **From Idealism to Materialism**, *he approves of Lenin's viewpoint. I have also remarked that in this article Deborin clearly states that like Feuerbach, Marx, Engels, and Plekhanov, Lenin first emphasized that the sum of human practice was the basis of epistemology[13]. In fact, in terms of his understanding of Feuerbach's views on practice, Plekhanov was originally correct. As Marx points out in* **Theses on Feuerbach**, *Feuerbach the philosophical materialist spoke of practice merely as man's abstract natural existence and emotional relationships and thus could not understand the significance of revolutionary, critical, social historical practice. Deborin's words were obviously meant to placate the omnipresent ideological* **Great Others**.

The **second** portion of deleted content was Deborin's placement of Lenin and Plekhanov within the context of the history of thought. Deborin wrote that Plekhanov was first a theoretician while Lenin was first a practician, politician, and leader. Under the ideological discourse framework that we have outlined here, to say that Lenin was a practician in relation to Plekhanov the theoretician called into question Lenin's identity as a thinker. This was obviously unacceptable. Why could Lenin have not also first been a theoretician? Therefore, this sentence was also deleted[14]. *Artificially causing history to cease to exist or creating false history is another, even more ridiculous method of ideological oppression.* It is not difficult to see that in this incident of textual deletion we find the first subtle foreshadowing of Lenin's later ideological deification.

---

13   Deborin, Abram. 1965. "Militant Materialist Lenin." *Philosophy and Politics.* Beijing Joing Publishing Company, volume 2, page 422 (Chinese).

14   The original text of this footnote can be found in Deborin, Abram. 1965. Philosophy and Politics. Beijing Joing Publishing Company, volume 2, pages 817-818 (Chinese). To see the post-deletion footnote, please refer to the second footnote on pages 422-423.

The second important deletion of content in this text touches on Lenin's definition of matter. As we all know, in *Materialism and Empirio-criticism* Lenin had already given a definition of matter; however in Deborin's original text, he dared to assert that he would provide a "more comprehensive and detailed definition of matter." This statement surely had deeper connotations, because if he was going to give a "more comprehensive and detailed" definition, then whose definition was insufficiently comprehensive and detailed? I believe that at the time, it was certain that others suggested this problem. Deborin's "comprehensive and detailed" definition can be found below:

Matter exists in time and space, acting on our senses and reflecting in them objective existence. In a broader sense, matter is the summation of all infinite, concrete "media," the summation of relations and connections. Each specific branch of science – mathematics, mechanics, physics, chemistry, biology, etc. – are the study of the different movement forms and "media" of matter, *i.e.*, the different stages of process, relation, and connection of the same matter[15].

The first half of Deborin's definition of matter was similar to Lenin's definition of matter, but the latter half, where he mentions "media" and "summation of relations" in a "broader" sense are his own ideas, because Lenin obviously did not mention them before. From Deborin's new definition here, he was attempting to include Lenin's definition of matter into a new logical scope, trying to break through the framework of substantive theory and allow matter to include the concept of relational objective existence. This attempt was reasonable to a certain extent, conforming also to the basic idea that the essence of social existence is social relations in Marx's The German Ideology. However, this thought-reform of classical expressions was not permissible in the Other ideological mirror-image discourse framework of the time. If Lenin did not say it, what gives you the right to say it? Therefore, the portions of this definition of matter that differed from Lenin were completely deleted[16]. This deletion served as a warning to Deborin's contemporaries and successors that **they were not to suggest anything that differed from classical expressions.**

---

15 The original text of this definition can be found in Deborin, Abram. 1965. *Philosophy and Politics.* Beijing Joing Publishing Company, volume 2, page 818 (Chinese).

16 The post-deletion definition of matter can be found in Deborin, Abram. 1965. *Philosophy and Politics.* Beijing Joing Publishing Company, volume 2, page 440 (Chinese).

The next article to have content deleted was the third article in *Lenin the Thinker*, "Revolutionary Dialectician Lenin" (1925). This article underwent numerous deletions. First, the title was changed to "Dialectician Lenin." Second, two terms were changed throughout. Deborin's truly imprecise assertion that dialectical materialism was the "dialectical reconciliation" of objectivism and subjectivism was deleted. Next, one of his assessments of imperialism was deleted, *i.e.*, "politically, imperialism is **reactionary**, but economically it is **progress**. This is the most profound contradiction in dying imperialism." In the criticism of Deborin that took place in the 1930s, this sentence was criticized as "Kautsky-style imperialist theory"[17]. It is my personal opinion that Deborin's statement on imperialism is basically correct; the problem was that his statement was not in line with Lenin's own view on imperialism. Third, most of the content of the second sub-section ("Identity of Opposites") was deleted, leaving only the fourth paragraph which was later included with the first sub-section. Most of the content of this sub-section related to Deborin's assessment of Lenin's *Bern Notebooks*[18]. This section was perhaps meant as the earliest research essay on Lenin's notes. Deborin's basic viewpoint here was that of his 1929 translator's preface to the Bern Notebooks; there was no disrespectful language, but likely because his assessment seemed overly objective it did not fit into the ideological intentions of purposefully elevating Lenin. For instance, when Deborin discusses Lenin's critique of Plekhanov, he carefully uses the word "censure." Even using the exigent eyes of Stalinist ideology, it seems there is very little to fault here. As such, it is still very hard for me to understand why this text was deleted.

---

17   To see more on these deletions, refer to Deborin, Abram. 1965. *Philosophy and Politics*. Beijing Joing Publishing Company, volume 2, page 819 (Chinese).
18   Both the 1925 *Under the Banner of Marxism* as well as The Bolshevik published portions of Lenin's *Bern Notebooks*.

2 THE ERADICATION OF HISTORY: THE ABSENCE OF PREVIOUSLY EXISTING TEXT

Here we will focus on examining Deborin's "Lenin and the Modern Age," which he wrote in 1924 but was deleted in 1961. There are three sections in this article, "Marxism and Bourgeois Thought," "Marxism and History," and "Bourgeois Society, Communism, and New Men." The most important of these is the second section, which will also be the centre of our analysis at this time.

In the first section, Deborin focuses his discussion on explaining the heterogeneity between Marxist philosophy and the ideas of bourgeois thinkers. There are three theoretical points worthy of our analysis here. **First**, in Deborin's opinion at this time, neither Marx nor Lenin were "philosophers" who created some philosophical system in the traditional sense. However, they did create "the only scientific worldview" which **dealt with life**. This worldview was "filled" with life, *i.e.*, practice in its true sense. I sense that there is a change implied within these ideas, that **practice** and **actual life** have become key words in Deborin's definition of Marxist philosophy. Deborin believed that Marx's worldview was "full of life," and that this life was not natural matter **external to man**, but historical social life. Here we do not find natural material existence, nor do we find reference to Feuerbachian materialist texts; this was obviously not completely in line with Deborin's past philosophical materialist viewpoint and logical circuit. **Second**, in the first section we also find this expression: "the materialism of Marxism and all of Marxist philosophy is, without an exception, the revolutionary critique of the sum of all social relations"[19]. This was also a completely new expression. Although Deborin's words were imprecise, through this statement we are able to get a sense of what Deborin was attempting to express. Marxist philosophy is a **revolutionary social critical theory**. *This viewpoint was brought forward at almost the same time by three of the founders of Western Marxism, Lukacs, Gramsci, and Korsch. I am not certain whether or not Deborin was aware that his viewpoint approached Bogdanov's mistaken understanding of Marx's critical theory of fetishisms 10 years earlier.* Third, the most important essential characteristic of bourgeois ideology was its **non-historical nature**. To use Deborin's original words, this was "contempt of history." Bourgeois

---

19 Deborin, Abram. 1965. *Philosophy and Politics.* Beijing Joing Publishing Company, volume 2, page 830 (Chinese).

thinkers always view their own ideas as eternal, built on foundations that surpass history. History as an important qualitative standard becomes for Deborin the watershed between Marxist philosophy and all past bourgeois thought. These three theoretical points form the central support points for the completely new thought situating expressed by Deborin in the second section of the text. I should also point that Deborin made a fatal mistake in the first section: he **repeatedly cited Hegel**. In Stalin's criticism of the "Deborin School," this was another of Deborin's major crimes[20].

The second section is evidently the central text of this article, and the key word here is **history**. This objectively existing social history, as **differentiated from natural material existence**, becomes for Deborin the essence of Marxist philosophy. This is evidence of a logical shift in Deborin's thought. I have deduced that this was not Deborin's own self-reflection, but rather a rupture in thought caused by the force of powerful external discourse. I believe that the primary reason for Deborin's shift in thought was apparently Marx and Engels' 1845-1846 text *The German Ideology. At this time, this text was already published in the 1924 first volume of the German edition of the* **Works of Marx and Engels**. *It is not hard to imagine that as an important party theorist, Deborin would have been one of the first to have read this text. This critical text, so vital to the understanding of the essence of Marxist philosophy, was never read by Lenin (who passed away that year) and all of the 20th century Marxists.* I also believe that the emergence of this text led to the complete deconstruction of the false interpretation of Marxist philosophy promulgated since the Second International, and that Deborin was the first to be conscious of this.

It was precisely in his study and research of this newly emerged text, written by Marx and Engels to establish the new philosophical worldview of Marxism, that Deborin gradually realized that Marx's new materialism "did not divorce cognition from life." The "life" to which he alluded here was no longer the natural matter spoken of by traditional philosophical materialists such as Plekhanov, Feuerbach, and Dietzgen,

---

20 In 1930, during Stalin's discourse at the Red Teachers' Academy, he claimed that the "Deborin School" was worse than Plekhanov. For the "Deborin School," dialectics were a ready-made box, Hegel was their idol. They blindly restore Hegel, setting him up as their God. See Stalin's *Conversations with the committee of the Philosophical and Natural Science Red Teachers' Institute. In Translated Philosophical Works* (1999) volume 2 (Chinese).

but rather the historical circumstances that Marx described as **actively constructed** by social existence. Deborin's new understanding was that **historicism** was Marxism's unique characteristic and social life was its central question. This expression is obviously incorrect. Marxism is not historicism, and its central issue is not merely **social life**. This is not a question of the dimension of **chronology** or the **realm** of social history. The historical nature of Marx's new philosophy was a question of *ontology*.

Furthermore, as Deborin again examines the question of practice, the content of practice itself also changes. He writes that in Marxism, it is man's practical life that first becomes the fundamental content of **theory**; the ultimate basis and roots of this worldview lie in practical life, in cultural creation, in social historical life[21]. Please note that here Deborin uses the words "ultimate basis and roots of this worldview." It is my understanding that this was a reference to the position of philosophical materialism. Philosophical materialism was the pre-foundation of Marxist philosophy, but the ultimate source used by Marx to examine nature and man's social existence **historical practice**. In Deborin's own "Militant Materialist Lenin," which he had written not long before, practice was still nothing more than a narrow **epistemological** category. Here, however, practice has become an **ontological** concept. This is an extremely important progression of theoretical logic. In this sense, Deborin was the first among Soviet scholars to understand *The German Ideology*. Placing this within the context of the 1920s, this was truly a remarkable achievement. Furthermore, I believe that this new understanding clearly surpassed Lenin's final philosophical scope. I say "surpassed" not because Deborin was deeper or more intelligent than Lenin, but because he was able to read the manuscript of Marx and Engels' *German Ideology*. Ironically enough, in the 1985 edition of *History of Soviet Philosophy*, the authors actually accuse the "Deborin School" of not according sufficient attention to the question of history during the 1920s[22].

Of course, here Deborin also re-interprets the ontological significance of history, building on the purely **past-facing**, foundational dimension of history a dimension that **faces the future**:

---

21 Deborin, Abram. 1965. *Philosophy and Politics*. Beijing Joing Publishing Company, volume 2, page 835 (Chinese).
22 See page 25 of Soviet *Philosophical History*, Commercial Press (1998) (Chinese).

The characteristic of the process of history is its trend towards the *future*. The object of history is not merely the past, but also the future. The present does not only disappear into a past that can never be reclaimed, but also faces the future. The present gives birth to the future. History often enters the present and thus generates the future. The present moves towards the future. The present is the result of the past and the guarantee of the future. Time is the basic category of history and even all of life. This is precisely why, precisely because all is changing, that all of history is able to exist. Marx's statement that history is the only science should be understood in this sense[23].

Deborin is correct on this point. Later, he went on to assert that man lives historical life; this is a demonstration of man's superiority over other natural creatures. Therefore, for Marx, historical time is a unique category[24]. Marx's concept of historical time is not time in a material sense, but rather unique life-time in historical social existence. The idea of history in Marx's historical materialism is internally identical to time in the sense of man's life existence. The historical existence of this idea of time in an ontological sense is not simply the past, **but rather a present that refutationally sublates the past and the future in itself.** This idea of history and time which Marx bases on modern conditions of production was later expressed again by Heidegger in a speculative way. *I mentioned this point in **Marx Revisited***[25]. Here, Deborin demonstrates that he discovered and understood this point before Heidegger or any other Western Marxist. *Among Western Marxists, Benjamin's concept of "now" most nearly approaches this context.*

---

23   Deborin, Abram. 1965. *Philosophy and Politics.* Beijing Joing Publishing Company, volume 2, page 836 (Chinese).
24   *Ibid.,* page 837.
25   Refer to chapter six of my *Marx Revisited.*

3 HISTORY AND THE ESSENCE OF MARXIST PHILOSOPHY

Deborin also turned his important new logical perspective to philosophy itself. He writes,

> **In philosophy and theory, all rationalism and absolutism assert that the truths they uphold are independent of time; thus they attain an absolute, abstract character. From a historical perspective, all suppositions and all beings have only relative value. Nothing can escape from the concrete conditions of history, all has only temporary existence[26].**

Deborin goes on to arrive at this conclusion: Marxism is **historical** in its own substance. This expression is quite profound. However, Deborin also states that Lenin is a historical thinker, because through his whole life there was interwoven the "spirit" of history. This is correct and incorrect. It is correct because Lenin's life was truly that of a revolutionary filled with the spirit of history; he untiringly pushed Russia's eastern society towards world history, surpassing the hegemonic logic of capital. He is incorrect because Lenin never read *The German Ideology*, and therefore his understanding of Marxist philosophy, including his final understanding of practical dialectics in the *Bern Notebooks*, did not include concrete, actual, social historical logic.

It was through this unique understanding of the concept of history that Deborin discovered: "man, in his own historical life, creates a kind of independent world"[27]. For Marx, this is also an objective material world, only one that is different from the natural material world that Deborin and Plekhanov had advocated from a philosophical materialist standpoint. Here Deborin is basically correct. However, Deborin also argues that this world only refers to "religion, rule of law, art, philosophy, science, economics, etc.," or in other words, to the objects that Hegel identified as belonging to the "spiritual sciences." Evidently, Deborin mistakenly and simply understands Marx's social historical existence as the phenomenon of social ideas. It is also in this sense that he asserts that these things are the **creation** of collective man. Furthermore, these products, created by man's vitality, are alienated from man and opposite

---

26   Deborin, Abram. 1965. *Philosophy and Politics*. Beijing Joing Publishing Company, volume 2, page 836 (Chinese).
27   *Ibid.*, page 837.

him, becoming objective existence, an independent world. This is certainly a logical mess.

First, it was Hegel's idealist view that the mutation of the ideal life of social history into independent objective existence was a kind of alienation. For Hegel, the Idea falls into natural material existence, becoming the "second nature" and only returns to spirit in the ultimate self-sublation of the Absolute Idea. Deborin did not know that this idea could not be simply regurgitated within the materialist logic of Marx's philosophy. Next, in the 19th century debate between Bogdanov and the philosophical materialism of Plekhanov and Deborin, Bogdanov erroneously made use of Marx's critical context of fetishisms, completely refuting philosophical materialism as a fetishism. Deborin's understanding here fell precisely into Bogdanov's logical trap. Unfortunately, Deborin was completely unaware of this. I believe that it is in this sense that Deborin did not yet truly understand Marx's historical materialism, or in other words, Deborin fundamentally misunderstood Marx's concept of history.

Also because of this, Deborin saw the new "independent world," which was separate from the natural, material world, as simply the ideology which Marx criticized. In Deborin's view, Marx believed the following:

At the same time that people develop their own material production, they also develop and change their own thoughts and the products of those thoughts in their own activity. All the content of man's historical life and activity can be summarized as changing nature, continually changing himself, and correspondingly changing "spirit" or all ideology. It is obvious that all ideology is the product of history, as well as the product of man's particular relation to nature and to other man in a specific period of time. Under these conditions, history becomes the central issue in the entire scientific world[28].

Deborin constantly exposes his own theoretical weaknesses in his expressions. Every time he cites Marx's views, there are always considerable areas of misunderstanding. For instance here, Deborin's conclusion is correct in that history is the central question in Marx's scientific worldview. However, man's material production which changes nature does not correspond directly to ideology. Between these there is still the great medium of social historical life and historical social existence.

---

28   *Ibid.*, page 837.

According to Marx's original meaning, the essence of consciousness is "my relationship to my environment" in historical time. However, the essence of ideology is not the general result of man's particular relationship with nature and with other men; rather it is **Ideal existence, which appears invertedly and in distorted form**. This could refer to man's non-historical understanding of nature (such as the concept of nature in Feuerbach's philosophical materialism) or it could refer to the slave relationships of social dominance that are veiled by false relationships. Evidently for Marx, ideology was not a neutral, descriptive concept, but a critical one. Fetishisms are one of the greatest bourgeois ideologies. *In this sense, the Machist Bogdanov's malicious understanding in his "The Idol State and Marxist Philosophy is actually correct*[29].

After understanding this point, Deborin engages in profound self-reflection, and finally returns to the epistemology of philosophical materialism. However, this time he also begins to penetrate beneath the surface level of philosophical materialism.

> **The relation between the subject and the object cannot be resolved through *direct observation*, but through grasping the object in practice. Only through *labour*, through *activity* can man expose the essence of things and penetrate to the secrets of existence. The victory of the subject over the object is accomplished through technology and labour. Past philosophers imagined that our relation with the world ends with thought. Now we know that our real relation with the world is *activity*[30].**

Our relation to the external world is no longer the fixed relation between man and nature of philosophical materialism, but rather the relation between man and the objects he uses. Furthermore, our relation with the object does not begin with direct observation (sensuous experience), but rather with subjective practice (subjective labour production activity). In "Militant Materialist Lenin," which he had written not long before, Deborin emphasizes that material is **reflected** in our senses; in other words, material is understood by us through the impressions that it creates in our senses[31]. At this point, man's understanding is no

29   Bogdanov, Alexandr. 1981. "The Idol State and Marxist Philosophy," In *Translated Marxist-Leninist Works*, volume 14 (Chinese).
30   Deborin, Abram. 1965. *Philosophy and Politics*. Beijing Joing Publishing Company, volume 2, pages 837-838 (Chinese).
31   *Ibid.*, page 839.

longer directly used by external material in the consciousness that we form, but **must proceed from subjective activity**. Only through subjective practical activity can the existence and essential mysteries of all objective things, including natural material existence, be exposed. Thus Deborin was able to make great progress in his epistemological ideas. *We can see that Deborin's ideas here already approach the new understanding that Lenin reached in his thought-reform in the* **Bern Notebooks**. *He finally understood that existence includes both nature and history*[32]. More importantly, as the object of man's activity, nature exposes its own secrets through history. This is a correct, Marxian response to this Kantian problem. When Kant said that nature appears before us in a certain form, Marx believed that **this appearance itself was created and situated by man's historical practice**. Because of this, from the time of Marx, world history has constituted the central problem of life and philosophical thought, because in historical activity, like a focal point, concentrates all the relations between us and the natural world and the spiritual world, concentrating all life[33]. However, Deborin's expressions often lack completeness; here he omits the social life that he just barely came to understand.

In explaining the historical science that Marx and Engels described, Deborin writes:

> **Dialectical materialism is primarily a *historical* worldview. The nature of existence, of all existing things, is revealed in their formative process – their historical development – because the world is forever changing. It is not a dead, unchanging thing. The history of the world is a special form of the development of the world. Therefore, history is the existential form of the universe, and so necessarily becomes a most fundamental science**[34].

Deborin's first sentence is correct. However, his explanation of the concept of history in the new Marxist philosophical worldview is still problematic. Although the concept of history is no longer merely a category in the realm of the study of history, neither does it simply have the connotation of change and development as he describes. It is my understanding that this point is not the major qualitative determination

---

32   *Ibid.*, page 838.
33   *Ibid.*, page 838.
34   *Ibid.*, page 838.

of Marx's concept of history. As I have already pointed out, the concept of history in Marx's historical materialism is an ontological category based on **modern material production**; it primarily expresses **actuality, concreteness, and real chronology within a certain historical context**. Here, history manifests a kind of profound **limited generative nature** of social existence, not the general characteristic of change and development that all material existence possesses.

Interestingly enough, Deborin's own logic in his exposition is often quite chaotic. At the very end of this text, he again redefines the concept of history in Marx's new worldview. This time, he connects it to the historical logic of Hegel's philosophy, thus interweaving truth and fallacy. I believe that Deborin's discussion of Hegel here was also one of his "crimes." In Stalin's opinion, he certainly over-emphasized the connections between Marxism and Hegel.

Deborin asserts that the content of human history is human activity, because human activity is first expressed in the production of material activity. This is correct. He also saw that in Hegel's philosophy, economics and labour were already included within a rational system. Therefore, "history is actually the kingdom of labour, because through labour is realized the process of development, the ascending towards the advanced stages of civilization." However, Deborin believed that although Hegel understood the significance of economics more profoundly than his contemporaries, he was unable to truly understand the internal life and development of the economy. "Marx was a true social philosopher, a **labour philosopher**"[35]. This was because Marx elevated labour to a principle of world history, a principle of his world view. Therefore, in a certain sense, labour is a principle of dialectics. Deborin writes:

> **The significance of economics is not only in satisfying our material needs. It is also the means by which human society appropriates the natural world and becomes the master of nature. The economy is the great objective creation of organized, connected humanity. The ultimate basis of human understanding and science is this creation, this activity. At the same time, Marx elevated concrete social practice to the level of philosophical theory. Man's practical life and practical activity became, for the first time, the object – the very**

---

35   *Ibid.*, page 839.

important object – of theoretical work. Here, the object is no longer alienated and opposed to the subject. In other words, as external objects – nature – change, man changes also. The production of material life becomes the connection between the object and the subject, between nature and society[36].

What Deborin was attempting to convey is somewhat correct. However, there is a great deal of logical confusion in his expression. For Deborin, practical activity and material production are the same things as the "economy." For Marx, on the other hand, these were three qualitatively different social activities that took place on different levels. Historical social material practice was the basis of the whole of the new Marxist philosophical world view; material production is the most basic condition practical activity, as well as the determining material premise to social existence; social activity is nothing more than a certain stage, a social phenomenon that appears in the historical development of human social material life. However, related to the theoretical realm of Marx's historical materialism, this important differentiation of theoretical logic advocated by Marx was always conceived vague and was confused, ever since the Second International.

The third sub-section of this text primarily discusses the bankruptcy of bourgeois ideology as well as the historical experience of the international communist movement, in particular the significance of Lenin's October Revolution for the future of communism. Here Deborin expects and hopes for the emergence of new communists. However, there is nothing here to really arouse our interest.

This was the historical text which Deborin wrote in the 1920s and which was later deleted. Though the text includes correct identifications of Marx and Engels' historical materialism, these discoveries were ideologically eradicated, disappearing into the depths of history. Today we are finally able to once again face this historical truth, allowing us to more accurately see the historical timeline of Marxist thought.

---

36   *Ibid.*, page 839-40.

CHAPTER TWELVE

THE UNITY OF IDENTICAL LOGIC, EPISTEMOLOGY, AND SUBJECTIVE DIALECTICS IN OBJECTIVE PRACTICAL DIALECTICS

As we know, in his research of Marxist epistemology, Lenin had a firm foundation in philosophical materialism. These firm beliefs in material-ist epistemological theory were hardened in the furnace of the modern philosophical battle against Machism. As we have already pointed out, on the eve of the October Revolution Lenin engaged in the profound study of Hegelian philosophy primarily in order to more fully under-stand dialectics. In the process of reading which he undertook for the *Bern Notebooks*, epistemological problems became a secondary think-ing point for him. However, hampered as he was by his Other reading framework, Lenin often found that Hegel's speculative epistemology often led to logical obstructions in the process of "inversion." Until he was later able to attain a new détournement of theoretical logic and re-constructed a sovereign thought context was he finally able to change his understanding of epistemology. His most important achievement was the **re-identification** of Hegel's views on the unity of dialectics, epistemology, and logic from the perspective of Marxism. *I must point* *out that because Lenin's efforts to resolve this problem stretched over the course of all his research on Hegelian philosophy, this chapter will appear more like a topical investigation.*

1 "TRIPLE IDENTITY" AND HEGEL'S LINE OF PHILOSOPHICAL THOUGHT

It is my conjecture that **first**, the so-called "triple identity" was not something that Lenin had decided to understand before he began his research. Rather, it was the side-product of his attempt to understand Marx's materialist dialectical logic through studying Hegelian dialectics. **Second**, the "triple identity" was not Lenin's independent creation; in fact, this is the natural structure of Hegel's philosophical logic, and after Marx had recreated Hegel's idealist dialectics, he applied it to his research of capitalist economic structures. **Third**, in Lenin's process of reading, he first rejected Hegel's idealist "triple identity," then understood the significance of the "dual identity," and finally united identical subjective dialectics, epistemology, and dialectical logic on the **basis of objective, practical dialectics**.

I should first emphasize the fact that the **"triple identity" was not a viewpoint that Lenin had always upheld**. *In reading the philosophical works of Dietzgen, though Lenin had read his similar viewpoints, he did not accept them.* These were not ideas that Lenin affirmatively identified, not only in his original philosophical thought, but also in the early stages of his research of Hegel's *The Science of Logic* (and even for most of the latter stages). I believe that the affirmative identification of this viewpoint was almost the last great achievement of Lenin's process of reading. I believe this because the Other reading framework under which Lenin operated as he entered the study of Hegelian philosophy contained a **subsidiary**, **auxiliary** foundational background of awareness that is often ignored. This was a strict dividing line between epistemology and methodology (dialectics) of philosophical, **ontological structure**. This view held that dialectics are the **object** of epistemology, and that **the two could certainly not be the same thing**. Here I employ the important qualifications set out by the modern British philosopher Michael Polanyi embodied in his idea of subsidiary awareness. In Polanyi's philosophical framework, the realm of cognitive structures is always created by subjective focal awareness in tandem with subsidiary awareness. Subsidiary awareness is the important background to the subjective cognitive process[1]. A good understanding of this point is critical to our later analysis.

As we have already seen, in the early stages of Lenin's study of Hegelian philosophy and under the pressure of his Other mirror-image reading framework, he actually stood against Hegel. This meant that as he frequently encountered Hegel's philosophical qualifications, he was astonished each time. Lenin accorded a great deal of importance to epistemology, and so when he read the introduction to The Science of Logic, he quickly grasped many of the reasonable aspects of its epistemology, for instance that the substance of epistemology was the "**movement** of scientific cognition"[2]. To illustrate with another example, he also identified with Hegel's proposal that this movement was not external, but rather the way by which self constitutes self, the way of true cognition, of continual cognition, of moving from unknown to known[3]. Lenin affirmatively pointed out that this was the key to epistemology. Furthermore, when he read Hegel's assertion that categories are the knots in the web of consciousness, he writes in a box:

Man is confronted by a *web* of natural phenomena. Instinctive man, the savage, does not distinguish himself from nature. Conscious man does distinguish, categories are stages of distinguishing, *i.e.* of cognizing the world, focal points in the web, which assist in cognizing and mastering it[4].

Here Hegel's original words are that as categories, "these are firm knots which give stability and direction to the life and consciousness of spirit"[5]. I believe that Lenin's critical interpretation of Hegel's idealism is correct; I especially believe that his reconstruction of materialist epistemological views is very accurate and profound. Categories are the stairways leading to our cognition of the world, knots in the cognitive web we use to understand and grasp external objects. However, Lenin did not know at this time whether these knots were based on the external world or on man's practical structures. Although not long before this, he followed in Hegel's steps in affirmatively pointing out

---

1   Refer to my work "Underlying Structural Analysis of Polanyi's Theory of Conscious Cognition" in the *Jiang Hai Academic Journal* (1991).
2   *The Collected Works of Lenin* (Chin. 2. Ed.), volume 55, page 73.
3   *Ibid.*, page 73.
4   *Ibid.*, page 78.
5   Hegel, Georg Wilhelm Friedrich. *The Science of Logic*. Commercial Press (1977), volume 1, page 15 (Chinese).

that logical categories were "simplifications" of external existence and activity, and that these categories also serve man in practice[6]. This problem was not resolved until he began to truly understand logical figures and the relations between practical structures.

It is commonly known that in Hegel's objective idealist philosophical cognitive framework, the Absolute Idea as an a priori subject was actually the result of the objectification and mystification of man's universal cognitive structures. Hegel inverted the idea logic by which man cognizes the world and confirms it as the essence and movement laws of the world; the entire existence and development of the world is thus mutated into the process of self-realization and self-consciousness of the Absolute Idea. Nature, society, and man all become the tools by which the Absolute Idea transitions and elevates itself. In this process, the Absolute Idea is its own self-connection and development (dialectics), its own internal structure (logic), and its own consciousness (epistemology) – it is the unified subject of these three. Besides this, there is no second process. In Hegel's idealist thought situating, **logic, dialectics, and epistemology were naturally the same thing; this triple identity is evidently unified in the subjective dialectics of the idea**. The science of logic is its dynamic conceptual system, dialectics are the self-contradiction and movement process of the concept, and epistemology is the subjective consciousness and continual deepening and self-reflection of the Absolute Idea. Thus the "triple identity theory" extends through the basic foundation of the situating of Hegel's logic, though this was something that Lenin, as a materialist, was unable to accept. As we have said, in the early stages of Lenin's study of *The Science of Logic*, because some of the expressions in the book ran counter to Lenin's own Other interpretive framework (**which separated epistemology and objective dialectics**), therefore the results of his philosophical materialist epistemology obviously came into conflict with Hegel's triple identity theory. Some of Hegel's points were difficult for Lenin to accept, even leading at times to profound, persistent logical white spaces.

Lenin found that Hegel's logic here was not the formal logic that he already understood. Hegel critically argued that Aristotle's traditional logic merely took the form of thought as an external, formal instrument,

---

6   *The Collected Works of Lenin* (Chin. 2. Ed.), volume 55, page 75. For Hegel's views see Hegel, Georg Wilhelm Friedrich. The Science of Logic. Commercial Press (1977), volume 1, page 11 (Chinese).

devoid of thought content. On the other hand, "What Hegel demands is a Logic, the forms of which would be forms with content, forms of living, real content, inseparably connected with the content"[7]. Here Lenin writes a particularly interesting expression:

Logic is the science not of external forms of thought, but of the laws of development "of all material, natural and spiritual things", *i.e.*, of the development of the entire concrete content of the world and of its cognition, *i.e.*, the sum-total, the conclusion of the *History* of knowledge of the world[8].

This is obviously the result of Lenin's typical materialist "inversion" under the influence of his early Other mirror image framework. *Just on the previous page Lenin wrote: "Objectivism: the categories of thought are not an auxiliary tool of man, but an expression of laws both of nature and of man."* This expression of Lenin's is worthy of further consideration. On the surface, it expresses the important thought of the "triple identity theory," that logic is dialectics, and that dialectics are epistemology. However, I believe that this was not Lenin's conscious thinking, but rather the result of his materialist recreation of Hegel's thought. In my opinion, here we find expressed some doubt as to the epistemology of Hegel's logic. **It was Hegel's logic to use epistemology to unify the world.** *I have noticed that after the 1960s, there emerged in the scholarly world of the former Soviet Union a school of thought called "Epistemological Centralism." However, I cannot be sure whether the views of this school of thought are related to Lenin's inchoate understanding at this point.*

Also at the beginning of his process of reading, when facing different problems Lenin becomes confused again. This is because even materialistically inverting some of Hegel's expressions of the dialectic can lead to suspicion. As we have already mentioned, for instance, in Hegel's chapter on being-for-self he criticizes the idealist duality of Kant and Fichte. Hegel's original intention was to oppose the idealism of Kant and Fichte, criticizing the latter for supposing a thing-in-itself (Fichte's "not self") and for supposing an other-sided world and a for-self phenomenological world. Hegel himself proposed that being-for-self was monistic. Phenomena are the "many," but this "many" is actually an expression of the abundant characteristics of the "one" (essence). Thus,

---

7 *The Collected Works of Lenin* (Chin. 2. Ed.), volume 55, page 77.

8 *Ibid.*, page 77.

"many" is merely the "many of one." Of course, looking at the level of logic of Hegel's expression here, "one" and "many" were also the means of changing from the concept of quality to the concept of quantity in logical structures. Lenin's understanding at this time was temporarily stuck at the latter, and so he naturally was unable to understand Hegel's "monistic" logic here[9].

As Lenin began to read the second book of *The Science of Logic*, titled "Essence," the logical contradiction that had lain dormant in his mind suddenly surged into relevance. Hegel's **ontological** logic (dialectics and epistemology) came into a conflict of **divergent structure** with Lenin's epistemological framework. This conflict was primarily expressed in the issues of semblance and appearance. As we know, The *Science of Logic* sets forth three levels of logical qualifications for essence. First, the pure self-reflection (*scheint*) of essence itself; Second, the appearance of self (*erscheint*); third, the synthesis of appearance and essence, or actuality (*wirklichkeit*). This is actually the historical **progression** by which the human subject cognizes external things. First it develops a subjective semblance, then a completely fixed overall appearance, and finally after grasping the essence of the thing, it unifies and returns the whole. However, Hegel **ontologizes** this cognitive process, describing actual movements as movements of the Idea itself. Hegel removes the actual historical relationship between the true subject (man) and the object, thus objectifying the subject. Thus the object becomes nothing more than an externalization of the Idea. Here epistemology is ontological dialectics, and the logical translation of the Idea is also the development of self-cognition. This is still Hegel's idealist "triple identity."

However, Lenin did not understand this at the time. He still maintains his Other mirror-image "inverted" logical interpretation of Hegel. First, Lenin takes semblance to be the expression of essence; this is merely an epistemological perspective, and his understanding according to this perspective is passable. However, when he reaches the second step, "reflection," he begins to have trouble. Is "die reflexion" an expression of essence itself? Invertedly speaking, semblance and appearance can be explained as cognizing the object externally, while "reflection" cannot be easily inverted. **Who is reflecting?** If man is reflecting, then this implies a separation from the object, epistemologically speaking; but

9   *Ibid.*, page 96.

how can reflection separated from object express the essence of the object? It is obvious that Hegel's idealist logical situating is impossible to invert in the mirror-image of Lenin's philosophical materialism. This made Lenin very confused. I believe that the root of the problem was still Lenin's Other interpretive framework: **the separation of epistemology from ontological dialectics**. According to Hegel's logic, "reflection" is self-cognition, a moment in the dialectical transition of the Idea. Thus epistemology and dialectics are the same thing. Lenin is unable to enter Hegel's logic at this point.

At this point in our discussion, we must again bring up an underlying question: **what would simply "turned on its head" Hegelian logic actually look like?** If "turned on its head" only means using material concepts to replace those of Absolute Spirit, then is the result materialist dialectics? We often directly align the laws and categories of materialist dialectics with the objective laws of the external world. Thus there emerges a great **invisible logical paradox**; because Hegel's line of thought invertedly objectifies man's cognitive structures as the original structure of the world, concepts and their movement become the essence and laws of objective things. But our "inversion" only says that these things are not "concepts" but "matter"! However, substantively speaking so-called dialectical "laws" are actually **still** human cognitive structures and **latent idealism** is not gone yet. We have merely fooled ourselves into thinking that we have materialistically recreated Hegel's idealist dialectics. This is a complex **false situating**. We think ourselves to be materialists, but in essence, our situating is actually completely homogeneous with Hegel's objective idealist thought situating. The most typical example is that in our dialectical theoretical framework, we always begin be explaining quality, then by explaining the logical transition to quantity as well as the dialectical categories of essence and appearance. However, these are not actually the **original** structure of things, but rather the **logical sequence** of human cognition, despite our rigid insistence that they be anchored in the objective world. *We will later find that Lenin began to gradually understand Hegel's philosophical logical sequence in a new thought situating.* It is evident that it is impossible to resolve the contradiction brought on by the separation of ontological dialectics from epistemology. Thus Lenin at this time found himself mired in an inescapable logical dilemma.

Not long after, Lenin began to notice that *The Science of Logic* always directly studied epistemology; Hegel always compared the study of logic to modern epistemology. He writes: "Hegel takes his self-development of concepts, of categories, in connection with the entire history of philosophy. This gives still a *new* aspect to the whole *Logic*"[10]. In other words, Lenin had already realized that for Hegel, **epistemology and logic were inextricably linked**.

2 THE DISCOVERY OF THE "DUAL IDENTITY" OF EPISTEMOLOGY AND LOGIC

As he delved deeper in his reading, Lenin's attitude towards Hegel began to change. He gradually began to understand that in Hegel's Logic, the internal connections between concepts and transitional dialectical movements formed a comprehensive dialectical logic. Lenin writes:

> **Movement and *"self-movement"* (this NB! arbitrary (independent), spontaneous, *internally-necessary* movement), "change," "movement and vitality," "the principle of all self-movement," "impulse" to "movement" and to "activity"— the opposite to *"dead Being"*[11].**

Next, Lenin begins to consciously demand that he, like Hegel and Marx, engage in "**dialectical** elaboration of the history of human thought, science and technique"[12]. What he means by "dialectical elaboration" was an epistemological task **proceeding from dialectics**, not merely searching for the results of the ontological existence of dialectics.

I have found that in the rest of his reading, Lenin continues to **unconsciously** accept Hegel's logical framework (however, I must emphasize that Hegel's logical framework of which we speak is the triple identity line of thought, not the logic of idealism). He also begins to separate himself from the constraining framework of the strict separation of epistemology and dialectics. *This kind of **unconscious deviation** in his logic situating was fundamentally parallel and identical to the shift in his basic view of Hegel's philosophy.* Lenin understood that "Hegel turned on his head" did not equal external laws; though the "laws" formed by men, including the contradictions, quality-quantity

---

10   *Ibid.*, page 97.
11   *Ibid.*, page 117.
12   *Ibid.*, page 122.

changes, and negation of the negation in dialectics, may have been the profound reflections of man towards the movement of external things, but as **subjective** dialectics, **they were not absolute** and thus could not be simplified or idolized. This is the first point to which science must pay attention (modern physics). *We have already identified this point in earlier discussion; however, it was only at this point in Lenin's epistemological situating that he was able to directly understand it.* Lenin points out that "**law** and **essence** are concepts of the same kind (of the same order), or rather, of the same degree, expressing the deepening of man's knowledge of phenomena, the world, etc." Here we can see that Lenin already maintains the **unity of epistemology and dialectics**. Any of the "laws" or "essence" that we encounter are nothing but the **limited, relative reflections of the essence and movement of the external world under certain historical conditions**. As such, "every law is narrow, incomplete, and approximate"[13]. *Lenin evidently is not referring to external objective laws in an ontological sense at this point, but rather to narrow and approximate "laws." This is the manifested form of this kind of law in man's subjective situating, the knots in the web of cognition that Lenin discussed earlier.*

Lenin writes that "the world of appearances and the world in itself are **moments** of man's knowledge of nature, stages, **alterations** or deepenings (of knowledge)." In the realm of human knowledge, the division between appearance and essence is relative, because laws are essential relations; this mainly refers to the unity of essence and appearance. However, I have found that here Lenin is already thinking from Hegel's point of view. The assertion that laws are essential relations implies epistemology, though Lenin reiterates this sentence in terms of **ontology**. It is my opinion that Lenin has unconsciously unified epistemology and dialectics, necessarily leading to a new contradiction in the thinking of the book.

Lenin's thought soon experienced his first great shift in theoretical logic, parallel to the continual deepening of the epistemological thought mentioned above. He thus developed a completely new thought situating, causing a great change to the place of Hegel's philosophy in all of Lenin's reading and thought. This also provided an immediate, completely new logical premise to the epistemological shift in Lenin's thinking. I have also found that not long later, Lenin's own epistemological thought also experienced an important shift.

---

13 *Ibid.*, page 127.

Lenin quickly discovered that logic is the science of cognition[14]. Lenin draws an arrow pointing to a box, writing "the general laws of movement of the world and of thought," referring to the problem of truth. *In fact, here it is not* **dual identity** *but rather* **triple identity! It is merely that here Lenin only notices that for Hegel, epistemology and logic are identical!** Lenin's understanding of this point progressed rapidly. When reading Hegel's words on syllogism, he excerpts Hegel's description of philosophical framework: "The three branches of philosophy, the Logical Idea, Nature, and Mind." We can see here that Hegel referred to nature as the medium connecting the Logical Idea and Spirit. Under these words, Lenin uses a large box to express his own important thoughts and feelings:

> **Nature, this immediate totality, unfolds itself in the Logical Idea and Mind." Logic is the science of cognition. It is the theory of knowledge. Knowledge is the reflection of nature by man. But this is not simple, not an immediate, not a complete reflection, but the process of a series of abstractions, the formation and development of concepts, laws, etc., and these concepts, laws, etc., (thought, science = "the logical Idea")** *embrace* **conditionally, approximately, the universal, law-governed character of eternally moving and developing nature. Here there are** *actually*, **objectively,** *three* **members: 1) nature; 2) human cognition = the human brain (as the highest product of this same nature), and 3) the form of reflection of nature in human cognition, and this form consists precisely of concepts, laws, categories, etc. Man cannot comprehend = reflect = mirror nature** *as a whole*, **in its completeness, its "immediate totality," he can only** *eternally* **come closer to this, creating abstractions, concepts, laws, a scientific picture of the world, etc., etc.[15].**

Please note that here, knowledge is the reflection of nature by man, and Logic is the science of cognition. In Lenin's new theoretical situating, man's knowledge of nature is no longer a simple, direct, and complete reflection as postulated by the discourse of traditional philosophical materialism; rather, it is a process of concepts, laws, and abstractions that only permits a conditional, approximate grasp of nature. At the same time, the relation between nature, human knowledge, and the reflected form of nature in human knowledge (this is logic, but not a

---

14   *Ibid.*, page 127.
15   *Ibid.*, page 152.

formal logic, rather one that approaches man's *cognitive structures* or *schema paradigms* as we understand them in our scientific epistemology today). Logic is identical to the theory of knowledge, because it is the structure of the latter; this was the first great discovery that Lenin made in the course of his reading.

As we have already seen, in the *Bern Noteboks* Lenin also experienced a second important détournement of theoretical logic, which allowed him to develop a new view of materialist dialectics on the basis of **practice**. As Lenin read the third chapter ("Teleology") of the second section ("Objectivity") of the second volume of *The Science of Logic*, he recorded his first comparison of logical situating. In these experimental notes, Lenin conducts a comprehensive logical inversion of Hegel's philosophy. It was in this comparative thought experiment that we see Lenin's new understanding of epistemological questions. As we have already pointed out, here Lenin has already realized that objective processes do not refer to nature (this is the dividing line between Marxism and old materialism), but rather has two existential forms: "nature (mechanism and chemism) and man's purposive activity"[16]. In Lenin's opinion at this time, the relation between these two forms could be described thus: the former was the basis of the latter, but from the perspective of man's practical (purposive) activity, the former seems to be external and of secondary importance. Please note that the external world in Lenin's original thought logic has divided into two, to which he adds man's activity and results in **objective material practice**. Thus the great relational form of Lenin's logic is also changed; no longer is his focus on **nature**, **knowledge**, and **logic**, but rather **nature**, **practice**, and **knowledge (logic)**. *Of course, this new qualitative differentiation was still unconscious for Lenin.*

I believe that the emergence of practice was extremely important in Lenin's understanding of the "triple identity" relationship, because it signalled a more important progression of knowledge. At the same time, Lenin follows Hegel's line of thought, proposing a set of important categorical epistemological relations, i.e. the relation between the category of logic and human practice. In other words, Lenin had already begun to notice the issue of the **composition** of human cognitive structures themselves; not long before, Lenin stilled viewed this as the medium between nature and knowledge, viewing logic as the abstract tool which composed knowledge.

---

16 *Ibid.*, page 158.

After discovering the importance of practice, Lenin was on the verge of forming a new understanding. After reading the third section ("The Idea") of the second volume of *The Science of Logic*, Lenin excitedly writes: "**perhaps the best exposition of dialectics**. Here too, the coincidence, so to speak, of logic and epistemology is shown in a remarkably brilliant way"[17]. Lenin goes on to point out that "The relations (= transitions = contradictions) of notions = the main content of logic," the dialectics of the Idea[18]. It is evident here that Lenin had finally begun to notice that for Hegel, logic and epistemology were identical; this was the best exposition of dialectics. As such, were not **the three aspects** then identical? However, Lenin did not make a determination at this point, because there was still the question of the relationship between the three and the point of convergence. For Hegel, dialectics seemed to be expressed through the movement logic of knowledge. Thus from the perspective of the substance of Hegelianism, the three aspects converged at epistemology, because its philosophical being was composed of man's cognitive structures. If Lenin were to restructure Hegel's "triple identity," **where** should the convergence take place? This was the next difficult point for Lenin to tackle.

3 PRACTICAL DIALECTICS: THE SOLE FOUNDATION POINT OF "TRIPLE IDENTITY"

In the *Bern Notebooks*, Lenin's resolution of this problem was gradually realized through a series of profound reflections and realizations. Here let us re-examine Lenin's second comparative logical situating experiment he wrote as he read the introductory portion of the third section ("The Idea") of "The Doctrine of the Notion."

Beginning from the context of the discussion here, we can see that Lenin first explained three important points. First was the premise, *i.e.* knowledge is the identity of the objective and the subjective. Second, this identity was not the idealized, static identity of old materialism, and knowledge (the Idea) itself was expressed as the relation between man and the objective. Third, in this relation, man's subjectivity plays the role of eliminating this subjective antagonistic impulse. *This line of thought clearly tells us that Lenin was progressing along the lines of Hegel's logic.* In Lenin's new thought situating, the affirmation of this

---

17   *Ibid.*, page 162.
18   *Ibid.*, page 166

logical progression exhibited the convergence of the visions of Lenin and Marx. Lenin begins to oppose the directly observational nature of epistemology, stressing that knowledge is a **relationship** ("my relationship with my surroundings is my consciousness," to use Marx's words) and that relationships are not simple opposites, but rather the transition of man's dynamic activity to the object of knowledge. We find that there is a logical loop hidden here: first is subjective and objective and then relation, but the control of this relation again belongs to man's active subjectivity. We must admit that there are unsolved questions here.

According to the text, Lenin first writes: "he idea (read: man's knowledge) is the coincidence (conformity) of notion and objectivity (the "universal"). This—first"[19]. This is the **materialist** premise of Marxist epistemology. However, human knowledge is certainly not, as it is understood in the discourse of traditional philosophical materialism, a passive, negative direct observation of external objects. Therefore, "Secondly, the idea is the **relation** of the subjectivity (= man) which is for itself (= independent, as it were) to the objectivity which is **distinct** (from this Idea)..." This implies that consciousness is a kind of **relationship**. In traditional philosophical materialism, the object of knowledge is directly understood to be sensuous substance, and cognitive relations are mirrored, idealized direct reflections of objective objects. Here, on the other hand, Hegel points out that subjectivity is the impulse that "sublates" this division of object and subject[20], and Lenin rewrites this thought to read: "Subjectivity is the **impulse** to destroy this separation (of the idea from the object)." It is evident that Lenin did not agree with the idealist line of thought which one-sidedly exaggerated subjective dynamism, turning instead to emphasize man's purposive recreation of the objective world. His "subjectivity" actually refers to the **practical subjectivity** of man. *It is somewhat surprising to me that this point is identical to Marx's theoretical point in **Theses on Feuerbach**: "understood from the subjective aspect." Not long after, Lenin would clearly express this as the movement from the subject to the object.*

We know that when Marx and Engels gave their first complete expression of the essence of consciousness (knowledge), they wrote: "my relation to my surroundings is my consciousness"[21]. They give the

19 *Ibid.*, page 164.
20 Hegel, Georg Wilhelm Friedrich. *The Science of Logic*. Commercial Press (1977), volume 2, page 452 (Chinese).
21 *The Collected Works of Marx and Engels*, volume 3, page 34 footnote 2 (Chinese).

following description of the essence of human knowledge:

> **The ideas which these individuals form are ideas either about their relation to nature or about their mutual relations or about their own nature. It is evident that in all these cases their ideas are the conscious expression – real or illusory – of their real relations and activities, of their production, of their intercourse, of their social and political conduct[22].**

It is clear that Marx's exposition of consciousness as relationships does not refer to a subjective relation, but first to **practical relations that emerge from the human subject**. Knowledge does not directly reflect objects, but rather reflects **mediated** social historical relations. *Lenin was not able to read **The German Ideology**, but through his recreation of Hegel's dialectics, he was able to accurately grasp the true depth of Marx's philosophical worldview.*

Here, Lenin goes on to point out: "The coincidence of thought with the object is a **process**: thought (= man) must not imagine truth in the form of dead repose, in the form of a bare picture (image), pale (matt), without impulse, without motion, like a genus, like a number, like abstract thought"[23]. Why? Because knowledge is made up of relations mediated by practice. The relation between knowledge ("the Idea") and external objects is not, as old materialism understands it to be, simple "dead repose" relations, but rather a historical process that continually deepens and changes through the mediation of practical relations. Thus Lenin believes that Hegel's opposition to the solidification of concepts is correct: "Concepts are not immobile but—in and for themselves, by their nature = **transition**"[24].

Lenin proposes:

> **Cognition is the eternal, endless approximation of thought to the object. The *reflection* of nature in man's thought must be understood not "lifelessly," not "abstractly," *not devoid of movement, not without contradictions*, but in the eternal *process* of movement, the arising of contradictions and their solution[25].**

---

22 *Ibid.*, page 29, footnote 1 (Chinese).
23 *The Collected Works of Lenin* (Chin. 2. Ed.), volume 55, page 164.
24 *Ibid.*, page 194.
25 *Ibid.*, page 165.

Here, the entanglements in the process of knowledge are no longer the self-entanglements of the Idea as described by Hegel; rather, they are the eternal contradictions of man's movement towards objective material dialectics through practical dialectics. Only through a historical, practical dialectical progression can man continually cognize the essence of objects and continually approach objective truth. In Lenin's view at this time, **the substance of objective truth was the dialectical movement of practice.**

Next, Lenin opens volume six of Hegel's *Encyclopaedia of the Philosophical Sciences*, beginning his excerpts with paragraph 213 of the *Shorter Logic* as he continued his theoretical recreation of Hegel's philosophy. In response to Hegel's assertion that "the Idea is **truth**"[26], Lenin writes in the right-hand column: "The idea is **Cognition** and aspiration (volition) [of man]... The process of (transitory, finite, limited) cognition and action converts abstract concepts into **perfected objectivity**"[27]. I believe that here Lenin had already very profoundly restructured Hegel's view that truth is the relationship of individual beings. Lenin continues:

> **Individual Being (an object, a phenomenon, etc.) is (only) *one side* of the Idea (of truth). Truth requires still other sides of *reality*, which likewise appear only as independent and individual (existing specially for themselves). *Only in their totality*, (*zusammen*), and in their *relation* (*Beziehung*) is truth realized[28].**

I must specially point out that Lenin's use of the words "appear as" refer not to objectively existing substance for itself in an ontological sense, **neither are material objects for themselves appearances**. *As we have already seen, appearance is not a qualification of materialist philosophical ontology; it is only established as it relates to the subject.* Rather, this actually refers to the exposition of objective objects in the course of practice as appearance and individual beings. It is also only in practical dialectical deepening that man is able to gradually discover the relations between these beings, and ultimately, totally, and truly grasp their relations.

---

26 Hegel, Georg Wilhelm Friedrich. *The Shorter Logic*. Commercial Press (1980), page 397 (Chinese).
27 *The Collected Works of Lenin* (Chin. 2. Ed.), volume 55, page 165.
28 *Ibid.*, page 165-66.

Therefore Lenin writes:

The *totality of all* sides of the phenomenon, of reality and their (reciprocal) *relations*—that is what truth is composed of. The relations (= transitions = contradictions) of notions = the main content of logic, *by which* these concepts (and their relations, transitions, contradictions) are shown as reflections of the objective world. The dialectics of *things* produces the dialectics of *ideas*, and not vice versa[29].

According to Lenin's logic at this time, the statement "the dialectics of **things** produces the dialectics of **ideas**" does not mean that objective objects will automatically create the dialectics of knowledge, but rather that **objective dialectics actively creates subjective dialectics through practical dialectics**. This was a completely new thread of situating logic. Both objective dialectics and practical dialectics are objective dialectics; through the medium of practical dialectics, under certain conditions objective dialectics historically forms the human cognitive result – subjective dialectics.

In his last box in this chapter, Lenin confirms one of Hegel's views in *The Shorter Logic*, that "the essence of the Idea is **process**"[30]. However, he goes to interpret this materialistically, arguing that "truth is process," because "from the subjective idea, man advances towards objective truth **through** 'practice' (and technique)"[31]. There is no doubt that practical dialectics have already become the focus of Lenin's attention at this point.

We have already seen that the confirmation of practical dialectics appeared in the third comparative thought situating experiment of Lenin's notes. There Lenin repeatedly identifies the basis of epistemology and logic as objective practical dialectics. He realizes that "What is necessary is the **union of cognition and practice**"[32]. In the box on page 187 Lenin incredibly writes: "The activity of man, who has constructed an objective picture of the world for himself, **changes** external actuality, abolishes its determinateness (= alters some sides or other, qualities, of it), and thus removes from it the features of Semblance, externality and

---

29   *Ibid.*, page 166.
30   Hegel, Georg Wilhelm Friedrich. *The Shorter Logic*. Commercial Press (1980), page 403 (Chinese).
31   *The Collected Works of Lenin* (Chin. 2. Ed.), volume 55, page 170.
32   *Ibid.*, page 185.

nullity, and makes it as being in and for itself (= objectively true)"[33]. Here Lenin first declares that practice **constructs** a picture of the objective world. First, this is not a direct reflection of the external world. Second, the basic lines of latitude and longitude of this picture of the objective world constructed by man change external reality; according to man's purpose (needs), he alters "some sides or other, qualities, of it." This means that in man's practical reconstruction, he restrains or reduces the sides of external objects that are harmful to man (such as natural disasters), while preserving, prioritizing, and expanding those aspects that are useful to man. This eliminates the "externality" in nature that is unrelated to man, becoming instead **for-self** existence in terms of man's practical utility. We can see that Lenin has already discovered practice as his most important theoretical base point.

Soon after, Lenin profoundly realized that "dialectics is the epistemology of (Hegel and) Marxism"[34]. Here, Lenin does not refer simply to external material dialectics, but rather to all objective dialectics, in which man's practical dialectics is deeply embedded. Lenin later discovered that in Marx's *Capital*, the logic, dialectics, and epistemology of materialism can be expressed with a single word; they are the same thing. Using our line of thought here to understand this issue, this means that logic, dialectics, and epistemology coincide above objective **practical dialectics**.

Among scholars of the former Soviet Union, Lenin's "triple identity" viewpoint was identified as "the true pinnacle of [his] philosophical thought"[35]. I believe that this declaration is another example of exaggeration. Objectively speaking, Lenin's view of the coincidence of logic, dialectics, and epistemology was merely one of the important theoretical fruits acquired by Lenin as he realized a new thought situating in his *Bern Notebooks*. Furthermore, if we are to base our analysis on the facts, we must concede that this knowledge was not the original discovery of Lenin's philosophical thought; we can only say that it was the result of his re-creation and approval of Hegel's views in the context of Marxist philosophy.

---

33   *Ibid.*, page 187.
34   *Ibid.*, page 308.
35   Dynnik, ed. *History of Philosophy*, volume 5. 1975. Beijing Sanlian Press, 176.

CHAPTER THIRTEEN

DESANCTIFICATION:
LENIN'S "SIXTEEN ELEMENTS" OF DIALECTICS

When Lenin wrote his famous "sixteen elements" of dialectics and epistemology, he was already approaching the end of his study of Hegel's *The Science of Logic* (Lenin had already read to the last chapter "Absolute Idea"). At this time, Lenin had already acquired the knowledge that subjective dialectical structures were identical to epistemological structures (logic). He wished to go on to record a comprehensive list and summary of his thoughts up to that point, in order to understand how to subjectively, dialectically grasp the various aspects of the material dialectics of the external world. In his reflections and organizations of his recent thought, Lenin did engage in crude consideration of the internal connections between the various aspects (moments) of materialist dialectical theory. Thus, this was a **research logic line of thought**, certainly not the **theoretical expression** of some kind of system (structure). However, more importantly, in the great shift in thought that Lenin had already realized in the latter stages of his reading, the logic of practical dialectics was not directly reflected in these "sixteen elements." This is a question worthy of deeper consideration.

1 LOGICAL ANALYSIS OF TEXTUAL STRUCTURE

I have three new views on Lenin's "sixteen elements" of dialectics and epistemology. **First**, the content of these sixteen elements is no longer merely dialectical, but also directly touches on important epistemological content. *This is why I believe that we should qualify the "sixteen elements" with the adjectives "dialectical and epistemological."* **Second**, the sixteen elements were no more than a summary of the knowledge that Lenin had acquired pertaining to materialist dialectical theory. More specifically, they were only his partial summary of subjective dialectics, certainly not a conscious construction of an entire theoretical **system** of materialist dialectics. *It is against the original intent of Lenin's thought to depart from this special context and abstractly elevate the "sixteen elements," setting them as structures of objective dialectics.* **Third**, the content of the "sixteen elements" is mainly a summary of Hegel's dialectical thought, not **original** expressions of Lenin's own ideas on materialist dialectics. As such, the legitimacy of any attempt to positively construct the logical system of Marxist materialist dialectics from Lenin's "sixteen elements" is highly doubtful. *I have found that the first person to propose using Lenin's "dialectical elements" to construct a materialist system was actually Deborin. In his 1929 introduction to Lenin's* **Bern Notebooks** *he writes that Lenin's principles ought to enter Soviet dialectical materialist textbooks as the starting point of the whole study of materialist dialectics. All of us, under many circumstances, are accustomed to superficiality and simplification when dealing with materialist dialectics*[1].

I believe that Lenin did not consciously propose the "sixteen elements" in order to construct a logical model of materialist dialectical theory. Rather, this was a short, theoretical summary of his thoughts on the "Absolute Idea" towards the end of his reading of Hegel's *The Science of Logic*. In fact, in the third chapter of this last section of *The Science of Logic* ("The Absolute Idea"), after countless conceptual changes and theoretical developments, Hegel reaches the pinnacle of his thought: the Absolute Idea. Here we find a theoretical summary of dialectics, as well as the proposition of a series of important principles. After completing multiple leaps in his thought, Lenin was now able to easily and accurately grasp the basic significance of Hegel's dialectics. Thus as he read this chapter, Lenin followed Hegel's summary of dialectics by

---

1   Deborin, Abram. *Introduction to volume 9 of "The Lenin Papers"*. Soviet National Press (1929) appendix (Chinese).

providing a thought-experimental explanation of **subjective** dialectical logic as he understood it. Beginning with the "planned conception theory," Kedrov makes a strained interpretation of Lenin's "sixteen elements" by referring to these points as the "first plan" of a book on dialectics after reading Hegel's *The Science of Logic*[2]. I believe that this is an example of subjective assumption and **false situating**.

According to my understanding, the "sixteen elements" represent a two-layered progressive structure of logical thought and situating which existed in Lenin's thought at this time. After reading Hegel's dialectical analysis in the section titled "Absolute Cognition," Lenin first cites one of Hegel's passages in the original German, drawing two thick lines next to this paragraph along with the words "one of the definitions of **dialectics**"[3]. Next, in an open box, he translates and records the words: "This equally synthetic and analytic moment of the Judgment, by which (the moment) the original universality [general concept] determines itself out of itself as other in relation to itself, must be called dialectical"[4]. He also uses a large arrow to indicate the passage of original German text.

On the facsimile of the original document is it possible to see Lenin's words on the left-hand margin: "A determination which is not a clear one!!" Nevertheless, Lenin still proposes three overall viewpoints on Hegel's discussion of the method of the structure of conceptual logic at the beginning of this third chapter. *Kedrov argues that Lenin's summary here of the first level of dialectics comes directly from his analysis and consideration of this passage of excerpts[5]; I believe that Kedrov's interpretation here deviates from the truth. I assert that in Lenin's thought at this time, with the exception of the third viewpoint which does originate from this passage of excerpts, the first two viewpoints importantly summarize Hegel's overall explanation of dialectics in the third chapter ("Absolute Idea") of **The Science of Logic**. This is a micro textual detail.* These viewpoints are also three overall summaries, the first level of thought in Lenin's thought situating experiment at this time.

---

2   See Kedrov's *On Methods of Expressing Dialectics*. China Social Science Press (1986), page 330.

3   *The Collected Works of Lenin* (Chin. 2. Ed.), volume 55, page 189.

4   *Ibid.*, page 190.

5   See Kedrov's *Study of Lenin's "Philosophical Notebooks,"* Qiushi Press (1984), page 300 (Chinese).

The first viewpoint establishes the premise of subjective dialectics, i.e. objectively "considering the thing itself," while also explaining that there are two dimensions to the overall perspective of dialectical observation: "the thing in its relations and in its development" should form our knowledge. I find that we return to the textual context of *The Science of Logic,* this is Lenin's restructuring of Hegel's first principle of the dialectical method. Hegel's original words are: "things thus constituted of method are the determinations and relations of concepts themselves"[6]. This is the logical starting point of Hegel's objective idealism; for Hegel, the true basis of the concept (being) is the sole object of cognition. Here, Lenin materialistically restructures Hegel's expression as consideration of external objects, emphasizing that things themselves must be considered on the basis of relations and development. This naturally becomes the theoretical starting point of materialist dialectics. Traditional materialist dialectics theoretical systems establish "relations" and "development" as overall features of the notion of dialectics.

The second viewpoint explains the substance of this subjective dialectics as the grasp of "the contradictory nature of the thing itself." This is also Lenin's restructuring of the second principle of Hegel's methodology. In The Science of Logic, as Hegel discusses the overall logic that opens dialectics, he identifies the overall logic of notional dialectics as including differences and "the unity of different things." Lenin immediately develops this idea, realizing that contradictions were the essential aspect of all dialectics: "the contradictory forces and tendencies in each phenomenon." *Considering Lenin's assertion in "On the Question of Dialectics" that the synthesis of contradiction was the "centre" and "essence" of dialectical theory, this viewpoint becomes immediately over-exaggerated.*

The third viewpoint elucidates the comprehensive characteristic of this dialectical knowledge: "the union of analysis and synthesis"[7]. As we have already seen, this is a summary of Lenin's excerpt of Hegel's passage. Lenin writes: "Such apparently are the elements of dialectics." Please note that these are not elements of objective dialectics in an ontological sense, but theoretical **logical elements** of the identity of subjective dialectics, epistemology, and logic. *This is because in terms of*

6   Hegel, Georg Wilhelm Friedrich. *The Science of Logic.* Commercial Press (1976), page 533 (Chinese).
7   *The Collected Works of Lenin* (Chin. 2. Ed.), volume 55, page 190.

*subjective **epistemological** qualifications, the concepts of "considera-*
tion," "analysis," and "synthesis" cannot belong to ontological logic.

After writing his first general expression proceeding **directly from
the context of Hegel's original words**, Lenin suddenly comes upon
new thinking. He writes, "One could perhaps present these elements
in greater detail as follows," going on to achieve his second level of
thought "expression" (not "system"!) – The "sixteen elements." Careful
examination of facsimiles of the original manuscript reveals that these
"elements" were not written all at once, but were only completed
through the internal links between two different thought situatings, **re-
organized** through multiple, careful thought experiments.

After the three general summarizing statements given above, Lenin appears to have written **seven** elements all at once; this formed the **first
thought situating process** of the "sixteen elements." This thinking
was mainly a direct and concrete unfolding of the three broad summaries he gave earlier. Kedrov's analysis of this point is correct, which
he expresses using the heading "three points expanded into seven"[8].
Elements 1 to 3 expanded on two of the points made in the "summaries," while the first gave further confirmation of the premise ("consider
things themselves") of materialist dialectics: "the objectivity of consideration (not examples, not divergencies, but the Thing-in-itself)"[9]. Here
I believe that this was Lenin's rewriting of one of Hegel's passages on
the same page. Hegel's original words are: "[cognition] must consider
things in and for themselves, that is, should consider them partly in their
universality, but also that it should not stray away from them catching
at circumstances, examples and comparisons, but should keep before
it solely the things themselves and bring before consciousness what is
imminent in them"[10]. From our perspective now, Lenin's restructured
expression of Hegel's ideas is both accurate and profound.

Elements 2 and 3 concern the specific explanations of the two dimensions of the "overall features" of materialist dialectics as expressed in
the first "summary" (relations and developments of things): "the entire totality of the manifold **relations** of this thing to others," and "the

---

8   See Kedrov's *Study of Lenin's "Philosophical Notebooks,"* Qiushi Press (1984),
page 302 (Chinese).
9   *The Collected Works of Lenin* (Chin. 2. Ed.), volume 55, page 190.
10   Hegel, Georg Wilhelm Friedrich. *The Science of Logic.* Commercial Press (1976),
page 533 (Chinese).

development of this thing, (phenomenon, respectively), its own movement, its own life." I believe that it was beginning with these two elements that Lenin no longer proceeded from Hegel's textual context, but expressed relatively independently his own general knowledge of dialectics. Of course, the vast majority of important views here still originated from Hegel's **dialectical thought that he had already read**.

Elements 4 through 6 compose a categorized description of the essential definition of the contradictions of materialist dialectics of the second "summary" described above, approached on three different levels. This was obviously a more complex thought experiment and process of theoretical situating. *Lenin writes: "the internally contradictory tendencies (and sides) in this thing," and then "the thing (phenomenon, etc.) as the sum and unity of opposites." Lenin writes a # sign within parentheses in the fourth element; according to textual analysis of this manuscript as well as the traces of his writing, we are able to conclude that this symbol was an incorrectly written word that Lenin crossed out[11]. Lenin then separates the second half of the sentence, making it into element 5. In order to differentiate between the fourth and fifth elements, Lenin drew a # sign in between these two elements.* The sixth element reads: "the **struggle**, respectively unfolding, of these opposites, contradictory strivings, etc." The seventh is an explanation of the third element. In the seventh element, Lenin repeats the content of the third element, then writes a hyphen and the words: "the break-down of the separate parts and the totality, the summation of these parts." From the facsimile of the original document we can see that after writing these first seven elements, Lenin draws two lines in the left-hand margin, as well as the words: "Elements of Dialectics." This was a specially made theoretical heading. The name of this text originates from this marginal note. Furthermore, Lenin emphasizes each vertically written word with double lines to show emphasis. This is the first level of Lenin's thought experiment at this point.

An examination of the manuscript reveals that these were the first seven elements written by Lenin. He had drawn a horizontal dividing line, presumably to record some of his personal thoughts, but then later erased this line and instead drew a small box to the lower right. There he conducted his **second situating thought experiment**.

---

11   *The Collected Works of Lenin* (Chin. 2. Ed.), volume 55, page 192.

In this box Lenin uses a broad-tipped pen to write: "In brief, dialectics can be defined as the doctrine of the unity of opposites. This embodies the essence of dialectics, but it requires explanations and development"[12]. Please note that the Chinese edition of this text committed a grave mistake by moving this box to the end of the sixteenth element when it should have come after the seventh. The original intent of this move was to preserve the continuity of the "elements"; however, this seriously veils Lenin's true line of thought at this point. I have found that Kedrov actually restores this text to its original state in his analysis, moving it between the seventh and eighth elements[13]. Also, the double lines from the seventh to the sixteenth elements were originally drawn in the left-hand margin. I believe that the content of this box is extremely important. It not only reflects the central thinking of the first two levels of Lenin's dialectical elements, but it also touches on the "explanations and developments" of the third level. It was with this end in mind that Lenin wrote nine more elements (elements eight through sixteen). It is my view that the expression of this third level of knowledge can be divided into three orientations of significance.

First, under the small box discussed above, Lenin writes what are now known as elements 11 and 12. The direct theoretical intention of these statements was to provide further explanation of the seventh element, because in Lenin's second level of expression, the first two points were more fully developed while the epistemological perspective of dialectics was not. Lenin writes:

11. The endless process of the deepening of man's knowledge of the thing, of phenomena, processes, etc., from appearance to essence and from less profound to more profound essence.

12. From co-existence to causality and from one form of connection and reciprocal dependence to another, deeper, more general form[14].

This passage is extremely important, because it explains a view that I identified earlier in this book, i.e., the "sixteen elements" were not explanations of **objective** dialectical structures, but rather the definition of the features of dialectical cognition from a subjective perspective.

---

12 *Ibid.*, page 192.
13 See Kedrov's *On Methods of Expressing Dialectics*. China Social Science Press (1986), page 330-331.
14 *The Collected Works of Lenin* (Chin. 2. Ed.), volume 55, page 191.

Here this becomes very clear. Lenin emphasizes the limitless process of the **cognitive** deepening of subjective dialectics, stressing the change from "appearance to essence and from less profound to more profound essence." These qualifications cannot be rooted in objective structures. Appearance and essence – in particular "less profound essence" – can only be established relative to the subject (for us). This is an aspect that we often ignored in our past study of Lenin's materialist dialectics. Perhaps Lenin later thought that this expression was too long and so decided to forego the second half of it, leaving this as the twelfth element. According to my textual analysis I have found that the sequence of elements eight through twelve was added later. Lenin first wrote numbers eleven and twelve, and then wrote numbers eight through ten. Apparently after finishing, he first wrote the numbers eight through ten, and divided number ten from number twelve. Lastly, he added the numbers for number eleven and twelve.

Next, Lenin at once writes what we know today as elements eight through ten. The intention of these three elements was to "develop" further the points broached in the second level of the expression of the three dialectical summaries. Concretely speaking, the eighth was a further development of the relations described in the second: "The relations of each thing (phenomenon, etc.) are not only manifold, but general, universal. Each thing (phenomenon, process, etc.) is connected with **every other.**" *Textually speaking, this was a new result of Lenin's thought experiment. Next to the word "manifold" in the second element Lenin wrote an "X," which he also did next to the beginning of the eighth element. This marks logical link, indicating that the eighth element was a supplementary explanation of the idea of "manifold."* The ninth element is a development of the fifth: "not only the unity of opposites, but the **transitions** of **every** determination, quality, feature, side, property into every other." *From the text we can see that Lenin first drew a "#" sign next to the word "unity" in the fifth element, though he did not draw the same sign in the ninth element. The tenth element supplements the seventh[15], as are elements eleven and twelve, which* were written first.

Finally, Lenin wanted to supplement the dialectical elements that he had already developed three times, and so recorded elements thirteen through sixteen. These four elements were written afterwards. Elements

---

15   *Ibid.*, page 191.

thirteen and fourteen are explanations of the features of the negation of the negation, written to the left of the small box after the seventh element and above the eleventh element, respectively. "The repetition at a higher stage of certain features, properties, etc., of the lower and the apparent return to the old (negation of the negation)." The fifteenth element was added at the beginning of numbers eight through fourteen. Here Lenin uses double lines to separate its content, actually explaining the category of dialectics: "the struggle of content with form and conversely. The throwing off of the form, the transformation of the content." At this point, there is no longer room for the sixteenth element on the second half of the page, it can only be written after the comprehensive summaries of the first level of expression. This element concerns the transition between quality and quantity: "the transition of quantity into quality and **vice versa** ((**15** and **16** are **examples** of **9**))." In fact, the last four elements were added precisely for Lenin to explain and expand the different aspects of the law of antithesis-synthesis that forms the centre of dialectics[16].

2 THE DIALECTICAL AND EPISTEMOLOGICAL THOUGHT IN THE "SIXTEEN ELEMENTS"

Here I would like to reiterate that these "sixteen elements" were certainly not an outline of a preconceived structure of materialist dialectics that Lenin was constructing. Rather, they were an unconscious self-summary after his study of Hegel's *The Science of Logic*. In terms of the content, Lenin provides a thought-experimental explanation of the materialist dialectical **theory** or **subjective** dialectical logic according to his understanding at the time. However, this was still obviously not the complete structure of a logical system, or rather not a very mature expression of views, but rather simply the reflection of the thought experiment that Lenin conducted in his thought situating at that precise moment in time. I have already provided a more detailed discussion of the basic textual situation of these texts, and so here we will examine more specifically the basic logic of Lenin's theoretical summary as well as its deeper level of thought. In this process we will **return and touch on** the theoretical impressions and conclusions that Lenin reached on dialectics and epistemology in the whole of the *Bern Notebooks*.

---

16 *Ibid.*, page 191.

The first element: "the *objectivity* of consideration (not examples, not divergencies, but the Thing-in-itself)." Although this point was directly based on the corresponding context of Hegel's chapter "Absolute Idea," it was also an expression of Lenin's unwavering theoretical belief in materialism. Hegel's original words here are "the determinations and relations of the Idea itself." These same ideas can be expressed using Hegel's words in the preface to the second edition of his work: "the objective notion of things constitutes their essential import." Thus the starting point of dialectical investigation "is not **things** but their **import**, the Notion of them"[17]. This was Hegel's self-identification in the logic of idealism, because for Hegel, dialectics were the immanent logic of the self-movement of the Idea. However, for Lenin, dialectics are not the logic of the Idea itself, but rather the scientific method by which man, through practice, cognizes and considers the external world. Analysis of the discourse in this element reveals that for Lenin, the logical perspective of materialist dialectics is first the objective examination of the external world; this implies that the placement of this theoretical logic is not ontological, or in other words does not depart from subjective practice and cognition, but is rather a qualification of epistemology and logic that **proceeds from the subject**. It could be said that materialist dialectics is a **kind of doctrine**[18]. Its many qualifications are not direct attributes of the object, but the subjective result of our observation of the external world. Here Lenin emphasizes that the starting point of this dialectical thought is the objectivity of observation, not the a priori frameworks and concepts described by Kant and Hegel.

I have found that this viewpoint constitutes a theoretical axis that extends throughout the entirety of Lenin's study of Hegelian philosophy. At the beginning of his study of Hegel's *The Science of Logic*, Lenin repeatedly emphasized his materialist stance. As he read the preface, he clearly points out that cognition and logic do not directly emerge from notions, but must be "turned around" in order to be derived from natural life. The thought category of dialectics are expressions of the law-fulness of nature and man." He not only did not agree with Hegel's idealist judgments, but also rewrote them to read: "Not things, but the laws of their movement, materialistically." In another place he writes this same idea in a marginal note: "dialectics of things themselves, of

---

17   Hegel, Georg Wilhelm Friedrich. *The Science of Logic.* Volume 1. Commercial Press (1966), pages 13 and 17 (Chinese).
18   *The Collected Works of Lenin* (Chin. 2. Ed.), volume 55, page 90.

Nature itself, of the course of events itself"[19]. As he read the introduction, he clearly agrees with Hegel's appraisal of Kant: "The great merit of **Kant** was that he removed 'the semblance of arbitrariness' from dialectics"[20]. He continues, basing himself on Hegel's exposition to further express the theoretical starting point of dialectics as attention to the objective, necessary relations of things. As he read "Doctrine of Being," he writes in a large box: "Flexibility, applied **objectively**, *i.e.* reflecting the all-sidedness of the material process and its unity, is dialectics, is the correct reflection of the eternal development of the world"[21]. *As I have already pointed out, Levine makes a correct judgment of this point, indicating that Lenin never abandoned materialism.* I must emphasize one point, which is that even after Lenin's thought experienced an important logical détournement and leap in understanding, he never betrayed materialism.

The second element: "the entire totality of the manifold **relations** of this thing to others." The comprehensiveness of cognition and observation was something to which Lenin accorded great attention throughout his study; it was consistently made identical to the idea of universal relationships of the objective world in materialist dialectics in the process of Lenin's reading. As he read the preface, as Lenin explains that logic is the doctrine of the laws of development, he emphasizes that it is "the science not of external forms of thought, but of the laws of development "of all material, natural and spiritual things", *i.e.*, of the development of the entire concrete content of the world and of its cognition, *i.e.*, the sum-total, the conclusion of the **History** of knowledge of the world"[22]. Next, as he reads Hegel's proposition of two important principles of dialectics in the introduction to *The Science of Logic* ("necessary connection" and "immanent emergence of distinction"), he immediately expresses the first as "**Necessary** connection, the objective connection of all the aspects, forces, tendencies, etc., of the given sphere of phenomena"[23]. The most important expression of this point comes at the end of Lenin's reading of "Essence." Here he first repeats some of Hegel's arguments, explaining that things as the basis of objects refer to the whole of things or all their facets. Expressed materialistically, this means "the universal, all-sided **vital** connection of everything with

19   *Ibid.*, page 92.
20   *Ibid.*, page 82.
21   *Ibid.*, page 91.
22   *Ibid.*, page 77.
23   *Ibid.*, page 82.

everything and the reflection of this connection." He next gives the famous example of the "water drop."

A river and the *drops* in this river. The position of *every* drop, its relation to the others; its connection with the others; the direction of its movement; its speed; the line of the movement— straight, curved, circular, etc.—upwards, downwards. The sum of the movement. Concepts, as *registration* of individual aspects of the movement, of individual drops (="things"), of individual "*streams*," etc.[24].

As Lenin read the footnote to paragraph 143 of Hegel's Shorter Logic, he summarizes Hegel's thought in a box: "The sum-total, the entirety of the moments of Actuality, which, in its unfolding discloses itself to be Necessity." Hegel's original words are: "Whether a thing is possible or impossible, depends altogether on the subject-matter: that is, on the sum total of the elements in actuality, which, as it opens itself out, discloses itself to be necessity"[25]. Lenin rewrites this as: "The unfolding of the sum-total of the moments of actuality N B = the essence of dialectical cognition"[26].

The third element: "The *development* of this thing, (phenomenon, respectively), its own movement, its own life."

Lenin accords a great deal of attention to Hegel's views on the self-movement of things, because this is also an important basis of the internal contradictory forces of the movement and development of things described in dialectics. At the beginning of his study, as Lenin read the preface to the first edition, he remarked that Hegel's theory of the movement of scientific knowledge was actually the "path of self-construction." He approved of Hegel's view that the reason for the development of things was the internal, contradictory movement of things themselves. When Lenin came upon Hegel's related discussion of the laws of contradiction in "Essence," he passionately expresses his approbation. For Hegel, "all things themselves are contradictory in themselves." Furthermore, this view is more able to express the truth and essence of things[27]. Hegel believes that contradiction is the source of all

---

24   *Ibid.*, page 122-3.
25   Hegel, Georg Wilhelm Friedrich. *The Shorter Logic*. Commercial Press (1980), page 300 (Chinese).
26   *The Collected Works of Lenin* (Chin. 2. Ed.), volume 55, page 132.
27   Hegel, Georg Wilhelm Friedrich. *The Science of Logic*. Volume 1. Commercial

movement and vitality; only because things themselves are contradictory are they able to move, do they have dynamism and vitality[28]. It is on this point that Lenin excitedly writes, "'Movement and '*self-movement*' (this NB! arbitrary (independent), spontaneous, **internally-necessary** movement), 'change,' 'movement and vitality,' 'the principle of all self-movement,' 'impulse' (Trieb) to 'movement' and to 'activity,'" as all things that Hegel's philosophy had to rescue and reveal[29]. Of course, the cause of the self-movement of things was contradiction.

The fourth element: "The internally contradictory **tendencies** (*and* sides) in this thing." The fifth element: "The thing (phenomenon, etc.) as the sum and **unity of opposites**." The sixth: "The **struggle**, respectively unfolding, of these opposites, contradictory strivings, etc."

In the introduction, Lenin approves of Hegel's idea of "immanent emergence of distinctions," going on to identify the "necessity of contradiction" and propose "the inner objective logic of evolution and of the struggle of the differences, polarity"[30]. I have already cited Lenin's well-known statement that dialectics are the science of how to unify opposites, and under certain conditions "mutually change" them[31]. However, this was not Lenin's original idea; rather, it came from a passage of Hegel's analysis. There, Hegel clearly proposes that the nature of speculative philosophy is the embrace of opposites in the unity of opposite moments[32].

The seventh element: "the union of analysis and synthesis—the breakdown of the separate parts and the totality, the summation of these parts."

The eighth element: "the relations of each thing (phenomenon, etc.) are not only manifold, but general, universal. Each thing (phenomenon, process, etc.) is connected with **every other**." Logically speaking, these two elements are internally linked; the comprehensiveness of analysis and synthesis in epistemology relies precisely on actually existing universal connections. In the first section of "The Doctrine of Essence,"

Press (1966), page 65 (Chinese).

28 *Ibid.*, page 66.

29 *The Collected Works of Lenin* (Chin. 2. Ed.), volume 55, page 117.

30 *Ibid.*, page 82.

31 *Ibid.*, page 89.

32 Hegel, Georg Wilhelm Friedrich. *The Science of Logic*. Volume 1. Commercial Press (1966), page 153 (Chinese).

Lenin agrees with Hegel's exposition of the law of opposites, writing: "Every concrete thing, every concrete something, stands in multifarious and often contradictory relations to everything else, ergo it is itself and some other"[33]. Lenin is very much in agreement with such Hegelian phrases as "the necessary connections of the entire world" and "the connection of the mutual determinations of all things," etc. Lenin even excerpts the example that Hegel uses in his discussion of "measure": "in developed civil society aggregates of individuals belonging to different trades are in a certain relation to one another"[34]. This is why Lenin was able to so affirmatively assert: "The **totality of all** sides of the phenomenon, of reality and their (reciprocal) **relations**—that is what truth is composed of"[35]. This is the actual, concrete meaning of the seventh "element" (epistemological proposition).

The ninth element: "not only the unity of opposites, but the **transitions** of **every** determination, quality, feature, side, property into **every** other [into its opposite?]." In "The Doctrine of Being," as Lenin read Hegel's discussion of the transition of "being-for-self" to "being-for-other," he affirms that Hegel's analysis contains "very profound" elements, because "in life, in movement, each thing and everything **is usually** both "in itself" and "for others" in relation to an Other, being transformed from one state to the other"[36]. When Lenin came across Hegel's discussion of the movements and negations of contradictions themselves, he writes: "Ordinary imagination grasps difference and contradiction, but not the **transition** from one to the other, **this however is the most important**[37]. However, the focused discussion of this point did not come until the last section of "The Doctrine of the Notion," corresponding to Lenin's second great shift in thought and the completion of his second comparative knowledge; here he re-opens *Shorter Logic* to the 213th section on the "Idea." Here Lenin excerpts large passages of Hegel's expressions of the Idea. Lenin's thinking here was still primarily focused on the idea that the actualization of the Concept could only take place in the "summation" of actual things, as well as in their "mutual relations"[38]. Following this, Lenin writes two long passages of his own

---

33 *The Collected Works of Lenin* (Chin. 2. Ed.), volume 55, page 115.
34 Hegel, Georg Wilhelm Friedrich. *The Science of Logic*. Volume 1. Commercial Press (1966), page 360 (Chinese).
35 *The Collected Works of Lenin* (Chin. 2. Ed.), volume 55, page 166.
36 *Ibid.*, page 90.
37 *Ibid.*, page 119.
38 Hegel, Georg Wilhelm Friedrich. *The Shorter Logic*. Commercial Press (1980),

assessment. Here, the most interesting point is Lenin's summary of Hegel's arguments. He first writes a question on the left-hand side of the page ("What constitutes dialectics?") and then goes on to write:

Mutual dependence of notions

Mutual dependence of all notions without exception

Transitions of notions from one into another

Transitions of all notions from one into another without exception

The relativity of opposition between notions...

The identity of opposites between notions[39].

After this, Lenin points to the right hand side of the page using a thin line, writing an "=" sign and the words: "**NB** Every notion occurs in a certain **relation**, in a certain connection with **all** the others"[40]. Interestingly enough, we are unable to find textual references to this idea in the 213th paragraph of *Shorter Logic*, which Lenin was reading at the time. Thus we can conclude that Lenin was conducting a **constructive** thought experiment, in other words, Lenin believed that in Hegel's ideas there existed logical structures concerning notional dialectics. At this point Lenin very solemnly writes:

> **This aphorism should be expressed more popularly, without the word dialectics: approximately as follows: In the alternation, reciprocal dependence of *all* notions, in the *identity of their opposites*, in the transitions of one notion into another, in the eternal change, movement of notions, Hegel brilliantly *divined* PRECISELY THIS RELATION OF THINGS, OF NATURE[41].**

The tenth element: "The endless process of the discovery of new sides, relations, etc." The eleventh element: "The endless process of the deepening of man's knowledge of the thing, of phenomena, processes, etc., from appearance to essence and from less profound to more profound essence."

Strictly speaking, the content of these two "elements" is not directly related to dialectical theory, pointing instead towards the dialectical

---

page 398 (Chinese).

39   *The Collected Works of Lenin* (Chin. 2. Ed.), volume 55, page 167.

40   *Ibid.*, page 167.

41   *Ibid.*, page 166.

movements of knowledge, which was Lenin's speciality. Actually, this is the highlight of all the *Bern Notebooks*. At the beginning of his study of *The Science of Logic*, Lenin writes: "The "path of self-construction" = the **path** (this is the crux, in my opinion) of real cognition, of the process of cognizing, of movement from ignorance to knowledge"[42]. Thus when Lenin read Hegel's critique of Kant's "thing-in-itself" in the preface to the second edition, he was naturally very pleased. In a large box, Lenin writes two of his own views:

(1) In Kant, cognition demarcates (divides) nature and man; actually it unites them; (2) In Kant, the 'empty abstraction' of the Thing-in-it-self instead of living progress, the movement, deeper and deeper, of our knowledge about things[43].

Lenin clearly understands that "categories are stages of distinguishing, i.e. of cognizing the world, focal points in the web, which assist in cognizing and mastering it"[44].

At the very end of the introduction, Lenin reads Hegel's discussion of the movement from sensuous concrete to abstract, then to concrete abstract logic, as well as his famous example of proverbs. As we know, in Hegel's system, The *Phenomenology of Spirit* as the phylogenetic pre-history of the Idea had already disproved the false legitimacy of sensuousness; as such, the beginning of speculative logic is already abstraction devoid of all sensuous concreteness[45]. However, Hegel goes on to tell us that this logical notion that proceeds from abstraction will progress to become abstraction of concrete historical qualification. To use Hegel's own words:

> **It is only after profounder acquaintance with the other scienc-es that logic ceases to be for subjective spirit a merely abstract universal and reveals itself as the universal which embraces within itself the wealth of the particular — just as the same proverb, in the mouth of a youth who understands it quite well, does not possess the wide range of meaning which it has in the mind of a man with the experience of a lifetime behind him, for whom the meaning is expressed in all its power[46].**

42   *Ibid.*, page 73.
43   *Ibid.*, page 76.
44   *Ibid.*, page 78.
45   el, Georg Wilhelm Friedrich. *The Science of Logic*. Volume 1. Commercial Press (1966), page 42 (Chinese).
46   *Ibid.*, page 41.

Lenin points out that Hegel's explanation here is a historical comparison that approaches materialism. Knowledge becomes ever deeper as man's life experiences grow richer; this is a limitless developmental progression. He finds that Hegel correctly explains the relation between the limited and limitless nature of knowledge in the process of cognition[47]. This makes him think of his discussion of the continual deepening of material concepts in Materialism and Empirio-criticism: "The limitlessness of the essence of matter"[48].

After reading the "Doctrine of the Notion," Lenin left a complete and focused passage of text on the methodological problem of "abstract to concrete." In reading the opening section of "The Doctrine of the Notion," in the textual context of that section, Hegel seems to want to explain the place of the Notion itself within the whole of "the science of logic." He declares that such things as direct observation and imagination are **self-conscious** spirit – in fact, this was content that he had already dealt with in *Phenomenology of Spirit*, where the emergence of the Notion was in abstract, speculative logical movements. However, the Notion was still not the Idea, because the Idea is the unity of the Notion and actuality[49]. Lenin first affirms Hegel's viewpoint in a large box, then surpasses the concrete context of the text and proposes his own complete view of the problem:

Thought proceeding from the concrete to the abstract— provided it is *correct* (NB) (and Kant, like all philosophers, speaks of correct thought)—does not get away *from* the truth but comes closer to it. The abstraction of *matter*, of a *law* of nature, the abstraction of value, etc., in short all scientific (correct, serious, not absurd) abstractions reflect nature more deeply, truly and *completely*. From living perception to abstract thought, *and from this to practice,*—such is the dialectical path of cognition of truth, of cognition of objective reality[50].

The most important understanding gained in the course of Lenin's research on deepening knowledge is mainly focused in the outline

47 *Ibid.*, page 125-57.
48 *The Collected Works of Lenin* (Chin. 2. Ed.), volume 55, page 76. Also see *The Collected Works of Lenin* (Chin. 2. Ed.), volume 18, pages 271-275.
49 Hegel, Georg Wilhelm Friedrich. *The Science of Logic*. Volume 1. Commercial Press (1966), page 251 (Chinese).
50 *The Collected Works of Lenin* (Chin. 2. Ed.), volume 55, page 142.

he made as he read the opening section of "Essence" in Hegel's *The Science of Logic*. We are immediately able to see Lenin's particular thought experiment exhibited in his textual excerpts. On the third page of the fourth volume of *The Collected Works of Hegel*, Lenin first sees the phrase "the truth of being is essence." He immediately criticizes it, writing: "sounding thoroughly idealistic and mystical." However, he goes on to assert that "a fresh wind" is blowing:

Being is the immediate. Knowledge seeks to understand that truth which Being, *in and for itself*, is, and therefore it does not halt (*does not halt* NB) "at the immediate and its determinations, but *penetrates* (NB) through (NB) it, assuming that *behind* (Hegel's italics) this Being there is something other than Being itself, and that this background constitutes the truth of Being[51].

It is in this extremely special textual experiment that Lenin uses underlining to highlight the details that he feels are important. Only the words "in and for it" and "behind" were emphasized by Hegel, and the rest of the highlights were added by Lenin. We can see that Lenin accorded special attention to the following concepts: knowledge "does not halt" at immediate things; "through" immediate things we can "penetrate" "behind" immediate things to find the **essence** of cognitive things. Lenin approves of Hegel's idea that this is a passage from "external outside being" to "inside being." Lenin specifically writes the word "passage" to the right of this passage of excerpted text, double-underlining it to show its importance. Lenin was actually very familiar with the aspect of his study, profoundly understanding Hegel's critique of Kant, that appearance is the expression of essence. He also agrees with Hegel on the concept of the identity of the order of the identity of essence and laws. Lenin writes that "law and essence are concepts of the same kind (of the same order), or rather, of the same degree, expressing the deepening of man's knowledge of phenomena, the world, etc." Next Lenin writes an "X" and a triangle in the right-hand margin, following it with the words: "NB Law is essential appearance"[52]. On the next page, Lenin affirms Hegel's words: "**Law is essential relation**"[53]. *The double underlines under these words were added by*

---

51   Hegel, Georg Wilhelm Friedrich. *The Science of Logic*. Volume 2. Commercial Press (1976), page 3 (Chinese).

52   *The Collected Works of Lenin* (Chin. 2. Ed.), volume 55, page 127.

53   Hegel, Georg Wilhelm Friedrich. *The Science of Logic*. Volume 2. Commercial Press (1976), page 127 (Chinese).

Lenin; Hegel's original text only emphasizes "essential relation." After this Lenin writes his own assessment inside large parentheses: "Law is **relation**. This N B for the Machists and other agnostics, and for the Kantians, etc. Relation of essences or between essences"[54]. Essence is synchronic while law is essential relation in movement, change, and development, *i.e.*, the relation between diachronic essences. As he read the second section of "The Doctrine of the Notion," Lenin came across a passage in Hegel's chapter "Mechanism" in which he discusses laws; at this point Lenin again gives a focused summary of law: "The concept of law approximates here the concepts 'order' (Ordnung); uniformity (Gleichförmigkeit); necessity; the 'soul' of objective totality, the 'principle of self-movement'"[55].

In fact, before this point Lenin had already affirmed this view: "The concept of **law** is **one** of the stages of cognition by man of **unity** and **connection**, of the reciprocal dependence and totality of the world process." He also writes that categories are stages of man's cognition of the external world or knots in the web of knowledge of nature. At this point, as Lenin reads Hegel's assertion in *Shorter Logic* that **substance is an important stage in the developmental process of the Idea**[56], he immediately writes in a box: "Read: an important stage in the process of development of **human knowledge** of nature and **matter**"[57]. *A textual detail that merits our attention is that in Hegel's original text, no emphasis was placed on this passage, but in excerpting it, Lenin double underlines those portions that are particularly important to him.* Please note that this important knowledge became deeper and more penetrating after his leap in understanding.

The twelfth element: "from co-existence to causality and from one form of connection and reciprocal dependence to another, deeper, more general form." The words "from co-existence to causality" seem to explain two relations. The first is the co-existence relation that is external and scattered among things while the second is the relation of causality. *I have noticed that in the sections of The Bern Notebooks, causality is a question that Lenin does not treat much.* From the text we are able to see that as Lenin discusses causal relations in his notes, most of the

---

54 *The Collected Works of Lenin* (Chin. 2. Ed.), volume 55, page 128.

55 *Ibid.*, page 155.

56 Hegel, Georg Wilhelm Friedrich. *The Shorter Logic.* Commercial Press (1980), pages 313-314 (Chinese).

57 *The Collected Works of Lenin* (Chin. 2. Ed.), volume 55, page 133.

discussion centres on his assessment of Hegel's corresponding explanations. When Lenin reads the third section of "The Doctrine of Essence"
in *The Science of Logic*, on the one hand he takes excerpts from Hegel's
exposition of causal relations, and on the other hand expresses some of
his own opinions: "The all-sidedness and all-embracing character of the
interconnection of the world." As we normally understand them, causal
relations are merely a small part of the interconnectedness of the world,
"Cause and effect, ergo, are merely moments of universal reciprocal dependence, of (universal) connection, of the reciprocal concatenation of
events, merely links in the chain of the development of matter[58]. Lenin
understands that the causality of the Idea to which Hegel refers is actually a subjective reflection of the causal nature of the objective world:
"The movement of the relation of causality" = in fact: the movement of
matter, respective the movement of history, grasped, mastered in its inner connection up to one or other degree of breadth or depth…"[59]. Lenin
also remarks that in Hegel's *The Science of Logic,* causal relations are
not worshipped as the Kantians do; it could even be said that relative
to other categories, Hegel mentions causality very infrequently. Lenin
believes that this may be because for Hegel, "causality is only **one** of
the determinations of universal connection, which he had already covered earlier, in his **entire** exposition, much more deeply and all-sidedly;
always and from the very outset emphasising this connection, the reciprocal transitions, etc., etc."[60].

The thirteenth element: "The repetition at a higher stage of certain
features, properties, etc., of the lower and…" The fourteenth element:
"The apparent return to the old (negation of the negation)."

These two elements are only the external characteristics of the law of
the negation of the negation. I believe that Lenin was never really able
to truly grasp Hegel's negation of the negation. *This was certainly true
when Lenin first came into contact with Hegelian philosophy at the end
of the 19th century, such as in his "What the 'Friends of the People'
Are."* In the beginning portion of "The Doctrine of Being," when Lenin
first encounters Hegel's negation of the negation, he writes that it is
"abstract and abstruse." Up until he wrote the "sixteen elements" he
was still unclear as to his identification of the basic determinations and
complex relations of Hegel's discussion of the affirmation and negation

58   *Ibid.*, page 134.
59   *Ibid.*, page 135.
60   *Ibid.*, page 137.

of things and appearances[61]. It was not until later, when Lenin read "The Absolute Idea," the last chapter in *The Science of Logic* that he began to be moved by the theory of the negation of the negation. At that point he first draws a large box and then writes the words:

Not empty negation, not futile negation, *not sceptical* negation, vacillation and doubt is characteristic and essential in dialectics,—which undoubtedly contains the element of negation and indeed as its most important element — no, as a moment of development, retaining the positive, *i.e.*, without any vacillations, without any eclecticism[62].

Lenin notices that in Hegel's philosophy, this so-called dialectical negation is the source of the self-movement of matter formed by internal contradictions on which Lenin himself focuses. Thus he is able to affirmatively write that this is the "brilliance of dialectics." However, despite these passages Lenin is never becomes truly excited by the triad of the negation of the negation; at the most he merely describes all of scientific development as a "circle of circles" on the basis of Hegel's negation of the negation, thus expressing reserved approval[63]. *In his later "On the Question of Dialectics," Lenin would again affirm this comparison.*

The fifteenth element: "the struggle of content with form and conversely. The throwing off of the form, the transformation of the content." In the beginning of his study, Lenin saw Hegel's discussion of the relation between form and content in the preface to the second edition. There Hegel criticizes the assertion that forms of thought were merely supplements to the "external forms" of conscious objects. He proposes that forms are precisely the common essence of objective content[64], and that as such, forms are also the immanent form of content. Lenin agrees strongly with Hegel's view here: "forms of content, forms of living, real content, inseparably connected with the content"[65]. In fact, Hegel's so-called forms are conceptual essence as material universals; as such, when Hegel later discusses again the relation between form and essence, Lenin affirmatively echoes his words[66].

---

61 *Ibid.*, page 89.
62 *Ibid.*, page 195.
63 *Ibid.*, page 201.
64 Hegel, Georg Wilhelm Friedrich. *The Science of Logic*. Volume 1. Commercial Press (1966), page 14 (Chinese).
65 *The Collected Works of Lenin* (Chin. 2. Ed.), volume 55, page 91.
66 *Ibid.*, page 120.

Last is the sixteenth element: "the transition of quantity into quality and *vice versa ((15 and 16 are examples of 9))*."

In the beginning of his reading of "The Doctrine of Being," Lenin at first simply repeats Hegel's determinations of quality; for instance, determinateness is the existence of concrete determination, "determinations are already quality"[67], separated from other matter. By the third chapter, "Being-for-Self," he begins to have his own ideas about Hegel's "transition from quality to quantity." Lenin points out that "quality is determinateness, determinateness for self, the posited, it is the One—this gives the impression of being very farfetched and empty"[68]. Furthermore, Lenin also calls into question Hegel's exposition of quantity and measure[69].

Some of the other important problems that Lenin discusses in his notes but that are not included in his summary here of dialectics are the following. The relation between freedom and necessity[70], the relation between possibility and reality, between end and means[71], the relation between limitedness and limitlessness[72], the relation between absolute and relative[73], the relation between whole and part[74], the relation between general and special[75], the relation between subject and object[76], the concept of measure[77], the concept of ground[78], and more. There are even more profound epistemological problems in his research and discussion that Lenin did not include in this summary of "sixteen elements" of dialectics and epistemology but were discussed elsewhere in his notes. This has already been discussed in the previous chapter, and so we will not redundantly repeat them here.

---

67 *Ibid.*, page 87.
68 *Ibid.*, page 97.
69 *Ibid.*, page 99-105.
70 *Ibid.*, page 132.
71 *Ibid.*, page 186.
72 *Ibid.*, page 78, 91-5 and 99.
73 *Ibid.*, page 131.
74 *Ibid.*, page 129.
75 *Ibid.*, page 147-50.
76 *Ibid.*, page 172.
77 *Ibid.*, page 101-3.
78 *Ibid.*, page 119.

3 A GENERAL REVIEW

As I have already pointed out, the Soviet scholar Kedrov argues that these "sixteen elements" constituted the "first plan" of a work by Lenin on materialist dialectics. The authors of the fifth volume of the Soviet History of Philosophy, on the other hand, assert that the "sixteen elements" were the "the fullest and most comprehensive abbreviated summary of the various aspects or elements of dialectics after Marx and Engels"[79]. I am basically opposed to these arguments. This is because, as we have seen in the discussion of this chapter, these "sixteen elements" merely made up an **incomplete** summary of those elements of dialectics and epistemology that left the deepest impression on Lenin, as directly acquired in his study of Hegelian philosophy. I disagree with the assertions of Soviet scholars that this was a "plan" of the construction of a dialectical system of logic or the "fullest" expression of the many aspects of dialectical theory.

There is another question for me at this point: why did Lenin completely avoid touching on the new discovery of his research and thought experimentation – **the logic of practice** – in this shorter theoretical summary? I have found that the Chinese scholar Cong Dachuan astutely discovered this detail in his own research. Professor Cong conducted a comparative study of Lenin's "sixteen elements" and Marx's "Theses on Feuerbach"[80]. He conducted a specific comparative analysis of six aspects of these two texts: philosophical objects, basic philosophical questions/logical foundations, logic axes, epistemology, worldview/conception of history, and line of thought. He found that there was a great difference between these two works. In short, Marx's theses represented "practical materialism," while Lenin's "sixteen elements" represented "the dialectical materialism of material ontology." Professor Cong argues that Lenin's elements lack the discussion of practice and the existence of social history that Marx elucidated in his "theses." I believe that Professor Cong's conclusions are basically correct. But what was the actual reason why Lenin's overall summary of dialectics did not include a discussion of the logic of practice, of which Lenin was already aware? Cong Dachuan's answer is that Lenin had the mode of thought of material ontology, which made him unable

---

79 Dynnik, ed. *History of Philosophy*, volume 5. 1975. Beijing Sanlian Press, 81.
80 Unfortunately, Cong Dachuan continues the Soviet, non-reflective line of thought, identifying the "sixteen elements" as an "essential blueprint of the dialectical system of a worldview and epistemological understanding." See Cong Dachuan's "Dialectical System: Marx and Lenin." *Yunnan Social Sciences* (1995), volume 2.

to introduce practical views into his "sixteen elements"[81]. I cannot agree with this explanation. I suspect that Professor Cong has not conducted an in-depth, systematic, comprehensive study of the *Bern Notebooks*, and thus has not found the great changes in Lenin's philosophical thought over the course of his studies. Thus although Cong Dachuan was able to astutely grasp the question raised by Lenin's "sixteen elements," he was unable to truly answer it. My own conclusion is that because this short summary was not consciously devised by Lenin to be a writing plan for the construction of a materialist dialectical theoretical system, but was rather merely a condensed summary of his own impressions and thoughts over the course of his reading (especially the basic viewpoints of dialectics and epistemology), therefore he did not go on to discuss the practical basis of dialectics and epistemology. Lenin would never have thought that his reading summary, the "sixteen elements," would ever have directly become an important logical framework for the dialectical materialism and materialist dialectical system of future generations.

After reading *The Science of Logic*, Lenin arrived at a conclusion that ran counter to his beliefs at the beginning of his reading: "The sum-total, the last word and essence of Hegel's logic is the **dialectical method**—this is extremely noteworthy. And one thing more: in this **most idealistic** of Hegel's works there is the least idealism and the **most materialism**. "Contradictory," but a fact!"[82]. *This passage was naturally very difficult for many Western scholars who do not understand dialectics; they were unable and unwilling to believe that Lenin was able to read materialism from Hegel's book!*[83]. However, Lenin ultimately understood Engels' words: "Hegel's system is materialism turned on its head"[84]. Thus the materialist dialectics of Marxism were not the inversion of Hegel's terminology, but rather a **logically** inverted "Hegelian system" proceeding from the practical subject. It is evident that Lenin's understanding at this point is already completely different from his earlier assessment of Hegelian philosophy, that "nine-tenths" of Hegel's thought is "chaff, rubbish," and that one must "**extract** the materialist dialectics from it"[85].

---

81   Cong Dachuan. "On the Theoretical Thought of Lenin's 'Philosophical Notebooks.'" *Yanbian University Journal* (1997) volume 4.

82   *The Collected Works of Lenin* (Chin. 2. Ed.), volume 55, pages 202-203.

83   Wittle. 1963. *Dialectical Materialism*. The Commercial Press, page 145 (Chinese Edition).

84   *The Collected Works of Lenin* (Chin. 2. Ed.), volume 55, page 202.

85   *Ibid.*, page 129.

CHAPTER FOURTEEN

THE CONCLUSION OF LENIN'S STUDY ON HEGELIAN PHILOSOPHY

The object of research of Lenin's *Bern Notebooks* was Hegel's *The Science of Logic*; Lenin's two great leaps in understanding and logical situating of philosophical thought also took place as he read *The Science of Logic*. However, after reading *The Science of Logic*, Lenin continued to study some of Hegel's important philosophical work, ultimately forming his own new thought and understandings. After this new process of thought, Lenin again reflected on and summarized his philosophical research. I have remarked that many of Lenin's thoughts were, to different degrees, deepened and developed in this process of reflection, composing a more profound level of his new thought situating. In this chapter we will specifically see the thought and ideas that Lenin developed at the end of his *Bern Notebooks*.

1 CONFIRMING PRACTICAL DIALECTICS IN THE HISTORY OF PHILOSOPHY

As we already know, Lenin's profound understanding of Hegelian philosophy and therefore Marxist materialist dialectics was completed as he read *The Science of Logic* through a series of remarkable leaps in understanding. After reading *The Science of Logic*, Lenin did not terminate his study, but rather turned next to Hegel's *Lectures on the Philosophy of History* and *Lectures on the History of Philosophy*. However, he never finished reading either of these books. *Volume four of **Lectures on the History of Philosophy** takes up books 13 through 16 of the **Collected Works of Hegel**, while Lenin's excerpts of this book only go through the beginning of book 15 (page 33). Volume nine of the **Collected Works of Hegel** contains **Lectures on the Philosophy of History**, and Lenin's notes indicate that he did not read beyond page 175.* In addition, Lenin found a good number of writings on Hegelianism, but in the end only elected to read Georges Noel's *Hegel's Logic* (other works include four by E Beaussire and others)[1]. In the reading process at this stage in his research, the volume of Lenin's notes did indeed decrease. In his notes on *Lectures on the History of Philosophy* and *Lectures on the Philosophy of History*, Lenin only recorded 71 page numbers; for *The Science of Logic* he wrote 137.

I believe that this was the case because Lenin's attitude in his reading here was already very much different from that of the early stage of his reading of *The Science of Logic*. At this time, he had already profoundly grasped the essence of Hegelian philosophy (dialectics) and so in his reading here, he primarily searches for new things that he may have missed in his past reading in order to **strengthen** the theoretical viewpoints that he has already developed. *Dunayevskaya has also remarked that upon entering his study of philosophical history, Lenin was not as excited as he was during his reading of **The Science of Logic**[2].*

The focus of Lenin's reading of Hegel's works on the history of philosophy was still dialectics. At the beginning of his reading of Greek philosophical history, he highlights the "negative determination of dialectics," *i.e.*, "Hence the determinations are dry, destitute of process,

---

1   *The Collected Works of Lenin* (Chin. 2. Ed.), volume 55, page 285.
2   Dunayevskaya, Raya. *Philosophy and Revolution*. Liaoning Education Press (2000), page 174 (Chinese Edition).

undialectical, and stationary"[3]. *These are the basic characteristics of metaphysics, as later scholars usually identify them.* When Lenin comes upon Hegel's discussion of Eleatic philosophy, his attention is caught by one of Hegel's overall assessments. Hegel believes that the philosophical thought of the Eleatic School is "the beginning of dialectics," because it is "simply the pure movement of thought in Notions; likewise we see the opposition of thought to outward appearance or sensuous Being, or of that which is implicit to the being-for-another of this implicitness, and in the objective existence we see the contradiction which it has in itself, or dialectics proper"[4]. Lenin goes on to engage in profound discussion and concrete analysis of this passage. He writes that this "fragment" of Hegel's thinking on dialectics could be expressed "without idealist connotations" in the following ways:

First, "human concepts are not fixed but are eternally in movement, they pass into one another, they flow into one another, otherwise they do not reflect living life. The analysis of concepts, the study of them, the 'art of operating with them' (Engels) always demands study of the **movement** of concepts, of their interconnection, of their mutual transitions." Here we can see that Lenin has already accepted Hegel's views on the triple identity of dialectics, epistemology, and logic; thus when he writes "the art of operating with [concepts]," he is referring to subjective dialectics as well as epistemology.

Second, "In particular, dialectics is the study of the opposition of the Thing-in-itself (*an sich*), of the essence, substratum, substance—from the appearance, from 'Being-for-Others.' (Here, too, we see a transition, a flow from the one to the other: the essence appears. The appearance is essential.) Human thought goes endlessly deeper from appearance to essence, from essence of the first order, as it were, to essence of the second order, and so on **without end**." *This is a very well-known passage of the Bern Notebooks.* The dialectics to which Lenin referred here did not mean, of course, external objective laws, but rather a dialectical knowledge of the dialectical movement of the external world. Especially important is the fact that Lenin had already realized that the objective being of things was not absolutely identical to **the form in which they manifest themselves to us.** *This was Kant's contribution to epistemology, an important aspect that the original philosophical*

---

3   *The Collected Works of Lenin* (Chin. 2. Ed.), volume 55, page 209.
4   Hegel, Georg Wilhelm Friedrich. *Lectures on the Philosophy of History.* Volume 1. Commercial Press (1959), page 253 (Chinese).

materialist mirror-image did not and was unable to see. Furthermore, the **internal** essence and **external** appearance of the thing-for-itself were in constant flux. From appearance to essence, then to **first order essence sublated into second order appearance**, then to second order essence and so on, *ad infinitum.* This is an extremely profound dialectical understanding.

Third, "Dialectics in the proper sense is the study of contradiction **in the very essence of objects**: not only are appearances transitory, mobile, fluid, demarcated only by conventional boundaries, but the **essence** of things is so as well"[5]. This sentence seems to be a theoretical summary of the important analysis that Lenin has just completed. The line of demarcation between appearance and essence is continually being redrawn by our **historical**, practical progress. I believe that Lenin's thinking here is generally identical to Engels' assertion that man's understanding can only attain the level of his practice. At this time, Lenin is confirming "a dialectics of concepts and a dialectics of cognition which has objective significance"[6]. Later, Lenin profoundly realized that this dialectics of concepts did not simply originate from natural matter, because "actual history is the basis, the foundation, the Being, which is **followed** by consciousness"[7]. This actual history is practical social life as described by Marx. This understanding is structurally similar to the notion of practical dialectics that Lenin had just acquired not long before.

As Lenin read Hegel's review of Zeno's dialectics[8], he recorded a concentrated exposition in his notebook of excerpts, focusing on the developmental view of dialectics. He writes: "

As Lenin opened the second volume of *Lectures on the History of Philosophy*, we find that his thought situating space continued to be filled with new thinking. An interesting textual detail here is that as Lenin read Hegel's discussion of Gorgias' relation between being and non-being, he actually writes: "'Vanishing moments' = Being and not-Being. That is a magnificent definition of dialectics!!"[9]. *Please remember that when Lenin began studying Hegel's **The Science of Logic**, the*

---

5   *The Collected Works of Lenin* (Chin. 2. Ed.), volume 55, pages 212-213.

6   *Ibid.,* page 215.

7   *Ibid.,* page 224.

8   *Ibid.,* page 232.

9   *Ibid.,* page 235.

question of being and non-being was very confusing to Lenin; here, on the other hand, it has become a "magnificent definition" that he easily understands. This is the result of a completely heterogeneous thought situating. In the section "The Philosophy of Socrates," Lenin writes: "Intelligent idealism is closer to intelligent materialism than stupid materialism. Dialectical idealism instead of intelligent; metaphysical, undeveloped, dead, crude, rigid instead of stupid"[10]. This is another of Lenin's famous lines in the Bern Notebooks. The semantic meaning of this expression is very complex. His use of the words "intelligent" and "stupid" have specific references. Evidently Socrates and others are "intelligent" here, while dialectical idealism refers to Hegel and other classical German philosophers; I believe that he is attempting to elucidate the important significance of dialectics in philosophical logic. *Even more interestingly, in a later box Lenin actually writes: "Objective (and still more, absolute) idealism came very close to materialism by a zigzag (and a somersault), even partially* **became transformed into it**"[11]. *Here Dunayevskaya believes that Lenin's understanding demonstrates the finality of the rupture between Lenin and his* **philosophical past**[12]. *This conclusion is basically correct. However, when she goes on to assert that Lenin's shift indicates a complete acceptance of Hegel's idealism and fundamental refutation of Lenin's materialist philosophical foundation, she falls into fallacious conclusions. In addition, Levine has published a lengthy critique of Lenin's reading of the first volume of Hegel's* **Lectures on the History of Philosophy**. *His argument is that the standard by which Hegel judges ancient Greek dialectical thought is the* **primacy of universality**, *but Lenin's interpretation of classical dialectics is based on the notions of movement and change*[13]. *From the perspective of Hegel's objective idealist primacy of ideas, Levine's conclusions are correct. Hegel truly does focus on Pythagoras' abstract "number," on the Eleatic School's "being" (the universality that remains unchanging in the midst of continuous change, i.e., the "One"), and even on Heraclitus' non-sensuous "fire." The universality of this idea is actually the basis of Hegel's idealist dialectics. However, does Levine really expect that Lenin, the materialist philosopher who has no intention to become a follower of Hegel, would actually ignore the*

10   *Ibid.*, page 237.
11   Dunayevskaya, Raya. *Marxism and Freedom.* Liaoning Education Press (2000), page 157 (Chinese Edition).
12   Levine, Norman. *Dialogue within the Dialectic.* Yunnan People's Press (1997), pages 370-372 (Chinese).
13   *The Collected Works of Lenin* (Chin. 2. Ed.), volume 55, page 236.

dialectical characteristics ascribed to the movement and change of things by ancient philosophers and instead focus on the erroneous logical starting point of this speculative dialectics?

Under the heading "To be elaborated," Lenin goes on to clarify his line of thinking:

> **Plekhanov wrote on philosophy (dialectics) probably about 1,000 pages (Beltov + against Bogdanov + against the Kantians + fundamental questions, etc., etc.). Among them, *about* the large Logic, *in connection with* it, its thought (i.e., dialectics *proper*, as philosophical science) nil!!**[14].

It is my understanding that this was the final dissolution of Lenin's original Other mirror image. It is also here that he ultimately accounts for his teacher – Plekhanov. The works on dialectics by Plekhanov that Lenin lists here comprise nearly all of his philosophical books[15]. The different elements connected by Lenin's "plus" signs may refer to Plekhanov's books such as *Monist View of History*, all his works criticizing Bogdanov, his works criticizing Bernstein, and finally his *Fundamental Problems of Marxism*, which positively elucidates the basic views of Marxism. *Dunayevskaya believes that the philosophical rupture between Lenin and Plekhanov took place here . Dunayevskaya's words are not without their validity. Of course, more precisely this rupture began to take place in the first epistemological leap in Lenin's reading of **The Science of Logic**; his words "none of the Marxists understood Marx" were certainly profound reflection. I do, however, believe that this rupture was expressed more thoroughly at this point.* As we know, in these books which all purported to proselytize and defend Marxist philosophy Plekhanov would often bring up materialist dialectics. Given this fact, why would Lenin accuse him (and all the Marxists of the past half-century) of not having any thought on the Large Logic (materialist dialectics)? I believe that here Lenin had already profoundly realized that his teacher Plekhanov in fact did not really understand the essence of Marx's materialist dialectics, especially the Large Logic (and epistemology) based on objective practical dialectics. Lenin acquired this viewpoint in his second important leap in understanding in his new theoretical situating.

---

14   *Ibid.*, page 637, footnote 125.
15   Dunayevskaya, Raya. *Philosophy and Revolution*. Liaoning Education Press (2000), page 94 (Chinese Edition).

I believe that Lenin's thinking here immediately activated another underlying thought situating. On the next page of his notes, Lenin again provides a deep expression of this large practical dialectical logic.

As he read "The Philosophy of Plato," Lenin wrote in a large box:

> **The significance of the universal is contradictory: it is dead, impure, incomplete, etc., etc., but it alone is a stage towards knowledge of the concrete, for we can never know the concrete completely. The *infinite* sum of general conceptions, laws, etc., gives the concrete in its completeness[16].**

To the right of this large box, he writes the letters "NB" before and after the words "The dialectics of cognition," and then an arrow pointing to another box in which he writes:

> **The movement of cognition *to* the object can always only proceed dialectically: to retreat in order to hit more surely— to fall back, the better to leap (to know?) Converging and diverging lines: circles which touch one another. Nodal point = the practice of mankind and of human history. (Practice = the criterion of the coincidence of one of the infinite aspects of the real)[17].**

This passage is quite profound and also extremely important because it reveals a complex and rich layer of theoretical situating in Lenin's thought. We can see that Lenin's thinking point here proceeds from the subject ("the movement of cognition *to* the object"), a viewpoint that is immediately connected to Marx's first thesis of *Theses on Feuerbach*. At the same time, this movement can "only proceed dialectically"; unlike the claims of the old materialists, it does not immediately conform to the object. Even in the process of cognition, it "retreat[s] in order to hit more surely— to fall back, the better to leap (to know?)." *We remember that in the political struggle of the early revolution, Lenin proposed the dialectical tactic of "advancing one step and retreating two steps" and "retreating in order to better advance."* What does Lenin mean by "retreat"? Examining the specific content of the dialectical thought of the philosophical history that Lenin had read up to this point, "retreat" most likely means that when the true reflection of man on external laws cannot be attained all at once, it can only be **actualized indirectly,**

---

16 *The Collected Works of Lenin* (Chin. 2. Ed.), volume 55, page 239.
17 *Ibid.*, page 239.

gradually. It is evident that this medium, which lies between subjective and objective dialectics, is objective social practice that proceeds from the subject. Here Lenin selects a very apt term: nodal point. "**Nodal point** = the practice of mankind and of human history." In Lenin's logic situating at this time, he has already constructed a thought space based on the fundamental theoretical circuit of practice. Substantive matter yields to the medium of relational practice. Practice as a nodal point constitutes a new dialectical thought situating.

It is also here that we see Lenin's confirmation of the logic structures of the theory of materialist dialectics: **under the mediation of moving, practical dialectics**, man's subjective and objective dialectics constitute a certain fundamental logical framework. Here **subjective dialectics are not immediately of the same structure as objective dialectics, but rather move with practical dialectical structures**, and through **concrete, actual, historical** human practice, coinciding with "one of the infinite aspects of the real." His words "one of the aspects" here refer to the historical dimension and depth of certain social practice. Thus subjective dialectics and objective dialectics form a historical point of contact ("nodal point") or "circles which touch one another." We are almost able to imagine the thought situating level of Lenin at this time: the curve of understanding of subjective dialectics and the for-itself baseline of objective dialectics intersect through practical relations. This "line of convergence" quickly becomes a "line of divergence" through the historical point of practice. The line of divergence in subjective dialectics is the elevation from the sensuous concrete to abstract reason; at the same time, abstract dialectics is the concrete return of objective dialectics. *The best explanation of the so-called "line of divergence" is Hegel's: "the abstract, the more concrete."* In the original theoretical circuit of philosophical materialism, subjective dialectics is merely the direct reflection of objective dialectics, while in Lenin's logical situating at this time, this simple reflectional relation exhibits a more complex relational system.

In the third box, Lenin writes: "These nodal points represent a unity of contradictions, when Being and not-Being, as vanishing moments, coincide for a moment, in the given moments of the movement (= of technique, of history, etc.)"[18]. It is not hard to see that as Lenin continues his reading, his thought theoretical situating centred on practical dialectics

---

18   *Ibid.*, page 240.

becomes ever more profound and ever richer. Hegel's dialectic of being and not-being is restructured in Lenin's epistemological logic. In Lenin's view, subjective dialectics do not directly reflect objective dialectics; it is only through continually developing practical dialectics (technology and history) and under the **practical levels of function** of certain historical conditions that man can reflect certain determinations of objective dialectics "in a given moment." It is evident that this reflection is necessarily a process; it seems as though the objective dialectics grasped by man in these vanishing moments that coincide for a moment are not all the content of objective laws. However, in the entire historical summation of practice, man is able to gradually approach objective truth. It is my opinion that this is a completely new level of thought in the philosophical thought situating of Lenin's *Bern Notebooks*.

In his subsequent reading notes, Lenin criticizes Hegel's idealist logical slant in his narration of the history of philosophy. Not long after Lenin began his reading of the third volume, his excerpts suddenly cease. Here he opens *Lectures on the Philosophy of History*, but does not continue reading for long. He only took a few excerpts and recorded a small number of thoughts and commentaries after reading this text. Lenin explains this himself: "In general the philosophy of history yields very, very little—this is comprehensible, for it is precisely here, in this field, in this science, that Marx and Engels made the greatest step forward. Here most of all, Hegel is obsolete and antiquated"[19].

At this point Lenin completes all of his research on Hegelian philosophy. He believed that he had gained much and felt that there was need to conduct another theoretical summary. It was at this time that he began to read related secondary philosophical texts, such as Noel's *Hegel's Logic*[20], though most of his energy was devoted to his own thought situating experiment and theoretical summary.

---

19   *Ibid.*, page 277.
20   Lenin only took a small amount of notes on this book. See *The Collected Works of Lenin* (Chin. 2. Ed.), volume 55, page 279-285.

2 AN IMPORTANT READING SUMMARY AND RECORD OF THOUGHTS

After basically completing his study of Hegelian philosophy, Lenin re-corded three focused passages in which he summarizes what he has learned (remember that these passages do not represent a "plan" or "conception" for the construction of any kind of materialist dialecti-cal system). These three texts are "Plan of Hegel's *Dialectics* (*Logic*)," "Conspectus of Lassalle's Book *The Philosophy of Heraclitus the Obscure of Ephesus*," and "On the Question of Dialectics." I believe that of these three texts, the first was a **reading summary**, the sec-ond was a **re-evaluation** of Lenin's own theoretical logical situating of practical dialectics, and the third discussed and expanded on **what Lenin had learned** in the course of his learning and study. From the research perspective of this book, I believe that the first text is the most important, because it represents the pinnacle of Lenin's thought situat-ing as he summarizes and analyzes the entire course of his reading and research.

In the thought outline that is "Plan of Hegel's *Dialectics* (*Logic*)," Lenin first analyzes the entire theoretical framework of *The Science of Logic* (the headings of the Shorter Logic) and then writes in a large box:

> **The concept (cognition) reveals the essence (the law of cau-sality, identity, difference, etc) in Being (in immediate phe-nomena)—such is actually the *general course* of all human cognition (of all science) in general. Such is the course also of *natural science* and *political economy* [and history]. *Insofar* Hegel's dialectic is a generalization of the history of thought. To trace this more concretely and in greater detail in the *his-tory of the separate sciences* seems an extraordinarily reward-ing task. In logic, the history of thought *must*, by and large, coincide with the laws of thinking[21].**

Here Lenin first proposes the important idea that human cognition is a process **oriented towards the subject** that continually reveals essence in "immediate phenomena." It is not difficult to see that Lenin no longer adheres to the epistemology of philosophical materialism in assuming that the subject immediately faces material being. He defines "being" as **immediate phenomena revealed through practical history**. This

---

21 *The Collected Works of Lenin* (Chin. 2. Ed.), volume 55, page 289.

was a completely new understanding of Lenin's in relation to the general progression of human cognition and science. After this point, human cognition (subjective dialectics) is no longer simply and directly correlated to the object, but is rather a dialectical movement full of contradiction. Lenin discovers that Hegel's dialectics are the expression of this thought progression, *i.e.*, the extraction of the true logic structure and historical thread of **all** of the history of human thought. *This viewpoint of Lenin's only strengthened gradually after reading Hegel's **Lectures on the History of Philosophy**. However, I must also point out that the foundation of Hegel's history of thought was mainly the **Western** history of philosophy centred on Europe.* In other words, the structure of subjective dialectics was not immediately equated with the structure of external objects, but was rather immediately the **logical structure of the history of thought**. Thus, "the history of thought **must**, by and large, coincide with the laws of thinking." This was an extremely important scientific confirmation of all of Hegel's *Logic* (dialectics) by Lenin: Hegel's dialectics (logic) was not merely nonsense, but rather objectified, mystified, and transformed *human cognitive logic* into a thing-in-itself. This viewpoint is already completely different from the views based on his Other framework of his earlier reading. We can see that this was a summary and re-evaluation of his thought situating (this was the leap in thought in his first logical détournement) with regards to Hegelian philosophy.

Next, Lenin goes on to analyze two opposing logical orientations in the movement of Hegel's philosophy: "sometimes passes from the abstract to the concrete (Being (abstract)—Determinate Being (concrete)—Being-for-self) and sometimes the other way round (the Subjective Notion—the Object—Truth (the Absolute Idea))"[22]. *In fact, these two logical figures are not opposite. They are both movements from abstract to concrete, only the first is an ontological conception of being, while the latter is a logical figure in the overall cognitive progression of the Absolute Idea.* Lenin first asks if this logical inconsistency is caused by the lack of thoroughness or mysticism of Hegel's idealism. But he quickly revises his question: "or are there deeper reasons?" *We can see that Lenin does not deal simply with Hegel by this point, he is already accustomed to experiencing the profoundness of Hegel's discourse in his own deep thought.*

---

22   *Ibid.*, page 289-99.

We can see that Lenin goes on to construct an extremely important line of logical analysis and underlying discourse:

First of all impressions *flash* by, then *Something* emerges, —afterwards the concepts of *quality*# (the determination of the thing or the phenomenon) and *quantity* are developed. After that study and reflection direct thought to cognition of identity—of difference—of Ground—of the Essence versus the Phenomenon—of causality, etc. All these moments (steps, stages, processes) of cognition move in the direction from the subject to the object, being tested in practice and arriving through this test at truth (= the Absolute Idea)[23].

This is an obvious deepening of thought situating. Lenin deepens the true essence of cognitive dialectics in concretely synthesizing the **whole logic structure** of Hegel's logic.

In these thought circumstances, Lenin finds that the world we face is not a directly observable, static object as described by philosophical materialism, but rather the unity of being and non-being in practical relations. This unity is also the developmental process of the dialectical movement of the objective world. *This was a point that greatly confused him as he began to read Hegel's* **The Science of Logic**. This is the **object** of human cognition, and in the beginning all objects are abstract. At this point Lenin uses large parentheses around the words: "Abstract 'being' only as a moment in 'everything flows." In human cognition progressing in practice, what takes place first is the "flashing by" of the impressions of different changes. These are fragments of human sensuous experience, the composite (consciousness) of which leads to the emergence of Something. This particular thing is concrete determinate being (*Dasein*). *There is no textual evidence to show that Lenin had read Hegel's* **Phenomenology of Spirit**, *but the brilliance of Lenin's thinking here constructs a narrative logic that is remarkably similar to that of Hegel's* **Phenomenology of Spirit**. When the human subject confirms this thing from the dual aspects of **difference** and **scope**, then emerge the determinations of quality and quantity. The process that Lenin describes here is an abstract expression of the **progression of the human (individual experience) cognitive object**.

---

23   *Ibid.*, page 290.

A particularly important textual detail is that Lenin added a "#" sign after the word "quality," and then on the left-hand side of the page he writes an explanation of the word "quality": "#Quality and sensation (Empfindung) are one and the same, says Feuerbach. The very first and most familiar to us is sensation, and **in it** these is inevitably also **quality**..."[24]. *Feuerbach expresses this viewpoint at the very end of the tenth lecture of* **Lectures on the Essence of Religion**. *Here he proposes that human sensation is "the first, immediately reliable thing." He goes on to argue that it is precisely this sensation, which has concrete attributes, which composes human existence and the inverted nature of god*[25]. *Interestingly enough, in the excerpted notes on Feuerbach's* **Lectures** *which we have already examined, Lenin only excerpts and comments on this as a basic* **materialist** *view*[26], *while here it is activated as* **underlying scholarly memory** *in re-entering the thought structure of Lenin's practical dialectical logical structure*. Lenin suddenly remembers Feuerbach's views on the coincidence of sensation and quality, then goes on to realize that sensation is the beginning of all human cognition, while quality inevitably **emerges first** in sensation. *This view is completely different from his focal point during his first reading of Feuerbach's* **Lectures**, *when he was still operating within the framework of philosophical materialism*. Therefore, the logical place of quality in Hegel's *The Science of Logic* is **identical to the progression of human cognition, not simply equated to a characteristic of the object**. Reading up to this point, Lenin reaches a new level of thought situating. He immediately realizes that the movement from the identity (quality) of one thing to the difference between one thing and another, then from the internal contradictions (ground) that confirm this thing to the expression of this essence through appearance and ultimately including the thing's departure from the connection between itself and the entire world ("causality, etc.") – **the fundamental logical sequence of all of this does not belong to the objective structure assumed by philosophical materialism**, but is rather made up of moments of cognition (steps, stages, processes) from the **subject to the object**, *i.e.*, the cognitive structure and logical progression of man. Hegel merely arbitrarily objectifies this cognitive logic into the essence of the material

---

24 *Ibid.*, page 290.
25 Feuerbach, Ludwig. "Lectures on the Essence of Religion," in *Selected Philosophical Works of Feuerbach*, volume 2, The Commercial Press (1984 edition), page 588 (Chinese).
26 Lenin, Vladimir Ilyich. "Conspectus of Feuerbach's Book The Essence of Religion." In *The Collected Works of Lenin*, volume 55, pages 40-41 (Chin. 2. Ed.).

world. Although the logical basis of Hegel's dialectics is idealist, the internal logic structures of his dialectics are not "nonsense," but rather truly reflect human cognitive progress and logic structures. As such, Marx's restructuring of Hegel was not a simple inversion of Hegel's dialectical terminology, nor did it immediately view Hegel's idealized **logic** of the dialectics of concepts as the objective structure of material dialectics. This is because such a simple treatment will result in something that appears to be materialist but will actually be latently idealist, and thus will **directly establish** Hegel's dialectics of concepts (of which the substance is cognitive structure) as objective laws. I believe that it was here that Lenin was able to truly realize the underlying problems with the Other framework under which he worked at the beginning of his study. *In Deborin's first introduction to the **Bern Notebooks,** he seems to have clearly read and understood Lenin's overall penetration of Hegel's philosophical structures in a completely new situating. He points out that this reflects human cognitive activity (the summation of human cognition and all the historical progress of scientific development) changes from immediate being (quality, quantity, measure) to substance, concept, and the Absolute Idea, which Lenin sees as **comprehensive** truth. This explains how Lenin's view on the overall progression of human cognition is identical to Hegel's. Placed here, this viewpoint is not incorrect. However, Deborin erroneously places this viewpoint as the **preconditional** cognitive framework of Lenin's reading of Hegel, not the **result** of multiple logical détournements and cognitive shifts*[27].

In fact, in Lenin's earlier reading of *Lectures on the History of Philosophy*, Lenin had already clearly warned himself: "Hegel's logic cannot be *applied* in its given form, it cannot be *taken* as given"[28]. At this point, he evidently clearly understands that Hegel's dialectical structure is the **logical reflection** of human subjective cognitive structures; his mistake was in idealistically confirming this **subjective cognitive structure** of the subject as the fundamental essence of the structure of objective existence. Thus our critical restructuring of Hegel should not immediately call this subjective cognitive structure an objective structure itself, but should reconfirm the true foundation of subjective cognitive structures within the subject. This foundation is practice! Man's

---

27   Deborin, Abram. *Introduction to volume 9 of "The Lenin Papers"*. Soviet National Press (1929) page 3 (Chinese).

28   *The Collected Works of Lenin* (Chin. 2. Ed.), volume 55, page 225.

subjective cognitive structures (logic) are constrained by the structure and logic of the progression of his objective practice. Thus the **progressive sequence of logic** described by Hegel is merely the **progression of practice** from the subject to the object. Only through the medium of practical structures can objective structures by historically expressed. This is also a summary and reflection by Lenin of his second great leap in understanding.

I believe that Lenin's thought situating here is the **pinnacle** of the progression he made in the course of reading Hegel's philosophical works. It is on this point that he profoundly and comprehensively grasped the substance of Marxist materialist dialectics. He writes:

> **If Marx did not leave behind him a *"Logic"* (with a capital letter), he did leave the *logic* of *Capital*, and this ought to be utilised to the full in this question. In Capital, Marx applied to a single science logic, dialectics and the theory of knowledge of materialism [three words are not needed: it is one and the same thing] which has taken everything valuable in Hegel and developed it further[29].**

Here Lenin is actually deepening the thoughts that he acquired in his earlier leaps of understanding. We find here the convergence of Lenin's thinking on Hegel's cognition, on Marx's dialectics, and on the triple identity of epistemology, dialectics, and logic. It is also at this point that Lenin truly understood Marx and Engels' discussion as they corresponded on the first volume of *Capital*, *i.e.*, why Marx and Engels would have such a positive appraisal of Hegel's *The Science of Logic*. Lenin is already able to profoundly see that, in a certain sense, the logic structure of Marx's *Capital* was similar to that in Hegel's The Science of Logic. "The beginning—the most simple, ordinary, mass, immediate "Being": the single commodity ("Being" in political economy)"[30]. This describes the existence of "quality," which Hegel first revealed; this is also the sensuous appearance of market economics. However, this concrete was set up in Marx's theoretical logic as an **abstract null**. Commodities are not things, but rather a kind of invisible ("null"), special social economic relation. This is what causes commodities to possess the mysticism of material phenomena. This is also because commodities "as social relations" are the "simplest **summary**" of capitalist

---

29   *Ibid.*, page 225.
30   *The Collected Works of Lenin* (Chin. 2. Ed.), volume 55, page 291.

relations of production. Thus proceeding from this point and based on the unified thread of logic and history, we can gradually reveal **all** the major contradictions that have not been unfolded in capitalism. It is precisely in this logic situating that Marx "copies" Hegel's *The Science of Logic*. However, unlike Hegel, in the entire logical progression of Capital, Marx proves each step using facts, using practice. All of this was newly acquired theoretical thought by Lenin at this time.

In his excerpts on Lassalle's book *Heraclitus the Obscure of Ephesus*, Lenin records his second summary of what he learned[31]. Compared with his earlier thought and summaries, this text is somewhat simpler, written from the **perspective of the history of thought**.

Lenin writes: "In Marx there is a mass of *new material*, and what interests him is only the movement forward *from* Hegel and Feuerbach *further, from* idealistic to materialistic dialectics"[32]. In Lenin's view at this time, this "new material" contains the true significance of the Marxist philosophical revolution, an idea not only directed towards Hegel but also towards Feuerbach. "Marx in 1844-47 went from Hegel to Feuerbach, and further beyond Feuerbach to historical (and dialectical) materialism"[33]. *We can see that Lenin has greatly pushed forward his understanding of Marxist history of philosophy from the time he wrote the article "Karl Marx." His division of the history of philosophy into different eras is more accurate here. Most importantly, Lenin no longer moves in step with Dietzgen and Plekhanov in describing the historical genesis of Marxism as "first the establishment of dialectical materialism, then the application of it to the field of social history to form historical materialism." At this point, Lenin identifies Marx's supersession of Feuerbach and then subsequent move towards "historical (dialectical) materialism." Here historical materialism and dialectical materialism are the **same thing**! How did Marx surpass Feuerbach? In the past, scholars argued that it was the sum of Hegel's dialectics and Feuerbach's materialism, concluding that Marx provided nothing more than a "+" sign; this is fundamentally wrong.* Lenin realizes that the key point in Marx's realization of his philosophical revolution was the establishment of the determination of **practice**.

---

31   Lenin read this book because it was mentioned repeatedly in the *Marx-Engels Correspondence*. See *The Collected Works of Lenin* (Chin. 2. Ed.), volume 58, pages 36-39.
32   *The Collected Works of Lenin* (Chin. 2. Ed.), volume 55, page 293.
33   *Ibid.*, page 293.

This is why Lenin criticizes Lassalle for basically not understanding dialectics, pointing out his "reactionism" with relation to "Marx's 1845 theses on Feuerbach"[34]. *At this point, remember that some Chinese scholars have followed in the footsteps of Western Marxologists in debasing Marx's **Theses on Feuerbach** as merely an extension of his 1844 **The Holy Family**, thus eradicating the significance of this important thought revolutionary experiment. To use Lenin's words here, this is extremely "reactionary."* In fact, as the brilliant seeds of a new worldview, the **new Marxist worldview** ("**new material**") revealed in these *Theses* are **practical** materialism and **practical** dialectics in the context of history. Here these form the scientific view of nature, scientific conception of history, and scientific epistemology of Marxist philosophy. It is in this sense that Marx surpasses all old materialist philosophy. Scientific epistemology and dialectical theory do not correspond directly to objective objects, but rather form in the realm of complete cognition above the progression of **human practice**. The history of philosophy is based on "the history of the diverse sciences," including the history of the mental development of the child, the mental development of animals, languages, psychology, and the physiology of the sense organs...the "history of cognition in general"[35]. *Of course, because Lenin did not read The German Ideology written by Marx and Engels between 1845 and 1846, he was naturally not able to understand the theoretical shift of Marx and Engels from practice to "man's immediate life and production and reproduction." He was also unable to understand the further deepening and development of all historical materialism in Marx's later economics research (**Grundrisse** and **Capital**).*

Thus we can see how laughable and superficial was Dunayevskaya's claim that Lenin's shift in thought in the *Bern Notebooks* was approval of Hegel's idealist notions.

---

34 *Ibid.*, page 301.
35 *Ibid.*, page 302.

3 "ON THE QUESTION OF DIALECTICS": THE MAJOR ACHIEVEMENT OF LENIN'S STUDY OF DIALECTICS

The third summary that Lenin wrote at this time is the unfinished manuscript "On the Question of Dialectics." *This is a document to which many scholars have devoted a great deal of attention.* In this article Lenin appears to want to jump out of the trap of following in the footsteps of others in his reading, attempting to independently organize the major achievements of his study of dialectics. *Dunayevskaya believes that strictly speaking, this is the ultimate conclusion to the philosophical evaluations written by Lenin between 1914 and 1915[36]. I have also noticed that in Deborin's 1924 "Revolutionary Dialectician Lenin," the second section specifically discusses Lenin's "On the Question of Dialectics." In that essay his critique is somewhat restrained, basically repeating Lenin's points without anything of real scholarly value. In our earlier discussion we saw that this section was completely deleted from* **Philosophy and Politics**[37].

First, Lenin highlights the important questions he had discovered as he wrote his "Sixteen Elements" of dialectics and epistemology, *i.e.*, that opposition and unity are the **substance** and **centre** of materialist dialectical theory. *Lenin also identified this viewpoint in his earlier notes on Hegel's* **Lectures on the History of Philosophy**, *proposing it as he discussed Zeno's paradox: "And precisely* **this essence** *is expressed by the formula: the unity, identity of opposites"*[38]. At this point, Lenin again writes: "The splitting of a single whole and the cognition of its contradictory parts is the essence (one of the "essentials," one of the principal, if not the principal, characteristics or features) of dialectics"[39]. Lenin indicates that this point corresponds directly to a passage by Lassalle on Philo in the third section of his book on Heraclitus. In the original text, Philo proposes: "For the One is that which consists of two opposites, so that when cut into two the opposites are revealed." To illustrate his point, Philo discusses the One in nature as being composed of opposites, mentioning the mountains and plains, winter and summer, and

36   Dunayevskaya, Raya. *Philosophy and Revolution.* Liaoning Education Press (2000), page 96 (Chinese Edition).
37   Deborin, Abram. *Philosophy and Politics.* Beijing Sanlian Press (1965) volume 2, pages 819-828 (Chinese).
38   *The Collected Works of Lenin* (Chin. 2. Ed.), volume 55, page 219.
39   *Ibid*, page 305.

fresh water and salty water[40]. Lenin points out that the correctness of the contradictory determination of opposite-unity as the essence of dialectics can only be "tested by the history of science"[41]. He believed that past Marxists used too many examples in making this point, giving the sense that the law of contradiction was "the sum-total of **examples**." *In reading the Marx-Engels Correspondence, Lenin saw Marx's critique of Lassalle: "Hegel never referred to the practice of inducing a great number of 'examples' into a general principle as dialectics"*[42]. Lenin immediately identifies his old teacher Plekhanov and Engels. One of the examples he gives is borrowed from Engels, the "negation of the negation" which appears in the growth of a "seed." Lenin criticizes him for not taking the appearance of contradiction as a "**law of cognition (and** as a law of the objective world)." *This is a very interesting phenomenon. Both Engels and Plekhanov were important theoretical mirror-image support points in the Other reading framework of Lenin's early reading, and now they have become the objects of his criticism.*

In Lenin's opinion, the study of the identity of opposites can be summarized as follows:

> **The recognition (discovery) of the contradictory, *mutually exclusive*, opposite tendencies in *all* phenomena and processes of nature (*including* mind and society). The condition for the knowledge of all processes of the world in their "*self-movement*," in their spontaneous development, in their real life, is the knowledge of them as a unity of opposites[43].**

This text is also a scholarly summary. In the different textual contexts that Lenin experienced in the course of his reading, Lenin encountered the Hegel's contradictory structures of different concepts. This is because Hegel's entire logical framework was based on the synchronic structure or diachronic relations of the triad of the identity of opposites of the **self-contradiction** of the Concept. Lenin seems to accord special attention to Hegel's important dialectical views here, and after materialistically restructuring them, immediately identifies them as the essence and centre of materialist dialectics.

---

40   *Ibid.*, page 300.
41   *Ibid.*, page 305.
42   *Ibid.*, page 318.
43   *Ibid.*, page 306.

Next, Lenin shifts the angle of his examination, considering the issue from the developmental process of the thing. He goes on to point out that "Development is the 'struggle' of opposites." In other words, the contradictions which had already been identified as the essence of dialectics are the **source** and **driving force** of the movement of things themselves. Also, because all phenomena and processes possess immanent contradiction, therefore the movement of objective things is spurred by the contradictions within themselves. Lenin writes that historically, there are two common views of development. The first believes that development is addition and subtraction, repetition, moving the source and force of development outside man, to God, the subject, etc. Lenin refers to this as a "lifeless, pale, and dry" conception of development. *These definitions of different conceptions of development were proposed in Lenin's reading of Zeno's discussion of the dialectic in Hegel's* **Lectures on the History of Philosophy***; his summary at the time was "simple, general, and eternal growth, addition (or subtraction)"*[44]. The second view of development contends that development is the identity of opposites. Its "chief attention is directed precisely to knowledge of the source of *"self"*–movement." In fact, this so-called "self" movement as the source and developmental force of the movement of things is the contradiction within things. "The unity (coincidence, identity, equal action) of opposites is conditional, temporary, transitory, relative. The struggle of mutually exclusive opposites is absolute, just as development and motion are absolute…The second *alone* furnishes the key to the 'self-movement' of everything existing; it alone furnishes the key to 'leaps,' to the 'break in continuity,' to the 'transformation into the opposite,' to the destruction of the old and the emergence of the new."[45] *In his notes in* **Lectures on the History of Philosophy** *this thought is summarized as the conception of development based on "the emergence and destruction of all things, the mutual transition of all things"*[46].

Lenin of course realized that for Hegel, the self-contradiction of spirit spurs the logical progression of the self movement of the Idea; in the objective world, it is the self-contradiction of objective things that spur all movements, changes, and developments. Here Lenin suddenly thinks of the thought experiment he had just conducted, because in Capital, Marx profoundly revealed the essence of capitalist modes of production

---

44   *Ibid.*, page 215.
45   *Ibid.*, page 306.
46   *Ibid.*, page 215.

through revealing the immanent contradictions of capitalist society.

In his *Capital*, Marx first analyzes the simplest, most ordinary and fundamental, most common and everyday *relation* of bourgeois (commodity) society, a relation encountered billions of times, viz., the exchange of commodities. In this very simple phenomenon (in this "cell" of bourgeois society) analysis reveals *all* the contradictions (or the germs of all contradictions) of modern society. The subsequent exposition shows us the development (*both* growth *and* movement) of these contradictions and of this society in the Σ of its individual parts[47].

Here it is clear that Lenin is in the process of deepening his earlier thought situating. His concrete analysis identifies a new level of the problem, that of human cognition. Lenin proposes that essential and lawful cognition reveal the complex contradictory relations within objects.

Third, again using the example of Marx's *Capital*, Lenin asserts that "the method of exposition (*i.e.*, study) of dialectics in general…[should begin] with what is the simplest, most ordinary, common, etc., with any proposition"[48]. This appears to be an abstract general, but this "general" can only exist through the individual. Thus any individual is general. The individual, through numberless changes, abandons contingency and appearance, moving towards the necessary and essential. This is the **epistemology of dialectics**. Lenin writes: "dialectics is a property of all human knowledge in general…Dialectics is the theory of knowledge of (Hegel and) Marxism"[49]. However, "This is the 'aspect' of the matter (it is not 'an aspect' but the essence of the matter) to which Plekhanov, not to speak of other Marxists, paid no attention."

Fourth, Lenin discovers that this theory of knowledge, which is identical to dialectics, is a "series of circles" in the history of knowledge:

Dialectics as *living*, many-sided knowledge (with the number of sides eternally increasing), with an infinite number of shades of every approach and approximation to reality (with a philosophical system growing into a whole out of

---

47 *Ibid.*, page 307.
48 *Ibid.*, page 307.
49 *Ibid.*, page 308.

each shade)—here we have an immeasurably rich content as compared with 'metaphysical' materialism, the fundamental *misfortune* of which is its inability to apply dialectics to the theory of reflection, to the process and development of knowledge[50].

Here Lenin accurately uses the term "metaphysical materialism" (in the past he used "vulgar materialism"), pointing out that "Philosophical idealism is only nonsense from the standpoint of crude, simple, metaphysical materialism." *Let us not forget that it was in Lenin's early reading for the **Bern Notebooks** that he referred to Hegel's philosophy as "nonsense." This is why Vranicki, when critiquing this viewpoint, wrote, "here Lenin again corrects his previous views, at the same time brilliantly explaining the 'epistemological roots' of idealism, pointing out that idealism is not merely the ideology of a class, but rather the result of certain knowledge, though it is one-sided and linear, etc. "[51].* On the contrary, "From the standpoint of dialectical materialism, on the other hand, philosophical idealism is a *one-sided*, exaggerated, excessive (Dietzgen) development (inflation, distension) of one of the features, aspects, facets of knowledge, into an absolute, *divorced* from matter, from nature, apotheosized."

Human knowledge is not (or does not follow) a straight line, but a curve, which endlessly approximates a series of circles, a spiral. Any fragment, segment, section of this curve can be transformed (transformed one-sidedly) into an independent, complete, straight line, which then (if one does not see the wood for the trees) leads into the quagmire[52].

The idea that the general cognitive process of man is a circle composed of multiple circles was evidently influenced by Hegel's similar views. At the end of his *The Science of Logic*, Hegel compared the development of science to a circle: "the science exhibits itself as a circle returning upon itself, the end being wound back into the beginning, the simple ground, by the mediation; this circle is moreover a circle of circles, for each individual member as ensouled by the method is reflected into itself, so that in returning into the beginning it is at the same time the

50   *Ibid.*, page 311.
51   Vranicki, Predrag. *History of Marxism* (volume 2), People's Press: 1988, page 30 (Chinese).
52   *The Collected Works of Lenin* (Chin. 2. Ed.), volume 55, page 311.

beginning of a new member"[53]. Lenin excerpts this entire passage, noting in the margin, "science is a circle of circles"[54]. In reading the introduction to Lectures on the History of Philosophy, Lenin came across a similar idea: Hegel compares the history of philosophy to a great circle, on the edges of which are more circles. In a marginal box, Lenin affirmatively writes, "Every shade of thought = a circle on the great circle (a spiral) of the development of human thought in general." He refers to this as "A very profound correct comparison!!"[55]. For Lenin, the epistemological roots of idealism are "Rectilinearity and one-sidedness, woodenness and petrifaction, subjectivism and subjective blindness"[56]. Idealism is not groundless: "it is a sterile flower undoubtedly, but a sterile flower that grows on the living tree of living, fertile, genuine, powerful, omnipotent, objective, absolute human knowledge." This was Lenin's final evaluation of Hegel's philosophy. *Levine writes that when Lenin wrote "On the Question of Dialectics" in 1915 he became a Hegelianized Leninist[57]. This is obviously an oversimplified, erroneous statement.*

Here I would like to raise another question: in this short essay on dialectics, as with his "sixteen elements," why did Lenin again avoid discussion of **practical dialectics**, which he had discovered in the course of his research? Professor Cong Dachuan also raised this question[58]. Furthermore, this new knowledge had reached new theoretical heights in the short summary that Lenin had just written not long before. This is a theoretical question that truly baffled me for a long time. It was not until I entered Lenin's later notes that my doubts as to this question began to gradually become clear.

I believe that after completing his reading and philosophical research, Lenin's way of thinking about problems changed greatly. Not only did he want to apply the fruits of his learning to the practice of actual revolution, but he necessarily focused on another question, i.e., how to help the Russian proletariat gradually understand the scientific thought that

---

53   Hegel, Georg Wilhelm Friedrich. *The Science of Logic.* Volume 2, Commercial Press (1976), page 551 (Chinese).
54   *The Collected Works of Lenin* (Chin. 2. Ed.), volume 55, page 201.
55   *Ibid.,* page 207.
56   *Ibid.,* page 207.
57   Levine, Norman. *Dialogue within the Dialectic.* Yunnan People's Press (1997), page 382 (Chinese).
58   Cong Dachuan. "On the Theoretical Thought of Lenin's 'Philosophical Notebooks.'" *Yanbian University Journal* (1997) volume 4.

he had acquired. In "On the Question of Dialectics," the four points that he chose to discuss are all popular and concise thought; he does not use "figures of logic and practice," "Logic," or any other Hegelian speculative philosophical concepts. *Lenin was ever opposed to pedantry*[59]. This is why Lenin does not discuss the revolution in thinking that he realized in the *Bern Notebooks*. After the victory of the October Revolution, he not only believed that he had to study "all the philosophical works" of Plekhanov, but he also re-published *Materialism and Empirio-criticism*. *Dunayevskaya also remarks this point*[60]. *Other scholars have written that Lenin courageously and publicly recognized that he had already rejected as useless some of the important aspects of his philosophy of 1908*[61]. It is my view that Lenin is not abandoning the important thought he had developed in the *Bern Notebooks*, but that he is considering how to more broadly introduce Marxism, making it more palatable to the Russian proletariat.

After the October Revolution, Lenin did not have the time to return to philosophical research, but the impression left on him of Hegelian philosophy and its dialectics was too deep. In his last essay that dealt directly with dialectics, written in 1922, we can read his final testament. In January 1922, the Soviet Union began publishing *Under the Banner of Marxism* in order to proselytize materialism and atheism. *Deborin was the editor-in-chief of this journal*. In March 1922, Lenin completed "On the Significance of Militant Materialism," which was published in the third issue of *Under the Banner of Marxism*. In this article, Lenin primarily upholds materialism and opposes religious theology. He entreats readers to understand philosophy, writing:

A conscious adherent of the materialism represented by Marx, i.e., must be a dialectical materialist. In order to attain this aim, the contributors to *Pod Znamenem Marksizma* [*Under the Banner of Marxism*] must arrange for the systematic study

---

59   In reading Lenin's later reading notes, I have found that he repeatedly criticizes the pedantry of the research of Bucharin and others. In 1915, when revising "Pacifism or Marxism: An Unfortunate Slogan," Lenin writes: We cannot leave untranslated German sentences in the newspaper for Russian workers. In 1920, Lenin read Bucharin's *Transitional Economics*, repeatedly criticizing his pedantry using the words "institutionalism" and "false classicism."

60   Dunayevskaya, Raya. 2000. *Philosophy and Revolution*. Liaoning Education Press, page 105 (Chinese Edition).

61   Nikolay Valentinov's *Encounter with Lenin*, as cited in Dunayevskaya, Raya. 2000. *Philosophy and Revolution*. Liaoning Education Press, page 105 (Chinese Edition).

of Hegelian dialectics from a materialist standpoint, *i.e.*, the dialectics which Marx applied practically in his *Capital* and in his historical and political works[62].

Lenin calls on other scholars to "print in the journal excerpts from Hegel's principal works, [and] interpret them materialistically." He even goes on to assert that the editors and writers of *Under the Banner of Marxism* "should be a kind of 'Society of Materialist Friends of Hegelian Dialectics'"[63]. *Dunayevskaya goes on to say that Lenin's "Conspectus of Hegel's Book The Science of Logic" became the philosophical basis for all of his later serious works. From on Imperialism to the State and Revolution written on the eve of the 1917 October Revolution, from all his works written during the revolution to his Last Testament[64].* Evidently Lenin wanted to continue his theoretical thought in the *Bern Notebooks*, but the flow of history callously interrupted this pleasant wish. It is even more unfortunate that Stalin transformed Lenin's philosophical research into a kind of false situating within an external, political-ideological framework. To this day, though we concede that there was certain inevitability to the emergence and existence of this kind of ideology, it has gravely veiled the actually existing, profound content of Lenin's philosophical thought; we cannot but conclude that this is a great tragedy.

---

62 Lenin, Vladimir. "On the Significance of Militant Materialism." *The Collected Works of Lenin* (Chin. 2. Ed.) volume 43, page 29 (Chinese).

63 *Ibid.*, page 30.

64 Dunayevskaya, Raya. 2000. *Philosophy and Revolution.* Liaoning Education Press, page 89 (Chinese Edition).

ABOUT THE AUTHOR

Zhang Yibing (originally named Zhang Yibin) was born in Nanjing in 1956. In August of 1981, he graduated with a degree in philosophy from Nanjing University. He later went on to receive a doctorate in philosophy, and currently teaches philosophy and tutors doctoral candidates at Nanjing University. He is vice president of Nanjing University and director of the Marxist Social Theory Research Center. Additionally, he is a permanent member of the Chinese Academy of Marx-Engels Research, Chinese Academy of Dialectical Materialism, a permanent member of the Chinese Academy of the History of Marxist Philosophy, chairman of the Philosophy Academy of Jiangsu Province, and chairman of the Marxist Academy of Jiangsu Province. His representative works include: *The Impossible Truth of Being: Image of Lacanian Philosophy* (The Commercial Press, 2006), *A Deep Plough: Unscrambling Major Post-marxist Texts* (Vol. 1, Renmin University Press, 2004; Vol. 2, RUC Press, 2008); *Problématique, Lecture Symptomale et Idéologie: A Textological Reading of Althusser* (Central Edition and Translation Press, 2003); *The Subjective Dimension of Marxist Historical Dialectics* (Nanjing University Press, 2002, 2nd Edition); *Atonal Dialectical Fantasia: A Textological Reading of Adorno's 'Negative Dialectics'* (Beijing Sanlian Bookstore, 2001), and *Marx Revisited: Philosophical Discourse in an Economics Context* (Jiangsu People's Press, 1999).

His books published in English by Canut Publishers Intl-London-Berlin include *A Deep Plough: Unscrambling Major Post-marxist Texts*, *The Subjective Dimension of Marxist Historical Dialectics* and *Problématique, Lecture Symptomale et Idéologie: A Textological Reading of Althusser* and *Contra Baudrillard: Déconstruction of a Post-modern Academic Myth*.

www.ingramcontent.com/pod-product-compliance
Lightning Source LLC
Chambersburg PA
CBHW050852150626
46549CB00013B/1422